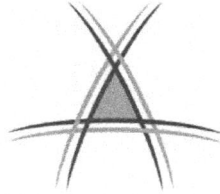

ASCENT®
CENTER FOR TECHNICAL KNOWLEDGE

# Creo Simulate:
# Structural and Thermal Analysis

## Student Guide

*Revision 1.0*
*July 2013*

# ASCENT - Center for Technical Knowledge®
## Creo Simulate
## Structural and Thermal Analysis
## Revision 1.0

Prepared and produced by:

ASCENT Center for Technical Knowledge
630 Peter Jefferson Parkway, Suite 175
Charlottesville, VA 22911

866-527-2368
www.ascented.com

ASCENT
CENTER FOR TECHNICAL KNOWLEDGE

ASCENT - Center for Technical Knowledge is a division of RAND Worldwide Inc., providing custom developed knowledge products and services for leading engineering software applications. ASCENT is focused on specializing in the creation of education programs that incorporate the best of classroom learning and technology-based training offerings.

We welcome any comments you may have regarding this training manual, or any of our products. To contact us please email: education@ASCENTed.com.

# Table of Contents

Class Files .......................................................................................... vii

Chapter 1  Introduction to Creo Simulate ................................. 1-1

   1.1  Finite Element Analysis (FEA) ........................................ 1-3

   1.2  FEA Solution Refinement ................................................ 1-7

   1.3  P-Elements ...................................................................... 1-9

   1.4  Convergence Methods ................................................... 1-10

   1.5  Types of Analysis in Creo Simulate ............................. 1-13

   1.6  FEA Process .................................................................. 1-14

   1.7  CAD Model Preparation ................................................ 1-15

   1.8  Creo Simulate Modes of Operation ............................. 1-16

Chapter 2  Basic Creo Simulate Modeling ................................. 2-1

   2.1  Launching Creo Simulate ............................................... 2-3

       Structure Ribbon ............................................................. 2-4

   2.2  Modeling Steps ............................................................... 2-6

       Defining Model Type ........................................................ 2-6

       Creating Idealizations ..................................................... 2-7

       Applying Material ............................................................. 2-7

       Applying Constraints ....................................................... 2-9

       Applying Loads .............................................................. 2-10

       Meshing the Model ........................................................ 2-10

   2.3  Analysis ........................................................................ 2-12

       Analysis Types .............................................................. 2-12

       Convergence Methods ................................................... 2-13

       Design Studies .............................................................. 2-14

   2.4  Results .......................................................................... 2-15

       Files and Directories ...................................................... 2-15

       Result Verification .......................................................... 2-16

       Result Visualization ....................................................... 2-17

       Practice 2a Static Stress Analysis of a Bracket ................... 2-19

       Practice 2b Static Stress Analysis of a Bike Crank .............. 2-54

Chapter 3  Loads and Constraints ............................................. 3-1

   3.1  Constraints ...................................................................... 3-3

       Rigid Body Motions ......................................................... 3-4

       Constraint Sets ............................................................... 3-4

       Displacement Constraint ................................................. 3-5

       Planar, Pin, and Ball Constraints .................................... 3-7

Symmetry Constraints ............................................................3-8

**3.2 Loads ......................................................................3-12**
    Load Sets.............................................................................3-13
    Force/Moment Load.............................................................3-14
    Pressure Load .....................................................................3-15
    Bearing Load .......................................................................3-17
    Gravity Load ........................................................................3-18
    Centrifugal Load ..................................................................3-19
    Temperature Load ...............................................................3-20
    Preload ................................................................................3-21

**3.3 Surface Regions ..................................................3-23**

**3.4 Singularities ........................................................3-24**
    Types of Singularities ..........................................................3-24
    Excluded Elements..............................................................3-25
    Guidelines............................................................................3-27
    Practice 3a Stress Analysis of a Crank................................ 3-28
    Practice 3b Cyclic Symmetry Constraints............................ 3-54
    Practice 3c Surface Regions ............................................... 3-68
    Practice 3d Excluded Elements ........................................... 3-88

**Chapter 4 Shell Idealizations ............................................4-1**

**4.1 Shell Idealizations.................................................4-3**

**4.2 Midsurface Shells ................................................4-5**
    Shell Pair Creation...............................................................4-6
    Manual Shell Pairs ..............................................................4-7
    Automatic Shell Pairs...........................................................4-8
    Shell Pair Compression .......................................................4-8

**4.3 Standard Shells....................................................4-10**
    Standard Shell Creation.......................................................4-10

**4.4 Applying Loads and Constraints to Shell Models ...........4-12**
    Practice 4a Automatic Shell Creation .................................. 4-13
    Practice 4b Manual Shell Creation ..................................... 4-39
    Practice 4c Shells from Surfaces........................................ 4-68
    Practice 4d Shell and Solid Combination............................ 4-85

**Chapter 5 Beams and Frames...........................................5-1**

**5.1 Beam Elements ...................................................5-3**
    Beam Definitions..................................................................5-6
    Beam Sections.....................................................................5-7

**5.2 Beam Coordinate Systems ................................5-8**

**5.3 Beam Action Coordinate System (BACS) .............5-9**

**5.4 Beam Shape Coordinate System (BSCS) .......................5-12**
    Practice 5a Beam Analysis ................................................. 5-14

Practice 5b 2D Frame Analysis ............................................. 5-38
Practice 5c 3D Frame Analysis............................................. 5-58

**Chapter 6 Sensitivity and Optimization Design Studies** ...............6-1

**6.1 Design Considerations**...............................................6-3
Objectives .................................................................6-4
Measures ..................................................................6-4
Design Variables.......................................................6-4

**6.2 Types of Design Studies** ...........................................6-5
Standard Studies ......................................................6-5
Sensitivity Studies....................................................6-5
Optimization Studies ................................................6-5
Setting Up Design Studies.........................................6-6

**6.3 Design Variables**.......................................................6-7
Practice 6a Sensitivity and Optimization Studies................... 6-8

**Chapter 7 Assembly Interfaces**.........................................7-1

**7.1 Types of Interfaces** .................................................7-3

**7.2 Bonded Interface** ....................................................7-5

**7.3 Free Interface** .........................................................7-6

**7.4 Contact Interface** ....................................................7-7
Automatic Contact Detection .................................7-10

**7.5 Reviewing Interfaces** ...............................................7-12

**7.6 Setting Up Contact Analysis**.....................................7-14

**7.7 Mesh Refinement**....................................................7-16
Practice 7a Door Handle Assembly .................................. 7-17
Practice 7b Pin-Jointed Assembly .................................... 7-34

**Chapter 8 Thermal Analysis**..............................................8-1

**8.1 Modes of Heat Transfer**...........................................8-3
Conduction..............................................................8-3
Convection...............................................................8-4
Radiation..................................................................8-4

**8.2 Creo Simulate Thermal**...........................................8-5
Thermal Ribbon .......................................................8-6

**8.3 Modeling Steps** ......................................................8-7
Idealizations.............................................................8-7
Applying Boundary Conditions.................................8-8
Applying Heat Loads...............................................8-11

**8.4 Analysis** ...............................................................8-13
Analysis Types........................................................8-13

8.5 **Results**................................................................**8-14**
Result Visualization .................................................8-14

8.6 **Thermal Load Transfer**................................**8-15**
Practice 8a Thermal Steady State Analysis.......................... 8-17

**Chapter 9 Modal Analysis** .........................................**9-1**

9.1 **Natural Frequency** ....................................**9-3**

9.2 **Natural Modes**.........................................**9-4**

9.3 **Defining a Modal Analysis** .........................**9-5**
Practice 9a Modal Analysis of a Bracket .............................. 9-7

**Chapter 10 Welds, Springs, and Masses** ........................**10-1**

10.1 **Weld Connections** ....................................**10-3**
Spot Welds ..............................................................10-3
End Welds ...............................................................10-4
Perimeter Welds .......................................................10-5

10.2 **Springs** .................................................**10-6**
Stiffness...................................................................10-8
Orientation ...............................................................10-9

10.3 **Masses**.................................................**10-10**
Practice 10a Spot Welds ............................................ 10-11
Practice 10b Perimeter Welds ...................................... 10-22
Practice 10c Springs and Masses Analysis ....................... 10-32

**Chapter 11 Fasteners and Rigid Links**..........................**11-1**

11.1 **Rigid Links** ............................................**11-3**
Creating Rigid Links...................................................11-4

11.2 **Fasteners**..............................................**11-6**
Prerequisites ............................................................11-6
Part Separation.........................................................11-6
Fastener Preload .......................................................11-8
Creating Fasteners ....................................................11-9
Fastener Measures....................................................11-10
Practice 11a Modal Analysis of a PCB Assembly............... 11-12
Practice 11b Static Analysis of a Mixed Solid/
Shell/Beam Model.................................................... 11-25
Practice 11c Fasteners with Preload .............................. 11-34
Practice 11d Handling Surface Separation Issues When
Using Fasteners...................................................... 11-46

**Chapter 12 Buckling Analysis**....................................**12-1**

12.1 **Theory of Buckling** ..................................**12-3**

12.2 **Creo Simulate Buckling Analysis**................**12-5**
Practice 12a Buckling Analysis of a Pole.......................... 12-7

**Appendix A  Basics of Structural Analysis** ....................................... **A-1**

    **A.1  Quantities and Units**........................................................**A-3**
       Fundamental Quantities............................................................ A-3
       Derived Quantities ................................................................... A-3
       Units........................................................................................ A-3

    **A.2  Newton's Laws**...............................................................**A-4**
       Equilibrium & Free-Body Diagrams ......................................... A-4
       Stresses................................................................................. A-10
       3D Stresses ........................................................................... A-12
       Failure Theories.................................................................... A-13

**Appendix B  Poisson's Ratio Project** ...............................................**B-1**

    **B.1  Poisson's Ratio**.............................................................**B-3**

**Appendix C  Verification and Practice Examples Set 1** ..................**C-1**

    **C.1  Structural Analysis**........................................................**C-3**
       Case 1 - Cantilevered I-Beam ................................................ C-4
       Case 1 - Plate with a Hole...................................................... C-6
       Case 1 - Stepped Circular Bar................................................ C-7
       Case 1 - Loaded Plate with Hole ............................................ C-9
       Practice C1 Structural Analysis Examples - Set 2.............. C-10
       Case 1 - Straight Beams....................................................... C-10
       Case 2 - Rectangular Plate................................................... C-11

**Appendix D  Conversion Factors** .....................................................**D-1**

    **D.1  Conversion Factors**.......................................................**D-3**

# Class Files

To download the Class Files that are required for this training guide, type or click the following in the address bar of your web browser:

**ftp://ftp.ascented.com/cware/genus.zip**

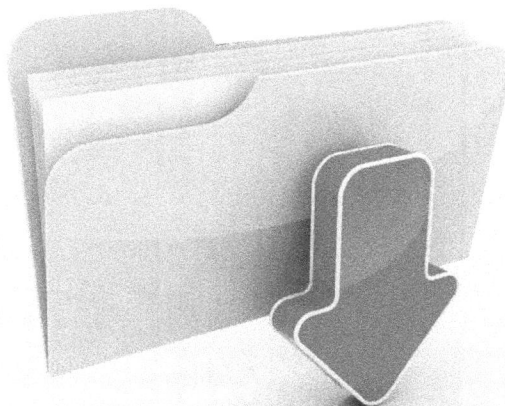

# Chapter 1

## Introduction to Creo Simulate

Creo Simulate is a powerful software tool that enables you to simulate structural and thermal behavior of your design to understand and improve the design's performance.

This chapter contains the following topics:

- **Finite Element Analysis (FEA)**
- **FEA Solution Refinement**
- **P-Elements**
- **Convergence Methods**
- **Types of Analysis in Creo Simulate**
- **FEA Process**
- **CAD Model Preparation**
- **Creo Simulate Modes of Operation**

# 1.1 Finite Element Analysis (FEA)

**Learning Objective**

Understand the concept of FEA.

Finite Element Analysis is a numerical mathematical method based on the following process:

*Creo Simulate contains the **AutoGEM** tool, which automatically meshes a model.*

*In 2D models, finite elements are triangles or quadrilaterals. In 3D models, finite elements are 4-node tetra, 6 node wedge or 8-node bricks.*

- Discretize (i.e., divide) the model into smaller and more simplified volumes (tets, bricks, etc.) called *finite elements*. The collection of finite elements approximates the shape of the model, and is called *finite element mesh*, or just *mesh*. An example of a meshed model is shown in Figure 1–1.

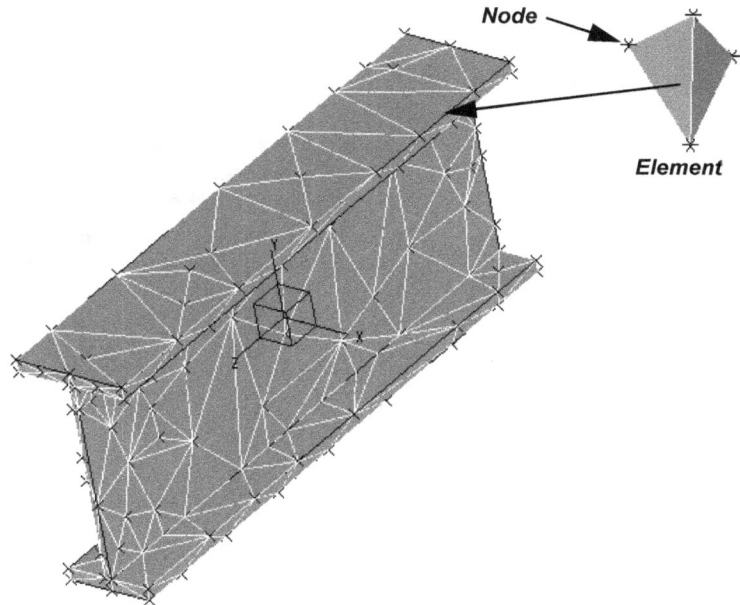

**Figure 1–1**

- Approximate the variation of the principal quantity of interest (such as displacement, stress, etc.), within each finite element with polynomials. These polynomials are typically called *local approximation functions*, or *shape functions*.

- Connect the finite elements at the mesh nodes, thus effectively *sewing* elemental polynomials together. The *sewn* local polynomials now approximate a variation of the quantity of interest over the entire model, and therefore comprise the global approximation function in the form of a piece-wise polynomial.

- Solve the governing equations and boundary conditions for the global approximation function, and find the best fitting solution. In structural mechanics, the principle of minimum total potential energy is typically used to find the best fitting solution, which results in solving a large number (sometimes hundreds of thousands), of simultaneous linear equations.

- Present the results for this approximate solution.

Therefore, the key FEA concept is the use of piece-wise polynomials to approximate the sought field quantity in the model, which effectively replaces a continuum problem with an infinite number of degrees of freedom (DOF) by a discrete problem with a finite number of DOF (i.e., *finite elements* and *discretization*).

For example, consider how the FEA method works when applied to calculate deflections in a simple beam as shown in Figure 1–2. The beam is clamped at the left end, has a couple of supports in the middle, and is loaded by a couple of transversal forces and a moment. The bottom graph shown in Figure 1–2 represents the unknown true deflection of the beam, which you are trying to determine using the FEA method.

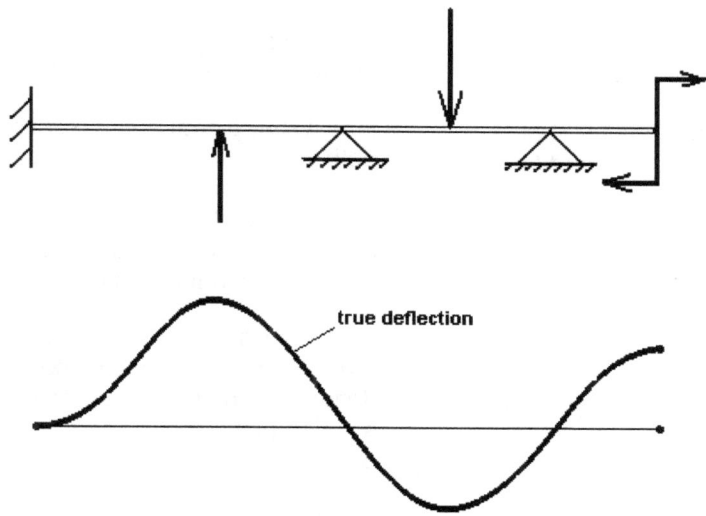

Figure 1–2

The first step in the process (shown in the example in Figure 1–3) is to mesh the beam by breaking it into a collection of shorter pieces (i.e., finite elements) connected at their ends (i.e., the nodes).

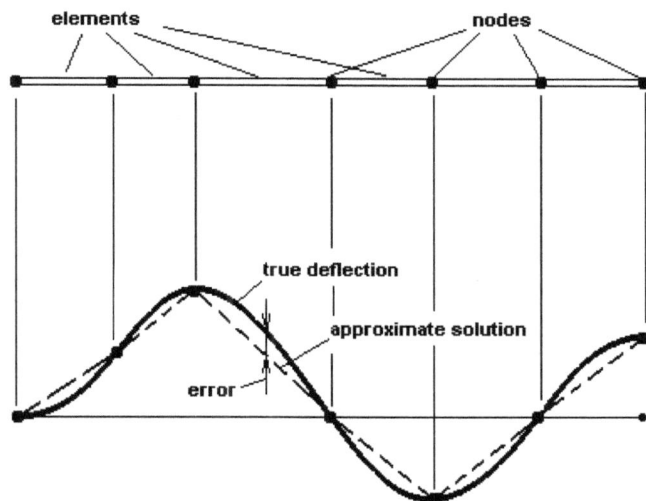

Figure 1–3

Next, the deflection **Y** within each finite element is approximated by a polynomial. In this example, you use linear polynomial $Y = a_0 + a_1X$, which means that deflection within each element is approximated by essentially a straight line.

*Note that sewing local polynomials at the nodes ensures continuity of the global approximation function, and therefore of the FEA solution for the deflection over the entire beam*

Next, the local linear polynomials are sewn together at the nodes, creating a global approximation function in the form of a piece-wise linear polynomial, which is a polyline.

Finally, the global approximation function is best-fit to satisfy both the bending differential equations and beam boundary conditions (loads and constraints). The resulting function (the dashed line shown in Figure 1–3) now represents the FEA solution for the true deflection (the solid line shown in Figure 1–3) in the beam.

It is important to note that your FEA result contains a certain amount of error, which is the deviation between the true deflection (the solid line shown in Figure 1–3) and the FEA solution (the dashed line shown in Figure 1–3), and which is called a *discretization error*.

Any FEA solution is just an approximation, which means it always contains a discretization error. Therefore, in the FEA process, it is critical to know how to estimate, how to control, and how to reduce this unavoidable approximation error to acceptable levels.

# 1.2 FEA Solution Refinement

**Learning Objective**

Understand the concepts of H-refinement and P- refinement.

The process of bringing the FEA approximation error to acceptable levels is typically called *solution refinement*. There are two alternative ways in which an FEA solution can be refined.

The first option involves making the finite elements in the mesh progressively smaller while maintaining the order of polynomials within each element in the same order.

For example, consider the beam shown in Figure 1–3. If you make the finite elements smaller without changing anything else, the approximation error becomes smaller as well, as shown in Figure 1–4.

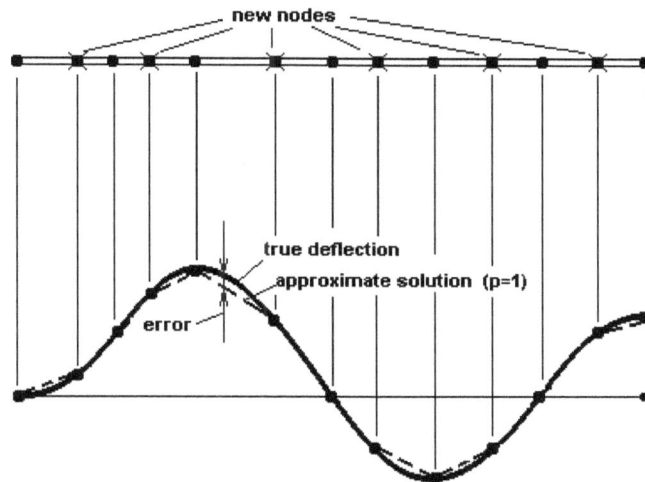

**Figure 1–4**

This approach is called *h-refinement* because the letter *h* in FEA literature typically refers to the size of the finite elements in the mesh. It is also worth noting that h-refinement requires re-meshing the model every time you need a more accurate solution.

The h-refinement approach is used by most FEA software systems that are commercially available today. However, this is not the only available option.

An alternative strategy involves increasing the order of polynomials within the finite elements, without changing the elements' sizes.

Again, consider the example of the beam shown in Figure 1–3. If you use second-degree polynomials $Y = a_0 + a_1X + a_2X^2$ to approximate the deflection within each element, this results in a more accurate solution, without needing to make the finite elements smaller, as shown in Figure 1–5.

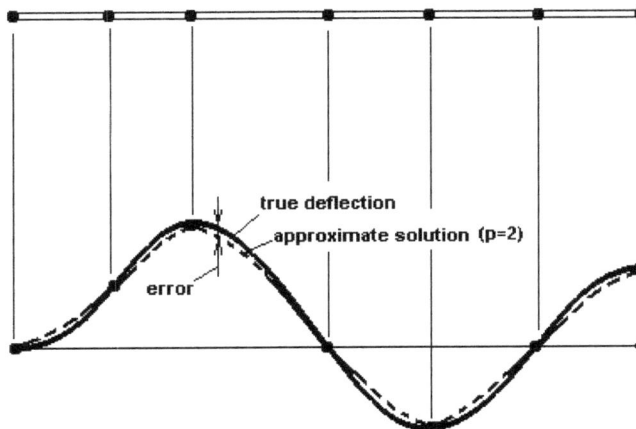

**Figure 1–5**

This approach is called *p-refinement*, because the letter *p* in FEA literature typically refers to the order of polynomials, and the process of progressively increasing the polynomial order is called *polynomial escalation*.

The p-refinement mathematical apparatus has been historically developed much later than the h-refinement. Today, the p-refinement approach is only used by a few commercial FEA software systems, one of which is Creo Simulate.

# 1.3 P-Elements

**Learning Objective**

Understand the advantages of P-elements.

Creo Simulate exclusively uses p-elements and p-refinement technology to ensure the accuracy of the solution. The maximum polynomial order in Creo Simulate can be as high as 9. (The maximum polynomial order in the h-version of FEA is typically 2.)

The advantages of p-technology over h-technology are as follows:

- Solution accuracy can be improved without having to re-mesh the model.

*The rate of convergence refers to how quickly the refinement process converges to the true solution.*

- P-elements use hierarchical polynomials, which permits the use of different polynomial orders in different areas of the model for better efficiency.

- The rate of convergence to the true solution is greater than that of the h-technology.

- High stress gradients, such as in stress concentrators, are simulated extremely well.

- The restrictions on the shape of elements (aspect ratio, skewness, etc.) are less stringent. Therefore a p-mesh always contains fewer elements that an h-mesh.

- P-elements have curvilinear boundaries and tend to approximate CAD geometry very well.

# 1.4  Convergence Methods

**Learning Objective**

Understand solution convergence methods in Creo Simulate.

Convergence in FEA (also called *adaptivity*) is a process of automatic solution refinement to achieve the required accuracy. In other words, the FEA software automatically *adapts* the solution parameters to better fit the true solution.

One of the key advantages of p-refinement over h-refinement is that p-elements permit an adaptive solution improvement without re-meshing the model. Instead, the maximum orders of polynomials used to approximate the solution are increased as needed. The solution process can then be repeated on the same mesh, with the new increased polynomial orders. Such an adaptive step (called *pass* in Creo Simulate) can be repeated until the required accuracy is achieved.

In p-elements, the polynomial orders (called *P-levels* in Creo Simulate) can be assigned independently to each edge, face, or solid in the mesh. Using the convergence algorithm, Creo Simulate can pick P-levels independently for each mesh edge in the model, the goal being to select just the correct P-levels to achieve the required solution accuracy at minimum computational expense.

Multi-Pass Adaptivity (MPA) is the most commonly used convergence method in Creo Simulate. To identify the edges that warrant a P-level increase, the MPA algorithm compares displacements and element strain energies on the current solution pass with the corresponding values on the previous pass. Where the difference is larger than the user-specified percentage (i.e., convergence percentage), the P-level is increased and otherwise left unchanged. This process is repeated until the user-specified convergence percentage for the solution is met. The convergence criteria might include percentages on the default local and global quantities, such as displacement, strain energy, and RMS stress, but could also involve user-defined solution parameters.

The MPA convergence graphs can be visualized once the analysis has finished, as shown in Figure 1–6.

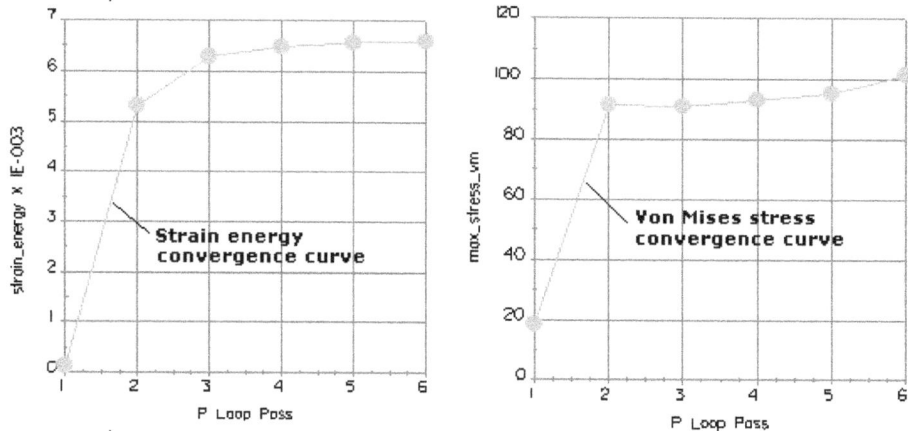

**Figure 1–6**

Since convergence percentage(s) are selected by the user, the MPA algorithm provides the user with maximum control, and is best used if the accuracy of the solution is critical.

The second convergence algorithm in Creo Simulate, called *Single-Pass Adaptivity* (SPA), uses a different theoretical foundation reach an accurate solution.

The SPA algorithm is based on the fact that, although displacements in an FEA solution are continuous between elements, stresses are not, and the magnitude of stress jump at the discontinuity is a good indicator of the solution accuracy (i.e., the greater the stress jump, the less accurate the solution).

In the SPA algorithm, Creo Simulate first calculates the solution for P-level 3, assigned uniformly to all edges, and average stress discontinuities around each element (element error indicators) are computed. The P-levels of edges belonging to elements with large stress jumps are increased. Edges of elements with larger errors receive a higher P-level increase than edges of elements with lower errors. The solution is then repeated, and the result obtained at this point is taken as the final answer. The element error indicators are recomputed to indicate the overall stress accuracy.

Since only two convergence passes are performed in SPA, the computation time is typically much shorter than in MPA.

No convergence graphs are available in the SPA algorithm. Instead, the RMS stress error estimate is printed out to the Creo Simulate report file, as shown in Figure 1–7.

```
RMS Stress Error Estimates:

Load Set          Stress Error   % of Max Prin Str
---------------   ------------   -----------------
LoadSet1          1.26e+01          10.3% of  1.22e+02
```

**Figure 1–7**

The SPA algorithm has been optimized by PTC with the goal of obtaining as good or better result as using the MPA convergence with the default (10%) convergence percentage.

The SPA convergence method does not provide control over the accuracy of the solution. Therefore, it should be reserved for quick design-analysis iterations when solution accuracy is not critical.

The third convergence method in Creo Simulate is called *Quick Check*, and does not perform a convergence process. The model is only run once, with all of the P-levels fixed at 3. The results of a Quick Check should not be trusted. The intention of a Quick Check analysis is to quickly run the model through the solver to detect any potential modeling errors (such as in constraints), before committing to a more lengthy analysis run (such as when using MPA).

# 1.5 Types of Analysis in Creo Simulate

**Learning Objective**

Understand the analysis abilities of Creo Simulate.

Creo Simulate analysis capabilities straddle two physics domains:

- **Structural:** Determines deformations, stresses, and strains in solid bodies caused by external forces, moments, and other types of loading.

- **Thermal:** Determines temperatures and heat fluxes in solid bodies due to heat sources and/or sinks.

The Structural part of Creo Simulate can perform the following types of analysis:

- Static (including nonlinear material models, large displacements, and contact)

- Pre-stress Static

- Buckling

- Fatigue

- Modal (Natural Vibrations)

- Pre-stress Modal

- Dynamic Time Response

- Dynamic Frequency Response

- Dynamic Random Response

- Dynamic Shock Response

The two options for the Thermal analysis are as follows:

- Steady State Thermal analysis

- Transient Thermal analysis

The models in Creo Simulate can be analyzed in 3D formulations (purely solids, or combinations of solids, shells, and beams) or 2D formulations (plane stress, plane strain, or axisymmetric).

# 1.6 FEA Process

**Learning Objective**

Understand the steps involved in a Creo Simulate analysis.

A typical FEA analysis process in Creo Simulate consists of three principle steps, as shown in Figure 1–8:

- **Pre-processing:** All input data for the analysis is prepared, such as material properties, loads, and constraints.

- **Solution:** The convergence type and criteria are specified and the analysis computation is performed.

- **Post-processing:** The analysis results are reviewed and verified. A report is prepared.

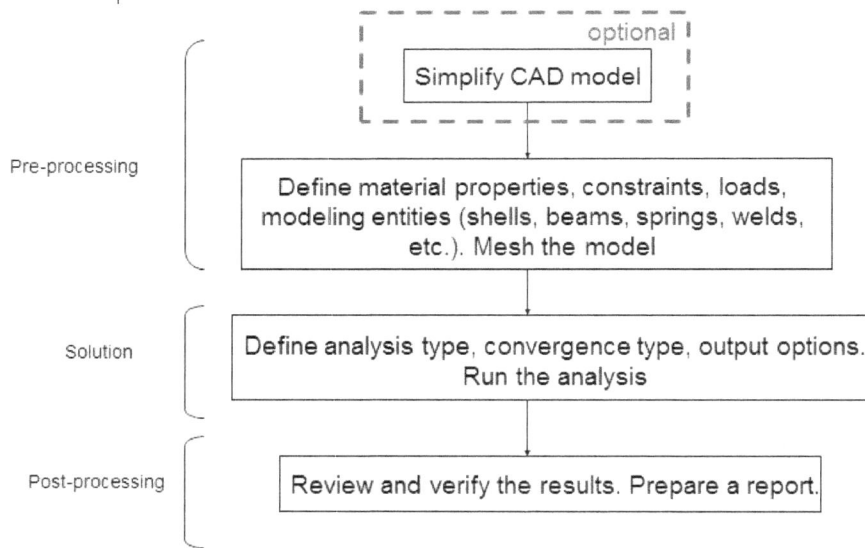

**Figure 1–8**

The CAD model simplification step is optional. It might not be needed, depending on the complexity of the model.

# 1.7 CAD Model Preparation

**Learning Objective**

Learn the recommendations for CAD model preparation.

A CAD model is developed to provide detailed information for manufacturing. All of the required information related to fillets, rounds, holes, and threads must be included. Processing steps and surface finishes are indicated and dimensions are fully specified.

An FEA model is developed to determine model behavior under a specific set of loading and boundary conditions. To analyze a model effectively, an FEA model is often different from a model developed for manufacturing. The symmetry of a model can often be used. Minor features, such as rounds, fillets, chamfers, and holes, can often be ignored unless they have a large effect on the result. Therefore, the general recommendation is to use the simplest model possible that is going to yield reliable results at the lowest computational time and cost.

In the example shown in Figure 1–9, the area of interest is the stress in the weld between two pipes due to high pressure. The FEA model within the component is shown on the right. In this case, the symmetry of the component (1/2 of the component) is used for the FEA model. The minor rounds, fillets, chamfers, and holes are ignored. The CAD model prepared for FEA would be different if the area of interest was the stress at the intersection of lips and pipes.

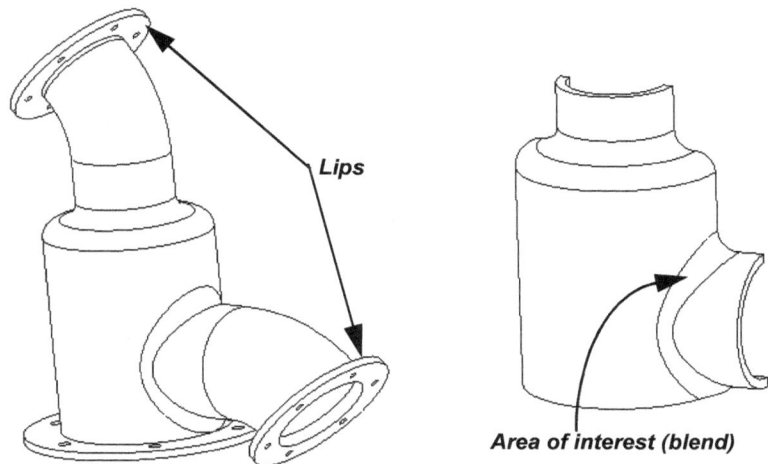

*Lips*

*Area of interest (blend)*

**Figure 1–9**

# 1.8 Creo Simulate Modes of Operation

**Learning Objective**

Understand the Creo Simulate modes of operation.

Creo Simulate can operate in the following modes:

- **Integrated:** The simulation is fully integrated within the Creo Parametric design process (i.e., the models can be analyzed without ever leaving the Creo Parametric user interface). This is the most common way to use Creo Simulate.

- **Standalone:** Enables the loading of CAD models directly into Creo Simulate, without first loading Creo Parametric. This is useful if models originating from different software than Creo Parametric need to be analyzed.

- **Independent:** Uses the legacy MECHANICA interface (predecessor to Pro/MECHANICA and Creo Simulate, circa 1986).

- **FEM:** Provides pre- and post-processing capabilities only. The model has to be exported to a neutral fuile format and then solved by a 3rd party FEA solver (ANSYS, NASTRAN, etc.). H-elements meshing is used.

- **Simulate Lite:** Limited model size of up to 200 surfaces and also has a limited user interface. Does not require a Simulate license.

This training guide focuses on the Integrated mode, which provides the most streamlined approach to part or assembly simulation and optimization within the Creo environment.

# Chapter 2

## Basic Creo Simulate Modeling

This chapter contains the following topics:

- **Launching Creo Simulate**
- **Modeling Steps**
- **Analysis**
- **Results**

# 2.1 Launching Creo Simulate

**Learning Objectives**

✓ Understand the Creo Simulate analysis steps and options.

✓ Launch Creo Simulate from Creo Parametric.

✓ Learn to use the Creo Simulate user interface.

The Finite element analysis process contains three different components: pre-processing, analysis, and post-processing. Each component contains a number of steps, as shown in Figure 2–1.

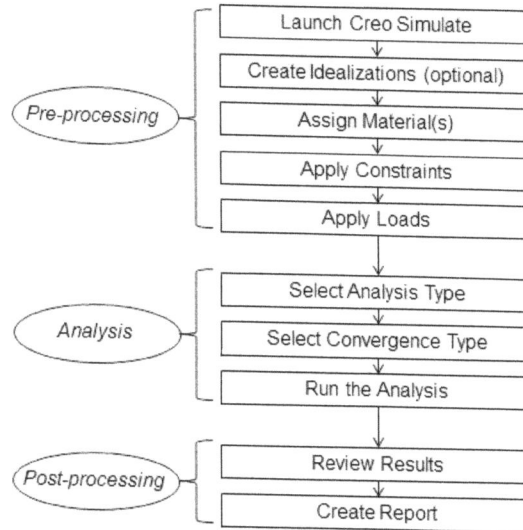

Figure 2–1

Each step in the structural analysis process requires a selection of the following options.

| Model Analysis Steps | Creo Simulate Structure Options | |
|---|---|---|
| Model Type | 3D<br>Plane Stress<br>Axisymmetric | Plane Strain<br>2D |

| Element Type | Shell | Springs |
| --- | --- | --- |
| | Beams | Mass |
| | Solid | |
| Analysis Methods | Static | Dynamic Time |
| | Modal | Dynamic Frequency |
| | Buckling | Dynamic Random |
| | Prestress modal | Dynamic Shock |
| | Prestress static | Fatigue |
| Convergence Methods | Multi-Pass Adaptive | Quick Check |
| | Single-Pass Adaptive | |
| Design Studies | Standard | Sensitivity |
| | Optimization | |

To launch Creo Simulate in Integrated mode, open the model in Creo Parametric, select the *Applications* tab, and click (Simulate). The Creo Simulate environment opens, the Ribbon appearance changes as shown in Figure 2–2, and a coordinate system labeled **WCS** is automatically added to the model.

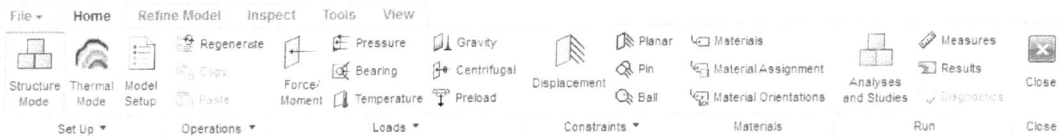

**Figure 2–2**

By default, Creo Simulate opens in Structure mode. To switch to Thermal mode if needed, click (Thermal Mode).

## Structure Ribbon

The Structure mode ribbon contains five tabs: *Home*, *Refine Model*, *Inspect*, *Tools*, and *View*.

The *Home* tab (shown in Figure 2–2) contains all of the most frequently used analysis tools, such as model setup, loads, constraints, analysis setup, and access to the analysis results.

The *Refine Model* tab contains tools, such as idealizations, connections, regions, and meshing as shown in Figure 2–3.

**Figure 2–3**

The *Inspect*, *Tools*, and *View* tabs contain common Creo tools, such as measurements, layers, views, appearances, etc.

# 2.2 Modeling Steps

**Learning Objectives**

✓ Understand how to define the model type.

✓ Learn how to create idealizations.

✓ Learn how to apply material.

✓ Learn how to apply constraints.

✓ Understand how to apply loads.

✓ Understand how to mesh the model.

✓ Understand how to create a design study.

## Defining Model Type

By default, Creo Simulate assumes that the model you want to analyze is 3D. To change the analysis model type to 2D, click

☐ (Model Setup) and click  Advanced <<  to open the Model Setup dialog box as shown in Figure 2–4.

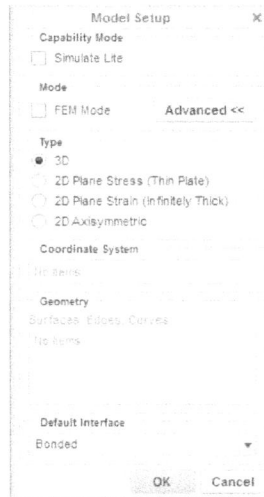

Figure 2–4

## Creating Idealizations

Idealizations are tools that simplify your FEA model, resulting in a faster analysis. Idealizations are optional. If your model is not overly complex and solves in a reasonable time, Idealizations might not be needed.

The following types of Idealizations are available in Creo Simulate, as shown in Figure 2–5:

- Beams

- Springs

- Masses

- Shells

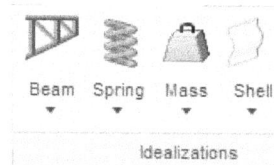

**Figure 2–5**

## Applying Material

In Creo Simulate, applying a material to your analysis model must be done in two steps:

- Import material definition into the model.

- Assign the imported material to your part.

If a material has already been applied to your part in Creo Parametric, it is automatically imported into the Creo Simulate model as well, but not assigned.

*The **Material Orientation** option only applies to non-isotropic materials, such as laminates, etc.*

To assign the imported material, click  (Material Assignment) to open the Material Assignment dialog box as shown in Figure 2–6. Select **References**, select a material, and click

OK to close the dialog box.

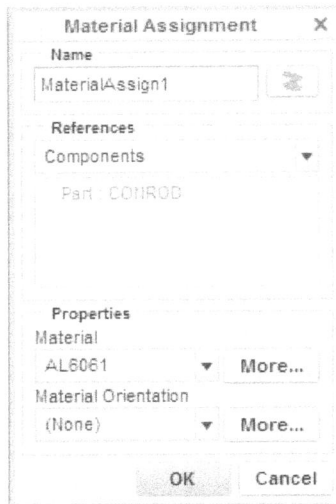

**Figure 2–6**

If a material has not been applied in the Creo Parametric environment, you must import a material definition into your model from within the Creo Simulate environment.

To import a material definition, click  (Materials) to open the Materials dialog box as shown in Figure 2–7. Select a material in

the library (on the left in the dialog box) and click ▶▶ to import it into the model. If needed, the material properties can be viewed and/or edited in the Materials dialog box.

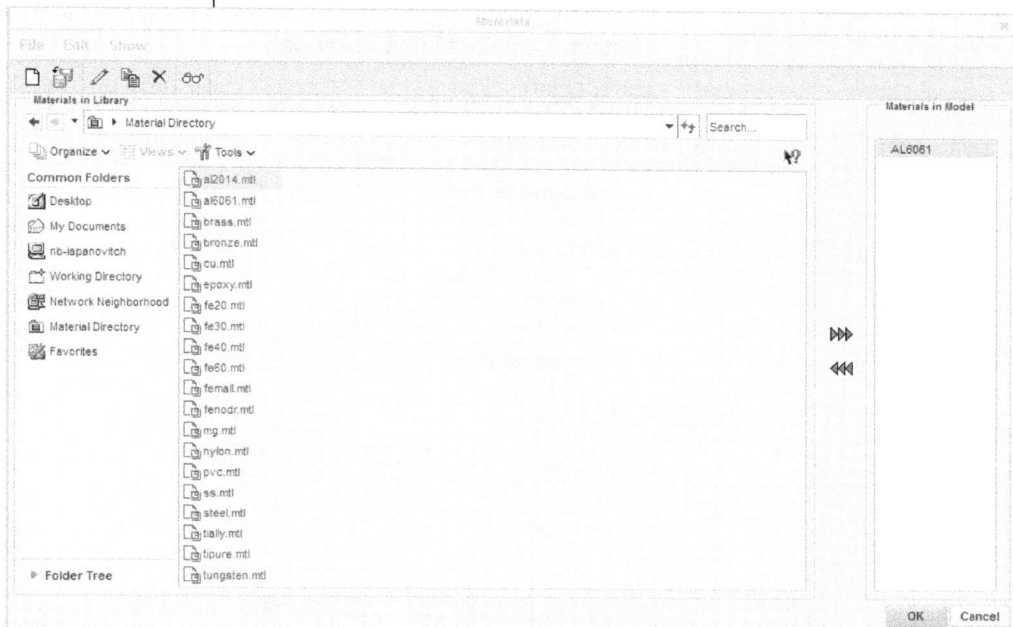

**Figure 2–7**

# Applying Constraints

Constraints simulate supports and other boundary conditions in your model. Constraints can be applied to the part's surfaces, edges/
curves, or points.

The following types of Constraints are available in Creo Simulate, as shown in Figure 2–8:

• Displacement

• Planar

• Pin

• Ball

• Symmetry

**Figure 2–8**

# Applying Loads

Loads in your analysis are intended to simulate the actual loading conditions in your model.

The following types of Loads are available in Creo Simulate, as shown in Figure 2–9:

- Force/Moment

- Pressure

- Bearing

- Temperature

- Gravity

- Centrifugal

- Preload

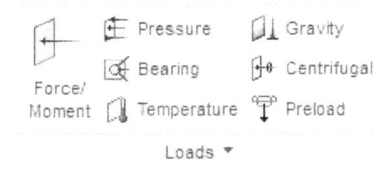

**Figure 2–9**

The type of geometry you can apply a Load to depends on the type of load selected. For example, Force/Moment loads can applied to surfaces, edges/curves, or points, while Pressure or Bearing loads can only be applied to surfaces.

# Meshing the Model

Meshing the model before running the analysis is optional in Creo Simulate. If not pre-meshed, the model is automatically meshed during the analysis computation.

However, pre-meshing the model helps to indicate whether Creo Simulate can mesh your model successfully, and to roughly estimate the analysis runtime based on the number of elements in the mesh.

To mesh the model before the analysis, click  (AutoGEM) in the *Refine Model* tab to open the AutoGEM dialog box, as shown in Figure 2–10.

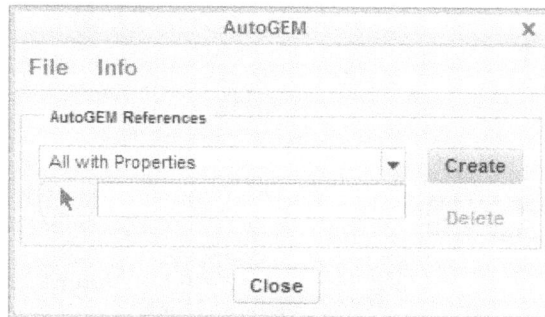

**Figure 2–10**

The options in the References drop-down list are as follows:

*   **Volume:** Creates Solid mesh for selected volumes.

*   **Surface:** Creates Shell mesh for selected surfaces.

*   **Curves:** Creates Beam mesh for selected curves.

*   **All with Properties:** An all-in-one option, which automatically meshes all volumes with materials assigned, all surfaces with shell properties assigned, and all curves with beam properties assigned. This option is used if mesh is created during the analysis run.

In the AutoGEM dialog box, you can review, save, and highlight areas in which the mesh fails.

# 2.3  Analysis

**Learning Objectives**

Create a structural analysis.

Learn how to select a convergence method.

**Analysis Types**

Creo Simulate can perform several types of structural analysis on a model. You select an analysis type based on the type of simulation that you want to perform. Click ⬜ (Analyses and Design Studies) and select the appropriate option in the **File** menu, as shown in Figure 2–11.

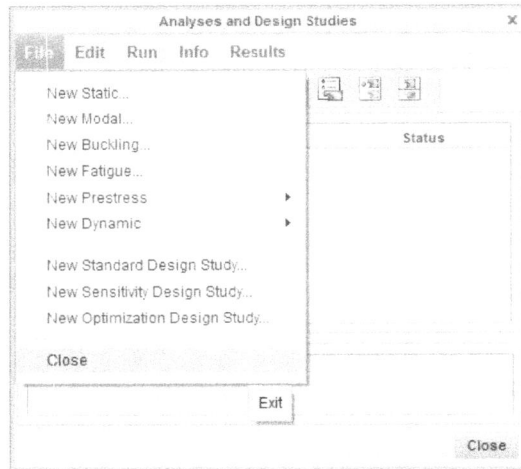

**Figure 2–11**

The types of structural analysis available in the Analyses and Design Studies dialog box are as follows:

| Analysis Type | Description |
|---|---|
| **New Static** | Static analyses calculate the stresses and deformations in the model, that are caused by static loads. |
| **New Modal** | Modal analyses calculate the mode shapes (i.e., characteristic deformed shapes of natural frequencies) and natural frequencies of a model. |

| | |
|---|---|
| **New Buckling** | Buckling analyses calculate the Buckling Load Factor (BLF), a magnification factor of the applied load that causes critical buckling to occur. When applying a load of 1 unit to the model, the BLF equals the critical buckling load. |
| **New Fatigue** | Fatigue analyses calculate the effect of repeating or varying loads on a model. |
| **New Prestress** | • **Static:** Prestress Static analyses calculate the effect of a prestressed structure on a model's stresses, strains, and deformations.<br>• **Modal:** Prestress Modal analyses use results from static analyses to provide specific data for natural frequencies and modes. |
| **New Dynamic** | • **Time:** Dynamic Time analyses calculate displacements, velocities, accelerations, and stresses in response to a load that varies with time.<br>• **Frequency:** Dynamic Frequency analyses determine the response of a system that is subjected to cyclical excitation (a frequency dependent input).<br>• **Random:** Dynamic Random analyses calculate the power spectral density (PSD) and the root mean square (RMS) values of displacements, velocities, accelerations, and stresses in a model subjected to a random loading.<br>• **Shock:** Dynamic Shock analyses calculate the peak values of displacement and stresses in a model in response to a base excitation defined by a response spectrum curve. This type of analysis subjects a model to an earthquake-like motion. |

## Convergence Methods

The three analysis convergence options in Creo Simulate are as follows:

| Option | Description | Uses |
|---|---|---|
| **Quick Check** | Runs a model through the solver to detect errors (e.g., in the constraints). The model is only run once for a single fixed low polynomial order.<br><br>If an error occurs, Creo Simulate displays an error message prompting you with: *Run completed with a fatal error.* | • Use to determine whether an analysis has been set up correctly.<br>• Use to generate proper elements.<br>• Use to check problem areas in the model. |

| Single Pass Adaptive | Runs a model through the solver at a low polynomial order (default 3), evaluates the accuracy of the solution, and modifies the p-element values accordingly. The model is run through the solver a second time with the new p-element values. This provides reasonable results in a short computation time. | • Use for preliminary calculations.<br>• Use when system resources are low. |
|---|---|---|
| Multi-Pass Adaptive | Runs a model through the solver, with the order of unconverged elements being increased with each run. The runs continue until the solution converges or the maximum order is reached (default 6 and maximum 9). Base your final decisions on the results obtained using this method. | • Use for accurate analysis.<br>• Use when you have enough time and system resources. |

# Design Studies

Design studies enable you to find better design alternatives using simulation and analysis tools. Creo Simulate can run the following three types of design studies.

| Study | Description |
|---|---|
| Standard | This study calculates the results for a standard analysis (e.g., Static analysis) for an alternative set of dimensions. Analogous to running a single *what if* scenario. |
| Sensitivity | This study calculates the results for several alternative sets of dimensions within a user-specified range. Analogous to running multiple *what if* scenarios. |
| Optimization | This study adjusts a model's parameters to meet a specified goal or to test the feasibility of a design. For this study, you assign a goal (e.g., minimum mass of the model) and one or more Creo Parametric dimensions (design variables), which can vary over assigned ranges. |

# 2.4 Results

**Learning Objectives**

Understand the files and directories created by Creo Simulate.

Understand the concepts of result verification.

Understand how to visualize analysis results.

## Files and Directories

Creo Simulate generates many output files that are written to an automatically created directory. The name of the result directory is the same as that of the analysis study. By default, the result directory is placed in the Creo working directory, which can be changed when you set up an analysis.

Create Simulate solver also creates many temporary files, which are only needed when the solver is running, and which are automatically deleted on completion of the analysis run. The default location for the temporary files is in the Creo working directory, which can also be changed when you set up an analysis.

The typical files created by Creo Simulate in the result directory are as follows. The names *model*, *study*, and *filename* represent your specified names.

| File Type | File/Directory Name | Description |
|---|---|---|
| Model Files | *model*.mdb | The .MDB file contains the last-saved model database. |
| Solver File | */study/study*.mdb | The engine file contains the entire model database from the time a design study is started. |

| Solver Output Files | /study/study.cnv<br>/study/study.hst<br>/study/study.res<br>/study/study.rpt<br>/study/study.ro1 | The .CNV file contains convergence information. The .HST file is a backup file that updates the model during optimization. The .RES file is a measure at each pass. The .RPT file is an output report that contains information about a run including measure values and warning messages. The .RO1 file contains information about the resultant reaction of loads applied to the model. |
|---|---|---|
| Exchange Files | filename.dxf<br>filename.igs | The exchange files are in formats that are used for the import or export of geometry information. |
| Temporary Files | /study.tmp/*.tmp<br>/study.tmp/*.bas | Temporary files contain the data that is needed to solve analyses. They are deleted automatically on completion of the design. |
| Results Files | filename.rwd | The .RWD files store your Result Window plot window for later use. |
| AutoGEM Files | model.agm | The .AGM files store information about the most recent AutoGEM operation. |
| AutoMesh Files | modelname.mmp<br>modelname.mma | This file stores a mesh database. The system allocates an .MMP extension to a part model mesh file and an .MMA extension to an assembly model. |

# Result Verification

Creo Simulate can produce several types of results to help determine the validity and soundness of your model. Take the following considerations into account when interpreting your results.

| Result | Description |
|---|---|
| **Reaction Verification** | The resultant reaction of loads applied to the model is automatically generated in the .RO1 file. To satisfy the equilibrium criteria, the resultant reaction must equal the resultant loads applied to the model. |
| **Model Integrity** | Model integrity determines the integrity of your model by checking the model entities (i.e., material properties, constraints, loads, and unit systems), geometry, and part accuracy before starting the run. You can also use the **Check Model** option to check for errors in the model. If the model fails the check, the model entities were probably incorrectly defined. |

| Displacement Animation | Displacement animation verifies whether your model is deflecting correctly and that your constraints are correct. The animation simulates the effect of real-world conditions on the model and enables you to compare them to the applied boundary conditions. |
|---|---|
| Shape Animation | Shape animation (performed after a sensitivity or optimization study) takes the geometry through the entire range of relevant parameters. This ensures that no unexpected regeneration failures occur and that the design intent is sound. |
| Computational Solution Quality | Computational solution quality is the percentage of error that the system calculates on the maximum principle stress. A low percentage indicates that the model is sound. This error estimate can be found in the .RPT file in the analysis directory. |
| Convergence Criteria | Provides an idea of the accuracy of your results. Convergence results with specific limits set by the user can be found in the .RPT file. You can create graphs based on predefined measures for strain energy and displacement. |

## Result Visualization

Creo Simulate enables you to visualize many different types of results:

- Displacements

- Stresses

- Strains

- Reactions

- Strain Energy

- P-Levels

The results can be displayed as a fringe plot or as a graph along an edge or curve. Fringe plots can be animated for better understanding of the model deformation.

The results are visualized and manipulated in the Creo Simulate Results environment. An overview of the icons and options available in the Creo Simulate Environment is shown in Figure 2–12.

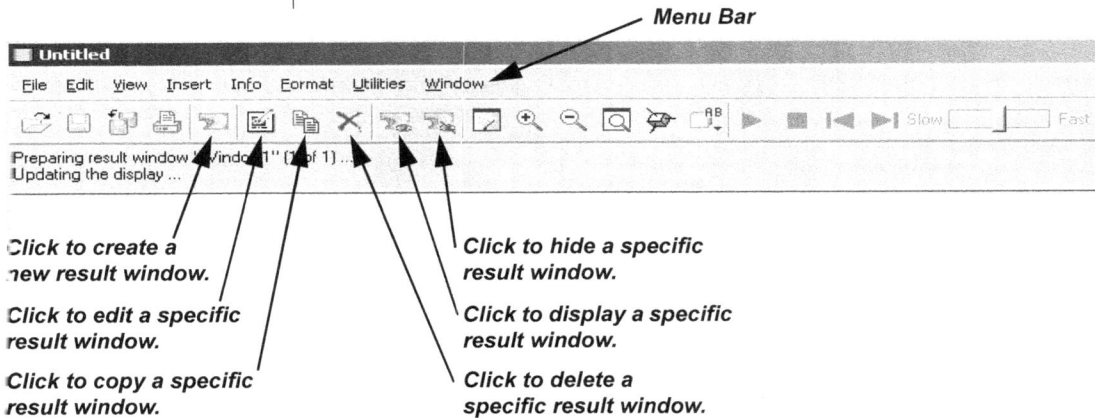

**Figure 2–12**

You can enter the Creo Simulate Results environment using one of the following options:

- Click ⬜ in the Analyses and Design Studies dialog box.

- Click ⬜ in the Creo Simulate interface, in the Home tab.

- Click ⬜ in the Creo Parametric interface, in the *Applications* tab. This options enables you to open the Creo Simulate results without having to open a corresponding Creo Simulate model first.

| Practice 2a | # Static Stress Analysis of a Bracket |
|---|---|

**Learning Objectives**

☑ Specify a 3D model type.

☑ Mesh the model.

☑ Set the loads, constraints, and material properties.

☑ Check the validity of the model.

☑ Set up and run a Quick Check analysis.

☑ Set up and run a Multi-Pass Adaptive analysis.

☑ Display the results.

☑ Animate and create sections through the part.

In this practice, you will mesh, set up, and run a static stress analysis on a simple solid bracket model. The model is shown in Figure 2–13.

**Figure 2–13**

## Modeling Tasks

In the following tasks, you will create the simulation entities needed to analyze your model.

## Task 1 - Open the solid_bracket_1 part in Creo Parametric.

1. Open **solid_bracket_1.prt**. The part displays as shown in Figure 2–14.

*The model has been defeatured. The rounds on the middle hole and bolt holes have been removed.*

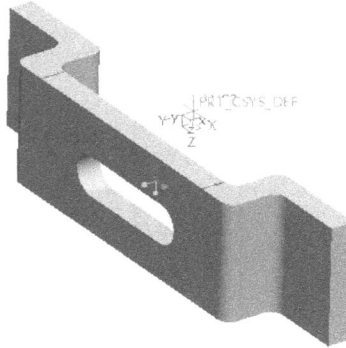

Figure 2–14

2. Select **File>Prepare>Model Properties** to check your unit system. The unit system for this practice is **mmNs**.

## Task 2 - Launch Creo Simulate.

1. Select **Applications>Simulate** to launch the Creo Simulate environment.

*WCS represents the World Cartesian System (the origin is at 0,0,0).*

2. Verify that ⬚ (Structure Mode) is active. The model displays as shown in Figure 2–15. Verify that the datum coordinate system visibility is toggled on. Note that the WCS coordinate system displays in the model window.

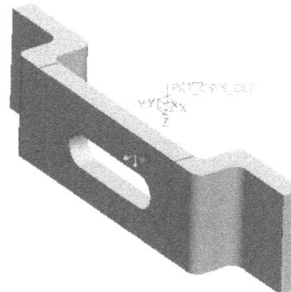

Figure 2–15

## Task 3 - Define the model type.

1. In the *Home* tab, select **Model Setup** and click Advanced << to expand the Model Setup dialog box.

2. In the Model Setup dialog box, verify that the **3D** option is selected and click OK .

## Task 4 - Mesh the bracket part.

In this task, you will mesh the bracket, which enables you to check whether Creo Simulate can mesh your model before analysis. Using this option before applying simulation entities (e.g., loads or constraints) highlights the areas (geometry) where the mesh has failed in your model. This option speeds up the analysis run time.

1. Select the *Refine Model* tab and expand the AutoGEM flyout and select **Settings**, as shown in Figure 2–16.

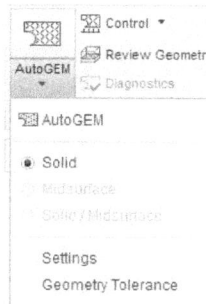

**Figure 2–16**

2. The AutoGEM Settings dialog box opens as shown in Figure 2–17.

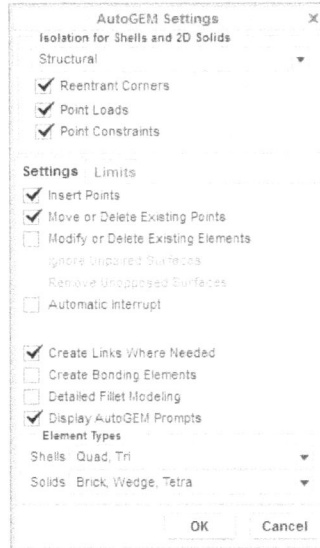

**Figure 2–17**

3. Expand the Solids drop-down list and verify that **Brick, Wedge, Tetra** is selected.

4. Select the *Limits* tab, as shown in Figure 2–18.

**Figure 2–18**

5.  In the AutoGEM Settings dialog box, four types of settings display in *Limits* tab: **Edge Angles**, **Face Angles**, **Edge Turn**, and **Aspect Ratio**.

    *   The allowable edge angles (**Edge Max** and **Edge Min**) between the edges of an element are shown in Figure 2–19.

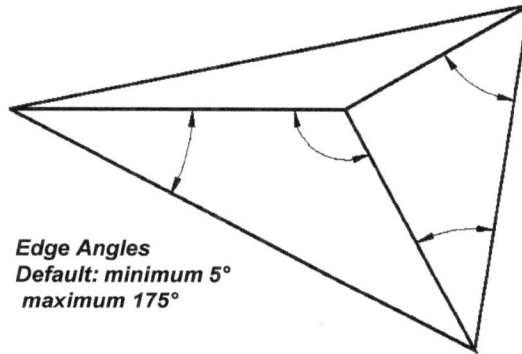

**Edge Angles**
**Default: minimum 5°**
**maximum 175°**

**Figure 2–19**

    *   The allowable face angles (**Face Max** and **Face Min**) between the faces of an element are shown in Figure 2–20.

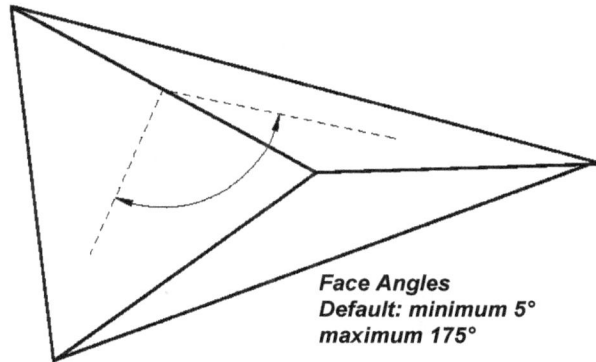

**Face Angles**
**Default: minimum 5°**
**maximum 175°**

**Figure 2–20**

*The maximum allowable Edge Turn enables you to create elements that better conform to the shape of the geometry on circles and cylinders.*

- The maximum allowable edge turns (**Max Edge Turn**) between 45° and 95° are shown in Figure 2–21. This limit has a valid range from 1° to 100°.

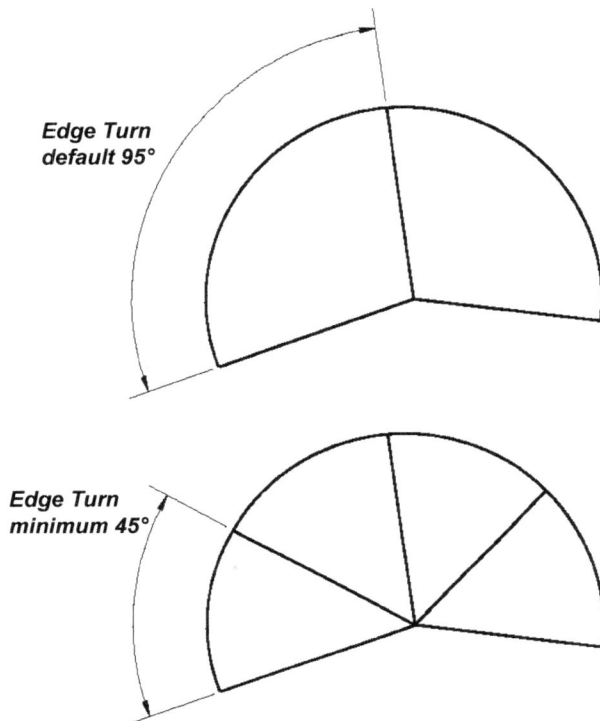

**Edge Turn default 95°**

**Edge Turn minimum 45°**

**Figure 2–21**

- The maximum allowable aspect ratio (**Max Aspect Ratio**), which is the ratio of length to width of an element, is shown in Figure 2–22.

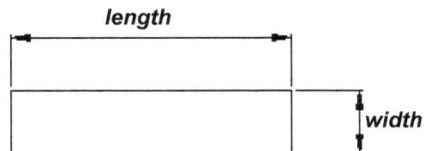

*length*

*width*

**Figure 2–22**

6. Click OK to close the AutoGEM Settings dialog box.

7. Click ⬚ . The AutoGEM dialog box opens as shown in Figure 2–23.

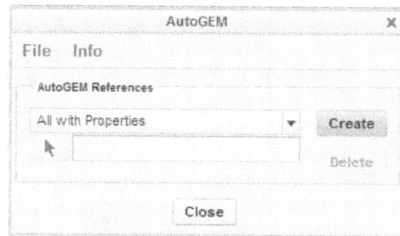

**Figure 2–23**

8. Expand the AutoGEM References drop-down list and select **Volume**.

9. Click ⬚ and select the entire model by drawing a box around it.

10. In the Surface Selection box, click **OK** or click the middle mouse button.

11. Click **Create** .

After you click **Create** , AutoGEM starts to pre-process the model and display these functions in the Creo message window. When initial precessing is finished, AutoGEM creates and optimizes elements. The AutoGEM optimization process reduces the number of elements by 50% on average. If any of these functions (e.g., pre-processing or creating elements) takes more than 30 seconds, the system displays a message indicating their progress. The message window for **solid_bracket_1** is shown in Figure 2–24.

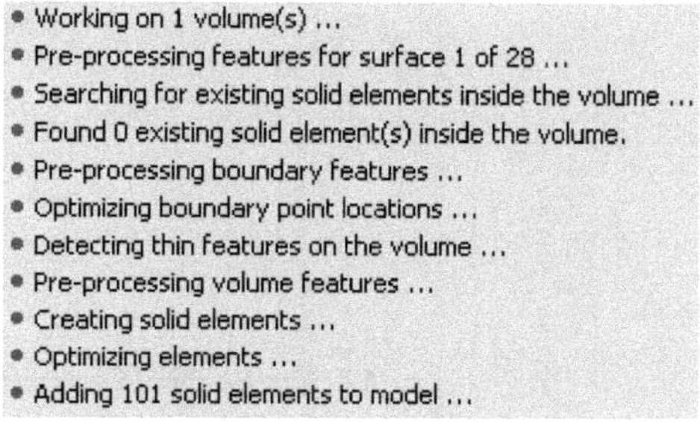

**Figure 2–24**

After a short time, the AutoGEM Summary and the Diagnostics dialog boxes open as shown in Figure 2–25.

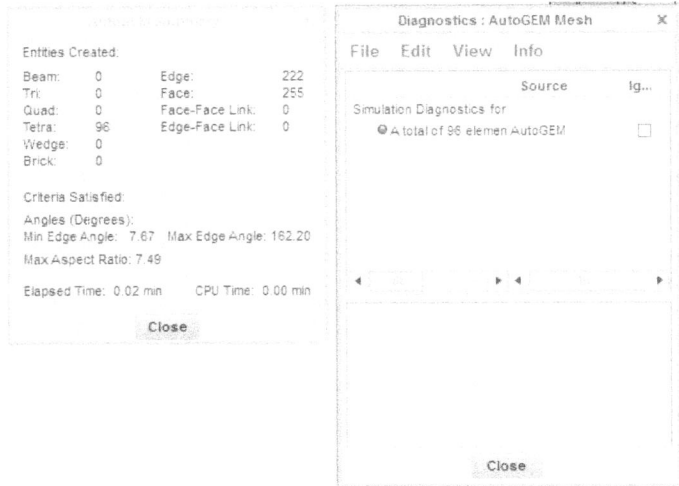

Entities Created:

| | | | |
|---|---|---|---|
| Beam: | 0 | Edge: | 222 |
| Tri: | 0 | Face: | 255 |
| Quad: | 0 | Face-Face Link: | 0 |
| Tetra: | 96 | Edge-Face Link: | 0 |
| Wedge: | 0 | | |
| Brick: | 0 | | |

Criteria Satisfied:

Angles (Degrees):
Min Edge Angle: 7.67   Max Edge Angle: 162.20

Max Aspect Ratio: 7.49

Elapsed Time: 0.02 min       CPU Time: 0.00 min

Close

Diagnostics : AutoGEM Mesh      X

File   Edit   View   Info

Source          Ig...

Simulation Diagnostics for

A total of 96 elemen AutoGEM       ☐

Close

**Figure 2–25**

Examine the information in the boxes. For example, note that the system has discretized the volume into approximately 96 tetrahedron solid elements and that the CPU time is 0.02 minutes.

12. Close both the AutoGEM Summary and Diagnostics boxes, but do not close the AutoGEM dialog box yet. The model displays as shown in Figure 2–26.

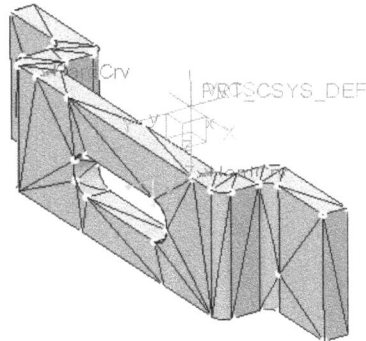

**Figure 2–26**

13. Click ⬚ (Simulation Display) in the floating toolbar. The Simulation Display dialog box opens.

The **Shrink Elements** option does not affect the analysis. It is a visualization tool that helps to display the mesh clearly.

14. Select the *Mesh* tab. In the *Mesh Display* area, select the **Shrink Elements** option and increase the shrinkage value to 20% as shown in Figure 2–27.

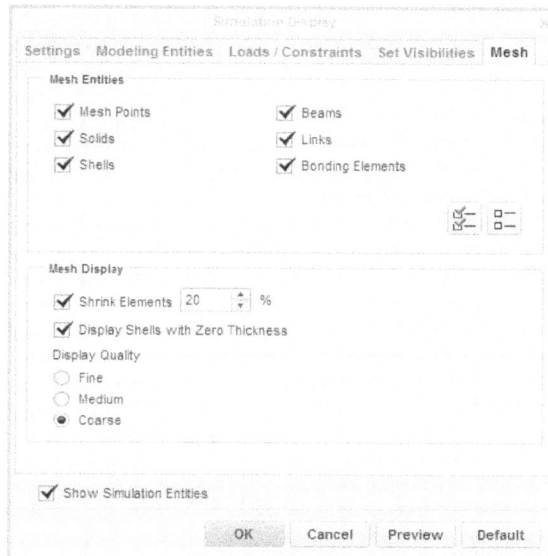

**Figure 2–27**

15. Click OK to close the Simulation Display dialog box. The model displays as shown in Figure 2–28. Spin the model and review the elements in various areas of the model.

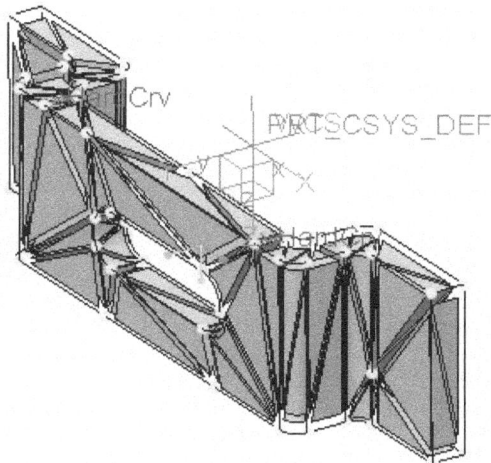

**Figure 2–28**

16. Click `Close` to close the AutoGEM dialog box and the warning shown in Figure 2–29 will display.

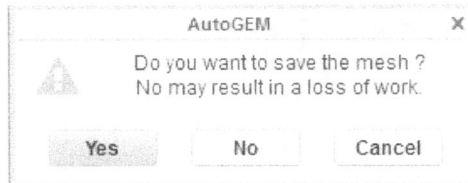

**Figure 2–29**

17. Click `Yes` to save the mesh.

The following three types of solid elements are commonly used:

| Element | Description | Example |
|---------|-------------|---------|
| **Hexahedron (brick)** | Brick has 12 edges, 8 nodes, and 6 quad faces. |  |
| **Pentahedron (wedge)** | Wedge has 9 edges, 6 nodes, 2 triangular faces, and 3 quad faces. |  |
| **Tetrahedron (Tetra)** | Tetra has 6 edges, 4 nodes, and 4 triangular faces. |  |

## Task 5 - Apply loads to the surface of the model.

In this task, you will apply loads to the surface of the model shown in Figure 2–30 to simulate the bracket loading. This task assumes that the bracket carries a load of 140kg (approx.) at 45° to vertical.

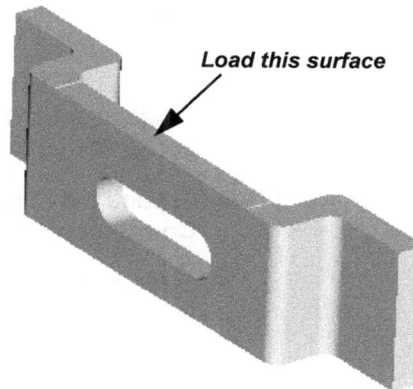

Load this surface

**Figure 2–30**

1. In the Home tab, click ⊞ . The Force/Moment Load dialog box opens as shown in Figure 2–31.

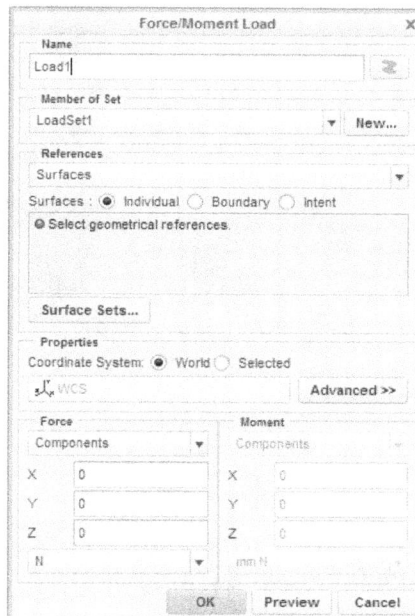

**Figure 2–31**

2. In the *Name* field, enter **surf_load**. For *Member of Set* accept the default **LoadSet1** option.

3. Select the surface shown in Figure 2–32 (select the surface region between the two lines shown in Figure 2–32).

4. In the Force/Moment Load dialog box, note that the loads are defined relative to the WCS coordinate system, as indicated in the *Properties* area.

5. Click ⟨ Advanced << ⟩ to display the distribution and spatial variation options. Expand the Distribution drop-down lists and accept the default options.

6. Expand the Force drop-down list and accept the default **Components** option.

7. In the *Force* area, in the *Y* field, enter **1000**.

8. In the *Force* area, in the *Z* field, enter **1000**.

9. Click ⟨ Preview ⟩ to display the applied load in the model.

10. Click ⟨ OK ⟩ to finish applying the load to the solid model. The load displays as shown in Figure 2–32.

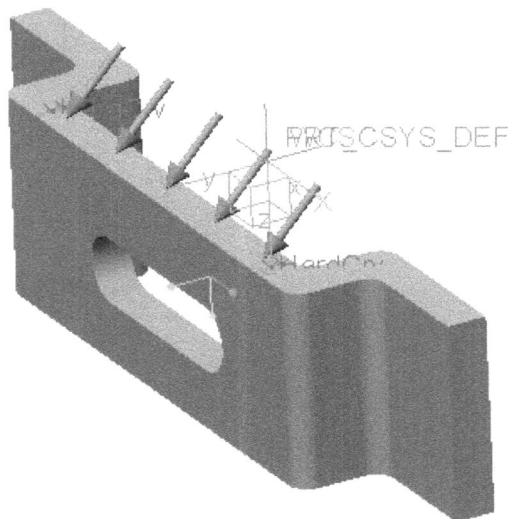

**Figure 2–32**

*Explore the different options in the Simulation Display dialog box.*

11. Click ⟨icon⟩ to open the Simulation Display dialog box.

12. In the *Settings* tab, in the Load/Constraint Display area, select the **Values** option.

13. Click [ OK ] to close the Simulation Display dialog box. The model displays as shown in Figure 2–33.

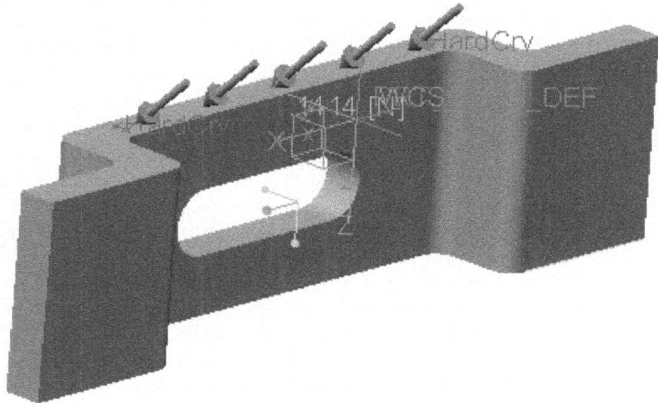

Figure 2–33

## Task 6 - Apply constraints to the surfaces of the model.

In this task, you will apply constraints to the entire end surfaces of the solid model, as shown in Figure 2–34, assuming that the load on the bracket is supported at the bracket flanges.

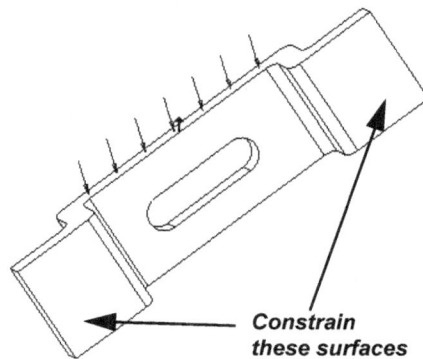

*Constrain these surfaces*

Figure 2–34

1. In the *Home* tab, click 📄. The Constraint dialog box opens as shown in Figure 2–35.

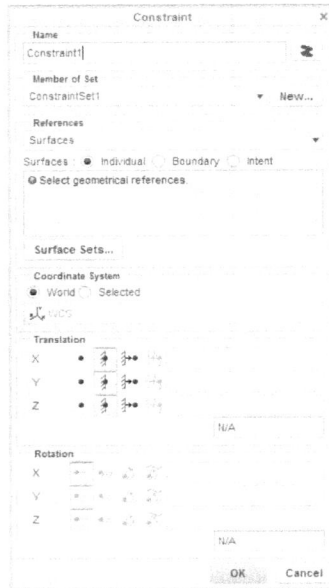

**Figure 2–35**

2. In the *Name* field, enter **fixed_faces**. For *Member of Set*, select the **ConstraintSet1** option.

3. Select the surfaces shown in Figure 2–34 (hold down <Ctrl> to select both surfaces).

4. The default coordinate system is WCS, as indicated in the Coordinate System area in the Constraint dialog box. Keep WCS as the coordinate system to be used.

*Solid element nodes only have three translational degrees of freedom. The rotation of a node cannot be specified or calculated.*

5. Six possible constraints are available at the bottom of the Constraint dialog box: three translations and three rotations. The icons for these constraints are as follows. Accept the default options for all of the translation and rotation directions.

| Translation Icons | Rotation Icons | Description |
|---|---|---|
| • | •— | Enables the constrained feature to move or rotate freely in the related direction. |
| ⨎ | •⁊⁊⁊ | Fixes the constrained feature so that it cannot move or rotate in the related direction. |

| | | Forces the constrained feature to move or rotate in the related direction by a specified amount. |
|---|---|---|

6. Click OK to finish applying the constraints. The model displays as shown in Figure 2–36.

*Depending on the orientation of your model, the load vectors might vary.*

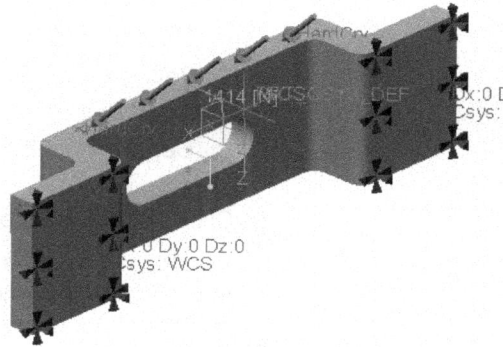

**Figure 2–36**

## Task 7 - Apply the material.

In this task, you will select the material for the solid bracket.

1. In the *Home* tab, click . The Materials dialog box opens as shown in Figure 2–37.

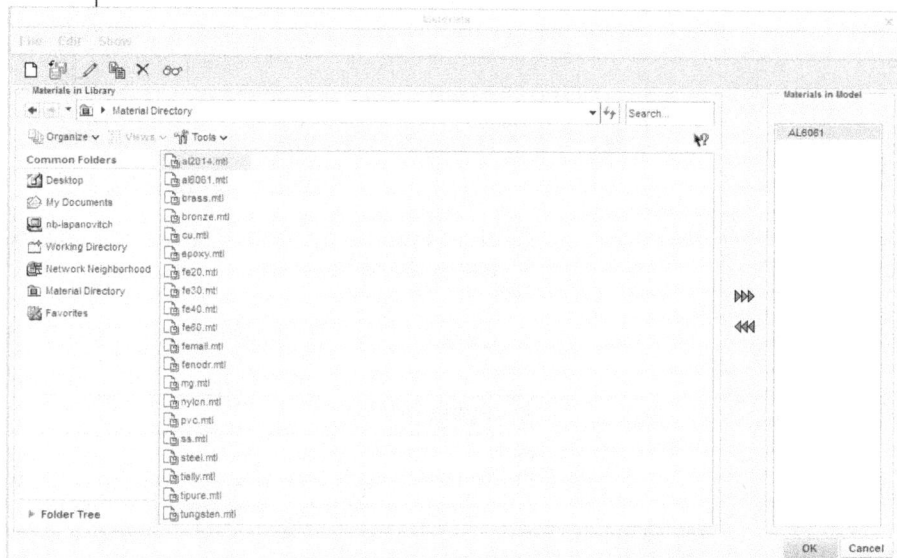

**Figure 2–37**

*The model's material should be as stated.*

2. In the *Materials in Library* area, select **STEEL**.

3. Click ▷▷▷ to transfer **STEEL** to the *Materials in Model* area.

4. Select **Edit>Properties** to check the material properties. The HS-low-alloy steel (STEEL) has the following default material properties:

   - Poisson's ratio = 0.27
   - Young's modulus = 199948 MPa
   - Coeff of thermal expansion = 1.17e-5 /C
   - Density = 7.82708e-9 tonne/mm^3

5. Click **OK** to close the Materials dialog box.

6. In the *Home* tab, click ⌐. The Material Assignment dialog box opens as shown in Figure 2–38.

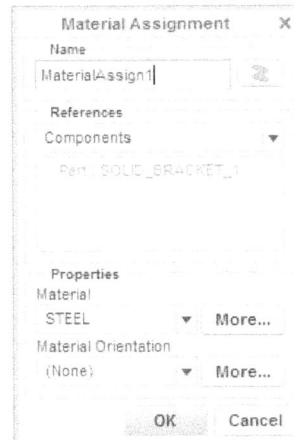

**Figure 2–38**

7. Note that the material **STEEL** has automatically been assigned to the part.

8. Click **OK** to close the Material Assignment dialog box.

## Analysis Tasks

In the following tasks, you will set the analysis type and convergence method, and then run the analysis.

## Task 8 - Set up and run the analysis.

In this task, you will specify the analysis type. First, the solid bracket is analyzed using the **Quick Check** convergence option to check for errors. The option gives you a general feel for the results and it indicates whether the model will behave as intended with the applied boundary conditions. The importance of this option increases with the size of your model.

1. In the *Home* tab, click . The Analyses and Design Studies dialog box opens as shown in Figure 2–39.

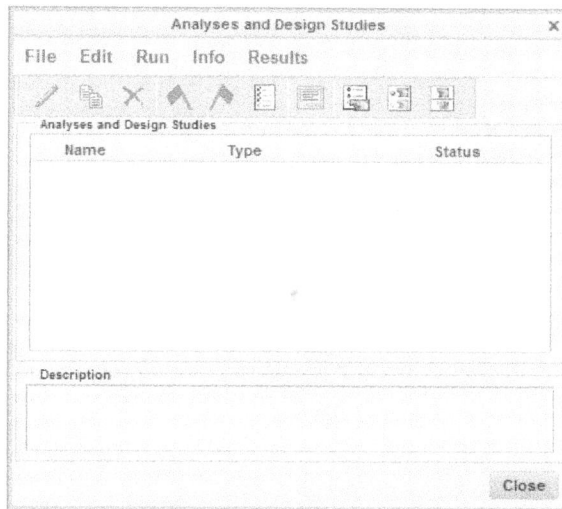

Figure 2–39

2. Select **File>New Static**. The Static Analysis Definition dialog box opens as shown in Figure 2–40.

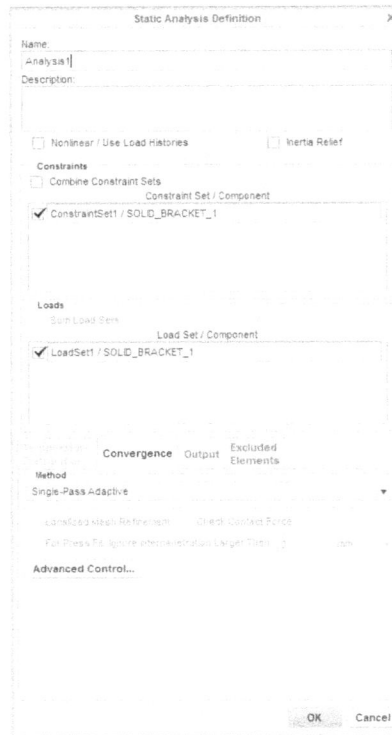

**Figure 2–40**

3. In the *Name* field, enter **solid_bracket** (this will be the name of a subdirectory containing all of your results files).

4. In the *Description* field, enter **Static analysis of a solid bracket**. This step is optional, but is helpful for identifying your analysis later.

*Each study can be set up with one constraint set and a single or multiple load sets.*

5. For a static stress analysis, you need to specify or select the constraint and load sets. These are the ones you created in the previous steps. In this case, they are **ConstraintSet1** and **LoadSet1**. Ensure that they are highlighted.

6. For the type of convergence, expand the Method drop-down list and select **Quick Check**. This option enables you to determine whether the analysis has been set up correctly in your first run.

7. Click ___OK___ in the Static Analysis Definition dialog box.

*By default, Creo Simulate files and directories are created in the Creo working directory. The recommended setting for the memory allocation is half the RAM in your computer.*

8. Click ⬚ in the Analyses and Design Studies box to set the locations for the temporary and output files, output files format, and RAM allocation. The Run Settings dialog box opens as shown in Figure 2–41.

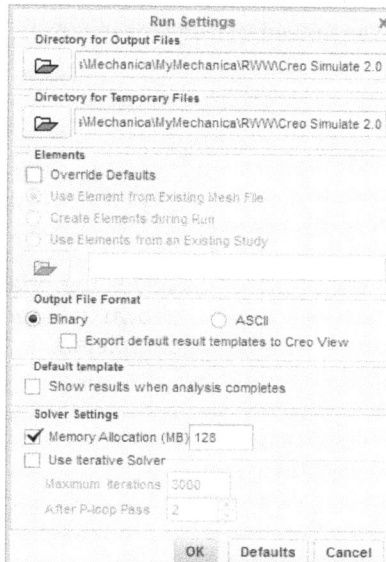

**Figure 2–41**

Note the format for the output files in the *Output File Format* area. The **ASCII** option needs a much larger disk space. The advantage of ASCII output files is that they are portable between Unix and Windows operating systems.

9. Accept the remaining default values, including the **Use Element from Existing Mesh File** option.

10. Click OK to close the Run Settings dialog box.

*The **Check Model** option highlights any modeling errors (e.g., load-constraint conflicts or unassigned material properties) and errors from modeling edits.*

11. Expand the Info menu and select **Check Model**. This command checks the validity of the simulation model. The Information dialog box opens (as shown in Figure 2–42), indicating that there are no errors.

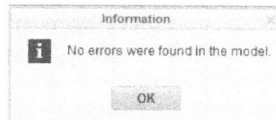

**Figure 2–42**

12. Click OK to confirm.

13. Click ⚐ in the Analyses and Design Studies dialog box to start your analysis. The Question dialog box opens as shown in Figure 2–43.

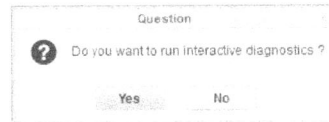

**Figure 2–43**

14. Click Yes in the Question dialog box. Creo Simulate solves the analysis. The Diagnostics dialog box opens as shown in Figure 2–44, stating that the analysis run has been completed.

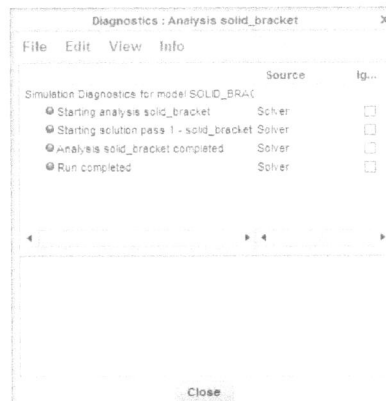

**Figure 2–44**

15. Click Close to close the Diagnostics dialog box.

16. Click 🗎 in the Analyses and Design Studies dialog box. The Run Status dialog box opens, displaying information regarding the analysis, such as the error estimates and mass moments of inertia, as shown in Figure 2–45. The very bottom of the window should indicate that the run has completed.

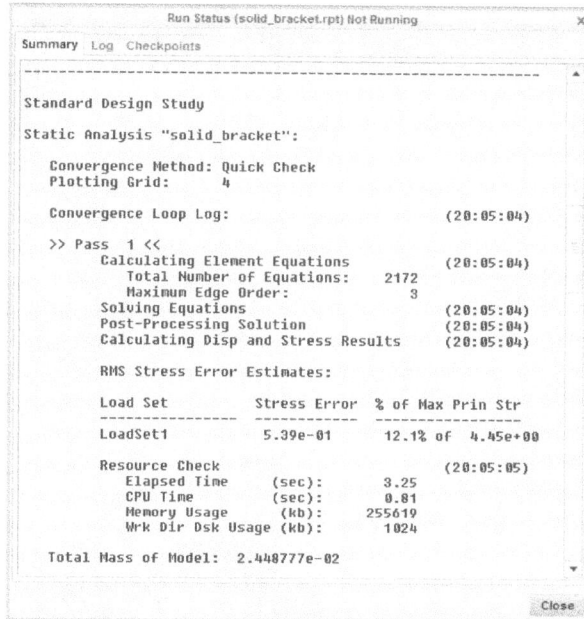

**Figure 2–45**

17. Click `Close` to close the Run Status dialog box.

18. Click `Close` in the Analyses and Design Studies dialog box. The **Quick Check** analysis is complete.

### Task 9 - Solve the solid bracket using the Multi-Pass Adaptive convergence option.

In this task, the model is run through the solver in multiple passes, with the element P-levels being increased with each pass. The passes continue until either the solution converges or the maximum polynomial order (default 6, maximum 9) is reached.

1. In the *Home* tab, click ⊞ . The Analyses and Design Studies dialog box opens as shown in Figure 2–46.

**Figure 2–46**

2. Highlight the **solid_bracket** analysis and click ✎ . The Static Analysis Definition dialog box opens as shown in Figure 2–47.

**Figure 2–47**

3. Expand the Method drop-down list and select **Multi-Pass Adaptive**.

4. In the *Polynomial Order* area, for the *Maximum value*, select **9**.

5. In the *Limits* area, in the *Percent Convergence* field, enter **5**. The Static Analysis Definition dialog box opens as shown in Figure 2–48.

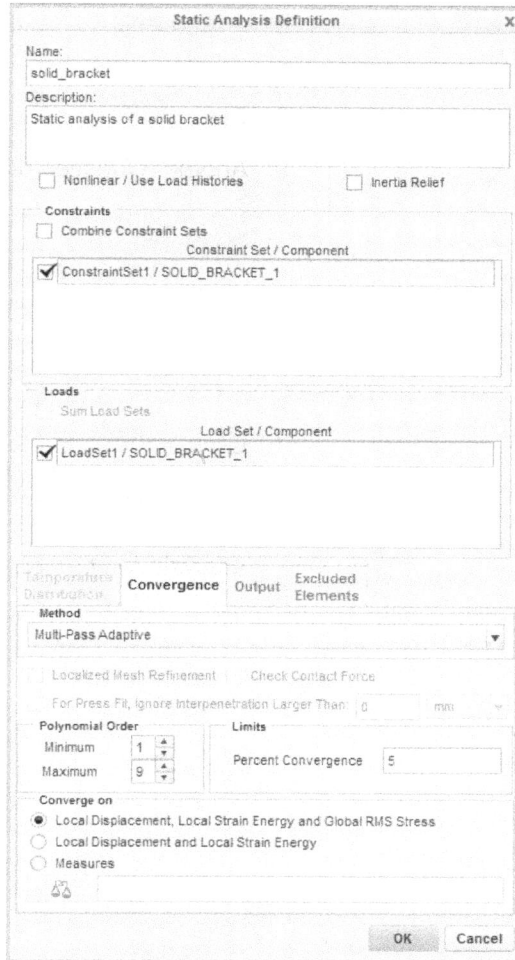

**Figure 2–48**

6. Click OK in the Static Analysis Definition dialog box.

7. Click ✎ in the Analyses and Design Studies dialog box to start the analysis. The Question dialog box opens as shown in Figure 2–49.

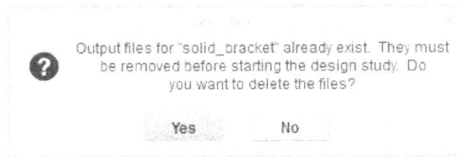

**Figure 2–49**

8. Click Yes in the Question dialog box.

9. Another Question dialog box opens as shown in Figure 2–50.

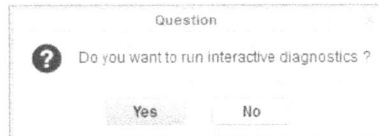

**Figure 2–50**

10. Click Yes in the Question dialog box. The message *The design study has started* displays in the Creo message window. Creo Simulate solves the problem. The Diagnostics dialog box opens as shown in Figure 2–51, stating that the analysis run has been completed.

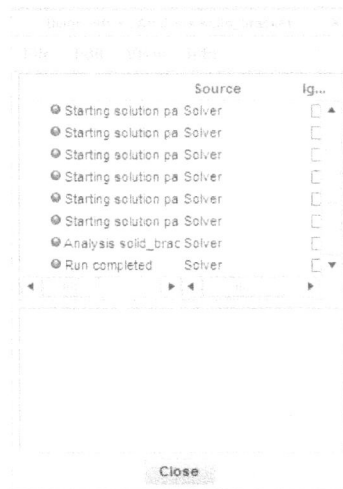

**Figure 2–51**

11. Click  Close  to close the Diagnostics dialog box.

12. Click ▦ in the Analyses and Design Studies dialog box. The Run Status window displays, displaying information regarding the analysis convergence. Examine the information in the window. Note that the analysis took six solution passes, up to the maximum edge order 6, to converge within the requested 5%.

13. Click  Close  to close the Run Status dialog box.

14. Do not close the Analyses and Design Studies dialog box.

## Results Tasks

In the following tasks, you will display and interpret the results of this analysis.

## Task 10 - Display the results.

In this task, you will create and show a von Mises stress plot.

1. Click 🔲 in the Analyses and Design Studies dialog box. The Result Window Definition dialog box opens as shown in Figure 2–52.

**Figure 2–52**

2. In the *Name* field, accept the default **Window1** option.

3. In the *Title* field, enter **VM_Plot**.

4. Select the *Display Options* tab and select **Show Element Edges**.

5. Click ⬚OK and Show⬚ . The Creo Simulate Results environment opens, with the Von Mises Stress fringe plot displayed.

6. In the **Format** menu, select **Result Window**. The Visibilities window displays, as shown in Figure 2–53.

**Figure 2–53**

7. Select **Loads** and **Constraints**.

8. Click ⬚OK⬚ . The results window displays as shown in Figure 2–54.

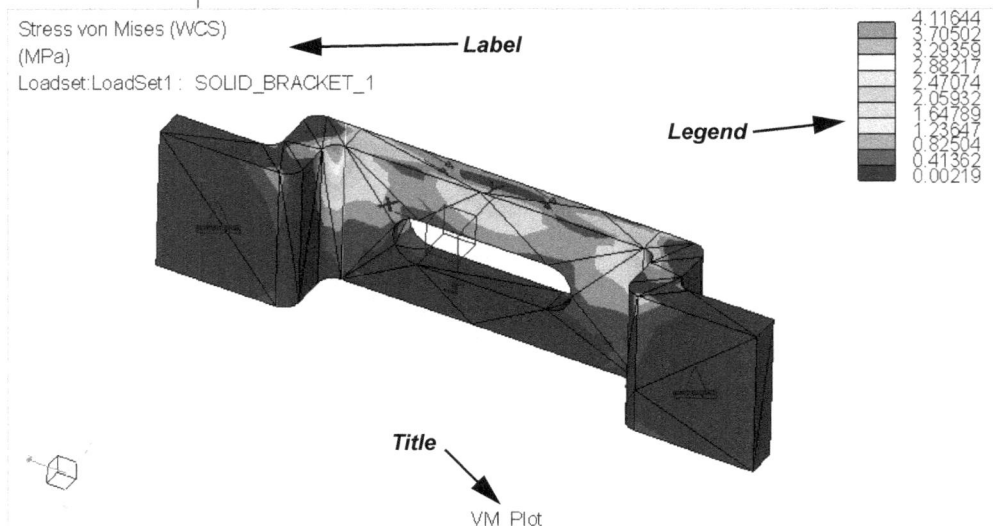

**Figure 2–54**

The stress values that you obtain when you run the analysis might be slightly different than those shown in Figure 2–54. This is because each new build of Creo Simulate produces slight variations in the creation of the mesh.

9. Click 🖾. The Result Window Definition dialog box opens. The *Display Options* tab is active, as shown in Figure 2–55.

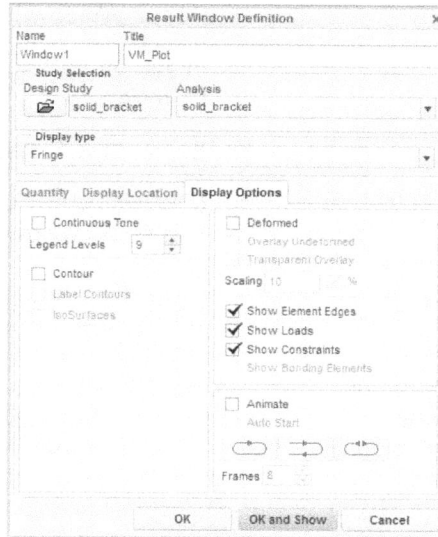

**Figure 2–55**

10. Select the **Continuous Tone** option and click OK and Show. Window1 displays as shown in Figure 2–56.

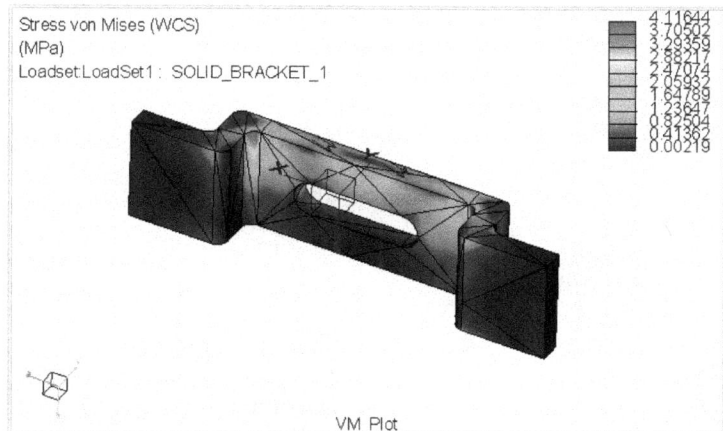

Stress von Mises (WCS)
(MPa)
Loadset:LoadSet1 : SOLID_BRACKET_1

VM_Plot

**Figure 2–56**

## Task 11 - Use predefined measures to study the convergence.

1. Click ⬚ to create a new results window. The Design Study for Result Window Definition dialog box opens.

2. Select the **solid_bracket** study and click `Open`. The Result Window Definition dialog box opens.

3. In the *Name* field, enter **Convm**, and in the *Title* field, enter **Convm**.

4. Expand the Display Type drop-down list and select **Graph**.

5. Expand the first Graph Ordinate (Vertical) Axis drop-down list and select **Measure**.

6. Click ⬚. The Measures dialog box opens as shown in Figure 2–57.

*A measure is a virtual gauge that can be attached to your model. For example, you can set a measure to obtain the stress at a specific point on a model.*

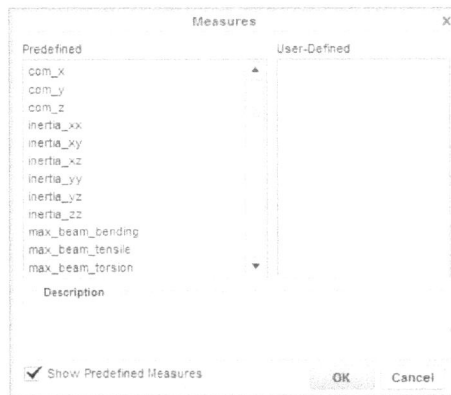

**Figure 2–57**

7. In the list of predefined measures, highlight **max_stress_vm** and click `OK`.

8. Click `OK` in the Result Window Definition box to confirm the creation of the graph without actually displaying it.

9. Repeat the previous eight steps to create graph measures for **max_disp_mag** and **strain_energy**. Enter **max_disp_mag** and **strain_energy**, respectively, for the names of the result window definitions.

10. Click 🔲. The Display Result Window dialog box opens as shown in Figure 2–58.

**Figure 2–58**

11. In the Display Result Window dialog box, highlight **Convm** only (disable any highlighting on others if necessary) and click OK to display **max_stress_vm**. The convergence plot displays as shown in Figure 2–59.

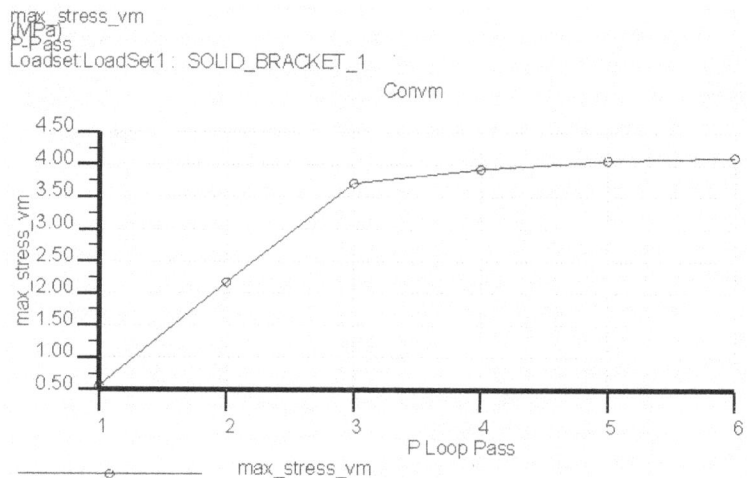

**Figure 2–59**

12. Select **Format>Graph**. The Graph Window Options dialog box opens as shown in Figure 2–60.

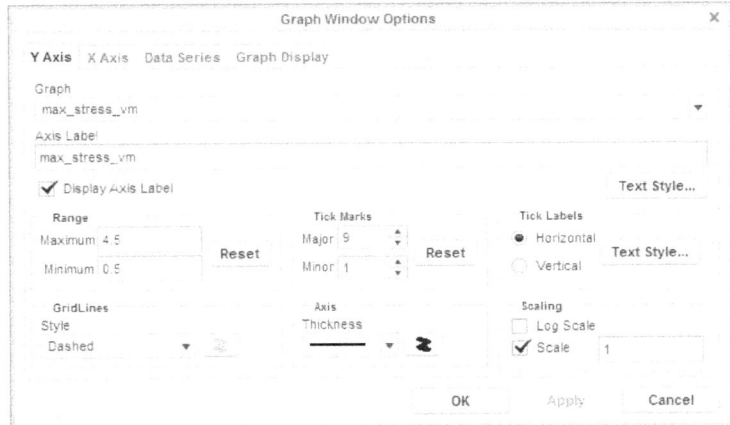

**Figure 2–60**

13. Explore the options in the Graph Window Options dialog box by making changes to the graph shown in Figure 2–59. Click OK when finished.

14. Click 🔲. The Display Result Window dialog box opens.

15. Highlight only **max_disp_mag** in the dialog box and click OK to display the next graph. The convergence plot displays as shown in Figure 2–61.

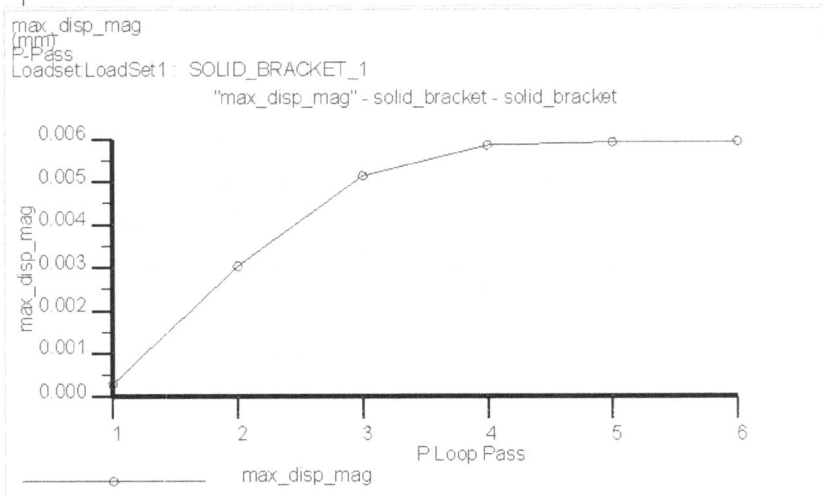

**Figure 2–61**

16. Repeat the previous two steps to display the **strain_energy** convergence plot, as shown in Figure 2–62.

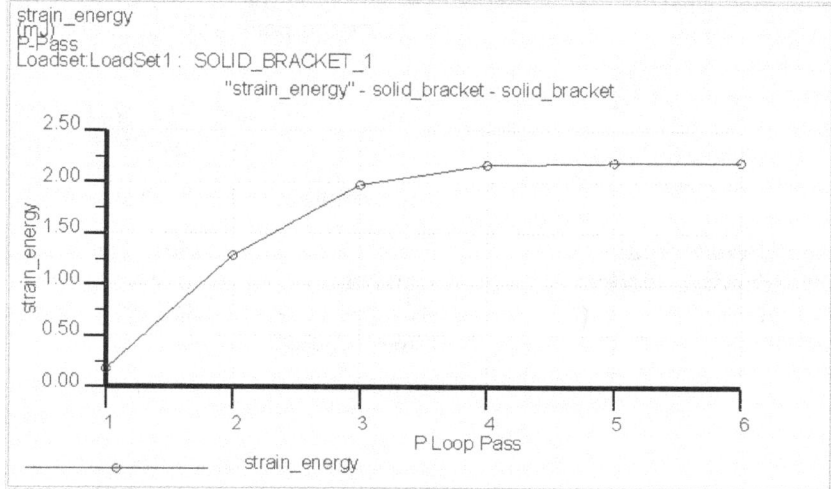

strain_energy
(mJ)
P-Pass
Loadset:LoadSet1 : SOLID_BRACKET_1
"strain_energy" - solid_bracket - solid_bracket

**Figure 2–62**

These plots indicate that the solution converges after six passes. The solution is practically unchanged after four passes.

## Task 12 - Animate the solid bar in Window1.

*Ensure that only **Window1** is selected in the Display Result Window dialog box.*

1. Click [icon], highlight **Window1** in the Display Result Window dialog box, and click OK. The Von Mises Stress fringe plot displays.

2. Click [icon]. The Result Window Definition dialog box opens.

3. Select the *Display Options* tab and clear the **Continuous Tone** option. Select the **Deformed** option and accept the default Scaling value (10%).

4. Select the **Animate** option. Clear the **Auto Start** option and accept the default Frames value (8).

5. Click OK and Show.

6. Click ▶ to start the animation. Click ▶| or |◀ to step through the animation frames. Click ■ to stop the animation.

Select **View>Span/ Pan/Zoom** to reorient the model.

## Task 13 - Explore the Info menu.

In this task, you will use the options in the **Info** menu. You will also locate the point and value of the maximum stress.

1. Click ⬚ or select **Edit>Result Window**. The Result Window Definition dialog box opens. Clear the **Deformed** and **Animate** options. Click OK and Show . Window1 displays.

2. Select **Info>Model Max**. The location and value of maximum von Mises stress displays, as shown in Figure 2–63. You can spin the model to display the location of the maximum von Mises stress.

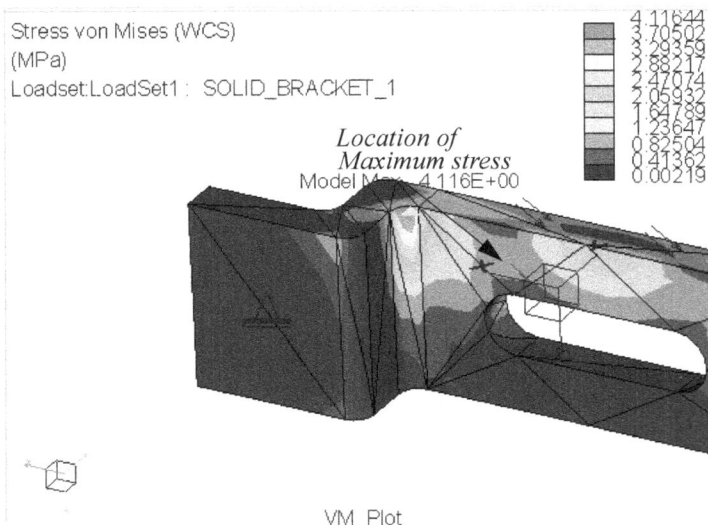

Figure 2–63

3. Investigate the other options in the **Info** menu. For example, the **Dynamic Query** option displays the stress values at the cursor location. Mark a specific location with its stress level by selecting the location while the Dynamic Query is running. Select **Info> Clear All Query Tags** when you are finished.

## Task 14 - Create sections through the solid bracket.

1. Select **View>Spin/Pan/Zoom**.

*Select **View>Shade** to remove any shading on the model.*

2. In the Orientation dialog box, click the **Front** button and then click **OK**.

3. Select **View>Shade** to add or remove the shade. The model displays as shown in Figure 2–64.

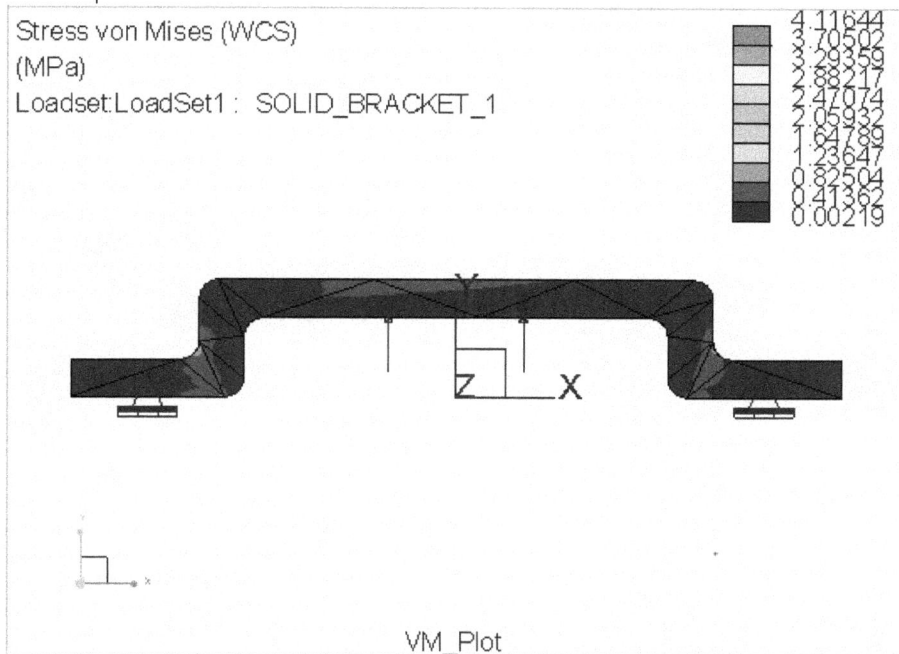

Stress von Mises (WCS)
(MPa)
Loadset:LoadSet1 :  SOLID_BRACKET_1

4.11644
3.70502
3.29359
2.88217
2.47074
2.05932
1.64789
1.23647
0.82504
0.41362
0.00219

VM_Plot

**Figure 2–64**

4. Select **Insert>Cutting/Capping Surfs**. The Results Surface Definition dialog box opens, as shown in Figure 2–65.

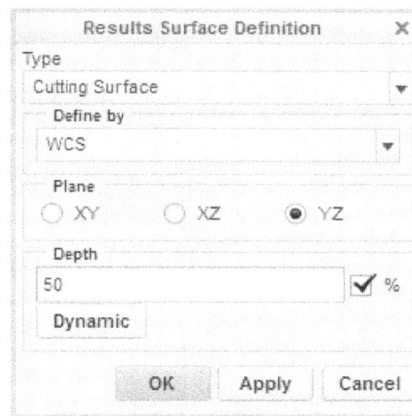

Results Surface Definition ✕
Type
Cutting Surface ▾
Define by
WCS ▾
Plane
○ XY   ○ XZ   ● YZ
Depth
50 ☑ %
Dynamic
OK   Apply   Cancel

**Figure 2–65**

5. Select the options in the Results Surface Definition dialog box as shown in Figure 2–65. Click <sup>Apply</sup> and reorient the model to display the section shown in Figure 2–66.

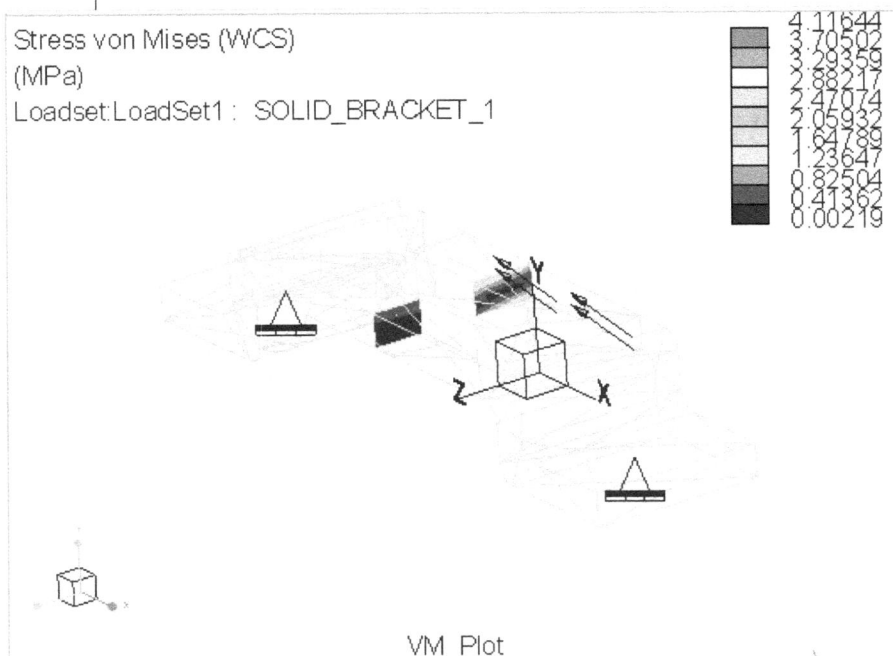

Stress von Mises (WCS)
(MPa)
Loadset:LoadSet1 : SOLID_BRACKET_1

4.11644
3.70502
3.29359
2.88217
2.47074
2.05932
1.64789
1.23647
0.82504
0.41362
0.00219

VM_Plot

**Figure 2–66**

6. In the *Depth* field, enter **60** and click <sup>Apply</sup>. Note that the section moves along the part.

7. Click <sup>Dynamic</sup> and select the cutting plane. By selecting the **Mouse** icon and dragging, you can move the section up and down in the model.

8. Click the middle mouse button to cancel the dynamic modification.

9. Expand the Type drop-down list and select the **Capping Surface**.

10. Select the **Below** option.

11. In the *Depth* field, enter **50** and click ~~Apply~~ . The capped section displays as shown in Figure 2–67.

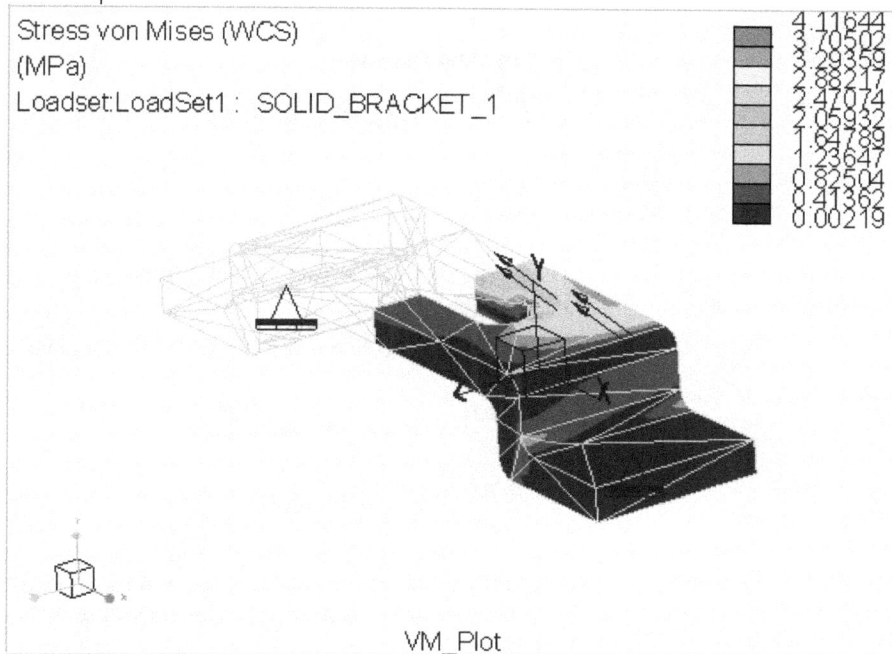

Figure 2–67

12. Click ~~OK~~ to close the Results Surface Definition dialog box.

13. Select **Edit>Delete Capping Surf**.

14. Select **File>Exit Results**. Click ~~No~~ in the Saving the Results window.

15. Close the Analyses and Design Studies dialog box.

16. Save the model and close the window.

# Practice 2b

# Static Stress Analysis of a Bike Crank

**Learning Objectives**

- Apply loads, constraints, and material properties.

- Mesh the model.

- Check the validity of the model.

- Set up and run a Single-Pass Adaptive analysis.

- Display the results.

- Prepare the report.

In this practice, you will set up and run a static stress analysis on a bicycle crank assembly. The model is shown in Figure 2–68.

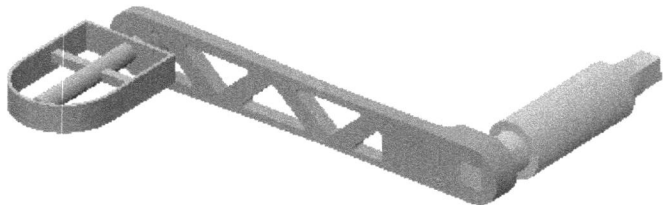

**Figure 2–68**

## Modeling Tasks

In the following tasks, you will create the simulation entities needed to analyze your model.

### Task 1 - Open the bike_crank assembly in Creo Parametric.

1. Open **bike_crank.asm**. The model displays as shown in Figure 2–69.

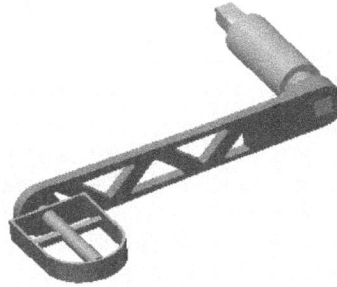

**Figure 2–69**

## Task 2 - Launch Creo Simulate.

1. Select **Applications>Simulate** to launch the Creo Simulate environment. Ensure that the ⬚ (Structure Mode) is active.

## Task 3 - Apply materials.

In this task, you will select materials for the parts in the assembly.

1. In the *Home* tab, click 🖵 . The Materials dialog box opens as shown in Figure 2–70.

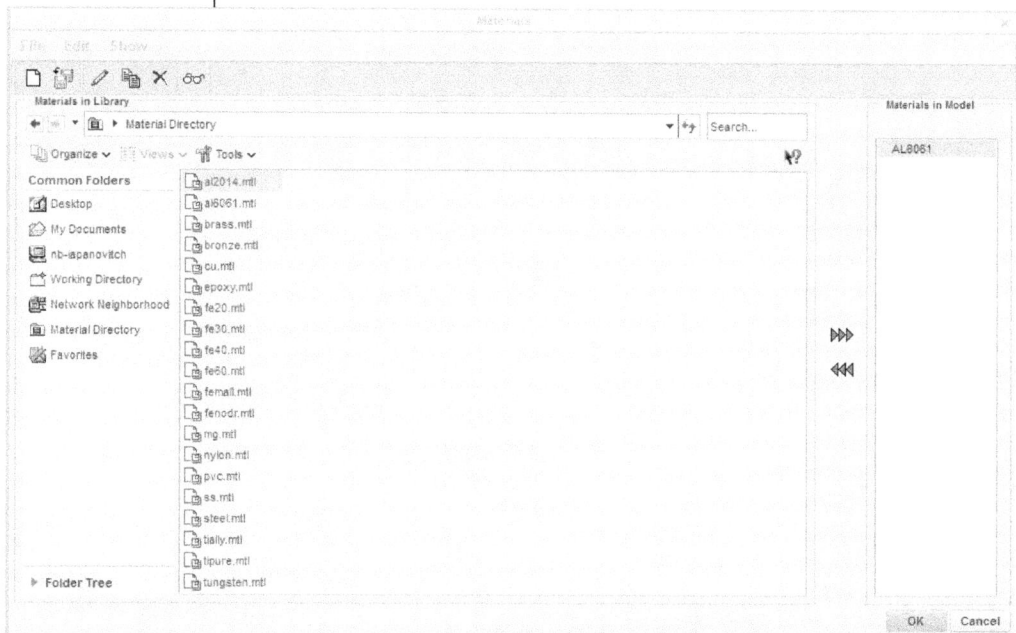

**Figure 2–70**

2. In the *Materials in Library* area, select **STEEL**.

3. Click ⋙ to transfer **STEEL** to the *Materials in Model* area.

4. In the *Materials in Model* area, highlight **STEEL** and click ✎ to edit the material.

5. In the Material Definition dialog box, make the changes shown in Figure 2–71:

   - Name: **STEEL AISI 304**
   - Tensile Yield Stress: **215 MPa**
   - Failure Criterion: **Distortion Energy (von Mises)**

**Figure 2–71**

6. Click **OK** to close the Material Definition box.

7. In the *Materials in Library* area, select **AL6061**.

8. Click ⋙ to transfer **AL6061** to the *Materials in Model* area.

9. In the *Materials in Model* area, highlight **AL6061** and click ✎ to edit the material.

10. In the Material Definition dialog box, make the changes shown in Figure 2–72:

- Name: **AL6061 T4**
- Tensile Yield Stress: **145 MPa**
- Failure Criterion: **Distortion Energy (von Mises)**

**Figure 2–72**

11. Click    OK    to close the Material Definition box.

12. Click    OK    to close the Materials dialog box.

13. In the *Home* tab, click ⬒. The Material Assignment dialog box opens as shown in Figure 2–73.

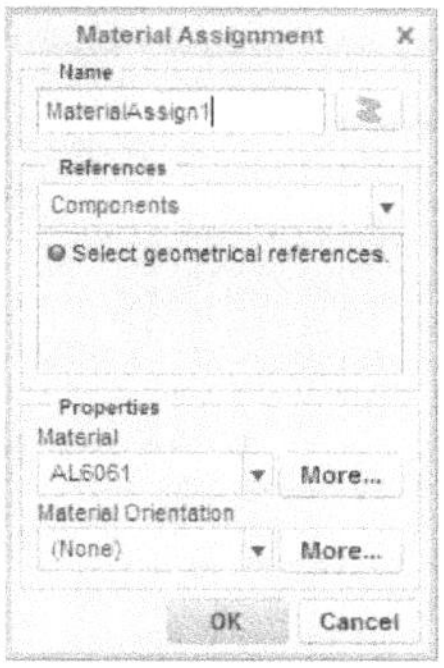

**Figure 2–73**

14. Select both **PEDAL** and **LHS CRANK** parts in the model (press and hold down <CTRL> for multiple selection) and click ____ OK ____ to assign **AL6061 T4** to both parts and close the Material Assignment dialog box.

15. In the *Home* tab, click ⌐ again. In the model, select the **BOTTOM_BRACKET** part and in the *Properties* area, select **STEEL AISI 304**, as shown in Figure 2–74.

Figure 2–74

16. Click ____ OK ____ to close the Material Assignment dialog box.

## Task 4 - Apply constraints.

In this task, you will constrain to the entire cylindrical surface of the **BOTTOM_BRACKET** part shown in Figure 2–75.

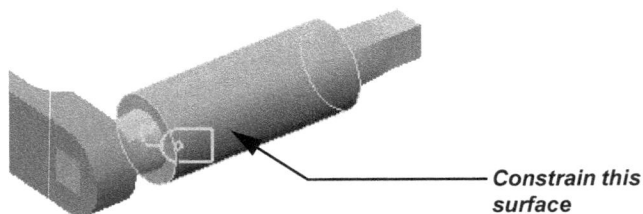

*Constrain this surface*

Figure 2–75

1. In the *Home* tab, click ▨ .

2. In the Constraint dialog box, rename the constraint as **fixed**, select the surface shown in Figure 2–75, and accept the defaults for all of the other values. The dialog box should open as shown in Figure 2–76.

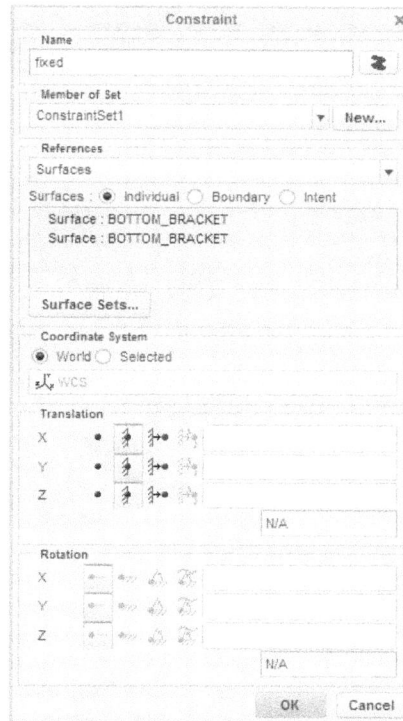

**Figure 2–76**

3. Click OK to close the Constraint dialog box. The model displays as shown in Figure 2–77.

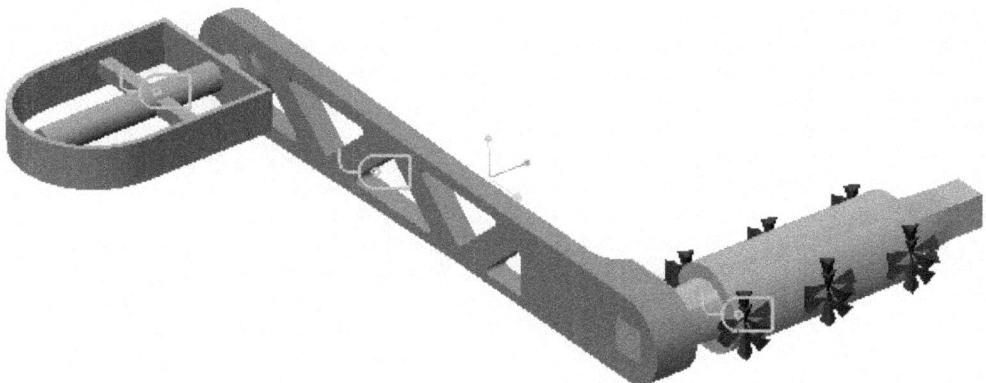

**Figure 2–77**

## Task 5 - Apply loads.

In this task, you will apply a 200N downward force to the top surface of the **PEDAL** part shown in Figure 2–78. The force simulates the average force a recreational bike rider applies to one pedal.

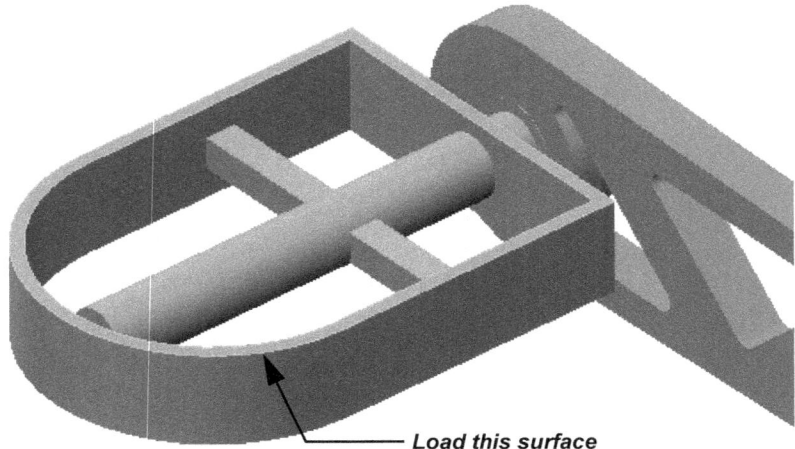

Load this surface

**Figure 2–78**

1. In the *Home* tab, click ⊞ .

2. In the Force/Moment dialog box, enter the following values (as shown in Figure 2–79):

   • Name: **downward_force**
   • References: Select the surface shown in Figure 2–78
   • Force Y: **-200**

**Figure 2–79**

3. Click **OK** to close the Force/Moment dialog box. The model displays as shown in Figure 2–80.

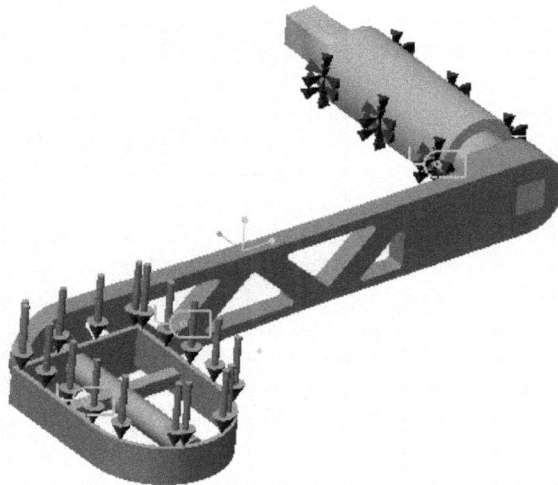

**Figure 2–80**

## Task 6 - Customize the simulation display.

1. Click ⬚ (Simulation Display) in the floating toolbar. The Simulation Display dialog box opens.

2. In the *Settings* tab, select **Values**. In the Load/Constraint Display area, set the *Distribution Density* to **3**, as shown in Figure 2–81.

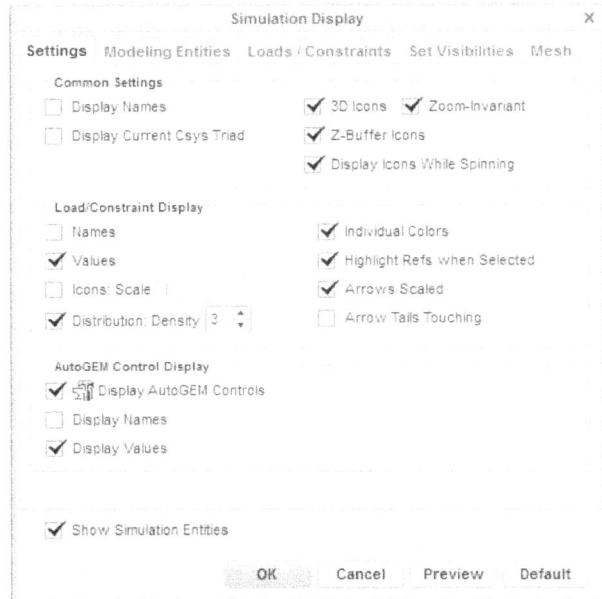

**Figure 2–81**

3. In the *Modeling Entities* tab, clear the **Material Assignments** option, as shown in Figure 2–82.

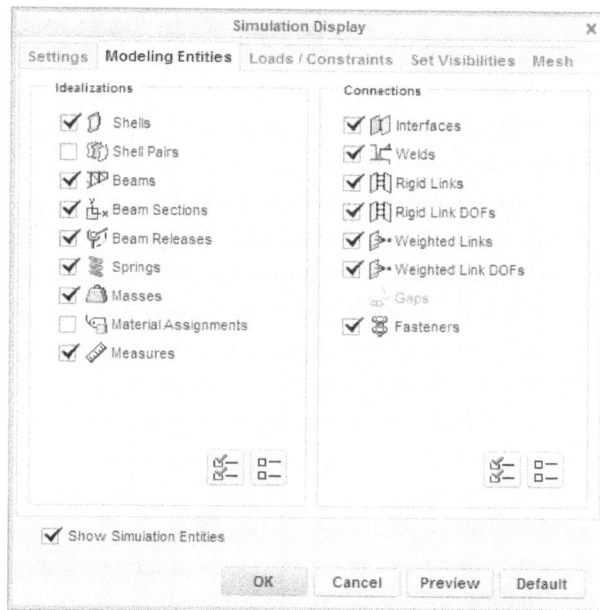

**Figure 2–82**

4. Click ![OK] to close the Simulation Display dialog box. The model displays as shown in Figure 2–83. Note that the **Material Assignment** icons are now hidden.

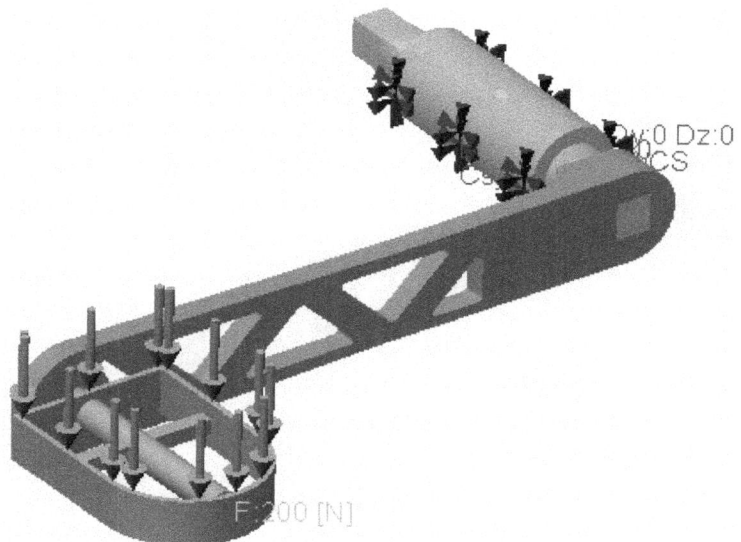

**Figure 2–83**

## Task 7 - Mesh the model.

1. In the *Refine Model* tab, click ⌗. The AutoGEM dialog box opens as shown in Figure 2–84.

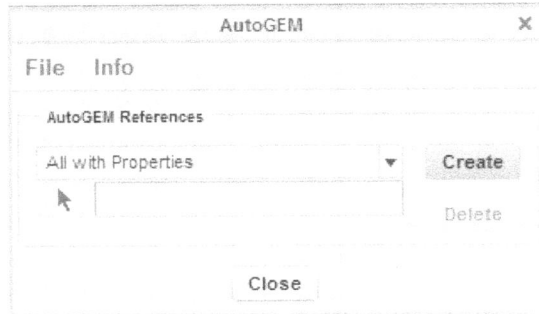

**Figure 2–84**

*The **All with Properties** option only meshes parts to which materials have already been assigned.*

2. Ensure that the **All with Properties** option is active and click Create .

*The number of elements might slightly vary, depending on the specific Creo build.*

3. The AutoGEM Summary and the Diagnostics dialog boxes open as shown in Figure 2–85. For this model, AutoGEM creates 999 tetrahedral elements.

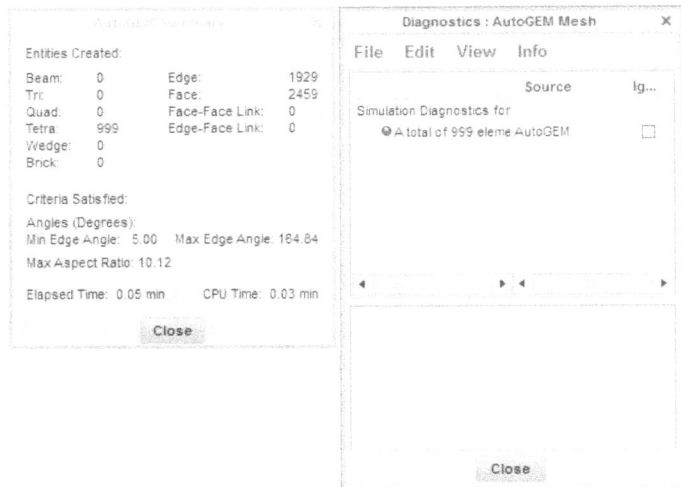

**Figure 2–85**

4. Close the AutoGEM Summary and Diagnostics boxes. The model displays as shown in Figure 2–86.

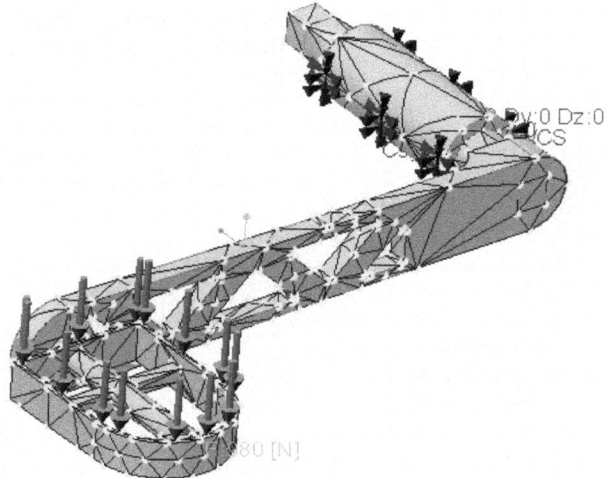

**Figure 2–86**

5. Click `Close` in the AutoGEM dialog box. The warning shown in Figure 2–87 displays.

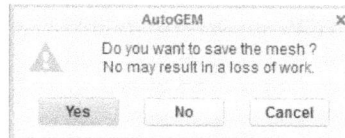

**Figure 2–87**

6. Click `No` to exit without saving the mesh.

The model will be meshed during the analysis run. Since meshing this model is fast, this will not impede the analysis runtime.

## Analysis Tasks

In the following tasks, you will set the analysis type and convergence method, and then run the analysis.

## Task 8 - Set up the analysis.

1. In the *Home* tab, click 🔲 . The Analyses and Design Studies dialog box opens as shown in Figure 2–88.

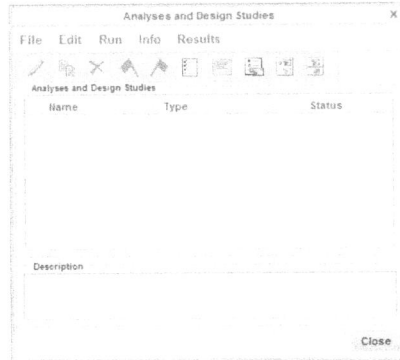

**Figure 2–88**

2. Select **File>New Static**. The Static Analysis Definition dialog box opens as shown in Figure 2–89.

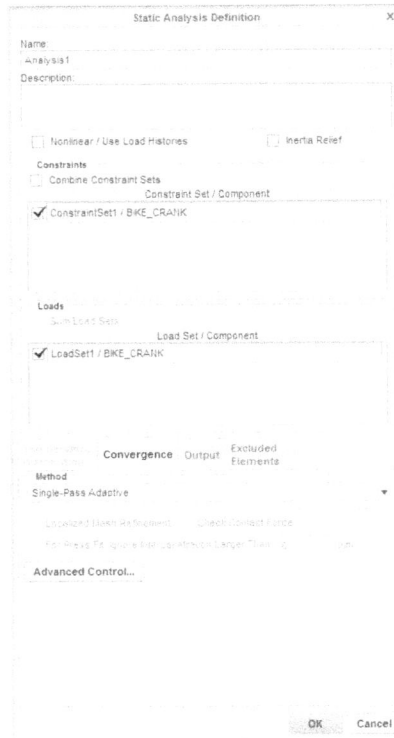

**Figure 2–89**

3. In the *Name* field, enter **bike_crank** (this will be the name of a subdirectory containing all of your results files).

4. For this analysis, you will use the Single-Pass Adaptive convergence method. Ensure that it is selected.

5. Click $\boxed{\text{OK}}$ to close the Static Analysis Definition dialog box.

6. Click $\boxed{\phantom{x}}$ in the Analyses and Design Studies dialog box. The Run Settings dialog box opens as shown in Figure 2–90.

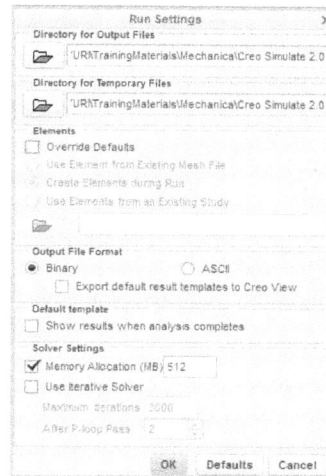

**Figure 2–90**

7. Note that, since you did not save the mesh file, the **Create Elements during Run** option is automatically selected in the *Element* area.

8. Set *Memory Allocation* to **512Mb**.

*The recommended setting for the memory allocation is half the RAM in your computer.*

9. Click $\boxed{\text{OK}}$ to close the Run Settings dialog box.

10. Expand the **Info** menu and select **Check Model**. This command checks the validity of the simulation model. The Information dialog box opens, as shown in Figure 2–91, stating that there are no errors.

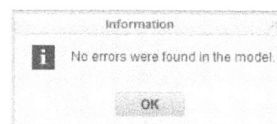

**Figure 2–91**

11. Click ⬜OK to confirm.

## Task 9 - Run the analysis.

1. Click ◣ in the Analyses and Design Studies dialog box to start your analysis. The Question dialog box opens as shown in Figure 2–92.

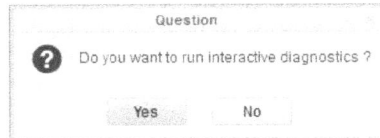

**Figure 2–92**

2. Click ⬜Yes in the Question dialog box. Creo Simulate solves the analysis. The Diagnostics dialog box opens as shown in Figure 2–93, stating that the analysis run has been completed.

Note that one warning message was issued during the analysis run, related to stress singularities.

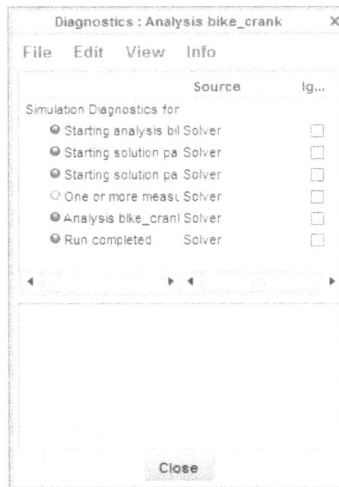

**Figure 2–93**

3. Click ⬜Close to close the Diagnostics dialog box.

4. Click [icon] in the Analyses and Design Studies dialog box. The Run Status dialog box opens, displaying various information regarding the analysis as shown in Figure 2–94. Scroll up or down to the area that prints the RMS Stress Error Estimates and note that the estimated RMS stress error in this analysis is approximately 16MPa, which is 8.6% of the maximum principal stress in the model.

Since this is a preliminary analysis, which is only intended to check for gross design errors, you will accept this amount of analysis error. For a design validation analysis run, a more accurate Multi-Pass Adaptive convergence method would be recommended, with a target RMS stress error under 5%.

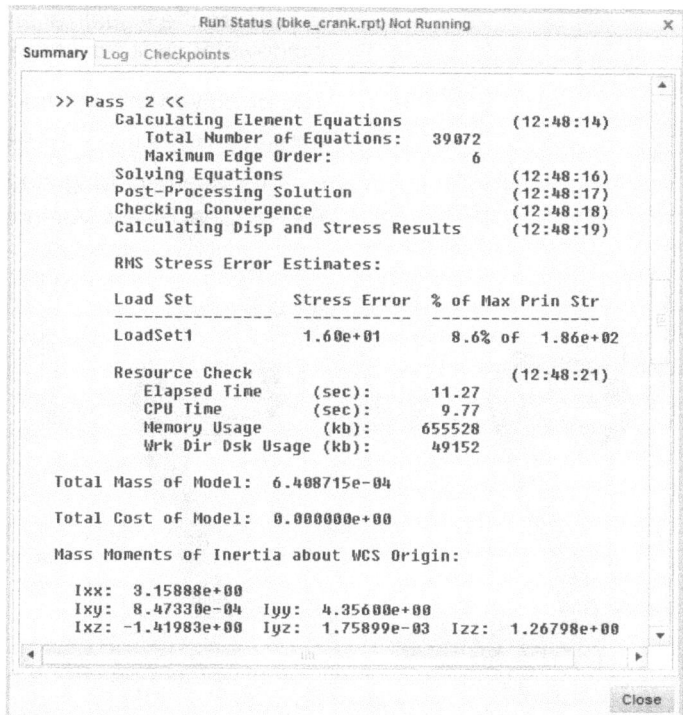

Figure 2–94

5. Click  Close  to close the Run Status dialog box, but do not close the Analyses and Design Studies dialog box yet.

## Results Tasks

In the following tasks, you will display and interpret the results of this analysis.

### Task 10 - Display the results using the Default Template.

In this task, you will display the analysis results using the Default Template.

1. Click ⬛ in the Analyses and Design Studies dialog box (the callout on the icon should say *Review Results of a Design Study from Default Template*). Creo Simulate takes a minute to prepare the visualization and then displays three result windows at once, as shown in Figure 2–95.

    The displayed result windows are as follows:

    * von Mises Stress Animation
    * Displacement Magnitude Fringe
    * Principal Stress Vectors

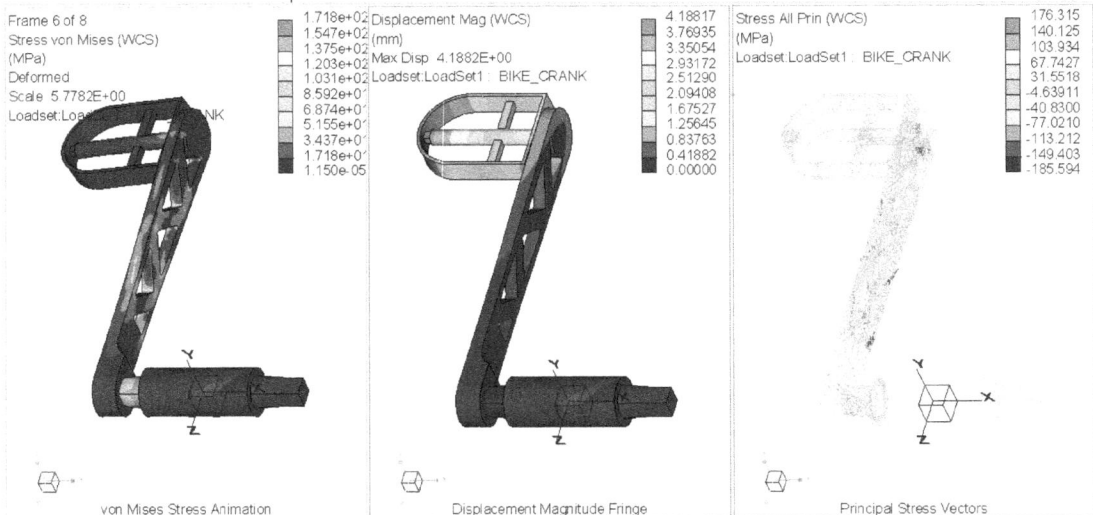

**Figure 2–95**

## Task 11 - Examine the Principal Stress results.

1. Click 🔍. The Display Result Window dialog box opens as shown in Figure 2–96.

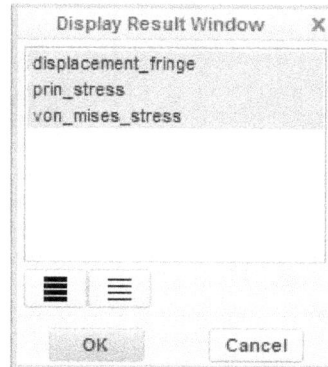

Display Result Window    X

displacement_fringe
prin_stress
von_mises_stress

OK      Cancel

**Figure 2–96**

2. Clear the **displacement_fringe** and **von_mises_stress** options and click OK. Only the principal stress vector plot is displayed as shown in Figure 2–97.

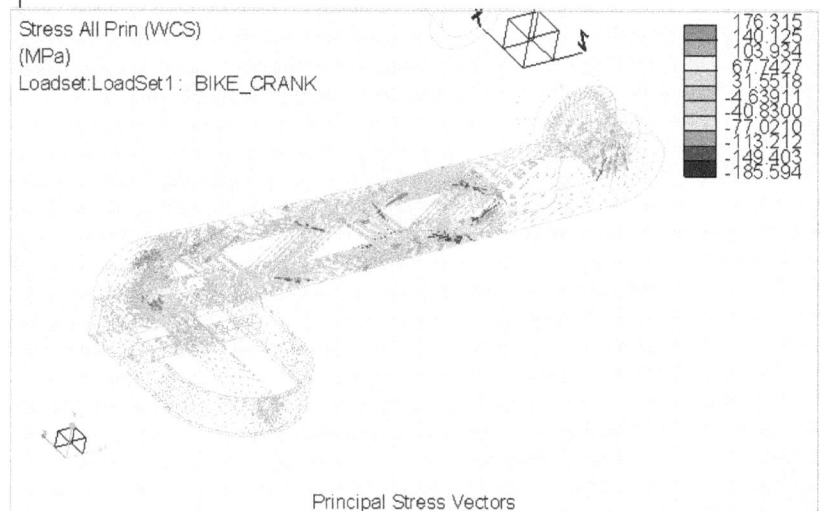

Stress All Prin (WCS)
(MPa)
Loadset:LoadSet1 : BIKE_CRANK

176.315
140.125
103.934
67.7427
31.5518
-4.63911
-40.8300
-77.0210
-113.212
-149.403
-185.594

Principal Stress Vectors

**Figure 2–97**

3. Click 🖾 . The Result Window Definition dialog box opens as shown in Figure 2–98.

| Result Window Definition | X |
|---|---|
| Name | Title |
| prin_stress | Principal Stress Vectors |

Study Selection

| Design Study | Analysis |
|---|---|
| 📂 bike_crank | bike_crank ▼ |

Display type

Vectors ▼

**Quantity**   Display Location   Display Options

| Stress ▼ | MPa ▼ |
|---|---|
| Component | |
| All Principals ▼ | |

OK        OK and Show        Cancel

**Figure 2–98**

4. Expand the Component drop-down list, select **Max Principal**, and click OK and Show . The result window now displays as shown in Figure 2–99.

The maximum principal stress component is typically the tensile stress in the model, and is critical for predicting fatigue or brittle failures of the material. Use the **Rotate** and **Zoom** tools to examine the tensile stresses in the model.

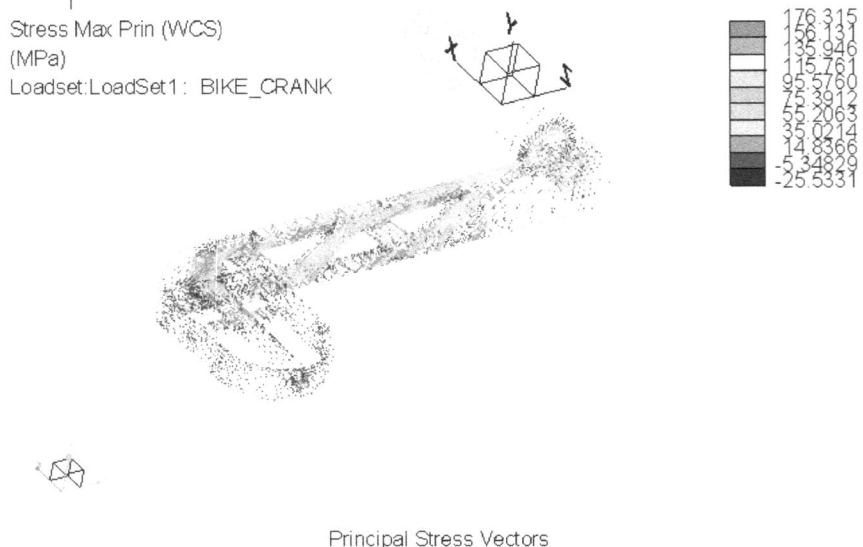

Stress Max Prin (WCS)
(MPa)
Loadset:LoadSet1 : BIKE_CRANK

176.315
158.131
135.946
115.761
95.5760
75.3912
55.2063
35.0214
14.8366
-5.34829
-25.5331

Principal Stress Vectors

**Figure 2–99**

5. Click 📇 to open the Display Result Window dialog box again. Clear the **prin_stress** option and click ⬛ OK ⬛ to hide all of the result windows for now.

## Task 12 - Display the Failure Index results.

*The Failure Index requires you to define a failure criterion. In the previous task you defined **von Mises** as the failure criterion, which means the material is predicted to fail in the areas in which the **von Mises** stress exceeds the material's **Yield Stress**.*

In this task, you will display and examine the Failure Index result plot. The Failure Index is used to determine whether or not the material is predicted to fail under the given loading conditions:

* If the Failure Index is less than 1, the material is not predicted to fail.

* If the Failure Index is equal to or greater than 1, the material is predicted to fail.

1. Click 📋 to create a new results window. The Design Study for Result Window Definition dialog box opens.

2. Select the **bike_crank** study and click ⬛ Open ⬛. The Result Window Definition dialog box opens.

3. In the *Name* field, enter **fail_index_pedal**.

4. Expand the Quantity drop-down list and select **Failure Index**. The Result Window Definition dialog box opens as shown in Figure 2–100.

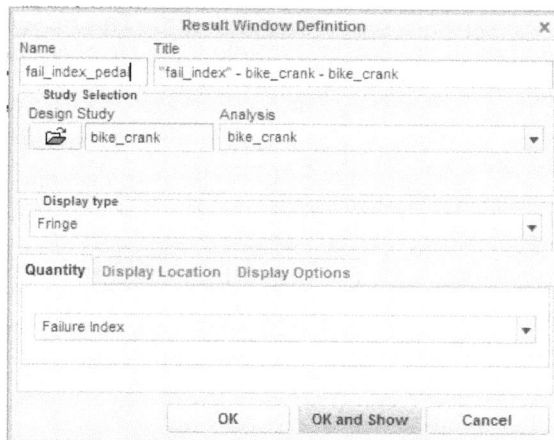

Figure 2–100

5. Click OK and Show . The result displays as shown in Figure 2–101.

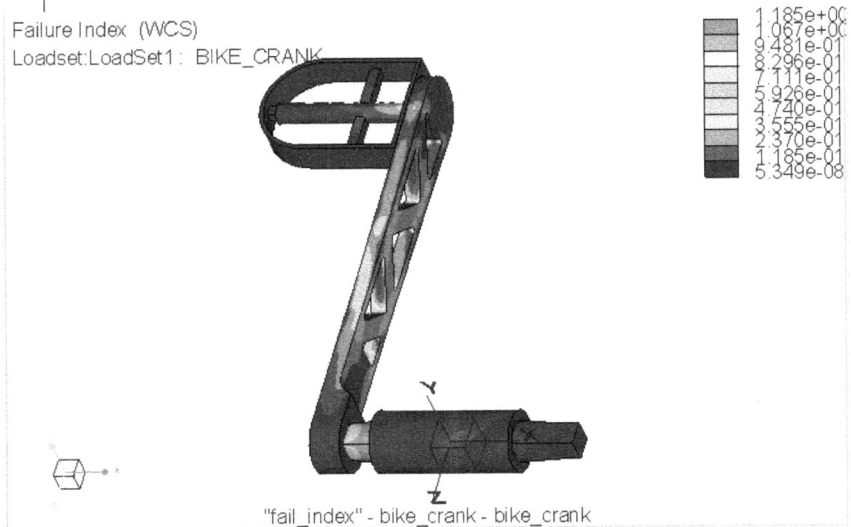

Failure Index (WCS)
Loadset:LoadSet1 : BIKE_CRANK

1.185e+00
1.067e+00
9.481e-01
8.296e-01
7.111e-01
5.926e-01
4.740e-01
3.555e-01
2.370e-01
1.185e-01
5.349e-08

"fail_index" - bike_crank - bike_crank

**Figure 2–101**

Note that the maximum failure index in the model is about 1.185, which is greater than 1, and means that in some areas in the model the material will fail under the given loading.

In the following steps, you will examine which areas in the model are predicted to fail.

6. Click [icon]. The Result Window Definition dialog box opens. Select the *Display Location* tab as shown in Figure 2–102.

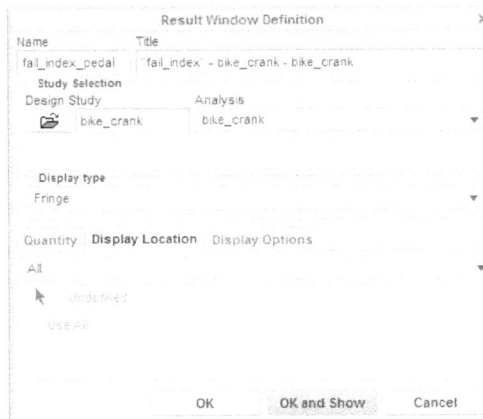

Result Window Definition ✕

Name                    Title
fail_index_pedal        "fail_index" - bike_crank - bike_crank
Study Selection
Design Study            Analysis
   bike_crank           bike_crank                            ▼

Display type
Fringe                                                        ▼

Quantity   **Display Location**   Display Options

All                                                           ▼

   Undefined

   Use All

              OK        OK and Show        Cancel

**Figure 2–102**

7. Expand the Display Location drop-down list and select **Components/Layers**. The Component and Layer Visibility dialog box opens as shown in Figure 2–103.

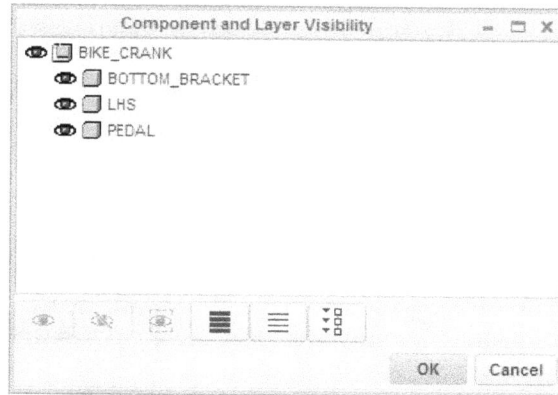

**Figure 2–103**

8. Set the visibility of **BOTTOM_BRACKET** and **LHS** to **Blanked**, as shown in Figure 2–104.

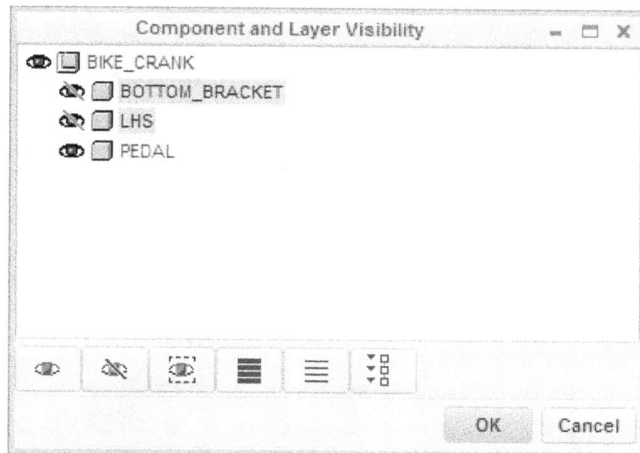

**Figure 2–104**

9. Click OK to close the Component and Layer Visibility dialog box and then click OK and Show to close the Result Window Definition dialog box. The result window displays as shown in Figure 2–105.

**Figure 2–105**

10. Select **Info>Model Max** to locate the maximum failure index in the pedal, as shown in Figure 2–106.

The failure index in the fillet near the pedal's main thread is approximately 1.006. Therefore, the material in the fillet is predicted to yield slightly.

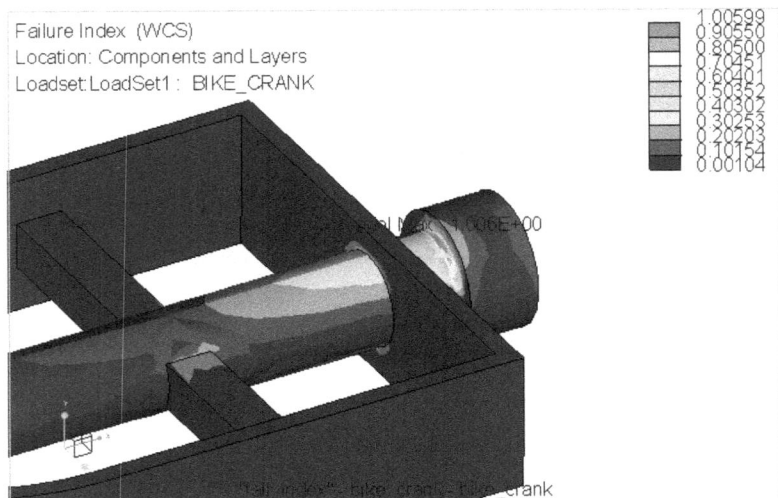

**Figure 2–106**

11. Click  to create a copy of the current result window. The Result Window Definition dialog box opens as shown in Figure 2–107.

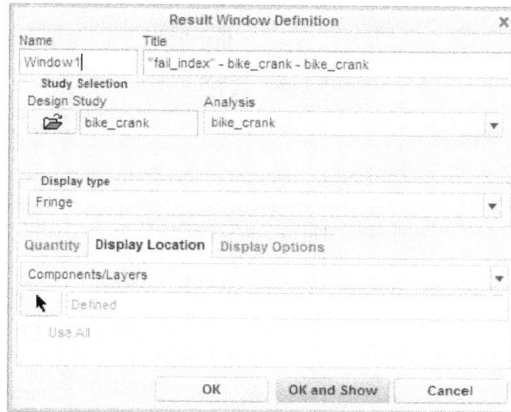

**Figure 2–107**

12. Rename the window as **fail_index_crank**.

13. Click  to open the Component and Layer Visibility dialog box. Set the visibility of the **LHS** component to **Shown** and of the **BOTTOM_BRACKET** and **PEDAL** parts to **Blanked**, as shown in Figure 2–108.

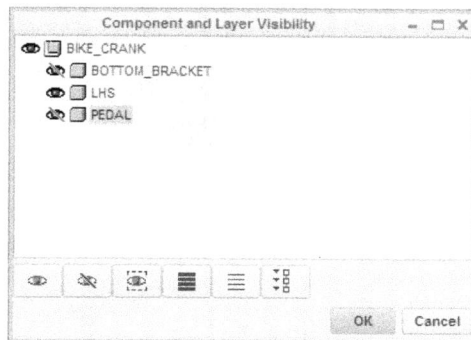

**Figure 2–108**

14. Click  to close the Component and Layer Visibility dialog box and then click  again to close the Result Window Definition dialog box and save the result definition without displaying.

15. Repeat Steps 11 to 14 to create a window named **fail_index_shaft** to display the failure index in the **BOTTOM_BRACKET** part.

16. Click [icon] to open the Display Result Window dialog box. Highlight the **fail_index_crank** line, and clear all of the others, as shown in Figure 2–109.

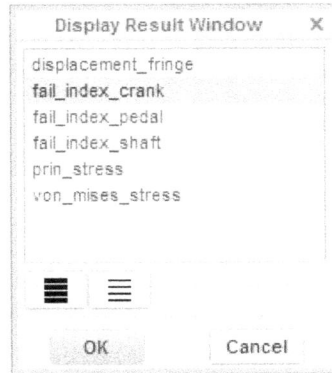

| Display Result Window                 X |
|---|
| displacement_fringe |
| **fail_index_crank** |
| fail_index_pedal |
| fail_index_shaft |
| prin_stress |
| von_mises_stress |

**Figure 2–109**

17. Click OK . The failure index result for the crank part displays as shown in Figure 2–110.

Failure Index (WCS)
Location: Components and Layers
Loadset:LoadSet1 : BIKE_CRANK

"fail_index" - bike_crank - bike_crank

**Figure 2–110**

18. Select **Info>Model Max** to locate the maximum failure index in the crank, as shown in Figure 2–111.

Note that the failure index in one of the fillets in the middle pocket is approximately 1.185. The stress in this area is 18.5% over the material's yield stress, which means the material in the fillet is predicted to substantially yield.

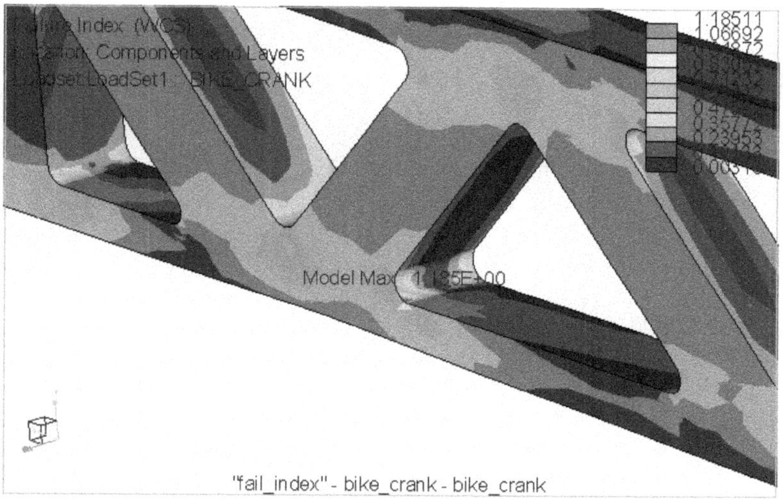

**Figure 2–111**

19. Click again. Highlight the **fail_index_shaft** line, and clear all of the others, as shown in Figure 2–112.

**Figure 2–112**

20. Click   OK   . The failure index result for the shaft part displays as shown in Figure 2–113.

Note that the maximum failure index in the shaft is approximately 0.711. Therefore, this part is safe under the given loading.

Failure Index (WCS)
Location: Components and Layers
Loadset:LoadSet1 :  BIKE_CRANK

7.114e-01
6.403e-01
5.691e-01
4.980e-01
4.268e-01
3.557e-01
2.846e-01
2.134e-01
1.423e-01
7.114e-02
5.349e-08

"fail_index" - bike_crank - bike_crank

**Figure 2–113**

## Report Tasks

In the following tasks, you will annotate the analysis results and prepare and export a report.

## Task 13 - Annotate the results.

1. Click 🔳 . The Result Window Definition dialog box opens as shown in Figure 2–114.

**Figure 2–114**

2. Expand the Display Location drop-down list, select **All,** and click OK and Show . The result window displays as shown in Figure 2–115.

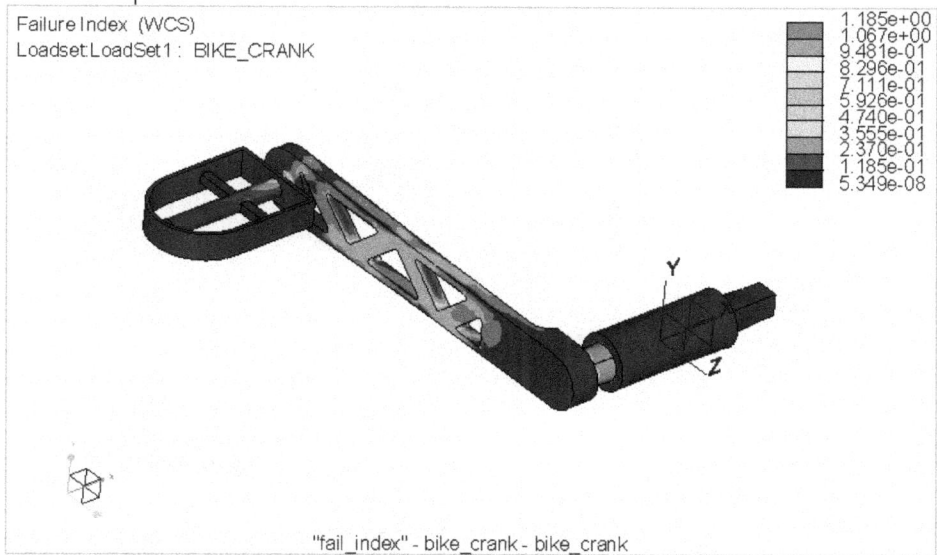

**Figure 2–115**

3. Select **Insert>Annotation**. The Note dialog box opens as shown in Figure 2–116.

**Figure 2–116**

4. In the *Text* field, enter **Unsafe area. Consider increasing the fillet radius and/or using stronger material**, as shown in Figure 2–117.

**Figure 2–117**

5. Click ↖ and select a location in the result window where you want to locate the top left corner of the annotation, as shown in Figure 2–118.

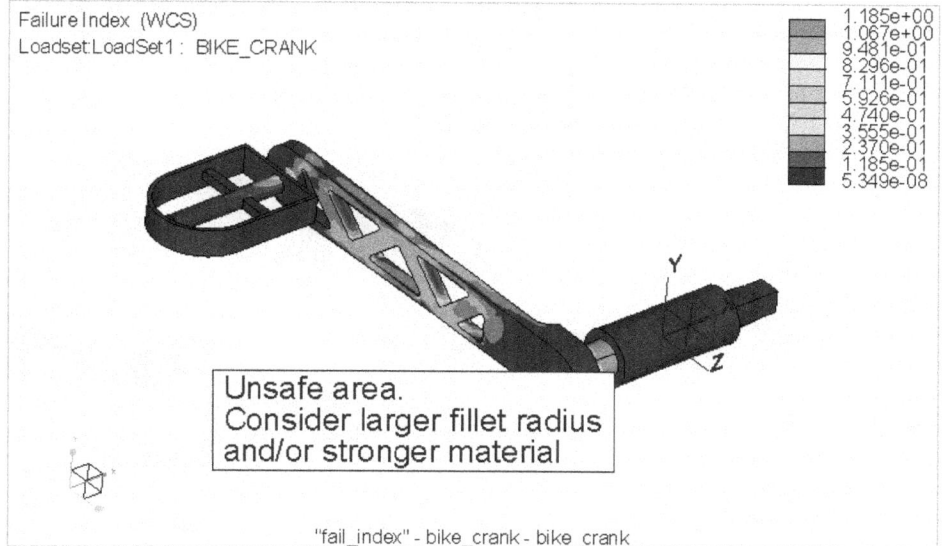

Failure Index (WCS)
Loadset:LoadSet1 : BIKE_CRANK

1.185e+00
1.067e+00
9.481e-01
8.296e-01
7.111e-01
5.926e-01
4.740e-01
3.555e-01
2.370e-01
1.185e-01
5.349e-08

Unsafe area.
Consider larger fillet radius
and/or stronger material

"fail_index" - bike_crank - bike_crank

**Figure 2–118**

6. Click ↙ in the Note dialog box, and select a location where the pedal joins the crank. The leader displays as shown in Figure 2–119.

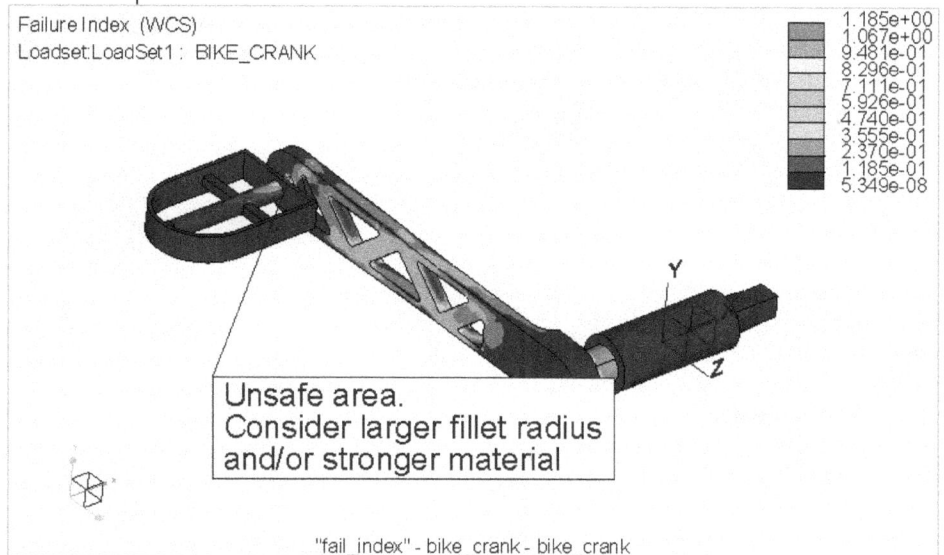

Failure Index (WCS)
Loadset:LoadSet1 : BIKE_CRANK

1.185e+00
1.067e+00
9.481e-01
8.296e-01
7.111e-01
5.926e-01
4.740e-01
3.555e-01
2.370e-01
1.185e-01
5.349e-08

Unsafe area.
Consider larger fillet radius
and/or stronger material

"fail_index" - bike_crank - bike_crank

**Figure 2–119**

7. Repeat Step 6 to add another leader as shown in Figure 2–120.

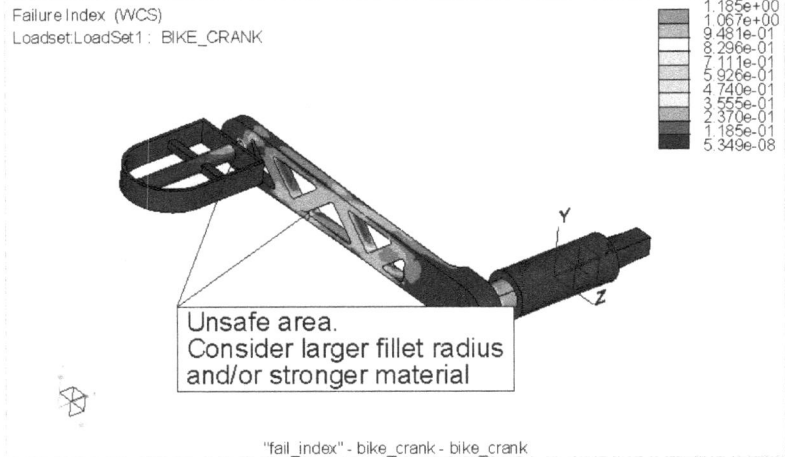

Failure Index (WCS)
Loadset:LoadSet1 : BIKE_CRANK

1.185e+00
1.067e+00
9.481e-01
8.296e-01
7.111e-01
5.926e-01
4.740e-01
3.555e-01
2.370e-01
1.185e-01
5.349e-08

Unsafe area.
Consider larger fillet radius
and/or stronger material

"fail_index" - bike_crank - bike_crank

**Figure 2–120**

8. Click **OK** to finish creating the annotation.

## Task 14 - Create a report.

1. In the top-level menu, select **File>Export>HTML Report**. The HTML Report dialog box opens as shown in Figure 2–121.

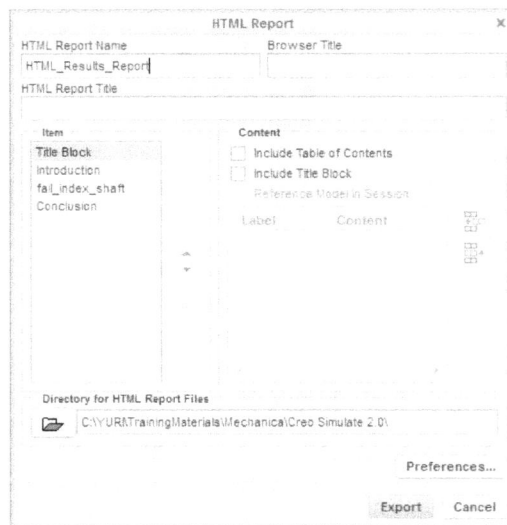

HTML Report

HTML Report Name                Browser Title
HTML_Results_Report
HTML Report Title

Item                  Content
Title Block           Include Table of Contents
Introduction          Include Title Block
fail_index_shaft      Reference Model in Session
Conclusion
                      Label        Content

Directory for HTML Report Files
C:\YURA\TrainingMaterials\Mechanica\Creo Simulate 2.0\

Preferences...

Export     Cancel

**Figure 2–121**

2. Rename the report as **Bike_Crank_Preliminary_Analysis**.

3. In the Item list, highlight **fail_index_shaft** and select the **Include modeling info** option, as shown in Figure 2–122.

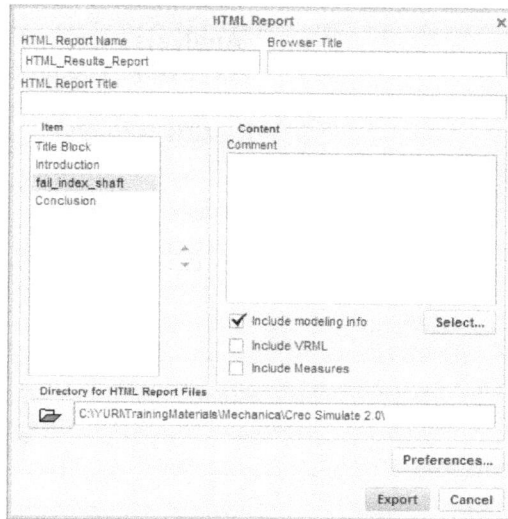

**Figure 2–122**

4. In the Item list, highlight **Conclusion** and enter **Bike crank predicted to fail at given loading conditions. Design modification is required**, as shown in Figure 2–123.

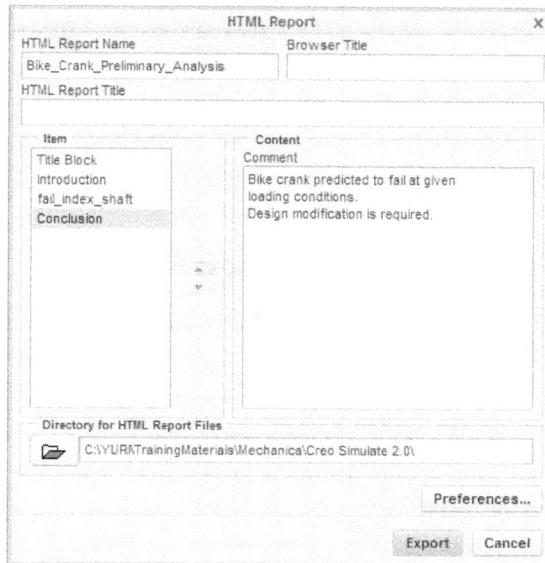

**Figure 2–123**

5. Click ___Export___ . The report is exported to the Creo working directory.

6. Open the *Bike_Crank_Preliminary_Analysis* directory in the Creo working directory and open **Bike_Crank_Preliminary_ Analysis.html** in a Web browser (such as Internet Explorer), for review. The report displays as shown in Figure 2–124.

## Results Report

fail_index_shaft

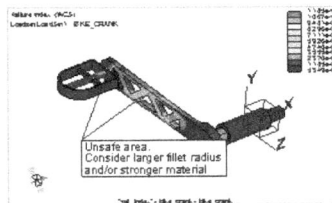

Figure 1. fail_index_shaft

Links

- Show Analysis Report File

BIKE_CRANK.ASM

Material Assignments

| Material Assignment "MaterialAssign1" | |
|---|---|
| References | Model (PEDAL.PRT) Model (LHS.PRT) |
| Material | AL6061 T4 |

**Figure 2–124**

7. Close the report.

8. Exit Creo Simulate Results. Save and close the model.

# Chapter 3

## Loads and Constraints

Loads and constraints are the boundary conditions that the model experiences in its working environment. Selecting the correct boundary conditions for your FEA model is a critical aspect of developing an accurate simulation. Therefore, when you are analyzing a model, the loads and constraints placed on it must realistically represent the operating conditions of your product.

This chapter contains the following topics:

- **Constraints**
- **Loads**
- **Surface Regions**
- **Singularities**

# 3.1 Constraints

**Learning Objectives**

- Understand the use of constraints.

- Understand rigid body motions.

- Understand constraint sets.

- Understand how to create a displacement constraint.

- Understand how to create planar, pin, or ball constraints.

- Understand how to create symmetry constraints.

In Creo Simulate, a constraint is a form of boundary condition in which a *prescribed displacement* is assigned to one or more geometrical entities in the model. Prescribed displacement means that the displacement of the geometrical entity to which it is applied stays constant (i.e., does not change during the analysis). A prescribed displacement (i.e., constraint) can be of a zero value, which is typically used to simulate all kinds of supports in the analysis model, or of a non-zero value, which is typically used to enforce a specific motion in the model.

Constraints are commonly used to model a true support, such as where a structure is fixed to a rigid foundation or adjoining structure. Another common use is to simulate various symmetry conditions, such as mirror symmetry, cyclic symmetry, or anti-symmetry.

Although constraints are essential for structural analyses, it is usually preferable to limit the use of constraints as much as possible. Since the essence of structural FEA is to calculate displacements (along with the corresponding strains and stresses), the prescribed displacements effectively force an assumed solution onto some of the geometrical entities in the model. Therefore, too many constraints might unnaturally stiffen the model, and, consequently, the stresses might typically err on the low side.

# Rigid Body Motions

In static analysis, it is necessary to provide sufficient supports to prevent rigid body motions (RBM), which are the movements of parts of the structure that do not produce strain. An example of a simply supported beam is shown in Figure 3–1.

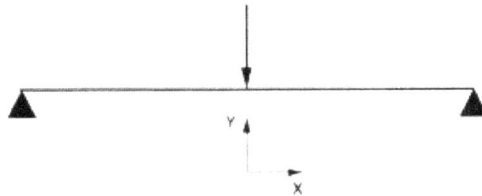

**Figure 3–1**

When using handbook formulas to calculate stresses, the only supports needed are those in the Y-direction. Since no loads are applied in the X-direction, a support in that direction is not necessary. However, in FEA the lack of support in X-direction results in a fatal error or inaccurate results. This is because a small load in the X-direction occurs during the FEA solution process, because of rounding errors.

*If possible RBMs are detected, Creo Simulate displays the error message:* **The model is insufficiently constrained for the analysis.**

The number of possible RBMs varies from one model to another. For a single part in 3D, there are six possible RBMs: three translations and three rotations. For an assembly, the number could be much greater, since each part now has six possible RBMs that have to be eliminated by applying constraints and connections between the parts.

# Constraint Sets

Every constraint in Creo Simulate belongs to a constraint set. A constraint set is a collection of constraints that act together on your model.

Constraint sets provide the means of organizing your modeling entities in a logical way, to have the additional flexibility of treating your constraints separately when setting up various analysis scenarios and load cases. A carefully considered approach to constraint sets simplifies the analyses definition.

To manage your constraint sets, select **Constraints>Constraint Sets** in the *Home* tab to open the Constraint Sets dialog box as shown in Figure 3–2.

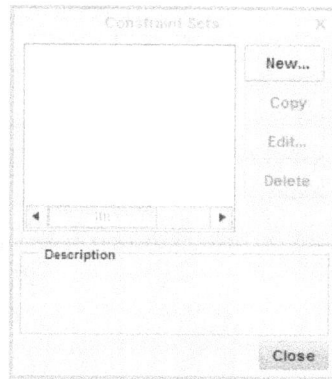

**Figure 3–2**

Constraint sets can be created, copied, edited, or deleted.

## Displacement Constraint

The displacement constraint is the most commonly used tool in Creo Simulate that is used to apply constraints. To apply a displacement constraint, click [icon] in the *Home* tab. The Constraint dialog box opens as shown in Figure 3–3.

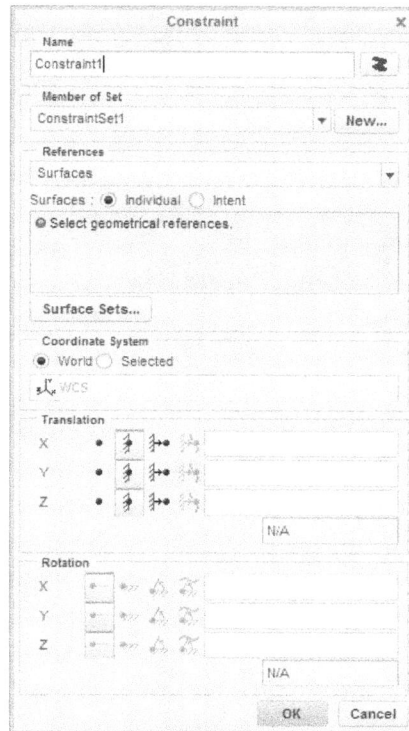

**Figure 3–3**

The options in the Constraint dialog box are as follows:

| Section | Option | Description |
|---|---|---|
| Name | N/A | Assigns a name to the constraint. |
| Member of Set | Constraint sets in the model | Selects a constraint set. |
| References | Surfaces | Assigns the constraint to surfaces. |
| | Edges/Curves | Assigns the constraint to edges or curves. |
| | Points | Assigns the constraint to vertices or points. |
| Coordinate System | World | The constraint directions are defined in WCS. |
| | Selected | Enables you to select another coordinate system to define constraint directions. The coordinate system can be cartesian, cylindrical, or spherical. |
| Translation | • | Enables the selected geometry to move in a direction. |
| | | Constrains the selected geometry in a direction. |
| | | Forces the selected geometry to move along a direction by a non-zero prescribed displacement value. |
| Rotation | | Enables the selected geometry to rotate about a direction. Not applicable to solid elements, which do not carry rotational degrees of freedom at their nodal points. |
| | | Constrains the selected geometry against rotations about a direction. Not applicable to solid elements, which do not carry rotational degrees of freedom at their nodal points. |
| | | Forces the nodes on the selected geometry into rotation about a direction by a non-zero prescribed angle. Not applicable to solid elements, which do not carry rotational degrees of freedom at their nodal points. |

## Planar, Pin, and Ball Constraints

The Planar constraint enables you to create a constraint that permits full planar movement, but constrains the off-plane displacement. Only planar surfaces can be selected.

To apply a planar constraint, click 🖑 in the *Home* tab. The Constraint dialog box opens as shown in Figure 3–4.

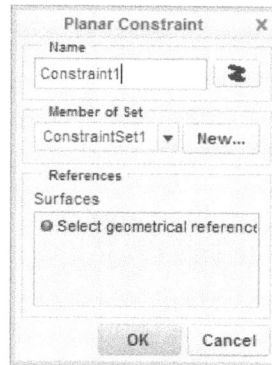

**Figure 3–4**

The Pin constraint enables you to control the translation or rotation about the axis of a cylindrical surface. Only cylindrical surfaces can be selected.

To apply a pin constraint, click 🖑 in the *Home* tab. The Constraint dialog box opens as shown in Figure 3–5. Use the buttons next to ⟲ to control the rotation about the cylinder's axis, and the buttons next to ⟶ to control the translation along the axis.

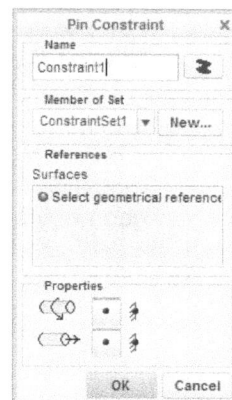

**Figure 3–5**

A Ball constraint simulates a ball support in which all of the translations are fixed while all of the rotations are free. Only spherical surfaces can be selected for this type of constraint.

To apply a ball constraint, click  in the *Home* tab. The Constraint dialog box opens as shown in Figure 3–6.

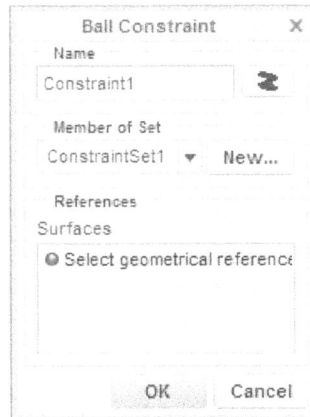

**Figure 3–6**

## Symmetry Constraints

There are two types of symmetry constraints in Creo Simulate:

*   Mirror Symmetry

*   Cyclic Symmetry

Using symmetry constraints, you can take advantage of the model's symmetry to reduce meshing and analysis time. In essence, symmetry constraints enable you to analyze a segment of the model and project the result onto the entire model.

### Mirror Symmetry

The mirror symmetry constraint requires that the model exhibits a *reflective* symmetry about a plane. The geometry and modeling entities on one side of the plane must mirror the geometry and modeling entities on the other side of the plane.

Use the following steps to apply a mirror symmetry constraint:

1. Cut your model in half along the plane of symmetry. The result is 1/2 of the geometry (it could be 1/4 or even 1/8 of the geometry if your analysis model exhibits more than one plane of symmetry).
2. In the *Home* tab, select **Constraints>Symmetry**. The Symmetry Constraint dialog box opens.
3. Expand the Type drop-down list and select **Mirror**. The Symmetry Constraint dialog box opens as shown in Figure 3–7.

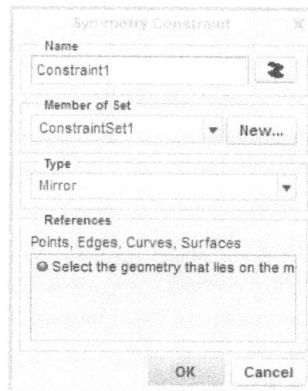

**Figure 3–7**

4. Select the surfaces, edges, curves, or points located on the symmetry plane.

5. Click   OK   to finish.

## Cyclic Symmetry

In a model with cyclic symmetry, a 3D geometric shape is repeated a number of times around the axis of rotation. The geometry is not continuous, but rather cyclic. For example, the fan shown in Figure 3–8 is an example of a cyclically symmetric geometry.

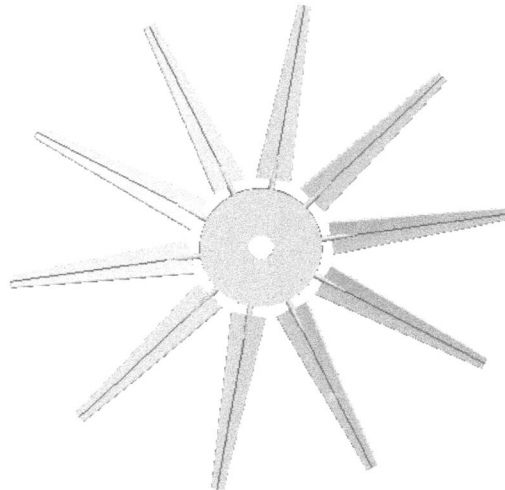

**Figure 3–8**

If loads, constraints, materials, etc., are cyclic as well, you can analyze a single blade, as shown in Figure 3–9, by properly isolating it and applying constraints that capture the cyclic symmetry.

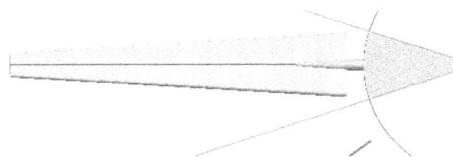

**Figure 3–9**

Use the following steps to apply a cyclic symmetry constraint:

1. Isolate the cyclic geometry by cutting it out of your model. The cutout surfaces do not have to be planar. The only requirement is that the cross-sections on the cutout surfaces must be identical.
2. In the *Home* tab, select **Constraints>Symmetry**. The Symmetry Constraint dialog box opens.

3. Expand the Type drop-down list and select **Cyclic**. The Symmetry Constraint dialog box opens as shown in Figure 3–10.

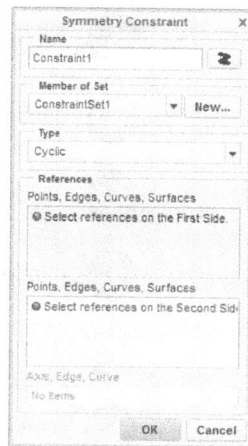

**Figure 3–10**

4. Select the geometry on the first cutout boundary.
5. Select the geometry on the second cutout boundary.
6. Depending on the selected geometry, Creo Simulate might or might not be able to automatically determine the axis of symmetry. If not, you need to select the axis of symmetry.

7. Click  OK  to finish.

Note that both the geometry and boundary conditions must meet the criteria of cyclic symmetry. If the constraints or loading is not repeated about the axis of rotation by the same number of repetitions as the geometry, the results are invalid.

# 3.2 Loads

**Learning Objectives**

Understand types of loads.

Understand load sets.

Understand how to create a force or moment load.

Understand how to create a pressure load.

Understand how to create a bearing load.

Understand how to create a gravity load.

Understand how to create a centrifugal load.

Understand how to create a temperature load.

Understand how to create a preload.

Unsatisfactory representation of the loading is a common cause of inaccurate analysis results. Therefore, gathering adequate information about the magnitude of the loads is a critical aspect of developing an accurate simulation. It should be noted that in a linear analysis the stresses and deformations are directly proportional to the magnitude of the loading. For example, a possible error in loading of 20% leads to a minimum 20% error in stresses and deflections.

There are two main types of loading in structural FEA:

- **Mechanical loads:** Consisting of concentrated or distributed forces or moments and body forces. The mechanical loads are typically related to a coordinate system, and consist of magnitude and orientation. The spatial distribution and time dependence of the load can also be defined. The following types of mechanical loads are available in Creo Simulate:

  - Force/Moment load
  - Pressure load
  - Bearing load

- Gravity load
- Centrifugal load
- **Initial strains:** Caused by thermal expansion, press-fit, or pre-stress. The following types of initial strain loads are available in Creo Simulate:

  - Temperature load
  - Preload

# Load Sets

Every load in Creo Simulate belongs to a load set. A load set is a collection of loads that act together on your model.

Load sets provide a means of organizing your modeling entities in a logical way, to have the additional flexibility of treating your loads separately when setting up various analysis scenarios and load cases. A carefully considered approach to load sets simplifies the analyses definition.

To manage your load sets, select **Loads>Load Sets** in the *Home* tab to open the Load Sets dialog box as shown in Figure 3–11.

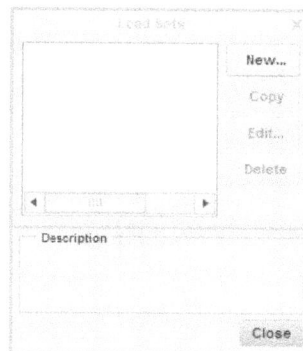

**Figure 3–11**

Load sets can be created, copied, edited, or deleted.

# Force/Moment Load

To apply a Force/Moment load, click ⊞ in the *Home* tab. The Force/Moment Load dialog box opens as shown in Figure 3–12.

**Figure 3–12**

The options available in the Force/Moment Load dialog box are as follows.

| Section | Option | Description |
|---|---|---|
| **Name** | **N/A** | Assigns a name to the load. |
| **Member of Set** | **Load sets in the model** | Selects a load set. |
| **References** | **Surfaces** | Applies the load to surfaces. |
| | **Edges/Curves** | Applies the load to edges or curves. |
| | **Points** | Applies the load to vertices or points. |
| **Coordinate System** | **World** | The load is related to the WCS. |
| | **Selected** | Enables you to select another coordinate system to define the load directions. The coordinate system can be cartesian, cylindrical, or spherical. |

| Distribution | Total Load | Applies a distributed load along the length or area of the entity, so that the sum of the distributed load equals the entered load value. |
|---|---|---|
| | Force Per Unit Area / Force Per Unit Length | The entered load value is interpreted as the load density (i.e., force per unit area or length) over the entity. |
| | Total Load At Point | Applies a distributed load (over the entity) that is statically equivalent to a load applied to a single point. |
| | Total Bearing Load At Point | Applies a distributed load (on a cylindrical surface) that represents the force and moment that one cylindrically shaped part exerts on another (e.g., a pin and a hole). The distributed load is made statically equivalent to the load applied at a point. |
| Spatial Variation | Uniform | Applies a uniform load over the entity. The load does not have a spatial variation. |
| | Function of Coordinates | The load's spatial variation is defined as a function of a coordinate system. Cartesian, Cylindrical, or Spherical coordinate systems can be used. |
| | Interpolated Over Entity | Applies a spatial variation that is either linear, quadratic, or cubic along the entity. |

# Pressure Load

A pressure load is a distributed load that acts in normal to the part surface direction, even if the surface is curved. The positive direction is toward the part body.

To apply a Pressure load, click ⊞ in the *Home* tab. The Pressure Load dialog box opens as shown in Figure 3–13.

**Figure 3–13**

The options available in the Pressure Load dialog box are as follows:

| Section | Option | Description |
|---|---|---|
| **Name** | **N/A** | Assigns a name to the load. |
| **Member of Set** | **Load sets in the model** | Selects a load set. |
| **Spatial Variation** | **Uniform** | Applies a uniform load over the entity. The load does not have a spatial variation. |
| | **Function of Coordinates** | The load's spatial variation is defined as a function of a coordinate system. Cartesian, Cylindrical, or Spherical coordinate systems can be used. |
| | **Interpolated Over Entity** | Applies a spatial variation that is either linear, quadratic, or cubic along the entity. |
| | **External Coefficients Field** | Imports a file containing the coefficients that specify the spatial variation of the load. The coefficients are automatically mapped onto the model surfaces. |

# Bearing Load

Bearing loads approximate the pressure applied on a cylindrical hole by a rigid pin or shaft passing through that hole.

To apply a Bearing load, click ⌖ in the *Home* tab. The Bearing Load dialog box opens as shown in Figure 3–14.

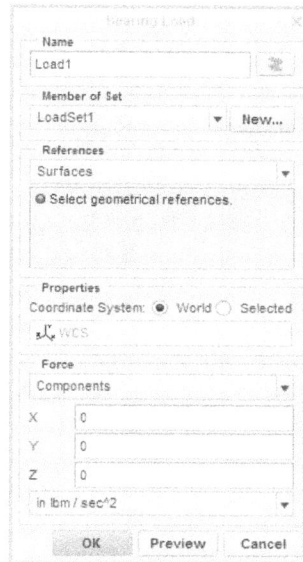

**Figure 3–14**

The options available in the Bearing Load dialog box are as follows:

| Section | Option | Description |
|---|---|---|
| **Name** | **N/A** | Assigns a name to the load. |
| **Member of Set** | **Load sets in the model** | Selects a load set. |
| **References** | **Surfaces** | Applies the load to surfaces. Only cylindrical surfaces are permitted. |
| | **Edges/Curves** | Applies the load to edges or curves in 2D models. |
| **Coordinate System** | **World** | The load is related to the WCS. |
| | **Selected** | Enables you to select another coordinate system to define the load direction. The coordinate system can be only Cartesian. |

| Force | Components | Load direction and magnitude is determined by the entered force components. |
|---|---|---|
| | Dir Vector & Mag | Load direction is defined by a 3D vector. |
| | Dir Points & Mag | Load direction is defined by selecting two points. |

## Gravity Load

A gravity load simulates the body force created by the acceleration or deceleration of your model.

To apply a Gravity load, click ⬚ in the *Home* tab. The Gravity Load dialog box opens as shown in Figure 3–15.

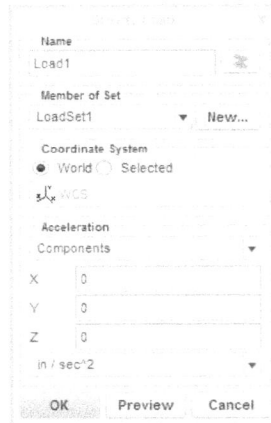

**Figure 3–15**

The options available in the Gravity Load dialog box are as follows:

| Section | Option | Description |
|---|---|---|
| Name | N/A | Assigns a name to the load. |
| Member of Set | Load sets in the model | Selects a load set. |
| Coordinate System | World | The load is related to the WCS. |
| | Selected | Enables you to select another coordinate system to define the load direction. The coordinate system can be only Cartesian. |

| Force | Components | Load direction and magnitude is determined by the entered force components. |
|---|---|---|
| | Dir Vector & Mag | Load direction is defined by a 3D vector. |
| | Dir Points & Mag | Load direction is defined by selecting two points. |

# Centrifugal Load

A centrifugal load applies a body force that is created by the rotation of your model. Both angular velocity and acceleration can be applied.

To apply a Centrifugal load, click ⤵ in the *Home* tab. The Centrifugal Load dialog box opens as shown in Figure 3–16.

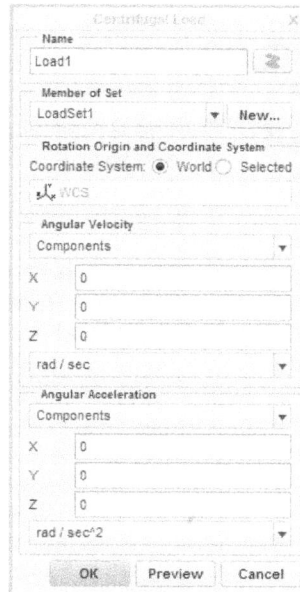

**Figure 3–16**

The options available in the Centrifugal Load dialog box are as follows:

| Section | Option | Description |
|---|---|---|
| Name | N/A | Assigns a name to the load. |
| Member of Set | Load sets in the model | Selects a load set. |

| Coordinate System | World | The load is related to the WCS. |
|---|---|---|
| | Selected | Enables you to select another coordinate system to define the load direction. The coordinate system can be only Cartesian. |
| Angular Velocity | Components | Axis of rotation and load magnitude are determined by the entered components. |
| | Dir Vector & Mag | Axis of rotation is defined by a 3D vector. |
| | Dir Points & Mag | Axis of rotation is defined by selecting two points. |
| Angular Acceleration | Components | Axis of rotation and load magnitude are determined by the entered components. |
| | Dir Vector & Mag | Axis of rotation is defined by a 3D vector. |
| | Dir Points & Mag | Axis of rotation is defined by selecting two points. |

## Temperature Load

The temperature load applies an initial strain to your model exerted by a change in the temperature of the selected geometric entities.

To apply a Temperature load, click 🗋 in the *Home* tab. The Structural Temperature Load dialog box opens as shown in Figure 3–17.

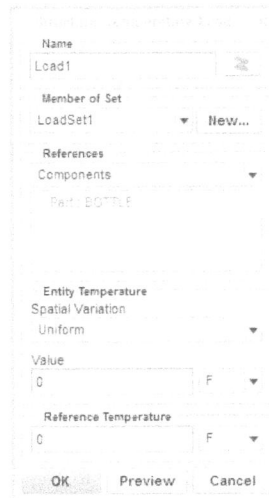

**Figure 3–17**

The options available in the Structural Temperature Load dialog box are as follows:

| Section | Option | Description |
|---|---|---|
| Name | N/A | Assigns a name to the load. |
| Member of Set | Load sets in the model | Selects a load set. |
| References | Components | Applies the temperature change to assembly components. |
| | Volumes | Applies the temperature change to solid volumes. |
| | Surfaces | Applies the temperature change to surfaces. |
| | Edges/Curves | Applies the temperature change to edges or curves in a 2D model. |
| Entity Temperature> Spatial Variation | Uniform | The temperature change is distributed uniformly over the entity. |
| | Function of Coordinates | The temperature change is defined as a function of a coordinate system. |
| | External Field | Imports the temperature field from a file. |
| Reference Temperature | N/A | Defines the zero strain temperature. |

## Preload

The Preload load simulates a bolt preload on a volume or components. The preload shortens the volume or component in the axial direction.

To apply a Preload, click ⊤ in the *Home* tab. The Preload dialog box opens as shown in Figure 3–18.

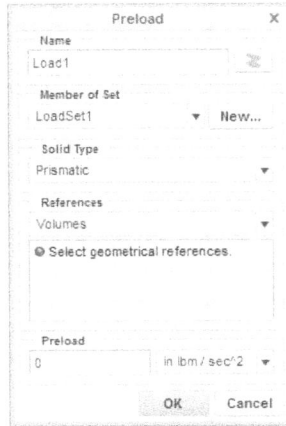

**Figure 3–18**

The options available in the Preload dialog box are as follows:

| Section | Option | Description |
|---|---|---|
| **Name** | **N/A** | Assigns a name to the load. |
| **Member of Set** | **Load sets in the model** | Selects a load set. |
| **Solid Type** | **Prismatic** | Requires the solid to be a prism. It should have two planar bases and all side edges normal to the two bases. |
| | **General** | Applies to any solid component or volume. Requires selecting the preload direction. |
| **References** | **Volumes** | Applies the preload to solid volumes. |
| | **Components** | Applies the preload to assembly components. |

# 3.3 Surface Regions

**Learning Objective**

Understand how to create surface regions.

Surface regions in Creo Simulate enable you to apply modeling entities to a portion of a surface. The creation of surface regions is useful in the following situations:

- Loads or constraints need to be applied to specific areas of the model.

- Specific contact regions between the faces or surfaces of a model must be analyzed.

- Refinement of the mesh is required in a specific area of the model.

For example, surface regions are required for the model shown in Figure 3–19 because the loads and constraints are only applied over small portions of the parts surface.

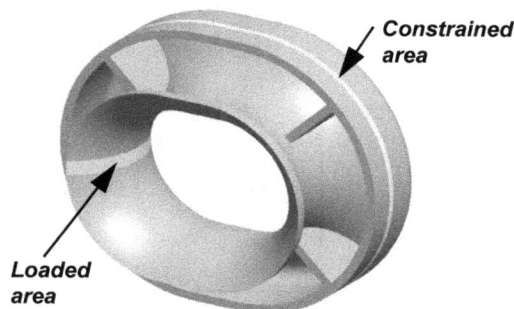

**Figure 3–19**

Surface region creation is a two-step process:

1. Define the boundary of the surface region. It can be created in Creo Parametric or Creo Simulate as a sketch or chain of datum curves. The datum curves must lie exactly on the parts surface, otherwise the creation of a surface region fails.
2. Define the parent surfaces for the surface region. The parent surfaces are then split by the surface region boundary, separating the surface region from the parent surface.

It is recommended that you create surface regions before you apply modeling entities, such as materials, loads, constraints, mesh controls, etc., to the model.

# 3.4  Singularities

**Learning Objective**

Understand how to handle models with stress singularities.

A singularity is the location on a model in which theoretically infinite stress and/or displacement occurs. A simple example of a singularity is a force applied at a point. The stress as calculated by the force over area formula is infinite because the area under a point is zero.

Physically, displacement and stress cannot be infinite. Mathematically, Creo Simulate tries to solve the model exactly as defined, which results in unrealistically high stresses or displacements at the singularities. Additionally, singularities disrupt and slow down the convergence process by requiring very high p-levels, and often causing the model to not converge.

**Types of Singularities**

Two types of singularities occur in Creo Simulate Structural: those due to loading and constraint conditions and those due to model geometry. Combinations of loads or constraints for types of elements that result in theoretically infinite stresses or displacements for 3D models are as follows.

| Load or Constraint | Beam | Shell | Solid |
|---|---|---|---|
| **Points** | Displacement: OK | Displacement: OK | Displacement: Infinite |
| | Stress: OK | Stress: Infinite | Stress: Infinite |
| **Edges and Curves** | Displacement: OK | Displacement: OK | Displacement: Infinite |
| | Stress: OK | Stress: OK | Stress: Infinite |
| **Faces and Surfaces** | N/A | Displacement: OK | Displacement: OK |
| | N/A | Stress: OK | Stress: Infinite |

Along with loads and constraints, sharp reentrant corners or other abrupt changes in geometry can cause singularities. It is recommended that you smooth out the discontinuous geometry to improve convergence.

# Excluded Elements

If a singularity cannot be avoided, the following technique can be used to improve convergence:

1. Mesh the close vicinity of the singularity with small elements, which can be done using the Isolate for Exclusion Auto GEM Control.
2. When setting up the analysis, request that those elements be ignored during the convergence process.

Collectively, this technique is called *excluding the elements*.

Use the following steps to exclude elements from convergence:

1. Once the loads and constraints have been set up, click ⬚ in the *AutoGEM* area to open the Isolate for Exclusion Control dialog box, as shown in Figure 3–20.

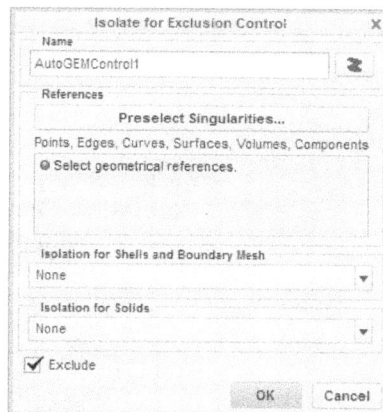

**Figure 3–20**

2. Manually select the singularities or click Preselect Singularities... to have Creo Simulate detect the potential singularities automatically.

3. Based on the dimensions of your model, enter the *Maximum Element Size* for the isolation. The Isolate for Exclusion Control dialog box should display similar to the one shown in Figure 3–21. Close the dialog box.

**Figure 3–21**

4. Alternatively, you can mesh the model and select **Info> Isolating Elements** in the AutoGEM dialog box to highlight the isolating elements in red, as shown in Figure 3–22.

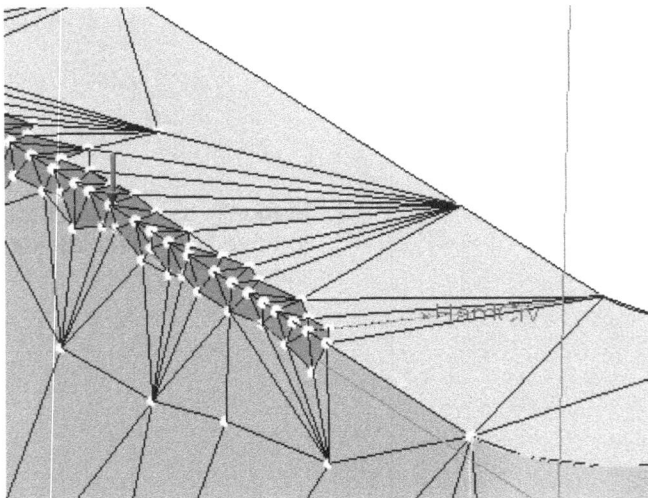

**Figure 3–22**

5. When setting up the analysis, in the *Excluded Elements* tab, select **Exclude Elements** as shown in Figure 3–23, and select other options as needed.

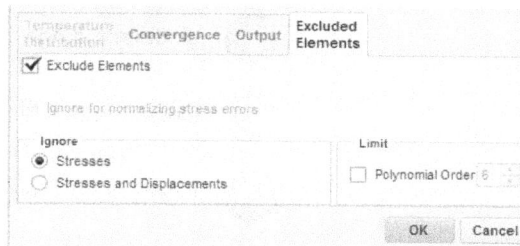

**Figure 3–23**

**Guidelines**

The general guidelines for improving convergence and obtaining more reliable analysis results are as follows:

- Spread the load or constraint over a larger area. Avoid using point or line loads and constraints in solid models.

- Use soft and flexible supports over rigid constraints.

- If possible, alter the geometry to smooth sharp reentrant corners or other geometrical discontinuities. It is recommended that you use fillets.

- In models that still have singularities, use excluded elements in the analysis.

# Practice 3a | Stress Analysis of a Crank

**Learning Objectives**

Understand how to create multiple load sets.

Understand how to apply pin constraints.

Understand how to apply a bearing load.

Understand how to apply a moment load using the **Total Load at Point** option.

In this practice, you will analyze the crank part shown in Figure 3–24 for two load cases:

- **Bending load case:** A force of 500N is applied to the hole in the upper boss, acting in-plane of the crank.

- **Torsional load case:** A twisting moment of 10,000 Nmm is applied to the upper boss.

The part is constrained by a pin support in the lower boss and by two bushing supports at the ends of the lower rod, as shown in Figure 3–24. This way, the lower beam of the part is not constrained against rotation at its ends, similar to a simply supported beam.

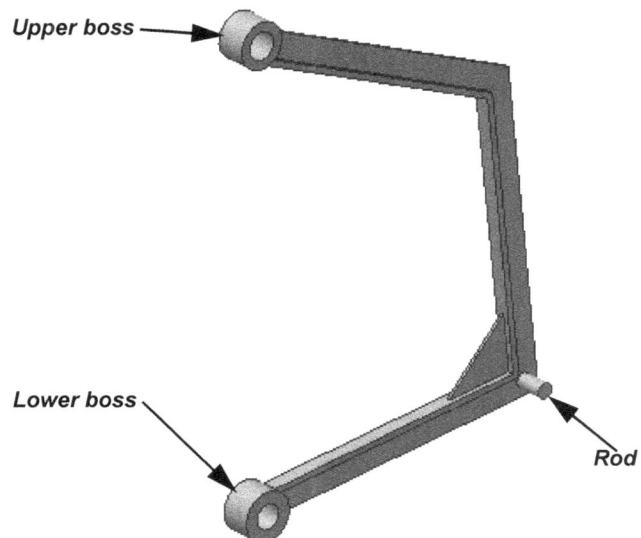

Figure 3–24

## Modeling Tasks

### Task 1 - Open the model.

1. Open **crank.prt** in Creo Parametric. The unshaded part displays as shown in Figure 3–25.

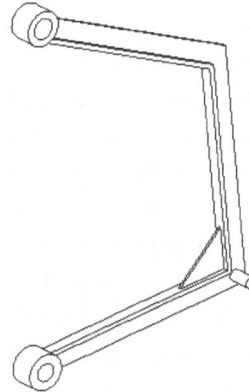

**Figure 3–25**

2. Ensure that the unit system is set to **mmNs**.

3. Switch to the Creo Simulate environment.

### Task 2 - Apply the material.

In this task, you will select the material for the part.

1. In the *Home* tab, click ⌐. The Materials dialog box opens as shown in Figure 3–26.

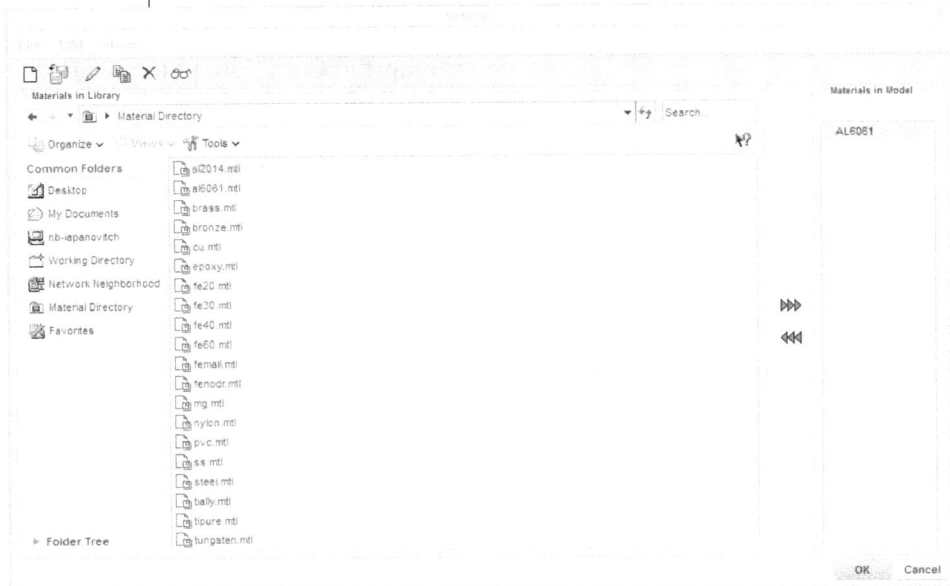

**Figure 3–26**

2. In the *Materials in Library* area, select **STEEL**.

*The model's material should be as stated.*

3. Click ▶▶▶ to transfer **STEEL** to the *Materials in Model* area.

4. Select **Edit>Properties** to check the material properties.

The HS-low-alloy steel (STEEL) has the following default material properties:

- Poisson's ratio = 0.27

- Young's modulus = 199948 MPa

- Coeff of thermal expansion = 1.17e-5 /C

- Density = 7.82708e-9 tonne/mm^3

5. Click OK to close the Materials dialog box.

6.  In the *Home* tab, click 🖫. The Material Assignment dialog box opens as shown in Figure 3–27.

**Figure 3–27**

7.  Note that the material **STEEL** has automatically been assigned to the part.

8.  Click OK to close the Material Assignment dialog box.

## Task 3 - Mesh the model.

1.  Click ▦. The AutoGEM dialog box opens as shown in Figure 3–28.

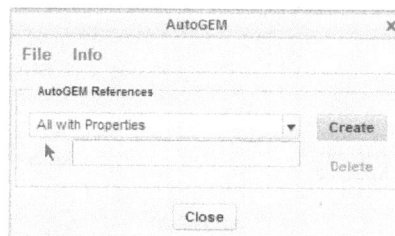

**Figure 3–28**

2.  Expand the AutoGEM References drop-down list and select **All with Properties**.

3.  Click Create.

4.  Creo Simulate meshes the model and displays the AutoGEM Summary and Diagnostics dialog boxes.

*The **All with Properties** option will automatically mesh all of the solid volumes in the model to which a material has been assigned.*

5. Close both the AutoGEM Summary and Diagnostics dialog boxes, but do not close the AutoGEM dialog box. The model displays as shown in Figure 3–29.

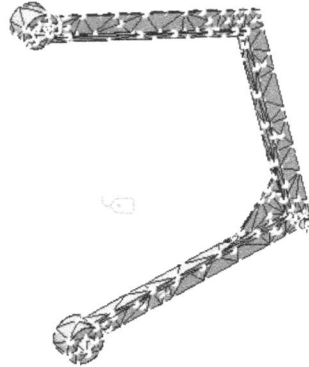

**Figure 3–29**

6. Click ⬚ (Simulation Display) in the floating toolbar. The Simulation Display dialog box opens.

7. Select the *Modeling Entities* tab and clear the **Material Assignments** option to hide the material assignment icon.

8. Select the *Mesh* tab and clear the **Mesh Points** option in the *Mesh Entities* area as shown in Figure 3–30.

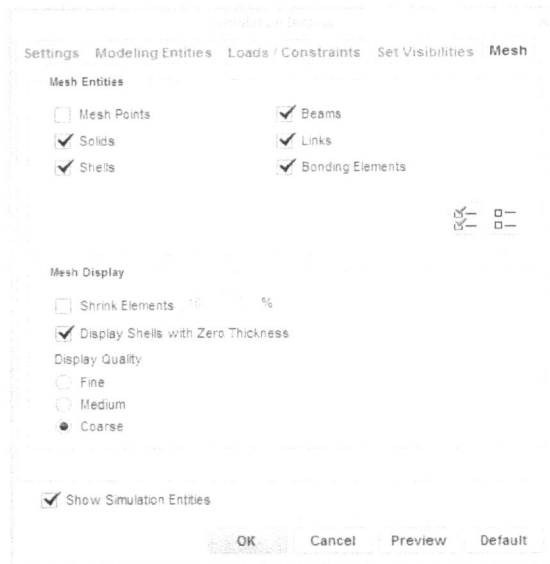

**Figure 3–30**

9. Click OK to close the Simulation Display dialog box. The model displays as shown in Figure 3–31. Rotate the model and review the elements in various areas of the model.

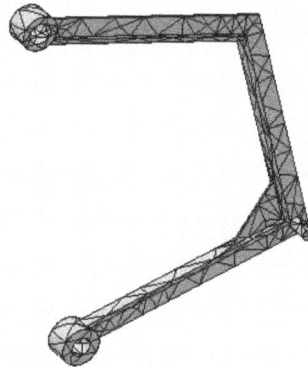

**Figure 3–31**

10. Save the mesh and close the AutoGEM dialog box.

## Task 4 - Create load sets.

In this task, you will create two load sets for the two load cases in this analysis.

1. Expand the *Loads* area, as shown in Figure 3–32.

**Figure 3–32**

2. Select **Load Sets**. The Load Sets dialog box opens as shown in Figure 3–33.

**Figure 3–33**

3. Click New… . The Load Set Definition dialog box opens as shown in Figure 3–34.

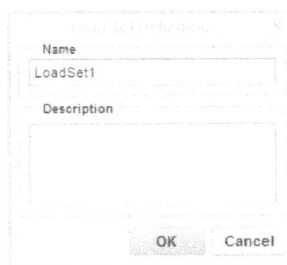

**Figure 3–34**

4. In the *Name* field, enter **bending** and click OK .

5. Repeat Steps 3 and 4 and create another load set named **torsion**.

6. Click Close to close the Load Sets dialog box.

---

### Task 5 - Apply a bending load.

---

In this task, you will apply a bearing load on the hole in the upper boss, acting in-plane of the part. The bearing load has a resultant force in a specified direction. The bearing load is applied normal to the surface in a non-uniform distribution, such as if a shaft placed in the hole would exert on the hole surface.

1.  Sketch two datum points with datum plane FRONT as the
    sketching plane and datum plane RIGHT as the reference
    plane. Sketch the first datum point (PNT0) at the center of the
    arm hole (add the edge of the hole as a reference to enable
    automatic snapping to the center) and the second datum
    point (PNT1) at the dimensions shown in Figure 3–35. These
    points define the bearing load direction.

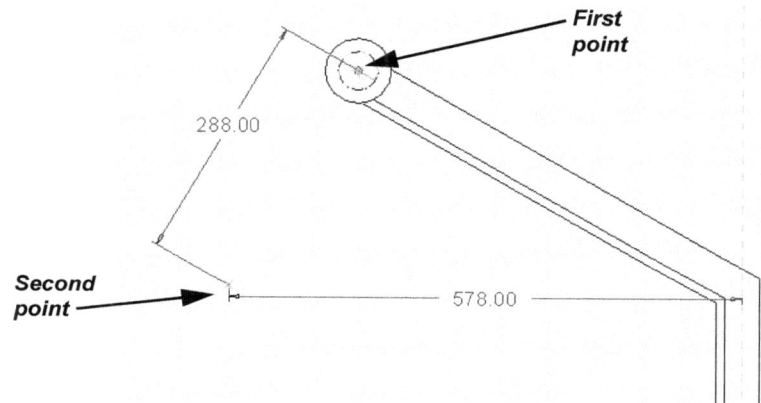

**Figure 3–35**

The model displays as shown in Figure 3–36.

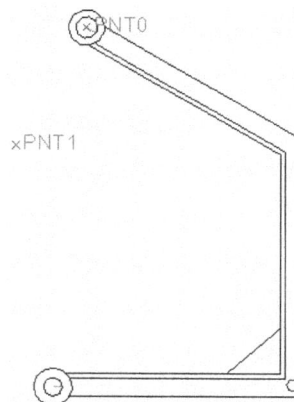

**Figure 3–36**

2. Click 🗐 . The Bearing Load dialog box opens as shown in Figure 3–37.

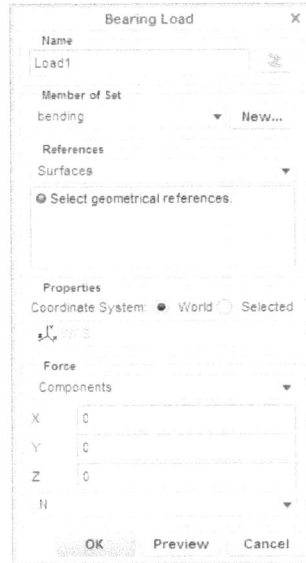

**Figure 3–37**

3. In the *Name* field, enter **bend_load**.

4. In the *Member of Set* field, select **bending**.

5. Select the hole shown in Figure 3–38.

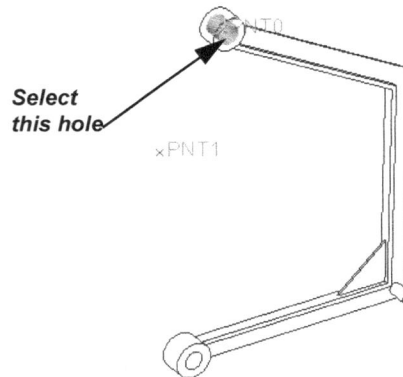

**Figure 3–38**

6. Expand the Force drop-down list and select **Dir Points & Mag**. The Bearing Load dialog box opens as shown in Figure 3–39.

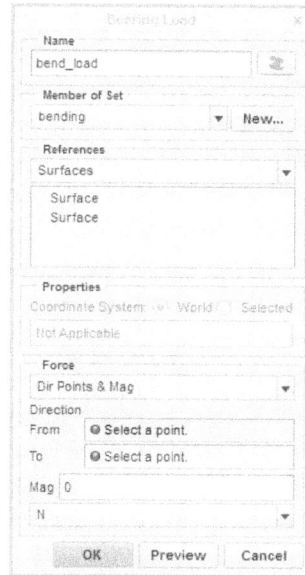

**Figure 3–39**

7. In the *Direction* area, for *From*, select **PNT0** and for *To*, select **PNT1** to define direction for the bearing load.

8. In the *Mag* field, enter **500**.

9. Click  Preview  to display the bearing load distribution, as shown in Figure 3–40.

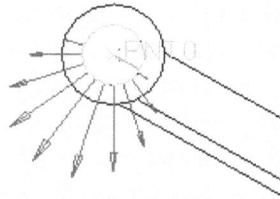

**Figure 3–40**

10. Click OK . The model displays as shown in Figure 3–41.

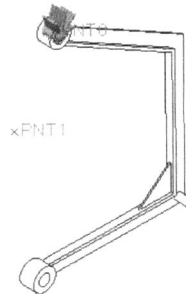

**Figure 3–41**

11. Use the Simulation Display dialog box to hide the bending load set.

---

## Task 6 - Apply a torsional load.

---

In this task, you will apply a twisting moment on the hole in the upper boss. The moment simulates the load exerted by a shaft placed in the hole and torqued about the X-axis of the WCS.

1. In the *Home* tab, click . The Force/Moment Load dialog box opens as shown in Figure 3–42.

**Figure 3–42**

2. In the *Name* field, enter **twist_load**.

3. In the *Member of Set* field, select **torsion**.

4. Select the hole in the upper boss (the same hole that you selected when applying a bearing load). The Force/Moment dialog box opens as shown in Figure 3–43.

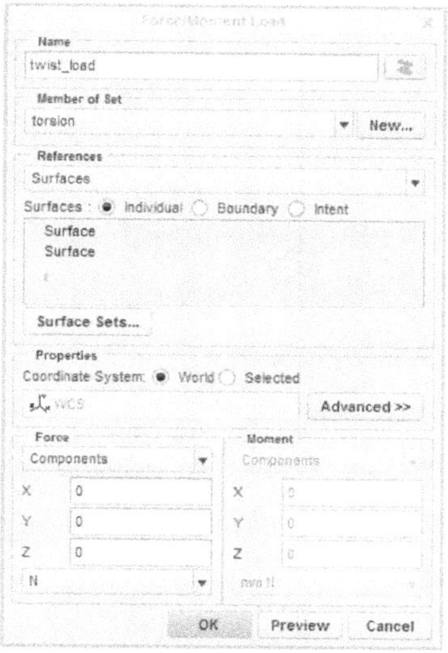

**Figure 3–43**

Note that the Moment fields in the dialog box are grayed out. This is because rotational degrees of freedom (i.e., moments) are not applicable to solid elements. Instead, a moment in a solid model must be applied as a collection of translational forces that are statically equivalent (i.e., exert the same effect) to the moment. In Creo Simulate, this can be done using the **Total Load at Point** option.

5. Click  Advanced >> .

6. Expand the Distribution drop-down list and select **Total Load at Point**. The Force/Moment dialog box opens as shown in Figure 3–44. Note that the Moment fields are no longer grayed out.

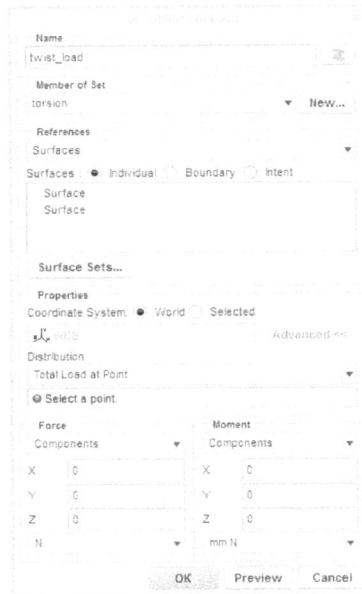

Figure 3–44

7. Select the **PNT0** point at the center of the hole.

8. In the *Moment* area, in the *X* field, enter **10000**.

9. Click Preview to display the load distribution, as shown in Figure 3–45.

*The load distribution is statically equivalent to the 10000 mmN moment applied at PNT0.*

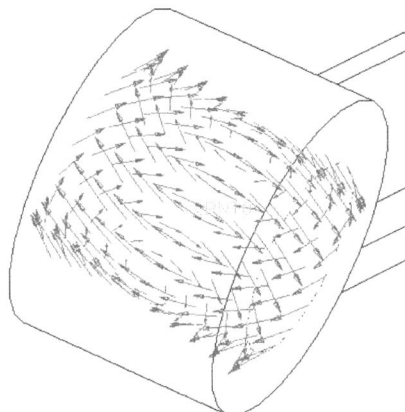

Figure 3–45

10. Click OK . The model displays as shown in Figure 3–46.

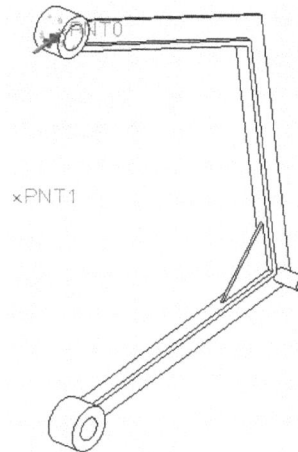

**Figure 3–46**

11. Use the Simulation Display dialog box to hide the torsion load set.

## Task 7 - Apply the constraints.

In this task, you will constrain the movement of the lower boss and of the rod, as shown in Figure 3–47.

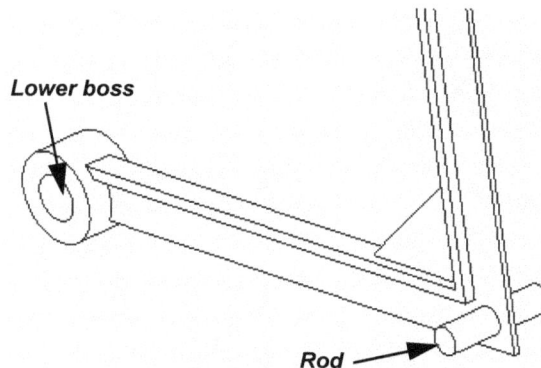

*Lower boss*

*Rod*

**Figure 3–47**

The boss is supported by a shaft and the rod is supported by two bushings. Both supports constrain translational motions, but permit rotation of the cylindrical surfaces about their respective axes. This type of support can be modeled using the Pin type of constraint.

1. Click ✎. The Pin Constraint dialog box opens.

2. In the *Name* field, enter **rod**.

3. Select the cylindrical surface of the rod shown in Figure 3–48, constrain the axial translation, and leave the rotation free, as shown in Figure 3–48.

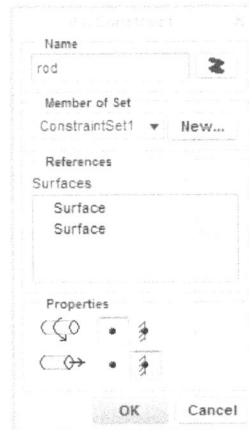

Name

rod

Member of Set

ConstraintSet1 ▼ New...

References

Surfaces

Surface
Surface

Properties

OK    Cancel

**Figure 3–48**

4. Click OK. The pin constraint displays as shown in Figure 3–49.

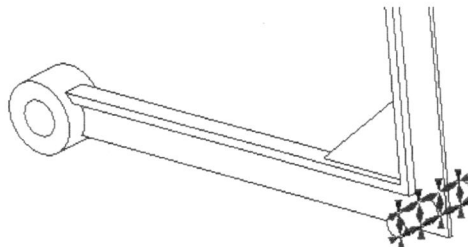

**Figure 3–49**

5. Click  again. Select the hole surface in the lower boss shown in Figure 3–50. In the *Name* field, enter **boss**. Constrain the axial translation and leave the rotation free, as shown in Figure 3–50.

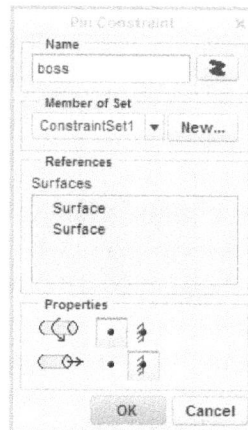

**Figure 3–50**

6. Click OK . The model displays as shown in Figure 3–51.

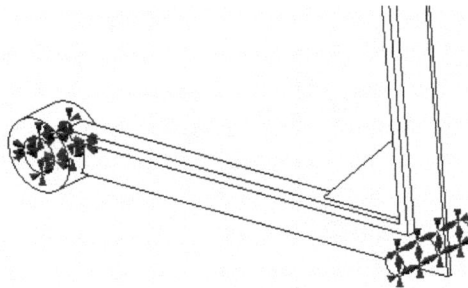

**Figure 3–51**

## Analysis Tasks

### Task 8 - Set up and run a Multi-Pass Adaptive analysis.

1. Create a new static analysis and name it **crank**.

2. Select both the **bending/CRANK** and **torsion/CRANK** load sets in the *Load Set / Component* area.

3. For the *Percent Convergence*, enter **10**. In the *Maximum Polynomial Order* field, enter **9**. The Static Analysis Definition dialog box opens as shown in Figure 3–52.

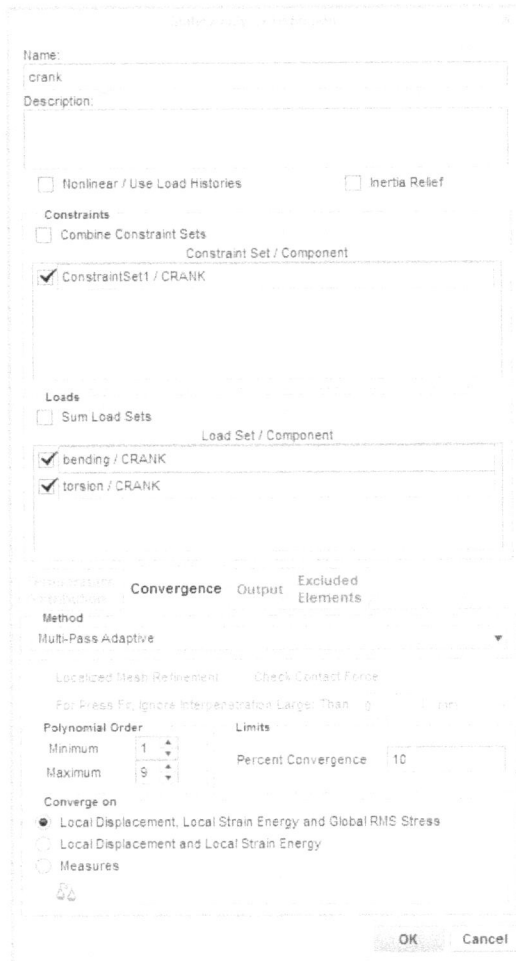

**Figure 3–52**

*You created and saved the mesh for the part in Task 3 of Modeling Tasks.*

4. Verify that the run settings are set so that the elements will be used from the existing mesh file. In the *Memory Allocation* field, enter **512**.

*The recommended memory allocation is 1/2 the RAM of your computer.*

5. Run the analysis. It should converge on pass 8. Note the warning in the Diagnostics box regarding the local reaction data. The warning displays because Creo Simulate uses the Cylindrical coordinate system on Pin constraints and the reaction forces could not be computed.

6.  Click ▣ in the Analyses and Design Studies dialog box to display the Run Status window. Scroll to the *RMS Stress Error Estimates* area and note that the analysis converged to under 1% RMS Stress Error, as shown in Figure 3–53.

```
RMS Stress Error Estimates:

Load Set          Stress Error  % of Max Prin Str
----------------  ------------  ------------------
bending           1.61e+00       0.8% of  1.97e+02
torsion           8.02e-01       1.0% of  8.14e+01
```

**Figure 3–53**

7.  Close the Run Status window.

## Results Tasks

### Task 9 - Animate the deformation for the bending load case.

1.  Click ▤ in the Analyses and Design Studies dialog box. The Result Window Definition dialog box opens.

2.  In the *Name* field, enter **deform_bending**.

3.  Clear the **torsion** load set option.

4.  Expand the Quantity tab drop-down list and select **Displacement**. The Result Window Definition dialog box opens as shown in Figure 3–54.

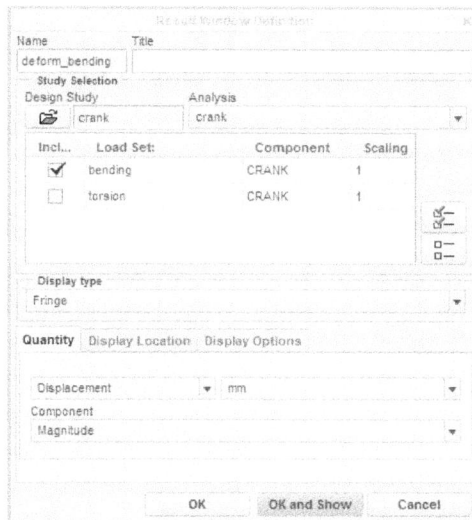

**Figure 3–54**

5. Select the *Display Options* tab. Select the **Deformed, Overlay Undeformed, Show Element Edges,** and **Animate** options. In the *Scaling* field, enter **20**, as shown in Figure 3–55.

**Figure 3–55**

6. Click ⟨OK and Show⟩. The Displacement Magnitude result plot is displayed and animated.

7. Zoom in on the rod. Note that the rod's rotation is not restricted, as if it was supported by sleeve bearings or bushings. This results from applying the Pin constraint to the rod's surface.

8. Stop the animation at Frame 5. The result plot displays as shown in Figure 3–56.

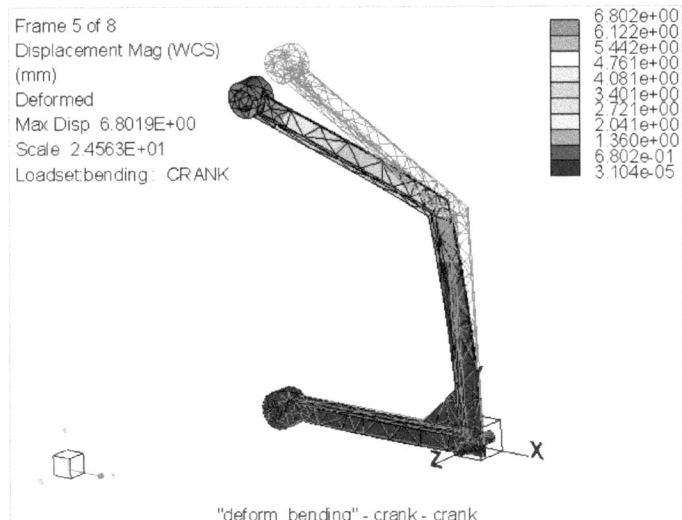

Frame 5 of 8
Displacement Mag (WCS)
(mm)
Deformed
Max Disp 6.8019E+00
Scale 2.4563E+01
Loadset:bending : CRANK

6.802e+00
6.122e+00
5.442e+00
4.761e+00
4.081e+00
3.401e+00
2.721e+00
2.041e+00
1.360e+00
6.802e-01
3.104e-05

"deform_bending" - crank - crank

**Figure 3–56**

## Task 10 - Animate the deformation for the torsional load case.

1. Click [icon]. The Result Window Definition dialog box opens.

2. In the *Name* field, enter **deform_torsion**.

3. Clear the **bending** load set and select the **torsion** load set. The Result Window Definition dialog box opens as shown in Figure 3–57.

Figure 3–57

4. Click OK.

5.  Click ⬚. In the Display Result Window dialog box, clear **deform_bending** and select **deform_torsion** as shown in Figure 3–58.

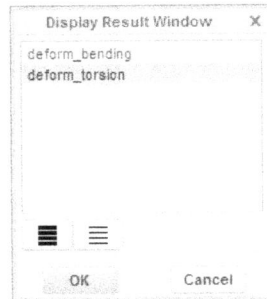

Display Result Window

deform_bending
deform_torsion

OK          Cancel

**Figure 3–58**

*Did the deformation display as you expected?*

6.  Click OK. The deformation plot for the torsional load case is displayed and animated.

---

**Task 11 - Create result windows for the von Mises stress.**

---

1.  Click ⬚. Select the **crank** design study in the Design Study for Result Window dialog box that opens and click

    Open. The Result Window Definition dialog box opens as shown in Figure 3–59.

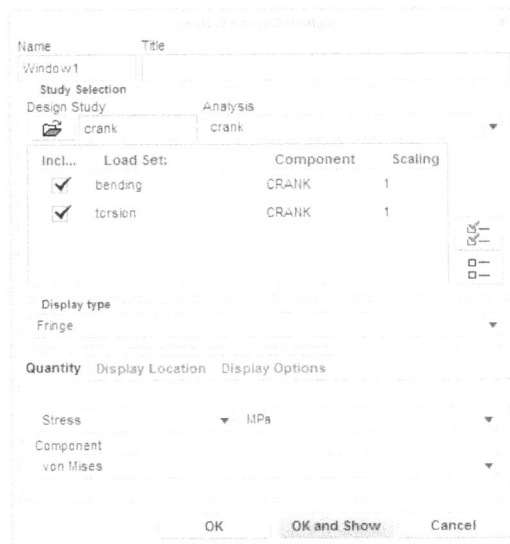

| Name | Title |
|------|-------|
| Window1 | |

Study Selection

| Design Study | Analysis |
|--------------|----------|
| crank | crank |

| Incl... | Load Set: | Component | Scaling |
|---------|-----------|-----------|---------|
| ✓ | bending | CRANK | 1 |
| ✓ | torsion | CRANK | 1 |

Display type
Fringe

Quantity   Display Location   Display Options

Stress          MPa
Component
von Mises

OK          OK and Show          Cancel

**Figure 3–59**

2. In the *Name* field, enter **stress_bending**.

3. Leave the **bending** load set selected and clear the **torsion** load set.

4. Select the *Display Options* tab. Select the **Deformed** and **Overlay Undeformed** options.

5. Click   OK   .

6. Repeat Steps 1 through 5, naming the window **stress_torsion** and selecting the **torsion** load set instead of the bending load set.

## Task 12 - Display the stress results.

1. Click 🔲 . In the Display Result Window dialog box that opens, select **stress_bending** and clear all of the other windows.

2. Click   OK   . The von Mises stress plot for the bending load case is displayed as shown in Figure 3–60.

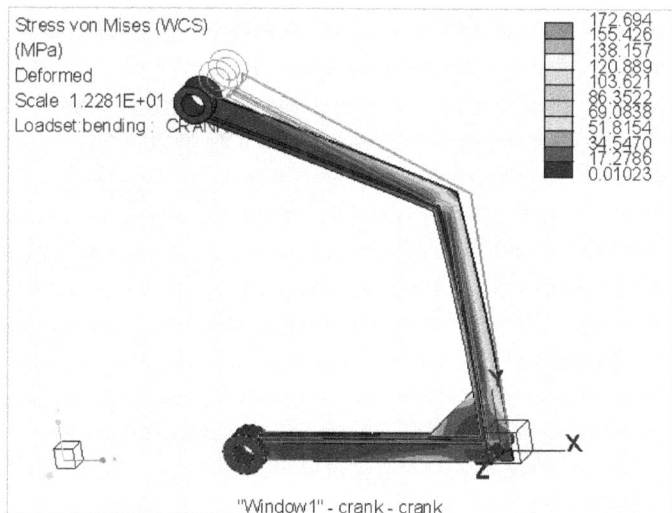

Figure 3–60

3. Locate the area of the maximum stress, as shown in Figure 3–61.

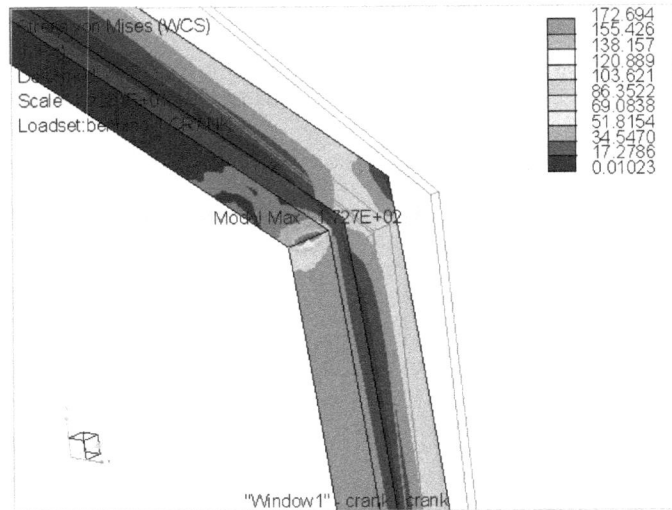

**Figure 3–61**

4. Click ![icon]. In the Display Result Window dialog box that opens, select **stress_torsion** and clear all of the other windows.

5. Click ![OK]. The von Mises stress plot for the torsional load case is displayed as shown in Figure 3–62.

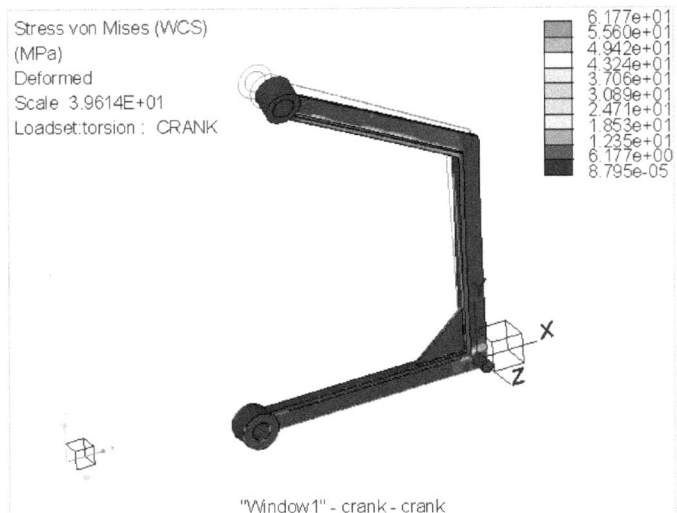

**Figure 3–62**

6. Locate the area of the maximum stress, as shown in Figure 3–63.

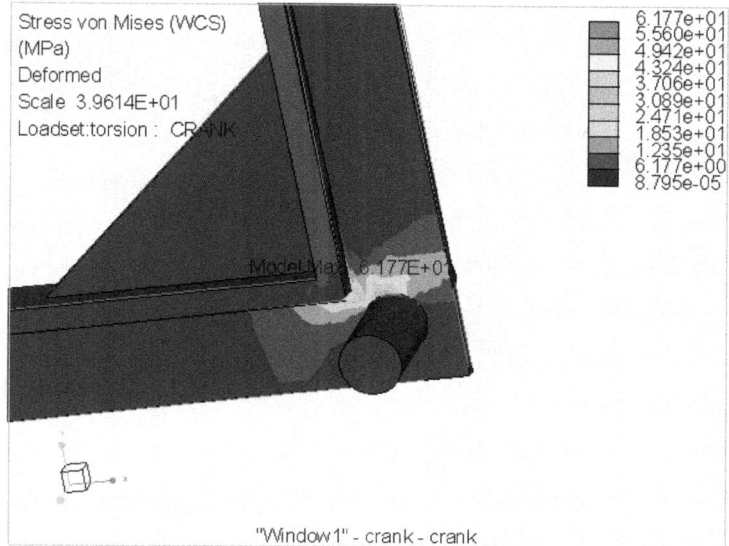

Stress von Mises (WCS)
(MPa)
Deformed
Scale 3.9614E+01
Loadset:torsion : CRANK

6.177e+01
5.560e+01
4.942e+01
4.324e+01
3.706e+01
3.089e+01
2.471e+01
1.853e+01
1.235e+01
6.177e+00
8.795e-05

"Window1" - crank - crank

**Figure 3–63**

Note that the maximum stress in the torsional load case displays at a different location than in the bending load case.

---

**Task 13 - Display the stress results for the combined load case.**

---

In this task, you will create and display a von Mises stress result plot for the combined load case, in which both the bending and twisting loads act together.

1. Click ⬚. The Result Window Definition dialog box opens.

2. In the *Name* field, enter **stress_combined**.

3. Select both the **bending** and **torsion** load sets. The Result Window Definition dialog box opens as shown in Figure 3–64.

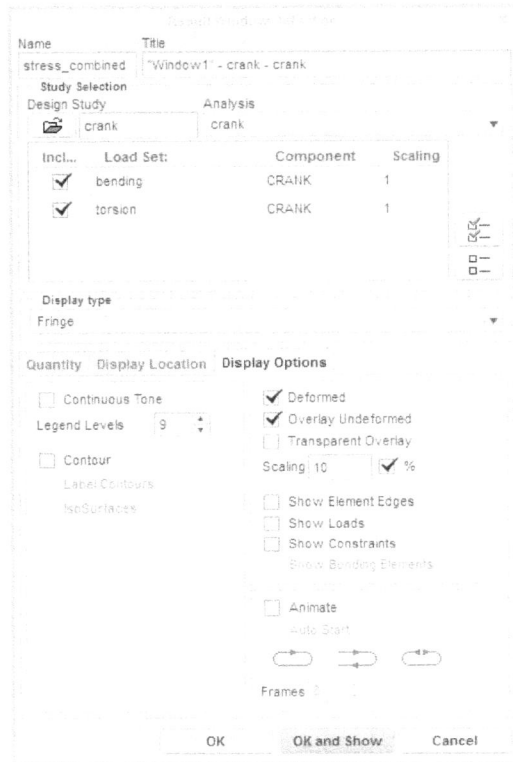

**Figure 3–64**

4. Click   OK   .

5. Click   . In the Display Result Window dialog box that opens, select **stress_combined** and clear all of the other windows.

6. Click   OK   . The von Mises stress plot for the combined load case is displayed as shown in Figure 3–65.

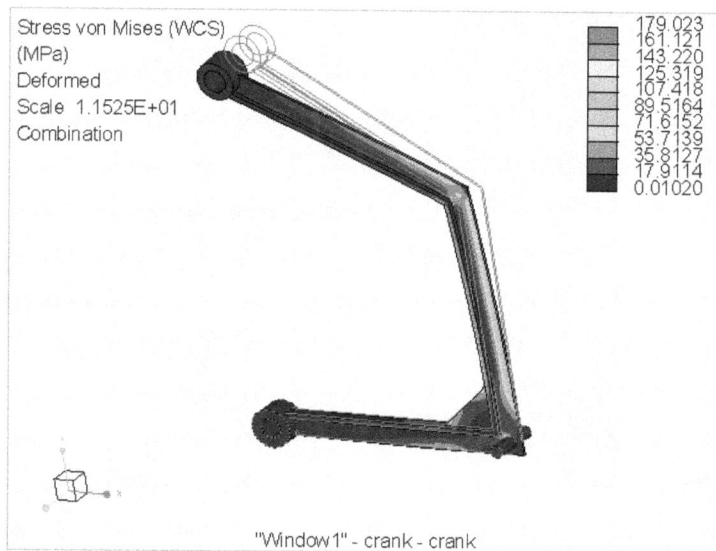

Figure 3–65

7. Examine the stress results. Locate the area of maximum stress.

8. Exit the Results. Save and close the model in Creo Parametric.

# Practice 3b

# Cyclic Symmetry Constraints

**Learning Objectives**

Understand how to apply cyclic constraints to a model.

Understand how to analyze a model using cyclic constraint types.

In this practice, you will use cyclic symmetry constraints to set up, run, and analyze the fan shown in Figure 3–66. The fan is rotating at 300rpm (5 rev/sec), and the fan blades are subjected to air pressure that varies linearly along the blade length, from 0.0008psi at the tip to 0psi at the center of the fan.

*You can only use cyclic symmetry constraints with solid and shell elements.*

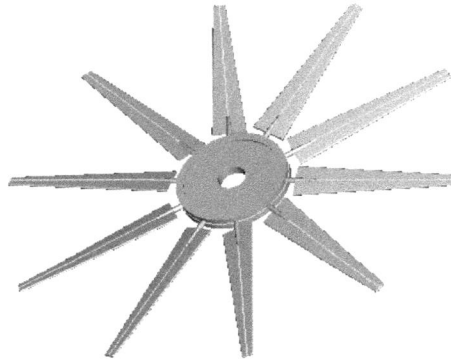

**Figure 3–66**

The intent of the cyclic symmetry constraint is to reduce the amount of geometry being analyzed, thus reducing the amount of time required to solve the analysis.

A model with cyclic constraints should be cyclically symmetric so that the entire model can be reproduced by rotating the symmetric section about an axis. The angle between cuts must equal 360° divided by the number of instances (the fan example is divided by ten). You will analyze the cyclic instance of the fan shown in Figure 3–67.

**Figure 3–67**

Note that both the geometry and boundary conditions must meet the criteria of cyclic symmetry. If the constraints or loading are not repeated about the axis of rotation by the same number of repetitions as the geometry, the results will be invalid.

## Modeling Tasks

### Task 1 - Open the model.

1. Open **fan.asm** in Creo Parametric and hide the datum planes. The model displays as shown in Figure 3–68.

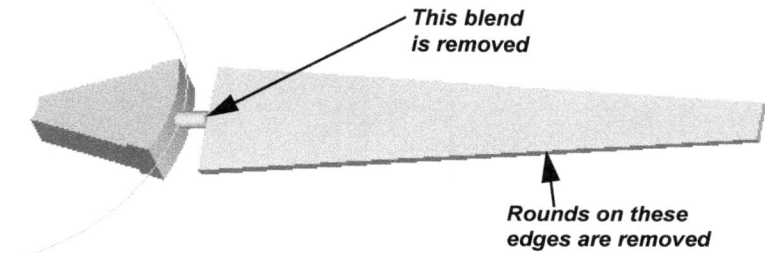

**Figure 3–68**

*For this practice, the FEA model has been de-featured (e.g., various rounds have been removed).*

*The material properties should be as stated.*

2. Ensure that the unit system is set to **IPS**.

3. Switch to the Creo Simulate environment.

### Task 2 - Apply the material.

1. Assign **AL6061** to both parts.

   The following values are the default material properties for the AL6061 aluminum alloy:

   • Poisson's ratio = 0.3
   • Young's modulus = 1e+07 psi
   • Density = 0.0002536 lbf sec^2/in^4

2. Using the Simulation Display functionality, hide the **Material Assignment** icons.

### Task 3 - Apply a centrifugal load.

The fan is rotating at a high speed (5 rev/sec equals 31.4 rad/sec) about the Y-axis. In this task, you will apply a centrifugal load to the model to simulate this rotational loading.

1. In the *Loads* area, click ⬚. The Centrifugal Load dialog box opens as shown in Figure 3–69.

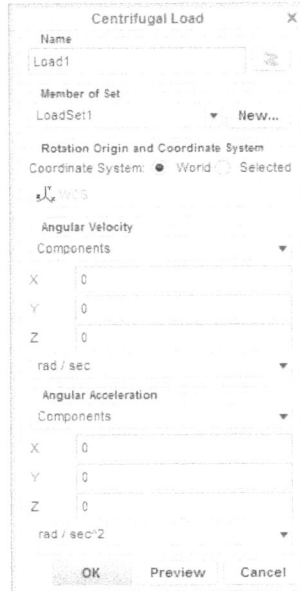

**Figure 3–69**

2. In the *Name* field, enter **c_force**.

3. For *Member of Set*, accept the default **LoadSet1** option.

*31.4rad/sec = 5 rev/sec*

4. In the *Angular Velocity* area, in the Y-field, enter **31.4**.

5. Click **OK**. The applied load in the model is represented as a vector at the origin (0,0,0), as shown in Figure 3–70.

**Figure 3–70**

## Task 4 - Create a cylindrical coordinate system.

In this task, you will create a cylindrical coordinate system. The radial direction of this coordinate system will be used later to define the air pressure variation along the length of the fan blade.

1. In the *Refine Model* tab, click ⬚.

2. In the Select a Component box that opens, click OK .
   The Coordinate System dialog box opens as shown in
   Figure 3–71.

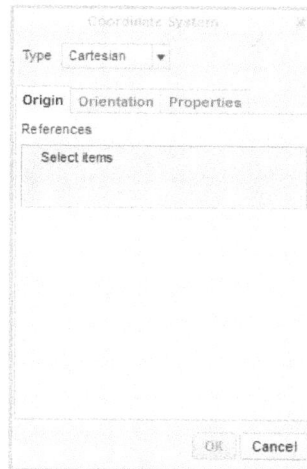

**Figure 3–71**

3. Expand the Type drop-down list and select **Cylindrical**.

4. Select the datum planes **ASM_RIGHT**, **ASM_TOP**, and
   **ASM_FRONT** to place the origin of the coordinate system at
   the intersection of the three planes. The Coordinate System
   dialog box opens as shown in Figure 3–72.

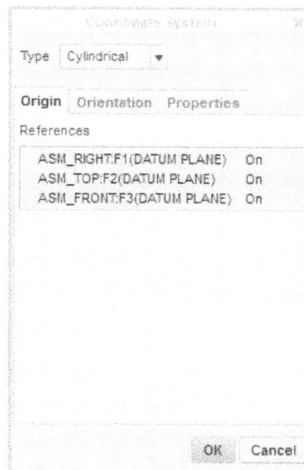

**Figure 3–72**

5. Select the *Orientation* tab. Use the ASM_TOP plane to orient the Z-axis of the new coordinate system and ASM_FRONT plane to orient the T = 0 axis. The Coordinate System dialog box opens as shown in Figure 3–73.

Figure 3–73

6. Click **OK** to finish. The new coordinate system ACS0 displays at the WCS origin, as shown in Figure 3–74.

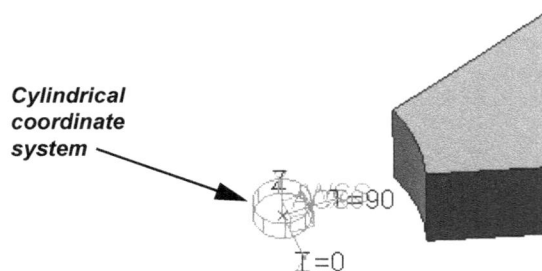

Figure 3–74

## Task 5 - Apply pressure load.

The fan blade is loaded with the air pressure that varies linearly along the length of the blade. In this task, you will apply a non-uniform pressure load to simulate the air pressure.

1. In the *Loads* area, click ⊑ . The Pressure Load dialog box opens as shown in Figure 3–75.

**Figure 3–75**

2. In the *Name* field, enter **pressure**.

3. For *Member of Set*, accept the default **LoadSet1** option.

4. Select the blade surface that is opposite to the Y-axis side, as shown in Figure 3–76.

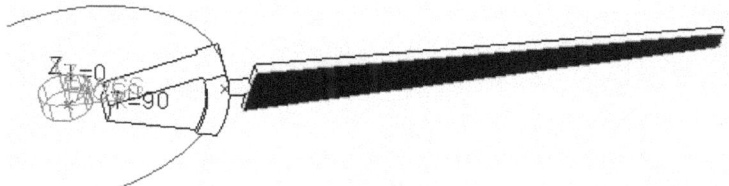

**Figure 3–76**

5. Click Advanced >> .

6. Expand the Spatial Variation drop-down list and select **Function of Coordinates**.

7. Click $f(x)$. The Functions dialog box opens as shown in Figure 3–77.

**Figure 3–77**

8. Click New... . The Function Definition dialog box opens as shown in Figure 3–78.

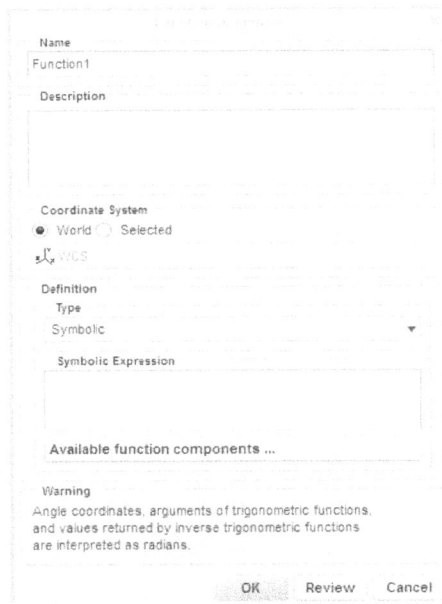

**Figure 3–78**

9. In the *Name* field, enter **linear**.

10. In the *Coordinate System* area, select the **Selected** option, and select the **ACS0** coordinate system.

11. Expand the Type drop-down list and select **Symbolic**.

12. Click Available function components ... . The Symbolic Options dialog box opens as shown in Figure 3–79.

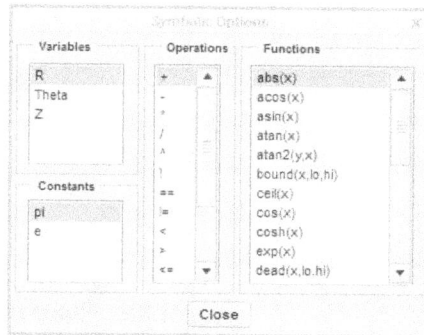

**Figure 3–79**

13. In the *Variables* area, double-click on the **R** and click Close . The Function Definition dialog box opens as shown in Figure 3–80.

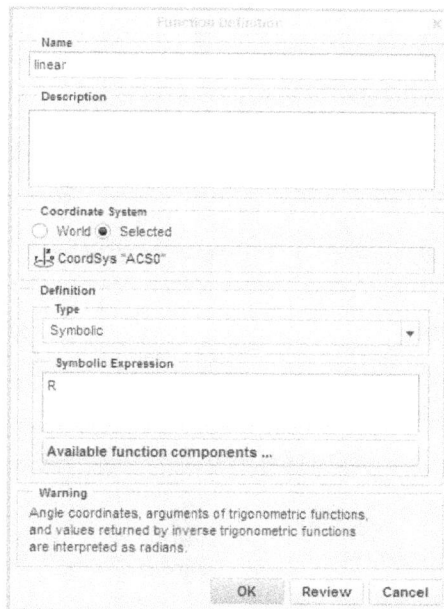

**Figure 3–80**

14. Click  Review . The Graph Function dialog box opens as shown in Figure 3–81.

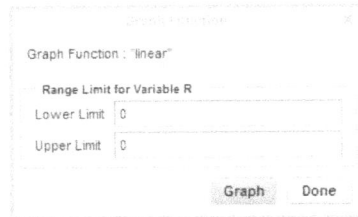

Graph Function

Graph Function : "linear"

Range Limit for Variable R

Lower Limit  0

Upper Limit  0

Graph    Done

**Figure 3–81**

15. For the *Upper Limit*, enter **100** and click  Graph . The Graphtool window displays as shown in Figure 3–82.

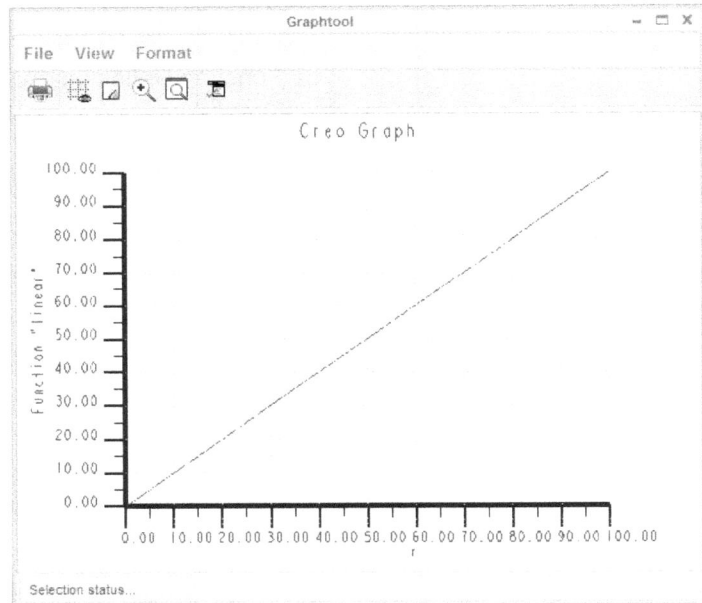

**Figure 3–82**

16. Verify that the function is linear and close the Graphtool window.

17. In the Graph Function dialog box, click  Done .

18. In the Function Definition dialog box, click  OK  and close the warning message that displays.

19. In the Functions dialog box, click  OK .

*The fan radius is 20.76in and the air pressure at the tip of the blade is 0.8psi. Given the linear R function, the value to be entered is 0.0008/20.76 = 0.00003846.*

20. In the *Value* field, enter **0.00003846**. The Pressure Load dialog box opens as shown in Figure 3–83.

| Pressure Load | X |
|---|---|
| Name | |
| pressure | |
| Member of Set | |
| LoadSet1 | ▼ New... |
| References | |
| Surfaces : ● Individual ○ Boundary ○ Intent | |
| Surface : PRT0018 | |
| Surface Sets... | |
| Pressure | |
| Advanced << | |
| Spatial Variation | |
| Function of Coordinates | ▼ |
| f(x)  linear | ▼ |
| Value | |
| 0.00003846 | psi ▼ |
| OK  Preview  Cancel | |

Figure 3–83

21. Click **Preview**. The model displays as shown in Figure 3–84.

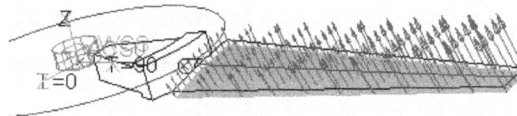

Figure 3–84

Note that the pressure increases linearly with the length of the blade.

22. Click **OK**. The model displays as shown in Figure 3–85.

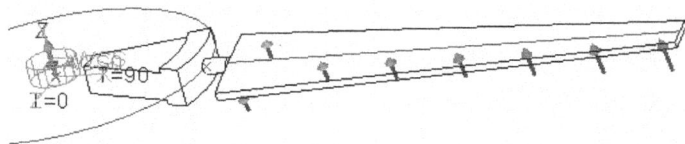

Figure 3–85

### Task 6 - Apply the constraints.

Apply cyclic constraints to the cut faces of the fan and fully constrain the fan hole surface.

1. Expand the *Constraints* area and click 衤. The Symmetry Constraint dialog box opens as shown in Figure 3–86.

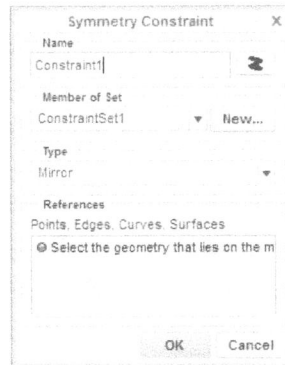

**Figure 3–86**

2. For the *Name*, enter **cyclic_const**.

3. Expand the Type drop-down list and select **Cyclic**.

4. Select the fan's First Side cut surface as shown in Figure 3–87.

5. Select the fan's Second Side cut surface, as shown in Figure 3–87.

*For the first or second side, you can select either side of the fan's cut surfaces.*

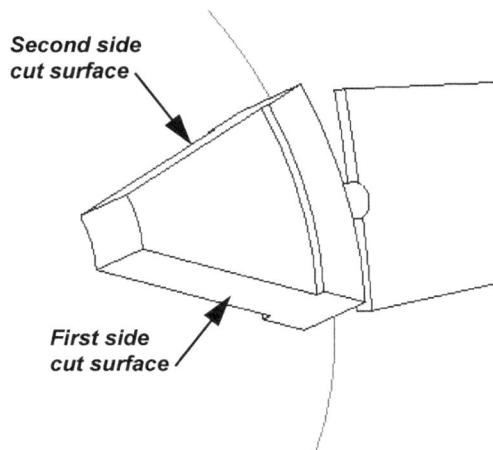

**Second side cut surface**

**First side cut surface**

**Figure 3–87**

6. Click OK to finish. The model displays as shown in Figure 3–88.

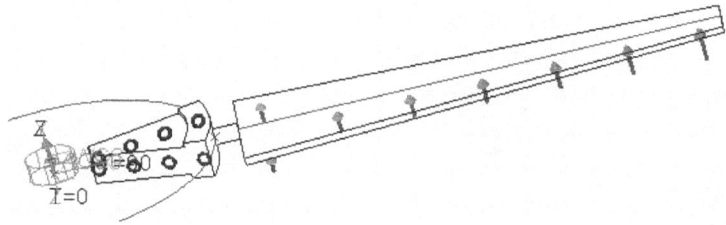

**Figure 3–88**

7. Click and constrain the fan's hole surface (all of the translations), as shown in Figure 3–89.

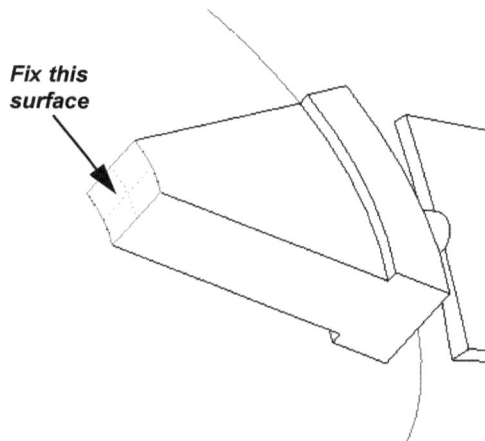

**Figure 3–89**

## Analysis Tasks

### Task 7 - Solve the model using the Single-Pass Adaptive convergence option.

1. Set up a Single-Pass Adaptive analysis. For the *Name*, enter **fan**.

2. Run the analysis.

3. In the Analyses and Design Studies dialog box, click ▤ .
The Run Status window opens. Extract the RMS Stress Error
Estimates as shown in Figure 3–90.

```
RMS Stress Error Estimates:

Load Set            Stress Error   % of Max Prin Str
----------------    ------------   -----------------
LoadSet1            6.59e+00        1.2% of  5.37e+02
```

**Figure 3–90**

## Results Tasks

### Task 8 - Display the results.

In this task you will create and display color plots for von Mises
stress and the deflection. Animate these plots to display the
effect of the loading on the model.

1. Create and display a color plot for the von Mises stress. The
von Mises fringe plot displays as shown in Figure 3–91.

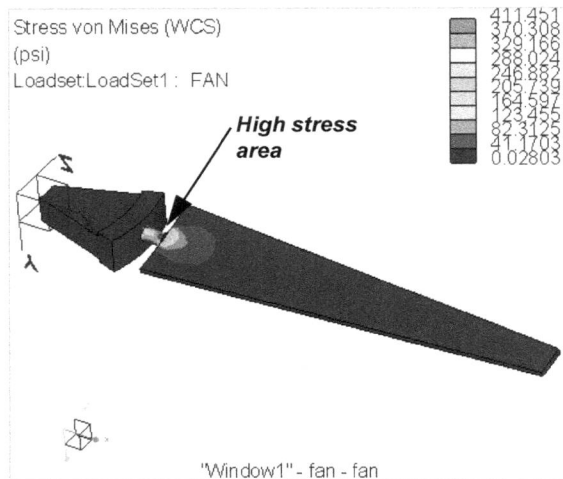

**Figure 3–91**

Locate the maximum von Mises stress. Note that the maximum
stress displays at the junction of the blade and shaft, which is a
re-entrant corner. This is expected, considering the load type
and the removal of the blend feature. Examine the stress in other
parts of your model. Create sections of the model in high stress
areas.

2. Animate the von Mises stress window and play the animation frames. Frame 5 is shown in Figure 3–92.

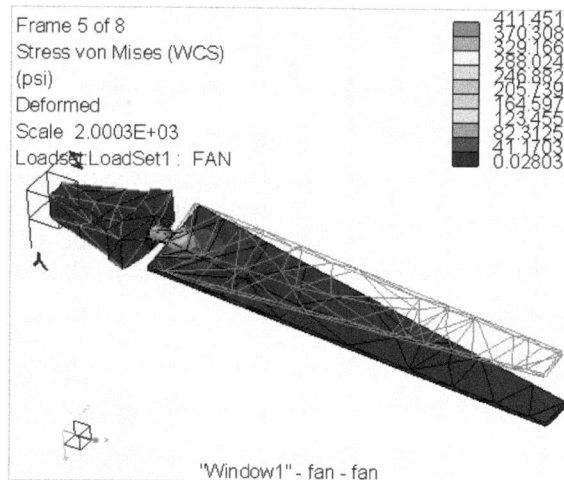

Frame 5 of 8
Stress von Mises (WCS)
(psi)
Deformed
Scale 2.0003E+03
Loadset:LoadSet1 : FAN

411.451
370.308
329.166
288.024
246.882
205.739
164.597
123.455
82.3125
41.1703
0.02803

"Window1" - fan - fan

**Figure 3–92**

## Task 9 - Create deflection windows.

1. Create and examine a Displacement Magnitude deflection window.

2. Create deflection windows for the X-, Y-, and Z-displacement components and animate the windows.

3. Note the value of deflection for each component.

4. Exit the Results. Save and close the model in Creo Parametric.

# Practice 3c

# Surface Regions

**Learning Objective**

Understand how to use Surface Regions to apply loads and constraints.

In this practice, you will analyze a mooring chock that is used for fastening ships to piers, etc. The model is shown in Figure 3–93. The chock is welded into the hull of the ship over an area 1" wide going around the outside surface, and loaded by a mooring line over a 2" area, as shown in Figure 3–93.

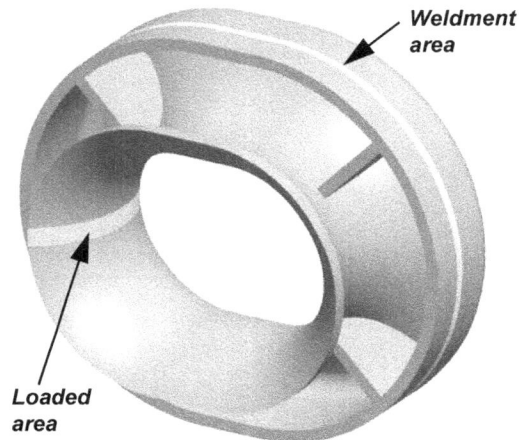

**Figure 3–93**

You will use surface regions to apply the loads and constraints over the areas shown in Figure 3–93.

---

**Modeling Tasks**

---

**Task 1 - Open the model.**

---

1. Open **chock.prt** in Creo Parametric. The part displays as shown in Figure 3–94.

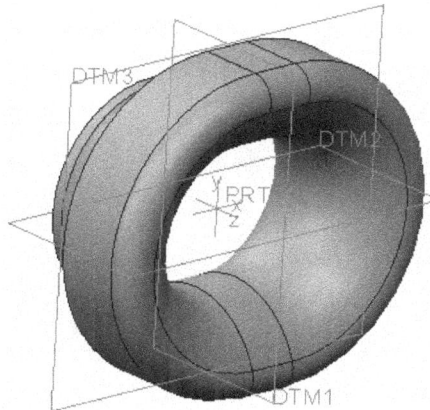

Figure 3–94

2. Ensure that the unit system is set to **IPS**.

3. Do not switch to Creo Simulate yet.

## Task 2 - Create boundary curves for the weldment region.

1. Click ▱ and create a DTM4 plane parallel to datum plane DTM3 at a distance of **3.5**, as shown in Figure 3–95.

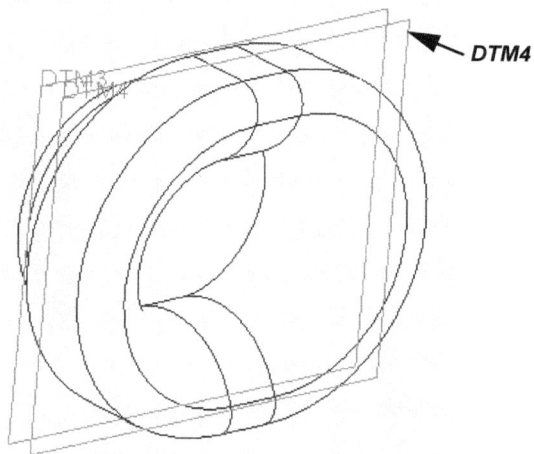

Figure 3–95

2. Click ▱ and create DTM5 plane parallel to datum plane DTM4 at a distance of **1**, as shown in Figure 3–96.

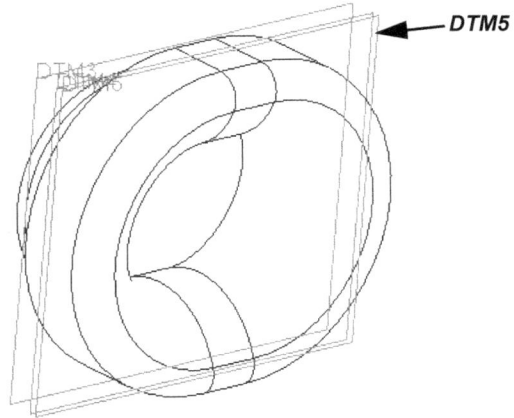

Figure 3–96

3. Select the DTM4 plane and click ⟍ (Intersect). The Surface Intersection dashboard opens.

4. Hold down <Ctrl> and select four surfaces on the outside of the chock, as shown in Figure 3–97.

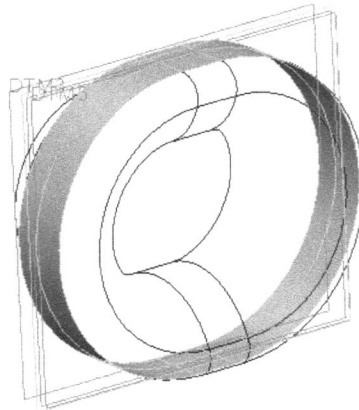

Figure 3–97

5.  Click  ✔  to finish. The new datum curve Intersect_1 displays in the model, as shown in Figure 3–98.

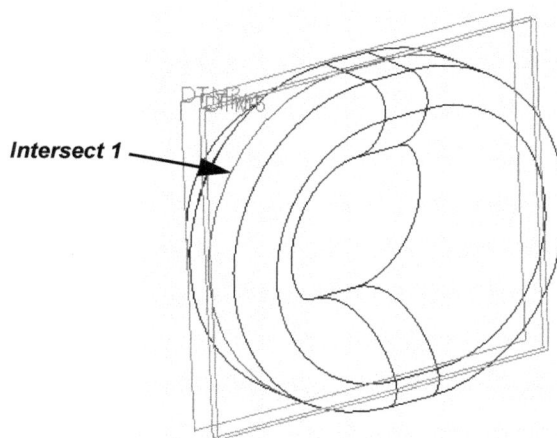

**Figure 3–98**

6.  Repeat Steps 3 to 5, now using the DTM5 plane. The model displays as shown in Figure 3–99.

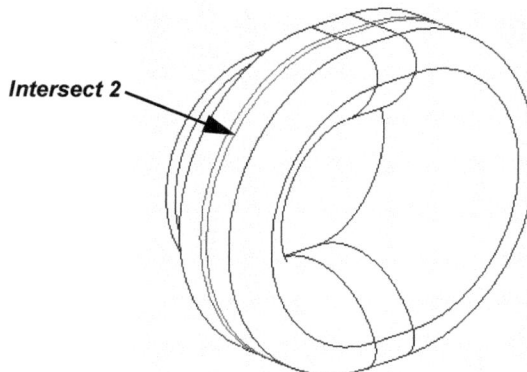

**Figure 3–99**

## Task 3 - Create boundary curves for the loaded region.

1.  Click  ⌒ . Select the DTM1 plane as the Sketch Plane and DTM2 plane as the Reference Plane for the Top orientation. Ensure that the sketch viewing direction is toward the positive X-direction.

2. Sketch the profile shown in Figure 3–100.

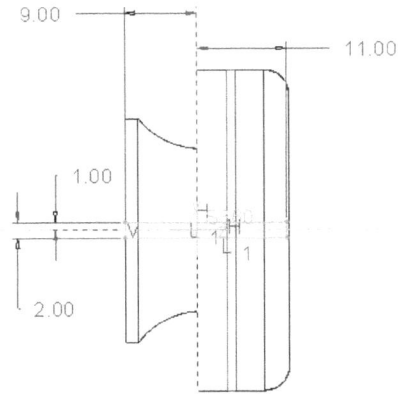

**Figure 3–100**

3. Select the sketch and click ⬄ (Project). The Projected Curve dashboard displays.

4. Select the inside surface of the chock, toward the positive X-direction, as shown in Figure 3–101.

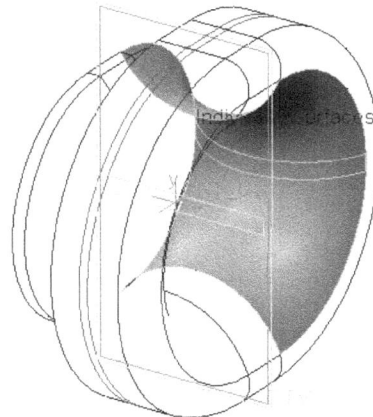

**Figure 3–101**

5.  Click ✔ to finish. The new datum curve Project_1 displays in the model, as shown in Figure 3–102.

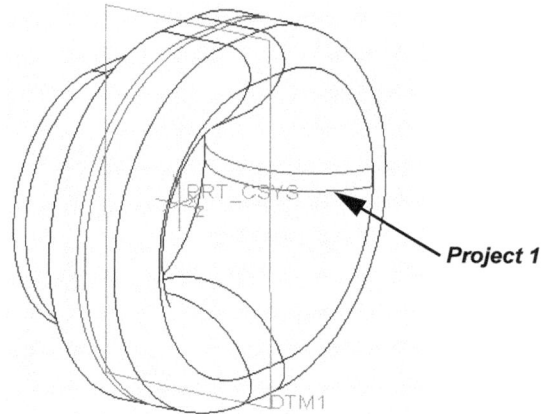

**Figure 3–102**

## Task 4 - Create a surface region for the weldment constraint.

1.  Switch to the Creo Simulate environment.

2.  In the *Refine Model* tab, click 🔲. The Surface Region dashboard opens as shown in Figure 3–103.

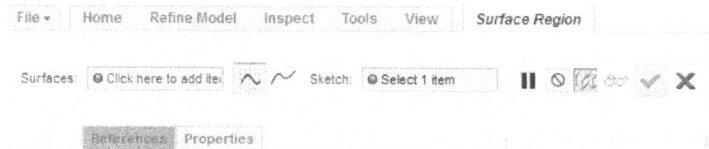

**Figure 3–103**

3. Select the **Surfaces** field. Hold down <Ctrl> and select four surfaces on the outside of the chock, as shown in Figure 3–104.

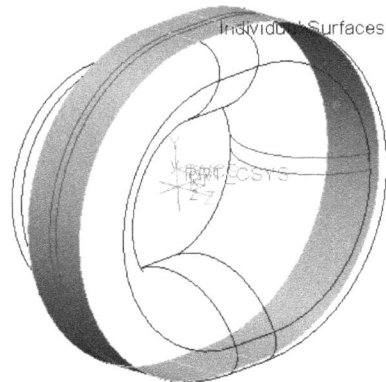

**Figure 3–104**

4. Click $\sim$ .

5. Select the *Chain* field, and select the **Intersect_1** curve. The model displays as shown in Figure 3–105.

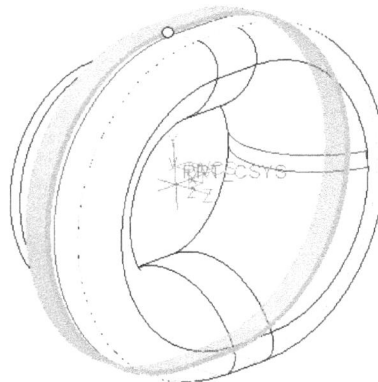

**Figure 3–105**

6.  Repeat Steps 2 to 5 using the curve Intersect_2. Two surface regions display in the Model Tree, as shown in Figure 3–106. Click the surface regions in the Model Tree to check how they highlight in the model.

> ▸ 〜 Project 1
> ➜ Insert Here
> ◥ Materials
> ▾ ⬚ Simulation Features
>     🗗 Surface Region 1
>     🗗 Surface Region 2

**Figure 3–106**

## Task 5 - Create a surface region for the load.

1.  Using Task 4 as a guideline, create another surface region, now using **Project_1** and the surface shown in Figure 3–107.

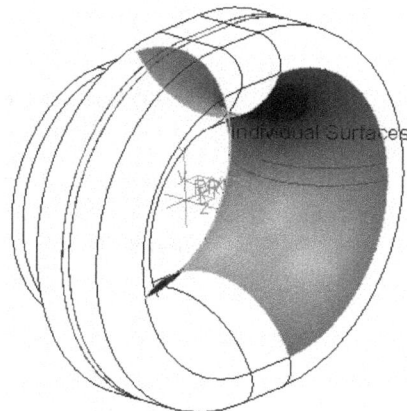

**Figure 3–107**

## Task 6 - Apply the material.

*The material properties should be as stated.*

1.  Assign **STEEL** to the part.

    The following values are the default material properties for the STEEL:

    *   Poisson's ratio = 0.3
    *   Young's modulus = 1e+07 psi
    *   Density = 0.0002536 lbf sec^2/in^4

2.  Using the Simulation Display functionality, hide the **Material Assignment** icon.

## Task 7 - Mesh the model.

1. Click ▦ . The AutoGEM dialog box opens as shown in Figure 3–108.

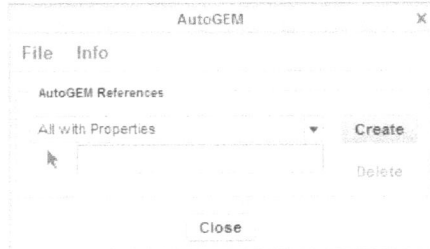

**Figure 3–108**

2. Expand the AutoGEM References drop-down list and select **All with Properties**.

3. Click Create .

4. Creo Simulate meshes the model and displays the AutoGEM Summary and Diagnostics dialog boxes.

5. Close both the AutoGEM Summary and Diagnostics dialog boxes, but do not close the AutoGEM dialog box. The model displays as shown in Figure 3–109.

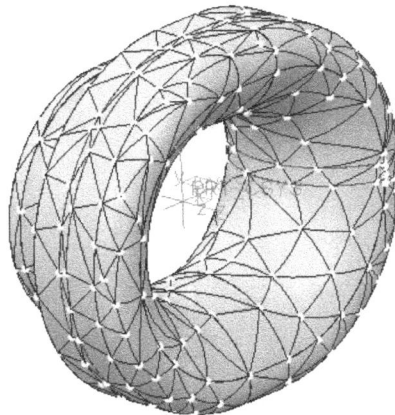

**Figure 3–109**

6. Review the mesh. Save the mesh and close the AutoGEM dialog box.

## Task 8 - Apply the constraints.

1. Fully constrain the weldment region (in all of the translations), as shown in Figure 3–110.

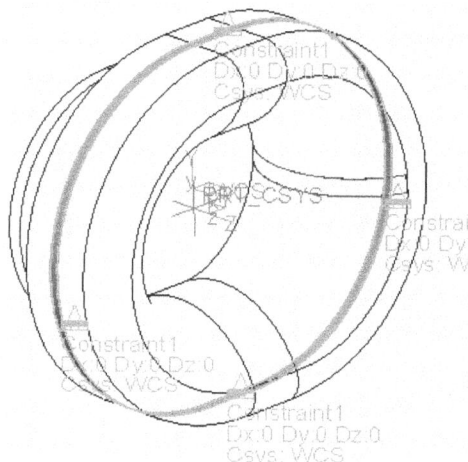

**Figure 3–110**

## Task 9 - Apply the load.

The force exerted by the mooring line onto the chock is 100,000 lbs. The force is distributed accordingly to the half-sine law. The load is maximum in the middle of the loaded region, and zero at the ends of the loaded region.

1. In the *Loads* area, click .

2. In the *Name* field, enter **line_load**.

3. Select the surface region for the load as shown in Figure 3–111.

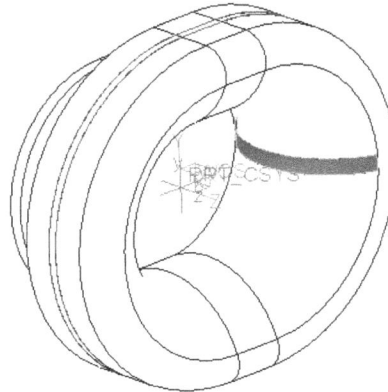

**Figure 3–111**

4. Click <sup>Advanced >></sup> . The Force/Moment dialog box opens as shown in Figure 3–112.

**Figure 3–112**

5. Expand the Spatial Variation drop-down list and select **Function of Coordinates**.

6. Click $f^{(x)}$. The Functions dialog box opens. Click New....

7. In the *Name* field, enter **halfsine**.

8. Expand the Type drop-down list and select **Table**.

9. In the *Row* field, select **Z**.

10. In the *Table* area, enter the tabular function as shown in Figure 3–113.

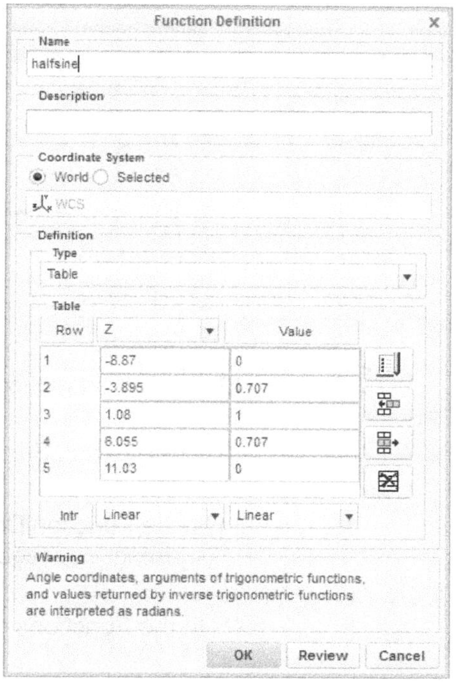

Figure 3–113

11. Click Review and click Graph . The Graphtool window displays as shown in Figure 3–114.

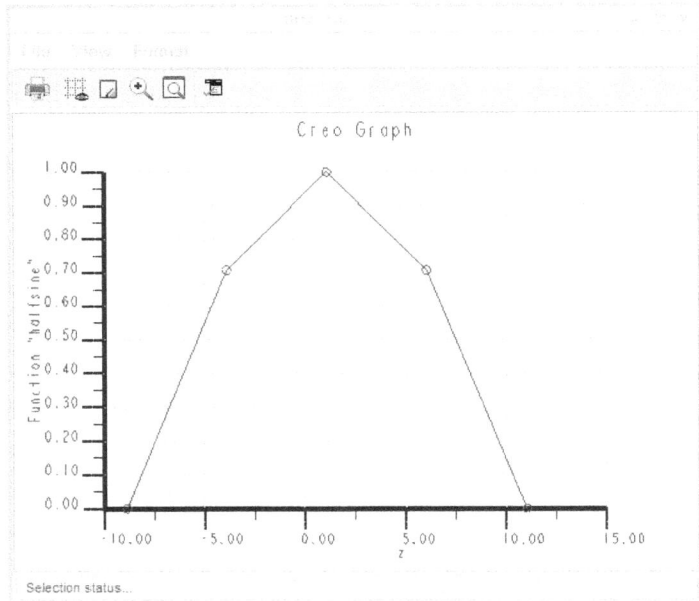

**Figure 3–114**

12. Verify the function and close the Graphtool window.

13. In the Graph Function dialog box, click Done .

14. In the Function Definition dialog box, click OK . Close the warning message that displays.

15. In the Functions dialog box, click OK .

16. In the *X* field, enter **100000**. The Force/Moment Load dialog box opens as shown in Figure 3–115.

**Figure 3–115**

17. Click   OK  . The model displays as shown in Figure 3–116.

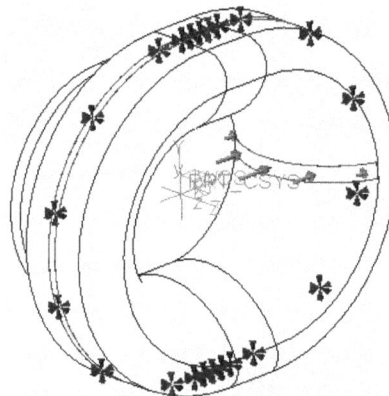

**Figure 3–116**

## Task 10 - Verify the load.

Since the load distribution you applied is non-uniform, in this task you will verify that total amount of load applied to the model is 100,000 lbs as required.

1. Expand the Loads area in the Ribbon and select **Review Total Load**. The Load Resultant dialog box opens as shown in Figure 3–117.

**Figure 3–117**

2. Click 🖢 and select the **line_load** load in the model. Click the middle mouse button to complete the selection.

3. Click Compute Load Resultant . The Load Resultant dialog box opens as shown in Figure 3–118.

**Figure 3–118**

Verify that the *FX* field reads **100000**.

4. Click OK to finish.

## Analysis Tasks

### Task 11 - Solve the model using the Multi-Pass Adaptive convergence option.

1. Set up a Multi-Pass Adaptive analysis. For the *Name*, enter **chock**. For the *Maximum Polynomial Order*, enter **9** and in the *Percent Convergence* field, enter **10**.

2. Run the analysis.

3. In the Analyses and Design Studies dialog box, click  to open the Run Status window. Extract the following information:

   - Number of solid elements in the model.
   - Number of passes to convergence.
   - Maximum P-Level on the last pass.
   - Number of equations on the last pass.
   - RMS Stress Error estimates.

## Results Tasks

## Task 12 - Display the deformation.

1. Create the displacement magnitude animation plot, as shown in Figure 3–119.

2. Start the animation. Check whether the applied boundary conditions behave correctly.

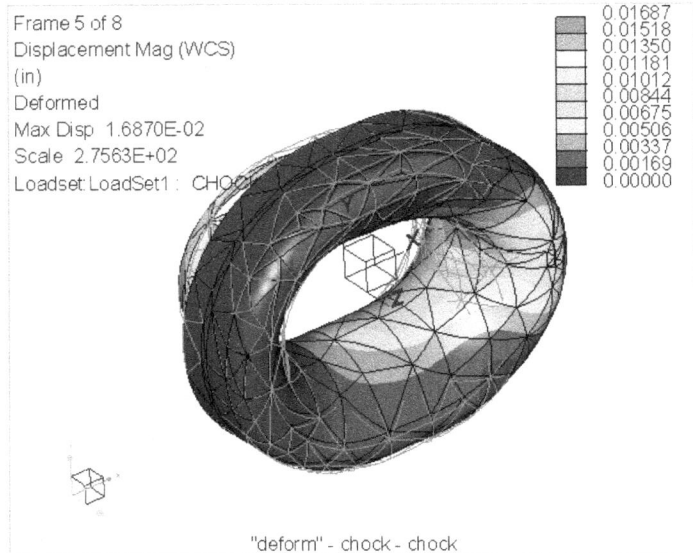

Figure 3–119

## Task 13 - Display the von Mises stress.

1. Create the von Mises stress undeformed plot, as shown in Figure 3–120.

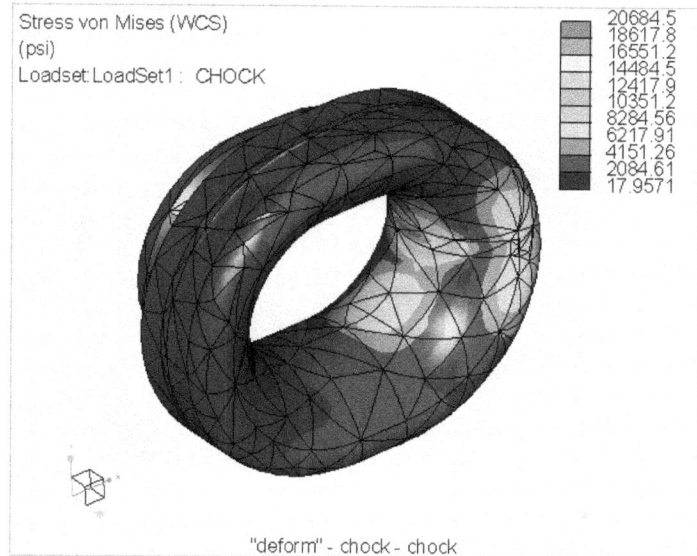

Figure 3–120

2. Using **Info>Model Max**, locate the area of maximum stress in the part, as shown in Figure 3–121.

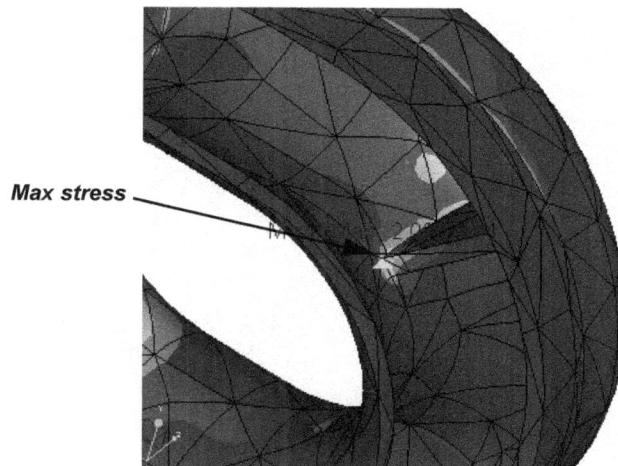

Figure 3–121

Note that the model maximum stress occurs in a hot spot at a sharp reentrant corner near one of the ribs. This is a stress singularity area, and stress result there should be disregarded.

3. Zoom in on the area under the load. Use **Info>View Max** to get a reading of the maximum stress in that area, as shown in Figure 3–122.

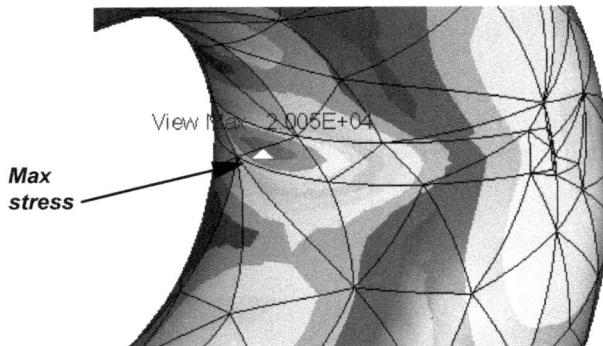

**Figure 3–122**

4. Select **Insert>Cutting/Capping Surfs**. In the Results Surface Definition dialog box, in the *Plane* area, select **XZ**, as shown in Figure 3–123.

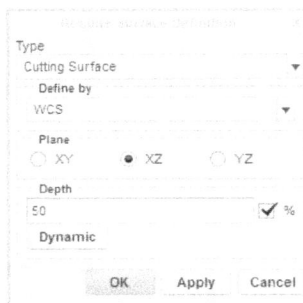

**Figure 3–123**

5. Click    Apply    . Zoom in on the cross-section. The model displays as shown in Figure 3–124.

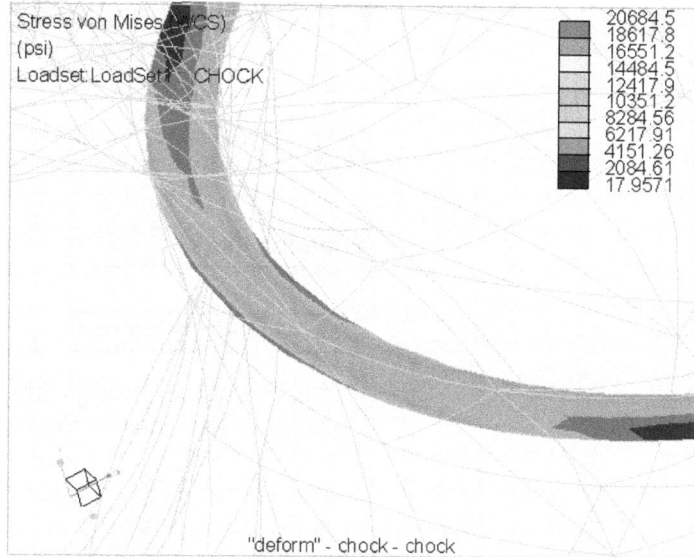

**Figure 3–124**

Note the characteristic bending pattern of stress through the thickness, with zero stress on the neutral fiber and maximum stress on the outermost fibers.

6. Click `Cancel` to close the Results Surface Definition dialog box.

7. Exit the Results. Save and close the model in Creo Parametric.

# Practice 3d

# Excluded Elements

**Learning Objective**

Understand how to use excluded elements to improve convergence.

## Modeling Tasks

### Task 1 - Open the model.

1. Open **solid_bracket_2.prt** in Creo Parametric. The part displays as shown in Figure 3–125.

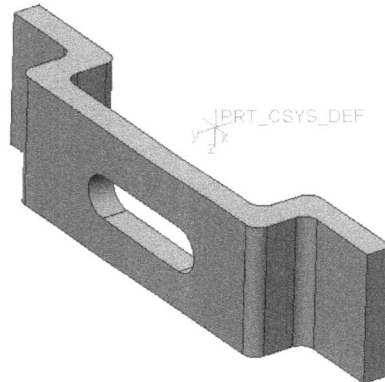

**Figure 3–125**

2. Switch to the Creo Simulate environment.

### Task 2 - Apply the material.

1. Assign **STEEL** to the part.

   The following values are the default material properties for the STEEL material:

   • Poisson's ratio = 0.27
   • Young's modulus = 199948 MPa

### Task 3 - Apply the constraints.

1. Constrain the two surfaces shown in Figure 3–126 in all translations.

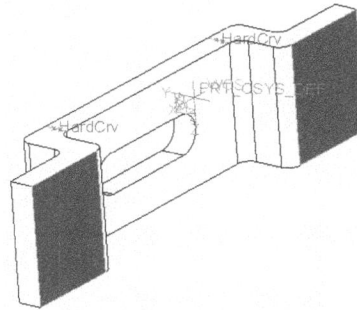

Figure 3–126

## Task 4 - Apply the load.

1. Apply a 500 N load in the Z-direction on the edge shown in Figure 3–127.

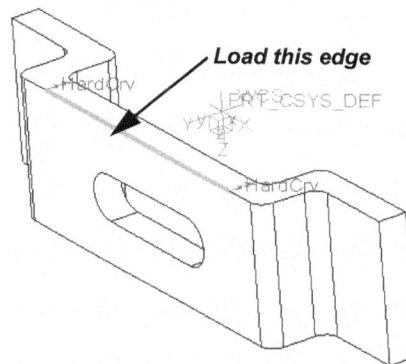

Figure 3–127

## Analysis Tasks

## Task 5 - Solve the model using the Multi-Pass Adaptive convergence option.

1. Set up a Multi-Pass Adaptive analysis. For the *Name*, enter **excluded**. For the *Maximum Polynomial Order*, enter **9** and for the *Percent Convergence* field, enter **10**.

2. Run the analysis.

3. The analysis does not converge. Note that the warning message in the Diagnostics window prompts you that *Convergence was not obtained because the maximum polynomial order of 9 was reached*.

## Results Tasks

### Task 6 - Display convergence graphs.

1.  Display convergence graphs for the **strain_energy** and **max_stress_vm** measures, as shown in Figure 3–128.

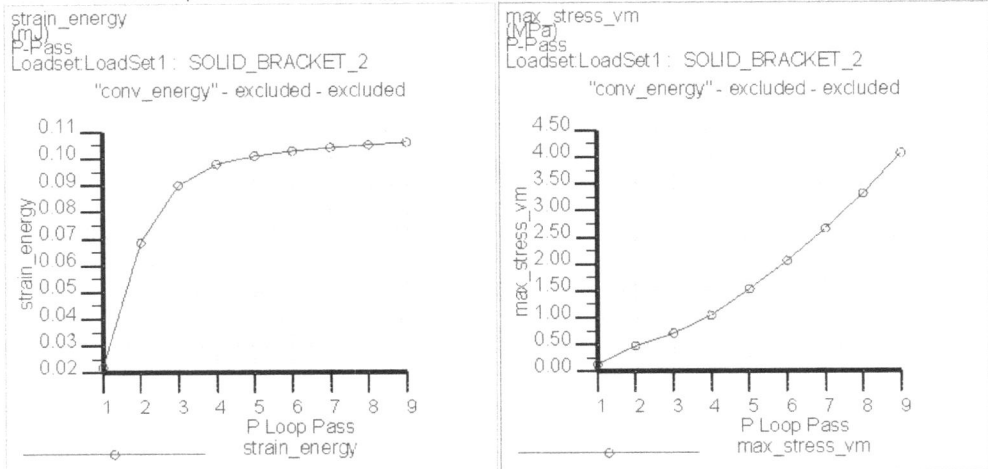

**Figure 3–128**

Note that the maximum stress does not exhibit any convergence. This is due to the singularity caused by the edge load in the model.

2.  Exit the Results.

## Modeling Tasks

In the following tasks, you will use the excluded elements to improve convergence.

### Task 7 - Isolate elements for exclusion.

1.  In the *AutoGEM* area, click ▨. The Isolate for Exclusion Control dialog box opens as shown in Figure 3–129.

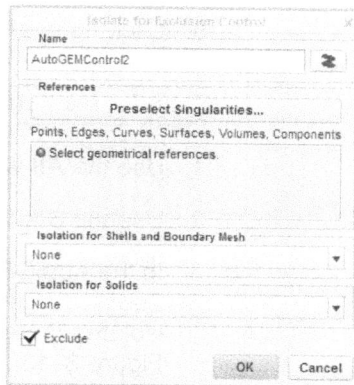

**Figure 3–129**

2. Click **OK** . In the Preselect Singularities dialog box, select the **Edge Loads** option, as shown in Figure 3–130.

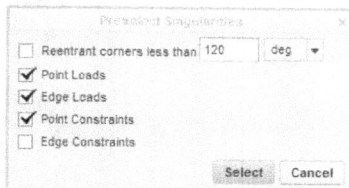

**Figure 3–130**

3. Click **Select** and Creo Simulate automatically selects the area of singularity.

4. Expand the drop-down list and select **Maximum Element Size**. In the *Isolation for Solids* area, enter **5** as shown in Figure 3–131.

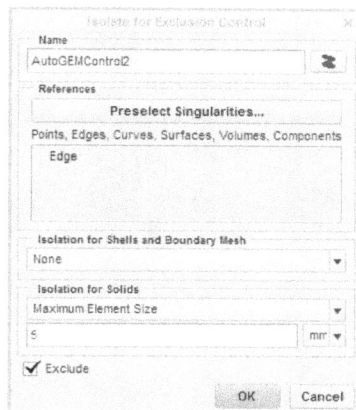

**Figure 3–131**

5. Click   OK   .

## Task 8 - Mesh the model.

1. Use the **All with Properties** option to mesh the model.

2. Use the **Simulation Display** tool to hide the mesh points.

3. In the AutoGEM dialog box, select **Info>Isolating Elements**. Zoom in on the loaded edge. Note that AutoGEM has isolated the edge with small elements, as shown in Figure 3–132.

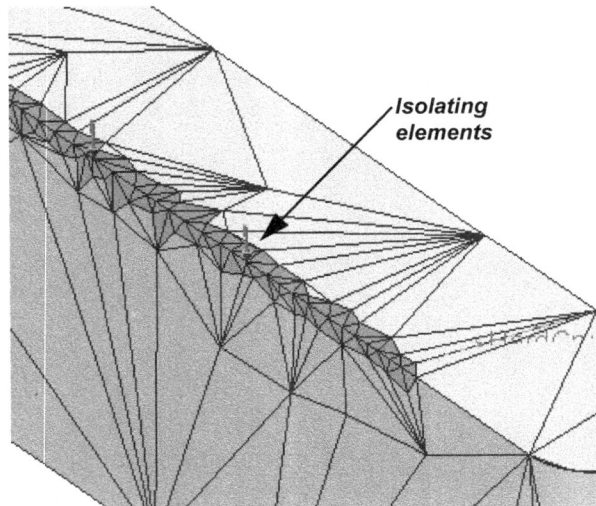

**Figure 3–132**

4. Close the AutoGEM without saving the mesh.

## Analysis Tasks

### Task 9 - Re-run the analysis.

1. Edit the **excluded** analysis study. In the *Excluded Elements* tab, select **Exclude Elements**. In the *Ignore* area, select **Stresses and Displacements**. In the *Polymonial field*, enter **3** as shown in Figure 3–133.

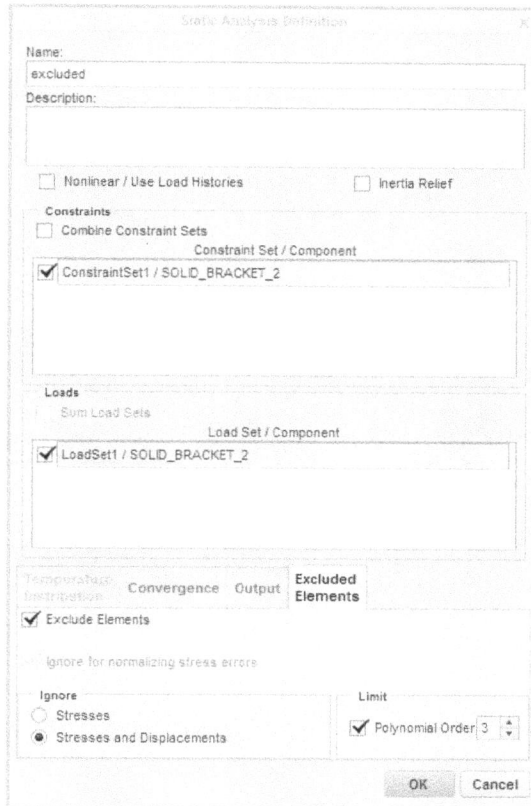

Static Analysis Definition

Name:
excluded
Description:

☐ Nonlinear / Use Load Histories          ☐ Inertia Relief

Constraints
☐ Combine Constraint Sets
Constraint Set / Component
☑ ConstraintSet1 / SOLID_BRACKET_2

Loads
Sum Load Sets
Load Set / Component
☑ LoadSet1 / SOLID_BRACKET_2

Temperature Distribution    Convergence    Output    **Excluded Elements**
☑ Exclude Elements

Ignore for normalizing stress errors

Ignore                                          Limit
○ Stresses                                      ☑ Polynomial Order 3
● Stresses and Displacements

OK        Cancel

**Figure 3–133**

2. Re-run the analysis.

3. Click 🖳 to open the Run Status window. Verify that the analysis has now converged on pass 5, as shown in Figure 3–134.

```
>> Pass  5 <<
      Calculating Element Equations                (17:55:32)
          Total Number of Equations:    34902
          Maximum Edge Order:               5
      Solving Equations                            (17:55:33)
      Post-Processing Solution                     (17:55:34)
      Calculating Disp and Stress Results          (17:55:35)
      Checking Convergence                         (17:55:36)
          Elements Not Converged:           0
          Edges Not Converged:              0
          Local Disp/Energy Index:        9.7%
          Global RMS Stress Index:        6.5%

      RMS Stress Error Estimates:

      Load Set            Stress Error   % of Max Prin Str
      ---------------     ------------   -----------------
      LoadSet1            3.88e-01       13.0% of  3.00e+00

      Resource Check                               (17:55:37)
          Elapsed Time    (sec):         14.24
          CPU Time        (sec):         11.26
          Memory Usage    (kb):         582310
          Wrk Dir Dsk Usage (kb):        49152

The analysis converged to within 10% on
edge displacement, element strain energy,
and global RMS stress.
```

**Figure 3–134**

## Results Tasks

### Task 10 - Display the convergence graphs.

1. Display convergence graphs for the **strain_energy** and **max_stress_vm** measures, as shown in Figure 3–135.

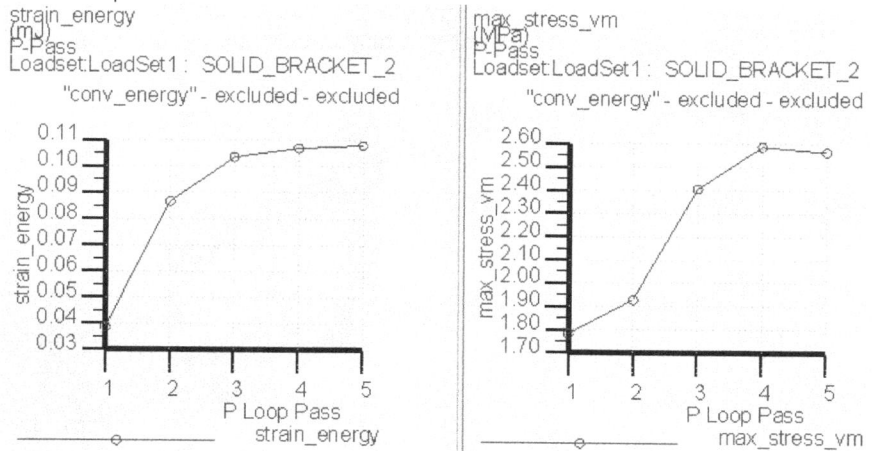

Figure 3–135

Note that the solution now displays perfect convergence on the strain energy and a reasonable convergence on stress.

## Task 11 - Display the stress results.

1. Display the von Mises Stress fringe plot, as shown in Figure 3–136.

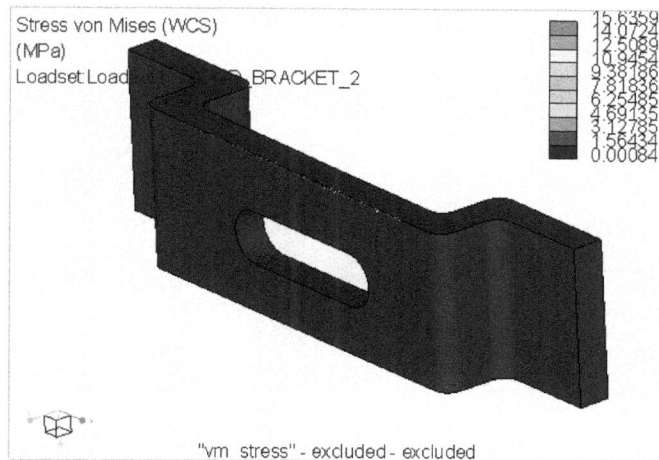

Figure 3–136

Note that the maximum stress is concentrated along the loaded edge. This is an area of singularity and the stress results are not realistic.

2. Change the *legend minimum* to **0** and *maximum* to **0.5**. The result plot displays as shown in Figure 3–137.

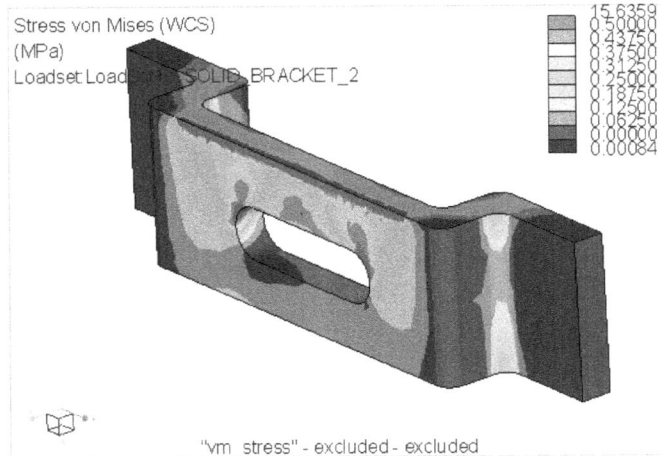

**Figure 3–137**

The stresses away from the loaded edge are now displayed. These values are not affected by the singularity and can be trusted.

3. Exit the Results. Save and close the model in Creo Parametric.

# Chapter 4

## Shell Idealizations

This chapter contains the following topics:

- **Shell Idealizations**
- **Midsurface Shells**
- **Standard Shells**
- **Applying Loads and Constraints to Shell Models**

# 4.1 Shell Idealizations

**Learning Objective**

✓ Understand shell idealization concepts.

Idealizations are tools that simplify a finite element model, resulting in faster analysis runtime. Creo Simulate has the following idealization options: **Beams**, **Masses**, **Shells**, and **Springs**.

The most common type of idealization is shell idealization. Shell idealizations are used to simplify a thin-walled solid model. Shell models are less CPU-intensive and can be analyzed faster than solid models.

Shell elements are 3D, surface-like elements that are used to represent features that are thin in comparison to the length and width of the surface in your part. The rule of thumb is to use shell elements when the thickness dimension is less than 1/10 of the length and width of the feature. Shell elements in Creo Simulate must be placed on the midsurface of the part, which is a surface that is equidistant from the side surfaces.

An example of a solid model that could be simplified using a shell idealization is shown in Figure 4–1. Portions of the solid model are composed of thin-walled features. The number of solid elements required to represent these features could be large. Therefore, the thin-walled features could be idealized as 3D shell elements represented by pairs of parallel surfaces.

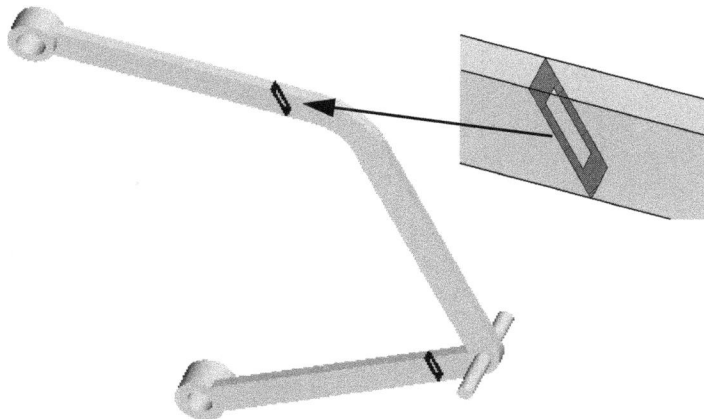

**Figure 4–1**

There are two types of shells in Creo Simulate:

- **Midsurface Shells:** The opposing faces of the solid model are paired and then compressed to form the midsurfaces for the shell element placement. Shell thickness is automatically imported from the solid model.

- **Standard Shells:** A solid model of the part is not required. Modeling the part geometry with datum surfaces is sufficient. You select surfaces that are assumed to be the midsurfaces for the shell element placement. You must assign shell properties, such as thickness. This option also enables you to define a shell as a laminate consisting of several layers of materials.

# 4.2 Midsurface Shells

**Learning Objectives**

Understand how to create shell models from solid Creo Parametric models.

Understand how to create shell pairs manually.

Understand how to automatically detect shell pairs.

Understand how to compress shell pairs to midsurface.

For midsurface shells, Creo Simulate pairs opposing surfaces of a thin-walled feature and compresses them to a midsurface, on which shell elements are placed.

The shell thickness is read directly from the Creo model. The paired surfaces can be parallel planar or non-planar surfaces, and the shell elements can be flat or curved as long as the pairing surfaces are parallel.

Use the following steps to create shell elements in Creo Simulate:

1. Pair two parallel surfaces. Two surfaces that can be paired are shown in Figure 4–2.

*Surface1 is parallel to surface2.*

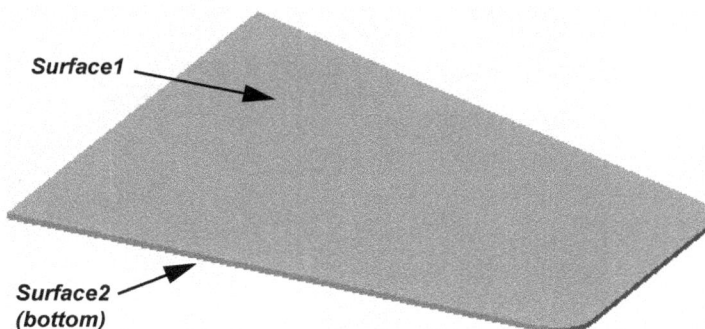

**Figure 4–2**

2. Compress the paired surfaces to a midsurface, as shown in Figure 4–3.

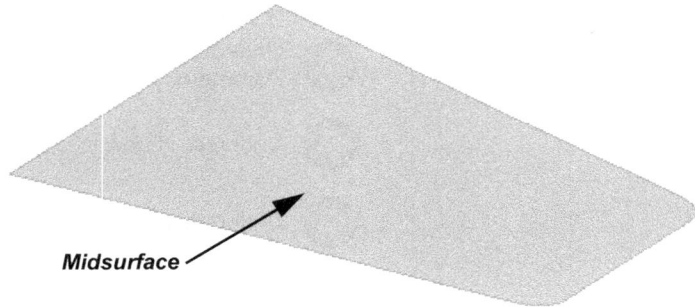

*Midsurface*

**Figure 4–3**

3. Create shell elements on the midsurface, as shown in Figure 4–4.

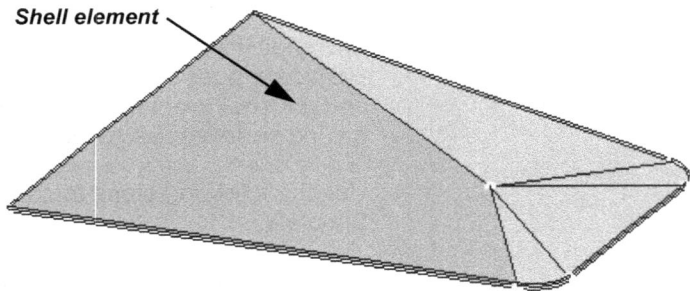

*Shell element*

**Figure 4–4**

## Shell Pair Creation

Shell pair creation tools are located in the *Refine* tab as shown in Figure 4–5.

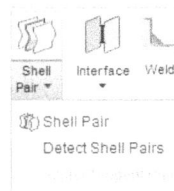

**Figure 4–5**

There are two options for creating shell pairs:

- **Manual:** You manually select opposing surfaces to be paired.

- **Automatic:** Creo Simulate detects and pairs surfaces based on feature types or feature thicknesses.

# Manual Shell Pairs

Manual shell pairing requires you to select opposing surfaces in the part. To create a manual shell pair, click 𝕊 to open the Shell Pair Definition dialog box, as shown in Figure 4–6.

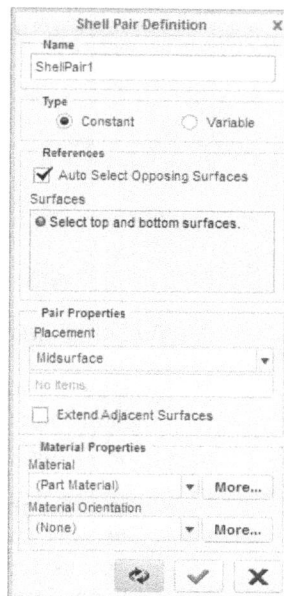

**Figure 4–6**

The Shell Pair Definition options are as follows.

| Option | Description |
| --- | --- |
| **Constant/Variable** | Thickness type of shell pair. |
| **Surfaces** | Selection collector for surfaces to be paired. |
| **Placement** | Enables you to change shell element placement for the pair. The default is **Midsurface**. Other options are: **Top**, **Bottom**, or **Selected Surface**. |
| **Material** | Enables you to apply materials to your shell model. By default, the part material is applied. |
| **Material Orientation** | Enables you to create and assign new material orientations in your shell model. Applies to non-isotropic materials only. |

## Automatic Shell Pairs

Creo Simulate can automatically pair surfaces using the **Detect Shell Pairs** option. Select **Shell Pair>Detect Shell Pairs** to open the Auto Detect Shell Pairs dialog box, as shown in Figure 4–7.

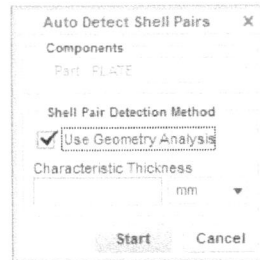

**Figure 4–7**

Two shell pair detection methods are available:

- **Use Geometry Analysis is toggled ON:** Creo Simulate searches for all shell pairs with a thickness of less than the Characteristic Thickness.

- **Use Geometry Analysis is toggled OFF:** Creo Simulate detects shell pairs based only on feature type. The following feature types are detected: Shells, Ribs, Thin protrusions, Ears, Sheet metal, and Plastic ribs.

When you click    Start   , Creo Simulate runs the detection algorithm, and displays all of the created shell pairs in the Model Tree. When you select the Shell Pairs in the Model Tree, they are highlighted in the model, one side in green and the other in cyan. These surfaces are compressed to create a midsurface.

## Shell Pair Compression

After you have defined the shell pairs, you need to check the compressed to midsurface geometry. Click 📄 in the *AutoGEM* area in the *Refine Model* tab to open the Simulation Geometry dialog box. Select the required options as shown in Figure 4–8.

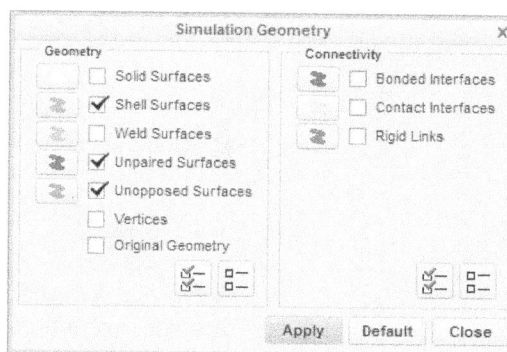

**Figure 4–8**

Click Apply . The midsurfaces are shaded in green, as shown in Figure 4–9.

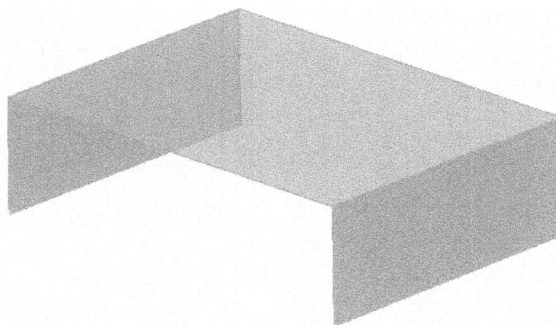

**Figure 4–9**

Alternatively, you can select **Original Geometry**, to display the original solid geometry (wireframe) over the compressed geometry (shaded), as shown in Figure 4–10.

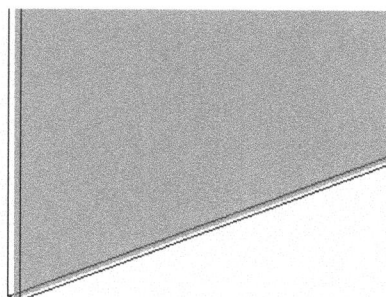

**Figure 4–10**

# 4.3 Standard Shells

**Learning Objective**

Understand how to create shell models from surface Creo Parametric models.

For Standard Shells, having a solid model of the part is not necessary. You select datum surfaces that are assumed to be the midsurfaces for the shell element placement. You must assign shell properties, such as thickness.

Standard Shells are useful in parts for which datum surfaces rather than solids are typically used to model part geometry, such as thin stampings, car body panels, aircraft skins, etc. An example of this type of model is shown in Figure 4–11.

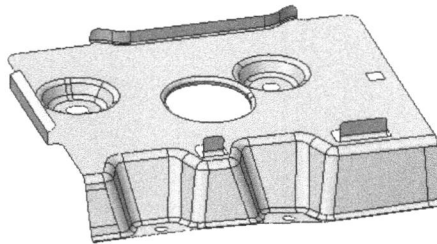

**Figure 4–11**

## Standard Shell Creation

To create a standard shell, click ⬨. The Shell Definition dialog box opens as shown in Figure 4–12.

**Figure 4–12**

Expand the Type drop-down list and select one of the following:

- **Simple:** Only **Thickness** and **Material** are required to define the shell properties.

- **Advanced:** Can be used to define shell properties for laminates.

Select surfaces for the shell, enter the shell properties as required, and click OK to finish.

# 4.4 Applying Loads and Constraints to Shell Models

**Learning Objective**

Understand how to apply loads and constraints to shell models.

Creo Simulate supports the same loads and constraints for both solid and shell models. However, because model geometry is automatically redefined during midsurface compression, you need to use caution when placing loads and constraints in shell models.

In general, loads and constraints applied to either side of the uncompressed model are automatically transferred by Creo Simulate to the midsurface. If you apply a load on both sides of the uncompressed model, the amount of load on the midsurface doubles. However, if you apply a constraint on both sides, Creo Simulate detects a conflict and aborts the analysis, because constraints in this case are effectively applied twice on the same midsurface.

The same applies to the edges. In the example shown in Figure 4–13, a load is applied to an edge on one side of the shell pair. After the midsurface compression, the load is transferred to the corresponding edge on the midsurface.

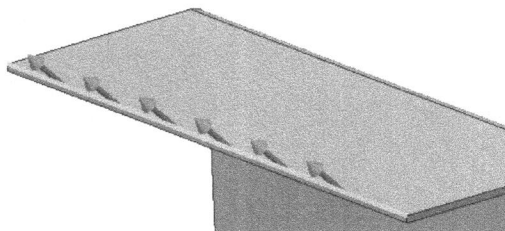

**Figure 4–13**

However, in the example shown in Figure 4–14, the same load is applied to the edges on both sides of the shell pair. After the midsurface compression, two loads are transferred and summed on the midsurface edge, which doubles the load in the analysis.

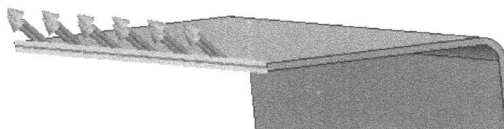

**Figure 4–14**

# Practice 4a

# Automatic Shell Creation

**Learning Objectives**

✓ Understand how to create shell element models.

✓ Set up loads, constraints, and material properties.

✓ Run and analyze a part.

In this practice, you will use shell element idealizations to set up and analyze the thin-walled pressure relief tank shown in Figure 4–15. You will use the **Detect Shell Pairs** option to create shell elements. The tank is created in Creo Parametric using surface features, and then the **Thicken** option is used to create a wall thickness of 0.5 mm.

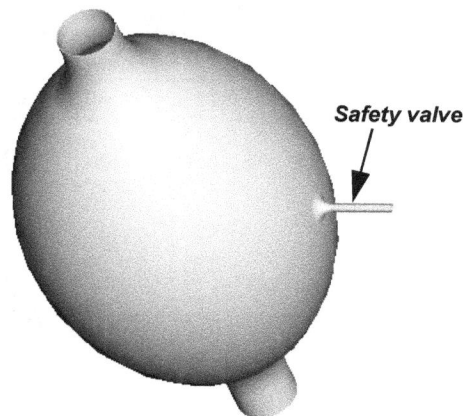

*Safety valve*

**Figure 4–15**

The existing symmetry is used to create a vertical cut through the tank to remove the front half of the tank. You will analyze 1/2 of the tank part shown in Figure 4–16, applying the Mirror Symmetry constraint on the cutting surface.

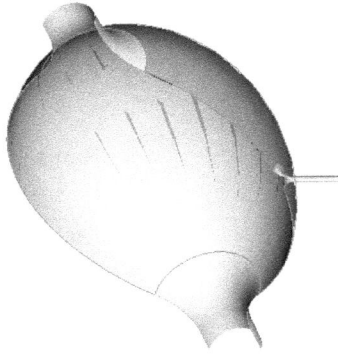

Figure 4–16

## Modeling Tasks

### Task 1 - Open the auto_p_t_02 part in Creo Parametric.

1. Open **auto_p_t_02.prt**. The part displays as shown in Figure 4–17.

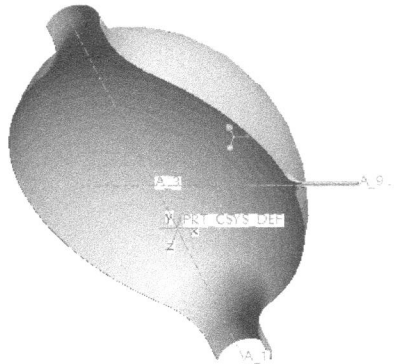

Figure 4–17

2. Ensure that the unit system is set to **mmNs**.

### Task 2 - Launch Creo Simulate.

1. Select **Applications>Simulate**.

2. Ensure that **Structure** mode is active.

3. Turn off the datum planes and datum axes.

## Task 3 - Define the shell elements.

1. In the *Refine Model* tab, in the *Idealizations* area, select **Shell Pair>Detect Shell Pairs**. The Auto Detect Shell Pairs dialog box opens as shown in Figure 4–18.

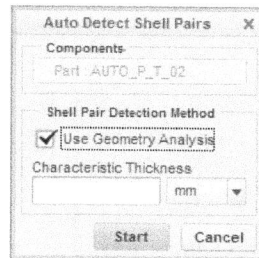

**Figure 4–18**

2. Clear **Use Geometry Analysis** and click ⬚Start . Creo Simulate creates six shell pairs that display in the Model Tree.

*Shells can be either flat or curved.*

3. In the *Refine Model* tab, in the *AutoGEM* area, click ⬚ to open the Simulation Geometry dialog box. Select the required options as shown in Figure 4–19.

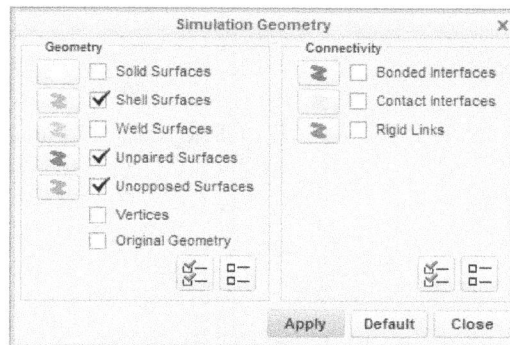

**Figure 4–19**

4. Click Apply . The model displays as shown in Figure 4–20.

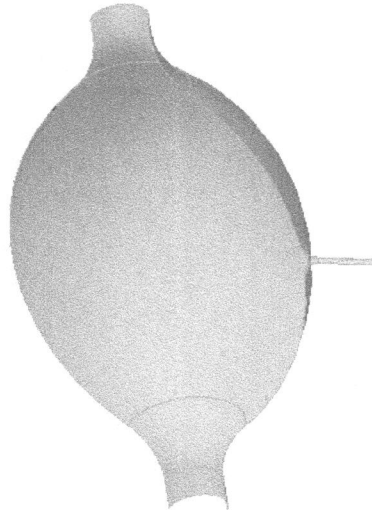

**Figure 4–20**

5. Select the **Original Geometry** option and click Apply . The midsurface is now shaded in green, while the solid edges are displayed as a black wireframe. Zoom in to display these edges more clearly, as shown in Figure 4–21.

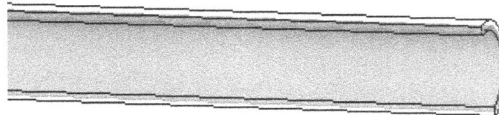

**Figure 4–21**

6. Click Close to finish.

## Task 4 - Mesh the model.

1. Expand the AutoGEM drop-down list and select **Midsurface**, as shown in Figure 4–22

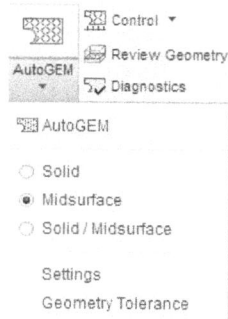

**Figure 4–22**

2. Click . The AutoGEM dialog box opens as shown in Figure 4–23.

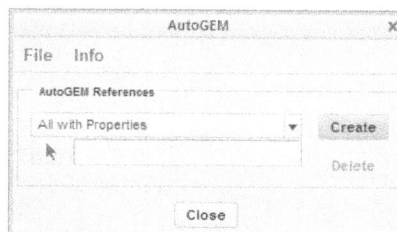

**Figure 4–23**

3. Expand the AutoGEM References drop-down list and select **Surface**.

4. Click . The Surface Selection box opens as shown in Figure 4–24.

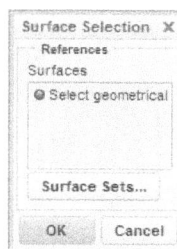

**Figure 4–24**

5. Draw a box around the model to select all of the surfaces.

6. In the Surface Selection dialog box, click   OK   or click the middle mouse button.

7. Click  Create . The AutoGEM Summary and Diagnostics dialog boxes open as shown in Figure 4–25.

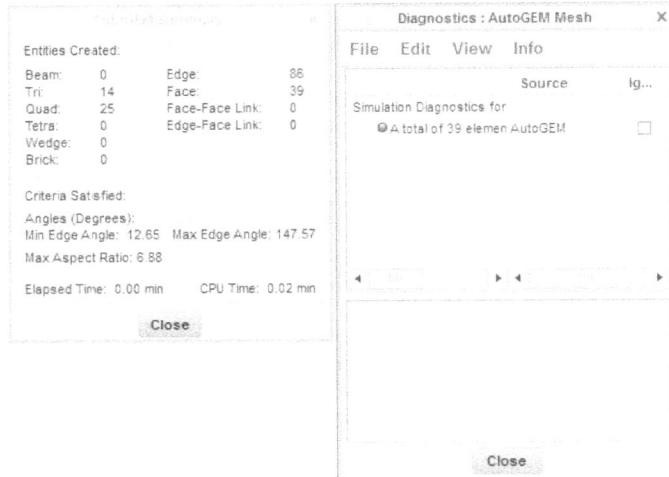

Entities Created:

| | | | |
|---|---|---|---|
| Beam: | 0 | Edge: | 86 |
| Tri: | 14 | Face: | 39 |
| Quad: | 25 | Face-Face Link: | 0 |
| Tetra: | 0 | Edge-Face Link: | 0 |
| Wedge: | 0 | | |
| Brick: | 0 | | |

Criteria Satisfied:

Angles (Degrees):
Min Edge Angle: 12.65   Max Edge Angle: 147.57
Max Aspect Ratio: 6.88

Elapsed Time: 0.00 min      CPU Time: 0.02 min

Close

Diagnostics : AutoGEM Mesh           X

File   Edit   View   Info

Source        Ig...
Simulation Diagnostics for
  ⊙ A total of 39 elemen AutoGEM         ☐

Close

**Figure 4–25**

Note the information displayed in this dialog box, such as the number of Tri and Quad shell elements.

8. Close both the AutoGEM Summary and Diagnostics boxes, but do not close the AutoGEM dialog box yet. The model displays as shown in Figure 4–26.

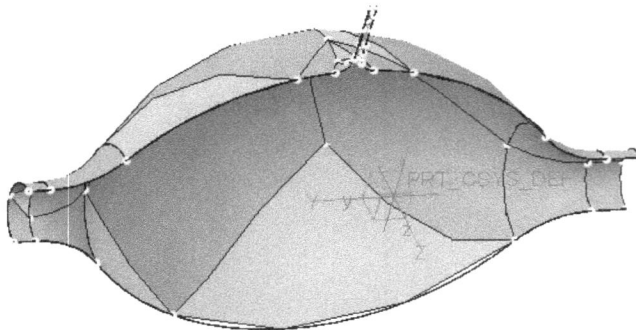

**Figure 4–26**

*The **Shrink Elements** option does not affect the analysis. It is only a visualization tool that helps to display the mesh more clearly.*

9. In the floating toolbar. click ⬚ (Simulation Display). The Simulation Display dialog box opens.

10. Select the *Mesh* tab, in the *Mesh Display* area, select the **Shrink Elements** option and increase the shrinkage value to 20%.

11. Click ⬚ OK ⬚ . The model displays as shown in Figure 4–27.

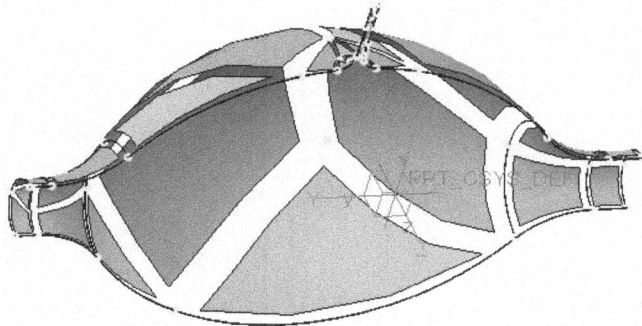

**Figure 4–27**

*The mesh is saved with model name and extension .MMP (**auto_p_t.mmp**).*

12. Click ⬚ Close ⬚ to close the AutoGEM dialog box and save the mesh.

## Task 5 - Apply a load to the model.

In this task, you will apply a pressure load to the interior surfaces of the model. This load represents the pressure exerted on the inside walls of the tank when the tank is pressurized.

1. In the *Loads* area, click ⊞ . The Pressure Load dialog box opens as shown in Figure 4–28.

**Figure 4–28**

*Load and constraint sets provide a logical means of organizing your modeling entities so that you can define the analyses clearly and effectively. A load set is a set of loads that act together on the model.*

2. In the *Name* field, enter **preload**.

3. For *Member of Set*, accept the default **LoadSet1** option.

4. Select the **Intent** option and select any interior surface of the tank. (This effectively selects all of the interior surfaces).

5. Click Advanced >>. Expand the Spatial Variation drop-down list and select **Uniform** (the other options are **Function Of Coordinates** and **External Coefficients Field**).

6. In the *Value* field for the pressure magnitude, enter **1**.

7. Click Preview to review the load.

8. Click OK to finish applying the load. The model displays as shown in Figure 4–29.

Figure 4–29

## Task 6 - Control load settings and visibilities.

1. In the floating toolbar, click ⬚. The Simulation Display dialog box opens as shown in Figure 4–30.

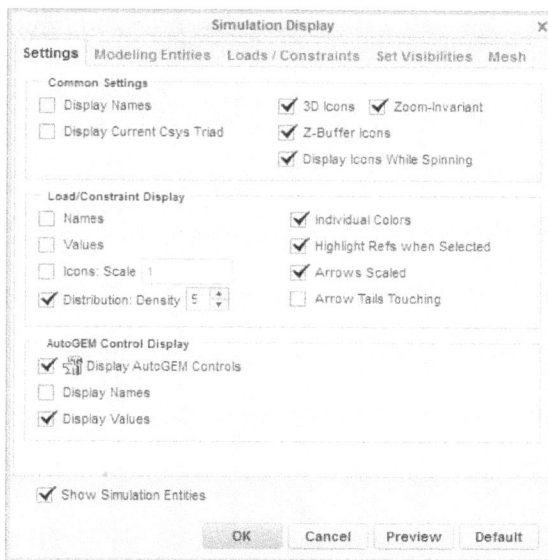

Figure 4–30

Examine the settings and visibilities in the Simulation Display dialog box. Note that in the *Settings* tab, the load arrows can be set to **Arrow Tails Touching** and **Individual Colors** to help visualize your loads. Additionally, you can remove the pressure load from the display (e.g., to see other constraints or loads more clearly).

2. Select the *Set Visibilities* tab.

3. Clear the **LoadSet1** option to turn off the pressure load.

4. Click  Preview  to display the model without the pressure load.

5. Click  OK  to close the Simulation Display dialog box.

### Task 7 - Apply constraints to the model.

In this task, you will constrain the edges at the top of the inlet/outlet pipes and the side of the safety valve pipe.

*Shell Elements have six degrees of freedom (three translations and three rotations).*

1. In the *Constraints* area, click  .

2. In the Constraint dialog box, in the *Name* field, enter **sidepipe**. For *Member of Set*, accept the default **ConstraintSet1** option.

3. Expand the References drop-down list and select **Edge(s)/ Curve(s)**.

4. Select the outer edges of the pipes (hold down <Ctrl> to select all of the outer edges of the pipes).

5. Constrain all of the Translation and Rotation directions. The Constraint dialog box opens as shown in Figure 4–31.

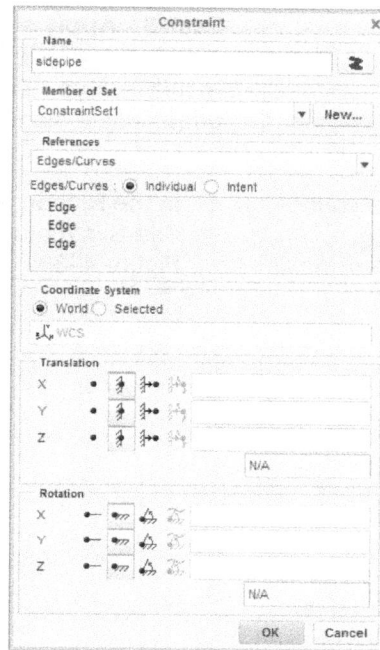

**Figure 4–31**

6. Click OK . The constraints display as shown in Figure 4–32.

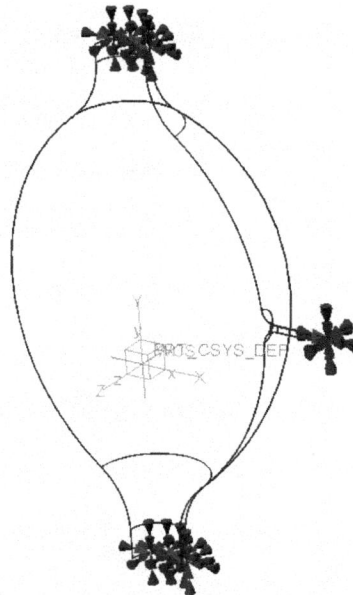

**Figure 4–32**

**Task 8 - Apply symmetry constraints.**

In this task you will apply a Mirror Symmetry constraint to the edges in the plane of symmetry to use the model's symmetry.

*To edit and delete your constraint sets, right-click and select the required option.*

1. In the Ribbon, expand the *Constraints* area, and click ⍨ . The Symmetry Constraint dialog box opens as shown in Figure 4–33.

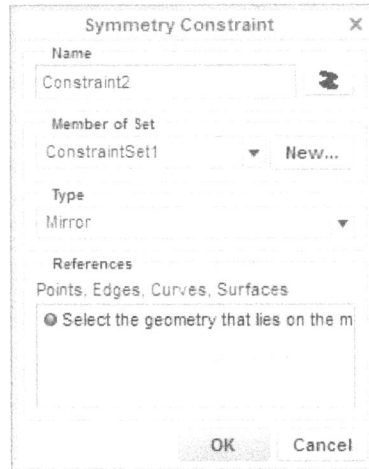

**Figure 4–33**

2. In the *Name* field, enter **sym_edges**. For *Member of Set,* select **ConstraintSet1**.

3. For the *Type*, select **Mirror**.

4. Select all of the outside edges of the model that are on the symmetry plane (do not select the interior edges). (Hold down <Ctrl> to select all of the edges.)

5. Click OK . The model displays as shown in Figure 4–34.

Figure 4–34

6. Click ⊞ . The Simulation Display dialog box opens.

7. In the *Setting* tab, select **Icons** and clear **Distribution**, as shown in Figure 4–35.

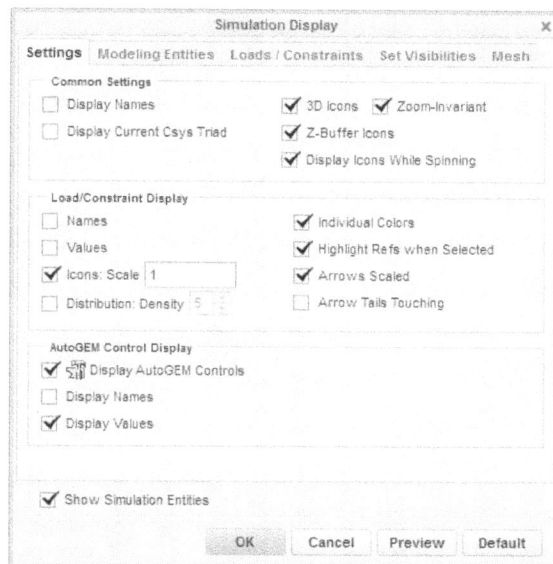

Figure 4–35

8. Click OK to close the Simulation Display dialog box. The constraints display as shown in Figure 4–36.

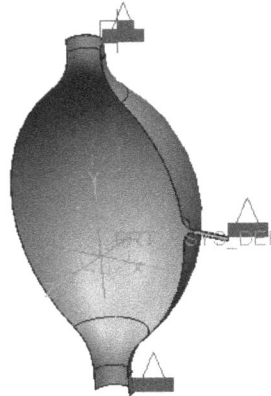

**Figure 4–36**

## Task 9 - Apply the material for the pressure tank.

1. Click ⌐. The Materials dialog box opens.

2. In the *Materials in Library* area, scroll through the list and select **SS** (stainless steel).

3. Click ▶▶▶ to transfer **SS** to the *Materials in Model* area.

4. Select **Edit>Properties** to check the material properties. Click OK when finished.

   The following values are the default material properties for stainless steel (SS):
   - Poisson = 0.3
   - Young's modulus = 193053 MPa
   - Density = 7.74372e-9 tonne/mm3

5. Click OK to close the Materials dialog box.

6. Click ⌐ to assign the material to the part. Click OK to close the Material Assignment dialog box.

7. In the Simulation Display dialog box, in *Set Visibilities* tab, toggle on the loads display.

## Analysis Tasks

### Task 10 - Set up and run the analysis.

1. Click [icon] . The Analyses and Design Studies dialog box opens as shown in Figure 4–37.

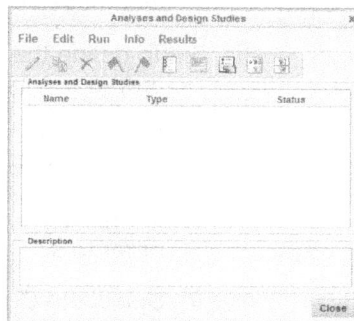

**Figure 4–37**

2. Select **File>New Static**. The Static Analysis Definition dialog box opens as shown in Figure 4–38.

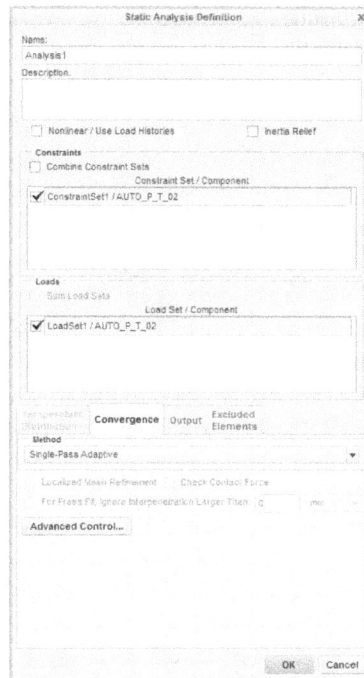

**Figure 4–38**

3. In the *Name* field, enter **tank**. (Tank becomes the name of a sub-directory containing all of your results files).

4. (Optional) In the *Description* field, enter **static analysis of a relieve pressure tank**. This help to identify your analysis.

5. For a static stress analysis, you need to specify or select the constraint and load sets, which have already been created. In this case, they are **ConstraintSet1** and **LoadSet1**. Ensure that these sets are highlighted.

6. To define the type of convergence, expand the Method drop-down list and select **Multi-Pass Adaptive**.

7. In the *Limits* area, in the *Percent Convergence* field, enter **5** percent convergence.

8. In the *Polynomial Order* area, set the *Maximum polynomial order* to **9**.

9. Select the *Output* tab and set the *Plotting Grid* to **9**. The Static Analysis Definition dialog box opens as shown in Figure 4–39.

*The Plotting Grid is a grid of points that Creo Simulate uses to display results within the elements. A higher density plotting grid is recommended to obtain smoother looking result plots.*

Figure 4–39

10. In the Static Analysis Definition dialog box, click OK.

*The **Check Model** option highlights any modeling errors (e.g., load-constraint conflicts or unassigned material properties) and errors from modeling edits.*

11. Expand the **Info** menu and select **Check Model**. This command checks the validity of the simulation model.

12. The Information dialog box opens, as shown in Figure 4–40, prompting you that there are no errors.

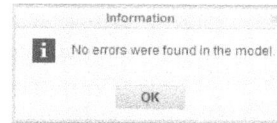

**Figure 4–40**

13. Click OK to finish checking the validity of the model.

14. Click in the Analyses and Design Studies dialog box to start your analysis. The Question dialog box opens as shown in Figure 4–41.

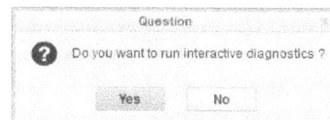

**Figure 4–41**

15. In the Question dialog box, click Yes. The prompt: *The design study has started*, displays in the message window.

16. The Diagnostics dialog box opens, displaying information about the analysis progress. Wait until the last line in the box says *Run completed*, as shown in Figure 4–42.

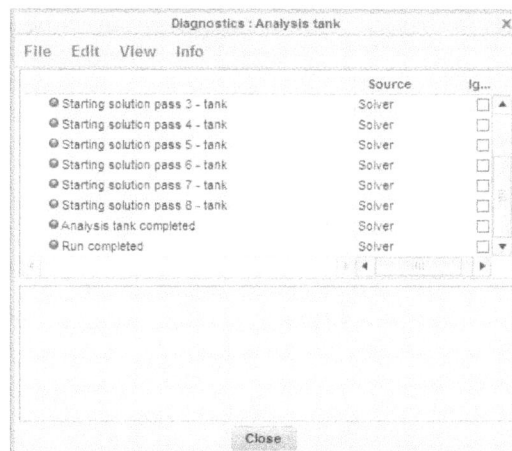

**Figure 4–42**

17. Click <u>Close</u> to close the Diagnostics dialog box.

## Task 11 - Explore the Run Status box.

1. In the Analyses and Design Studies dialog box, click ⊟.
   The Run Status window opens displaying a variety of
   information about the analysis.

2. Extract the following information from the dialog box:

   - Number of shell elements
   - Number of elements not converged at pass 4
   - Number of edges not converged at pass 7
   - RMS stress error estimates

   Did the solution converge at 5% (you set the convergence
   percentage in Step 7 of Task 1)?

## Results Tasks

## Task 12 - Display the results.

In this task, you will create and display von Mises stress and
Displacement color plots.

1. In the Analyses and Design Studies dialog box, click ▦.
   The Result Window Definition dialog box opens as shown in
   Figure 4–43.

**Figure 4–43**

2. In the *Name* field, accept the default of **Window1**.

3. In the *Title* field, enter **VM_PLOT**.

4. Select the *Display Options* tab and clear the **Show Element Edges**, **Show Loads**, and **Show Constraints** options.

5. Click OK and Show . The Creo Simulate Results environment displays, with the Von Mises Stress fringe plot displayed, as shown in Figure 4–44.

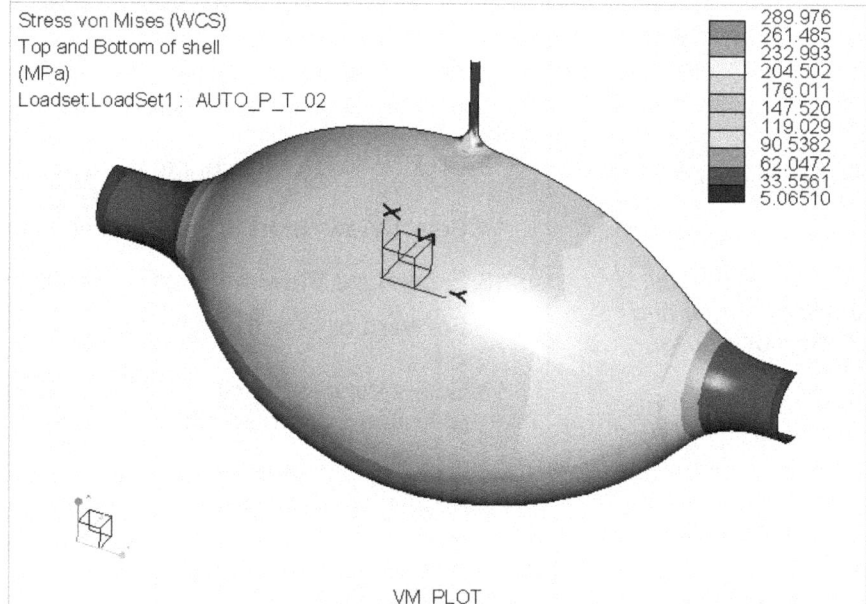

Stress von Mises (WCS)
Top and Bottom of shell
(MPa)
Loadset:LoadSet1 :  AUTO_P_T_02

289.976
261.485
232.993
204.502
176.011
147.520
119.029
90.5382
62.0472
33.5561
5.06510

VM_PLOT

**Figure 4–44**

6. Click 🗐 . The Result Window Definition dialog box opens.

7. In the *Name* field, enter **deformation**.

8. In the *Title* field, enter DEF_PLOT.

9. Expand the Quantity drop-down list and select **Displacement**.

10. In the *Display Options* tab, select the **Deformed** and **Animate** options.

11. Clear the **Auto Start** option and click OK .

12. Click [icon]. In the Display Result Window dialog box, clear **Window1** and select **deformation**, as shown in Figure 4–45.

Display Result Window ✕

Window1
deformation

≡  ≡

OK        Cancel

**Figure 4–45**

*Did the deformation display correctly?*

13. Click    OK   . The deformation plot displays.

14. Select **View>Start** to start the animation or click ▶.

*Use animations to check for errors and verify your results.*

15. Expand the **View** menu and select **Step Back** or **Step Forward** or click ◀ or ▶▌ to step through the animation.

16. Select **View>Stop** or click ■ to stop the deformation window at Frame 5 of the animation, as shown in Figure 4–46.

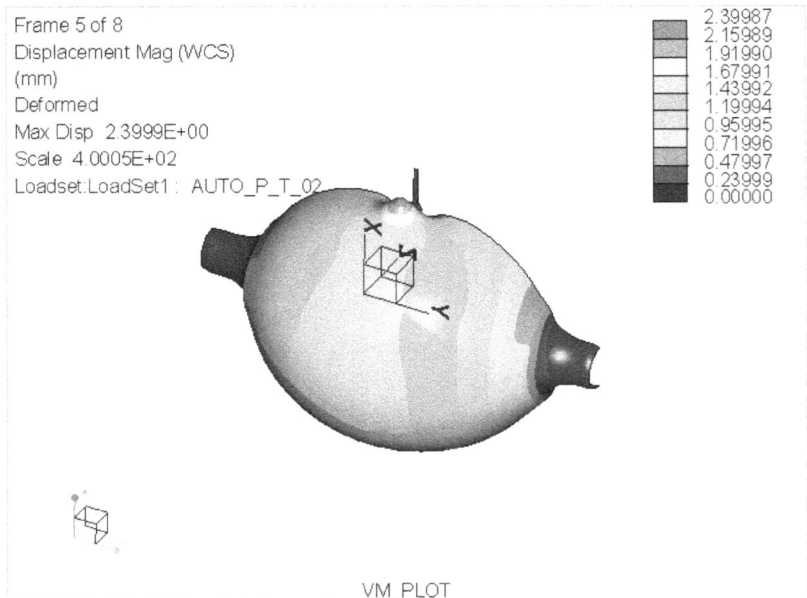

Frame 5 of 8
Displacement Mag (WCS)
(mm)
Deformed
Max Disp 2.3999E+00
Scale 4.0005E+02
Loadset:LoadSet1 : AUTO_P_T_02

2.39987
2.15989
1.91990
1.67991
1.43992
1.19994
0.95995
0.71996
0.47997
0.23999
0.00000

VM_PLOT

**Figure 4–46**

Note that the area around the small pipe seems to have excessive deformation. This is only a visual effect, due to Creo Simulate magnifying the amount of displayed deformation, for better clarity. Note the Scale value (shown in the top left corner in Figure 4–46), which is approximately 400, this is the deformation magnification factor. Therefore, the displayed deformation is 400 times the actual deformation (which is actually approximately 2.4mm).

17. Click ⊞ .

18. In the *Display Options* tab, select the **Overlay Undeformed** and **Transparent Overlay** options.

*If % is selected, the magnification factor is automatically set by Creo Simulation, based on the size of the model.*

19. Near the *Scaling* field, clear the **%** option. In the *Scaling* field, enter **50**. This is the magnification factor that is used to display deformation in the model.

20. In the *Display Options* tab, clear the **Animate** option. The Result Window Definition box opens as shown in Figure 4–47.

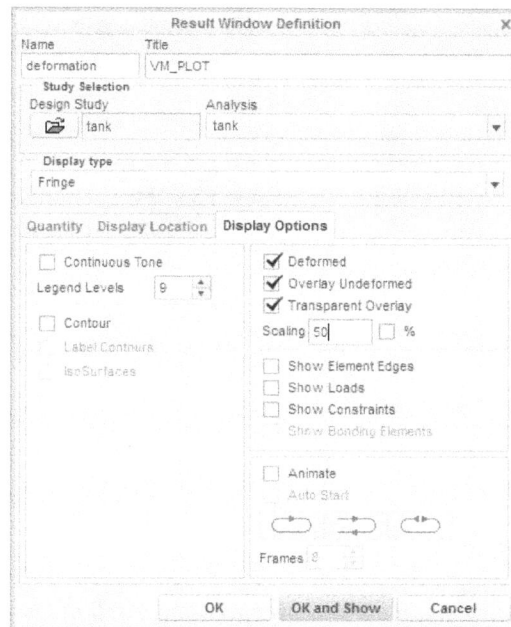

**Figure 4–47**

21. Click  OK and Show . The DEF_PLOT displays as shown in Figure 4–48. Note that the deformation around the small pipe is not now excessive (even though it is still magnified by the factor of 50).

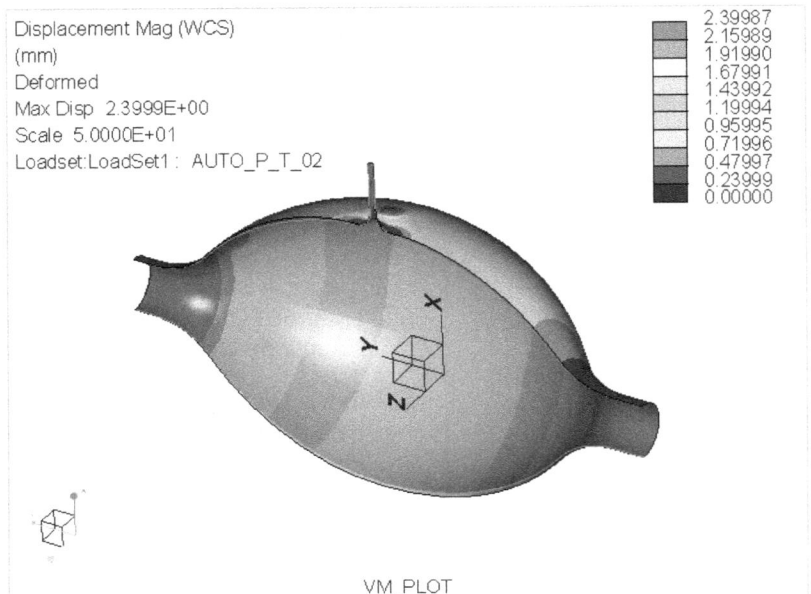

Displacement Mag (WCS)
(mm)
Deformed
Max Disp 2.3999E+00
Scale 5.0000E+01
Loadset:LoadSet1 : AUTO_P_T_02

2.39987
2.15989
1.91990
1.67991
1.43992
1.19994
0.95995
0.71996
0.47997
0.23999
0.00000

VM_PLOT

**Figure 4–48**

---

## Task 13 - Use predefined measures to study the convergence.

---

1. Click ⌗ to create a new results window. The Design Study for Result Window Definition dialog box opens.

2. Select the **tank** study and click  Open . The Result Window Definition dialog box opens.

3. In the *Name* field, enter **strain_energy**.

4. Expand the Display type drop-down list and select **Graph**.

5. Expand the first Graph Ordinate (Vertical) Axis drop-down list and select **Measure**.

6. Click 🗜. The Measures dialog box opens as shown in Figure 4–49.

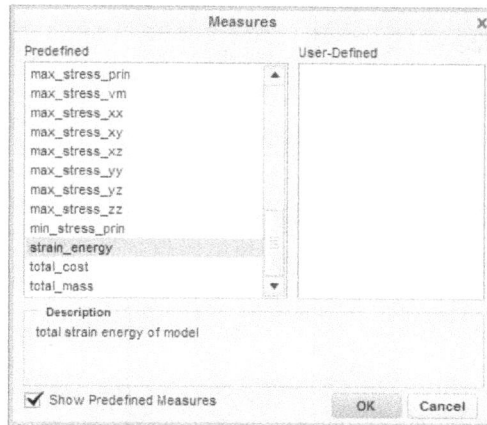

**Figure 4–49**

7. Highlight **strain_energy** (near the bottom of the list) and click OK . The Result Window Definition dialog box opens.

8. Click OK and Show .

9. Click 🗜. The Display Result Window dialog box opens as shown in Figure 4–50.

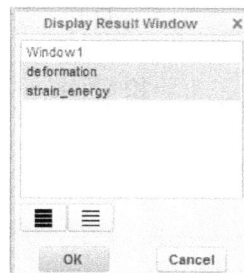

**Figure 4–50**

10. In the Display Result Window dialog box, select only

    **strain_energy** and click    OK   . The convergence plot
    displays as shown in Figure 4–51.

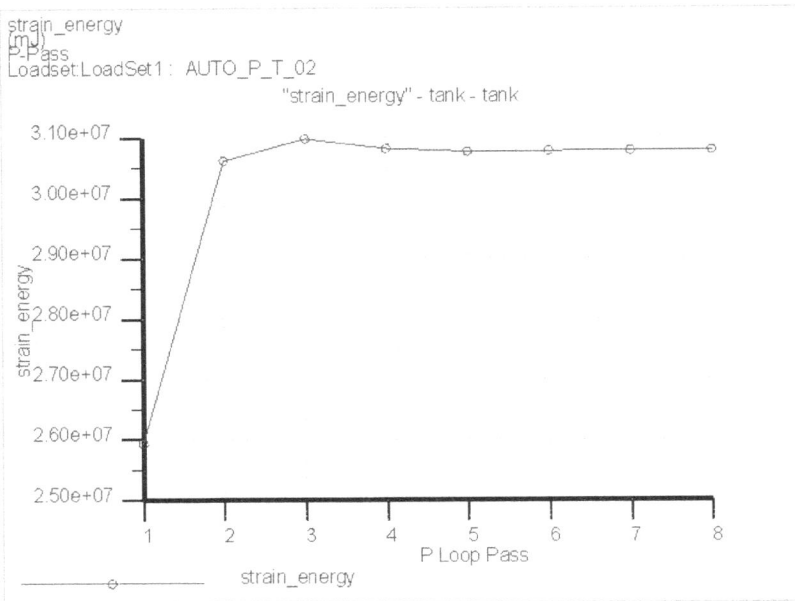

**Figure 4–51**

Note that the strain energy converges after pass 4.

11. Repeat the first eight steps of this task to create a
    convergence graph for the max_disp_mag measure.

12. Click    . The Display Result Window dialog box opens.

13. In the dialog box, highlight only **max_disp_mag** and then
    click ` OK `. The convergence plot displays as shown in
    Figure 4–52.

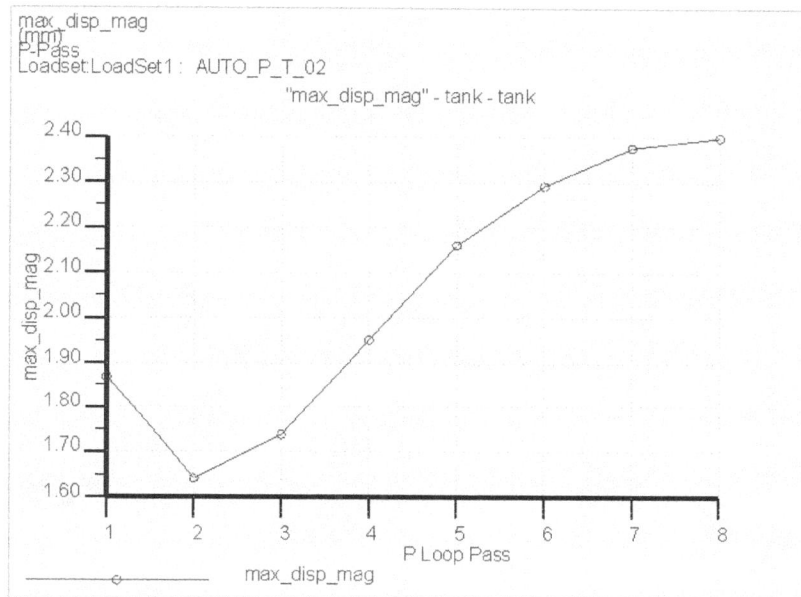

max_disp_mag
[mm]
P-Pass
Loadset:LoadSet1 :   AUTO_P_T_02

**Figure 4–52**

Note that the displacement curve converges after pass 7.

---
**Task 14 - Explore the Info menu.**
---

In this task, you will use the options in the **Info** menu. You will
also locate the point and value of the maximum stress.

1. Click ` `. In the Display Result window, highlight only
   **Window1** and then click ` OK `.

2. Select **Info>Model Max**. The location and value of maximum von Mises stress displays as shown in Figure 4–53. Rotate and/or zoom in on the model to display the location more clearly.

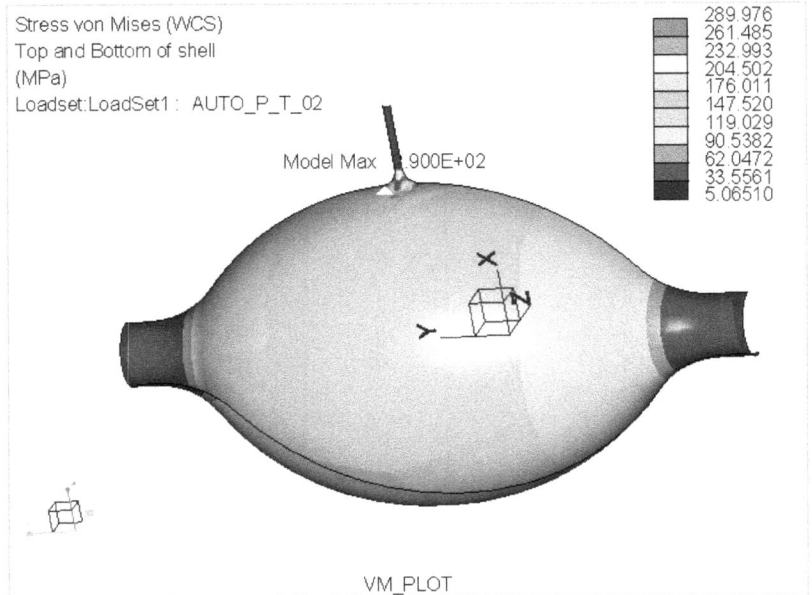

Stress von Mises (WCS)
Top and Bottom of shell
(MPa)
Loadset:LoadSet1 : AUTO_P_T_02

Model Max .900E+02

289.976
261.485
232.993
204.502
176.011
147.520
119.029
90.5382
62.0472
33.5561
5.06510

VM_PLOT

**Figure 4–53**

3. Investigate the other options in the **Info** menu. For example, the **Dynamic Query** option displays the part stress levels as you hold down the left mouse button and move the cursor along the model. In the Query dialog box. click `Close` when finished.

## Task 15 - Save and close the model.

1. Select **File>Exit Results**. In the dialog box, click `No` when prompted to save the results.

2. Close the Analyses and Design Studies dialog box.

3. Exit Creo Simulate. Save and close the model in Creo Parametric.

# Practice 4b | # Manual Shell Creation

**Learning Objective**

Set up and run an analysis on an assembly using shell element idealizations.

In this practice, you will use shell element idealizations to set up, run, and analyze a thin-walled assembly (a miniature model of a diving stand). The assembly consists of two cross members with a bend part, diving board, and supporting wedge. The assembly is shown in Figure 4–54.

In assemblies, shell pairs can be defined on component level or assembly level. In this practice, you will use both methods.

*All parts in the assembly must use the same unit system.*

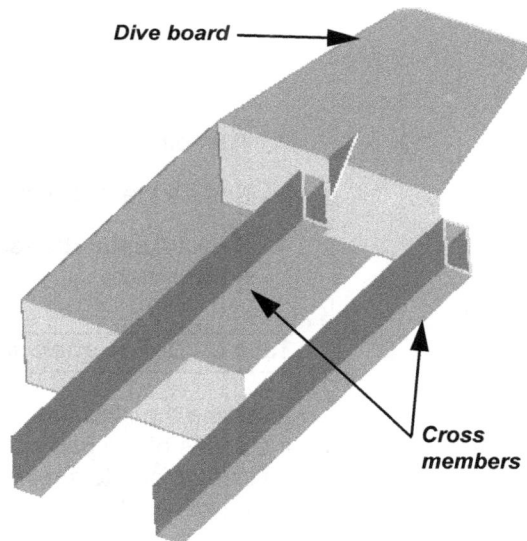

Dive board

Cross members

**Figure 4–54**

## Modeling Tasks

### Task 1 - Open the assembly.

1. Open **dive_board.asm** in Creo Parametric. The assembly displays as shown in Figure 4–55.

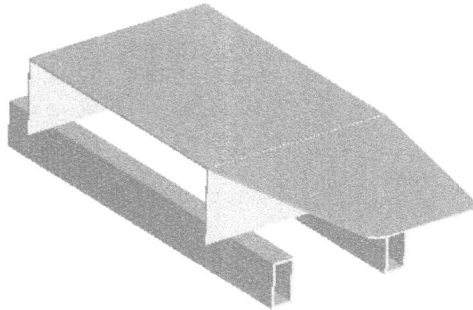

**Figure 4–55**

2. Turn off the datum planes and datum axes.

3. Ensure that the unit system is set to **mmNs**.

4. Select **Applications>Simulate** to enter the Creo Simulate environment.

### Task 2 - Define shell pairs for the part called BOX.prt.

Examine the structure of the assembly. Note that there are two instances of the part called BOX.prt. Therefore, it is more efficient to create shell pairs for this part on the component level, which will automatically apply the shell pairs to all of the instances of the part in the assembly.

1. In the Model Tree, right-click on **box.prt** and select **Open**. The part opens in a new window, as shown in Figure 4–56.

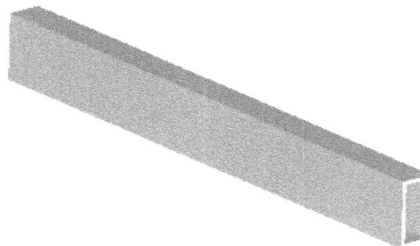

**Figure 4–56**

*Although it would be more efficient to use the automatic shell pair detection tool in this part, in this case you will use manual shell pair creation.*

2. Select **Applications>Simulate** to enter the Creo Simulate environment.

3. In the *Refine Model* tab, click . The Shell Pair Definition dialog box opens as shown in Figure 4–57. Ensure that the **Auto Select Opposing Surfaces** option is selected.

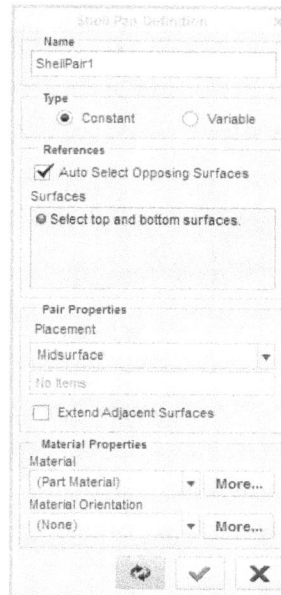

**Figure 4–57**

4. Select the outer surface of the top flange, as shown in Figure 4–58. Click to complete the shell pair and reopen the Shell Pair Definition dialog box.

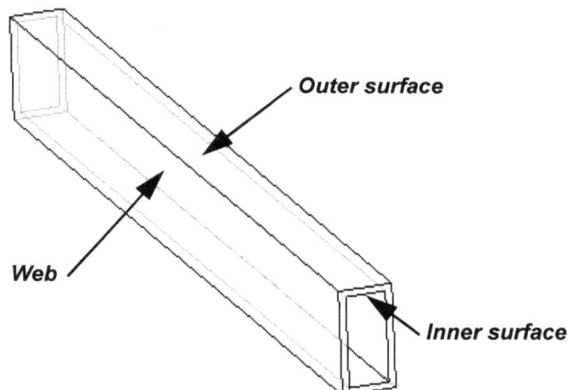

**Figure 4–58**

5. Repeat the previous Step for all other outer surfaces of the part. When selecting the last outer surface, click ✔ to close the Shell Pair Definition dialog box.

6. Four shell pairs should now be displayed in the Model Tree.

7. Click 🔲 and click Apply . The compressed model displays as shown in Figure 4–59.

**Figure 4–59**

8. Close the Simulation Geometry dialog box.

9. In the *Home* tab, click ❎ to exit Creo Simulate.

10. Save and close the part to return to the assembly window.

## Task 3 - Define shell pairs for all of the other parts.

Shell pairs for all of the other parts in the assembly will be defined on the assembly level. You will use the **Detect Shell Pairs** tool to automatically create the shell pairs.

1. In the *Refine Model* tab, expand the Shell Pair drop-down list and select **Detect Shell Pairs**. The Auto Detect Shell Pairs dialog box opens as shown in Figure 4–60.

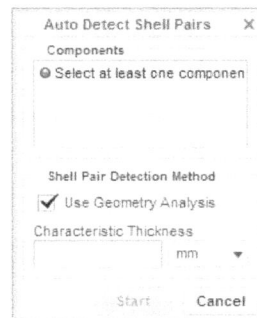

**Figure 4–60**

*The thickness of the parts in this assembly is 0.3mm.*

2. In the assembly, select the **TOP_SHAPE.PRT**, **PLATE.PRT**, and **WEDGE.PRT** parts (hold down <Ctrl> to multi-select).

3. Ensure that **Use Geometry Analysis** is selected. In the *Characteristic Thickness* field, enter **0.4**. The Auto Detect Shell Pairs dialog box opens as shown in Figure 4–61.

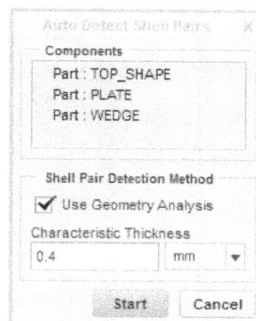

**Figure 4–61**

4. Click Start. Creo Simulate runs the automatic detection algorithm and closes the Auto Detect Shell Pairs dialog box.

5. Five shell pairs should now be displayed in the Model Tree on the assembly level.

## Task 4 - Test the midsurface compression.

1. In the *Refine Model* tab, in the *AutoGEM* area, click 🔲 to open the Simulation Geometry dialog box. Select the required options as shown in Figure 4–62.

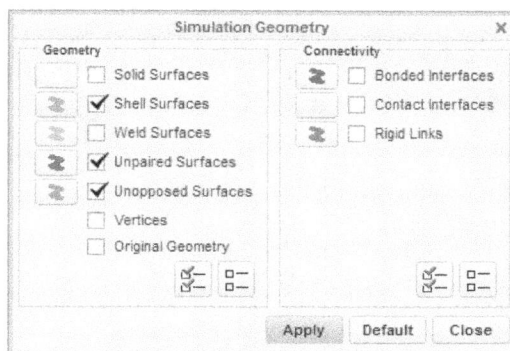

**Figure 4–62**

2. Click <sup>Apply</sup> . The model displays as shown in Figure 4–63. Ensure that there are no unpaired surfaces (displayed in red) or unopposed surfaces (displayed in orange) in the model.

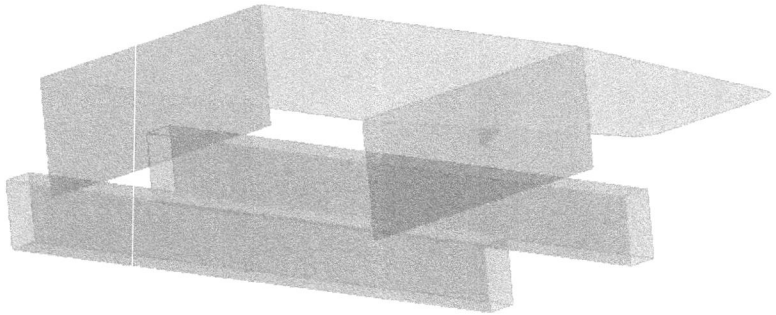

**Figure 4–63**

3. Zoom in on the areas where the parts join, and note that there are gaps between the midsurface, as shown in Figure 4–64. This is because the midsurfaces are obtained by offsetting the part surfaces by a half thickness. Therefore, even though the part surfaces being mated in the assembly, the midsurfaces are not mated.

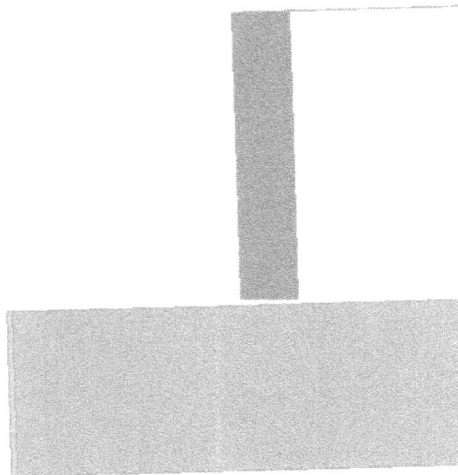

**Figure 4–64**

4. In the Simulation Geometry dialog box, select the **Bonded Interface** option, as shown in Figure 4–65.

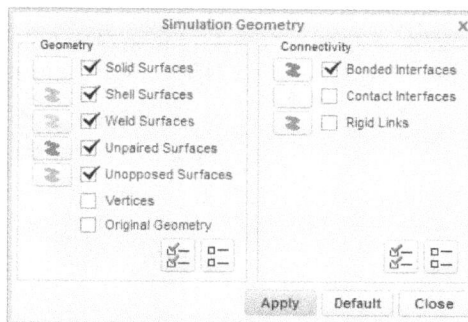

**Figure 4–65**

5. Click Apply . The model displays as shown in Figure 4–66.

Note that the areas of contact between the parts are now highlighted in magenta. Creo Simulate detects the mated in assembly surfaces, and assumes that the parts in those areas should be bonded during the analysis.

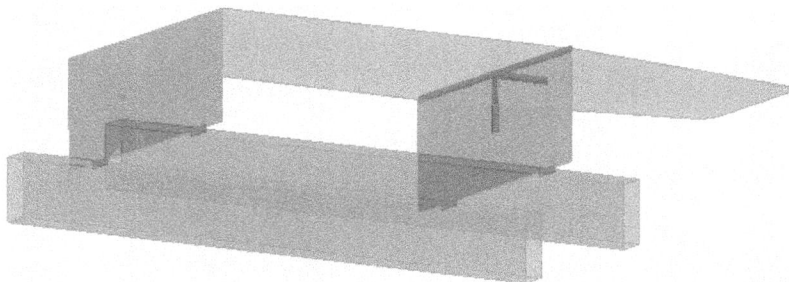

**Figure 4–66**

6. Click Close to finish.

## Task 5 - Apply material to parts in the assembly.

1. Click ⌐ . The Materials dialog box opens.

2. In the *Materials in Library* area, scroll down the list and select **STEEL** (HS-low-alloy steel).

3. Click ▶▶▶ to transfer **STEEL** to the *Materials in Model* area.

*The model's material properties should be as stated.*

4. Click ✎ to check your material properties and click `OK` when finished.

   The following values are the default material properties for HS-low-alloy steel (STEEL):

   - Poisson = 0.27
   - Young's modulus = 199948 MPa
   - Density = 7.82708e-9 tonne/mm3

5. Click `OK` to close the Materials dialog box.

6. Click ⬚ to assign the material to the parts.

7. Select all of the parts in the assembly (hold down <Ctrl> to multi-select). The Material Assignment dialog box should be as shown in Figure 4–67.

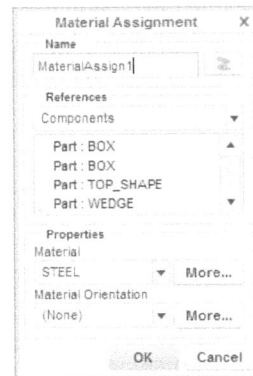

| Material Assignment | X |
|---|---|
| Name | |
| MaterialAssign1 | |

**References**
Components ▾

Part : BOX
Part : BOX
Part : TOP_SHAPE
Part : WEDGE

**Properties**
Material
STEEL ▾ More...
Material Orientation
(None) ▾ More...

OK     Cancel

**Figure 4–67**

8. Click `OK` to close the Material Assignment dialog box.

9. Click ⬚. The Simulation Display dialog box opens.

10. In the *Modeling Entities* tab, clear the **Material Assignments** option.

11. Click `OK` to close the Simulation Display dialog box.

---

**Task 6 - Mesh the model.**

---

1. Expand the AutoGEM drop-down list and select **Midsurface**, as shown in Figure 4–68.

---

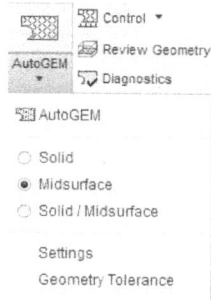

**Figure 4–68**

2. Click . The AutoGEM dialog box opens as shown in Figure 4–69.

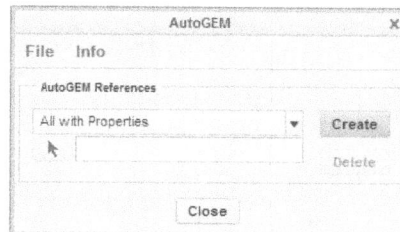

**Figure 4–69**

*The **All with Properties** option requires that materials be applied before meshing.*

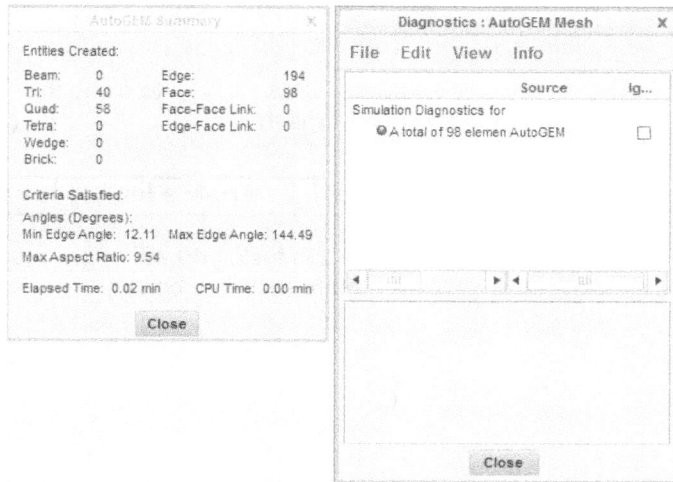

3. Expand the AutoGEM References drop-down list, select **All with Properties**, and click `Create`. The AutoGEM Summary and Diagnostics dialog boxes open as shown in Figure 4–70.

**Figure 4–70**

4. Close both of the AutoGEM Summary and Diagnostics boxes, but do not close the AutoGEM dialog box yet. The model displays as shown in Figure 4–71.

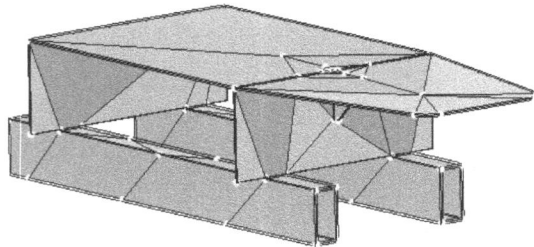

**Figure 4–71**

5. Zoom in on the model and examine the areas where the parts join, as shown in Figure 4–72.

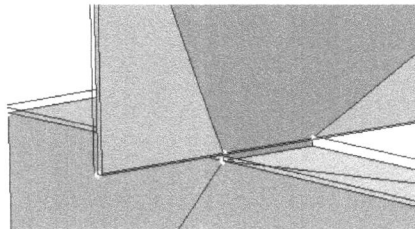

**Figure 4–72**

Note that the shell elements (displayed in green) in areas that are connected using grey elements, which are the Bonding elements. Bonding elements in Creo Simulate are specifically designed to connect compressed parts in shell assemblies.

6. Click `Close` to close the AutoGEM dialog box and save the mesh.

## Task 7 - Apply a load to the model.

In this task, you will apply a load of 15N to the top surface of **plate.prt** (dive board).

1. Click ⊞ . Enter the information in the Force/Moment dialog box, as shown in Figure 4–73.

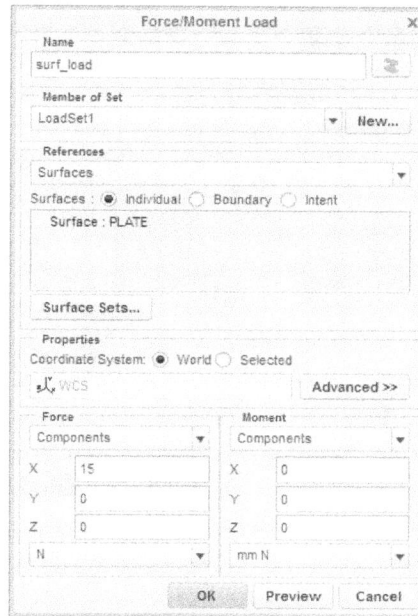

**Figure 4–73**

2. Click OK to finish. The assembly displays as shown in Figure 4–74.

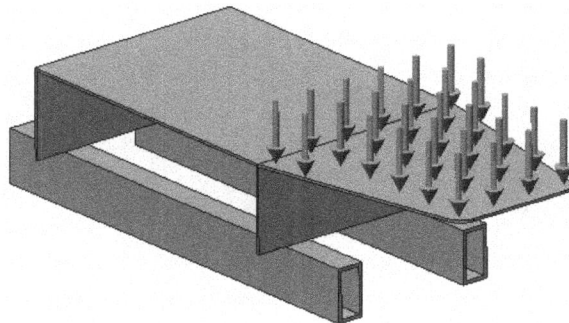

**Figure 4–74**

## Task 8 - Apply constraints to the model.

In this task, you will apply constraints to the ends of the beams shown in Figure 4–75.

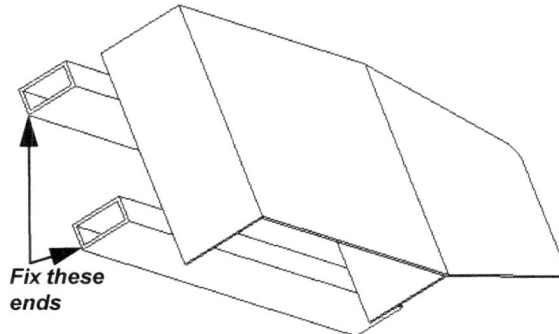

**Fix these ends**

**Figure 4–75**

1. Click 🖾. The Constraint dialog box opens.

2. In the *Name* field, enter **asm_const**. For *Member of Set*, accept the default **ConstraintSet1**.

3. Expand the References drop-down list and select **Edges/Curves**.

4. Select eight outer edges on the end faces, as shown in Figure 4–76. (Hold down <Ctrl> to multi-select.)

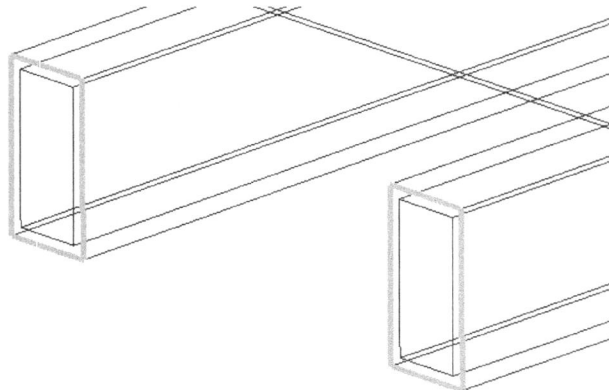

**Figure 4–76**

5. Fix all of the Translations and Rotations, as shown in Figure 4–77.

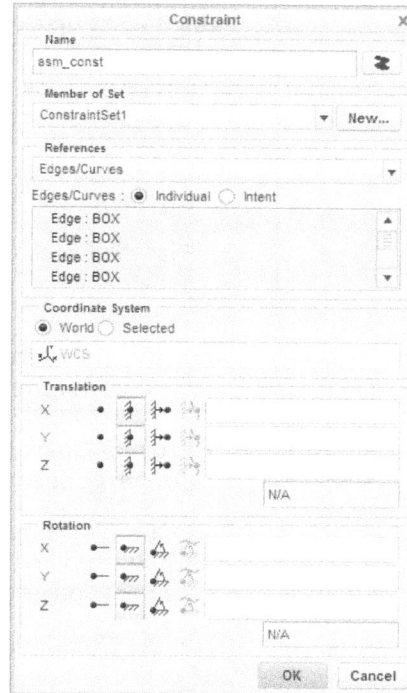

**Figure 4–77**

6. Click OK . The constraints display as shown in Figure 4–78.

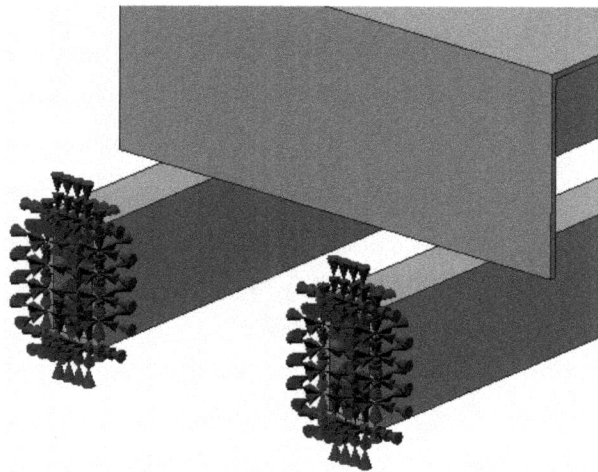

**Figure 4–78**

## Analysis Tasks

### Task 9 - Set up the analysis.

1.  Set up a Quick Check static analysis. For the name of the analysis, enter **dive_asm**.

2.  In the Analyses and Design Studies dialog box, run **Info> Check Model** to check the validity of the model.

3.  Run the Quick Check analysis to check for errors in loads or constraints.

### Task 10 - Solve the assembly using the Multi-Pass Adaptive convergence option.

1.  Change *Quick Check* to the **Multi-Pass Adaptive convergence** method.

2.  In the *Polynomial Order* field, enter **9** maximum and in the *Limits* area, in the *Percent Convergence* field, enter **10** percent convergence.

3.  In the *Output* tab, increase the *Plotting Grid* value to **10**.

4.  Start the analysis run and wait until it completes.

5.  In the Analyses and Design Studies dialog box, click ▤. The Run Status window opens displaying information about the analysis, as shown in Figure 4–79.

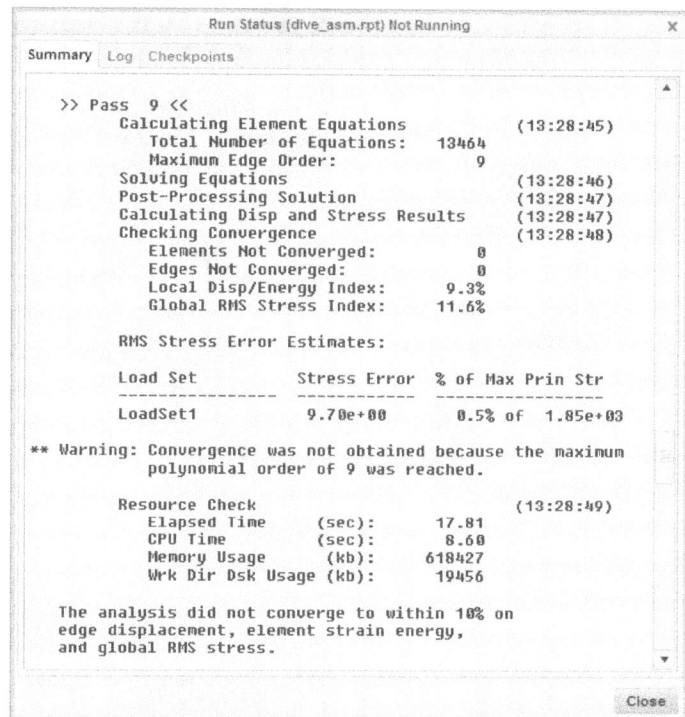

**Figure 4–79**

Note that the analysis did not converge on the Global RMS Stress to the required 10% because the maximum polynomial order 9 was not sufficient to obtain the convergence. In the following tasks, you will explore the elements that have not converged.

6. Close the Run Status window.

## Task 11 - Display the non-converged elements.

1. In the Analyses and Design Studies dialog box, click ⊞. In the Result Window Definition dialog box, expand the Quantity drop-down list and select **P-Level**, as shown in Figure 4–80.

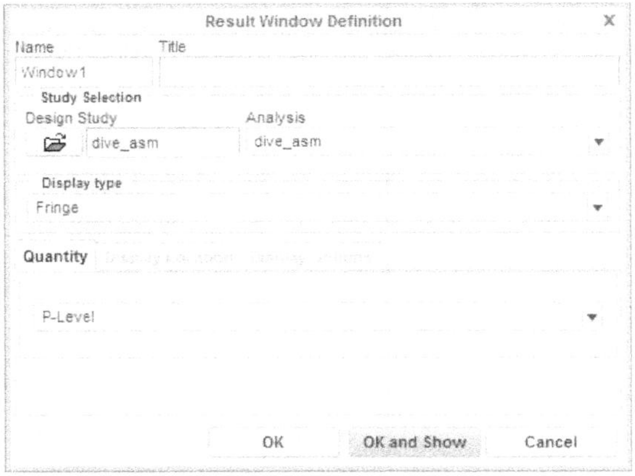

**Figure 4–80**

2. Click OK and Show. The P-Level plot displays as shown in Figure 4–81.

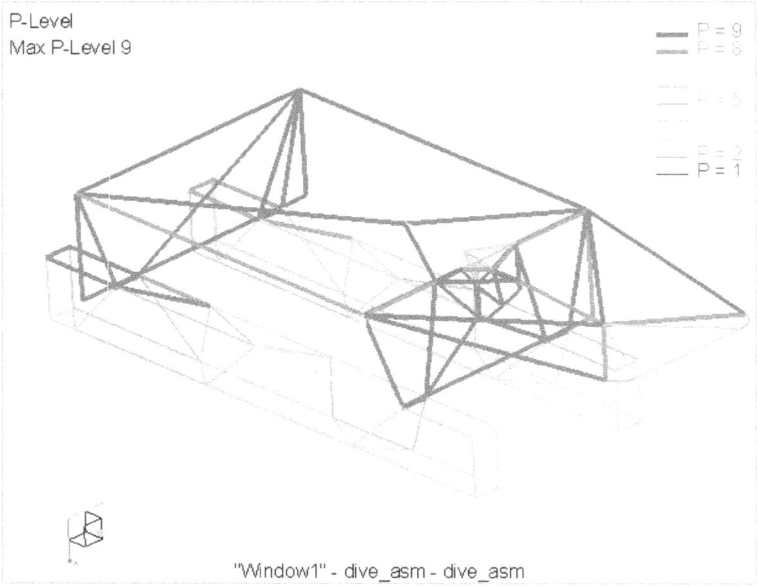

"Window1" - dive_asm - dive_asm

**Figure 4–81**

Examine the P-Levels and note that majority of the elements, in all but the beam parts, have their edges displayed in red, which corresponds to P-Level 9. These are the elements that are most likely to have not converged.

Note that the elements in the model are very large. Therefore, the non-convergence might be attributed to the elements being too large. In the following task, you will refine the mesh to obtain convergence.

3. Select **File>Exit Results** and exit without saving the result window.

4. Close the Analyses and Design Studies dialog box.

## Mesh Refinement Tasks

## Task 12 - Set up the AutoGEM Controls.

1. In the *Refine Model* tab, in the *AutoGEM* area, expand the Control drop-down list and select **Maximum Element Size**, as shown in Figure 4–82.

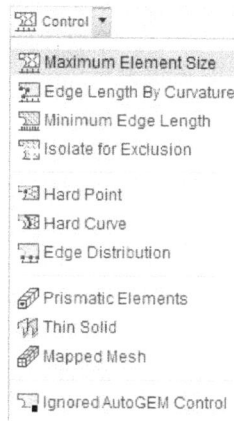

Figure 4–82

2. The Maximum Element Size Control dialog box opens. Expand the References drop-down list and select **Components**. Select all of the parts in the assembly (hold down <Ctrl> to multi-select), and in the *Element Size* field, enter **8** as shown in Figure 4–83.

**Figure 4–83**

3. Click OK to finish. Note that AutoGEM Control icons display in the model and in the Model Tree.

## Task 13 - Re-mesh the model.

1. Click [icon]. The Question box displays as shown in Figure 4–84.

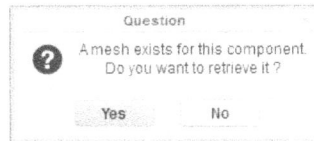

**Figure 4–84**

2. Click No . The AutoGEM dialog box opens as shown in Figure 4–85.

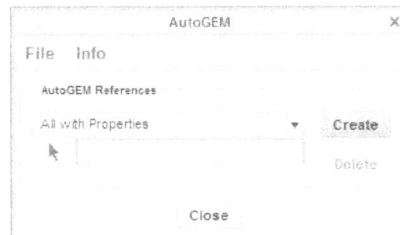

**Figure 4–85**

3. Click  Create . Once meshing is finished, close both the AutoGEM Summary and Diagnostics dialog boxes. The model displays (with loads and constraints hidden) as shown in Figure 4–86.

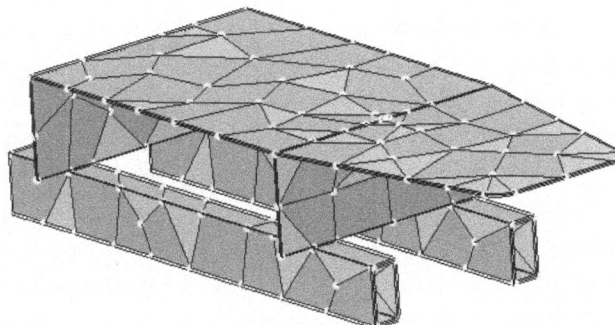

**Figure 4–86**

Note that AutoGEM now creates a much finer mesh, according to the element size that you specified in an earlier task.

4. Click  Close  to close the AutoGEM dialog box and save the mesh.

## Task 14 - Re-run the analysis.

1. Run the **dive_asm** analysis again and wait until it completes.

2. In the Analyses and Design Studies dialog box, click 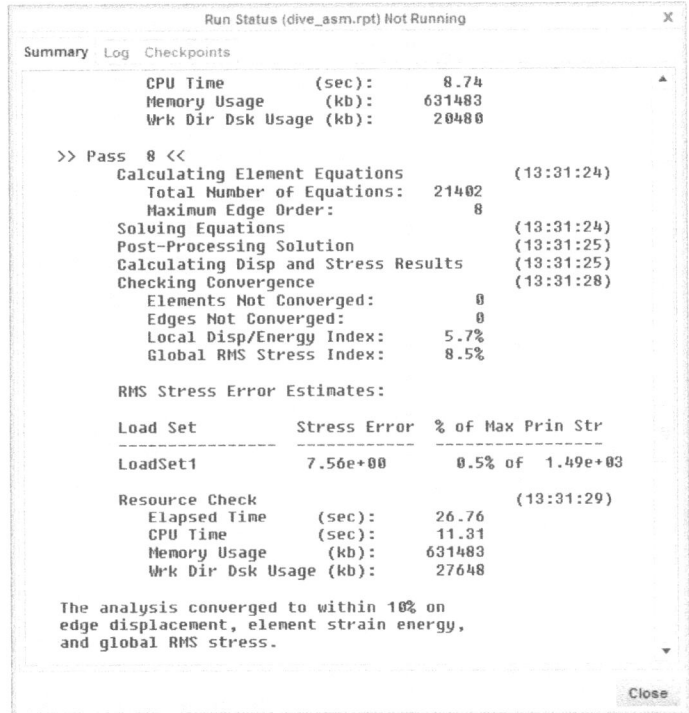 to open the Run Status window and check whether the analysis has converged, as shown in Figure 4–87.

```
Run Status (dive_asm.rpt) Not Running                          X

Summary  Log  Checkpoints
         CPU Time        (sec):      8.74                        ▲
         Memory Usage     (kb):    631483
         Wrk Dir Dsk Usage (kb):    20480

  >> Pass  8 <<
         Calculating Element Equations          (13:31:24)
             Total Number of Equations:   21402
             Maximum Edge Order:             8
         Solving Equations                      (13:31:24)
         Post-Processing Solution               (13:31:25)
         Calculating Disp and Stress Results    (13:31:25)
         Checking Convergence                   (13:31:28)
             Elements Not Converged:         0
             Edges Not Converged:            0
             Local Disp/Energy Index:      5.7%
             Global RMS Stress Index:      8.5%

         RMS Stress Error Estimates:

         Load Set          Stress Error   % of Max Prin Str
         ----------------  -------------  ------------------
         LoadSet1           7.56e+00       0.5% of  1.49e+03

         Resource Check                         (13:31:29)
             Elapsed Time    (sec):      26.76
             CPU Time        (sec):      11.31
             Memory Usage     (kb):    631483
             Wrk Dir Dsk Usage (kb):    27648

  The analysis converged to within 10% on
  edge displacement, element strain energy,
  and global RMS stress.                                        ▼

                                                        Close
```

**Figure 4–87**

Note that the analysis now converges on Pass 8, with the maximum P-level 8 (**Maximum Edge Order** in the Run Status window).

3. Click  Close  to close the Run Status window.

## Results Tasks

### Task 15 - Display the stress results.

1. Create and display a color plot of the von Mises stress. It should display as shown in Figure 4–88.

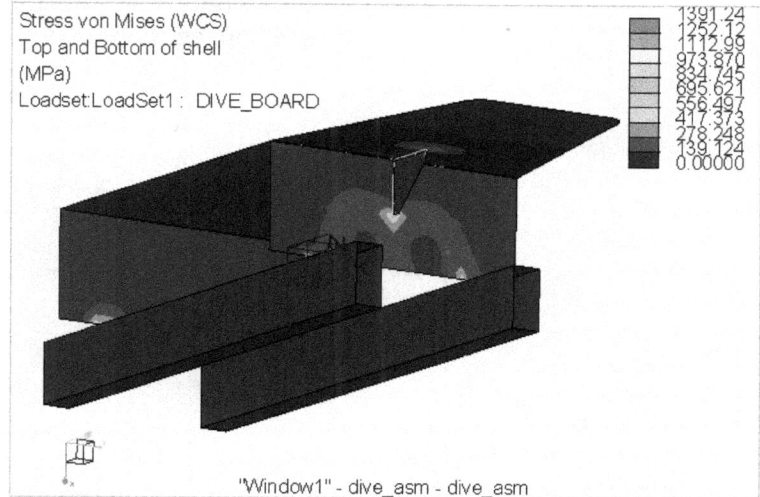

Stress von Mises (WCS)
Top and Bottom of shell
(MPa)
Loadset:LoadSet1 : DIVE_BOARD

1391.24
1252.12
1112.99
973.870
834.745
695.621
556.497
417.373
278.248
139.124
0.00000

"Window1" - dive_asm - dive_asm

**Figure 4–88**

The stress values that you obtain once you run the analysis
might be slightly different than those that have been provided.
This is because each build of Creo Simulate has a slightly
different solver, which will produce variations in the creation of
the mesh and the solution of the analysis.

2. Select **Format>Legend**. The Edit Legend dialog box opens
   as shown in Figure 4–89. Explore the options in the box.

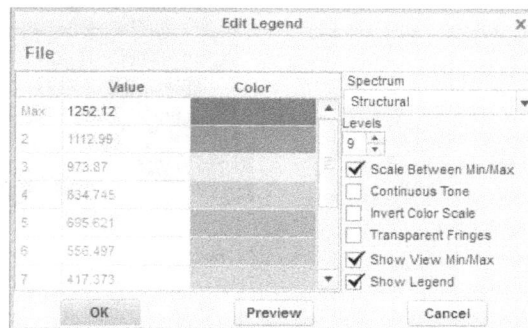

**Figure 4–89**

3. Clear the **Show View Min/Max** option and change the *Max* value to **500**, as shown in Figure 4–90.

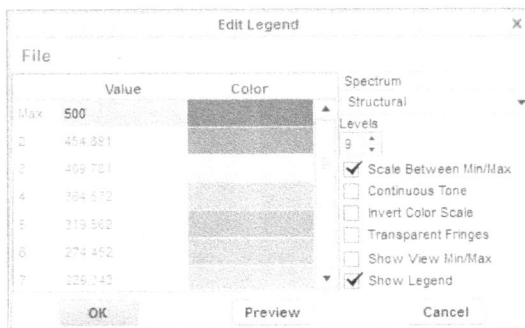

Figure 4–90

4. Click ___OK___ . The model displays as shown in Figure 4–91. Note that the changed legend enables the stress distribution in the model to be displayed more clearly.

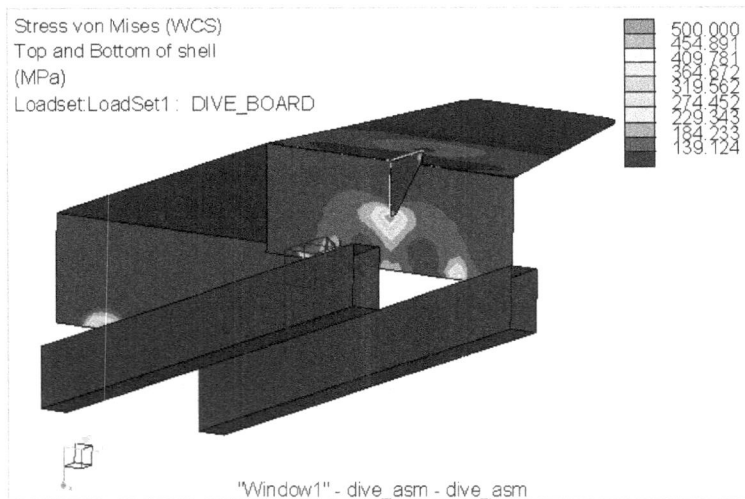

Figure 4–91

## Task 16 - Examine areas of high stress.

1. Select **Info>Model Max**. The result plot displays as shown in Figure 4–92. Zoom in on the location of the maximum stress.

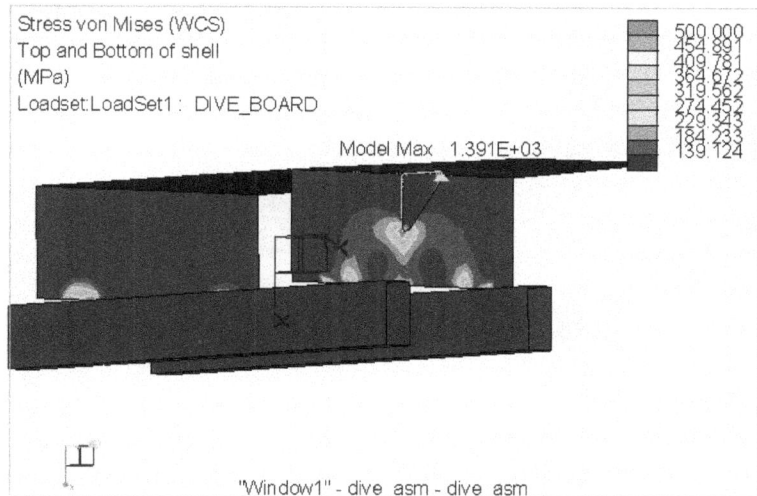

**Figure 4–92**

2. Zoom in on the area in which the top C-shape is attached to the left beam, and select **Info>View Max**. Creo Simulate now only displays the location of the maximum stress within the viewing area, as shown in Figure 4–93.

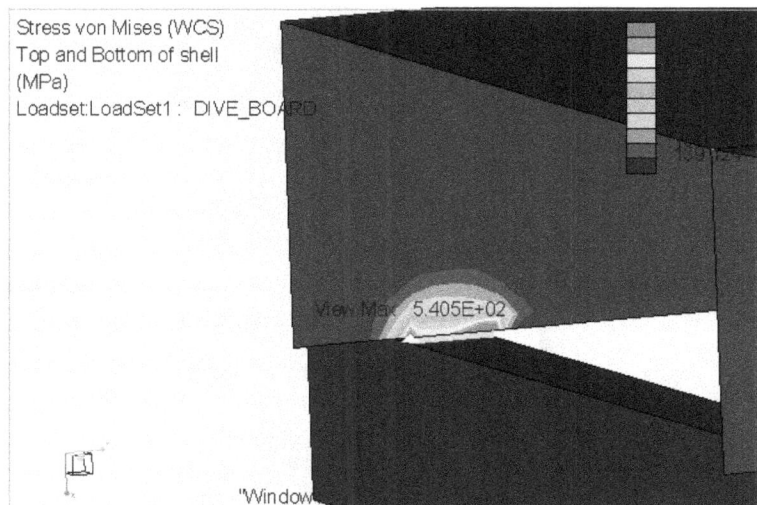

**Figure 4–93**

3. Select **Info** and then select **Location in Dynamic Query**.

4. Select **Info>Dynamic Query** and explore the stresses in the area by hovering the cursor over the model, as shown in Figure 4–94. Note that the Query box displays the coordinates of the queried point as well.

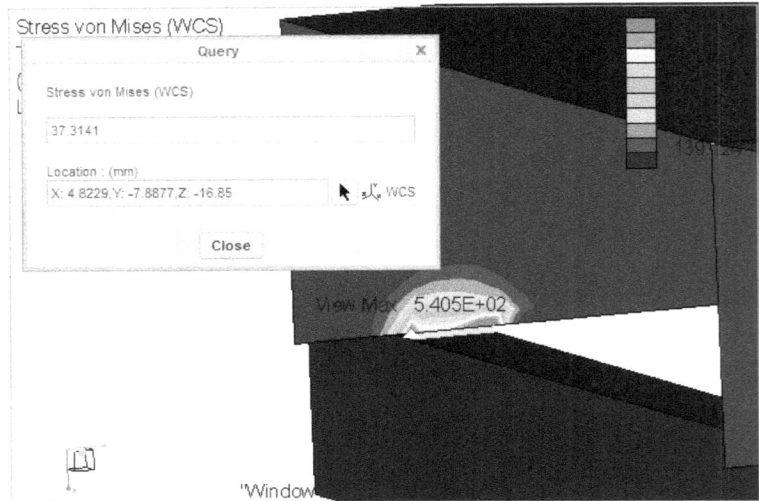

Figure 4–94

5. Click _Close_ in the Query box to finish.

## Task 17 - Display the displacement results.

1. Click . The Result Window Definition dialog box opens.

2. In the *Name* field, enter **deformation**.

3. In the *Title* field, enter **DEF_PLOT**.

4. Expand the Quantity tab drop-down list and select **Displacement**.

5. In the *Display Options* tab, select the **Deformed**, **Overlay Undeformed**, **Transparent Overlay**, and **Animate** options.

6. Clear the **Auto Start** option.

7. Click _OK_ .

*Ensure that only* **deformation** *is highlighted in the Display Result Window.*

8. Click 🔲. In the Display Result Window dialog box, highlight the **deformation** as shown in Figure 4–95.

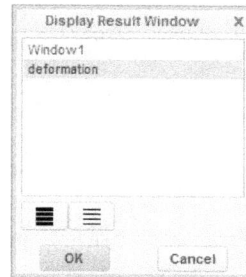

**Figure 4–95**

*Did the deformation display correctly?*

9. Click OK . The deformation plot displays.

10. Select **View>Start** to start the animation or click ▶.

*Use animations to check for errors and verify your results.*

11. Expand the **View** menu and select **Step Back** or **Step Forward** or click ◀ ▶ to step through the animation.

12. Select **View>Stop** or click ■ to stop the animation, as shown in Figure 4–96.

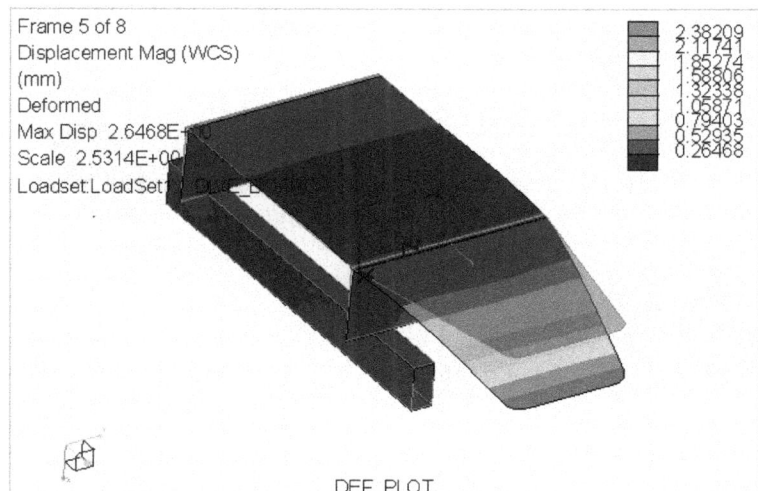

**Figure 4–96**

## Task 18 - Use predefined measures to study the convergence.

1. Create convergence graphs (i.e., against the P-loop pass) for the following predefined measures:

   - **max_stress_vm**
   - **max_disp_mag**
   - **strain_energy**

   The convergence plot for the **max_vm_stress** displays as shown in Figure 4–97.

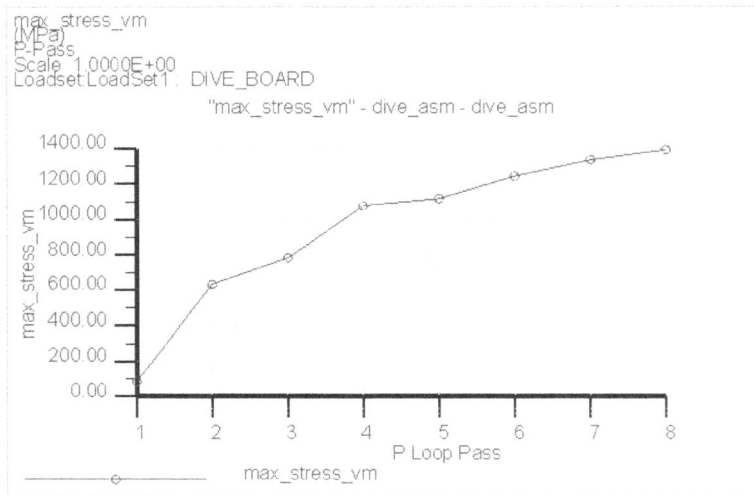

max_stress_vm
(MPa)
P-Pass
Scale 1.0000E+00
Loadset:LoadSet1 : DIVE_BOARD

"max_stress_vm" - dive_asm - dive_asm

**Figure 4–97**

2. The convergence plot for **strain_energy** displays as shown in Figure 4–98.

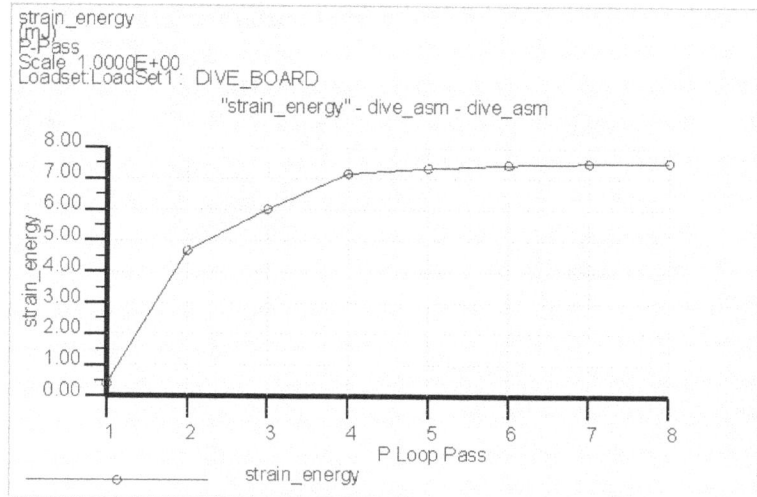

strain_energy
(mJ)
P-Pass
Scale 1.0000E+00
Loadset:LoadSet1 : DIVE_BOARD

"strain_energy" - dive_asm - dive_asm

Figure 4–98

3. The convergence plot for the **max_disp_mag** displays as shown in Figure 4–99.

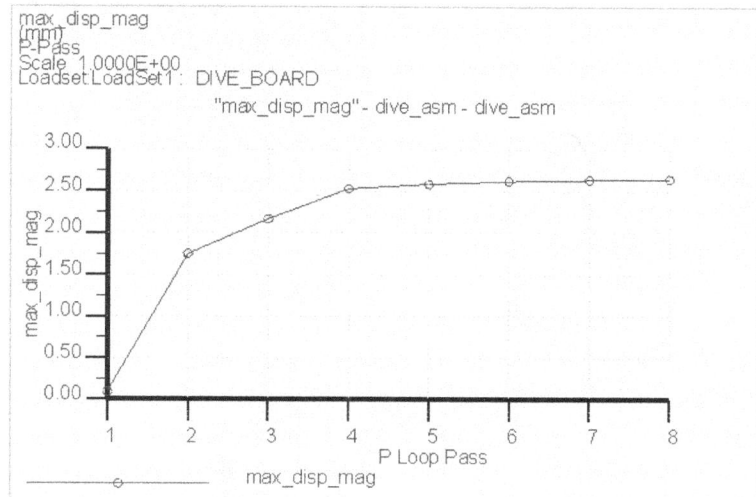

max_disp_mag
(mm)
P-Pass
Scale 1.0000E+00
Loadset:LoadSet1 : DIVE_BOARD

"max_disp_mag" - dive_asm - dive_asm

Figure 4–99

These plots indicate that the solution converges after eight passes.

**Task 19 - Use the Graph Window Options dialog box.**

1. Select **Format>Graph**. The Graph Window Options dialog box opens as shown in Figure 4–100.

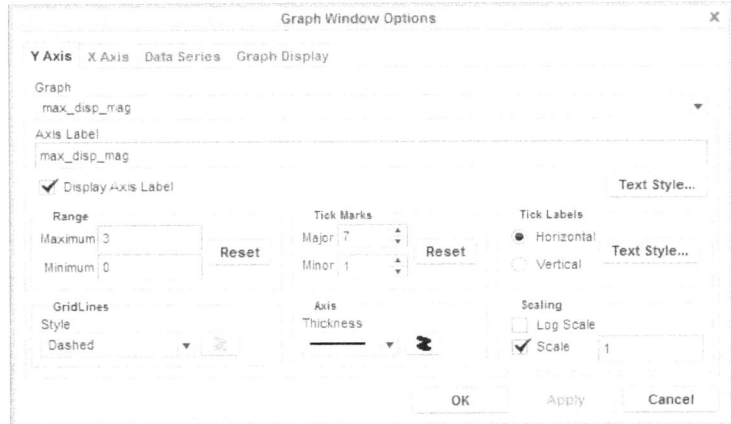

**Figure 4–100**

2. Select the *Data Series* tab. Change *Point Display* to **Rectangle** and *Interpolation* to **Smooth**, as shown in Figure 4–101.

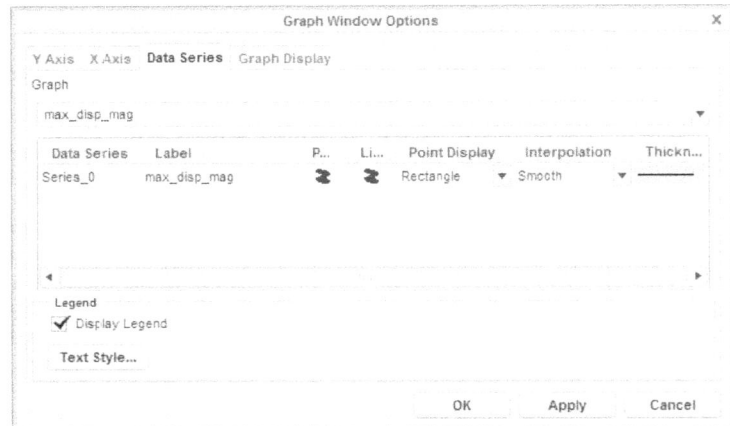

**Figure 4–101**

3. Click ___OK___ to finish. The graph displays as shown in Figure 4–102.

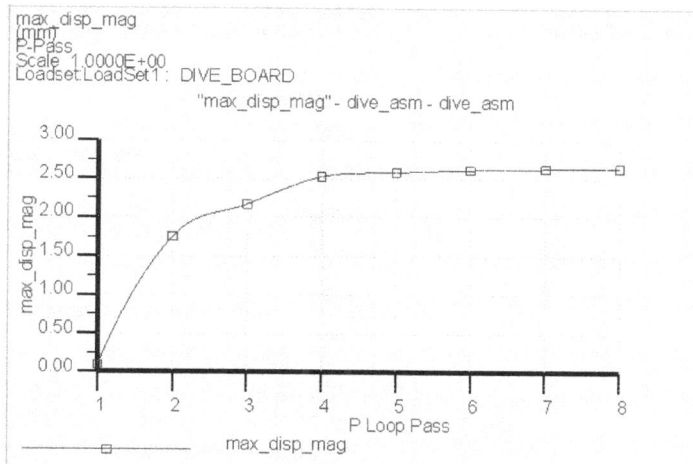

**Figure 4–102**

4. Double-click on the square symbol in the graph at P Loop Pass to obtain the **max_disp_mag** value in that analysis pass, as shown in Figure 4–103.

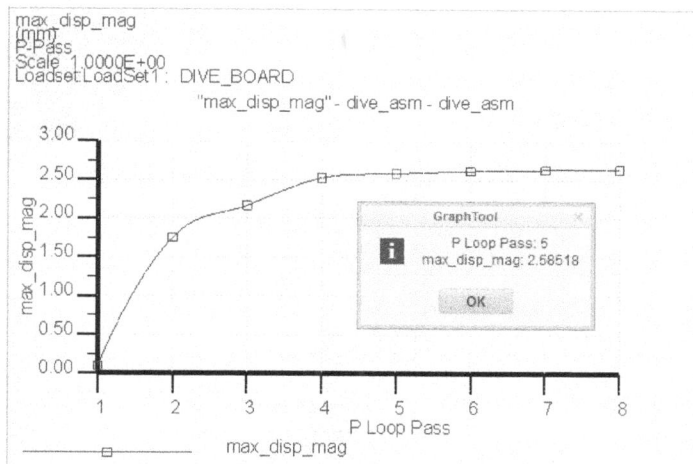

**Figure 4–103**

## Task 20 - Save and close the model.

1. Select **File>Exit Results**. Click    No    in the dialog box when prompted to save the results.

2. Close the Analyses and Design Studies dialog box.

3. Exit Creo Simulate. Save and close the model in Creo Parametric.

# Practice 4c

# Shells from Surfaces

**Learning Objectives**

Create shell elements from surface models.

Set up loads, constraints, and material properties.

Run and analyze a part.

In this practice, you will use shell element idealizations to set up and analyze the bent tube with flanges shown in Figure 4–104. The tube is created in Creo Parametric using surface features only (i.e., there are no solid volumes in the model). The tube is about 13in long and just over 3in in diameter. The tube wall thickness is 0.15in and flange thickness 0.4in.

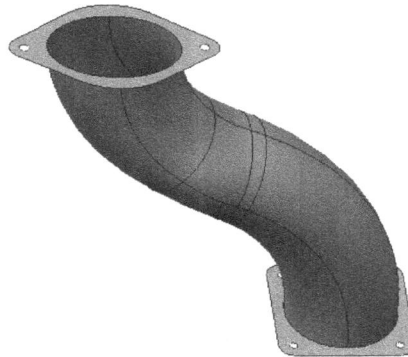

**Figure 4–104**

**Modeling Tasks**

**Task 1 - Open the tube_quilt part.**

1. Open **tube_quilt.prt** in Creo Parametric. The part displays as shown in Figure 4–105.

**Figure 4–105**

2. Select **Applications>Simulate** to switch to the Creo Simulate environment. Ensure that the **Structure** mode is active.

---

## Task 2 - Apply material.

---

1. Click ⌐ and transfer **STEEL** to the *Materials in Model* area.

2. Click ✎ to check your material properties and click OK when finished.

   *The model's material properties should be as stated.*

   The following values are the default material properties for HS-low-alloy steel (STEEL):

   - Poisson = 0.27
   - Young's modulus = 2.9e+7 psi
   - Density = 0.0007324 lbf sec2/in4

3. Click OK to close the Materials dialog box.

4. Click ⌐ to assign the material to the part.

5. Since there is only one material in the model, Creo Simulate automatically selects it for the part. Click OK to close the Material Assignment dialog box.

## Task 3 - Define the shells.

Since this part is not a solid model, the compression from solid to midsurface does not apply. In this task you will use the standard **Shell** option to define the shell elements.

1. In the *Refine Model* tab, in the *Idealizations* area, click 〔 . The Shell Definition dialog box opens as shown in Figure 4–106.

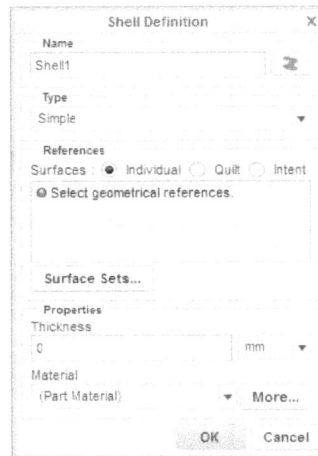

**Figure 4–106**

2. Select the **Quilt** option and select any surface in the tube portion of the part. This selects all of the individual surfaces that comprise the tube surface.

*Creo Simulate assumes the selected surface is the midsurface through the thickness of the part. The tube material in the analysis is extended by 0.075in to the inside and outside of the surface.*

3. In the *Thickness* field, enter **0.15**. The dialog box opens as shown in Figure 4–107.

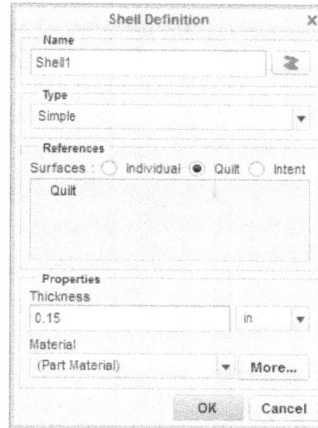

**Figure 4–107**

4. Click   OK   to finish.

5. Click 📄 again.

6. Select **Individual** and the multi-select both flange surfaces.

*Creo Simulate assumes the selected surfaces to be the midsurfaces of the part. The flange material is extended by 0.2in in either direction.*

7. In the *Thickness* field, enter **0.4**. The dialog box opens as shown in Figure 4–108.

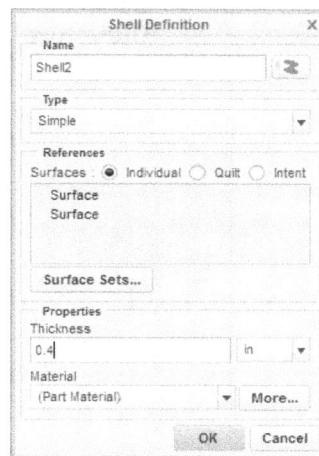

**Figure 4–108**

8. Click   OK   to finish.

9. In the *Refine Model* tab, in the *AutoGEM* area, click ⬚ to open the Simulation Geometry dialog box and then click Apply . The model displays as shown in Figure 4–109. Check whether all of the surfaces are highlighted in green.

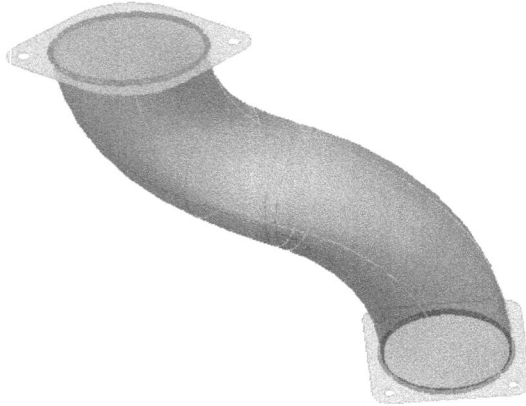

**Figure 4–109**

10. Click Close .

## Task 4 - Mesh the model.

1. In the *Refine Model* tab, in the *AutoGEM* area, expand the Control drop-down list and select **Edge Length By Curvature**, as shown in Figure 4–110.

Control ▼

Maximum Element Size
Edge Length By Curvature
Minimum Edge Length
Isolate for Exclusion

Hard Point
Hard Curve
Edge Distribution

Prismatic Elements
Thin Solid
Mapped Mesh

**Figure 4–110**

*The **Edge Length By Curvature** option is useful for accurate meshing of curved surfaces. Ratio 1.0 means that the mesh size will be made roughly equal to the radius of curvature of the surface.*

2. In the Edge Length By Curvature Control dialog box that opens, expand the References drop-down list and select **Components**. Select the part and in the *Edge Length / Radius of Curvature ratio* field, enter **1** as shown in Figure 4–111.

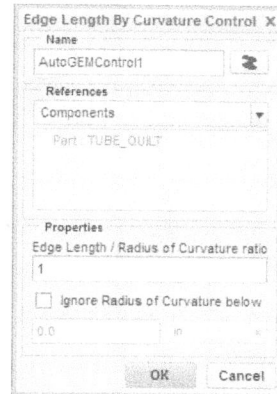

**Figure 4–111**

3. Click OK to finish.

4. Click [icon]. The AutoGEM dialog box opens. Click Create.

5. Once the meshing has finished, close both the AutoGEM Summary and Diagnostics dialog boxes. The model displays as shown in Figure 4–112.

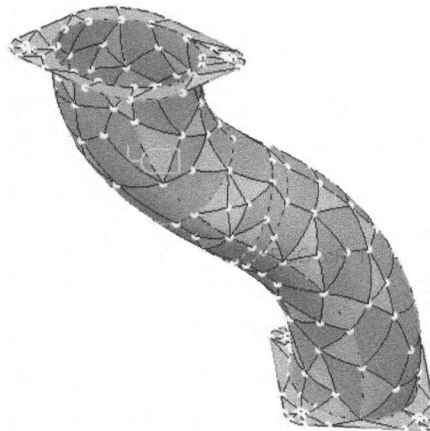

**Figure 4–112**

6. Click [icon] in the floating toolbar. The Simulation Display dialog box opens.

7. Select the *Mesh* tab and clear the **Display Shells with Zero Thickness** option, as shown in Figure 4–113.

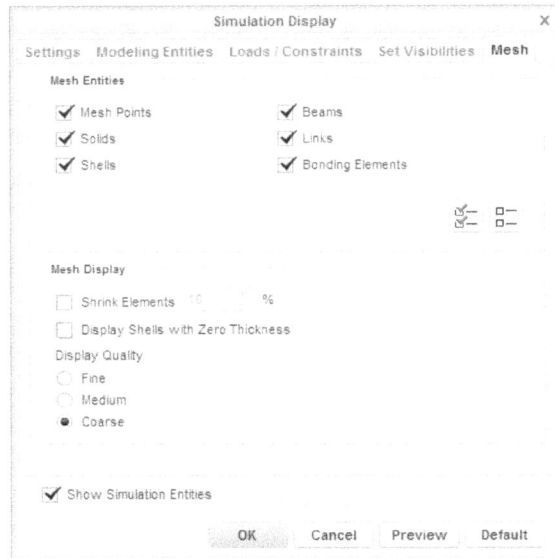

**Figure 4–113**

8. Click _____OK_____. The model displays as shown in Figure 4–114.

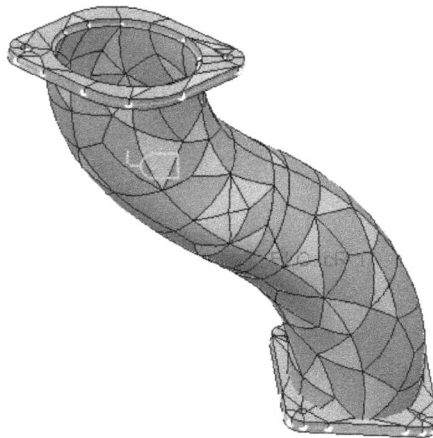

**Figure 4–114**

Note that the elements have now been thickened, using the thicknesses that you applied when creating the shells. Check whether the thicknesses are correct.

9. Click  Close  to close the AutoGEM dialog box and save the mesh.

## Task 5 - Apply a load to the model.

In this task, you will apply a load of 1000lb to the holes in the oval flange.

1. Click ⊩ . The Force/Moment dialog box opens.

2. Expand the References drop-down list, select **Edges/Curves**, and then multi-select the edges of the two holes in the oval flange, as shown in Figure 4–115.

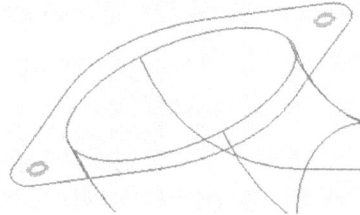

**Figure 4–115**

3. In the Force/Moment dialog box, enter the other required information as shown in Figure 4–116.

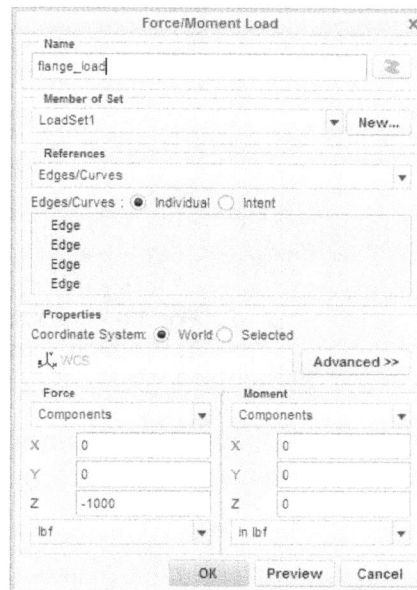

**Figure 4–116**

4. Click ⬛ OK . The model displays as shown in Figure 4–117.

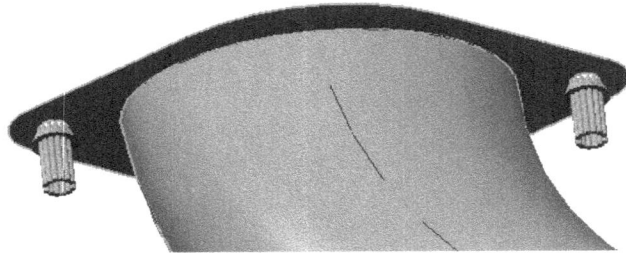

**Figure 4–117**

## Task 6 - Apply constraints to the model.

In this task, you will constrain the four holes in the square flange.

1. Click 🖾. The Constraint dialog box opens.

2. Expand the References drop-down list, select **Edges/Curves**, and then multi-select the edges of the four holes in the square flange, as shown in Figure 4–118.

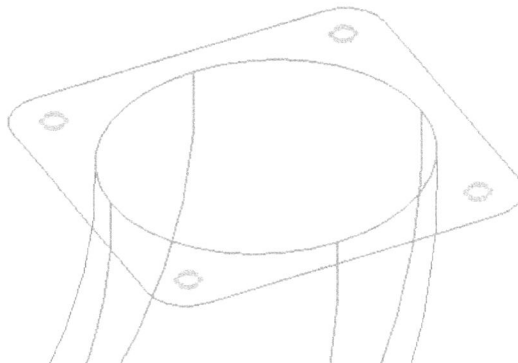

**Figure 4–118**

3. For the constraint, for the *Name*, enter **fixed**. Fix all of the Translations and Rotations, as shown in Figure 4–119.

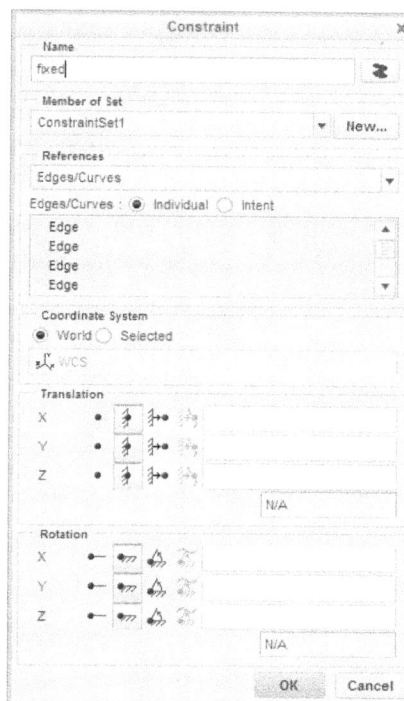

**Figure 4–119**

4. Click ___OK___ . The model displays as shown in Figure 4–120.

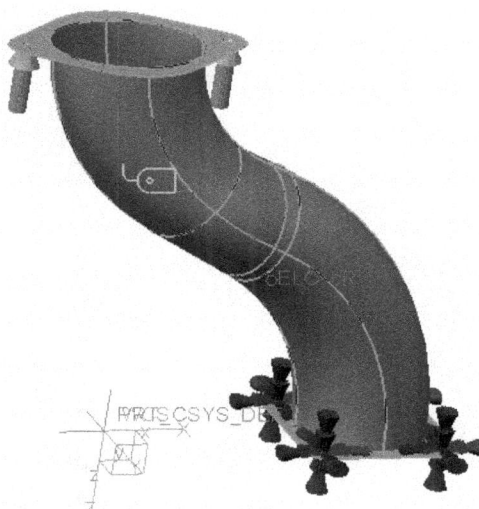

**Figure 4–120**

## Analysis Tasks

### Task 7 - Solve the model using the Multi-Pass Adaptive convergence option.

1.  Create a Static Analysis named **tube_shell**.

2.  Select the **Multi-Pass Adaptive** convergence method.

3.  In the *Polynomial Order* field, enter **9** Maximum and in the *Limits* area, in the *Percent Convergence* field, enter **5** percent convergence, as shown in Figure 4–121.

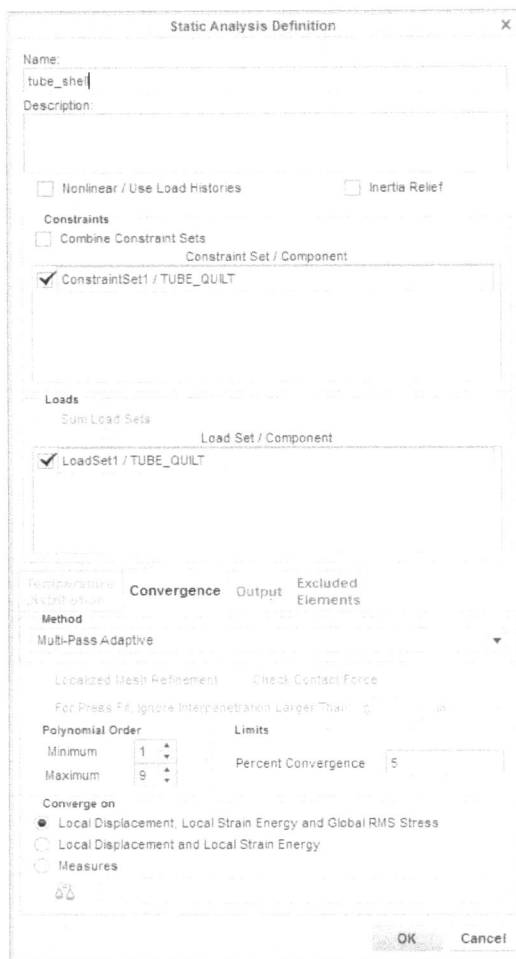

**Figure 4–121**

4.  Start the analysis run and wait until it finishes.

5.  In the Analyses and Design Studies dialog box, click 🗐. In the Run Status window, verify that the analysis has converged, as shown in Figure 4–122.

```
Run Status (tube_shell.rpt) Not Running                    ✕

Summary  Log  Checkpoints

        Memory Usage      (kb):      624827
        Wrk Dir Dsk Usage (kb):       27648

>> Pass  7 <<
        Calculating Element Equations            (17:31:15)
        Total Number of Equations:     31218
        Maximum Edge Order:                9
        Solving Equations                        (17:31:17)
        Post-Processing Solution                 (17:31:18)
        Calculating Disp and Stress Results      (17:31:19)
        Checking Convergence                     (17:31:20)
        Elements Not Converged:            0
        Edges Not Converged:               0
        Local Disp/Energy Index:         1.4%
        Global RMS Stress Index:         1.6%

    RMS Stress Error Estimates:

    Load Set          Stress Error  % of Max Prin Str
    ----------------  ------------  ------------------
    LoadSet1          4.76e+02       0.8% of  6.04e+04

        Resource Check                           (17:31:20)
        Elapsed Time    (sec):         18.47
        CPU Time        (sec):         13.62
        Memory Usage    (kb):        624827
        Wrk Dir Dsk Usage (kb):       40960

The analysis converged to within 5% on
edge displacement, element strain energy,
and global RMS stress.

                                               Close
```

Figure 4–122

## Results Tasks

## Task 8 - Display the displacement results.

1.  Create and display an animated fringe plot of the Displacement Magnitude. Use the animation controls to start, stop, and step through the frames of the animation. Note Frame 5 of the animation, it should display as shown in Figure 4–123.

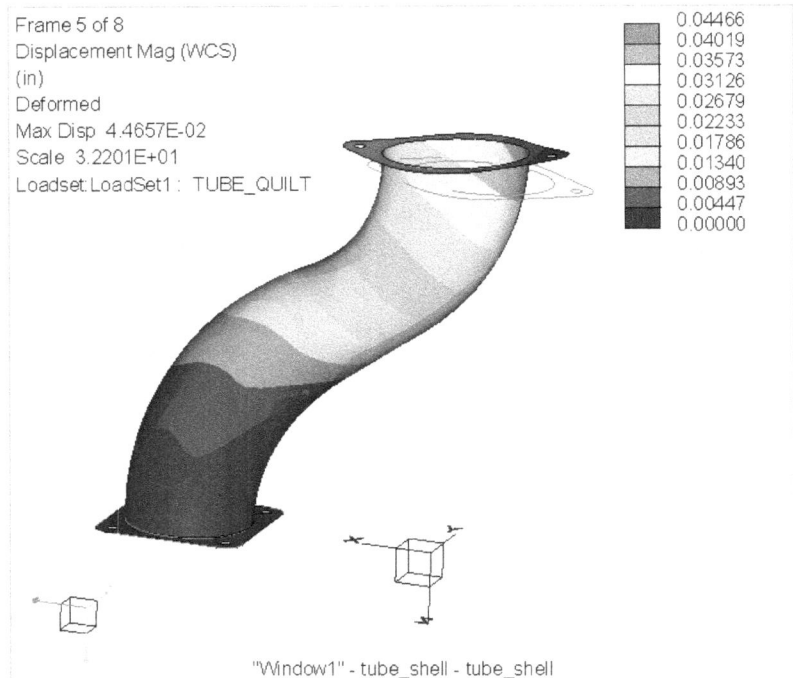

Frame 5 of 8
Displacement Mag (WCS)
(in)
Deformed
Max Disp 4.4657E-02
Scale 3.2201E+01
Loadset:LoadSet1 : TUBE_QUILT

0.04466
0.04019
0.03573
0.03126
0.02679
0.02233
0.01786
0.01340
0.00893
0.00447
0.00000

"Window1" - tube_shell - tube_shell

**Figure 4–123**

Note that the maximum displacement in the model is approximately 0.0447 inches.

2.  Create and display an undeformed fringe plot of the von Mises Stress. It should display as shown in Figure 4–124.

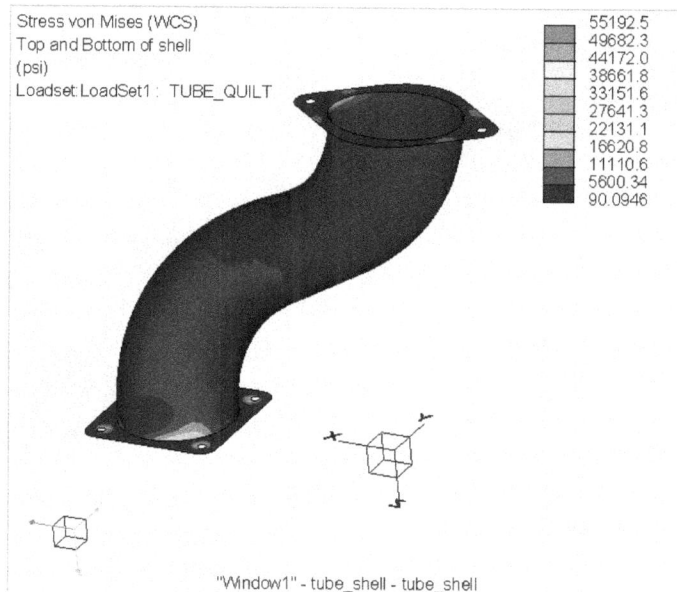

Figure 4–124

Note that the maximum stress is approximately 55ksi, and that it occurs at one of the holes in the square flange. (Use **Info>Model Max** to find the exact location if needed.)

3.  Click ⬛ to edit the von Mises Stress plot. In the Result Window Definition dialog box, in the *Quantity* tab, clear the **Bending** and **Transverse Shear** options, as shown in Figure 4–125.

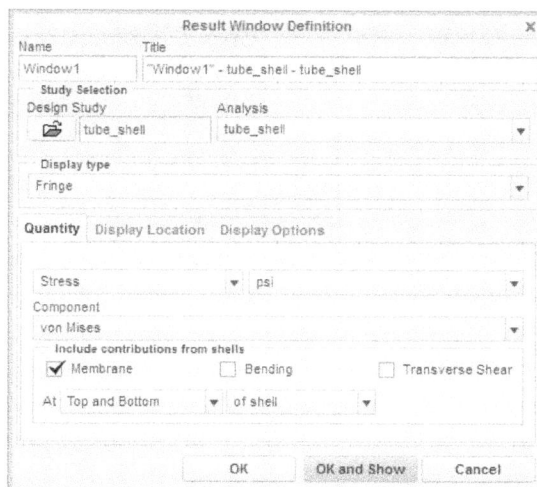

Figure 4–125

*The membrane component of the stress is constant through the shell thickness, and is due to loads acting in-plane of the midsurface.*

4. Click OK and Show . Now the result plot displays only the membrane component of stress in the part, as shown in Figure 4–126.

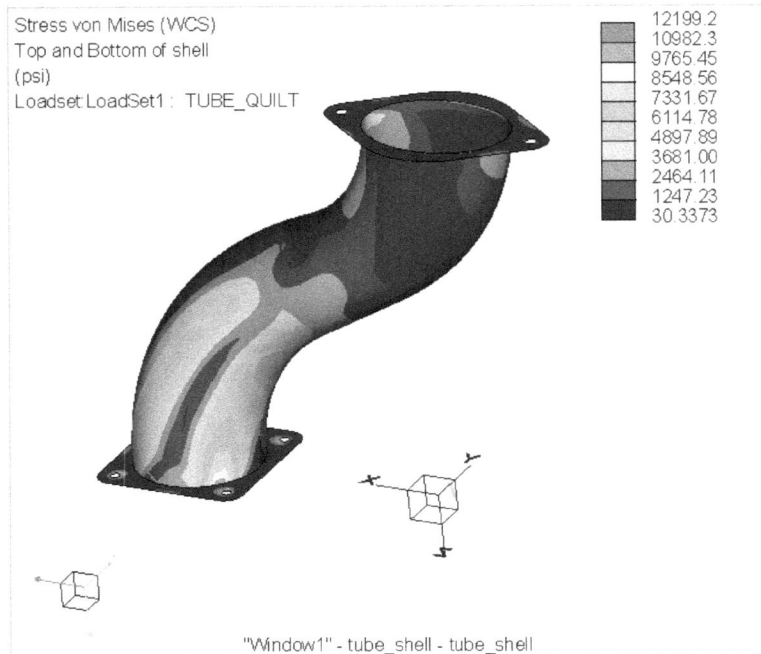

Stress von Mises (WCS)
Top and Bottom of shell
(psi)
Loadset: LoadSet1 : TUBE_QUILT

12199.2
10982.3
9765.45
8548.56
7331.67
6114.78
4897.89
3681.00
2464.11
1247.23
30.3373

"Window1" - tube_shell - tube_shell

**Figure 4–126**

Note that the maximum membrane stress occurs in the tube walls near the square flange.

5. Click 🖾 again. In the Result Window Definition dialog box, in the *Quantity* tab, clear the **Membrane** and **Transverse Shear** options, and select the **Bending** option, as shown in Figure 4–127.

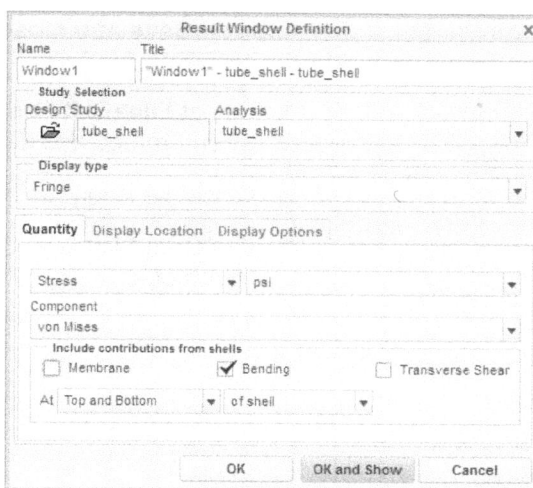

**Figure 4–127**

*The bending component of stress is anti-symmetric through the thickness, (i.e., it is tensile on one side and compressive on the other side). It is caused by the out-of-plane bending loads.*

6. Click OK and Show . Now the result plot only displays the bending component of stress in the part, as shown in Figure 4–128.

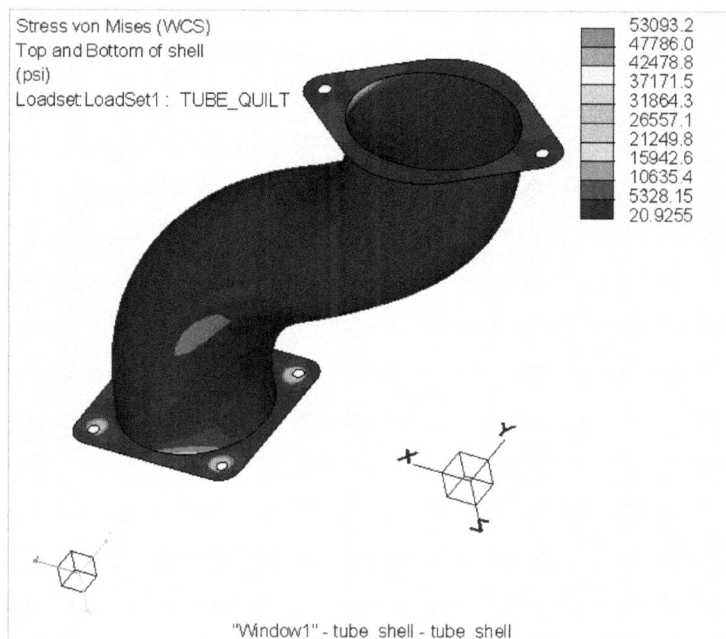

Stress von Mises (WCS)
Top and Bottom of shell
(psi)
Loadset:LoadSet1 : TUBE_QUILT

| 53093.2 |
| 47786.0 |
| 42478.8 |
| 37171.5 |
| 31864.3 |
| 26557.1 |
| 21249.8 |
| 15942.6 |
| 10635.4 |
| 5328.15 |
| 20.9255 |

"Window1" - tube_shell - tube_shell

**Figure 4–128**

Note that the bending stress (i.e., deformation) is most pronounced in the square flange of the part.

## Task 9 - Save and close the model.

1. Select **File>Exit Results**. Click    No    in the dialog box when prompted to save the results.

2. Close the Analyses and Design Studies dialog box.

3. Exit Creo Simulate. Save and close the model in Creo Parametric.

# Practice 4d

# Shell and Solid Combination

**Learning Objective**

Set up and run an analysis on a part using a combination of solid and shell elements.

*Shell elements can drastically reduce the number of elements in the model and computation time to obtain a solution.*

In this practice, you will use the shell element idealizations to set up and analyze a crank part, as shown in Figure 4–129. The crank arms are thin-walls. The part can be analyzed using solid elements. However, it is more efficient to idealize any thin-walled features using shell elements.

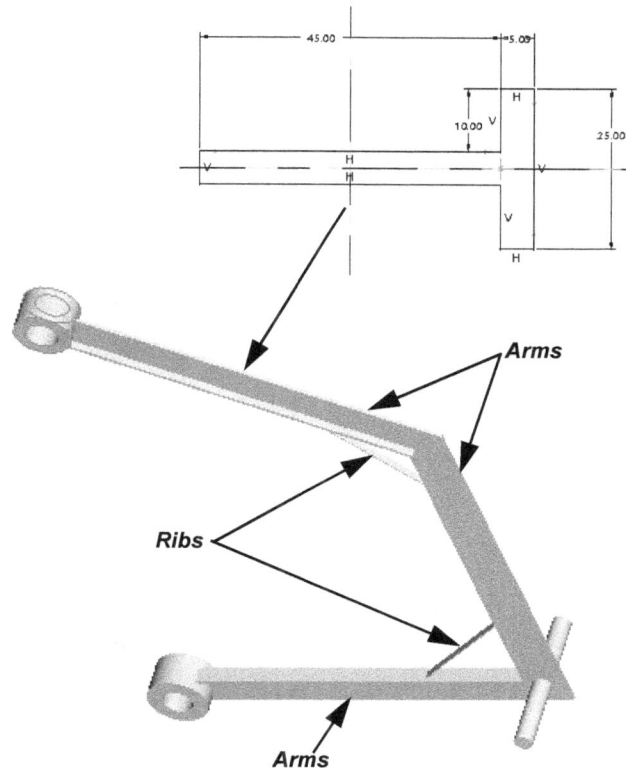

Figure 4–129

## Modeling Tasks

### Task 1 - Open the part.

1.  Open **solid_shell.prt** in Creo Parametric. The part displays as shown in Figure 4–130.

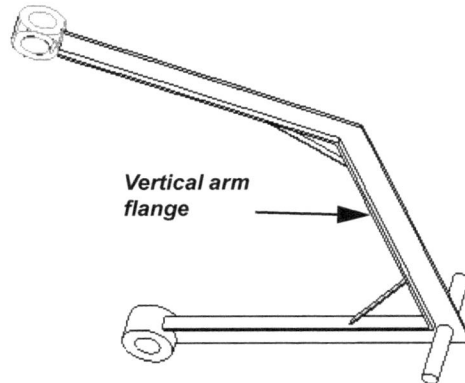

Vertical arm flange

**Figure 4–130**

2.  Turn off the datum plane and datum axis display.

3.  Ensure that the unit system is set to **mmNs**.

4.  Switch to Creo Simulate environment.

### Task 2 - Apply the material.

1.  Click ⌐. The Materials dialog box opens.

2.  In the *Materials in Library* area, scroll through the list and select **SS** (stainless steel).

3.  Click ▷▷▷ to transfer **SS** to the *Materials in Model* area.

4.  Select **Edit>Properties** to check your material properties and click    OK    when done.

    The following values are the default material properties for stainless steel (SS):

    *   Poisson = 0.3
    *   Young's modulus = 193053 MPa
    *   Density = 7.74372e-9 tonne/mm3

5. Click ▢ OK ▢ to close the Materials dialog box.

6. Click ⬐ to assign the material to the part.

7. Since there is only one material in the model, Creo Simulate automatically picks it for the part. Click ▢ OK ▢ to close the Material Assignment dialog box.

8. Using the Simulation Display dialog box, toggle off the Material Assignment visualization.

## Task 3 - Define the shell elements.

The wall and flange thickness in the arms of the crank is 5mm. You will use the **Detect Shell Pairs** tool to automatically create the shell pairs in those areas.

1. In the *Refine Model* tab, expand the Shell Pair drop-down list and select **Detect Shell Pairs**. The Auto Detect Shell Pairs dialog box opens as shown in Figure 4–131.

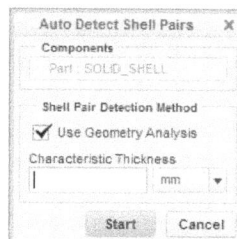

**Figure 4–131**

*Creo Simulate will pair all of the parallel surfaces in the model that are closer than 6mm.*

2. In the *Characteristic Thickness* field, enter **6** and click ▢ Start ▢. Creo Simulate runs the automatic detection algorithm and closes the Auto Detect Shell Pairs dialog box.

3. Check the Model Tree. Six shell pairs should be displayed in the Model Tree.

4. In the *Refine Model* tab, in the *AutoGEM* area, click ⬚ to open the Simulation Geometry dialog box. Select the required options as shown in Figure 4–132.

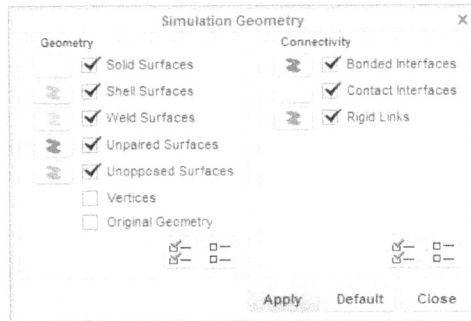

**Figure 4–132**

5. Click  Apply . The model displays as shown in Figure 4–133.

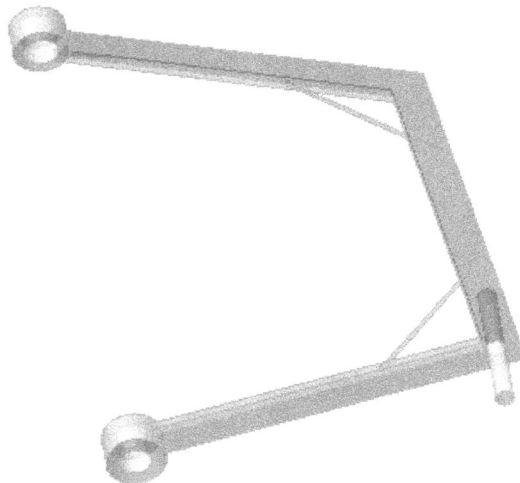

**Figure 4–133**

Verify that the end bosses and pin are displayed in grey (these are the uncompressed areas), and that the thin-walled arms are displayed in green (these are the shell pairs compressed to a midsurface).

6. In the Simulation Geometry dialog box, click  Close .

## Task 4 - Mesh the model.

1. Expand the AutoGEM drop-down list and verify that the **Solid/Midsurface** option is enabled, as shown in Figure 4–134.

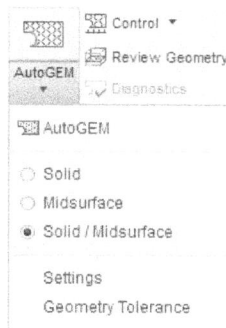

**Figure 4–134**

2. Expand the AutoGEM drop-down list and select **Settings**. The AutoGEM Settings dialog box opens. Clear the **Create Links Where Needed** option, as shown in Figure 4–135.

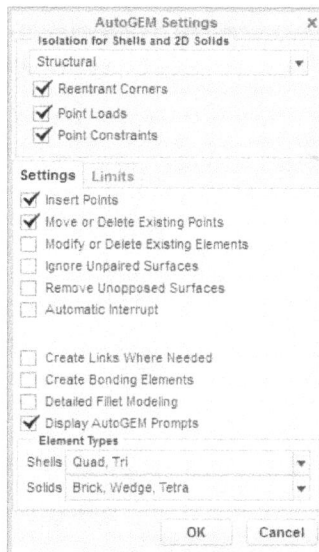

**Figure 4–135**

The Links in Creo Simulate are used to ensure the connectivity of the shell and solid elements along rotational degrees of freedom, so the shells attached to solids do not rotate like a hinge. The Links can significantly increase the analysis runtime.

Links are only needed if you have a shell in your model that is connected to a solid along a straight line. In the crank model, shells are connected to solids along T-shaped lines. Therefore, Links are not needed.

3. Click OK.

4. Click ⬚. The AutoGEM dialog box opens as shown in Figure 4–136.

**Figure 4–136**

*The **All with Properties** option requires that materials be applied before meshing.*

5. Expand the AutoGEM References drop-down list, select **All with Properties**, and click Create.

6. The AutoGEM Summary and Diagnostics dialog boxes open as shown in Figure 4–137.

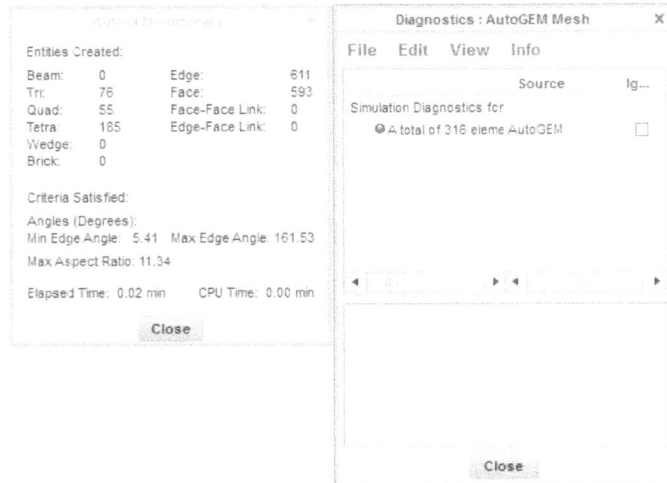

**Figure 4–137**

In the AutoGEM Summary box, note that the AutoGEM has now created both the solid elements (185 Tetra) and shell elements (76 Tri and 55 Quad).

7. Close both the AutoGEM Summary and Diagnostics boxes, but do not close the AutoGEM dialog box yet. The model displays as shown in Figure 4–138.

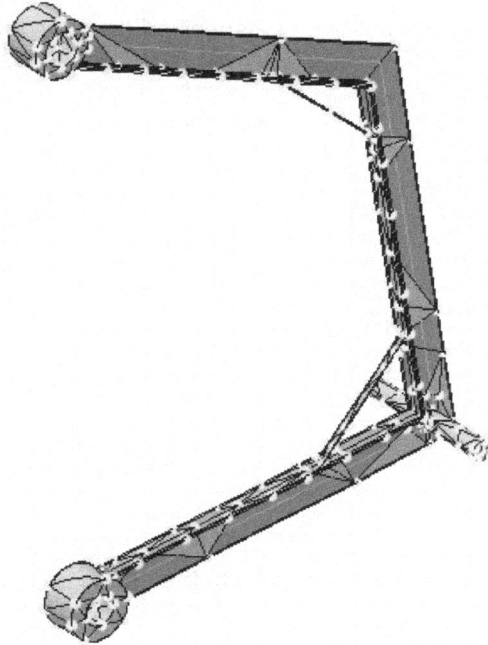

**Figure 4–138**

Note that two end bosses and the pin have been meshed onto solid elements (displayed in blue), while the arms have been meshed onto shell elements (displayed in green).

8. Click ⬚Close⬚ to close the AutoGEM dialog box and save the mesh.

## Task 5 - Apply loads to the model.

In this task, you will apply a bearing load on the hole in the boss shown in Figure 4–139. The bearing load has a resultant force in a specified direction (in this case, the negative Y-direction in the WCS). The bearing load is applied normal to the bearing surface in a non-uniform distribution. The bearing load simulates a lateral load that is exerted on a hole by a shaft placed in the hole.

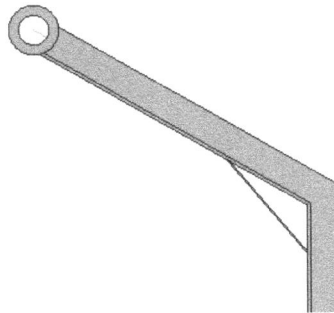

**Figure 4–139**

1. In the *Loads* area, click  . The Bearing Load dialog box opens as shown in Figure 4–140.

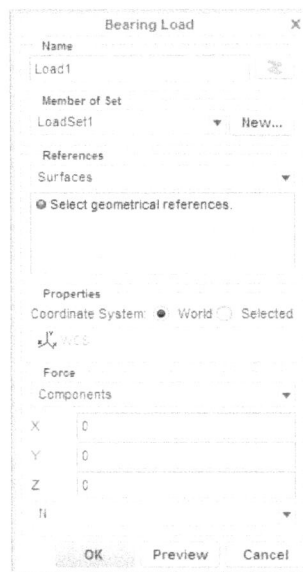

**Figure 4–140**

2. In the *Name* field, enter **b_load**.

3. Select the arm hole shown in Figure 4–141.

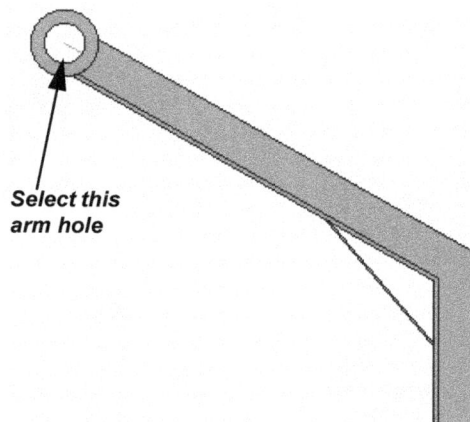

**Select this arm hole**

**Figure 4–141**

4. In the Y field, enter **-500**.

5. Click ⁣Preview⁣ to display the bearing load distribution, as shown in Figure 4–142.

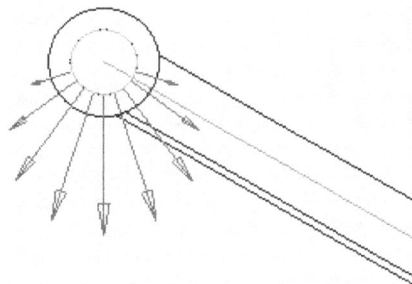

**Figure 4–142**

6.  Click ___OK___ . The bearing load displays as shown in Figure 4–143.

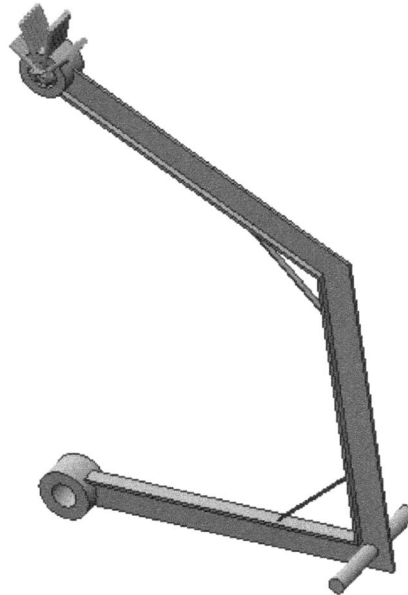

**Figure 4–143**

## Task 6 - Apply constraints.

In this task, you will constrain the movement of the central rod and the end boss of the crank arms, as shown in Figure 4–144.

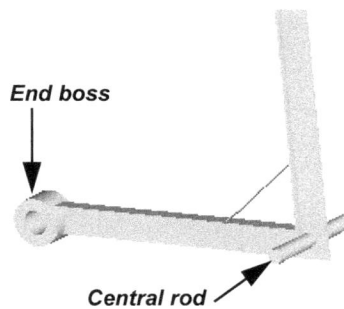

*End boss*

*Central rod*
**Figure 4–144**

You will constrain each cylindrical surface against radial and axial motion, but enable rotation around their axes. This can be done using **Pin** constraint.

1.  Click ⚲ . The Pin Constraint dialog box opens.

*Fixing the axial direction and freeing the rotation simulates the rod being supported by a sleeve bearing or bushing.*

2. Select the cylindrical surface of the central rod (shown in Figure 4–144). In the *Name* field, enter **rod**. Constrain the axial translation and leave the rotation free, as shown in Figure 4–145.

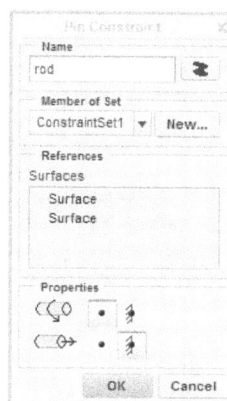

**Figure 4–145**

3. Click OK . The pin constraint displays as shown in Figure 4–146.

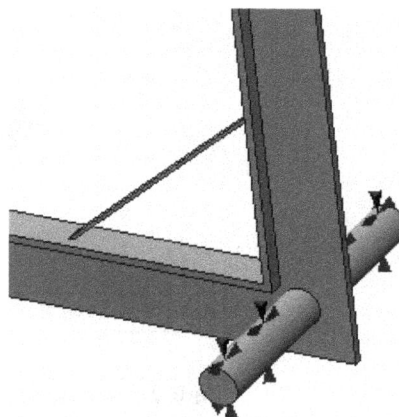

**Figure 4–146**

*Fixing the axial direction and freeing the rotation simulates the end boss being supported by a pin.*

4. Click 🔍 again. Select the hole surface in the end boss (shown in Figure 4–144). In the *Name* field, enter **end_boss**. Constrain the axial translation and leave the rotation free, as shown in Figure 4–147.

**Figure 4–147**

5. Click **OK**. The pin constraint displays as shown in Figure 4–148.

**Figure 4–148**

## Analysis Tasks

### Task 7 - Solve the model using the Single-Pass Adaptive convergence option.

1. Create a Static Analysis named **crank_shell**.

2. Select the **Single-Pass Adaptive** convergence method.

*The Plotting Grid is a grid of points that Creo Simulate uses to display results within the elements. A higher density plotting grid is recommended to obtain smoother looking result plots.*

3. In the *Output* tab, increase the *Plotting Grid* value to **10**.

4. Start the analysis run and wait until it finishes.

5. In the Analyses and Design Studies dialog box, click ▤. Examine the Run Status window that displays. Scroll up or down to the *RMS Stress Error Estimates* area and note that the analysis converged to approximately 6.6% RMS Stress Error, as shown in Figure 4–149.

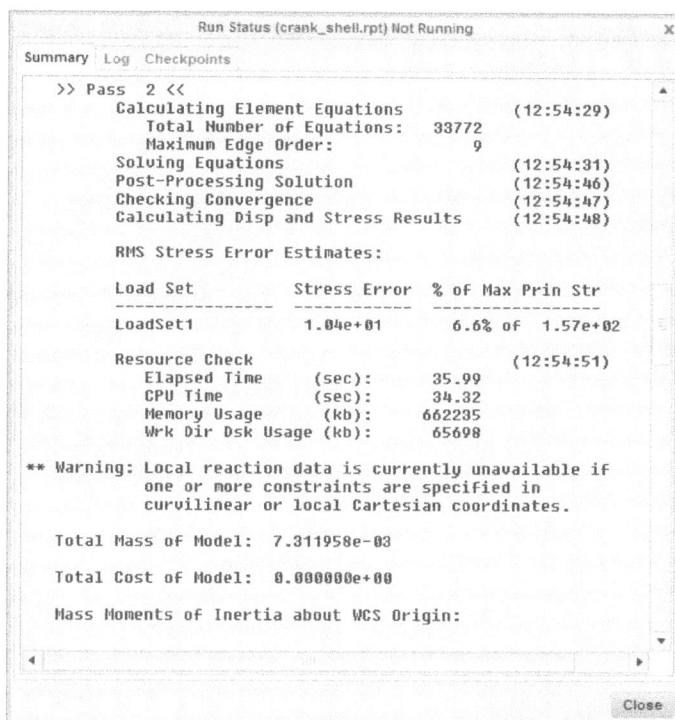

**Figure 4–149**

Ignore the warning prompting you about the local reaction data. This is just a notification that force reactions are not available on Pin constraints.

6. Close the Run Status window.

## Results Tasks

### Task 8 - Display and animate the displacement results.

1. In the Analyses and Design Studies dialog box, click 🖳. The Result Window Definition dialog box opens.

2. In the *Name* field, enter **deformation**.

3. Expand the Quantity tab drop-down list and select **Displacement**.

4. In the *Display Options* tab, select the **Deformed**, **Overlay Undeformed**, **Show Element Edges,** and **Animate** options.

5. Click OK and Show . The Displacement Magnitude result plot is displayed and animated.

6. Zoom in on the rod. Note that the rod's rotation is not restricted, as if the rod was supported by sleeve bearings or bushings. This is because you applied the Pin Constraint in a previous task.

7. Stop the animation at Frame 5. The result plot displays as shown in Figure 4–150.

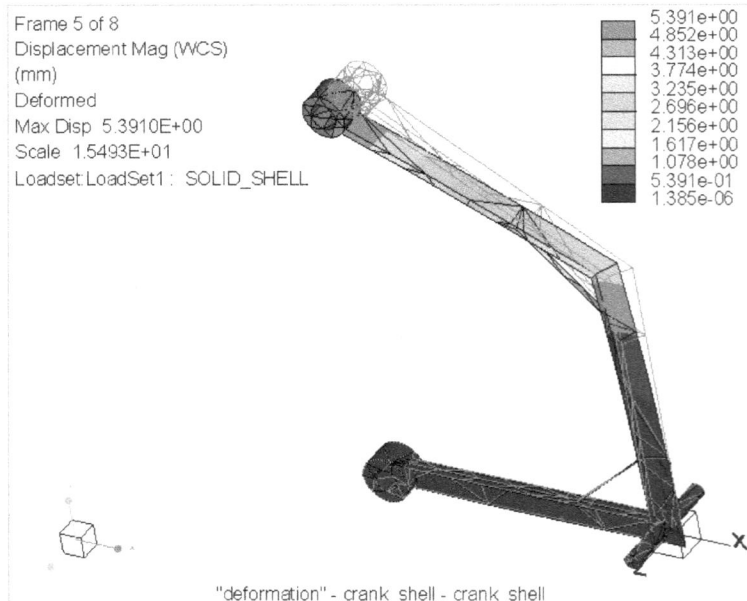

Frame 5 of 8
Displacement Mag (WCS)
(mm)
Deformed
Max Disp 5.3910E+00
Scale 1.5493E+01
Loadset:LoadSet1 : SOLID_SHELL

5.391e+00
4.852e+00
4.313e+00
3.774e+00
3.235e+00
2.696e+00
2.156e+00
1.617e+00
1.078e+00
5.391e-01
1.385e-06

"deformation" - crank_shell - crank_shell

**Figure 4–150**

Note that the maximum displacement magnitude under the given loading is approximately 5.4mm.

## Task 9 - Display the stress results.

1. Click 📋. The Result Window Definition dialog box opens.

2. In the *Name* field, enter **von_mises**.

3. Expand the Quantity tab drop-down list and select **Stress**.

4. Clear the **Overlay Undeformed**, **Animate Deformed**, and **Show Element Edges** options.

5. Click OK and Show. The Stress von Mises result plot is displayed with the Displacement Magnitude result plot.

6. Click 📊. In the Display Result Window dialog box, clear **deformation**, as shown in Figure 4–151.

Figure 4–151

7. Click OK . The von Mises stress plot displays as shown in Figure 4–152.

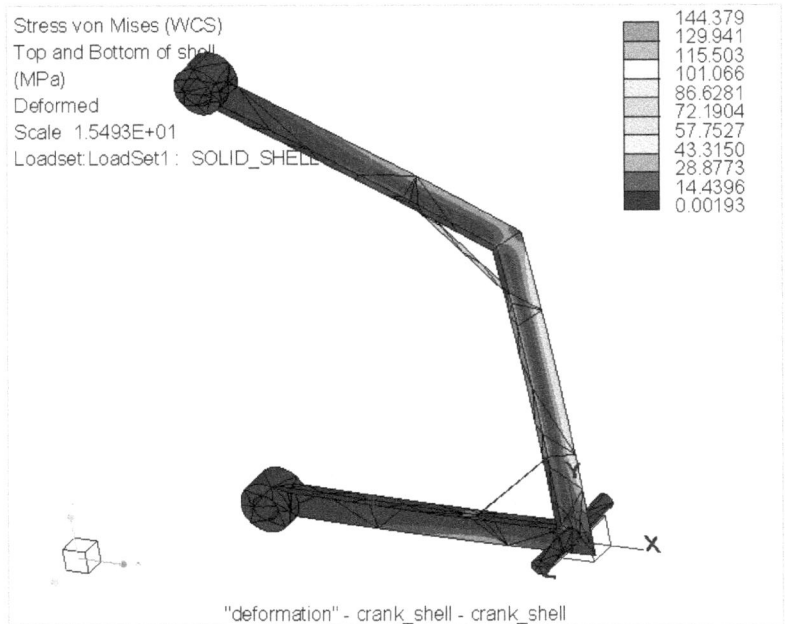

Stress von Mises (WCS)
Top and Bottom of shell
(MPa)
Deformed
Scale 1.5493E+01
Loadset:LoadSet1 : SOLID_SHELL

144.379
129.941
115.503
101.066
86.6281
72.1904
57.7527
43.3150
28.8773
14.4396
0.00193

"deformation" - crank_shell - crank_shell

**Figure 4–152**

8. Select **Format>Result Window**. In the Visibilities window, clear the **Label** and **Coordinate System** options, as shown in Figure 4–153. Click OK when finished.

Visibilities ×
Background Color
Creo ▼

Visibilties
✔ Title                Contour Labels
☐ Label               ☐ Loads
☐ Coordinate System   ☐ Constraints
✔ Legend              ✔ Annotations
✔ Csys Triad

OK

**Figure 4–153**

9. Select **Format>Legend**. In the Edit Legend dialog box, change the *Max value* to **80**, as shown in Figure 4–154.

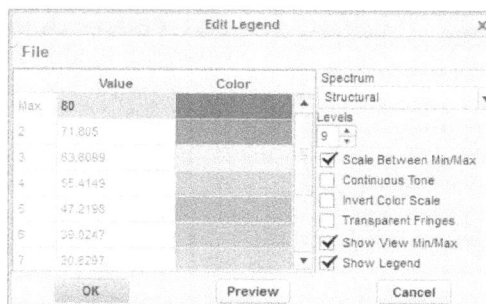

**Figure 4–154**

10. Click    OK    . The von Mises stress result plot displays as shown in Figure 4–155.

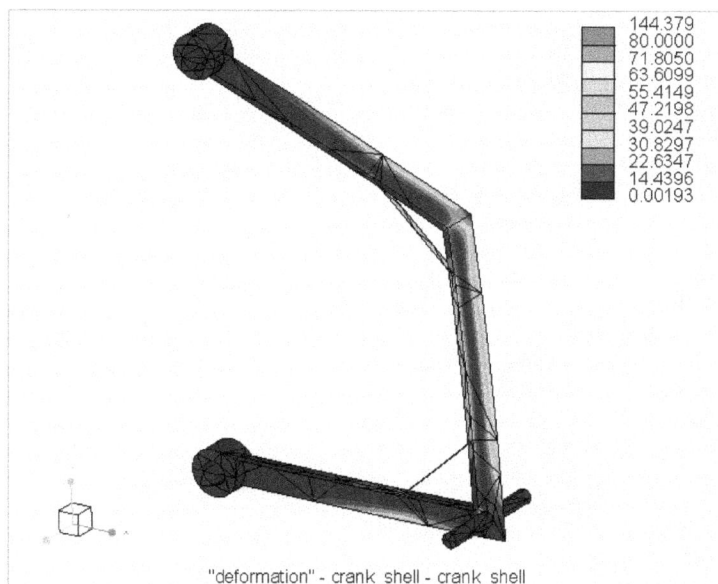

"deformation" - crank_shell - crank_shell

**Figure 4–155**

Note that the result window is now less cluttered and that it is easier to examine the results.

## Task 10 - Save and close the model.

1. Select **File>Exit Results**. In the dialog box, click    No    when prompted to save the results.

2. Close the Analyses and Design Studies dialog box.

3. Exit Creo Simulate. Save and close the model in Creo Parametric.

# Chapter 5

## Beams and Frames

This chapter contains the following topics:

- **Beam Elements**
- **Beam Coordinate Systems**
- **Beam Action Coordinate System (BACS)**
- **Beam Shape Coordinate System (BSCS)**

# 5.1 Beam Elements

**Learning Objectives**

✓ Understand beam idealizations.

✓ Understand how to create beam elements.

✓ Understand how to define beam sections.

Beam elements are one-dimensional elements, but represent 3D idealizations. An FEA model might only be composed of beam elements. Beam elements can also be mixed with shells and solids to represent a FEA model. An example of a simple beam is shown in Figure 5–1.

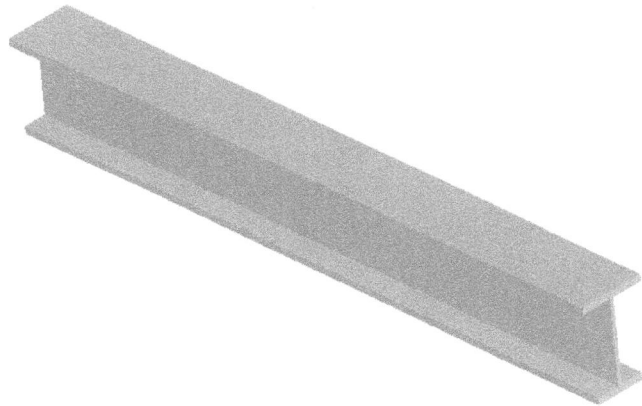

**Figure 5–1**

The idealized version of the beam shown in Figure 5–1 is shown in Figure 5–2.

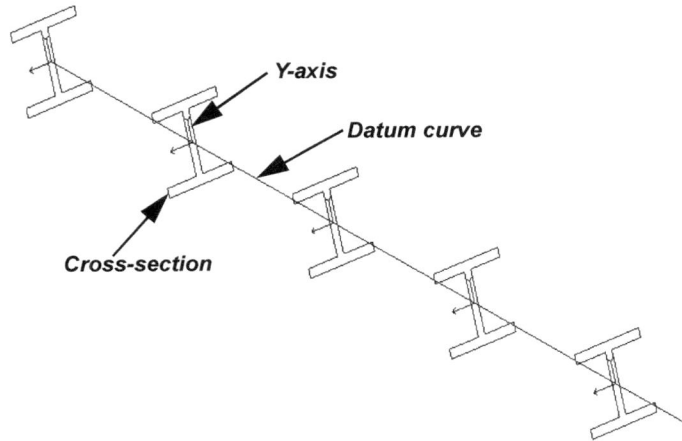

**Figure 5–2**

In Creo Simulate, a beam element is represented by a straight line or planar curve with an assigned cross-section. The line or curve can be created as a datum curve in Creo Parametric or as a simulation feature in Creo Simulate. In the example shown in Figure 5–2 an I-beam section is used and the straight line is a sketched datum curve.

Different beam section shapes can be used for different purposes. In the example shown in Figure 5–3, a hollow circle section and a sketched datum curve are used for a frame.

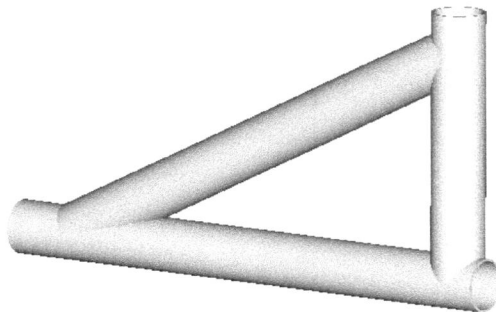

**Figure 5–3**

The idealized version of the frame is shown in Figure 5–4.

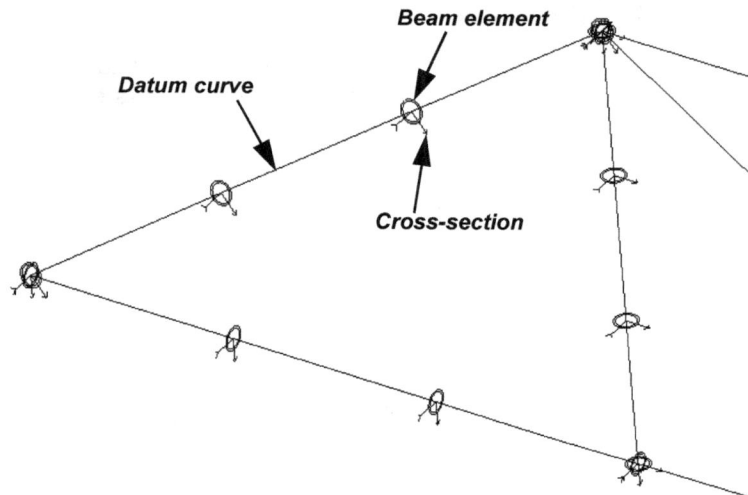

**Figure 5–4**

Creo Simulate automatically places beam elements on a specified datum curve or simulation feature. However, you must define the attributes of the beam element before running the analysis.

# Beam Definitions

Use the following steps to define the attributes (e.g., material, beam cross-section, etc.) of the beam:

1. In the *Refine Model* tab, click ⬚. The Beam Definition dialog box opens, as shown in Figure 5–5.

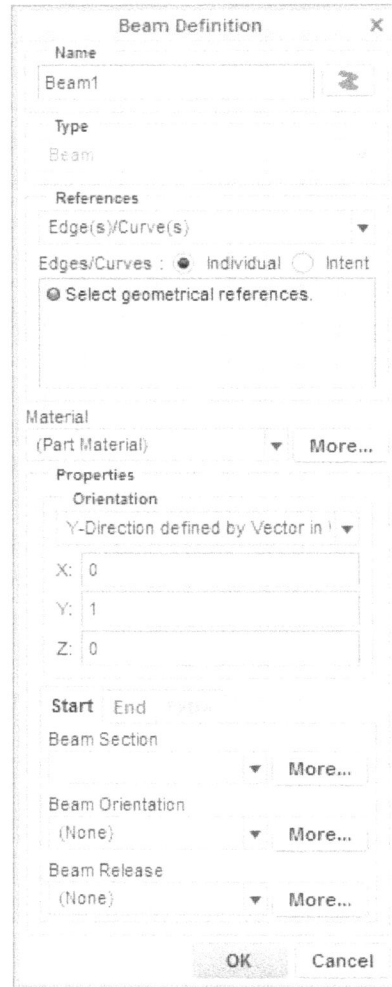

| Beam Definition | ✕ |
|---|---|
| **Name** | |
| Beam1 | 🔂 |
| **Type** | |
| Beam | |
| **References** | |
| Edge(s)/Curve(s) | ▼ |
| Edges/Curves : ● Individual ○ Intent | |
| ◎ Select geometrical references. | |
| **Material** | |
| (Part Material) ▼ More... | |
| **Properties** | |
| Orientation | |
| Y-Direction defined by Vector in ⁞ ▼ | |
| X: 0 | |
| Y: 1 | |
| Z: 0 | |
| **Start** End | |
| Beam Section | |
| ▼ More... | |
| Beam Orientation | |
| (None) ▼ More... | |
| Beam Release | |
| (None) ▼ More... | |
| OK Cancel | |

**Figure 5–5**

2. In the *Name* field, enter a name for the beam.
3. Define the geometry references. References define the underlying curve. The following types of geometry references are available:
   - Point-Point
   - Point-Surface (Projection)
   - Point-Edge (Projection)

- Chain
- Edge(s)/Curve(s)
- Point-Point Pairs

4. Expand the Material drop-down list and select an option to define the material of the beam.
5. Define the direction of the Y-axis by selecting a point, axis, or vector in WCS. If you use a vector to define the Y-axis, you must specify the X-, Y-, and Z-coordinates. The rotation of the beam around its local X-axis, relative to the World Coordinate System (WCS), is defined by specifying the direction in which the Beam Action Coordinate System (BACS) Y-axis is pointing.
6. Define the type of beam section.
7. Define the orientation of the beam relative to BACS.
8. Define the degrees of freedom to release at the beam's ends.
9. Click OK to complete the beam definition.

# Beam Sections

Creo Simulate has 11 standard types of beams that you can use for your analysis. These beams are shown in Figure 5–6.

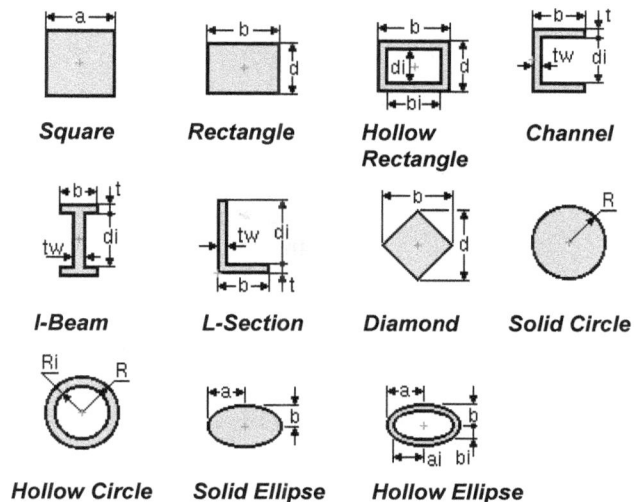

**Square**     **Rectangle**     **Hollow Rectangle**     **Channel**

**I-Beam**     **L-Section**     **Diamond**     **Solid Circle**

**Hollow Circle**     **Solid Ellipse**     **Hollow Ellipse**

Figure 5–6

You can also use a Creo sketch (.SEC file) as a beam cross-section.

# 5.2  Beam Coordinate Systems

**Learning Objective**

Understand beam coordinate systems.

Each beam model starts with a World Coordinate System (WCS), which is Creo Simulate's default coordinate system. Creo Simulate also uses two local coordinate systems to define the beam's cross-section orientation relative to the WCS. The local coordinate systems are oriented with respect to the WCS. This is notably valid for curved beams and beams whose cross-sections are asymmetrical about their centroid in at least one lateral direction. For example, these can include channels and angles, as shown in Figure 5–7.

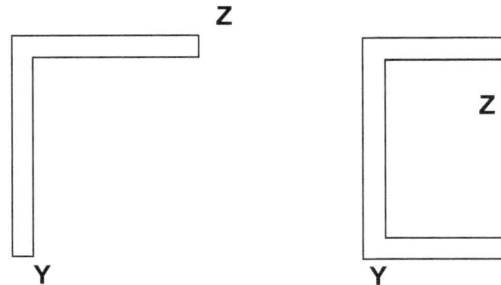

**Figure 5–7**

The two local coordinate systems used by Creo Simulate in beam analysis are as follows:

- Beam Action Coordinate System (BACS)

- Beam Shape Coordinate System (BSCS)

# 5.3 Beam Action Coordinate System (BACS)

**Learning Objective**

Understand how to define the beam action coordinate system.

Forces and moments applied to the beams are transmitted to the beams using the Beam Action Coordinate System (BACS). The underlying curve or points define the X-axis of the beam's BACS, as shown in Figure 5–8.

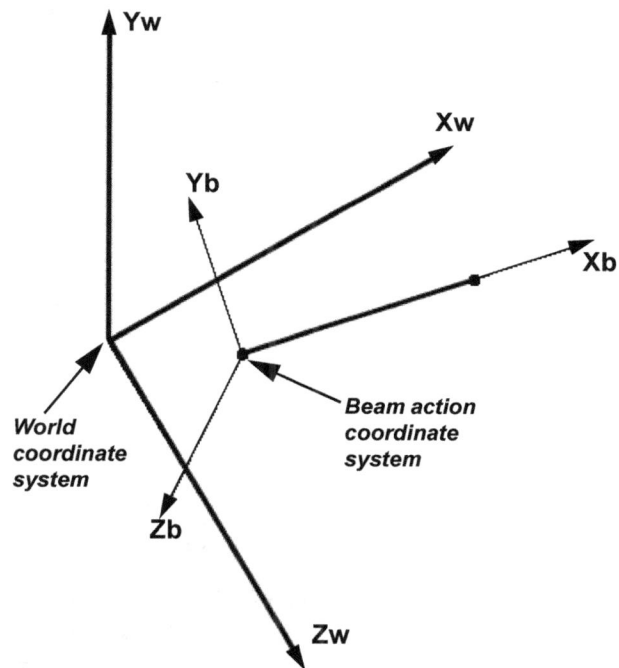

**Figure 5–8**

The beam's BACS Y- and Z-axes are perpendicular to the beam. The orientation of the beam relative to WCS is defined by the direction of the BACS Y-axis around the beam's BACS X-axis.

*Curves and points on a beam can be created as datum curves in Creo Parametric or as simulation features in Creo Simulate.*

*Several beams with the same properties can be created simultaneously.*

Beams are associated with geometry curves or by connecting two or more points defined in the WCS. For straight beams, the underlying curve or points define the X-axis of the beam's BACS, as shown in Figure 5–8. The beam's local Y- and Z-axes are perpendicular to the beam. The rotation of the beam around its local X-axis, relative to the WCS, is defined by specifying the direction of the BACS Y-axis.

This direction can be determined by specifying an axis direction, edge, or point, or providing vector components in the WCS. Some examples of the specification of the BACS Y-axis using vector components are shown in Figure 5–9.

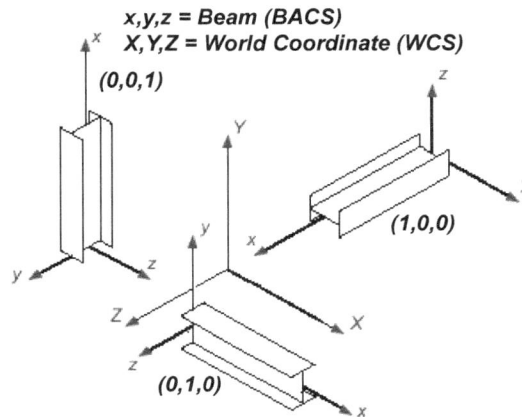

**Figure 5–9**

All of the properties of each beam element are set in the Beam Definition dialog box. For straight beams, the example in Figure 5–10 shows how the system assigns BACS coordinates relative to WCS using the **Vector in WCS** option.

The BACS X-axis always lies along the length of the beam. The specified orientation vector **0,-1,0** makes the BACS Y-axis at 90° to BACS X-axis. The system then uses the right-hand rule to determine the BACS Z-axis.

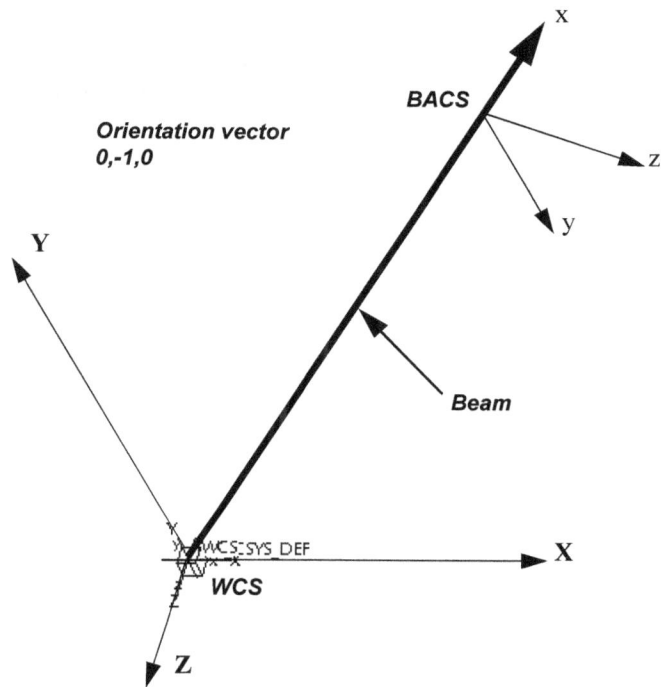

**Figure 5–10**

For curved beams (which must lie in a plane), the BACS X-axis lies along the length of the beam, tangent to the beam. The BACS Y-axis lies in the plane of the curved beam. The BACS Z-axis is perpendicular to the plane of the curved beam. The BACS Y-axis changes direction as the beam curves. Figure 5–11 shows an example of a curved beam.

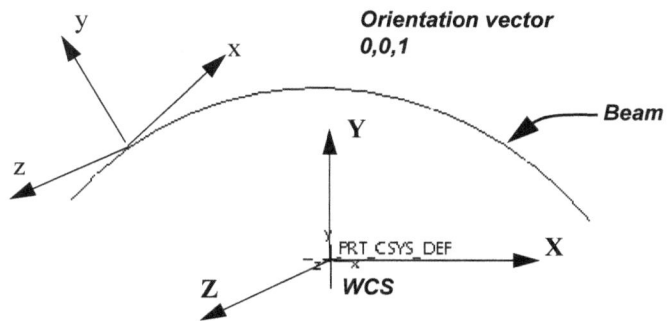

**Figure 5–11**

# 5.4 Beam Shape Coordinate System (BSCS)

**Learning Objective**

Understand how to define the beam shape coordinate system.

*For most standard shapes, the origin of the BSCS coincides with the centroid of the section.*

The beam cross-sectional shape and position are defined relative to the BSCS. The shape is defined in the BSCS YZ plane. The X-axis of the BSCS is always parallel to the BACS X-axis, as shown in Figure 5–12.

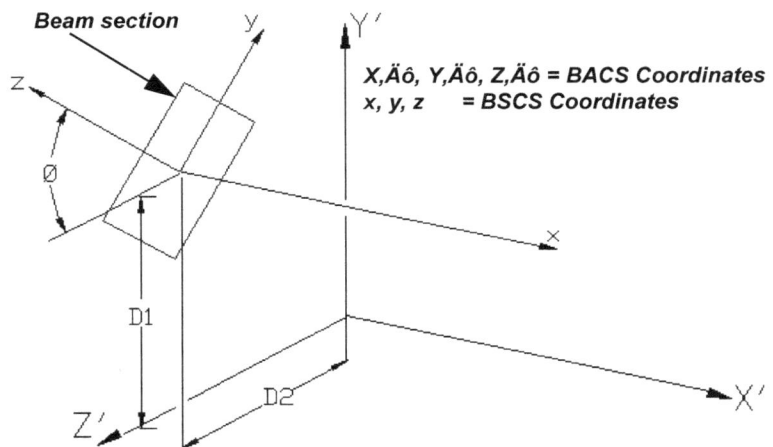

**Figure 5–12**

The BSCS origin (shear center) is defined by the offsets D1 and D2, measured from the origin of the BACS. In Creo Simulate, the orientation of the BSCS is determined by the angle (Ø). If Ø is zero, the BSCS is parallel to the BACS. If the offsets D1 and D2 are zero, the BSCS coincides with the BACS. Examples of standard Creo Simulate beam section shapes defined in the BSCS axes are shown in Figure 5–13.

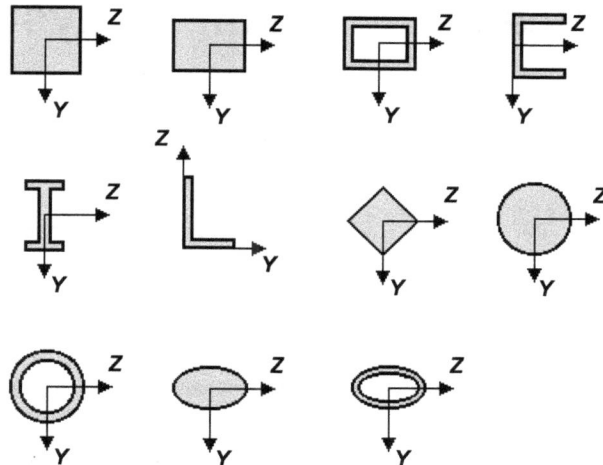

**Figure 5–13**

Use the following steps to position the origin of the BSCS relative to the BACS:

1. In the Beam Orientation Definition dialog box, enter the beam offset values for DY (i.e., D1) and DZ (i.e., D2). Alternatively, select the **Shear Center** option to position the beam section relative to the BACS. The Beam Orientation Definition dialog box is shown in Figure 5–14.

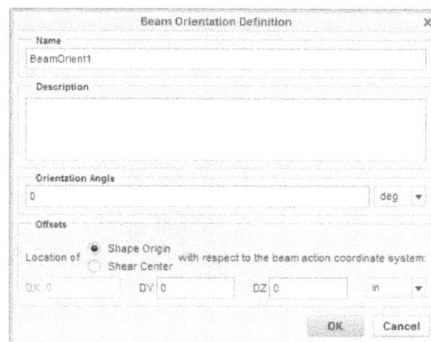

**Figure 5–14**

2. In the *Name* field, enter a name for the beam orientation.
3. Specify the angle about which you want the beam's X-axis to rotate.
4. Select the **Shape Origin** or **Shear Center** option to define the value used for the offset of the beam shape coordinate system (BSCS)
5. Define the values for each offset in the BACS X-, Y- and Z-directions.
6. Click ___OK___ to complete the beam orientation definition.

*Shear center is the point on a beam section about which the section rotates under deflection.*

# Practice 5a

# Beam Analysis

**Learning Objectives**

- Set up a beam model.

- Set up beam releases.

- Run a beam model.

- Analyze a beam model.

*The aspect ratio of the beam element should be greater than 10:1(the ratio of its length to its largest section dimension).*

In this practice, you will use beam element idealizations to set up, run, and analyze a beam model. The beam model is shown in Figure 5–15. The beam cross section is an I-beam. The beam's ends are fixed and the middle support is a roller.

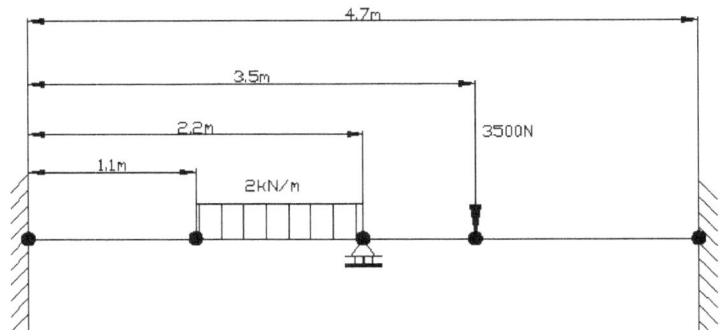

**Figure 5–15**

You will apply linear distributed loads to a section of the model and a point load 3.5 m from the left side of the beam, as shown in Figure 5–16.

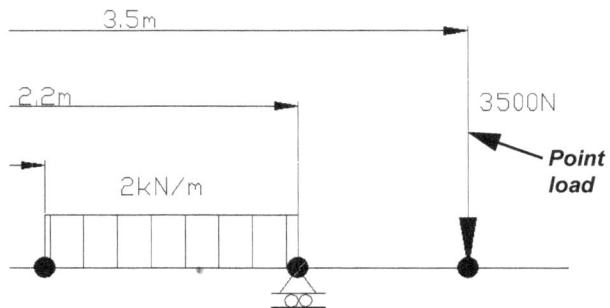

**Figure 5–16**

## Modeling Tasks

### Task 1 - Open 1d_beam.prt and start Creo Simulate.

1. Open **1d_beam.prt** in Creo Parametric. The part displays as shown in Figure 5–17.

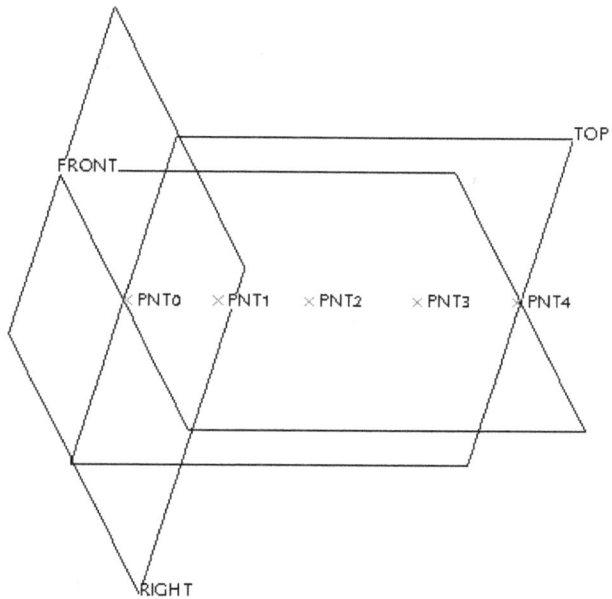

**Figure 5–17**

2. Ensure that the unit systems are **MKS**.

3. Switch to the Creo Simulate environment.

4. In the *View* tab, in the *Show* area, click ⟨icon⟩ to visualize the datum point tags. The model displays as shown in Figure 5–18.

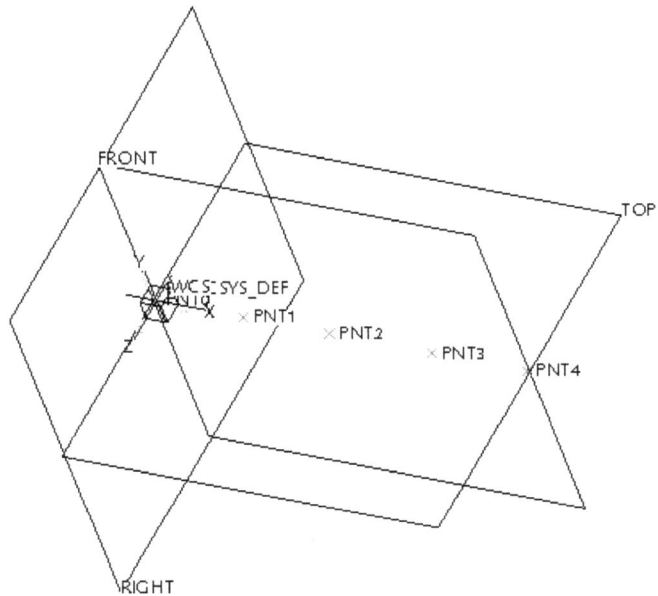

**Figure 5–18**

## Task 2 - Create a datum curve as a simulation feature.

In beam models, distributed loads can only be defined on datum curves. The load is transferred to the beam elements created on the curve.

1. In the *Refine Model* tab, expand the *Datum* area (as shown in Figure 5–19), and click ⟨icon⟩ .

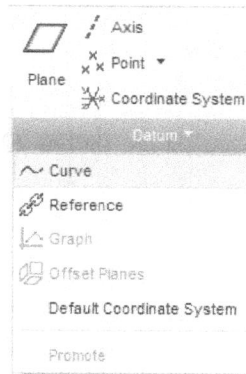

**Figure 5–19**

2. Create a datum curve between PNT1 and PNT2. The datum curve displays as shown in Figure 5–20.

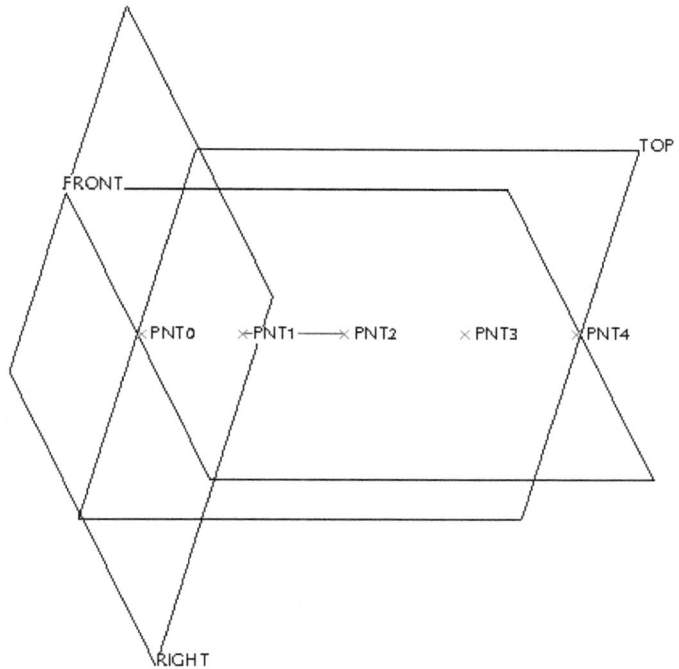

**Figure 5–20**

## Task 3 - Create a beam element between PNT0 and PNT1.

1. In the *Refine Model* tab, click ▷▷. The Beam Definition dialog box opens as shown in Figure 5–21.

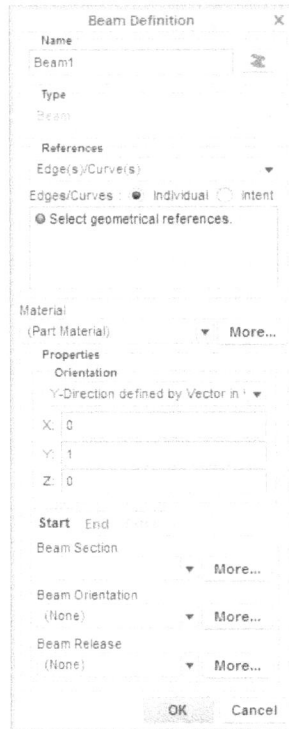

**Figure 5–21**

2. In the *Name* field, enter **beam_1**.

3. Expand the References drop-down list and select **Point-Point**.

4. Select **PNT0** and **PNT1**.

5. In the *Material* area, click More... . The Materials dialog box opens.

6. In the *Materials in Library* area, select **STEEL**. Click ▷▷▷ to transfer STEEL to the *Materials in Model* area.

*The model's material properties should be as stated.*

7. Select **Edit>Properties** to check the material properties. The following values are the default material properties for HS-low-alloy steel (STEEL):

- Poisson = 0.27
- Young's modulus = 1.99948 e11 Pa
- Density = 7827.08 Kg/m^3

8. Click OK in the Material Definition dialog box and Materials dialog box. STEEL displays in the *Material* area in the Beam Definition dialog box.

9. In the *Orientation* area, accept the default X-, Y-, and Z-values.

10. Next to the Beam Section drop-down list, click More... . The Beam Sections dialog box opens as shown in Figure 5–22.

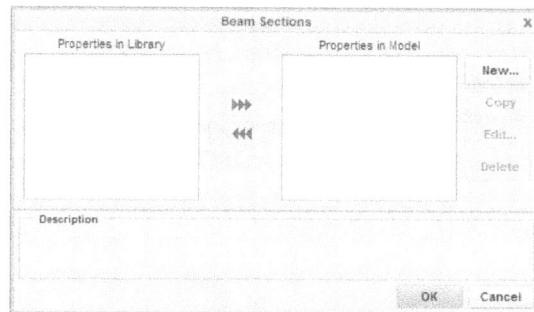

**Figure 5–22**

11. Click New... . The Beam Section Definition dialog box opens as shown in Figure 5–23.

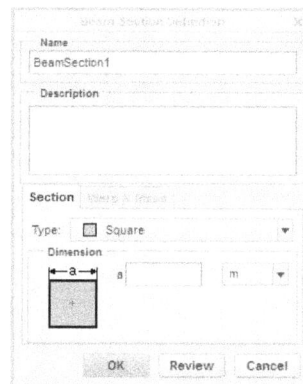

**Figure 5–23**

*If the section is not listed in the Type drop-down list, you can sketch it using the **Sketched Solid** and **Sketched Thin** sketch options in the Type drop-down list. These options open Sketcher in Creo Parametric.*

12. In the *Name* field, enter **I_beam_section**.

13. Expand the Type drop-down list and select **I-Beam** as shown in Figure 5–24.

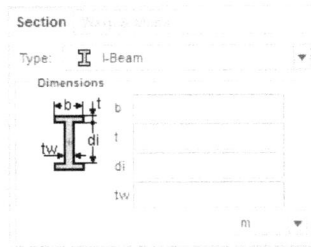

**Figure 5–24**

14. In the *b* field, enter **0.092**.

15. In the *t* field, enter **0.009**.

16. In the *di* field, enter **0.164**.

17. In the *tw* field, enter **0.006**.

18. Click    Review   . The Simulation Information window displays. The window contains the section properties shown in Figure 5–25.

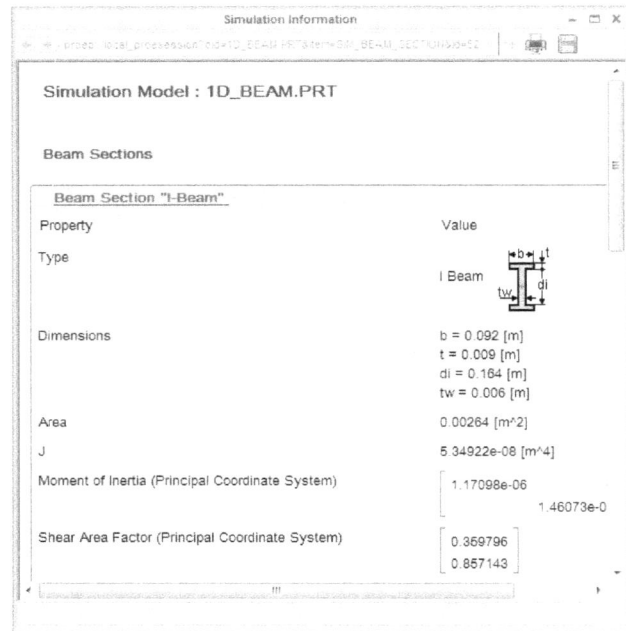

**Figure 5–25**

19. Close the Simulation Information window.

20. Click OK to close the Beam Section Definition dialog box.

21. Click OK to close the Beam Sections dialog box.

22. Click OK to close the Beam Definition dialog box. The model displays as shown in Figure 5–26.

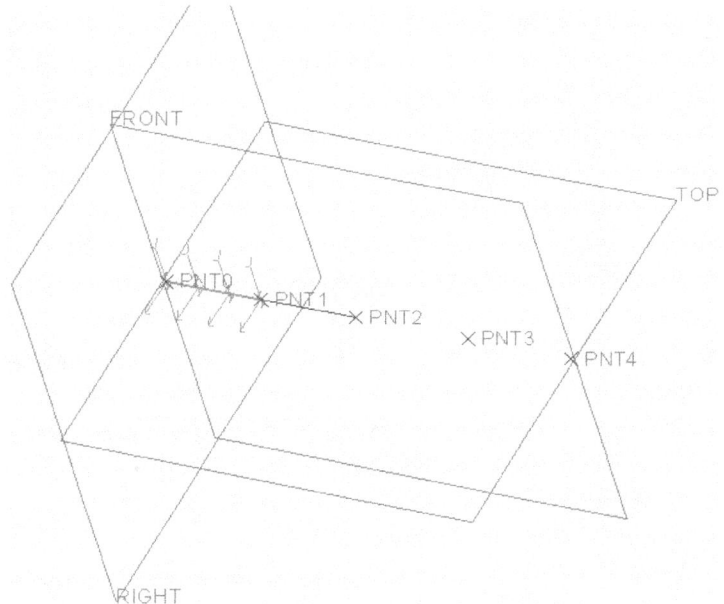

**Figure 5–26**

## Task 4 - Create a beam element between PNT1 and PNT2.

1. Click 🔀. The Beam Definition dialog box opens.

2. In the *Name* field, enter **beam_2**.

3. Expand the References drop-down list and select **Edge/Curve**.

4. Select the curve between PNT1 and PNT2.

5. Expand the Material drop-down list and select **STEEL**.

6. In the *Orientation* area, in the *X*, *Y*, and *Z* fields, accept the default values.

*The section property of the beam is the I_beam_section that you created in the previous task.*

7. Click OK to close the Beam Definition dialog box. The model displays as shown in Figure 5–27.

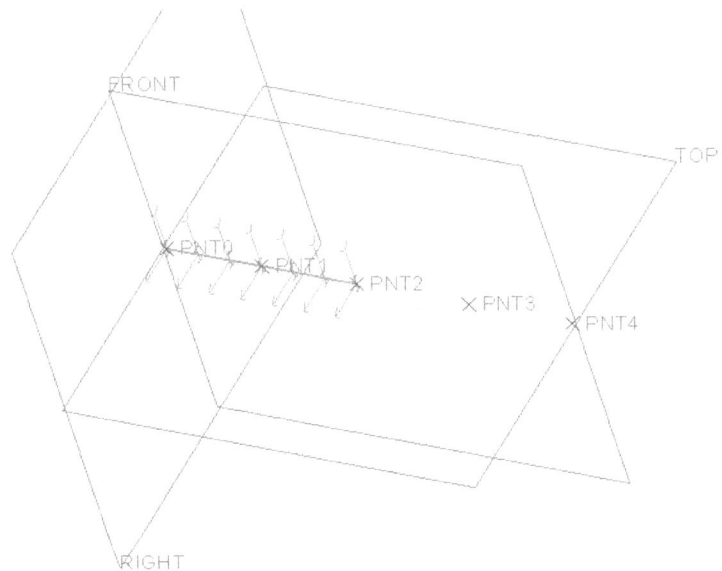

**Figure 5–27**

**Task 5 - Create a beam element between PNT2 and PNT3.**

1. Click [icon]. The Beam Definition dialog box opens.

2. In the *Name* field, enter **beam_3**.

3. Expand the References drop-down list and select **Point-Point**.

4. Select **PNT2** and **PNT3**.

5. Expand the Material drop-down list and select **STEEL**.

6. In the Beam Definition dialog box, accept the other defaults.

*To display the section icons, use the zoom function.*

7. Click ⬚ OK to close the Beam Definition dialog box. The model displays as shown in Figure 5–28.

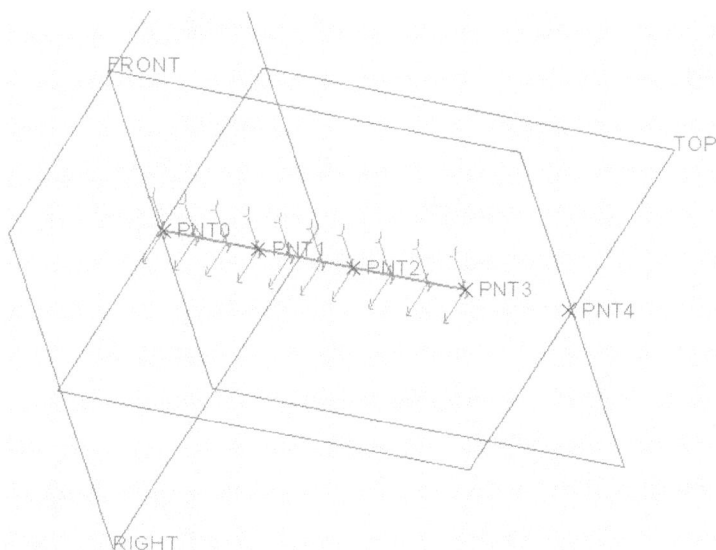

**Figure 5–28**

---

**Task 6 - Create a beam element between PNT3 and PNT4.**

1. Click ⬚ . The Beam Definition dialog box opens.

2. In the *Name* field, enter **beam_4**.

3. Expand the References drop-down list and select **Point-Point**.

4. Select **PNT3** and **PNT4**.

5. Expand the Material drop-down list and select **STEEL**.

6. In the Beam Definition dialog box, accept the other defaults.

7. Click ___OK___ to close the Beam Definition dialog box. The model displays as shown in Figure 5–29.

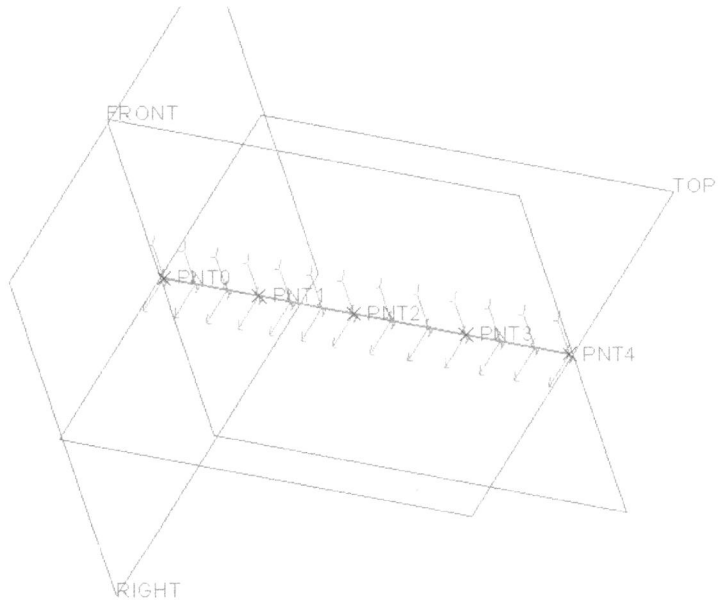

**Figure 5–29**

8. In the floating toolbar, click ⬚. The Simulation Display dialog box opens.

9. Select the *Modeling Entities* tab and clear the **Beam Sections** option.

10. Click ___OK___ to close the Simulation Display dialog box. The model displays as shown in Figure 5–30 with the default datum planes and coordinate systems turned off.

**Figure 5–30**

## Task 7 - Apply the loads.

The loading is uniformly distributed on the section between PNT1 and PNT2 of the model, and a point load is also applied at PNT3. In this task, you will apply the distributed load to the curve between PNT1 and PNT2.

1. Click ⊞. The Force/Moment dialog box opens as shown in Figure 5–31.

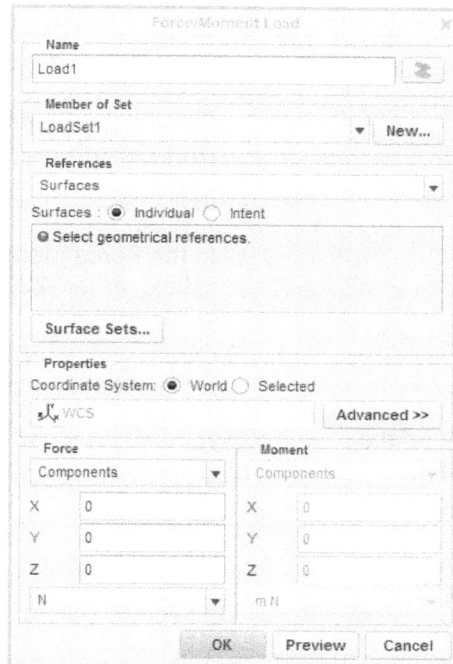

**Figure 5–31**

2. In the *Name* field, enter **uniform_load**.

3. For *Member of Set*, accept the default **LoadSet1** option.

4. Expand the References drop-down list and select **Edges/Curves**.

*The load is related to the WCS.*

5. Select the curve between PNT1 and PNT2, as shown in Figure 5–32.

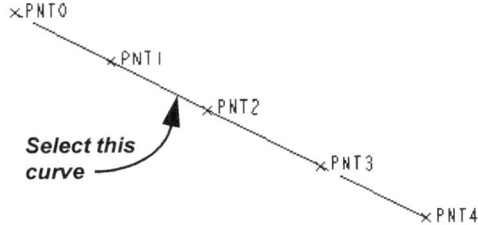

Figure 5–32

6. Click Advanced >> .

7. Expand the Distribution drop-down list and select **Force Per Unit Length**.

8. In the *Spatial Variation* area, select the **Uniform** option.

9. In the Force/Moment dialog box, in the *Force* area, in the Y field, enter **-2200**.

10. Click OK . The model displays as shown in Figure 5–33. Default datum planes are turned off.

*You can toggle off the load values in the Simulation Display dialog box.*

Figure 5–33

## Task 8 - Apply the point load to the PNT3.

1. Click . The Force/Moment Load dialog box opens.

2. In the *Name* field, enter **point_load**.

3. For *Member of Set*, accept the default **LoadSet1** option.

4. Expand the References drop-down list and select **Points**.

5. Select **PNT3**.

*The load is related to the WCS.*

6. In the Force/Moment dialog box, in the *Force* area, in the Y field, enter **-3500**.

7. Click **OK**. The model displays as shown in Figure 5–34 with the default datum planes turned off.

**Figure 5–34**

## Task 9 - Apply the constraints.

The beam ends (PNT0 and PNT4) are constrained (fixed) and the middle support (PNT2) is a roller (free Z-rotation and free X-translation). In this task, you will constrain the beam ends.

1. Click ⬚. The Constraint dialog box opens.

2. In the *Name* field, enter **end_constraints**.

3. For *Member of Set*, accept the default **ConstraintSet1** option.

4. Expand the References drop-down list and select **Points**.

5. Multi-select **PNT0** and **PNT4**.

6. Fix all of the Translations and Rotations.

7. Click **OK**. The model displays as shown in Figure 5–35.

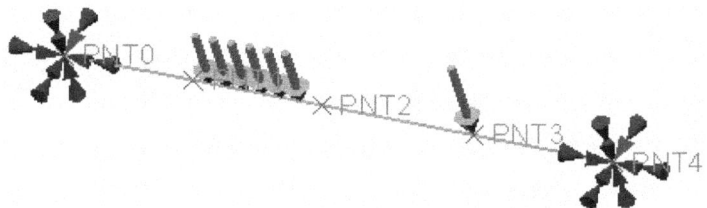

**Figure 5–35**

## Task 10 - Apply the constraints to PNT2.

1. Click ⬚. The Constraint dialog box opens.

2. In the *Name* field, enter **roller**.

3. For Member of Set, accept the default **ConstraintSet1** option.

4. Expand the References drop-down list and select **Points**.

5. Select **PNT2**.

6. Free X-translation and Z-rotation, and fix all of the other degrees of freedom, as shown in Figure 5–36.

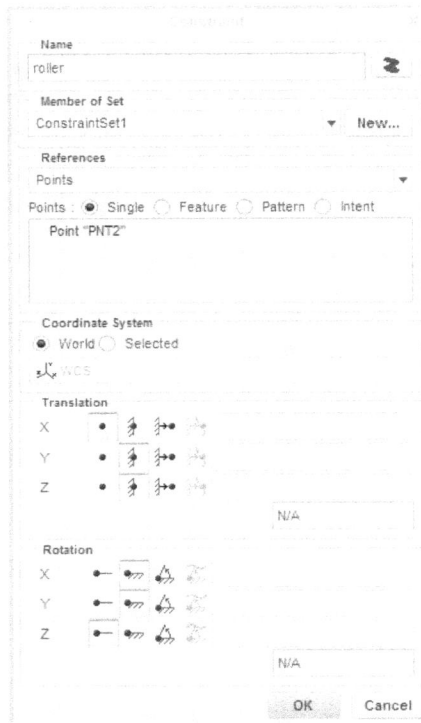

**Figure 5–36**

7. Click OK to close the dialog box. The model displays as shown in Figure 5–37.

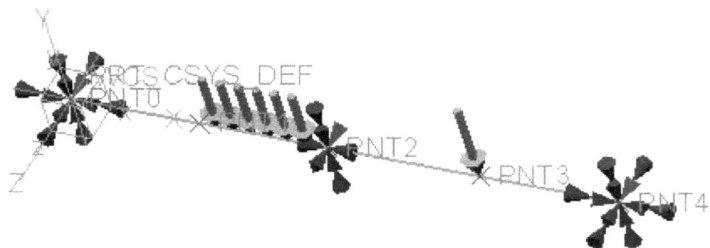

**Figure 5–37**

## Analysis Tasks

### Task 11 - Set up the analysis.

1. Set up a Quick Check analysis to check for errors. For the name of the analysis, enter **beam_q_c**.

2. In the *Output* tab, increase the plotting grid to **10**.

3. In the Analyses and Design Studies dialog box, in the **Info** menu, select **Check Model** to check the validity of the model.

4. Click and ensure that the **Create Elements during Run** option is selected in the Run Settings dialog box.

5. Click OK to close the Run Settings dialog box.

*The **Check Model** option highlights any modeling errors (e.g., load-constraint conflicts or unassigned material properties) and errors from modeling edits.*

### Task 12 - Run the Quick Check analysis.

1. Click to start the analysis.

2. Click to display the status of the run and any errors or warnings.

3. Close the Run Status dialog box when the run is complete.

### Task 13 - Solve the analysis using the Multi-Pass Adaptive convergence option.

1. Change the convergence method to Multi-Pass Adaptive. In the *Polynomial Order* field, enter **6**. In the *Limits* area, in the *Percent Convergence* field, enter **1**.

2. Re-run the analysis.

**Results Tasks**

**Task 14 - Display the results.**

Create and display the color plot for the displacement. Animate the plot to ensure that the boundary conditions are correct.

1. In the Analyses and Design Studies dialog box, click 🖻. The Result Window Definition dialog box opens.

2. Create, animate and display a fringe color plot for the displacement.

3. Stop the animation. Select **Format>Result Window**. Select **Loads** and **Constraints** and close the Visibilities dialog box.

4. Click ▶️ and ◀️ to step through the animation frames. Frame 5 is shown in Figure 5–38.

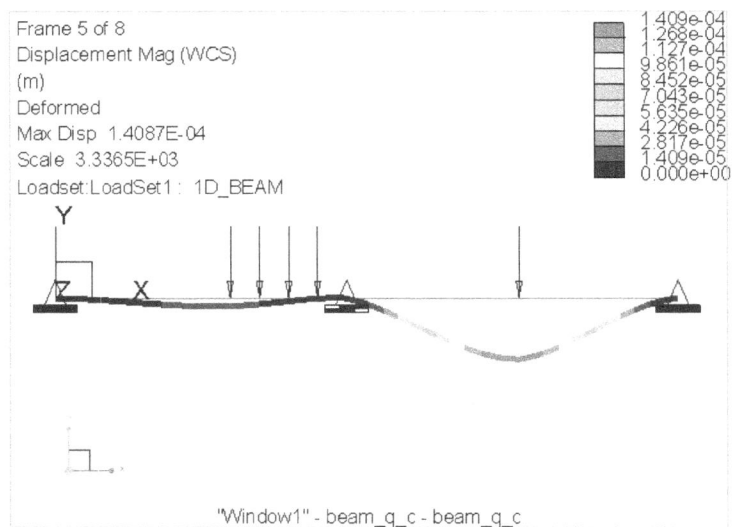

Figure 5–38

Note that the deflection is zero at the beam ends and at the roller support, which is correct.

5. Animate and display the components of displacement (X, Y, and Z). Note that the deflection of the model in the X- and Z-directions is zero.

## Task 15 - Create a shear and bending moment plot window for beam elements.

1. Click 🗈. The Result Window Definition dialog box opens.

2. In the *Name* field, enter **shear_moment_window**.

3. In the *Title* field, enter **shear_moment_graph**.

4. Expand the Display type drop-down list and select **Graph**.

5. Expand the first Quantity drop-down list and select **Shear & Moment**.

6. In the *Shear and Moment* area, clear all of the options except **Vy** and **Mz** in the *Beam* area.

7. Expand the Graph Location drop-down list and select **Beams**.

8. Click ▶ and select all four beam elements from left to right (hold down <Ctrl> to multi-select). Click the middle mouse button. The Information dialog box opens as shown in Figure 5–39.

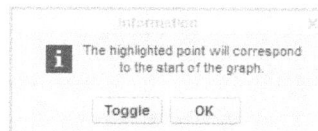

Figure 5–39

9. Read the information and verify that the start of the graph corresponds to the point PNT0.

10. In the Information dialog box, click OK . The Result Window Definition dialog box opens as shown in Figure 5–40.

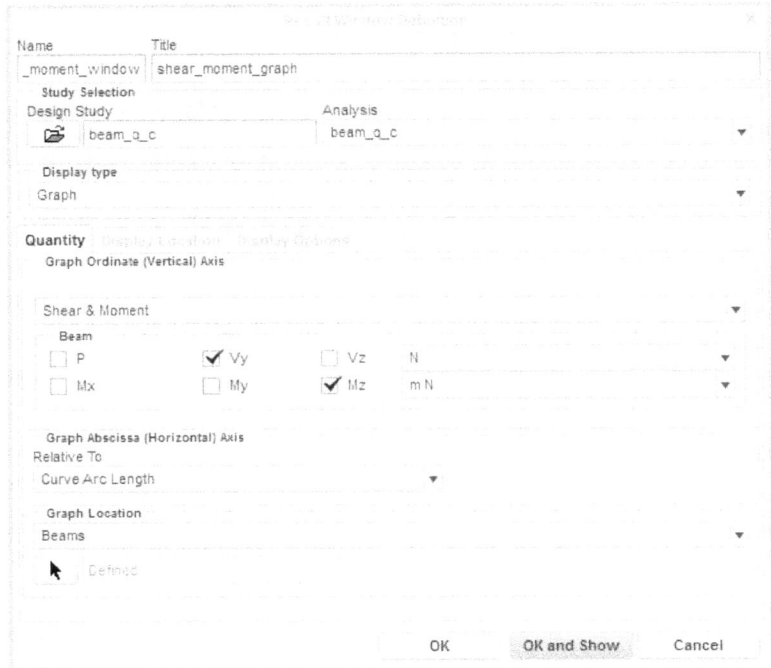

**Figure 5–40**

11. Click OK .

12. Click ⛋. In the Display Result Window dialog box, clear **Window1** and select **shear_moment_window**.

13. Click OK . The result window displays as shown in Figure 5–41.

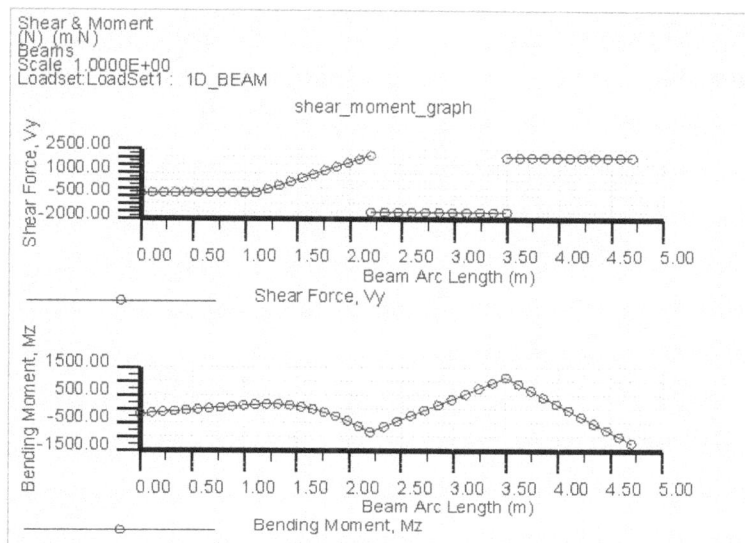

**Figure 5–41**

The plot shown in Figure 5–41 displays the shear and moment plots along the beam elements in the model. Note the bending moment continuity along the model. Note the shear force discontinuity at the roller support and at the point load.

14. Select **File>Exit Results**. Click    No    in the dialog box when prompted to save the results window.

15. Close the Analyses and Design Studies dialog box.

---

**Task 16 - Set up the beam releases.**

---

*Beam release is a term that describes the type of connections (pinned or rigid) between two beam elements.*

In this task, you will release the **beam_4** start point (free rotation in the Z-direction) to simulate a pinned connection between **beam_3** and **beam_4**.

---

*Release can only be applied directly to beam elements.*

1. Select **beam_4** (the curve between PNT3 and PNT4). The curve will highlight in green. Right-click and select **Edit Definition**. The Beam Definition dialog box opens as shown in Figure 5–42.

**Figure 5–42**

2. Next to the Beam Release drop-down list, click More... . The Beam Releases dialog box opens as shown Figure 5–43.

*Releases are handy when modeling trusses (because no moment is transmitted through a connection), modeling an expansion joint (because no axial load is transmitted), or when modeling dovetails (because all of the forces and moments are transmitted except shear in one direction).*

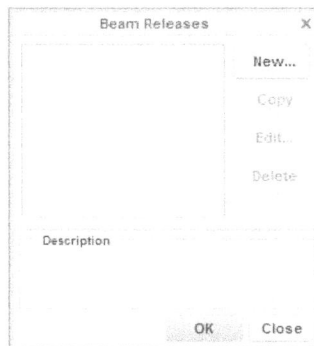

**Figure 5–43**

3. In the Beam Releases dialog box, click  New... . The Beam Release Definition dialog box opens as shown in Figure 5–44.

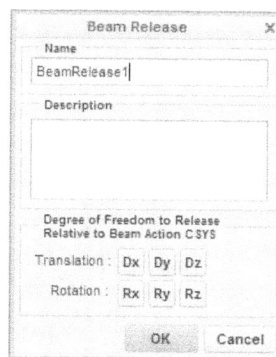

**Figure 5–44**

4. In the *Name* field, enter **beam_4_rz**.

5. Click Rz to release (free) the beam element rotation in the Z-direction at PNT3.

6. Click OK to close the Beam Release Definition dialog box.

7. Click OK to close the Beam Releases dialog box.

8. Click OK to close the Beam Definition dialog box.

9. Create and run a new Multi-Pass Adaptive analysis **d1_beam** for the modified model.

*(Beam Release) indicates the degrees of freedom and the end of the beam on which the release is acting.*

## Task 17 - Display the results.

1. Create and display a color plot for the displacement. Additionally, animate this plot to ensure that the boundary conditions are correct. The deformed shape is shown in Figure 5–45. Note the changes in the slope at the point of the release.

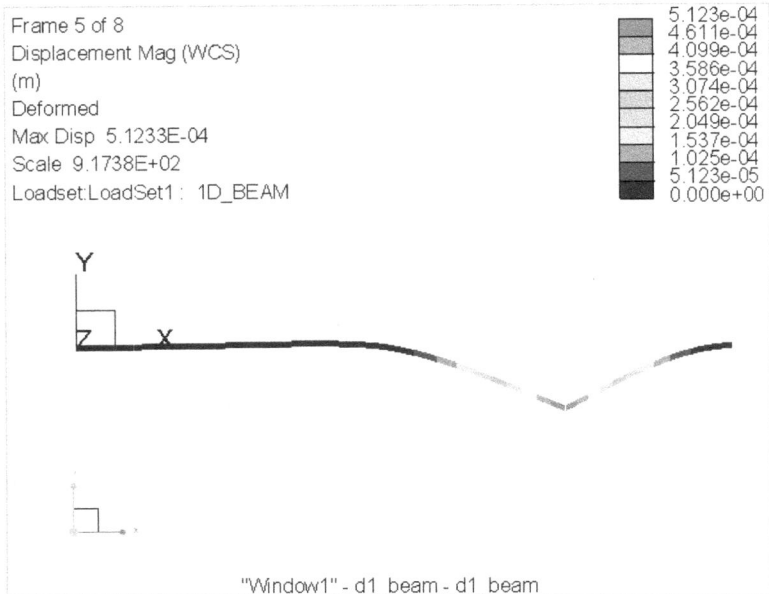

```
Frame 5 of 8                                    5.123e-04
Displacement Mag (WCS)                          4.611e-04
                                                4.099e-04
(m)                                             3.586e-04
                                                3.074e-04
Deformed                                        2.562e-04
Max Disp  5.1233E-04                            2.049e-04
                                                1.537e-04
Scale  9.1738E+02                               1.025e-04
Loadset:LoadSet1 :  1D_BEAM                     5.123e-05
                                                0.000e+00
```

Y

Z    X

"Window1" - d1_beam - d1_beam

**Figure 5–45**

2. Create shear and bending moment plot windows for the beam elements (four beam elements), as shown in Figure 5–46. Note that the shear is non-zero and that the bending moment is zero at the release.

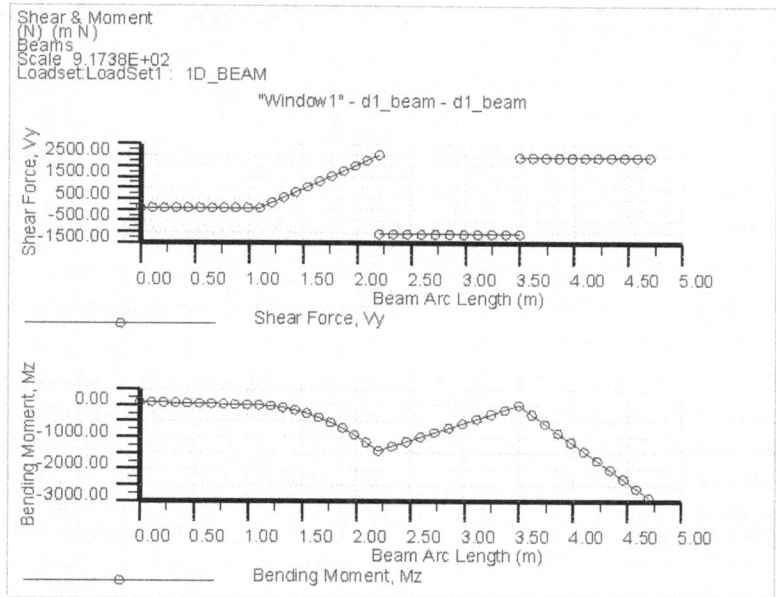

Figure 5–46

## Task 18 - Save and close the model.

1. Select **File>Exit Results**. Click    No    in the dialog box when prompted to save the results window.

2. Close the Analyses and Design Studies dialog box.

3. Exit Creo Simulate. Save and close the model in Creo Parametric.

# Practice 5b

# 2D Frame Analysis

**Learning Objectives**

Understand how to set up a 2D beam model.

Understand how to run a 2D beam model.

Understand how to analyze a 2D beam model.

*The aspect ratio of the beam element should be greater than 10:1(the ratio of its length to its largest section dimension).*

In this practice, you will use beam element idealizations to set up, run, and analyze a 2D frame. The frame part is shown in Figure 5–47. The beam section is a hollow circular pipe and the frame ends are fixed. The frame loading is a linearly distributed load in the Y-direction, a uniform total load in the Z-direction, a point load in the X-direction and a load due to gravity.

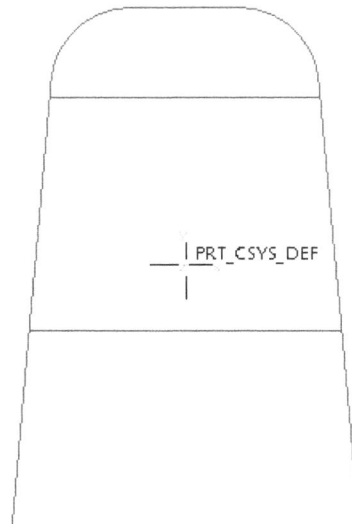

Figure 5–47

**Modeling Tasks**

**Task 1 - Open the d2_frame.prt.**

1. Open **d2_frame.prt** in Creo Parametric.

2. In the *View* tab, in the *Show* area, click to visualize the datum point tags. The part displays as shown in Figure 5–48.

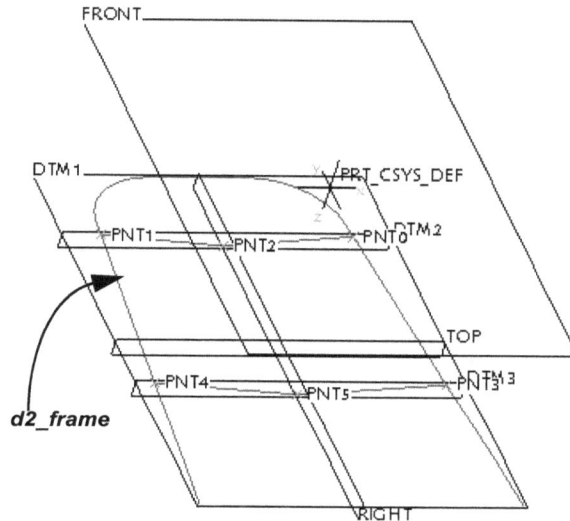

**Figure 5–48**

3. Ensure that the unit system is **IPS**.

4. Switch to the Creo Simulate environment.

5. Click . In the Simulation Display dialog box, clear the **Display AutoGEM Controls** option.

---

**Task 2 - Create a datum point as a simulation feature.**

---

In beam models, Creo Simulate can only define distributed loads on curves. The load is transferred to the beam elements created on the curve.

1. In the Refine Model tab, click .

2. Create a datum point at the end of the curve in the location shown in Figure 5–49.

**Simulation datum point feature**

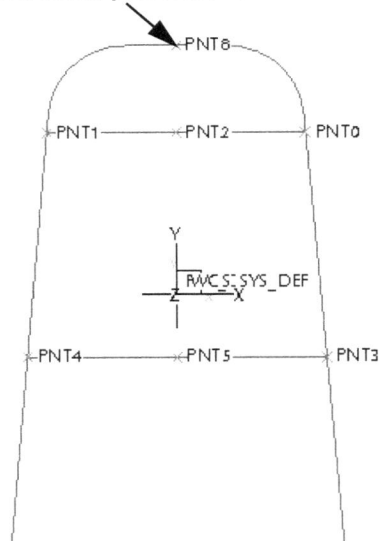

**Figure 5–49**

---

### Task 3 - Create beam elements.

---

1. Click ⬙. The Beam Definition dialog box opens.

2. In the *Name* field, enter **d2_beam_1**.

3. Expand the References drop-down list and select **Edge/Curve**.

4. Select the curve shown in Figure 5–50. As you select the curve, a direction arrow displays on the curve (clicking the curve again changes the direction of the arrow). The direction is shown in Figure 5–50.

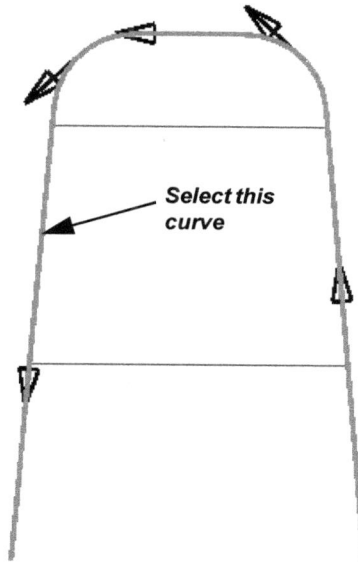

Select this curve

Figure 5–50

5. In the *Material* area, click More... . The Materials dialog box opens.

6. in the *Materials in Library* area, select **AL2014**. Click ▶▶▶ to transfer **AL2014** to the *Materials in Model* area.

7. Select **Edit>Properties** to check the material properties. The following values are the default material properties for Aluminum alloy 2014-T6:

   - Poisson = 0.33
   - Young's modulus = 1.06e+07 psi
   - Density = 0.0002614 lbf sec^2/in^4

8. Click OK in the Material Definition dialog box and Materials dialog box. AL2014 displays in the *Material* area in the Beam Definition dialog box.

9. In the *Orientation* area, in the *X* field, accept the default, in the *Y* field, enter **0**, and in the *Z* field, enter **1**.

10. Next to the Beam Section drop-down list, click More... . The Beam Sections dialog box opens.

11. Click ^New... . The Beam Section Definition dialog box opens as shown in Figure 5–51.

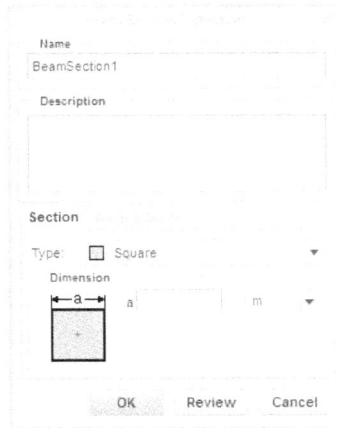

Name
BeamSection1

Description

Section

Type: ☐ Square ▾

Dimension

⊢—a—⊣  a          m    ▾

OK   Review   Cancel

**Figure 5–51**

12. In the *Name* field, enter **d2_frame_section_1**.

13. Expand the Type drop-down list and select **Hollow Circle**.

14. In the *R* field, enter **1.50**.

15. In the *Ri* field, enter **1.10**.

16. Click ^OK to close the Beam Section Definition dialog box.

17. Click ^OK to close the Beam Sections dialog box.

18. Click ^OK to close the Beam Definition dialog box. The model displays as shown in Figure 5–52.

*If the section is not in the Type drop-down list, you can sketch the section using the **Sketched Solid** and **Sketched Thin** sketch options in the Type drop-down list. These options open Sketcher in Creo Parametric.*

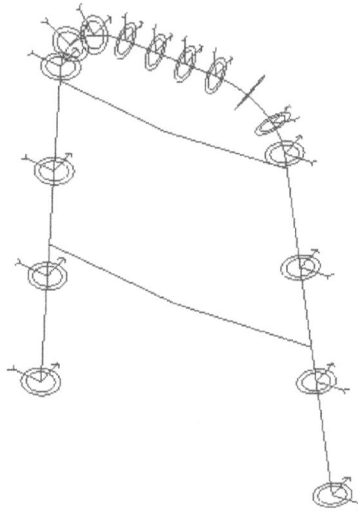

**Figure 5–52**

19. Click . The Beam Definition dialog box opens.

20. In the *Name* field, enter **d2_beam_2**.

21. Expand the References drop-down list and select **Edge/Curve**.

22. Select the curves shown in Figure 5–53. As you select each curve, a direction arrow displays on the curve (selecting the curve again will change the direction of the arrow). The direction is shown in Figure 5–53.

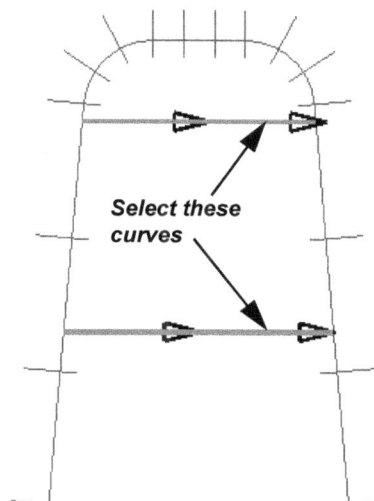

Select these curves

**Figure 5–53**

23. In the *Material* field, select **AL2014**.

24. In the *Orientation* area, in the *X* field, accept the default, in the *Y* field, enter **0** in the *Z* field, enter **1**.

25. Next to the Beam Section drop-down list, click More... . The Beam Sections dialog box opens.

26. Click New... . The Beam Section Definition dialog box opens.

27. In the *Name* field, enter **d2_frame_section_2**.

28. Expand the Type drop-down list and select **Hollow Circle**.

29. In the *R* field, enter **1.20**.

30. In the *Ri* field, enter **0.80**.

31. Click OK to close the Beam Section Definition dialog box.

32. Click OK to close the Beam Sections dialog box.

33. Click OK to close the Beam Definition dialog box. The model displays as shown in Figure 5–54.

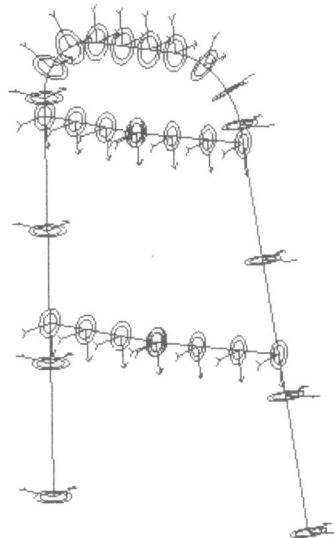

**Figure 5–54**

34. Click 🖳. The Simulation Display dialog box opens.

35. Select the *Modeling Entities* tab and clear the **Beam Sections** option.

36. Close the Simulation Display dialog box. The model displays as shown in Figure 5–55 with the default datum planes, points, and coordinate systems turned off.

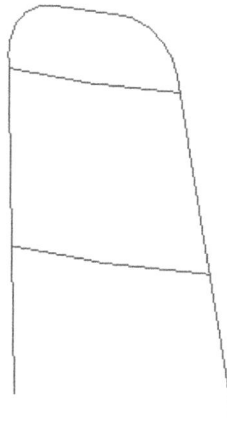

**Figure 5–55**

## Task 4 - Apply the loads.

The loading is a linearly distributed load in the Y-direction, a uniform total load in the Z-direction, a point load in the X-direction and a load due to gravity. In this task, you will apply the linear distributed load to the curve shown in Figure 5–56.

1. Click . The Force/Moment Load dialog box opens.

2. In the *Name* field, enter **distributed_load**.

3. For *Member of Set*, accept the default **LoadSet1** option.

4. Expand the References drop-down list and select **Edges/Curves**.

*The easiest way to select this section of the curve is to hover the cursor over the curve, right-click and select **Pick From List**. Then toggle through the items in the Pick From List dialog box, until the required curve highlights.*

5. Select the curve shown in Figure 5–56.

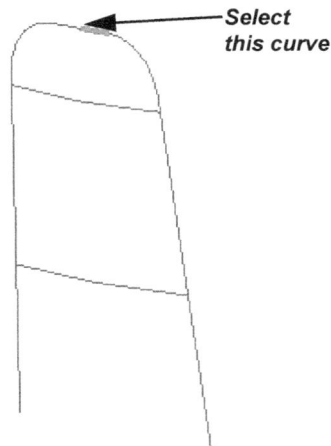

**Figure 5–56**

6. Click $^{Advanced >>}$ . Expand the Distribution drop-down list and select **ForcePerUnitLength**.

7. Expand the Spatial Variation drop-down list and select **InterpolatedOverEntity**.

8. In the 1st row of the *Value* column, enter **0.25**.

9. In the 2nd row of the *Value* column, enter **1.00**.

*The values (0.25, 1) are scale factors that Creo Simulate applies to the load at the ends of the curve.*

10. In the *Force* area, in the *Y* field, enter **-4350**. The Force/Moment dialog box opens as shown in Figure 5–57.

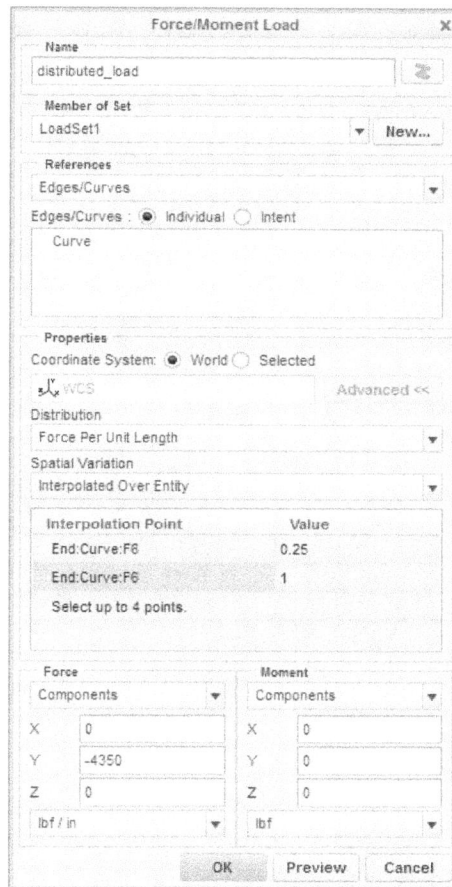

**Figure 5–57**

*If the load distribution is reversed, swap the **0.25** and **1** values defined in Steps 8 and 9.*

11. Click **Preview** to verify that the load distribution is linear, as shown in Figure 5–58.

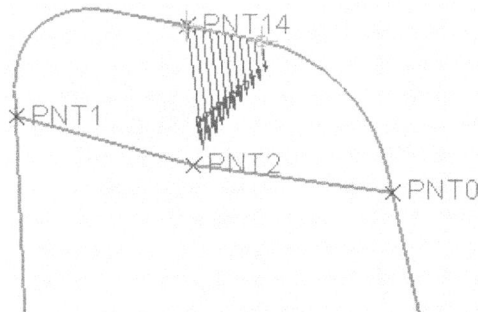

**Figure 5–58**

*You can turn the load values off in the Simulation Display dialog box.*

12. Click **OK**. The model displays as shown in Figure 5–59. Default datum planes are turned off.

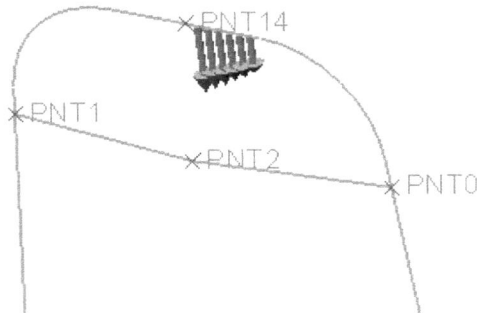

Figure 5–59

*Name the load* **distributed_load_1**.

13. Repeat Steps 1 to 7 of this task to apply the load to the curve shown in Figure 5–60.

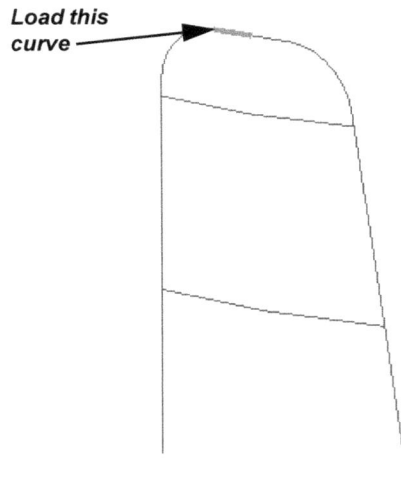

Figure 5–60

14. In the 1st row of the *Value* column, enter **1.00**.

15. In the 2nd row of the *Value* column, enter **0.25**.

16. Repeat Steps 10 to 12 to finish applying the loads. The model displays as shown in Figure 5–61.

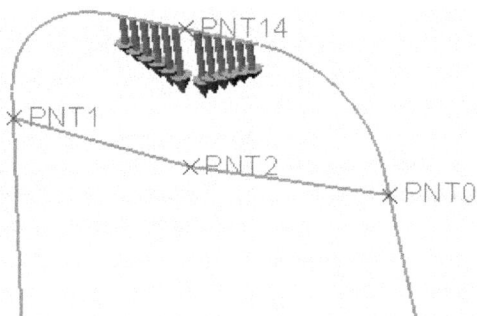

**Figure 5–61**

## Task 5 - Apply the point load.

1. Click 🔲 . The Force/Moment Load dialog box opens.

2. In the *Name* field, enter **point_load**.

3. For *Member of Set*, accept the default **LoadSet1** option.

*The load is related to the WCS.*

4. Expand the References drop-down list and select **Points**. Select **PNT14**, as shown in Figure 5–62.

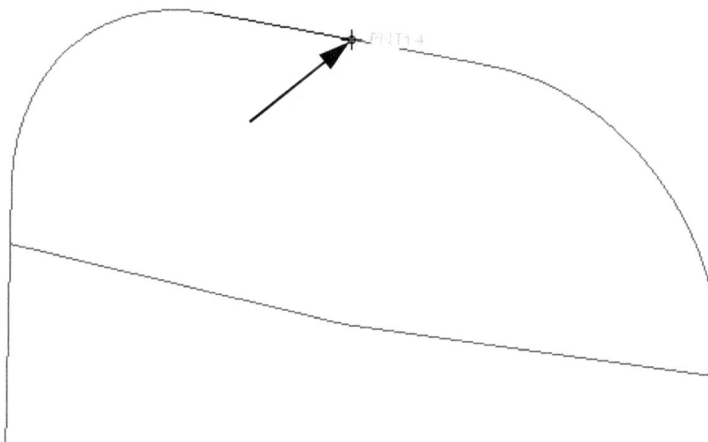

**Figure 5–62**

5. In the Force/Moment Load dialog box, in the *Force* area, in the *X* field, enter **-1930**.

6. Click OK to create the load.

## Task 6 - Apply a uniform total load in the Z-direction.

*The load is related to the WCS.*

1. Click  . The Force/Moment Load dialog box opens.

2. In the *Name* field, enter **total_uniform_load**.

3. In *Member of Set*, accept the default **LoadSet1** option.

4. Expand the References drop-down list and select **Edges/Curves**. Select the two curves shown in Figure 5–63.

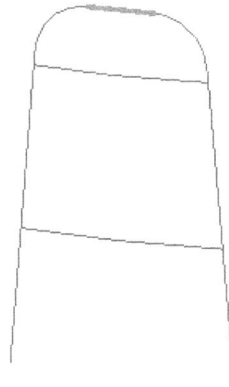

**Figure 5–63**

5. In the Force/Moment Load dialog box, in the *Force* area, in the *Z* field, enter **1930**.

6. Click    OK    to finish. The model displays as shown in Figure 5–64. Default datum planes and points are turned off.

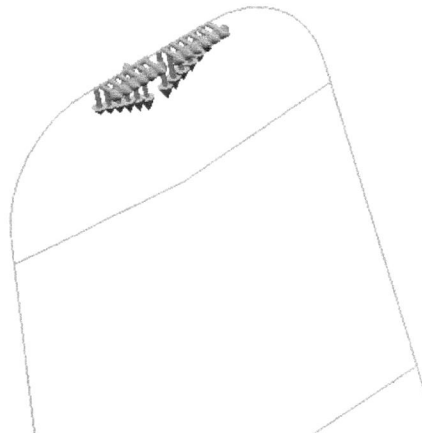

**Figure 5–64**

## Task 7 - Apply the gravity load.

1. Click ⬜⌐. The Gravity Load dialog box opens as shown in Figure 5–65.

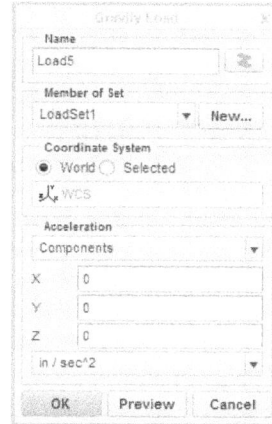

**Figure 5–65**

2. In the *Name* field, enter **gravity**.

3. Click New... to define a new load set. The Load Set dialog box opens as shown in Figure 5–66.

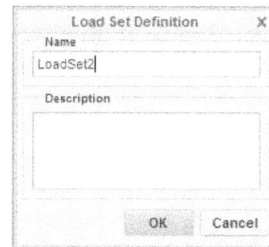

**Figure 5–66**

4. Accept the default name and click OK .

*The gravity load is related to the WCS.*

5. In the dialog box, in the *Acceleration* area, in the *Y* field, enter **-386**.

6. Click ___OK___ to finish defining the gravity load. The model displays as shown in Figure 5–67.

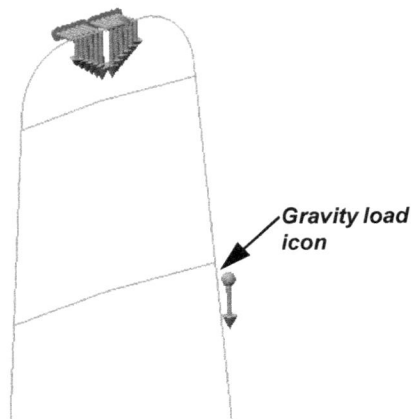

Gravity load icon

**Figure 5–67**

## Task 8 - Apply the constraints.

In this task, you will constrain the ends of the frame model (fix in translation and rotation). To constrain the ends, create two datum points as simulation features at the ends of the frame model.

*A beam end point has six degrees of freedom.*

1. In Creo Simulate, create the two datum points shown in Figure 5–68.

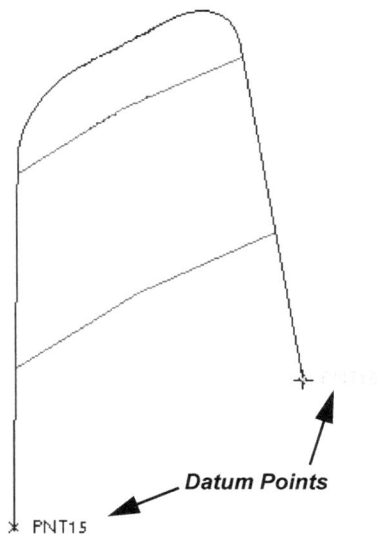

Datum Points

PNT15

**Figure 5–68**

2. Click ⬚. The Constraint dialog box opens.

3. In the *Name* field, enter **end_constraints**.

4. Expand the References drop-down list and select **Points**.

5. Select the points created in Step 1 of this task.

6. Fix all of the Translations and Rotations.

7. Click OK. The model displays as shown in Figure 5–69.

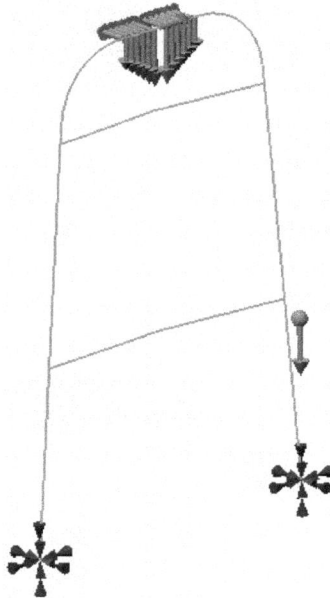

Figure 5–69

## Analysis Tasks

### Task 9 - Set up the analysis.

In this task, you will set up and run a Multi-Pass Adaptive convergence analysis.

1. For the name of the analysis, enter **d2_frame**.

2. Select both load sets.

3. In the *Limits* area, in the *Polynomial Order* field, enter **6** and in the *Percent Convergence* field, enter **1**.

4. In the *Output* tab, increase the *Plotting Grid* to **10**.

5. Run the analysis.

## Results Tasks

### Task 10 - Display the results.

In this task, you will create and display four result windows.

1. In the Analyses and Design Studies dialog box, click 🖳. The Result Window Definition dialog box opens as shown in Figure 5–70.

*Note that both load sets are included. You can display results for them individually or combined. The default combination factor is 1. You can change it for a different load combination ratio. Note the **Bending**, **Tensile**, and **Torsional** stress options.*

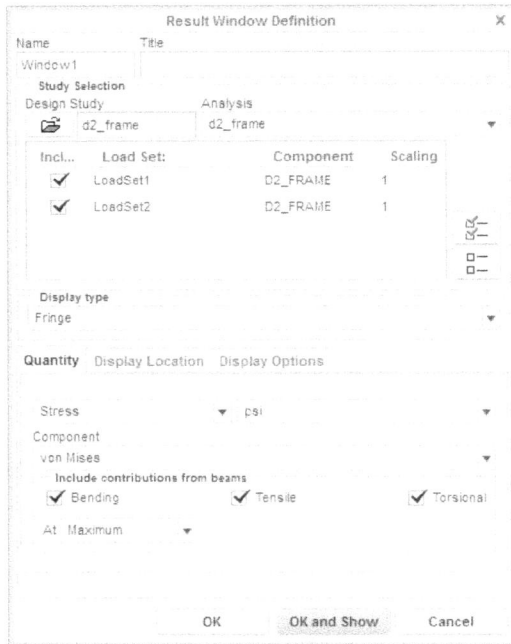

**Figure 5–70**

2. Create, display, and animate a displacement result window. Include both load sets. The display type is **Fringe** and the displacement component is **Magnitude**. The window displays as shown in Figure 5–71.

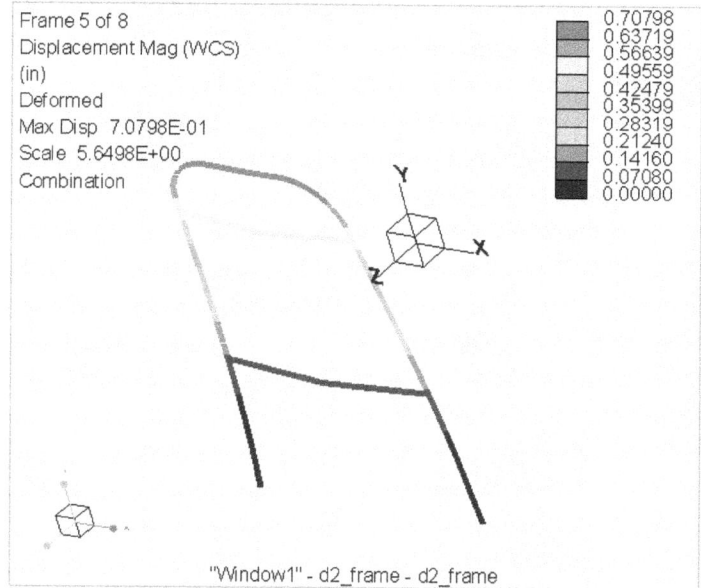

Frame 5 of 8
Displacement Mag (WCS)
(in)
Deformed
Max Disp 7.0798E-01
Scale 5.6498E+00
Combination

0.70798
0.63719
0.56639
0.49559
0.42479
0.35399
0.28319
0.21240
0.14160
0.07080
0.00000

"Window1" - d2_frame - d2_frame

**Figure 5–71**

Note that the displacements at the end points of the frame are zero, according to the applied constraints.

*The **Info>Model Max** option is not available in an animated result window.*

3. Create and display the beam bending stress plot for the combined load sets. Select **Info>Model Max** to display the maximum beam bending stress. The plot display as shown in Figure 5–72.

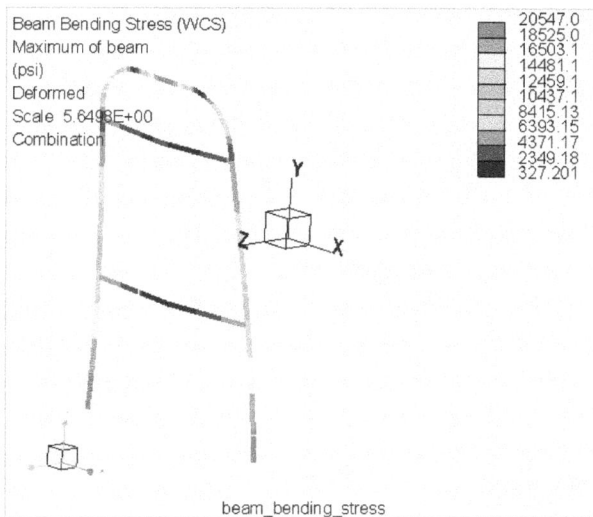

**Figure 5–72**

4. Create and display the deformed torsional stress plot for the combined load sets. Display the minimum and maximum torsional stress locations. The plot displays as shown in Figure 5–73.

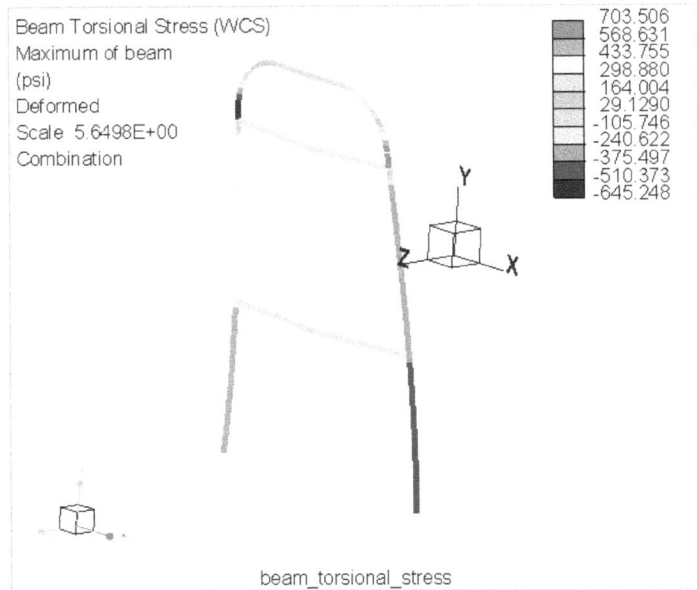

Beam Torsional Stress (WCS)
Maximum of beam
(psi)
Deformed
Scale 5.6498E+00
Combination

703.506
568.631
433.755
298.880
164.004
29.1290
-105.746
-240.622
-375.497
-510.373
-645.248

beam_torsional_stress

**Figure 5–73**

5. Create and display the reaction force Y at the point constraints. The plot displays as shown in Figure 5–74. Enter the information in the Result Window Definition dialog box, as shown in Figure 5–74.

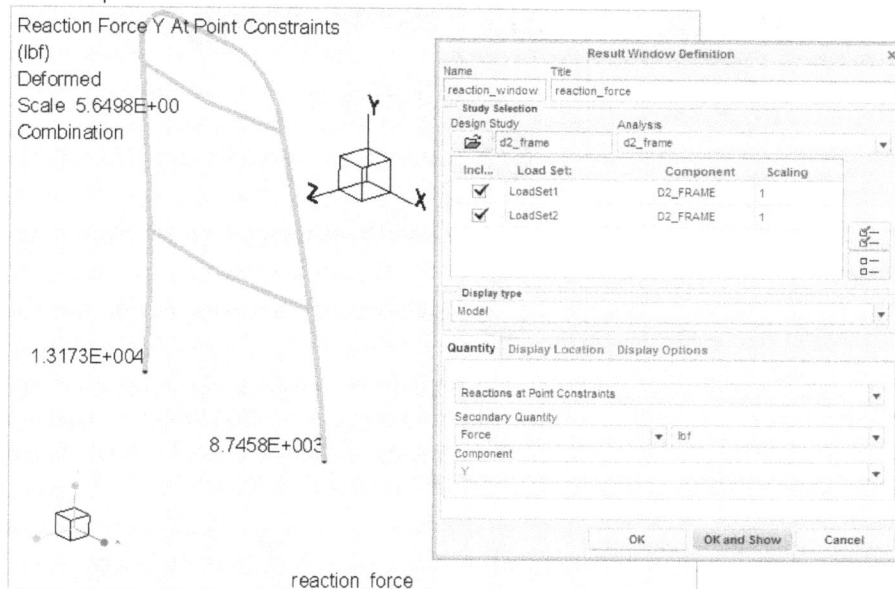

Reaction Force Y At Point Constraints
(lbf)
Deformed
Scale 5.6498E+00
Combination

1.3173E+004

8.7458E+003

reaction_force

**Result Window Definition**

Name          Title
reaction_window   reaction_force

Study Selection
Design Study              Analysis
d2_frame                  d2_frame

| Incl... | Load Set: | Component | Scaling |
|---|---|---|---|
| ✓ | LoadSet1 | D2_FRAME | 1 |
| ✓ | LoadSet2 | D2_FRAME | 1 |

Display type
Model

Quantity   Display Location   Display Options

Reactions at Point Constraints

Secondary Quantity
Force                          lbf
Component
Y

OK     OK and Show     Cancel

**Figure 5–74**

## Task 11 - Save and close the model.

1. Select **File>Exit Results**. Click   No   in the dialog box
   when prompted to save the results window.

2. Close the Analyses and Design Studies dialog box.

3. Exit Creo Simulate. Save and close the model in Creo
   Parametric.

# Practice 5c

# 3D Frame Analysis

**Learning Objectives**

Understand how to set up a 3D beam model.

Understand how to run a 3D beam model.

Understand how to analyze a 3D beam model.

*The walker supports a 225lb person.*

In this practice, you will use beam element idealizations to set up, run, and analyze a 3D Aluminum walker frame. The frame part is shown in Figure 5–75. The beam section is a hollow circular pipe and the frame ends are fixed.

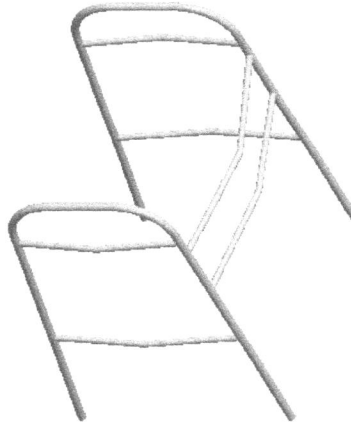

Figure 5–75

**Modeling Tasks**

**Task 1 - Open the d3_frame.prt.**

1. Open **d3_frame.prt** in Creo Parametric. The part displays as shown in Figure 5–76.

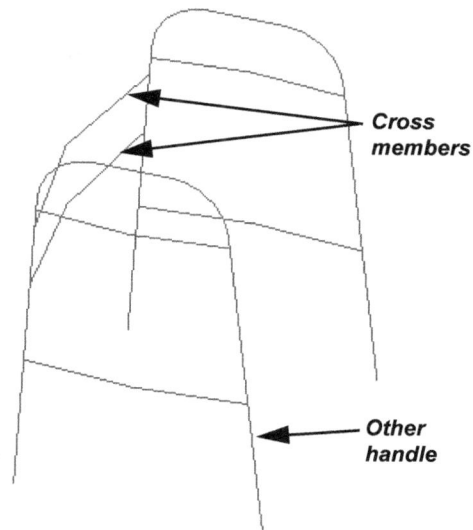

Figure 5–76

2. The unit systems are set to the Creo Parametric default.

3. Switch to the Creo Simulate environment.

4. Click ![icon]. In the Simulation Display dialog box, clear the **Display AutoGEM Controls** option.

5. The frame model displays as shown in Figure 5–77.

*The 2D frame (original curves) in the previous practice was used to create this 3D frame. The 2D frame sections and properties are maintained in this practice.*

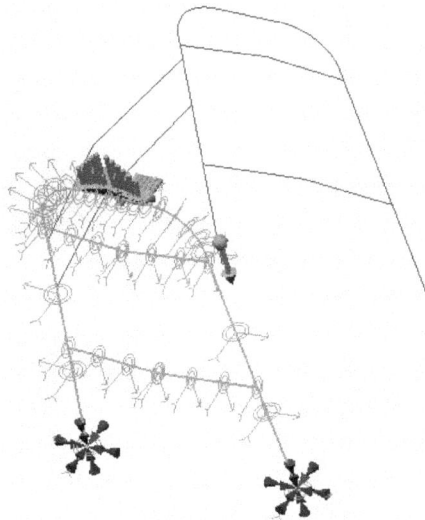

Figure 5–77

## Task 2 - Create the beam elements for the other walker handle.

1. Double-click on the curve shown in Figure 5–78. The Beam Definition dialog box opens.

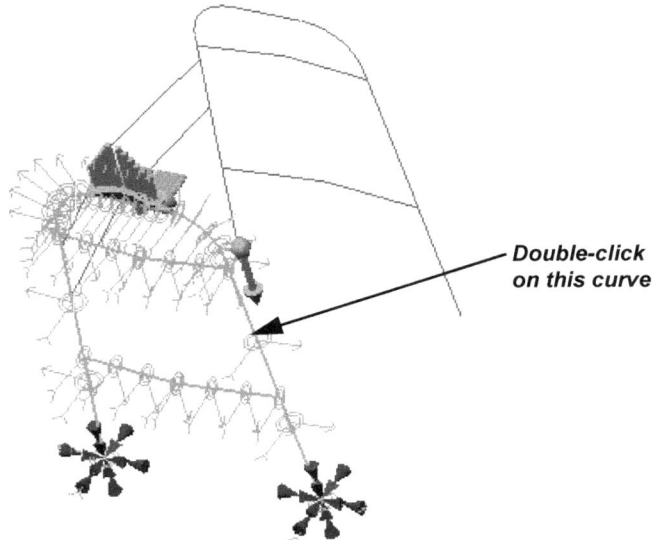

*Double-click on this curve*

**Figure 5–78**

2. Hold down <Ctrl> and select the other handle curve shown in Figure 5–79.

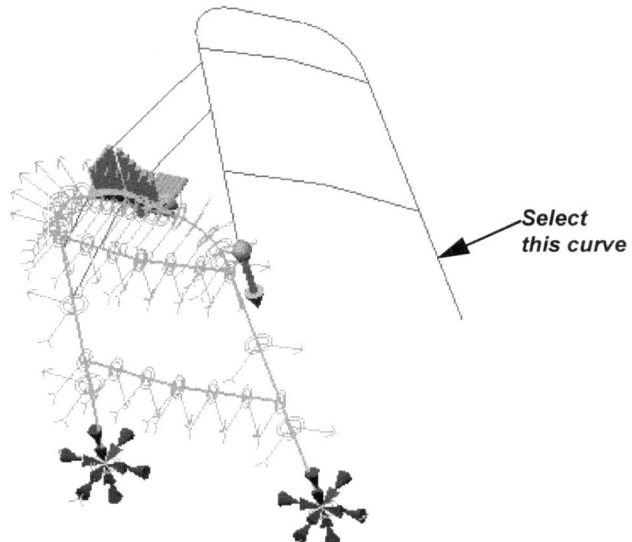

*Select this curve*

**Figure 5–79**

*The beam section is*
**d2_frame_section_1**.

3. Click OK to close the Beam Definition dialog box. The model (with loads and constraints turned off) displays as shown in Figure 5–80.

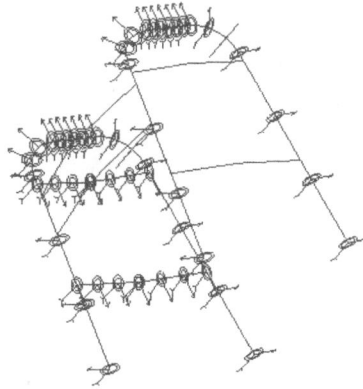

**Figure 5–80**

4. Double-click on the curve shown in Figure 5–81. The Beam Definition dialog box opens.

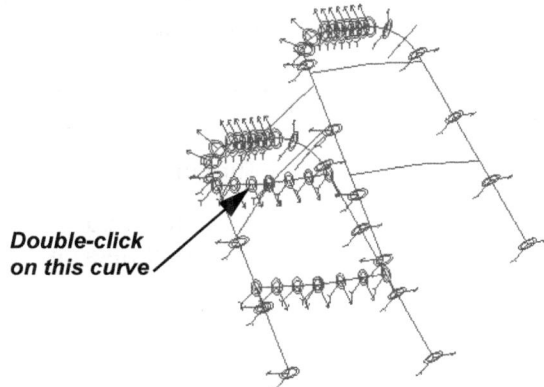

**Double-click on this curve**

**Figure 5–81**

5. Hold down <Ctrl> and select two cross member curves on the other handle and two cross member curves that connect the handles.

6. Click OK to close the Beam Definition dialog box. The model (with loads and constraints turned off) displays as shown in Figure 5–82.

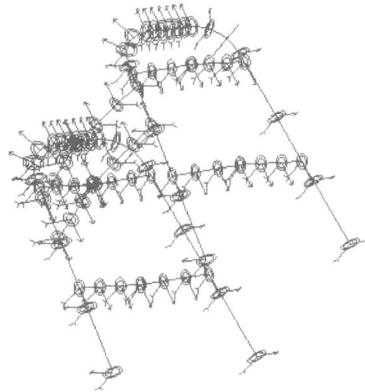

**Figure 5–82**

7. Click ⬛. The Simulation Display dialog box opens.

8. Select the *Modeling Entities* tab and clear the **Beam Sections** option.

## Task 3 - Delete the gravity load.

1. Turn the loads visualization on.

2. Expand the *Loads* area in the Ribbon and select **Load Sets**. The Load Sets dialog box opens as shown in Figure 5–83.

**Figure 5–83**

3. Highlight **LoadSet2** and click Delete . In the Question dialog box, click Yes .

4. Click **Close** to close the Load Sets dialog box.

## Task 4 - Copy the vertical load to the other handle.

*Assign **LoadSet1** to all of the loads.*

1. In the Model Tree, highlight the **distributed_load** load and click ⧉ (Copy).

2. Click ⧉ (Paste). The Force/Moment Load dialog box opens as shown in Figure 5–84.

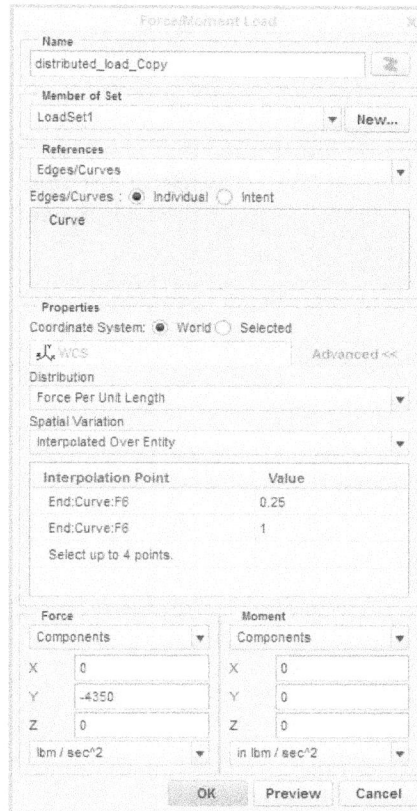

**Figure 5–84**

3. Right-click in the selection collector and select **Remove** to clear the selection.

4. Select the curve on the other handle, as shown in Figure 5–85

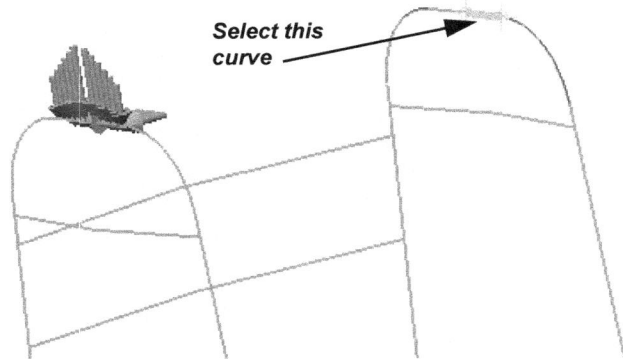

**Figure 5–85**

5. In the 1st row of the *Value* column, enter **0.25** and in the 2nd row of the *Value* column, enter **1.00**. The Force/Moment Load dialog box opens as shown in Figure 5–86.

**Figure 5–86**

6. Click ⬚ OK . The model displays as shown in Figure 5–87.

**Figure 5–87**

7. Follow Steps 1 to 6 to copy **distributed_load_1** to the other handle. The model displays as shown in Figure 5–88.

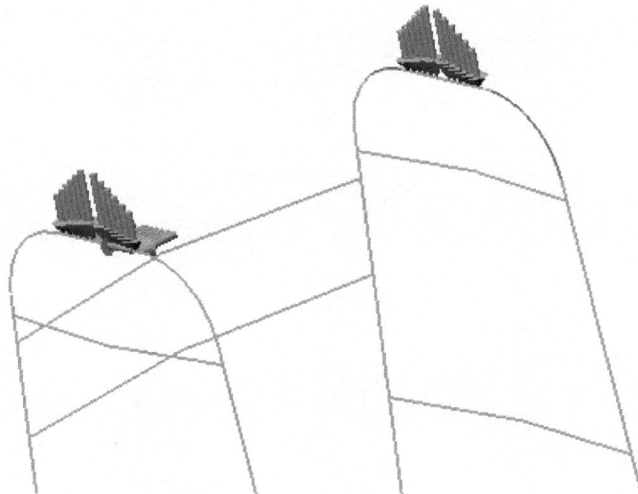

**Figure 5–88**

## Task 5 - Copy the side load to the other handle.

*Changing the sign of the force is necessary to maintain the symmetry of the loading.*

1. Follow Steps 1 to 6 in the previous task to copy **total_uniform_load** to the other handle. However, change the sign of the force in the Z-direction from *1930* to **-1930**. The model displays as shown in Figure 5–89.

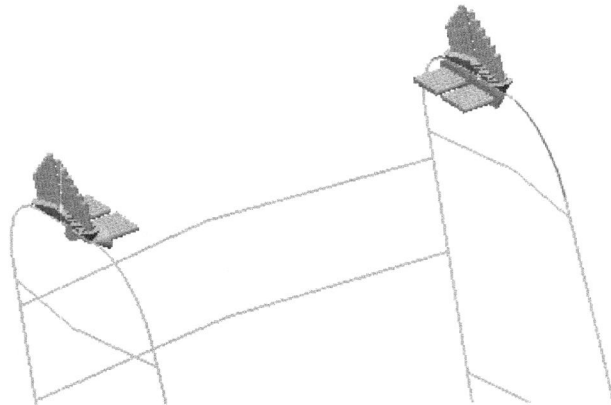

**Figure 5–89**

## Task 6 - Copy the point load to the other handle.

1. Create a datum point in the middle of the other handle, as shown in Figure 5–90.

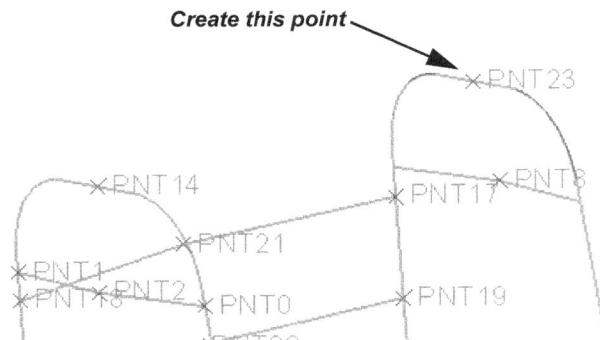

*Create this point*

PNT23

PNT14  PNT17  PNT

PNT21

PNT1  PNT19
PNT18  PNT2  PNT0

**Figure 5–90**

2. In the Model Tree, right-click on **point_load** load and select **Edit Definition**. The Force/Moment Load dialog box opens.

3. Hold down <Ctrl> and click the point you created in Step 1. The selection collector displays two points.

*The **Load Per Point** option applies the entered amount of load to each selected point. The other option is **Total Load**, which evenly divides the entered load among all of the points.*

4. Expand the Distribution drop-down list and verify that the **Load Per Point** option is selected. The Force/Moment Load dialog box opens as shown in Figure 5–91.

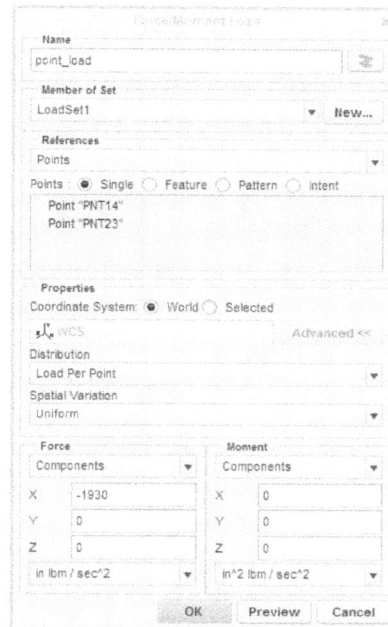

**Figure 5–91**

5. Click ⬜ OK . The model displays as shown in Figure 5–92.

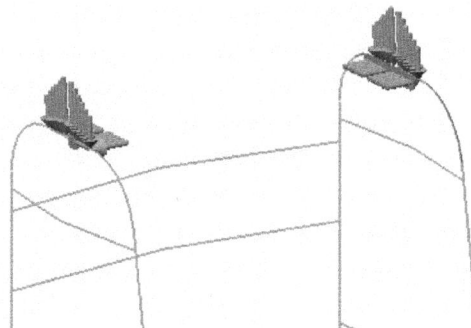

**Figure 5–92**

## Task 7 - Constrain the ends of the other handle.

1. In the Model Tree, right-click on the **end_constraints** load and select **Edit Definition**. The Constraint dialog box opens.

2. Hold down <Ctrl> and click the end points on the other handle. The selection collector displays the four selected points.

3. Click ⬚ OK ⬚ . The model displays as shown in Figure 5–93

**Figure 5–93**

## Analysis Tasks

## Task 8 - Set up the analysis.

Set up and run a Multi-Pass Adaptive convergence analysis.

1. For the name of the analysis, enter **d3_frame**.

2. In the *Limits* area, in the *Polynomial Order* field, enter **6**, and in the *Percent Convergence* field, enter **1**.

3. In the *Output* tab, increase the *Plotting Grid* to **10**.

4. Run the analysis. Ignore the warning messages in the Diagnostics window.

## Task 9 - Display the results.

1. Create and display a color plot of the displacement for the frame model. Animate this plot to verify that the boundary conditions are correct and the deformation is symmetrical.

2. Step through the animation. On Frame 5 the result window displays as shown in Figure 5–94.

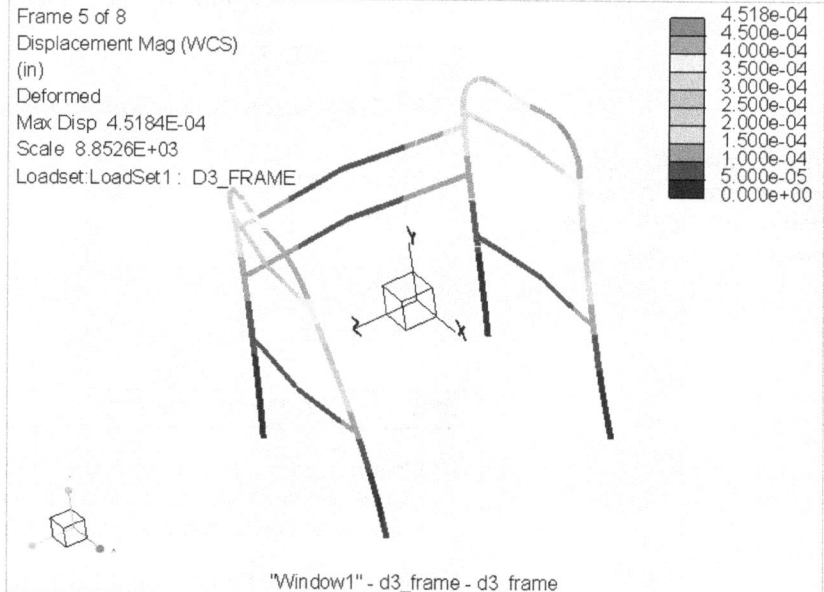

Frame 5 of 8
Displacement Mag (WCS)
(in)
Deformed
Max Disp 4.5184E-04
Scale 8.8526E+03
Loadset:LoadSet1 : D3_FRAME

```
4.518e-04
4.500e-04
4.000e-04
3.500e-04
3.000e-04
2.500e-04
2.000e-04
1.500e-04
1.000e-04
5.000e-05
0.000e+00
```

"Window1" - d3_frame - d3_frame

**Figure 5–94**

3. Start the animation. Note that each beam displays some bending.

### Task 10 - Modify the constraint on PNT15.

In this task, you will modify the constraint on PNT15 to simulate a settling foundation for the walker at this corner. This represents a forced displacement in the Y-direction for the constraint at PNT15.

1. Select **File>Exit Results**. Click   No   in the dialog box when prompted to save the results window. Close the Analyses and Design Studies dialog box.

2. In the Model Tree, right-click on the **end_constraints** load and select **Edit Definition**. The Constraint dialog box opens.

3. Right-click on the PNT15 in the selection collector and select **Remove**.

4. Click   OK   to close the Constraint dialog box.

5. Click 🗋. The Constraint dialog box opens.

6. In the *Name* field, enter **forced_constraint**.

7. Expand the References drop-down list and select **Points**.

8. Select **PNT15**.

9. Fix Translations X and Z and fix all of the Rotations.

*The frame at this corner will be forced to move down by 0.0625in (the unit length is inch).*

10. In the *Translation* area, for Y, click ⇥•. In the Y field, enter **-0.0625**.

11. Click ‎ OK ‎ to close the Constraint dialog box.

12. Re-run the analysis.

## Task 11 - Display the results.

1. Create and display a color plot of the displacement for the frame model. Overlay the undeformed model and animate the plot to verify that the boundary conditions are correct.

2. Step through the animation. On Frame 5 the result window displays as shown in Figure 5–95.

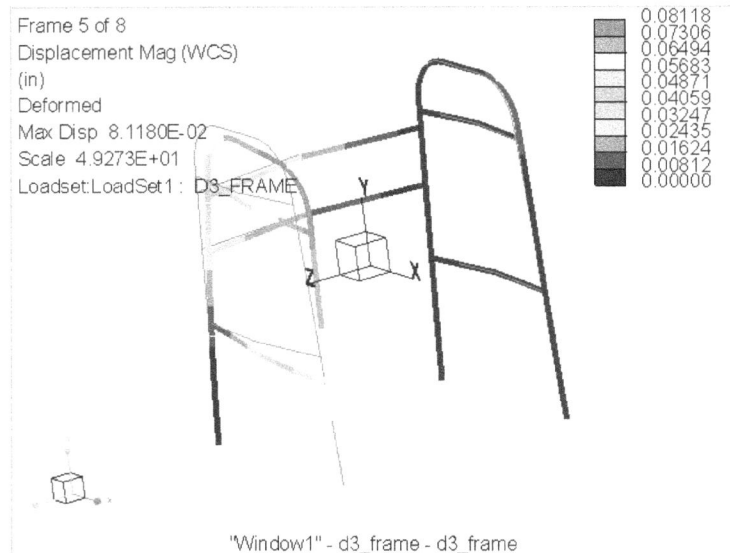

"Window1" - d3_frame - d3_frame

**Figure 5–95**

Note that the end of the frame with the enforced displacement constraint is moving down, as required.

3. Exit the Creo Simulate results. Save and close the model in Creo Parametric.

# Chapter 6

## Sensitivity and Optimization Design Studies

---

Design studies enable you to explore design alternatives and to optimize your model. You can perform three types of design studies in Creo Simulate: standard, sensitivity, and optimization. Standard design studies calculate results for an analysis with different design variable settings. Sensitivity design studies calculate results for several different values of design variables (e.g., dimensions). Optimization design studies adjust a model's parameters to meet a specified goal or to test the feasibility of a design.

This chapter contains the following topics:

- **Design Considerations**
- **Types of Design Studies**
- **Design Variables**

# 6.1 Design Considerations

**Learning Objective**

Understand the design study objectives and variables.

Before you set up a design study, it is recommended that you define your objectives, measures, and design variables. This enables you to organize and provide the correct data to Creo Simulate for the study.

The lift point shown in Figure 6–1 needs to be run through a design study. Before the design study is set up, an objective, a measure, and variables need to be defined.

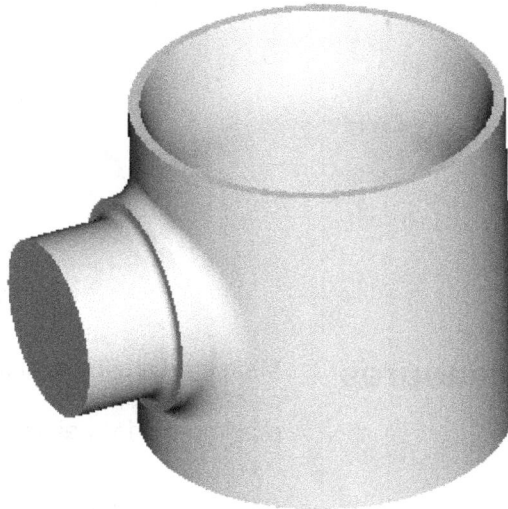

**Figure 6–1**

- The objective is to minimize the mass of the part.

- The measures include the von Mises stress and the total mass.

- The design variables include the diameter of the trunnion, and the diameter of the leg distance from the center of the trunnion to the center of the leg.

## Objectives

Objectives are the goals that you want to achieve with a design study (e.g., minimize weight, minimize reaction forces, etc.). You set your objectives during the setup of the optimization design studies. Your objective can be user-defined or system-defined using the options in the *Predefined* area in the Measures dialog box, as shown in Figure 6–2. For example, a system-defined objective would be to minimize stress (i.e., the system-defined parameter **max_stress_vm**). An example of a user-defined objective would be to ensure that clearance (i.e., a user-defined parameter calculated by subtracting 2D values) is maximized.

*Objectives are only required for optimization design studies.*

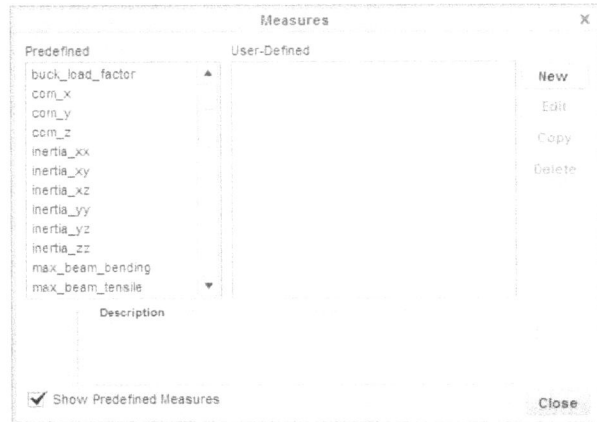

Figure 6–2

## Measures

Measures are the scalar quantities of interest that Creo Simulate calculates during analysis (e.g., maximum von Mises stress, maximum principal stress, etc.).

## Design Variables

Design variables are the Creo Parametric dimensions or parameters that you set to achieve your objective.

# 6.2 Types of Design Studies

**Learning Objective**

Understand the Standard, Sensitivity, and Optimization design studies.

## Standard Studies

Standard design studies evaluate the model for an alternative set of design variables, similarly to running a *what if* scenario.

## Sensitivity Studies

Sensitivity studies calculate how the variation in a design variable affects the results in which you are interested (i.e., the maximum stress or deflection). You might want to determine how a particular dimension or model property is going to affect the results of an analysis (i.e., you want to assess the sensitivity of the model to changes in this parameter). You could manually edit the model (i.e., geometry or properties) and perform the analysis many times. However, this method would be time-consuming and potentially inaccurate. A Creo Simulate sensitivity study automates this task.

You can perform two types of sensitivity studies: local and global. Local sensitivity studies assess which parameters have the greatest effect on a measure at the current parameter values (within a range of 2%). Local sensitivity studies are useful when you are testing small variations of data. They enable you to test the validity of your parameters and provide data on whether to increase or decrease them to meet your design goal. If the von Mises stress is not sensitive to one of the parameters, the parameter is not carried over to the next phase, which is the Global sensitivity study.

Global sensitivity studies vary a parameter over a user-defined range of values (the range is larger than that in a local sensitivity study). They are useful when you have done a local study and want to test a larger range of variables to get the best possible parameter values to achieve your design goal.

## Optimization Studies

Optimization studies manipulate parameters and determine an optimal solution to your design goal, within the specified design limits. It is necessary to have a design goal or design limit or both. If you do not have a goal, Creo Simulate searches for the first possible design while conforming to your design limit. This is called feasibility study.

Optimization studies are set up and run using the same procedure as sensitivity studies. The report generated by an optimization study contains the following information:

- Optimized value of each parameter

- Value of the goal and of each design limit measure

## Setting Up Design Studies

In Creo Simulate, design studies are set up and run in the following order:

1. Run an analysis to ensure that the model converges to a solution.
2. Set up the design parameters for the design studies.
3. Run a local sensitivity study and select the parameters that have an effect on the measure.
4. Run a global sensitivity study on the selected parameters and find the parameter values (maximum or minimum) that have the greatest effect on the measure (design limit).
5. Run an optimization study for the parameters that have the greatest effect on the measure. Select initial values for the parameters based on data from the global sensitivity study.

# 6.3 Design Variables

**Learning Objective**

Understand how to set up the variables for a design study.

Design variables are Creo Parametric dimensions and/or parameters that you want to change during a design study. Design variables are selected in the Design Study Definition dialog box, which is opened from the Analyses and Design Studies dialog box.

For example, the Optimization Study Definition dialog box is shown in Figure 6–3. ⊞ enables the selection of model dimensions to vary and ⊞ enables you to select the model parameters.

**Figure 6–3**

# Practice 6a

# Sensitivity and Optimization Studies

*Sensitivity and optimization design studies automate some of the repetitive work involved in design.*

**Learning Objectives**

✓ Set up and run sensitivity design studies.

✓ Set up and run an optimization design study.

In this practice, you will use sensitivity and optimization design studies to set up, run, and analyze a hinge plate part as shown in Figure 6–4. The part is made of steel.

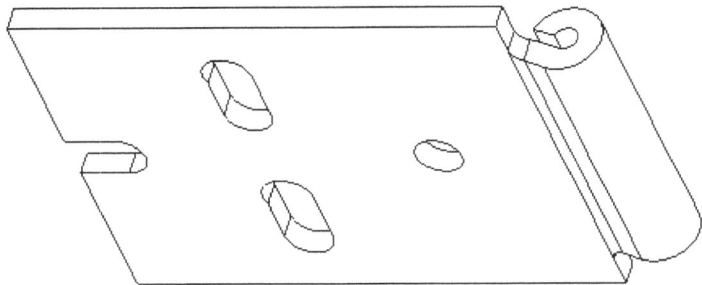

**Figure 6–4**

When setting up design studies, you need to define the following information:

- The goal for the study.

- The measure to be used to analyze the parameter's effect on the hinge part.

- The design variables (Creo Simulate dimensions).

These requirements are summarized as follows:

| Objective | Measure | Parameters |
|---|---|---|
| Minimize the weight of the part. | • Von Mises stress <br> • Total mass | • Dimension from left edge to center of vertical slots (40 mm) <br> • Holes and slots diameter (10 mm) <br> • Hinge Plate thickness (3 mm) <br> • Dimension from left edge to center of right hand side hole (75 mm) |

## Modeling Tasks

### Task 1 - Open hinge.prt.

1. Open **hinge.prt** in Creo Parametric. The part displays as shown in Figure 6–5.

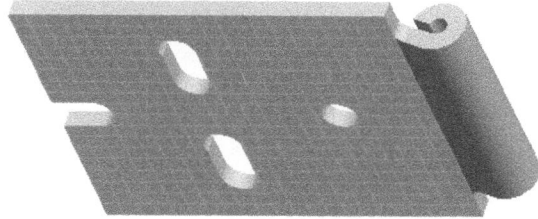

**Figure 6–5**

2. Ensure that the unit system is set to **mmNs**.

### Task 2 - Change the Dimension Symbol text.

In this task, you will rename the Creo Parametric dimensions to make it easier to identify the optimized variables in Creo Simulate.

*d7 =d23*

1. In the Ribbon, in the *Tools* tab, select **Relations**. The Relations dialog box opens. Enter the relation shown in Figure 6–6. It ties the plate thickness to the slot depth.

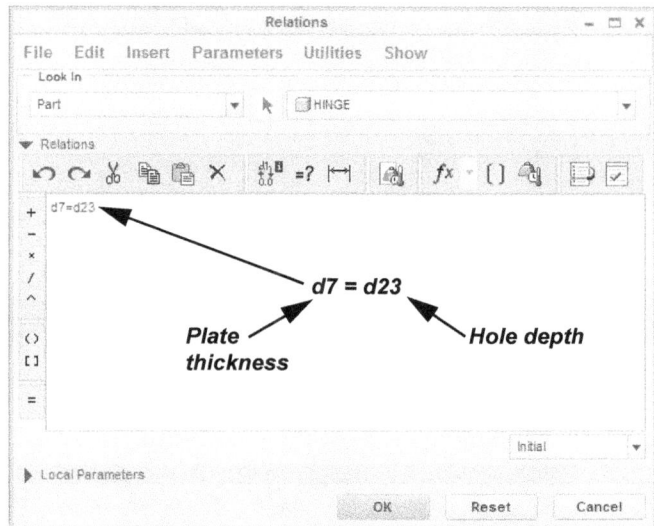

**Figure 6–6**

2. Click ▭ OK ▭ to close the Relations dialog box.

3. In the Model Tree, right-click on Cut id 226 and select **Edit**. The part displays. Select the 40 dimension as shown in Figure 6–7.

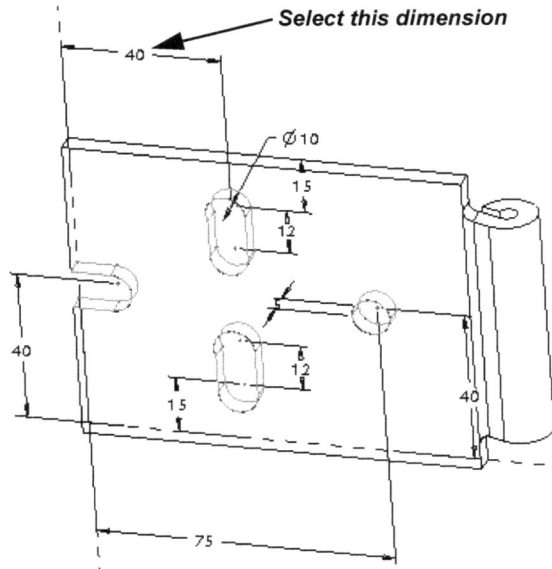

**Figure 6–7**

4. Right-click and select **Properties**. The Dimension Properties dialog box opens.

5. In the *Name* field, enter **slot_dim**, as shown in Figure 6–8.

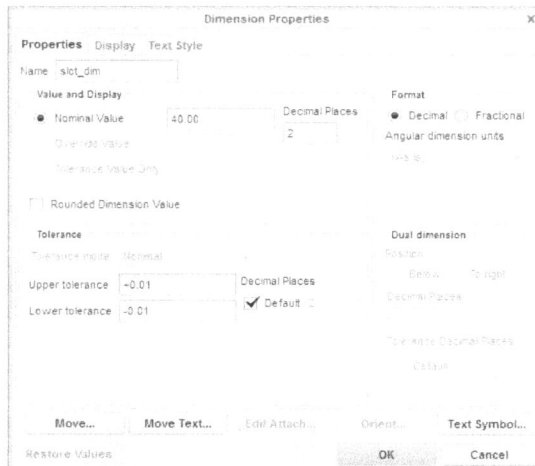

**Figure 6–8**

*The 3 dimension is the depth of the holes in the plate, which is equal to the plate thickness.*

6. Click  OK  .

7. Repeat Steps 3 to 7 for the 75, Ø10, and 3 dimensions. For the *75* dimension, enter **hole_dim**, for the *Ø10* dimension, enter **slot_diameter**, and for the *3* dimension, enter **depth**.

8. In the *Tools* tab, select **Switch Symbols**. The part displays as shown in Figure 6–9.

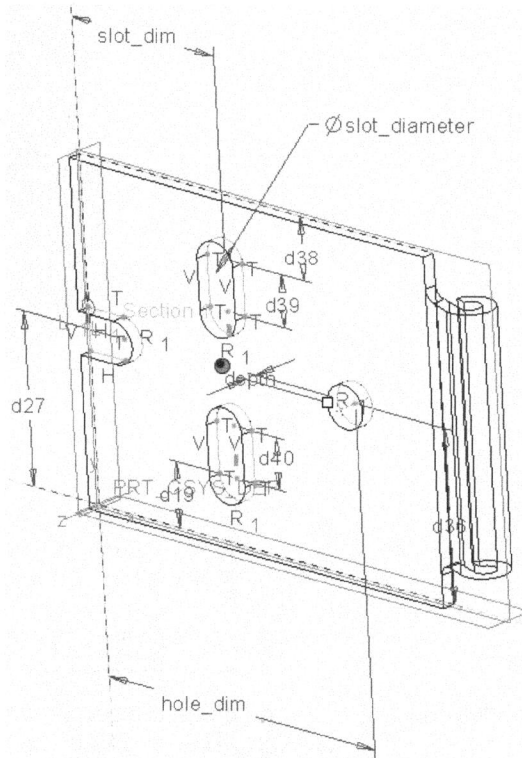

**Figure 6–9**

9. Save the part.

## Task 3 - Mesh the part with 3D solid elements.

1. Switch to Creo Simulate.

2. Click  .

3. Expand the AutoGEM References drop-down list and select **Volume**.

4. Select the part and click **Create** to create the mesh.

5. The AutoGEM Summary and Diagnostics dialog boxes open with a summary of the entities created, criteria satisfied, and time elapsed. Close both dialog boxes. The meshed model displays as shown in Figure 6–10.

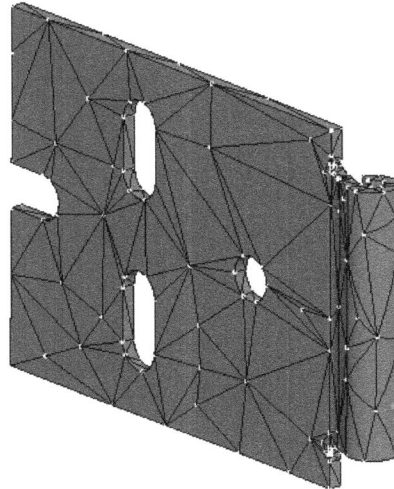

**Figure 6–10**

6. Close the AutoGEM dialog box and save the mesh. The mesh is saved with your model name and the .MMP extension (e.g., **hinge.mmp**) in your working directory.

## Task 4 - Apply loads.

*10° is an exaggerated measurement.*

The hinge supports a door of 200Kg = 2000N at 10° to the vertical. In this task, you will apply this force in two components.

1. Click . The Force/Moment Load dialog box opens.

2. In the *Name* field, enter **hinge _force_1** and select the surface shown in Figure 6–11.

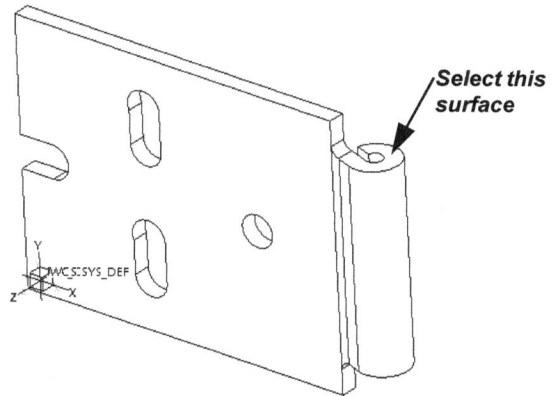

*Select this surface*

**Figure 6–11**

3. In the *Force* area, in the *Y* field, enter **-1970**.

4. Click **OK**. The model displays as shown in Figure 6–12.

*You can use the **Simulation Display** option to place the load vectors as **Tails Touching** and to toggle off the load values.*

**Figure 6–12**

5. Click ⊞ . The Force/Moment Load dialog box opens.

6. In the *Name* field, enter **hinge _force_2** and select the inside surface of the hinge hook as shown in Figure 6–13.

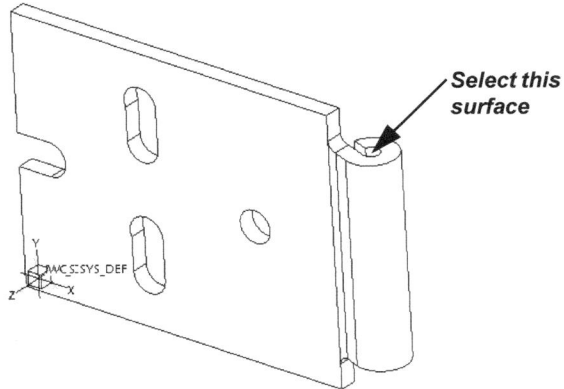

**Select this surface**

**Figure 6–13**

7. In the *Force* area, in the *X* field, enter **375**.

8. Click OK . The model displays as shown in Figure 6–14.

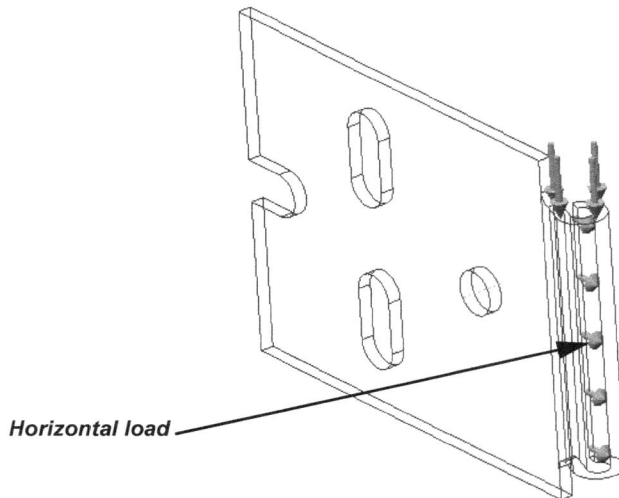

**Horizontal load**

**Figure 6–14**

**Task 5 - Constrain the surface of the hinge plate.**

1. Click . The Constraint dialog box opens.

2. In the *Name* field, enter **hinge_surface_const**. Select the surface shown in Figure 6–15, and fix all of the Translations.

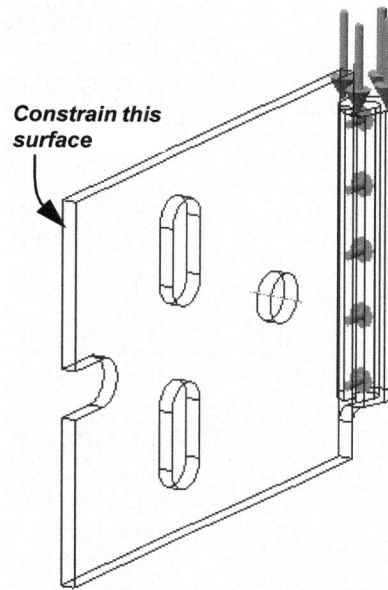

**Figure 6–15**

3. Click OK . The model displays as shown in Figure 6–16.

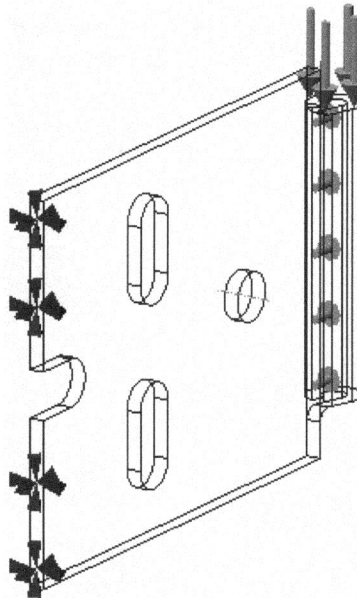

**Figure 6–16**

## Task 6 - Apply the material.

1. Assign STEEL to the model. The following values are the default material properties for HS-low-alloy steel (STEEL):

   - Poisson = 0.27
   - Young's modulus = 199948 MPa
   - Coeff of thermal expansion = 1.17e-5 /C
   - Density = 7.82708e-9 tonne/mm^3

## Analysis Tasks

## Task 7 - Set up and run the analysis.

1. Set up a Multi-Pass Adaptive analysis with a 5% convergence and a maximum polynomial order of 9. For the name of the analysis, enter **hinge_multi_pass**.

2. Run the analysis. It should converge after 6 passes.

## Task 8 - Display the results.

*The measure for this practice is von Mises stress.*

1. Create and display a fringe color plot of the von Mises stress for the hinge. It displays as shown in Figure 6–17.

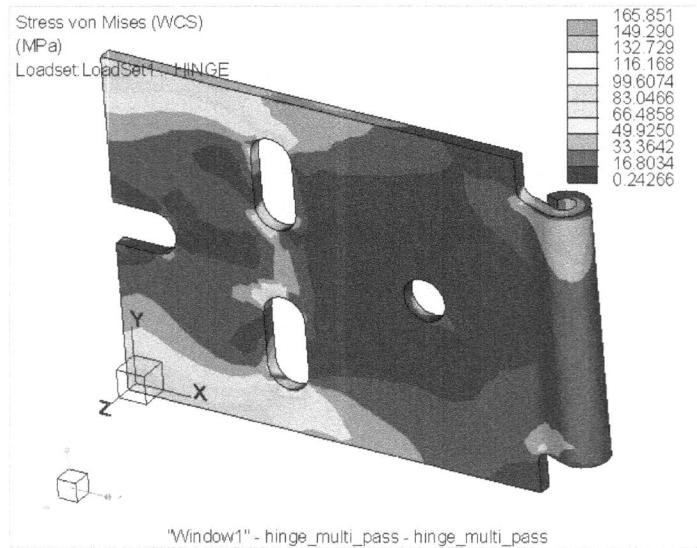

**Figure 6–17**

2. Exit the Creo Simulate Results.

*Design variables = Creo dimensions or parameters.*

## Summary

In the previous tasks, you ensured that no errors have occurred in the model and that convergence is achieved. In the following tasks, you will note that the changes in the measure indicate small variations in each parameter. This is a local sensitivity study.

The maximum von Mises stress is approximately 166MPa. The yield strength for the hinge material is 230MPa. The difference (230 - 166 = 64MPa) leaves a good margin for weight optimization.

## Task 9 - Run a local sensitivity study.

In this task, you will vary the parameters by a small amount ($\pm$ 2%) and examine the effect of the small parameter's variation on your measure (von Mises stress).

1. Open the Analyses and Design Studies dialog box and select **File>New Sensitivity Design Study.** The Sensitivity Study Definition dialog box opens.

2. In the *Name* field, enter **hinge_local**.

3. Expand the Type drop-down list and select **Local Sensitivity**.

4. In the *Analyses* field, highlight **hinge_multi_pass (Static)**.

5. In the Model Tree, click ⊢ᷓ and select **cut id 226**. In the *Tools* tab, select **Switch Symbols**. The model displays as shown in Figure 6–18.

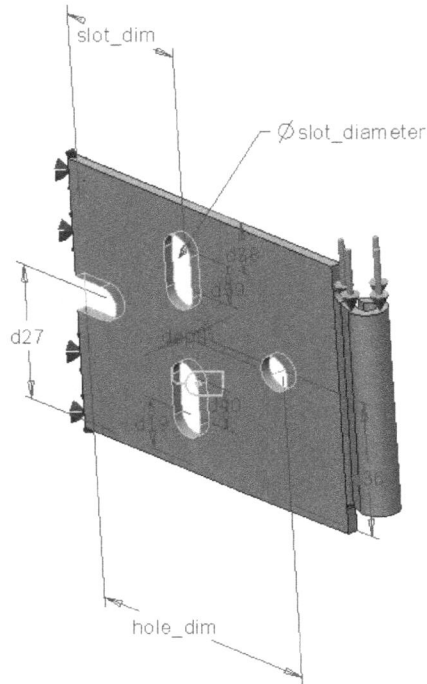

**Figure 6–18**

*Select the **Cut id 226** in the Model Tree. The dimensions display. Select the dimension symbol named **slot_dim**.*

6. Select **slot_dim (40mm)** of the Cut id 226.

7. Click ⊢ᷓ.

8. Select **hole_dim (75mm)** of the Cut id 226.

9. Click ⊢ᷓ.

10. Select **depth (3mm)** of the Cut id 226.

11. Click ⊢ᷓ.

12. Select **slot_diameter (10mm)** of the Cut id 226.

13. The Sensitivity Study Definition dialog box opens as shown in Figure 6–19.

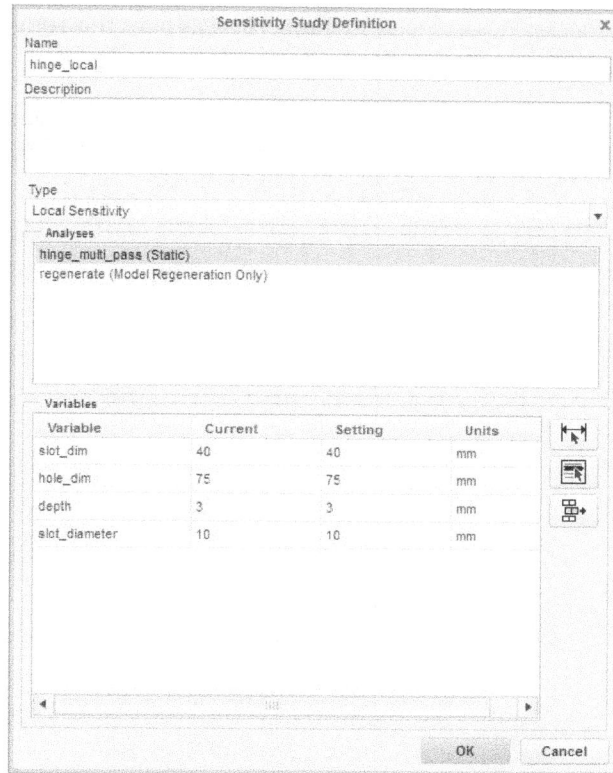

**Figure 6–19**

14. Click  OK  to close the Sensitivity Study Definition dialog box.

15. Run the design study. It should take a few minutes to solve.

## Results Tasks

## Task 10 - Display the results.

1. In the Analyses and Design Studies dialog box, click ⬚. The Result Window Definition dialog box opens, as shown in Figure 6–20.

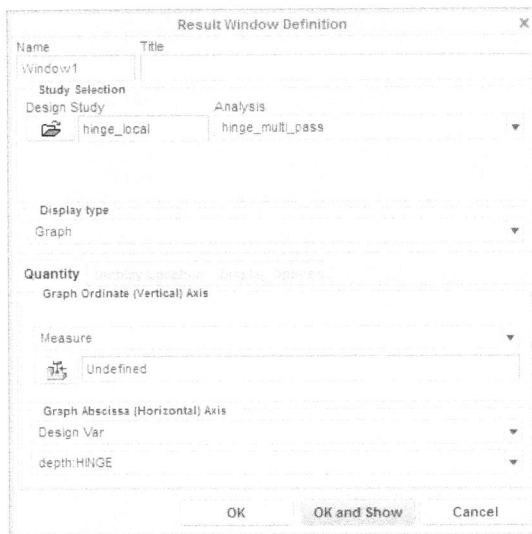

**Figure 6–20**

2. Click ⬚ and select **max_stress_vm** in the list of predefined measures.

3. Expand the drop-down menu at the bottom and select **slot_dim: HINGE**. The dialog box opens as shown in Figure 6–21.

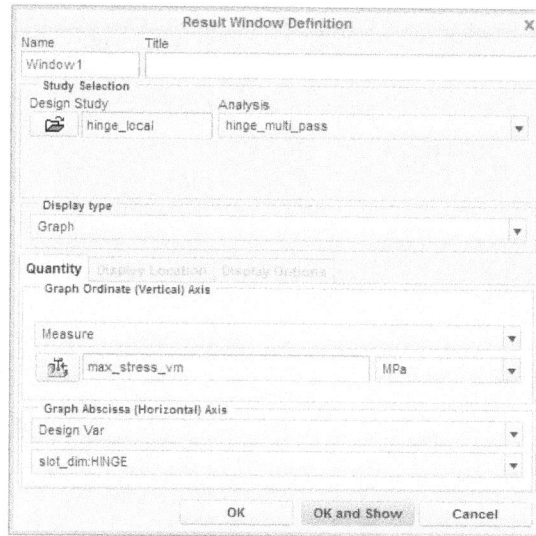

**Figure 6–21**

4. Click OK and Show . The result graph displays as shown in Figure 6–22.

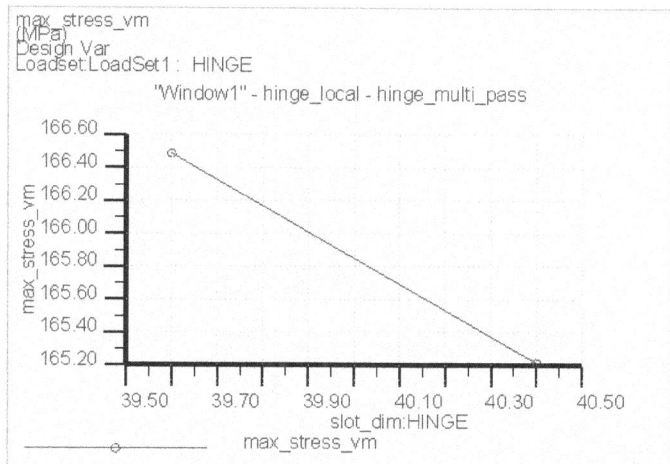

**Figure 6–22**

Examine the graph (you can double-click on the points in the graph to get exact readings). Note that the slot_dim dimension has been varied in the study from *39.6mm* to **40.4mm**, which is ± 2% of the nominal 40mm, while max_stress_vm changed from *166.5MPa* to **165.2MPa**, which is only ± 0.4% of the average 165.85MPa at 40mm. In other words, for every 1% change in the dimension value, there is a 0.2% change in the stress result.

5. Repeat Steps 1 through 4 to create **max_stress_vm** sensitivity graphs for the **depth, hole_dim,** and **slot_diameter** dimensions. The results are shown in Figure 6–23.

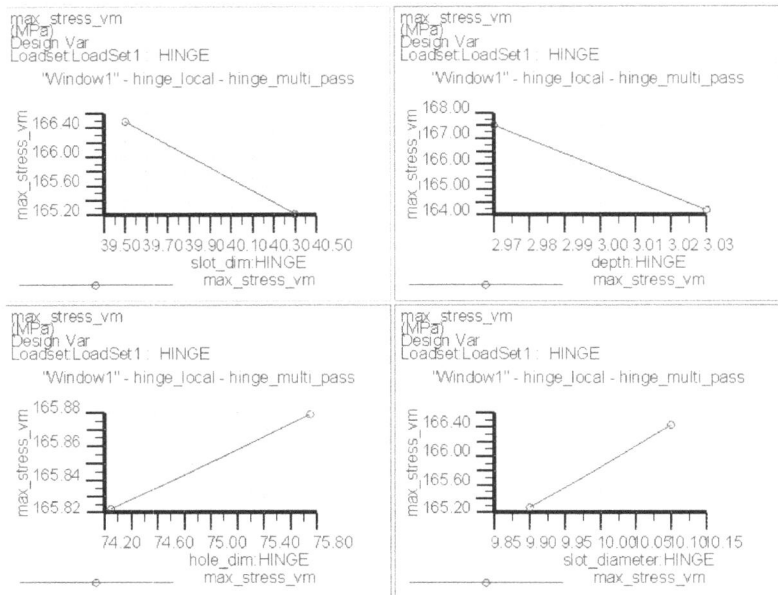

**Figure 6–23**

Examine the graphs and determine which dimensions have the greatest effect on the maximum stress in the model.

6. Close the results window.

## Summary

At this stage, you have completed the local sensitivity studies and created the result windows. Use local sensitivity studies to determine which parameters have the greatest effect on a measure (the maximum von Mises stress) with a small variation in the parameter values. The result windows indicate that the measure is sensitive to the **slot_dim**, **hole_diameter**, and **depth** parameters. Examining the graphs in Figure 6–23 determines that the measure is not sensitive to the **hole_dim** parameter. The difference in measure within the parameter range (4%) is only 165.88 -165.82 = 0.06MPa.

Three parameters are now available for the next task, in which you will run a global sensitivity study and note the variations of all of the parameters over a larger range of user-defined values.

*If the von Mises stress is not sensitive to a specific parameter, the parameter is not available for the next task.*

## Task 11 - Create a global sensitivity design study.

In this task, you will examine the variation of all of the parameters over a range of user-defined values and examine the effect of the parameter's variation on your measure (von Mises stress) by creating a global sensitivity analysis.

1. In the Analyses and Design Studies dialog box, select the **hinge_local** study and click .

2. Select the **Copy_of_hinge_local** study and click . The Sensitivity Study Definition dialog box opens as shown in Figure 6–24.

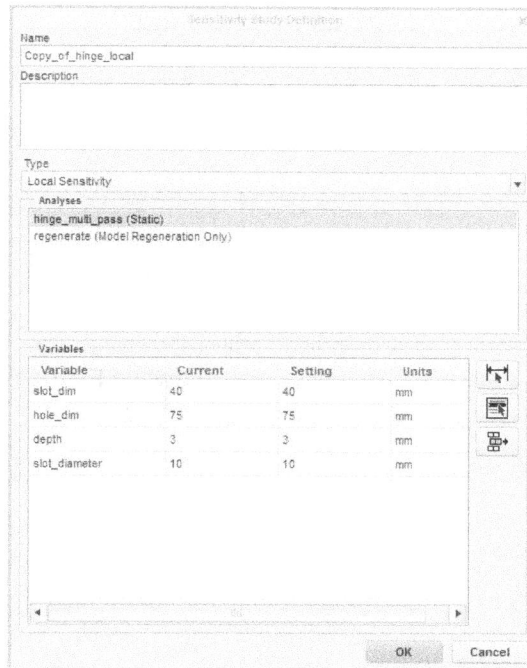

**Figure 6–24**

3. In the *Name* field, enter **hinge_global**.

4. Expand the Type drop-down list and select **Global Sensitivity**.

5. Select **hole_dim** from the variables and click to remove it.

*Use the **Options** button to set the **Repeat P-Loop Convergence** option when the parameter's range is high and the shape of the model changes considerably.*

6. In the Variables, select the **Start** and **End** value, as shown in Figure 6–25.

**Figure 6–25**

7. Click Options... . The Design Study Options dialog box opens as shown in Figure 6–26.

**Figure 6–26**

8. Click Shape Animate the Model and step through the model shape animation to ensure that the model regenerates on each sensitivity study step. Restore the model to its original shape in the end.

9. Click Close to close the Design Study Options dialog box.

10. Click OK to close the Sensitivity Study Definition dialog box.

11. Run the design study if time permits.

## Task 12 - Display the results.

*Select **hinge_global** as the Design Study in the canned_results directory.*

1. Create three von Mises stress sensitivity graph windows, one for each variable. The window for the slot_dim dimension displays as shown in Figure 6–27.

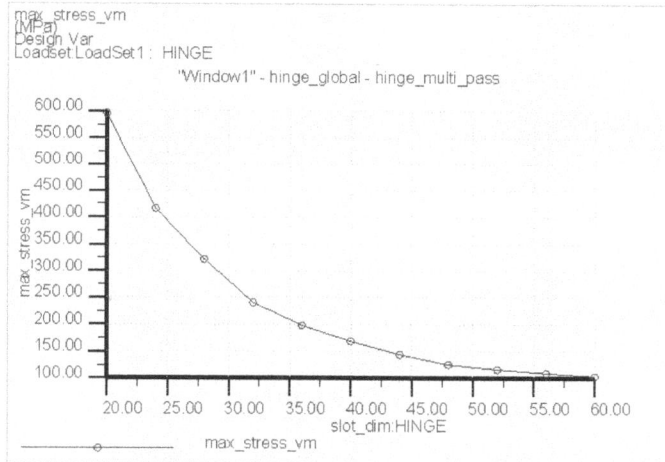

**Figure 6–27**

The window for the depth dimension displays as shown in Figure 6–28.

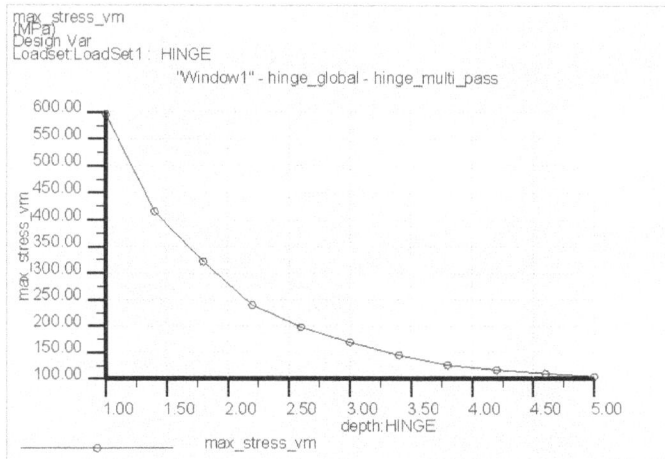

**Figure 6–28**

The window for the slot_diameter dimension displays as shown in Figure 6–29.

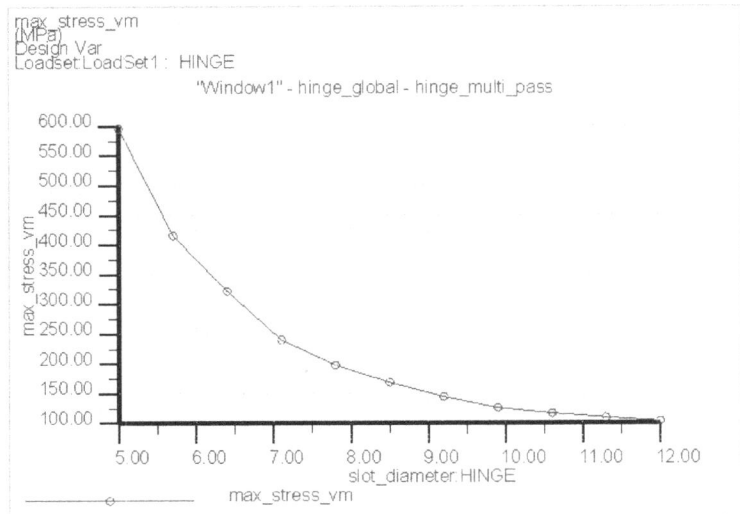

max_stress_vm
(MPa)
Design Var
LoadSet:LoadSet1 : HINGE

"Window1" - hinge_global - hinge_multi_pass

**Figure 6–29**

2. Close the results.

## Summary

At this stage, you have completed your global sensitivity study and examined the sensitivity graphs. The sensitivity graphs indicate that the following dimensions could be optimized for minimum von Mises stress:

- Maximum depth (plate thickness)

- Minimum slot_diameter (holes diameter)

- Maximum slot_dim

In the next tasks, you will locate the dimension values that result in the minimum weight of the hinge model without exceeding a set value of von Mises stress.

## Task 13 - Create an optimization design study.

In this task, you will create a design study to optimize your model weight.

*You ran this study to determine the best possible combination of parameters for the minimum von Mises stress.*

*This is the most calculation-intensive part of the practice.*

1. In the Analyses and Design Studies dialog box, select **File>New Optimization Design Study**. The Optimization Study Definition dialog box opens.

2. In the *Name* field, enter **hinge_optimize**.

3. Configure the Optimization Design Study Definition dialog box as shown in Figure 6–30.

**Figure 6–30**

4. Click **OK** to close the Optimization Study Definition dialog box.

5. Run the design study if time permits.

## Task 14 - Display the results.

In this task, you will locate the optimum model mass and dimension values. You will also create two graphs displaying the optimization process for measures: **max_stress_vm** and **total_mass.**

*Select **hinge_optimize** as the design study in the canned_results directory.*

*Note that the unit mass is metric tons and the unit length is mm.*

1. If you have run the design study, highlight **hinge_optimize** in the Analyses and Design Studies dialog box and click 🗐. The Run Status window displays.

2. Otherwise, locate and open **hinge_optimize.rpt** (with Notepad) in the *hinge_optimize* directory.

3. Locate the optimum model mass and parameter values as shown in Figure 6–31.

```
Best Design Found:
Parameters:
    depth                    2.85
    slot_diameter           10.5
    slot_dim                  40
Goal:  2.0017e-04
```

**Figure 6–31**

## Task 15 - Create two graphs for the measures:
## max_stress_vm and total_mass.

1. Create a graph for the **max_stress_vm** measure versus the **Optimization Pass**. The graph displays as shown in Figure 6–32.

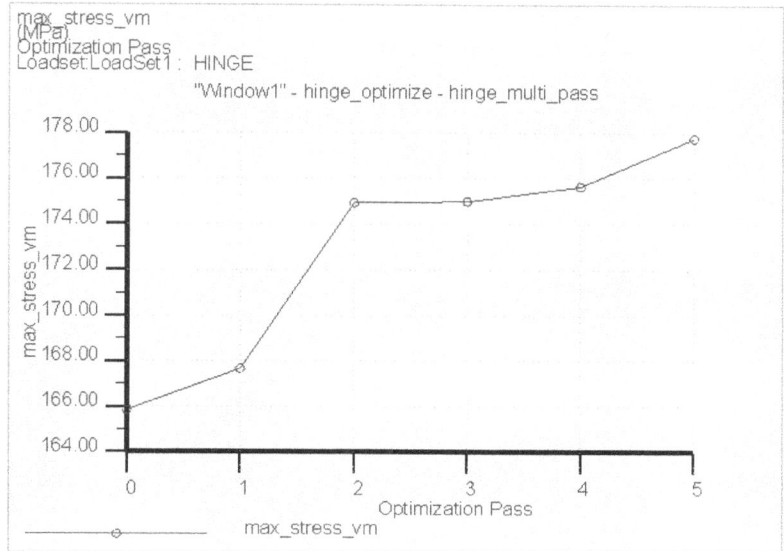

**Figure 6–32**

2. Create a graph for the **total_mass** measure versus **Optimization Pass**. The graph displays as shown in Figure 6–33.

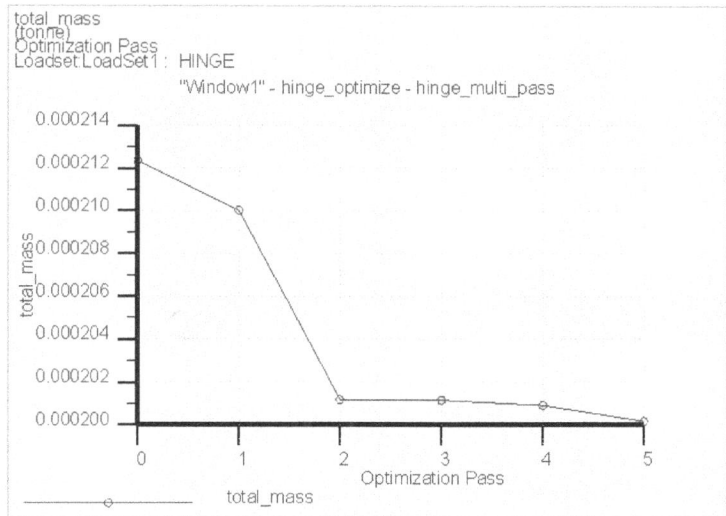

**Figure 6–33**

Note that the optimization algorithm reduced the weight of the hinge from approximately *0.000212* tonne to **0.000200** tonne, which is approximately 5.7% less than the original design.

## Task 16 - Display the stress plot.

1. Create and display a fringe plot for the von Mises stress in the optimized model. The result plot displays as shown in Figure 6–34.

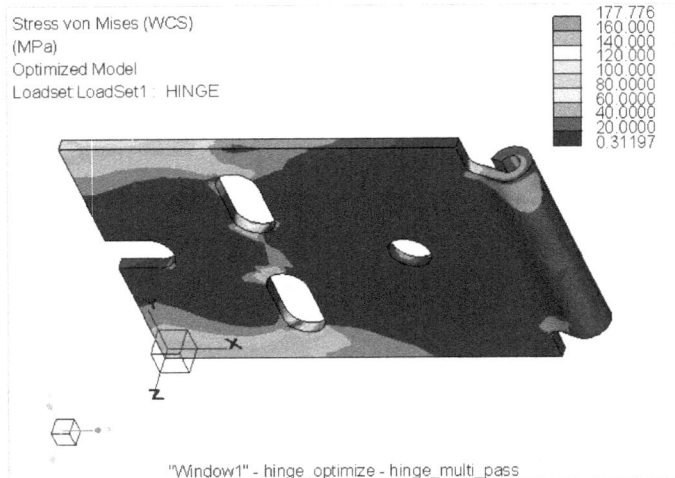

Figure 6–34

2. Close the results and save the model in Creo Parametric.

# Chapter 7

## Assembly Interfaces

This chapter contains the following topics:

- **Types of Interfaces**
- **Bonded Interface**
- **Free Interface**
- **Contact Interface**
- **Reviewing Interfaces**
- **Setting Up Contact Analysis**
- **Mesh Refinement**

# 7.1 Types of Interfaces

**Learning Objective**

Understand the types of part interfaces in Creo Simulate.

Interfaces in Creo Simulate define the treatment of mated or overlapping components or surfaces in an assembly model.

There are three types of Interfaces in Creo Simulate Structural:

- **Bonded:** The interfacing surfaces are essentially *glued* together.

- **Free:** The interfacing surfaces are not connected in any way.

- **Contact:** The interfacing surfaces cannot interpenetrate, but can still separate and/or slide along each other under the applied loading.

There are also three types of Interfaces in Creo Simulate Thermal:

- **Bonded:** Full transfer of heat, without any thermal resistance, through the interface.

- **Adiabatic:** No heat transfer through the interface.

- **Thermal Resistance:** Simulates a *thermal gap* between the surfaces, where the rate of heat transfer through the interface is determined by a thermal resistance coefficient.

## Default Interface

By default, Creo Simulate treats all of the mated surfaces in the model according to the option selected in the Default Interface drop-down list in the Model Setup dialog box, as shown in Figure 7–1.

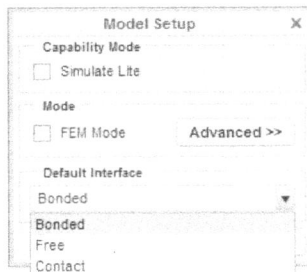

**Figure 7–1**

# 7.2 Bonded Interface

**Learning Objective**

Understand how to create Bonded Interfaces.

A Bonded Interface is a connection that essentially *glues* two parts together. Displacement continuity between the interfacing surfaces is ensured (i.e., the surfaces remain *attached* to each other during the analysis).

This type of interface is typically used for, but not limited to, bonded, glued, surface-welded, etc., connections between parts in an assembly. The key criterion for the correct use is either no or negligible separation or the sliding of the two surfaces under applied loading.

The applied forces are fully transmitted through the Bonded Interfaces. Creo Simulate automatically creates a simulation measure to calculate the resultant force over each Bonded Interface.

Use the following steps to create a Bonded Interface:

1. In the *Refine* tab, in the *Connections* area, click ⬚ to open the Interface Definition dialog box.
2. Expand the Type drop-down list and select **Bonded**. The Interface Definition dialog box opens as shown in Figure 7–2.

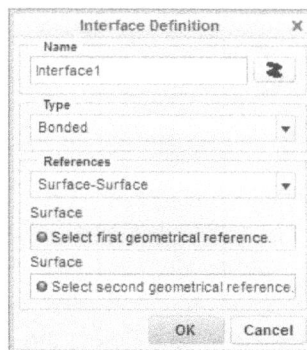

**Figure 7–2**

3. Select the geometrical references (**Surface-Surface** or **Component-Component**).
4. Click OK to finish.

# 7.3 Free Interface

**Learning Objective**

Understand how to create Free Interfaces.

A Free Interface does not connect the two surfaces in any way. The surfaces can freely separate or pass through each other under the applied loading, and no forces are transmitted through the interface. The surfaces ignore each other.

This type of interface should only be used for parts that are expected to separate and never to press against each other under the loading in the model. The analysis results should also be carefully reviewed afterward, to ensure there is no interpenetration of the surfaces in the model, which would otherwise render the analysis as incorrect.

Use the following steps to create a Free Interface:

1. In the *Refine* tab, in the *Connections* area, click 🔲 to open the Interface Definition dialog box.
2. Expand the Type drop-down list and select **Free**. The Interface Definition dialog box opens as shown in Figure 7–3.

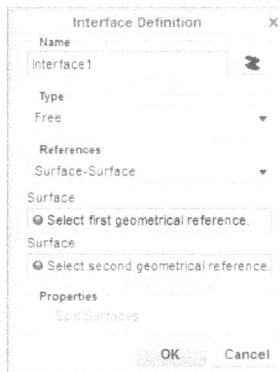

**Figure 7–3**

3. Select the geometrical references (**Surface-Surface** or **Component-Component**).

4. Click ⬚ OK ⬚ to finish.

# 7.4 Contact Interface

**Learning Objective**

Understand the Contact Interface properties.

Understand how to create Contact Interface manually.

Understand how to create Contact Interface automatically.

In a Contact Interface, the two surfaces are free to move apart and/or slide along each other under the applied loading, but they cannot interpenetrate. The surfaces are initially permitted to be at a clearance, but might come into contact during the analysis. Only compressive normal stresses are transmitted through the interface (i.e., the interfacing surfaces cannot *pull* each other).

The Contact Interface is the most realistic model for simulating parts that must remain separate from each other during the analysis, yet do not interpenetrate. From the FEA standpoint, the Contact Interface represents a boundary condition that changes during the loading. For example, when a chain roller is pressed against the sprocket, the line contact changes to an area contact.

In the example shown in Figure 7–4, there is a gap between the plate and block initially (configuration 1 in Figure 7–4). Once the load has been applied, the plate bends freely, until it comes into contact with the block, as shown in configuration 2 in Figure 7–4. If the load is further increased, the area of contact shifts from the edge of the plate to the edge of the block (configuration 3 in Figure 7–4). Therefore, the contact area and location change depending on the amount of load applied.

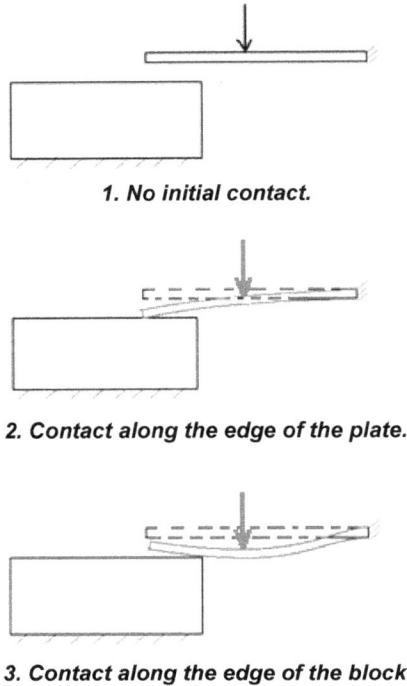

*1. No initial contact.*

*2. Contact along the edge of the plate.*

*3. Contact along the edge of the block.*

**Figure 7–4**

Contact in Creo Simulate can be frictionless or with infinite friction. The latter means that the surfaces can still separate, but they cannot slide along each other in the tangential direction under the loading.

Only compressive forces are transmitted through a frictionless Contact Interface. Creo Simulate automatically creates simulation measures to calculate the contact area and the resultant force over a Contact Interface.

Contact with infinite friction transmits tangential forces as well. Creo Simulate automatically creates a simulation measure to calculate the maximum traction in the contact, as well as slippage indicator measures. A positive value of a slippage measure indicates that the surfaces in contact might have slid relative to each other. Therefore, the assumption of infinite friction is not accurate.

To create a Contact Interface, click ⬚ to open the Interface Definition dialog box, and select **Contact** option in the Type drop-down list, as shown in Figure 7–5.

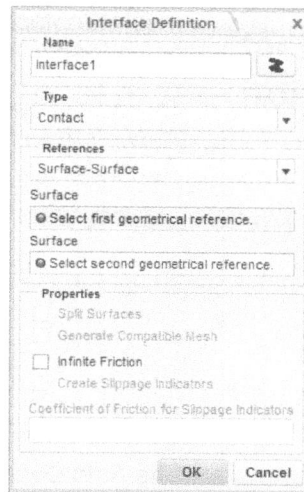

**Figure 7–5**

The options in the dialog box are as follows:

| Section | Option | Description |
|---|---|---|
| References | Surface-Surface | User selects the surfaces that are in contact, or might come into contact during the analysis. |
| | Component-Component | Creo Simulate creates Contact Interfaces between any two surfaces that satisfy the user-defined **Separation Distance** and **Angle** criteria. |
| Properties | Split Surfaces | Creo Simulate splits the contact surfaces along their boundaries. |
| | Generate Compatible Mesh | Creo Simulate creates geometrically coincident mesh node locations on the contact surfaces. |

| | | |
|---|---|---|
| | **Infinite Friction** | Creates a Contact with infinite friction. |
| | **Create Slippage Indicators** | Creates slippage measures. Only available with the **Infinite Friction** option. |
| | **Coefficient of Friction for Slippage Indicators** | Specify the friction coefficient that is used to calculate the slippage indicators. Only available with the **Infinite Friction** option. |

## Automatic Contact Detection

Creo Simulate has a tool that enables you to automatically create Contact Interfaces between parts in the assembly, based on user-specified criteria.

To start the auto detection, expand the *Interface* area in the *Refine Model* tab, as shown in Figure 7–6, and select **Detect Contacts**.

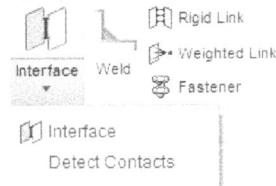

**Figure 7–6**

The Auto Detect Contacts dialog box opens as shown in Figure 7–7.

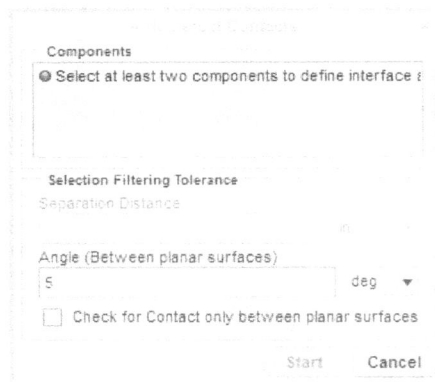

**Figure 7–7**

The options in the dialog box are as follows:

| Option | Description |
|---|---|
| **Separation Distance** | Maximum distance between surface pairs on which you want to define a contact. |
| **Angle (between planar surfaces)** | Only surfaces that are at an angle less than the specified are considered. |
| **Check for Contact only between planar surfaces** | Creates contacts only between planar surfaces. |

# 7.5 Reviewing Interfaces

**Learning Objective**

Understand how to review the interfaces in your model.

Once created, all of the interfaces display under **Connections> Interfaces** in the Model Tree, as shown in Figure 7–8. You can review and delete the interfaces in the model using the Model Tree.

**Figure 7–8**

You can also visualize the interfaces in your model by clicking

in the *Refine Model* tab, and selecting the Connectivity options as shown in Figure 7–9.

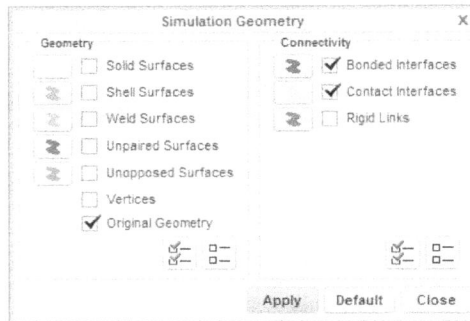

**Figure 7–9**

Once you click  Apply , the model displays in Wireframe mode, with all of the interfaces shaded and color-coded, as shown in Figure 7–10.

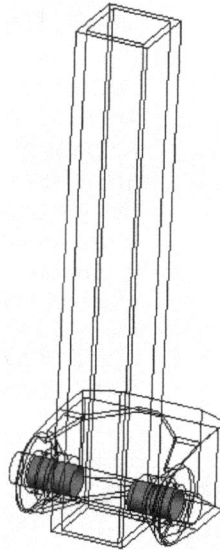

**Figure 7–10**

# 7.6  Setting Up Contact Analysis

**Learning Objective**

Understand how to set up an analysis with Contact Interfaces.

Structural analysis with Contact Interfaces is a non-linear FEA analysis. A non-linear analysis is solved in small steps (controlled by the FEA solver), with the applied loads gradually incremented from no load to the full load, and with the equation system solved on every load increment. A non-linear FEA takes much longer to solve than a comparable linear analysis. Therefore, use caution when setting up an analysis with many Contact Interfaces.

The Static Analysis Definition dialog box for an analysis with Contact Interfaces is shown in Figure 7–11.

Figure 7–11

The following options must be set to run a non-linear analysis with Contact Interfaces:

1. Ensure that the **Nonlinear/Use Load Histories** and **Contacts** options are selected.

2. In the *Constraints* and the *Loads* areas, use $f(x)$ to define the time histories for the constraints and loads in your model. The default time history is a simple ramp function with the load linearly increased from zero to the full load.

3. Set the Convergence options:

   • **Localized Mesh Refinement:** Automatically refines the mesh in the contact regions. Only available with the Single-Pass Adaptive convergence method.

   • **Check Contact Force:** Checks to ensure convergence on contact forces.

   • **For Press Fit, Ignore Interpenetration Larger Than:** Ignores interpenetrations at Contact Interfaces that are larger than the length specified.

4. In the *Output* tab, select the **Output Steps**. This setting defines the load intervals (also called *load percentage factors*) at which Creo Simulate calculates the full results for displaying.

   • **Automatic Steps within Range:** The results are only calculated for the full load.

   • **User-defined Output Steps:** Enables you to define the load intervals for which the output is to be calculated, as shown in the example in Figure 7–12.

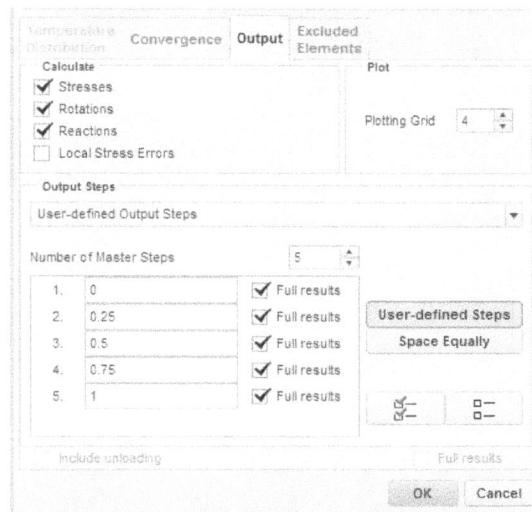

**Figure 7–12**

# 7.7 Mesh Refinement

**Learning Objective**

Understand how to refine the mesh in contact areas.

The accuracy of the Contact analyses are affected by the mesh density in the contact areas. The element size should be smaller than the contact region.

Use the following guidelines to achieve this condition:

- Create Surface Regions to separate areas of contact from the rest of the part surface.

- Use the **AutoGEM Control, Maximum Element Size Control** option, as shown in Figure 7–13, to apply a smaller element size in the contact areas

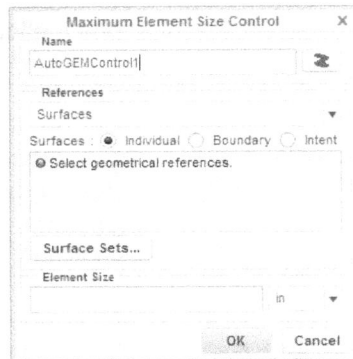

**Figure 7–13**

- Use 2D models when possible. Doing so improves accuracy, eases setup, and reduces run time.

# Practice 7a

# Door Handle Assembly

**Learning Objective**

✓ Understand how to create Free and Contact Interfaces.

✓ Understand how to set up and run a contact analysis.

In this practice, you will set up a contact analysis on a part of the door handle assembly. The assembly model is shown in Figure 7–14.

*The model has been defeatured (various rounds and blends have been removed).*

**Figure 7–14**

The area of interest is only the contact between the sleeve and barrel. The assembly that you analyze consists of a sleeve part, the barrel part, and the door slab part, as shown in Figure 7–15. The model will be solved using one possible simulation scenario.

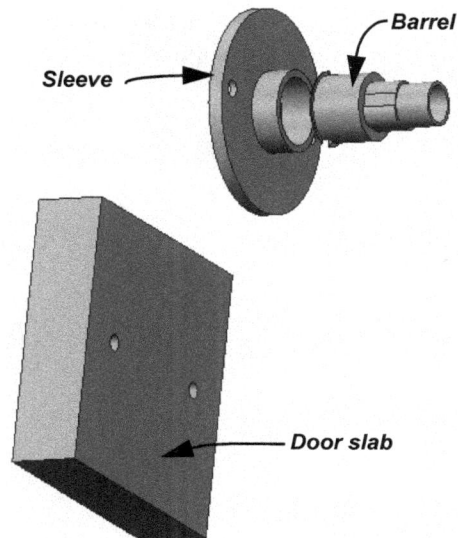

**Figure 7–15**

## Modeling Tasks

### Task 1 - Open the model and launch Creo Simulate.

1. Open **door_handle.asm** in Creo Parametric. The assembly displays as shown in Figure 7–16.

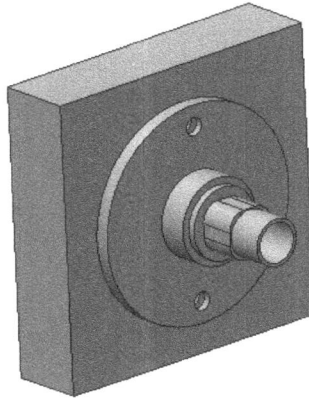

**Figure 7–16**

2. Ensure that the unit system is set to **IPS**.

3. Select **Applications>Simulate** to launch Creo Simulate.

### Task 2 - Apply the loads.

In this task, you will apply loads to the barrel end surface shown in Figure 7–17.

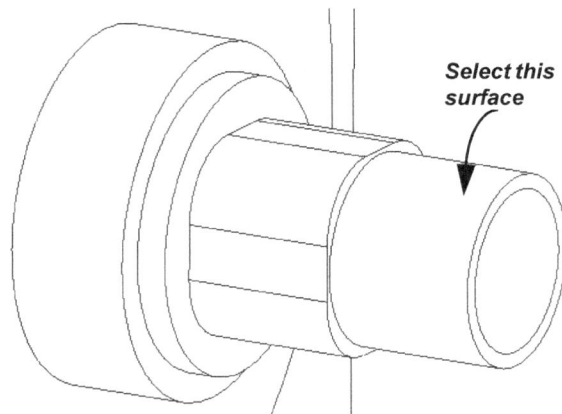

*Select this surface*

**Figure 7–17**

*To apply the load, use the **Uniform** and **Total Load** options in the Distribution area in the Force/Moment dialog box. Note that the load is applied in the Z-direction.*

1. Apply **100lbs** to the surface in the Z-direction. For the *Name*, enter **handle_load**. The model displays as shown in Figure 7–18.

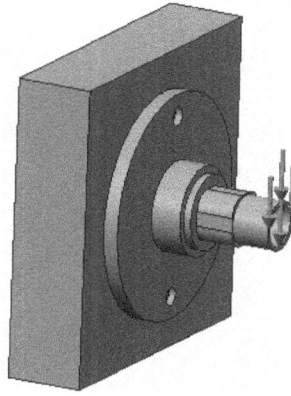

**Figure 7–18**

## Task 3 - Apply the constraints.

1. Fully constrain the door slab end surfaces, as shown in Figure 7–19.

2. For the *Name*, enter **door_const**. The model displays as shown in Figure 7–19.

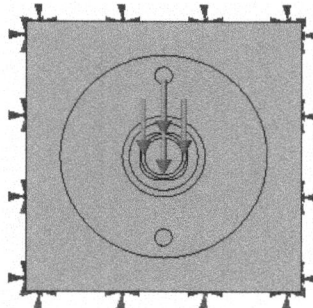

**Figure 7–19**

3. Constrain the barrel vertex shown in Figure 7–20 in the X- and Y-directions to prevent the rotation and slippage of the barrel (you will use a frictionless Contact Interface in this analysis). Ensure that the selected vertex lies on the ASM_RIGHT datum plane.

4. For the *Name*, enter **barrel_const**. The model displays as shown in Figure 7–20.

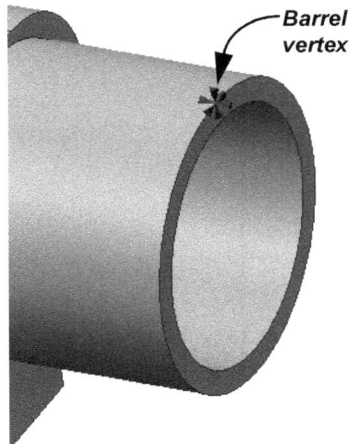

**Figure 7–20**

## Task 4 - Create a Contact Interface.

In this task, you will create a Contact Interface between the sleeve and the barrel.

1. Click [ ]. The Interface Definition dialog box opens as shown in Figure 7–21.

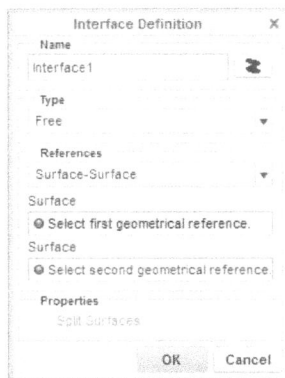

**Figure 7–21**

2. Expand the Type drop-down list and select **Contact**.

3. Expand the References drop-down list and select **Component-Component**.

4. Select the **SLEEVE** and **BARREL** parts as the references. The Interface Definition dialog box opens as shown in Figure 7–22.

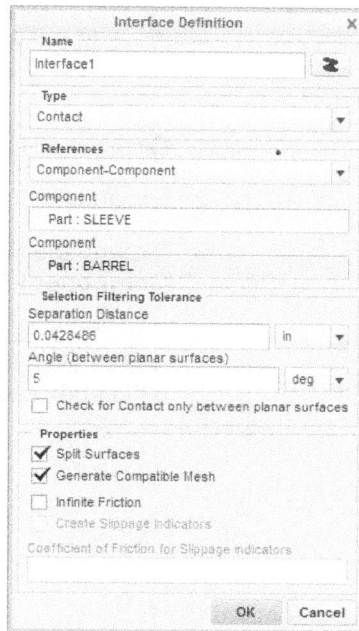

**Figure 7–22**

5. Accept all of the other defaults and click OK to finish. The model displays as shown in Figure 7–23.

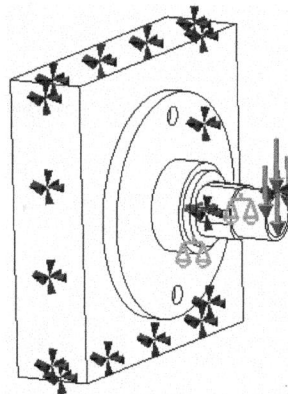

**Figure 7–23**

## Task 5 - Create a Free Interface.

The sleeve and door slab in this analysis are assumed to be only interacting through the screws. In this task, you will create a Free Interface to ensure that the barrel is not pressing against the door slab along their surfaces during the analysis.

1. Click 🗔. The Interface Definition dialog box opens.

2. Expand the Type drop-down list and select **Free**.

3. Expand the References drop-down list and select **Component-Component**.

4. Select the **SLEEVE** and **DOOR** parts as the references and accept all of the other default options. The Interface Definition dialog box opens as shown in Figure 7–24.

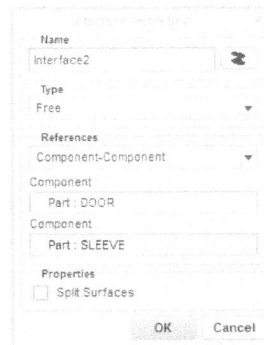

**Figure 7–24**

5. Accept all of the other defaults and click OK to finish. The model displays as shown in Figure 7–25.

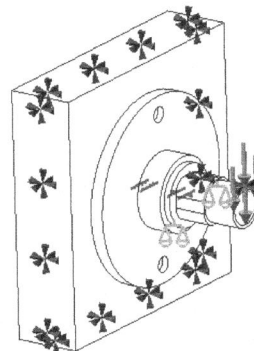

**Figure 7–25**

## Task 6 - Create rigid links.

In this task, you will create Rigid Links to model the screws that attach the sleeve to the door slab.

1. In the *Connections* area, click 🔲. The Rigid Link Definition dialog box opens as shown in Figure 7–26.

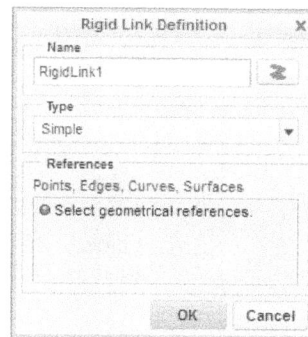

**Figure 7–26**

2. Select the inside cylindrical surfaces of the top hole in the sleeve and of the top hole in the door slab, as shown in Figure 7–27.

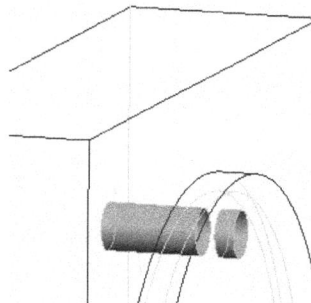

**Figure 7–27**

3. The Rigid Link Definition dialog box opens as shown in Figure 7–28.

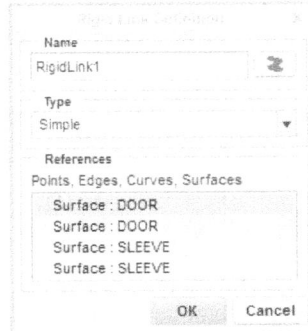

**Figure 7–28**

4. Click OK to finish. The Rigid Link displays as shown in Figure 7–29.

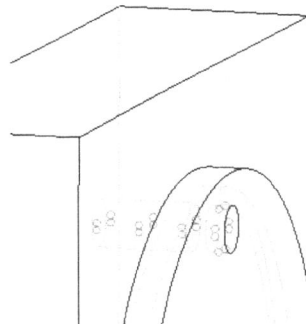

**Figure 7–29**

5. Repeat Steps 1 to 4 to create a Rigid Link for the bottom holes.

6. Use the Simulation Display box to hide the loads and constraints. The model displays as shown in Figure 7–30.

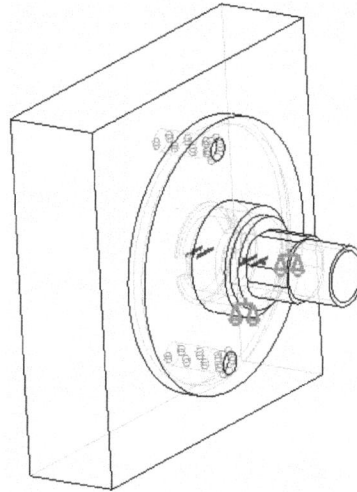

**Figure 7–30**

## Task 7 - Review the connections.

1. In the *Refine Model* tab, in the *AutoGEM* area, click ⬒ to open the Simulation Geometry dialog box.

2. Select the options shown in Figure 7–31.

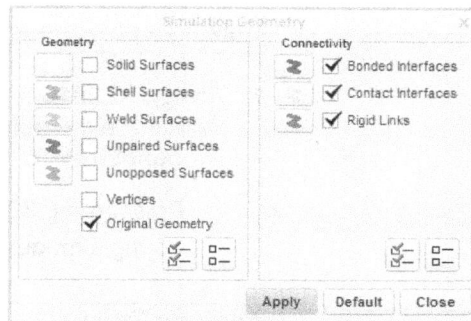

**Figure 7–31**

3. Click  Apply  . The model displays as shown in Figure 7–32.

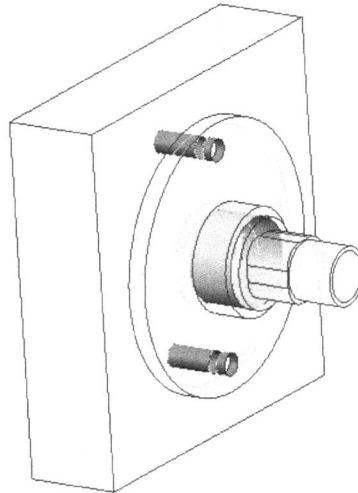

**Figure 7–32**

Examine the model display. Locate the Contact Interfaces and the Rigid Links. Ensure that there are no Bonded Interfaces in the model.

4. Click  Close  to finish.

## Task 8 - Apply the material.

1. Assign **AL2014** to all of the assembly parts. The following values are the default material properties for Aluminum, wrought 2014-T6:

   • Poisson = 0.33
   • Young's modulus = 1.06e+07 psi

## Analysis Tasks

## Task 9 - Set up and run the analysis.

1. Set up a Single-Pass Adaptive convergence analysis. For the analysis name, enter **door_handle** and keep all of the other defaults. The Static Analysis Definition dialog box opens as shown in Figure 7–33.

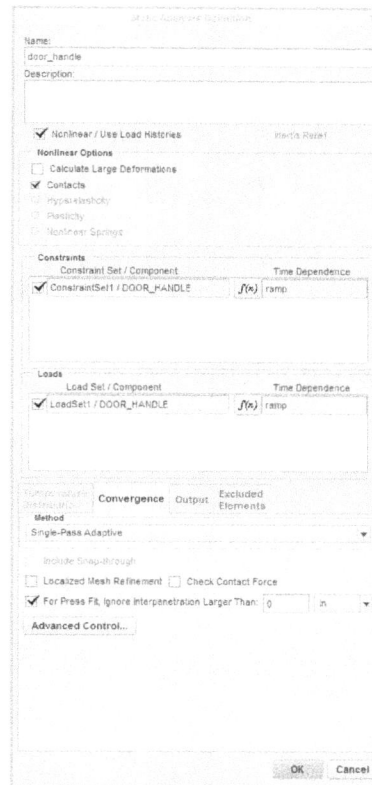

**Figure 7–33**

2. Select the *Output* tab.

3. Expand the Output Steps drop-down list and select **User-defined Output Steps**.

4. For the *Number of Master Steps*, select **5**.

5. Click **User-defined Steps** and **Space Equally**. In the Static Analysis Definition dialog box, the *Output* area displays as shown in Figure 7–34.

**Figure 7–34**

6. Click OK to close the Static Analysis Definition dialog box.

7. In the Analyses and Design Studies dialog box, in the **Info** menu, select **Check Model** to check the validity of the model.

8. Run this analysis if time permits.

## Results Tasks

## Task 10 - Display the deformation results.

*You can use*
***door_handle*** *as the design study in the canned_results directory.*

1. In the Analyses and Design Studies dialog box, click 🖳. In the Result Window Definition dialog box, in the Steps list, highlight the last row as shown in Figure 7–35.

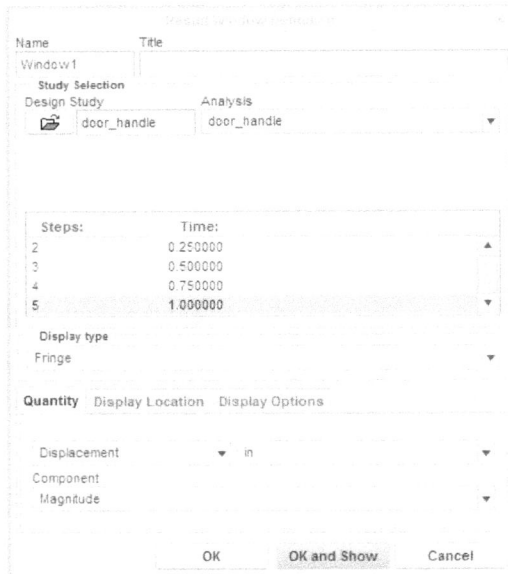

| Name | Title | |
|------|-------|--|
| Window1 | | |

Study Selection

| Design Study | Analysis | |
|--------------|----------|--|
| 🗁 door_handle | door_handle | ▼ |

| Steps: | Time: | |
|--------|-------|--|
| 2 | 0.250000 | ▲ |
| 3 | 0.500000 | |
| 4 | 0.750000 | |
| 5 | 1.000000 | ▼ |

Display type

Fringe ▼

**Quantity** Display Location Display Options

Displacement ▼ in ▼

Component

Magnitude ▼

OK    OK and Show    Cancel

**Figure 7–35**

2. Select the *Display Options* tab. Select the **Deformed**, **Overlay Undeformed**, and **Animate** options, as shown in Figure 7–36.

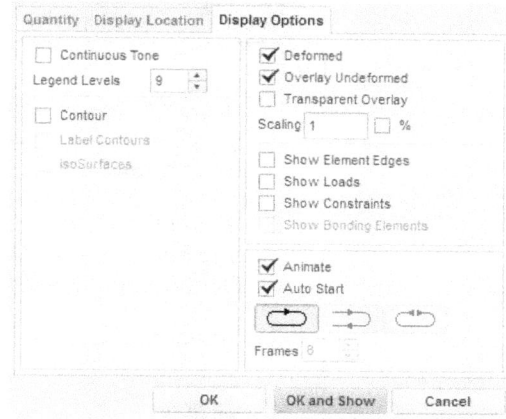

**Figure 7–36**

3. Click **OK and Show** to display and animate the Displacement Magnitude result.

4. Note that the animation frames correspond to the Load Factor, from 0 (no load) to 1 (full load). Stop the animation at Step 4. The model displays as shown in Figure 7–37.

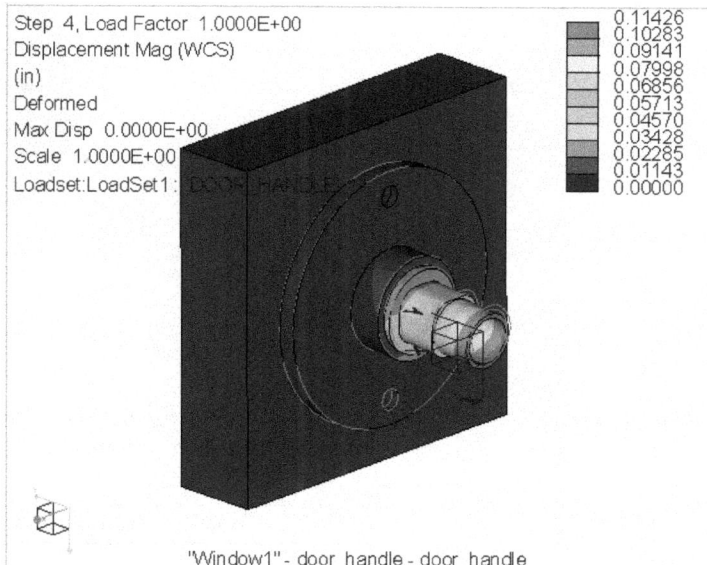

**Figure 7–37**

## Task 11 - Display the stress results.

1. Click 🖼 to edit the result window. In the *Steps* area, highlight the last row, and in the *Quantity* area, select **Stress, von Mises**.

2. Select the *Display Location* tab. Expand the drop-down list and select **Components/Layers**. Set the visibility of the **DOOR** component to **Blanked**.

3. Select the *Display Options* tab and clear the **Animate** option.

4. Click   OK and Show  . The von Mises stress plot displays as shown in Figure 7–38.

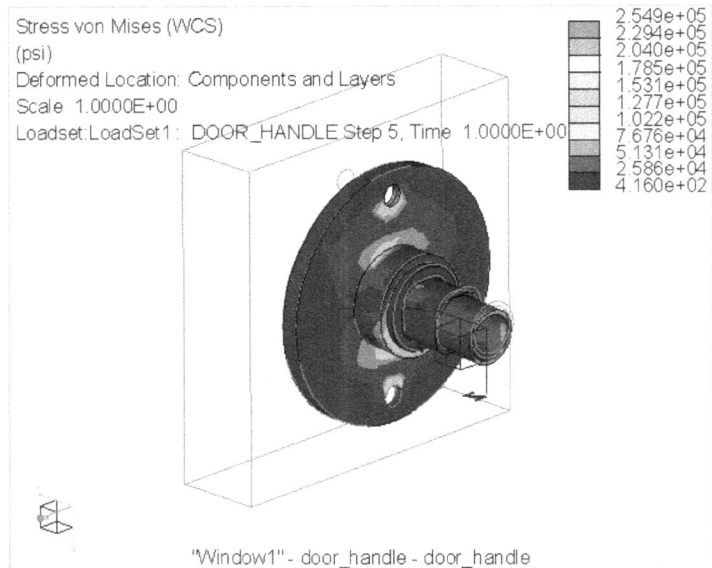

Stress von Mises (WCS)
(psi)
Deformed Location: Components and Layers
Scale 1.0000E+00
Loadset:LoadSet1 : DOOR_HANDLE Step 5, Time 1.0000E+00

2.549e+05
2.294e+05
2.040e+05
1.785e+05
1.531e+05
1.277e+05
1.022e+05
7.676e+04
5.131e+04
2.586e+04
4.160e+02

"Window1" - door_handle - door_handle

**Figure 7–38**

Examine the stress plot. Use the tools in the **Info** menu to locate the area of maximum stress.

## Task 12 - Display the contact pressure results.

1. Click 🖼 to edit the result window. In the *Steps* area, highlight the last row, and in the *Quantity* area, select **Contact Pressure**.

2. Click OK and Show . The Contact Pressure plot displays as shown in Figure 7–39.

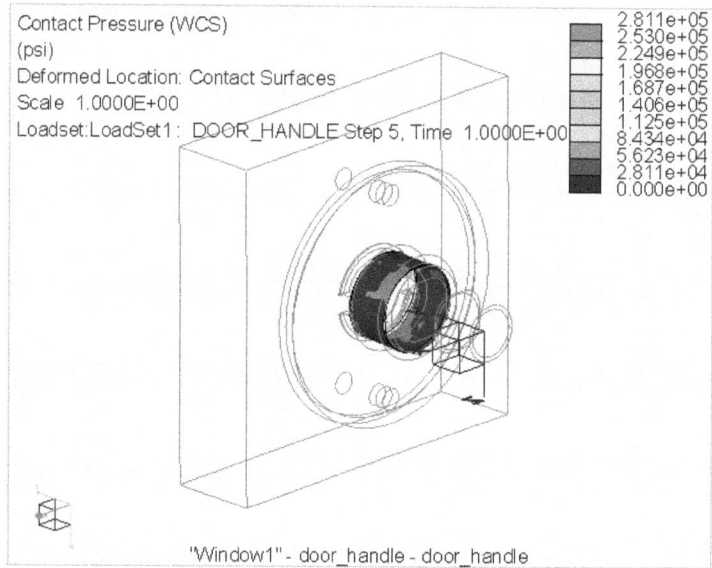

Contact Pressure (WCS)
(psi)
Deformed Location: Contact Surfaces
Scale 1.0000E+00
Loadset:LoadSet1 : DOOR_HANDLE Step 5, Time 1.0000E+00

2.811e+05
2.530e+05
2.249e+05
1.968e+05
1.687e+05
1.406e+05
1.125e+05
8.434e+04
5.623e+04
2.811e+04
0.000e+00

"Window1" - door_handle - door_handle

**Figure 7–39**

3. Select **Info>Model Max** to locate the maximum. Note that the maximum contact pressure occurs at the back of the top of the contact region, as shown in Figure 7–40.

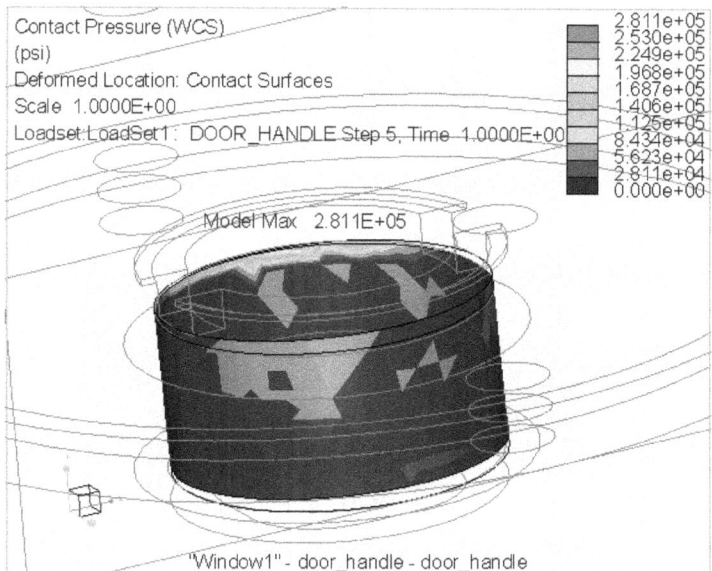

Contact Pressure (WCS)
(psi)
Deformed Location: Contact Surfaces
Scale 1.0000E+00
Loadset:LoadSet1 : DOOR_HANDLE Step 5, Time 1.0000E+00

2.811e+05
2.530e+05
2.249e+05
1.968e+05
1.687e+05
1.406e+05
1.125e+05
8.434e+04
5.623e+04
2.811e+04
0.000e+00

Model Max 2.811E+05

"Window1" - door_handle - door_handle

**Figure 7–40**

## Task 13 - Display the contact pressure graph.

1. Click ⊞ to edit the result window. In the Display type list, select **Graph** and in the *Quantity* area, select **Measure**. The Result Window Definition dialog box opens as shown in Figure 7–41.

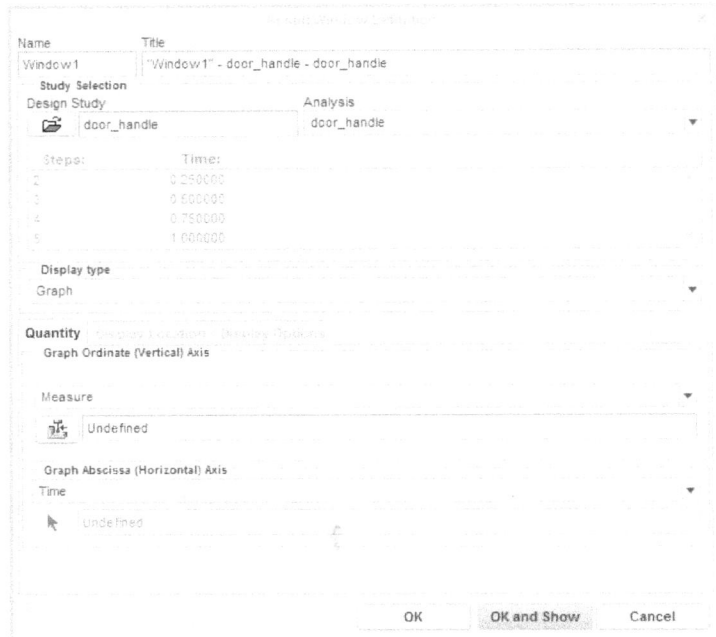

| Name | Title |
| --- | --- |
| Window1 | "Window1" - door_handle - door_handle |

Study Selection

| Design Study | Analysis |
| --- | --- |
| 📂 door_handle | door_handle ▾ |

| Steps: | Time: |
| --- | --- |
| 2 | 0.250000 |
| 3 | 0.500000 |
| 4 | 0.750000 |
| 5 | 1.000000 |

Display type

Graph ▾

Quantity

Graph Ordinate (Vertical) Axis

Measure ▾

📊 Undefined

Graph Abscissa (Horizontal) Axis

Time ▾

➤ Undefined

| OK | OK and Show | Cancel |

**Figure 7–41**

2. Click 📊. In the list of predefined measures, select **contact_max_pres**. Click OK to complete.

3. Click OK and Show . The **contact_max_pres** graph displays
   as shown in Figure 7–42.

contact_max_pres
(psi)
Time
Loadset:LoadSet1 : DOOR_HANDLE
"Window1" - door_handle - door_handle

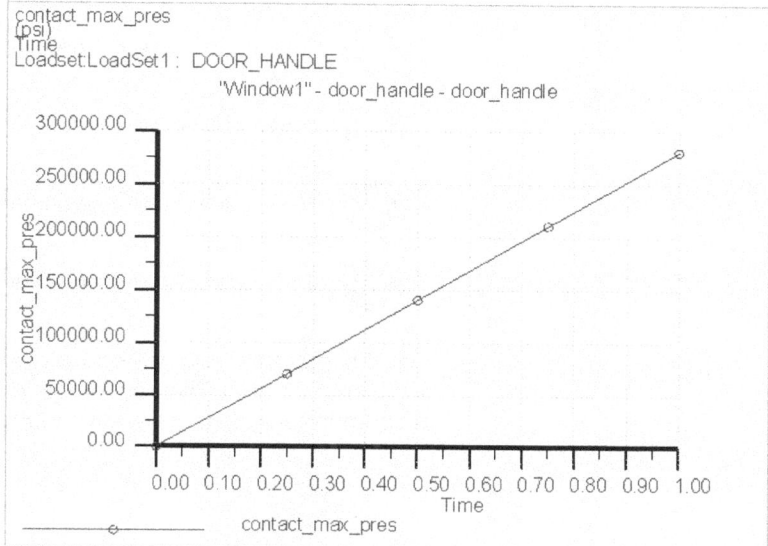

**Figure 7–42**

Note how the maximum contact pressure is increasing with the
load, from no load to the full load. Although the horizontal axis in
the graph displays *Time*, this is not a physical time because a
static analysis was solved. Rather, it is a load factor (i.e., the
0.50 value on the horizontal axis corresponds to the 50% load
applied, etc.).

4. Exit the Results and save and close the model.

# Practice 7b | Pin-Jointed Assembly

**Learning Objectives**

✓ Understand how to create surface regions.

✓ Understand how to create Contact Interfaces.

✓ Understand how to refine mesh in contact regions.

✓ Understand how to run a contact analysis.

In this practice, you will set up a contact analysis on a pin-jointed assembly model. The assembly model is part of a hydraulic boom mechanism, as shown in Figure 7–43.

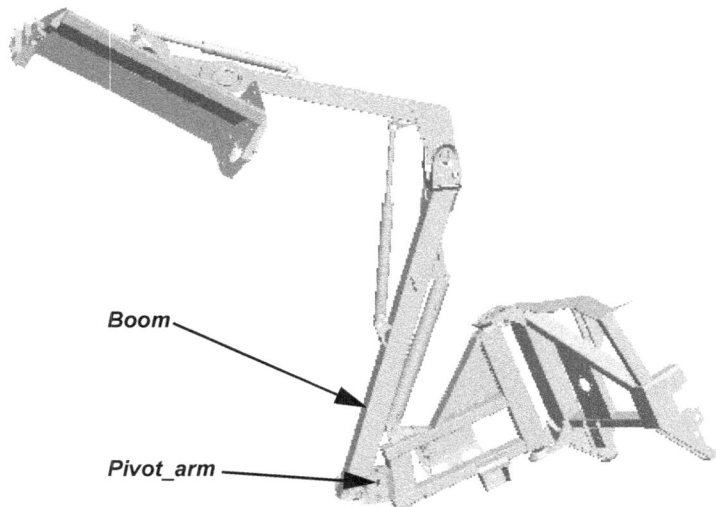

Boom

Pivot_arm

**Figure 7–43**

The contact analysis takes a long time and the area of interest is only the contact between the pin, boom, and pivot arm. The assembly that you will analyze consists of these parts, as shown in Figure 7–44. The model will be solved with one possible simulation scenario.

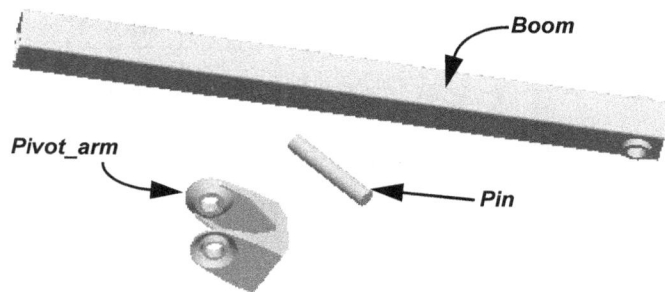

**Figure 7–44**

The pin is press-fit into the pivot arm holes. Therefore, the pin is fully fixed to the pivot arm. However, the boom is assembled on the pin with a small clearance, to be able to rotate around the pin when the mechanism (shown in Figure 7–43) is moving.

## Modeling Tasks

## Task 1 - Open the assembly and launch Creo Simulate.

1. Open **hydraulic.asm** in Creo Parametric. The assembly displays as shown in Figure 7–45.

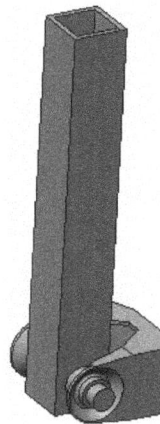

**Figure 7–45**

*All parts in the assembly must use the same system of units.*

2. Ensure that the unit system is set to **mmNs**.

3. Select **Applications>Simulate** to launch Creo Simulate.

## Task 2 - Create the surface regions.

In this task, you will define the surface areas that are used later to create Contact Interfaces between the pin and boom.

1. Open **pin_1.prt** in Creo Parametric. Do not switch to Creo Simulate. The pin displays as shown in Figure 7–46.

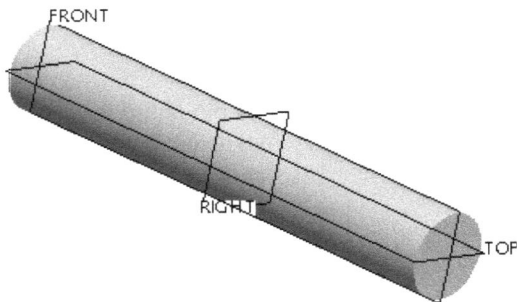

**Figure 7–46**

2. Click ⏢ and create **DTM1** plane parallel to datum plane RIGHT at a distance of **80**, as shown in Figure 7–47.

*The plane is created on the left side of datum plane RIGHT, using the pin orientation shown in Figure 7–47.*

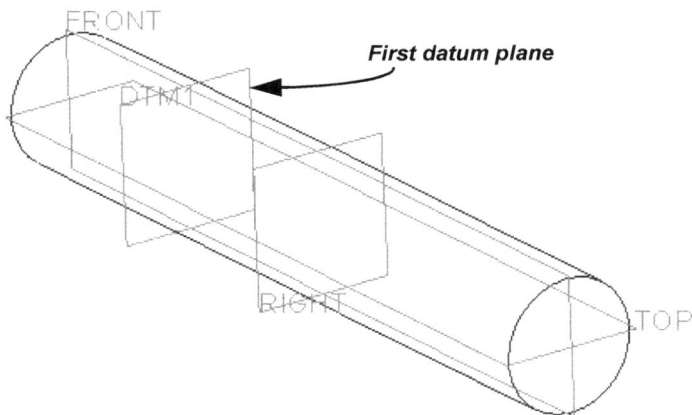

**Figure 7–47**

3. Create another plane (**DTM2**) on the same side of datum plane RIGHT, now at a distance of **48**, as shown in Figure 7–48.

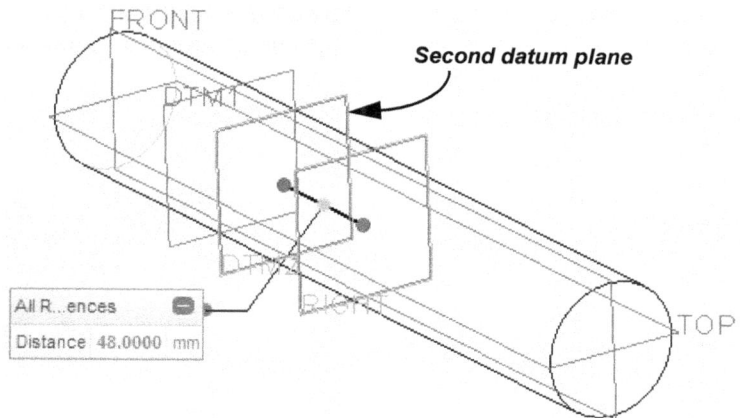

**Figure 7–48**

4. Create two more datum planes on the right side of datum
   plane RIGHT, as follows:

   • DTM3: **48mm offset from the RIGHT datum plane**
   • DTM4: **80mm offset from the RIGHT datum plane**

   The model displays as shown in Figure 7–49.

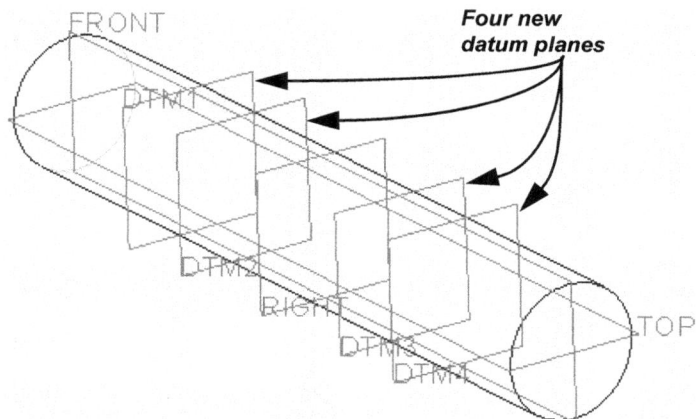

**Figure 7–49**

The datum planes you created have been placed at the ends of
the boom holes, where the pin contacts the boom. The planes
are symmetrical about the middle of the pin.

5. Select the DTM1 plane and click ⬡ (Intersect). The Surface
   Intersection dashboard opens.

6. Hold down <Ctrl> and select both halves of the cylindrical surface of the pin, as shown in Figure 7–50.

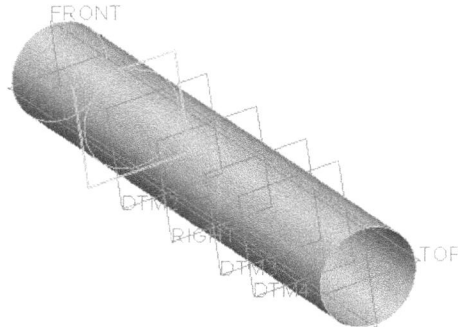

**Figure 7–50**

7. Click ✔ to finish. The new datum curve **Intersect_1** displays in the model, as shown in Figure 7–51.

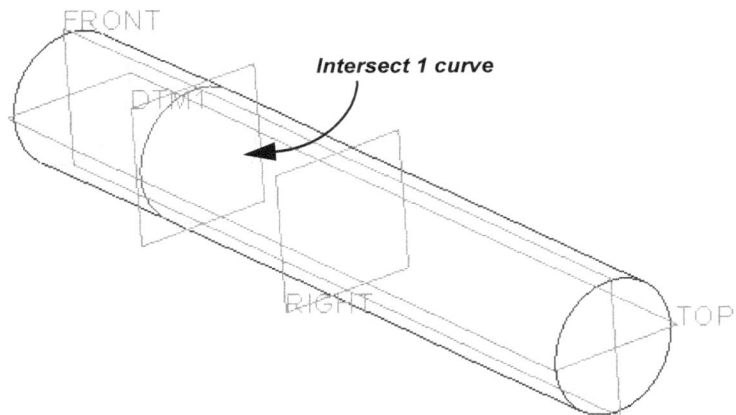

*Intersect 1 curve*

**Figure 7–51**

8. Repeat Steps 6 to 7 to create intersection curves between the pin surface and the planes DTM2, DTM3, and DTM4. The model displays as shown in Figure 7–52 (with the datum planes hidden).

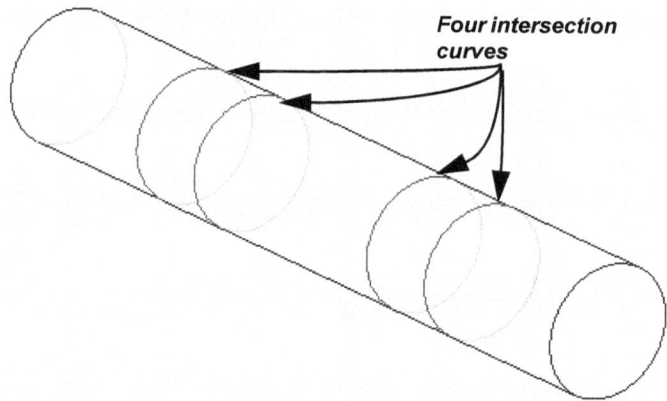

Four intersection
curves

**Figure 7–52**

9.  Switch to the Creo Simulate environment.

10. In the *Refine Model* tab, click ⬜. The Surface Region
    dashboard open as shown in Figure 7–53.

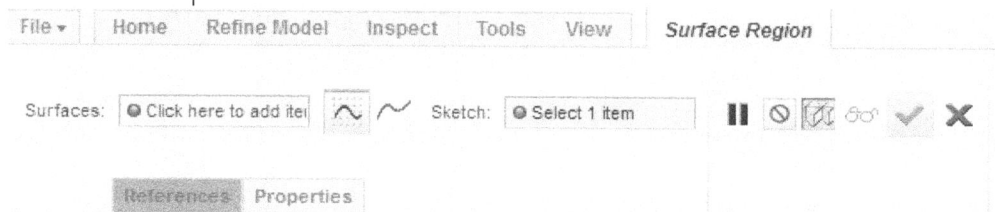

**Figure 7–53**

11. Select the **Surfaces** field and select both halves of the
    cylindrical surface of the pin, as shown in Figure 7–54.

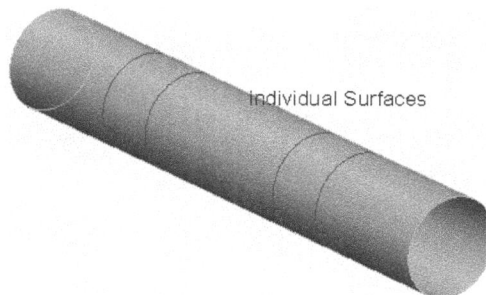

Individual Surfaces

**Figure 7–54**

12. Click 〜.

13. Select the **Chain** field and select the **Intersect_1** curve. The model displays as shown in Figure 7–55.

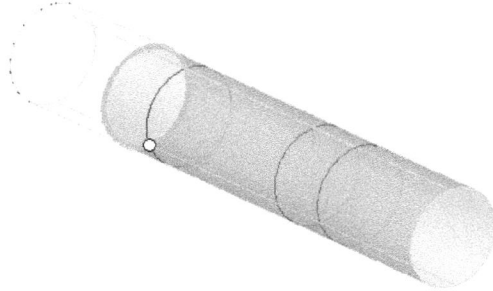

**Figure 7–55**

14. Click ✔ to finish.

15. Repeat Steps 10 to 14 to create surface regions using the curves **Intersect_2**, **Intersect_3**, and **Intersect_4**. The surface regions display in the Model Tree, as shown in Figure 7–56. Select the surface regions in the Model Tree and note how they highlight in the model.

   ▭ Materials
  ▼ ▦ Simulation Features
    ◙ Surface Region 1
    ◙ Surface Region 2
    ◙ Surface Region 3
    ◙ Surface Region 4

**Figure 7–56**

---

**Task 3 - Refine the mesh on the pin.**

---

*Refining the mesh in the contact areas improves the accuracy of the contact analysis.*

1. In the *AutoGEM* area, click ▦ . The Maximum Element Size Control dialog box opens, as shown in Figure 7–57.

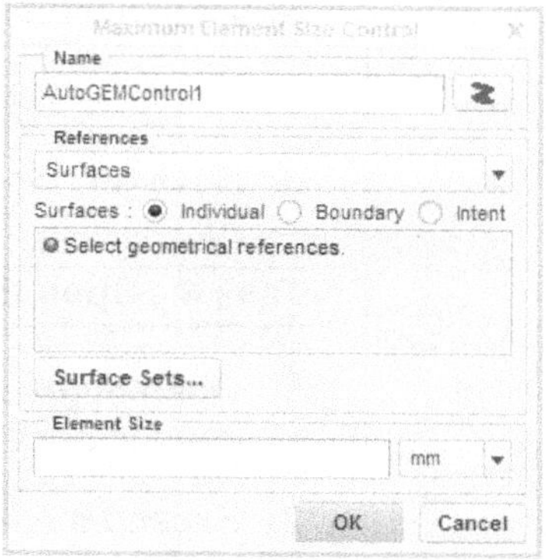

**Figure 7–57**

2. Select the two surface regions between the curves (these are the contact areas between the pin and the boom), as shown in Figure 7–58.

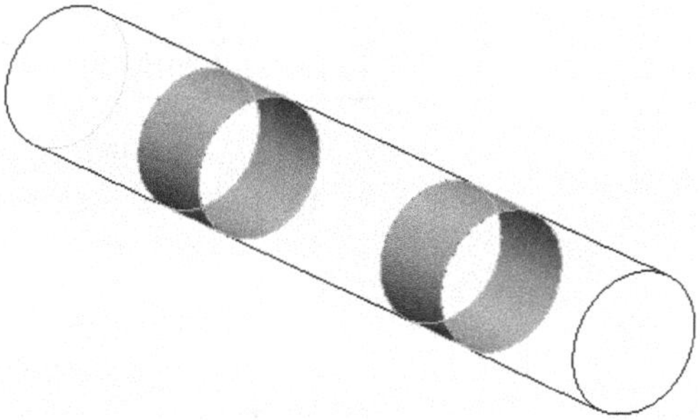

**Figure 7–58**

*The pin diameter is 50mm.*

3. In the *Element Size* field, enter **15** and click **OK** to finish.

4. Use the **Volume** option to mesh the pin. The mesh displays as shown in Figure 7–59.

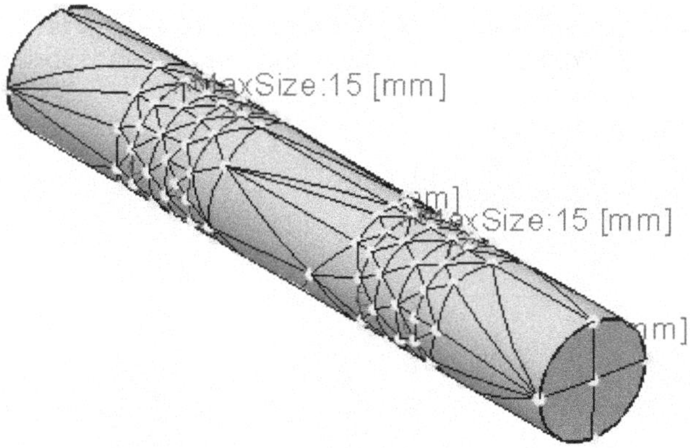

**Figure 7–59**

Note the finer mesh that has been created on the contact areas.

5. Exit AutoGEM without saving the mesh.

6. Save and close the **pin_1** part in Creo Parametric.

## Task 4 - Open the assembly.

1. Open **hydraulic.asm** and switch to the Creo Simulate environment.

2. Expand the Model Tree and note that the Surface Regions and AutoGEM Controls created on the part level in Tasks 2 and 3 have been propagated into the assembly analysis model.

3. Use the Simulation Display dialog box to turn off display of the AutoGEM Controls.

## Task 5 - Apply the material.

1. Assign **STEEL** to all of the parts in the assembly. The following values are the default material properties for HS low-alloy steel:

   - Poisson = 0.27
   - Young's modulus = 199948 MPa
   - Density = 7.82708e-9 tonne/mm^3

2. Using the Simulation Display dialog box, turn off the display of the Material Assignments.

## Task 6 - Create the interfaces.

*The pin is press-fit into the pivot arm holes, while the boom is assembled on the pin with a clearance.*

In this task, you will create Bonded Interfaces between the pivot arm and the pin, and Contact Interfaces between the pin and the boom.

*The default Bonded Interface will apply to the mated areas between the pin and the pivot arm.*

1. Click ▤. Expand the Default Interfaces drop-down list and verify that **Bonded** is selected, as shown in Figure 7–60.

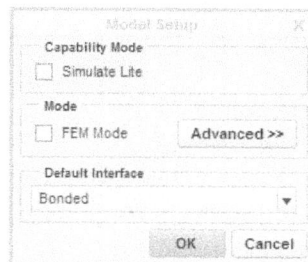

**Figure 7–60**

2. Click ▯. The Interface Definition dialog box opens as shown in Figure 7–61.

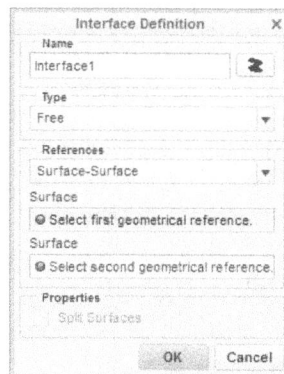

**Figure 7–61**

3. Expand the Type drop-down list and select **Contact**.

4. Expand the References drop-down list and select **Component-Component**.

5. Select the **PIN_1** and **BOOM_1** parts as the references. The Interface Definition dialog box opens as shown in Figure 7–62.

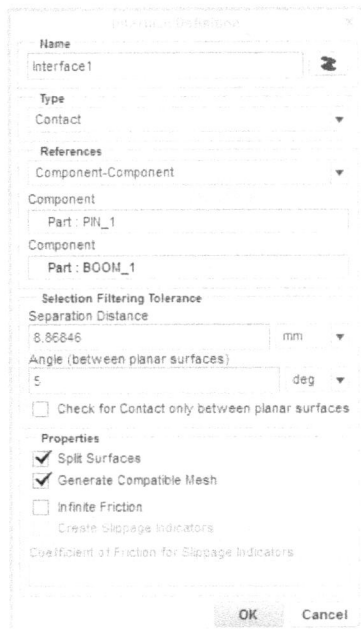

**Figure 7–62**

6. Accept all of the other defaults and click OK to finish. The model displays as shown in Figure 7–63.

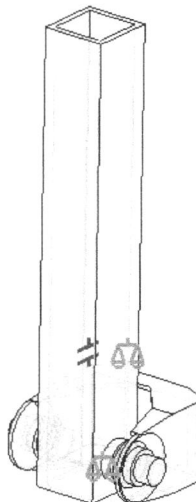

**Figure 7–63**

7. In the *Refine Model* tab, in the *AutoGEM* area, click 📋 to open the Simulation Geometry dialog box.

8. Select the options shown in Figure 7–64.

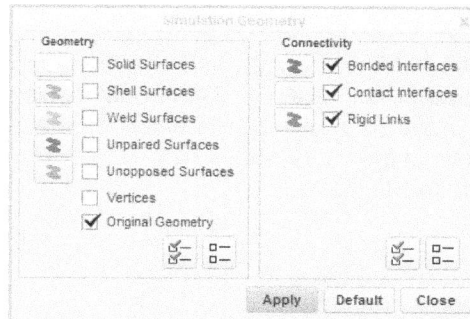

**Figure 7–64**

9. Click  Apply . The model displays as shown in Figure 7–65.

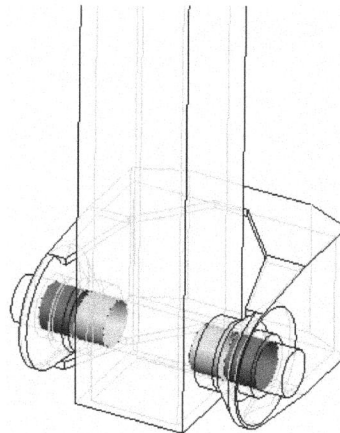

**Figure 7–65**

Compare the interface colors (shown as shaded in Figure 7–65) to the color scheme in the Simulation Geometry dialog box. Ensure that the Bonded Interfaces are shown between the pin and the pivot arm, and that the Contact Interfaces are shown between the pin and the boom.

10. Click  Close  to finish.

11. Using the Simulation Display dialog box, turn off the visibilities of the Measures and of the Interfaces.

## Task 7 - Apply loads.

In this task, you will apply loads to the top surface of the boom part.

*To apply the load, use the **Uniform** and **Total Load** options in the Distribution area in the Force/Moment Load dialog box.*

1. In the *Name* field, enter **boom_load**.

2. In Y-direction, apply **10,000N** to the top surface of the boom. The model displays as shown in Figure 7–66. WCS is the default coordinate system.

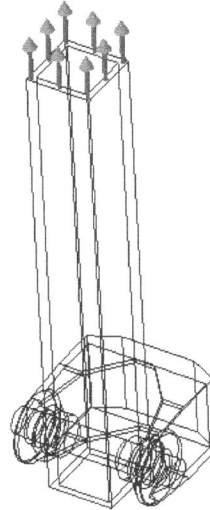

**Figure 7–66**

3. Using the Simulation Display dialog box, hide the loads.

## Task 8 - Apply the constraints.

1. Fully constrain the surface of the **pivot_arm** shown in Figure 7–67. Enter **pivot_const** as the constraint name.

*Ensure that the two named constraints are members of ConstraintSet1.*

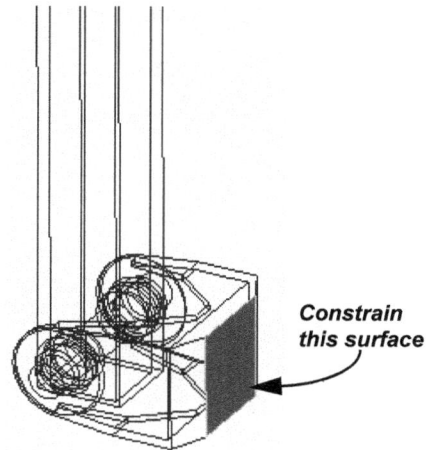

Constrain
this surface

**Figure 7–67**

The model displays as shown in Figure 7–68.

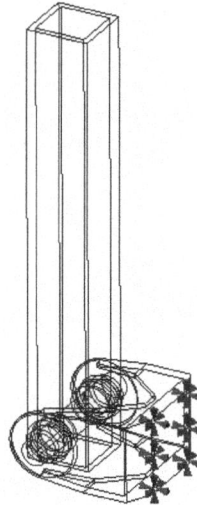

**Figure 7–68**

*This constraint is necessary to eliminate the rigid body rotation and sliding motions of the boom about the pin. The Contact Interface that you defined in Task 4 was frictionless.*

2. Constrain the X- and Z-directions on the end of the surface of the boom shown in Figure 7–69. Ensure that you leave the Y-direction free. Enter **boom_const** as the constraint name.

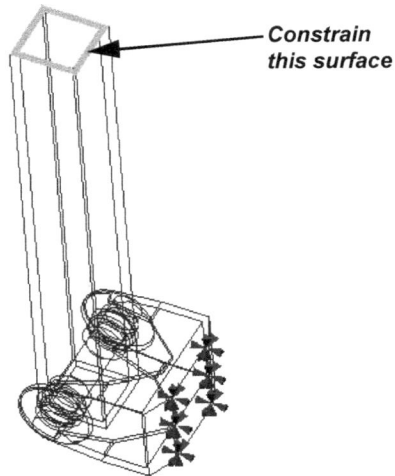

**Constrain this surface**

**Figure 7–69**

3. Turn on the loads visibility. The model displays as shown in Figure 7–70.

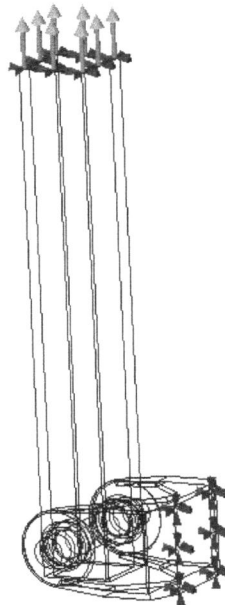

**Figure 7–70**

## Task 9 - Mesh the model.

1. Mesh the assembly using the **All with Properties** option. The mesh displays as shown in Figure 7–71.

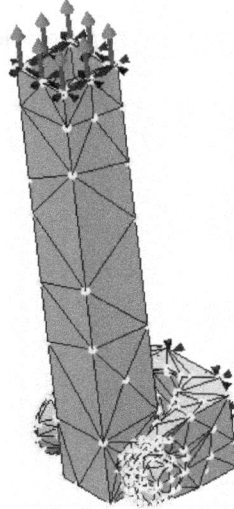

**Figure 7–71**

2. Save the mesh and exit the AutoGEM dialog box.

## Analysis Tasks

### Task 10 - Set up and run the analysis.

1. Set up a Single-Pass Adaptive convergence analysis. Enter **hydraulic** as the analysis name and keep all of the other defaults. The Static Analysis Definition dialog box opens as shown in Figure 7–72.

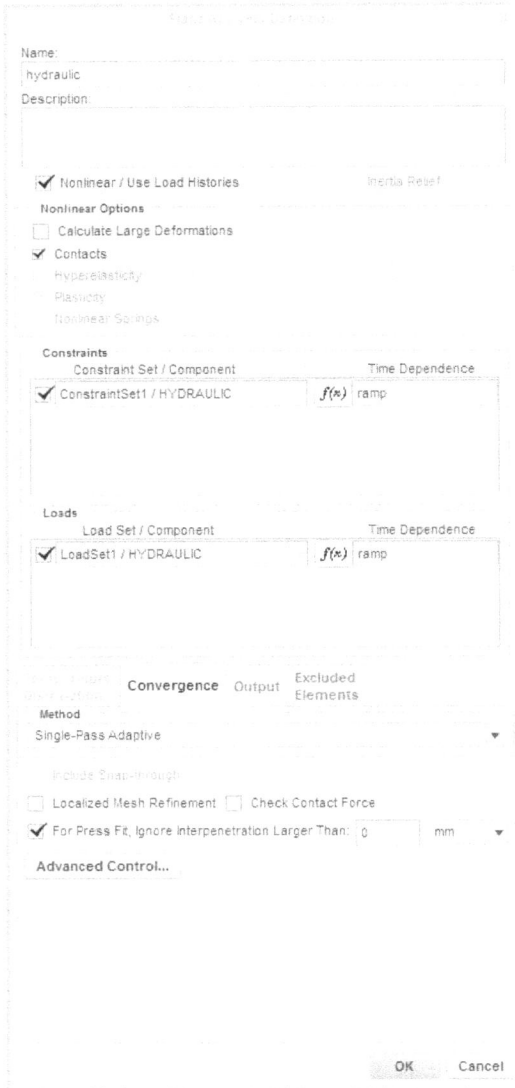

**Figure 7–72**

*The **Contacts** option is already selected.*

2. Click OK to close the Static Analysis Definition dialog box.

3. In the **Info** menu, select **Check Model** to check the validity of the model.

4. Run this analysis if time permits.

## Results Tasks

### Task 11 - Display the deformation results.

*You can use the hydraulic as the design study in the canned_results directory.*

1. Click in the Analyses and Design Studies dialog box. In the Result Window Definition dialog box, in the Steps list, highlight the second row as shown in Figure 7–73.

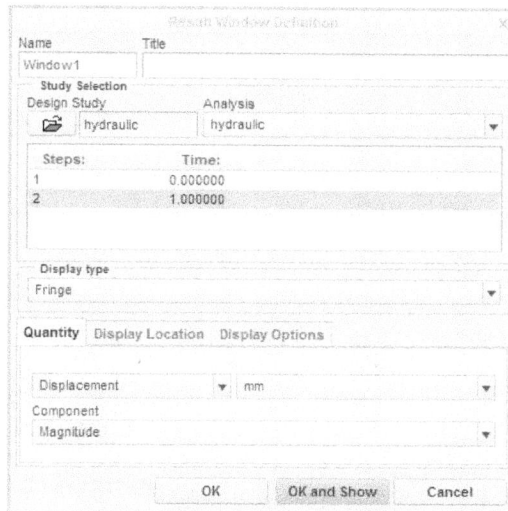

**Figure 7–73**

2.  Select the *Display Options* tab. Select the **Deformed** and **Overlay Undeformed** options, and set the *Scaling* to **5%**, as shown in Figure 7–74.

**Figure 7–74**

3.  Click  OK and Show  to display the Displacement Magnitude result. The model displays as shown in Figure 7–75.

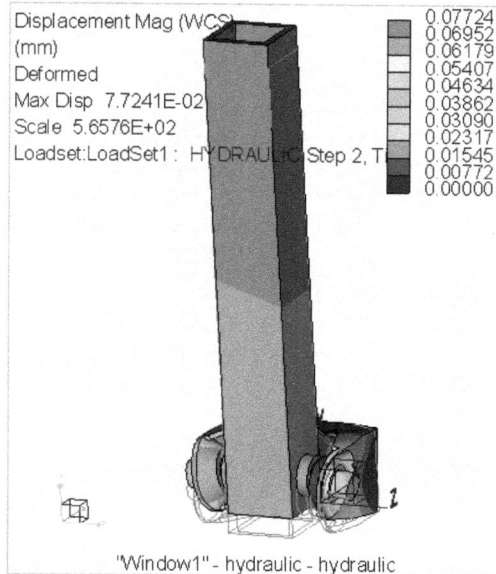

**Figure 7–75**

4. Select **View>Saved Views> EFT**. Zoom in on the bottom area. The model displays as shown in Figure 7–76.

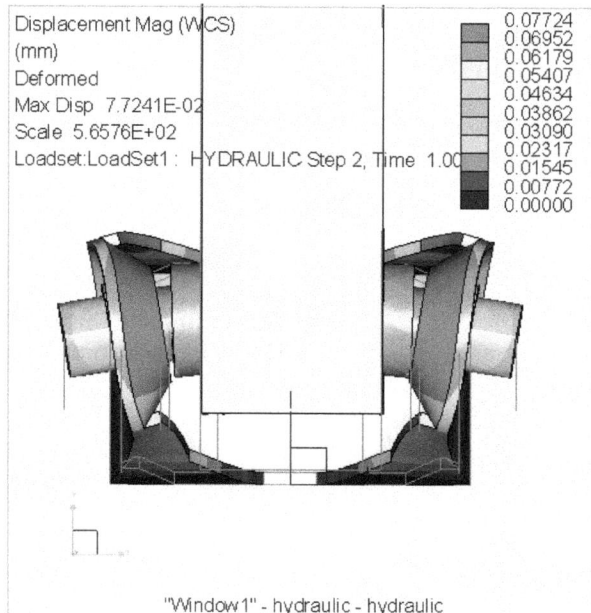

**Figure 7–76**

Examine the deformation of the parts under the load.

## Task 12 - Display the stress results.

1. Click 🖼 to edit the result window. In the *Steps* area, highlight the last row, and in the *Quantity* area, select **Stress, von Mises**.

2. In the *Display Options* tab, clear the **Overlay Undeformed** option.

3. Click OK and Show . In the menu, select **View>Default**. The von Mises stress plot displays as shown in Figure 7–77.

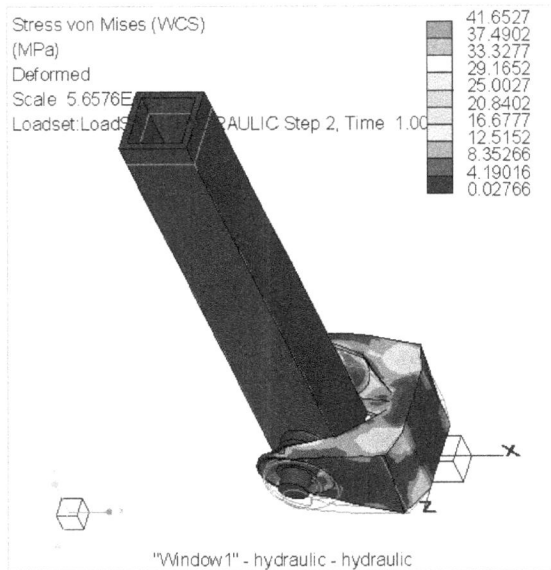

Figure 7–77

4. Select **Insert>Cutting/Capping Surfs**. The Results Surface Definition dialog box opens as shown in Figure 7–78.

Figure 7–78

5. In the *Plane* area, select **YZ**, and for the *Depth*, enter **-190mm** as shown in Figure 7–79.

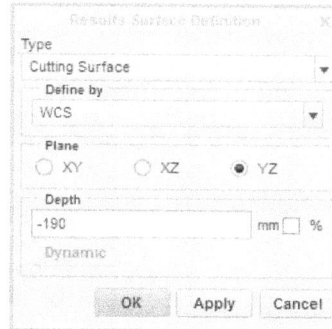

**Figure 7–79**

6. Click [ OK ] .

7. Select **View>Saved Views>LEFT** and clear **View>Shade**. Zoom in on the bottom area. The model displays as shown in Figure 7–80.

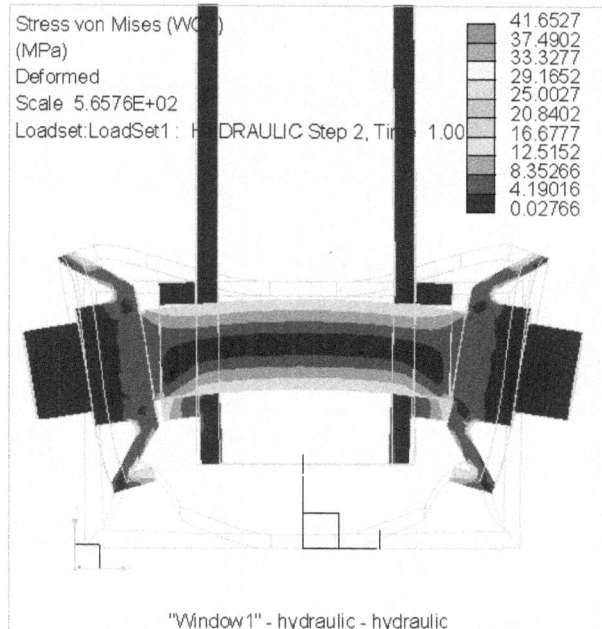

Stress von Mises (WCS)
(MPa)
Deformed
Scale 5.6576E+02
Loadset:LoadSet1 : HYDRAULIC Step 2, Time 1.00

41.6527
37.4902
33.3277
29.1652
25.0027
20.8402
16.6777
12.5152
8.35266
4.19016
0.02766

"Window1" - hydraulic - hydraulic

**Figure 7–80.**

Note the well-pronounced bending stress pattern in the pin under the applied load.

## Task 13 - Display the contact pressure results.

1. Click ⊞ to edit the result window. Highlight the last row in the Steps area. In the *Quantity* area, select **Contact Pressure**.

2. In the *Display Options* tab, select the **Overlay Undeformed** option.

3. Click  OK and Show . The Contact Pressure plot displays as shown in Figure 7–81.

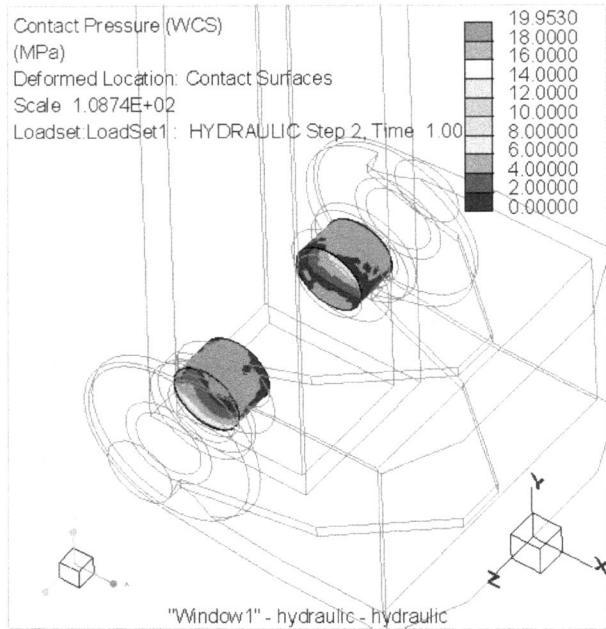

Contact Pressure (WCS)
(MPa)
Deformed Location: Contact Surfaces
Scale 1.0874E+02
Loadset:LoadSet1 : HYDRAULIC Step 2, Time 1.00

19.9530
18.0000
16.0000
14.0000
12.0000
10.0000
8.00000
6.00000
4.00000
2.00000
0.00000

"Window1" - hydraulic - hydraulic

**Figure 7–81**

Note that the maximum contact pressure occurs at the ends of the boom bushings.

4. Exit the Results and save and close the model.

# Chapter 8

## Thermal Analysis

This chapter contains the following topics:

- **Modes of Heat Transfer**
- **Creo Simulate Thermal**
- **Modeling Steps**
- **Analysis**
- **Results**
- **Thermal Load Transfer**

# 8.1 Modes of Heat Transfer

**Learning Objective**

Understand the concept of heat transfer.

Thermal analyses measure the effect of heat transfer rates on a model. Heat transfer is the flow of heat through a body in which there is a temperature variance. Heat transfer rates are an important part of engineering analysis in many industries. For example, heat transfer rates have a major role in the design of boilers, turbines, and combustion engines. The designer of these systems often needs to maintain high heat transfer rates while staying inside the material's limits for high temperatures. There are three modes of heat transfer: conduction, convection, and radiation.

**Conduction**

Conduction is the transfer of heat through a solid body or a body of stationary fluid (e.g., water or gas), in which temperature variance occurs. The conduction mode of heat transfer occurs in the atomic and molecular structures of a body. An example of conduction in a gas cylinder is shown in Figure 8–1.

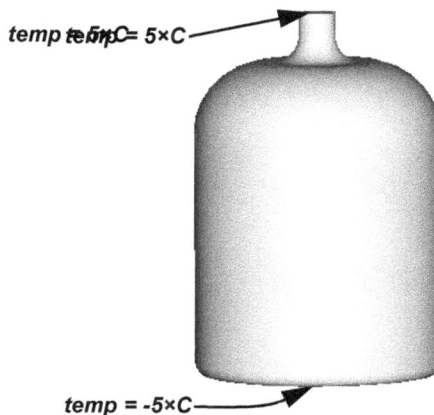

*temp = 5×C*

*temp = -5×C*

**Figure 8–1**

The temperature difference between the top and bottom of the gas cylinder is assumed to be 10°C. The molecules of the gas on the top of the cylinder have higher energies (i.e., they vibrate more freely) because of the higher temperature. Therefore, they collide with neighboring molecules and energy is transferred to these molecules. The process continues from high energy molecules to neighboring molecules from the top of the cylinder to the bottom until equilibrium is reached.

## Convection

Convection is the transfer of heat from a surface into a moving fluid (e.g., air) with a lower temperature than the surface. The heat must be conducted through material (e.g., heat exchanger) before it can be carried away by the outside air. There are two types of convection heat transfer: free and forced.

In free convection heat transfer, the moving fluid is free-flowing. For example, if a hot plate is left outside to be cooled on a day with little wind, the air in contact with the hot plate has a lower density than the air above the hot plate. This creates a circulation where warm air moves up and cooler air moves down.

In forced convection heat transfer, the moving fluid is pumped or fanned over a surface. Using the previous example, on a windy day, the primary transfer of heat is through the force of wind, while free convection still exists.

## Radiation

Radiation is the emission of energy from heated surfaces in the form of electromagnetic waves. Two heated surfaces at different temperatures transfer heat to each other by radiation if there is no other means of transport (e.g., molecular vibration or air). Heat transfer by conduction or convection requires a means of transport. Radiation heat transfer works best in a vacuum.

# 8.2 Creo Simulate Thermal

**Learning Objective**

Understand the Creo Simulate Thermal analysis steps and options.

Similar to the Structure mode, the Creo Simulate Thermal mode has three components for finite element analysis: analysis, pre-processing, and post-processing. Each component contains steps, as shown in Figure 8–2.

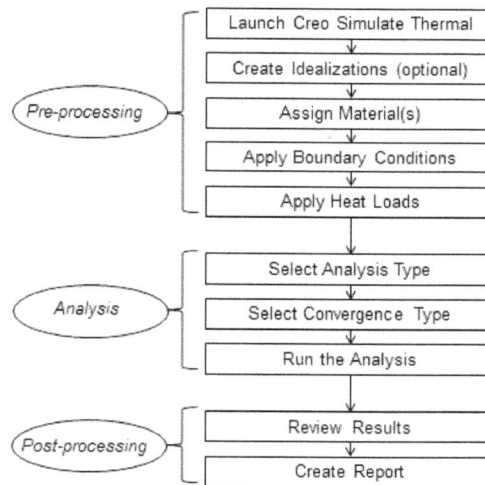

**Figure 8–2**

*Thermal mode is launched in the same way as Structure, However, instead of selecting **Structure**, you select **Thermal**.*

After you launch Thermal mode, each step in the model analysis process requires a selection of options. These options are as follows:.

| Model Analysis Steps | Pro/MECHANICA Thermal Options | |
|---|---|---|
| Model Type | 3D<br>2D Axisymmetric | 2D Plate<br>2D Unit Depth |
| Element Type | Solid<br>Shells<br>Beams | Connections |
| Analysis Methods | Steady State Thermal | Transient Thermal |
| Convergence Methods | Multi-Pass Adaptive<br>Single-Pass Adaptive | Quick Check |
| Design Studies | Standard Optimization | Sensitivity |

## Thermal Ribbon

*The Thermal interface is similar to the Structure interface.*

To enter the Thermal mode, click in the Creo Simulate Ribbon. The Ribbon changes as shown in Figure 8–3. The tools in the Thermal mode Ribbon are similar to those in the Structure mode. The Loads and Boundary Conditions areas are different.

**Figure 8–3**

# 8.3 Modeling Steps

**Learning Objectives**

Understand how to create idealizations.

Understand how to apply boundary conditions.

Understand how to apply heat loads.

The majority of the analysis steps in the Thermal mode are same or similar to those in the Structure mode. The following steps are identical:

* Defining model type

* Applying material

* Simulation features (datums, surface regions, etc.)

* Meshing the model

* Convergence methods

* Design Studies

The steps and options that are different from their counterparts in the Structure mode, are as follows:

**Idealizations**

Idealizations are tools that simplify your FEA model, resulting in faster analysis. Idealizations are optional. If your model is not overly complex and solves in a reasonable time, Idealizations might not be needed.

The following types of Idealizations are available in Thermal mode, as shown in Figure 8–4:

Beam    Shell    Shell
 ▼       ▼      Pair ▼

Idealizations

**Figure 8–4**

- **Beams:** These are 1D thermal elements (also called thermal rods) in which the temperature variation only occurs in the direction of the element's axis.

- **Shells:** These are 2D thermal elements, in which the temperature variation only occurs within the element's midplane.

## Applying Boundary Conditions

In thermal FEA, all of the surfaces default to perfect insulators unless you apply a heat load, specified temperature, convection condition, or radiation condition. A perfect insulator means that there is no heat transfer through the surface.

Four types of Boundary Conditions are available in Thermal mode, as shown in Figure 8–5:

- Prescribed Temperature

- Convection Condition

- Radiation Condition

- Symmetry

*Radiation Condition is only available with the Advanced Creo Simulate license.*

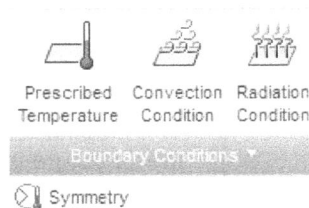

**Figure 8–5**

### Prescribed Temperature

Use the Prescribed Temperature boundary condition to enforce a specific temperature on one or more geometrical entities in your model. The specified temperature value is strictly maintained throughout the analysis.

The Prescribed Temperature dialog box is shown in Figure 8–6.

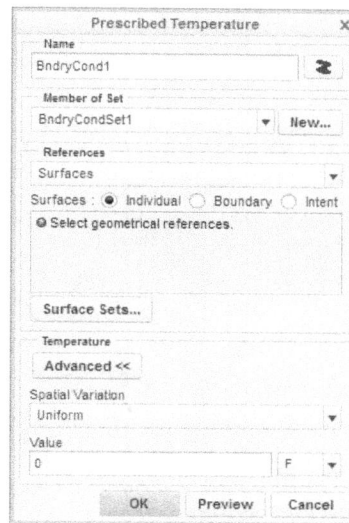

**Figure 8–6**

Prescribed Temperature can be applied to Surfaces, Edges/Curves, or Points. The options for the Spatial Variation are: Uniform, Function of Coordinates, and Interpolated Over Entity.

## Convection Condition

Use the Convection Condition to define a convective heat exchange for one or more geometric entities in your model.

The Convection Condition dialog box is shown in Figure 8–7.

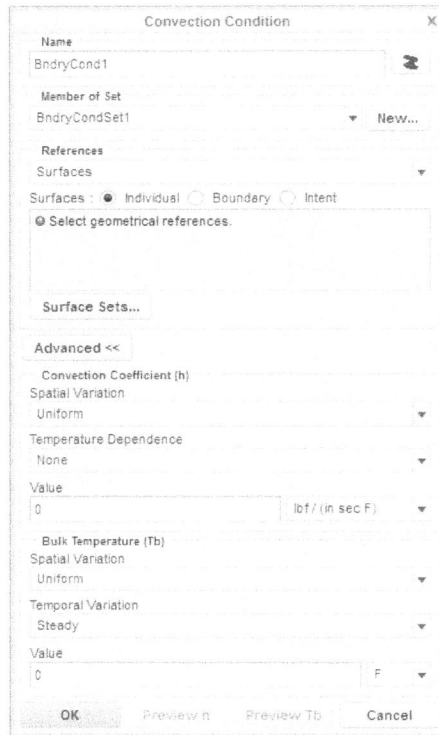

**Figure 8–7**

The Convection Condition can be applied to Surfaces, Edges/Curves, or Points.

The Convection Coefficient $h$ relates the amount of heat $Q$ transferred between the boundary surface of area $A$ at temperature $T$, and the moving fluid at Bulk Temperature $T_b$ in the following way:

$$Q = h A (T - T_b)$$

## Radiation Condition

Use the Radiation Condition to define a radiative heat exchange for one or more surfaces in your model.

The Radiation Condition dialog box is shown in Figure 8–8.

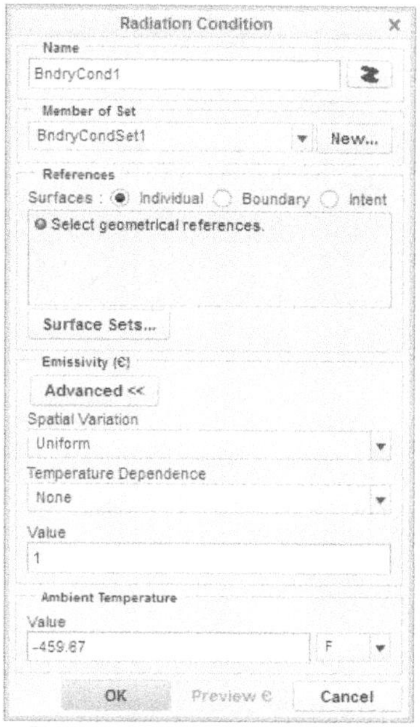

**Figure 8–8**

The Emissivity is the ratio of the energy radiated from a material's surface to that radiated from a blackbody (a perfect emitter) at the same surface temperature and viewing conditions. It is a dimensionless number between 0 (perfect reflector) to 1 (perfect emitter). The Ambient Temperature is the absolute temperature of the surrounding medium.

## Applying Heat Loads

Heat Loads provide local heat sources or heat sinks in your model. The icon to apply Heat Loads is located in the Loads area in the Ribbon, as shown in Figure 8–9.

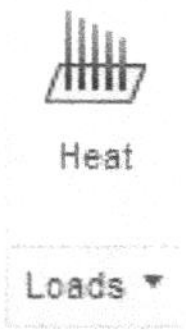

**Figure 8–9**

The Heat Load dialog box is shown in Figure 8–10.

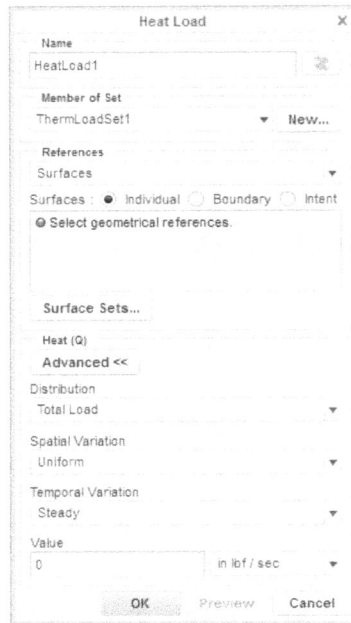

**Figure 8–10**

Heat Loads can be applied to Components/Volumes (to simulate internal heat generation), Surfaces, Edges/Curves, or Points.

# 8.4 Analysis

**Learning Objective**

Understand how to create a thermal analysis.

## Analysis Types

Creo Simulate enables you to perform two types of thermal analyses on a model. You select an analysis type based on the type of simulation you want to perform. Click ⬚ (Analyses and Design Studies) and select the appropriate option in the **File** menu, as shown in Figure 8–11.

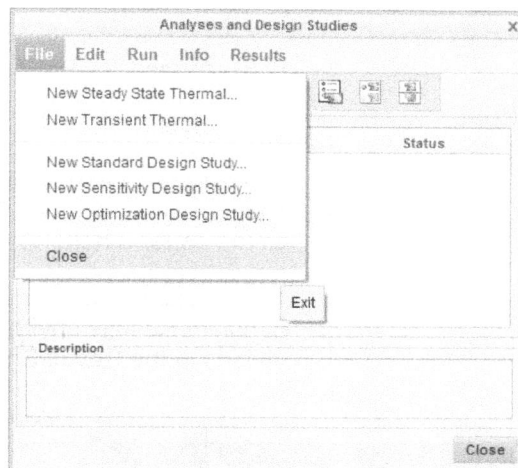

**Figure 8–11**

A Steady State Thermal analysis calculates the thermal response of a model to a heat load that is constant and does not vary over time. This type of analysis does not evaluate changes in temperature over time. For example, a turbine blade that is turned by steam and generates electricity would require this type of analysis because it is under constant pressure and temperature.

A Transient Thermal analysis calculates the thermal response in your model that is changing with time. The application of a heat load is not typically constant and varies over time. For example, the heat element in a toaster would require this type of analysis because it is time-dependent.

# 8.5 Results

**Learning Objective**

Understand how to visualize the thermal analysis results.

**Result Visualization**

Thermal mode enables you to visualize many different types of results:

- Temperatures

- Temperature Gradients

- Heat Fluxes

- Reactions

- P-Levels

The results can be displayed as a fringe plot, as a graph along an edge, or as a curve. Fringe plots for heat fluxes can be animated for a better understanding of the heat flows.

The results are visualized and manipulated from with the Creo Simulate Results environment. An overview of the icons and options in the Result Environment is shown in Figure 8–12.

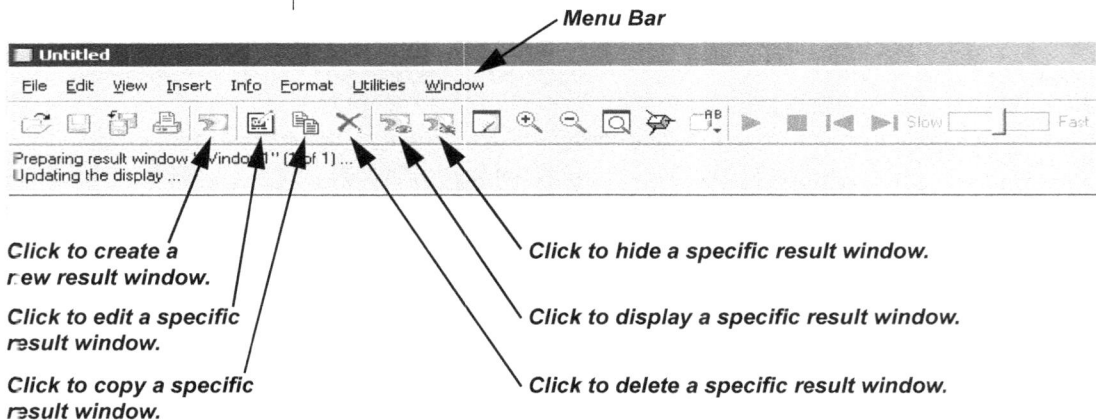

*Menu Bar*

Click to create a new result window.

Click to edit a specific result window.

Click to copy a specific result window.

Click to hide a specific result window.

Click to display a specific result window.

Click to delete a specific result window.

**Figure 8–12**

# 8.6 Thermal Load Transfer

**Learning Objective**

Understand how to import thermal results into a structural analysis.

You can transfer the temperature field from a thermal analyses to a structural analyses and apply it as a thermal load in your structure. For example, a heat sink is shown in Figure 8–13. The temperature distribution obtained in a thermal analysis can be transferred to structure mode to determine the deformations and stresses in the heat sink as it expands.

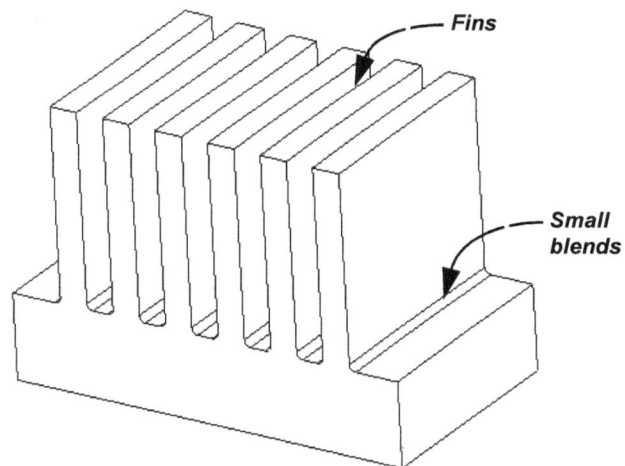

**Figure 8–13**

To transfer a temperature result from *Thermal* to **Structure**, expand the *Loads* area and select **MEC/T Load**, as shown in Figure 8–14.

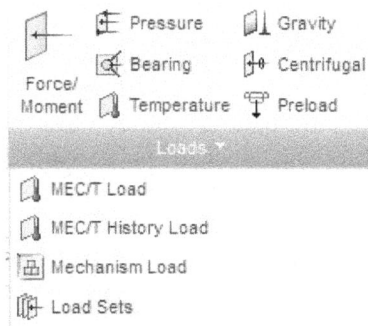

**Figure 8–14**

The MEC/T Temperature Load dialog box is shown in Figure 8–15.

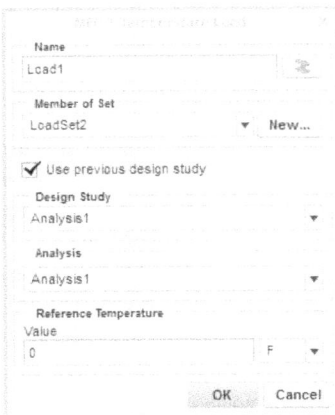

**Figure 8–15**

# Practice 8a

# Thermal Steady State Analysis

**Learning Objectives**

- Set up and run a thermal Quick Check analysis.

- Set up and run a thermal Multi-Pass Adaptive analysis.

- Display the results of each analysis.

- Use the Load Transfer function.

In this practice, you will set up and run a thermal steady state analysis on a heat transfer device, as shown in Figure 8–16. The heat transfer device sits on a 20W CPU (heat source) and a free convection is placed on the long vertical faces of fins. The device is aluminum and has a convection coefficient of 0.01 (lbf/in F° sec). Later, you will transfer the heat load to Structure mode to run a static analysis.

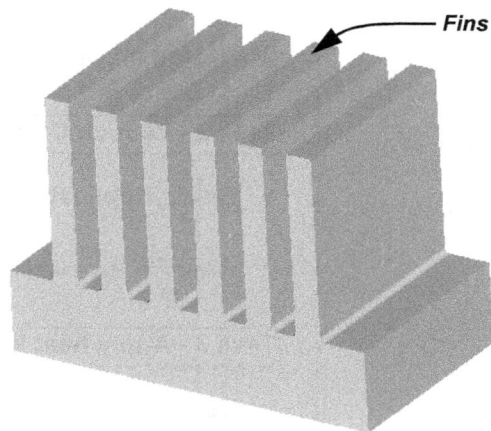

Figure 8–16

## Modeling Tasks

### Task 1 - Open the model.

1. Open **heat_device.prt** in Creo Parametric. The part displays as shown in Figure 8–17.

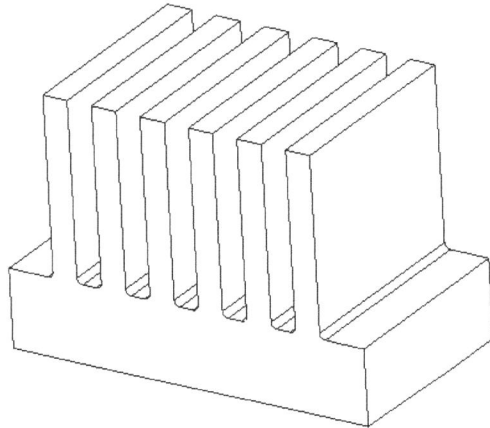

**Figure 8–17**

2. Ensure that the unit system is set to **IPS**.

### Task 2 - Launch Creo Simulate.

1. Select **Applications>Simulate**.

2. Click 🗔 to switch to the Thermal mode.

### Task 3 - Apply heat loads.

In this task, you will apply a heat load to the bottom surface of the heat device, as shown in Figure 8–18.

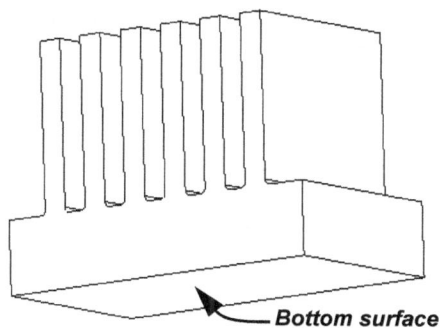

**Figure 8–18**

1. Click ⛩. The Heat Load dialog box opens as shown in Figure 8–19.

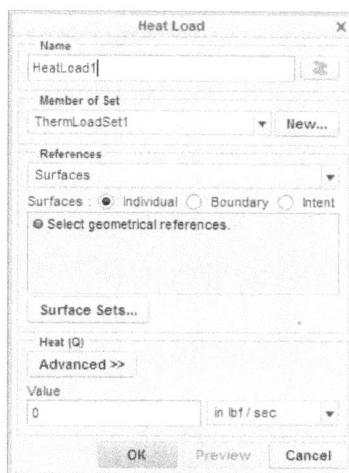

**Figure 8–19**

2. In the *Name* field, enter **end_heat_load**. For *Member of Set*, accept the default **ThermalLoadSet1** option.

3. Select the bottom surface shown in Figure 8–18.

*14.75lbf in/sec = 20Watt*

4. In the *Value* field, enter **14.75**.

5. Click Preview to preview the applied heat load.

6. Click  OK . The model displays as shown in Figure 8–20.

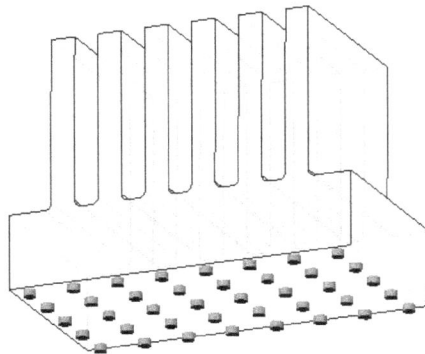

**Figure 8–20**

## Task 4 - Apply boundary conditions.

*Assume that the convection on the smaller surfaces is negligible.*

In this task, you will apply boundary conditions to the long vertical faces of the fins, the top faces of the fins, and the side faces, as shown in Figure 8–21.

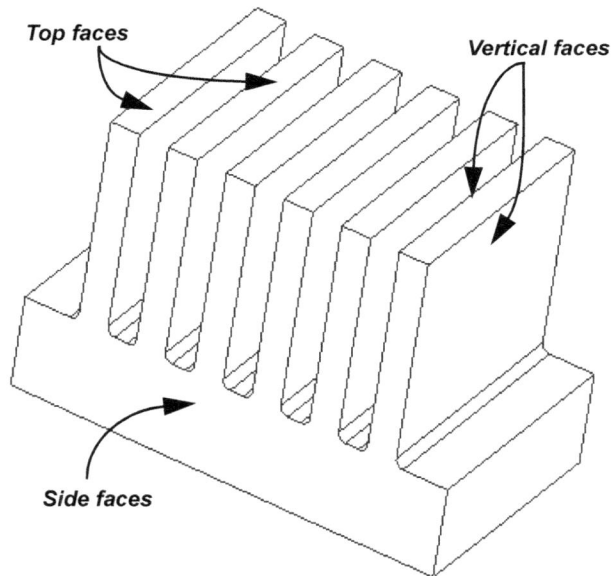

**Figure 8–21**

1. Click ⛀ . The Convection Condition dialog box opens as shown in Figure 8–22.

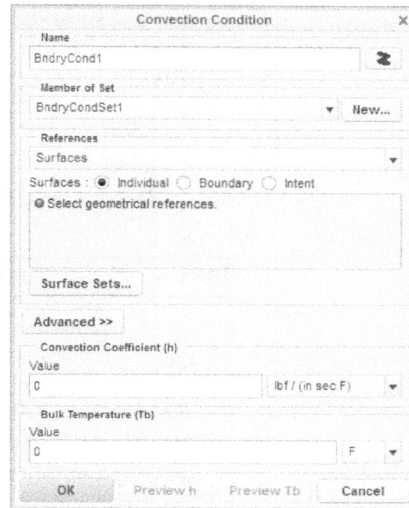

**Figure 8–22**

2. In the *Name* field, enter **long_face**. For *Member of Set*, accept the default **BndryCondSet1** option.

3. Select the 12 large vertical surfaces of the fins, the six top faces of the fins, and the two side faces. (Hold down <Ctrl> to multi-select.)

4. In the *Convection Coefficient* field, enter **0.01**.

5. In the *Bulk Temperature* field, enter **80**.

6. Click ▭ OK ▭ . The model displays as shown in Figure 8–23.

*The load values are turned off.*

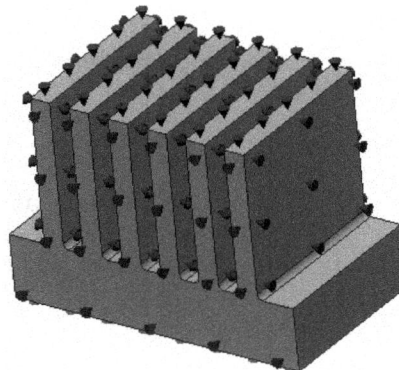

**Figure 8–23**

## Task 5 - Apply the material.

1. Assign **AL2014** to the heat device part. The following values are the default material properties for the aluminum alloy AL2014 (in the *Thermal* tab in the Material Definition dialog box):

   - Specific Heat capacity = 829900 in^2/(sec^2 F)
   - Thermal conductivity = 24 lbf/(sec F)
   - Density = 0.0002614 lbf sec^2/in^4

## Task 6 - Mesh the model.

1. Click ▦ . The AutoGEM dialog box opens.

2. Expand the AutoGEM References drop-down list and select the **All with Properties** option to mesh the model. The mesh displays as shown in Figure 8–24.

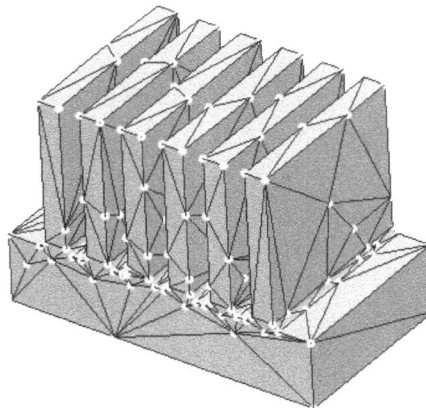

**Figure 8–24**

3. Close the AutoGEM dialog box and save the mesh.

## Summary

In the previous tasks, you created the simulation entities needed to analyze your model. In the following tasks, you will set the analysis type and the convergence method and run the analysis.

## Analysis Tasks

### Task 7 - Set up and run the analysis.

In this task, you will specify the analysis type. First, the **heat_device** is analyzed using the **Quick Check** convergence option to check for errors. The importance of this option increases with the size of your model (e.g., a model with a large number of elements). The option gives you a general feel for the results and indicates that the model behaves as intended with applied boundary conditions.

1. Click ▦. The Analyses and Design Studies dialog box opens.

2. Select **File>New Steady State Thermal**. The Steady Thermal Analysis Definition dialog box opens as shown in Figure 8–25.

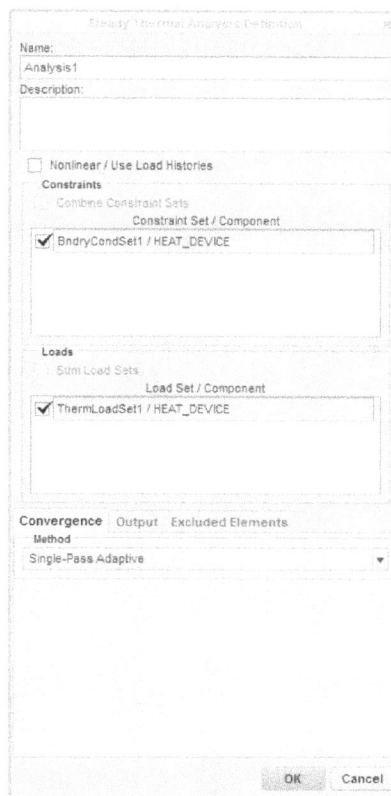

**Figure 8–25**

3. In the *Name* field, enter **heat_device** (heat_device is now the name of a subdirectory containing all of your results files).

4. In the *Description* field, enter **thermal analysis of a heat_device**. This step is optional, but it is helpful for identifying your analysis later.

5. For a thermal analysis, you must specify or select the boundary conditions and heat load sets. These were created in the previous steps. In this case, they are **BndryCondSet1** and **ThermalLoadSet1**. Verify that they are highlighted.

6. For the type of convergence, expand the Method drop-down list and select **Quick Check**. This option enables you to determine whether the analysis was set up correctly in your first run.

7. Click ___OK___ in the Steady Thermal Analysis Definition dialog box.

8. Verify that the Run Settings are correct, check the model, and run the analysis. Wait until it completes.

9. In the Analyses and Design Studies dialog box, click ▤. The Run Status dialog box opens. View the information in the window. Click ___Close___ when done.

---

**Task 8 - Run the analysis using the Multi-Pass Adaptive convergence option.**

---

1. With the **heat_device** analysis highlighted, select **Edit> Copy**. Double-click on **Copy_of_heat_device** to edit it. The Steady Thermal Analysis Definition dialog box for Analysis opens.

2. For the *Name*, enter **heat_device_multi_pass**.

3. Expand the Method drop-down list and select **Multi-Pass Adaptive**.

4. In the *Polynomial Order* area, expand the Maximum drop-down list and select **9**.

5. In the *Limits* area, in the *Percent Convergence* field, enter **10** percent convergence.

6. Click ___OK___ in the Steady Thermal Analysis Definition dialog box.

7. Start the analysis and wait until it finishes.

8. Click . The Run Status dialog box opens. The following results display in the dialog box:

   - The analysis converges on pass two.
   - The flux error is 17.1% of the Max Flux, as shown in Figure 8–26.

RMS Flux Error Estimates:

| Load Set | Flux Error | % of Max Flux |
|---|---|---|
| ThermLoadSet1 | 1.01e+01 | 17.1% of 5.90e+01 |

**Figure 8–26**

In the Run Status dialog box, the *Measures* area is shown in Figure 8–27.

Measures:

| Name | Value | Convergence |
|---|---|---|
| energy_norm: | 9.831981e+02 | 0.0% |
| max_flux_mag: | 5.900253e+01 | 55.9% |
| max_flux_x: | -5.021393e+01 | 41.5% |
| max_flux_y: | 4.078262e+01 | 100.0% |
| max_flux_z: | 7.135470e+00 | 100.0% |
| max_grad_mag: | 2.458439e+00 | 55.9% |
| max_grad_x: | 2.092247e+00 | 41.5% |
| max_grad_y: | -1.699276e+00 | 100.0% |
| max_grad_z: | -2.973112e-01 | 100.0% |
| max_temperature: | 2.133459e+02 | 0.0% |
| min_temperature: | 2.127240e+02 | 0.0% |

**Figure 8–27**

Note the maximum temperature (213.3 °F) and the minimum temperature (212.7 °F). The quantity of interest of the analysis is the temperature. Since the temperature measures converge, you could assume that the result of this analysis is valid, despite the flux error being 17.1% of maximum flux.

The values that you obtain when you run the analysis might be different than those that have been provided. This is due to the fact that each new build of Creo Simulate produces slight variations in the creation of the mesh.

9. Close the Run Status dialog box.

## Results Tasks

### Task 9 - Display the temperature results.

In this task, you will create and display a temperature plot for one of the long vertical surfaces.

1. In the Analyses and Design Studies dialog box, click . The Result Window Definition dialog box opens as shown in Figure 8–28.

**Figure 8–28**

2. In the *Name* field, accept the default **Window1**.

3. In the *Title* field, enter **SURFACE_PLOT**.

4. Click **OK and Show**. The Temperature fringe plot is displayed, as shown in Figure 8–29.

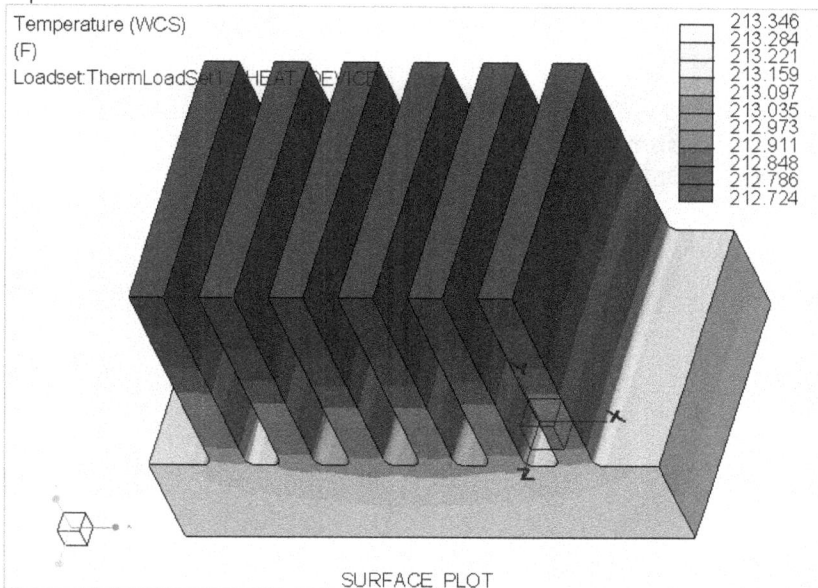

Temperature (WCS)
(F)
Loadset:ThermLoadSet1 : HEAT_DEVICE

213.346
213.284
213.221
213.159
213.097
213.035
212.973
212.911
212.848
212.786
212.724

SURFACE_PLOT

**Figure 8–29**

Note that the maximum temperature occurs at the bottom of the
heat sink, where the heat load is applied. The temperature
gradually decreases to the top of the heat sink, due to
convection on the fins.

5. Click 🖳 . The Result Window Definition dialog box opens.

6. Select the *Display Location* tab, expand the drop-down list
   and select **Surfaces**.

7. Click 🖢 and select the right vertical surface of the
   right-most fin. Click the middle mouse button when finished.

8. Click **OK and Show** . The result window displays as shown in Figure 8–30.

*Use the **View>Spin/ Pan/Zoom>Isometric** options to orient the plot.*

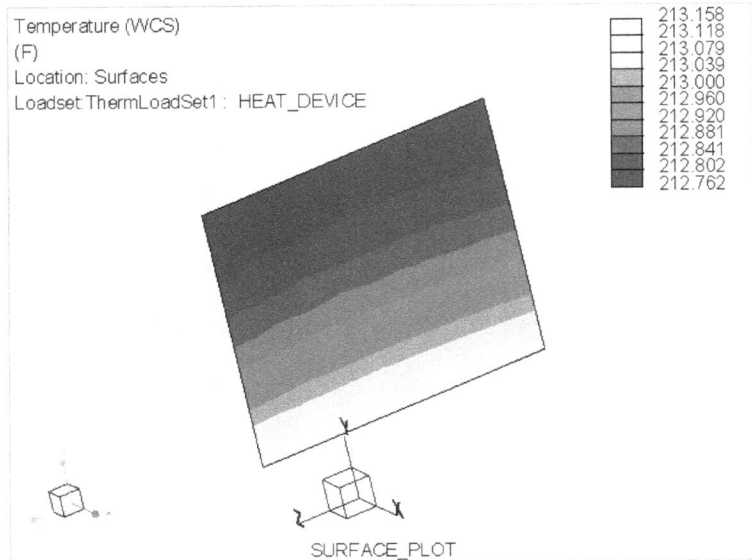

Temperature (WCS)
(F)
Location: Surfaces
Loadset: ThermLoadSet1 : HEAT_DEVICE

213.158
213.118
213.079
213.039
213.000
212.960
212.920
212.881
212.841
212.802
212.762

SURFACE_PLOT

**Figure 8–30**

*The higher the temperature gradient, the higher the heat transfer.*

The temperature gradient is very small (0.4°F) and the temperature is too high throughout the surface. These results indicate that the heat device is not convecting enough heat to cool the CPU. Possible solutions include either a forced convection by means of a fan or a different heat device with more fins and a higher fin height. A sensitivity study would be useful for the second solution. Additionally, the convection coefficient could be increased by introducing surface roughness to the **heat_device** fins to enhance turbulence.

## Task 10 - Display the heat flux results.

1. Click 🗔 . The Result Window Definition dialog box opens.

2. In the *Quantity* tab, select **Flux Magnitude**.

3. In the *Display Location* tab, select **All**.

4. In the *Display Options* tab, select **Animate** and **Auto Start**.

5. Click **OK and Show** . Step through the animation. On Frame 5, the result plot displays as shown in Figure 8–31.

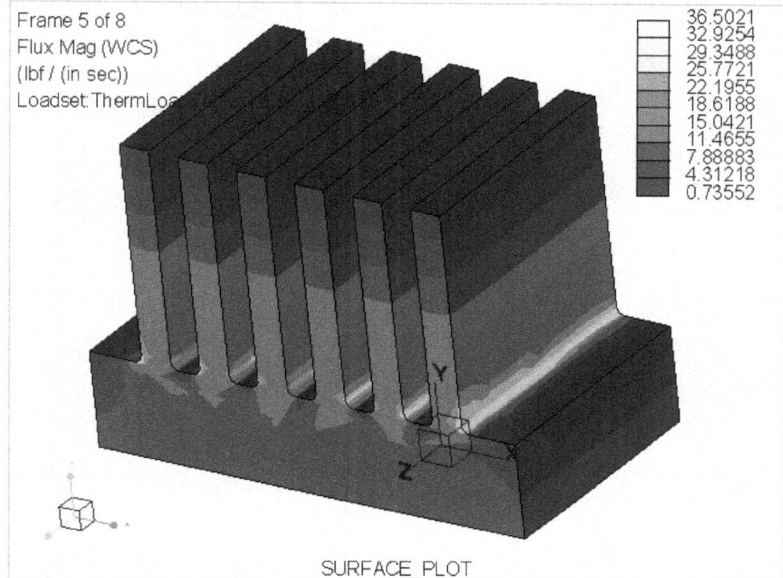

Frame 5 of 8
Flux Mag (WCS)
(lbf / (in sec))
Loadset: ThermLo

```
36.5021
32.9254
29.3488
25.7721
22.1955
18.6188
15.0421
11.4655
7.88883
4.31218
0.73552
```

SURFACE_PLOT

**Figure 8–31**

Note that the maximum heat flow occurs at the bottom of the fins. This area acts like a funnel, transferring heat from the heat source at the bottom surface to the tops of the fins.

6.  Exit the Results.

7.  Close the Analyses and Design Studies dialog box.

## Task 11 - Transfer loads from thermal to structure.

In this task, you will transfer the temperature distribution from Thermal analysis to Structural analysis and apply the temperature distribution's thermal load in Structure mode.

1.  Click ⬚ to switch to the Structure mode.

2. Expand the *Loads* area and select **MEC/T Load**. The MEC/T Temperature Load dialog box opens as shown in Figure 8–32.

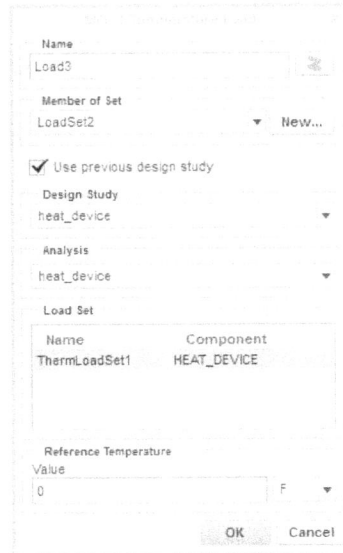

Figure 8–32

3. In the *Name* field, enter **transfer**.

4. For *Member of Set*, accept the default option.

5. In the *Reference Temperature* field, enter **50**.

6. Click   OK  . The model displays as shown in Figure 8–33.

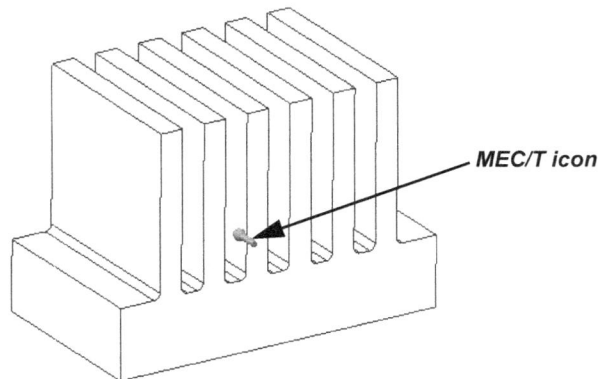

Figure 8–33

## Task 12 - Apply constraints.

The heat sink is bonded to the circuit board. In this task, you will apply the proper constraints.

1. Constrain the bottom surface of the heat sink in all of the translations, as shown in Figure 8–34.

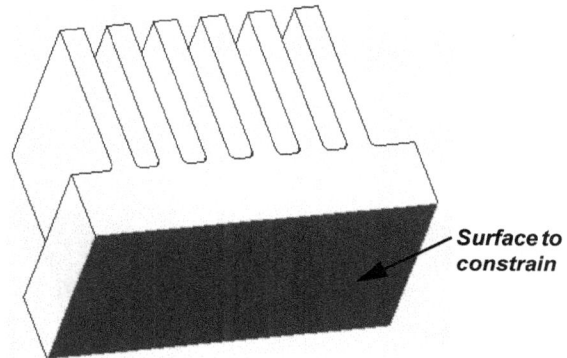

Figure 8–34

## Task 13 - Run the structural analysis.

1. Set up a static analysis using the **Single-Pass Adaptive** convergence option.

2. For the name of the analysis, enter **heat_structure**.

3. Run the heat_structure analysis.

## Task 14 - Display the results.

In this task, you will create and display two fringe plots: one for displacement and one for von Mises stress.

1.  Create the fringe plot for displacement, as shown in Figure 8–35.

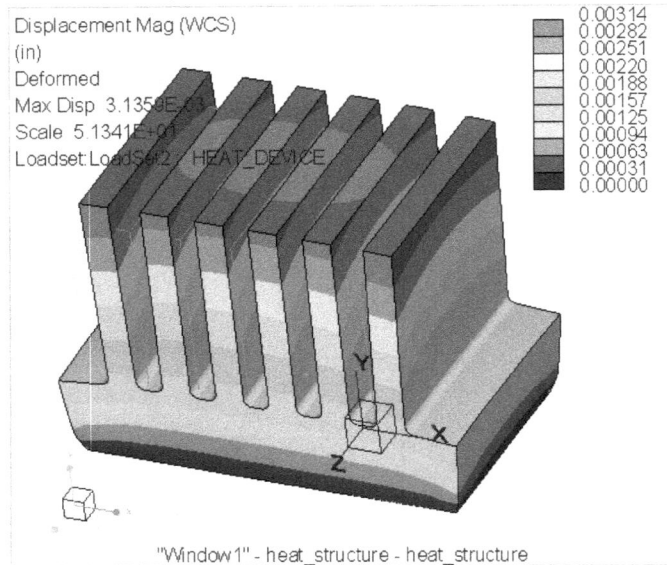

Figure 8–35

Note that the most deformation occurs in the fins, where material expansion due to heating is not constrained.

2.  Create the fringe plot for the von Mises stress, as shown in Figure 8–36.

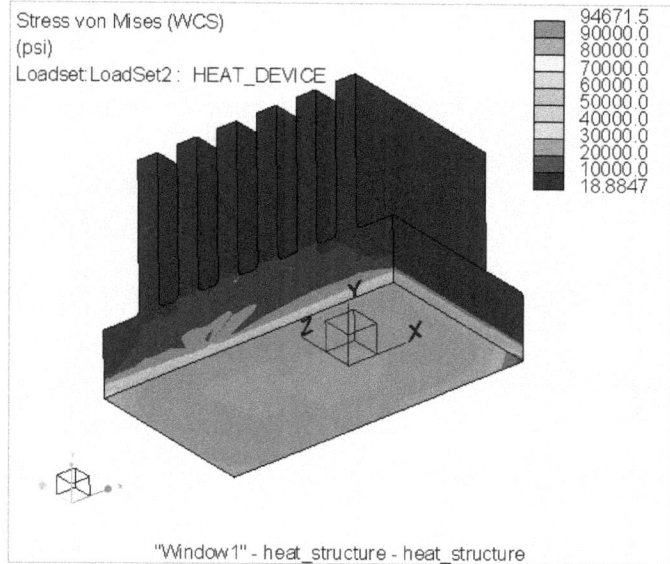

**Figure 8–36**

Note that the greatest stress occurs at the bottom of the sink, which is due to the constraint that restricts material expansion in that area.

3. Exit the Results. Save and close the model.

# Chapter 9

## Modal Analysis

A modal analysis in Creo Simulate helps you to determine the natural frequencies and natural modes of vibration for a model. These factors are important for models that are subjected to cyclic or vibration loads, because resonance occurs at vibrational loads that are at or close to the natural frequencies for the model. You can calculate natural frequencies and model shapes for the following types of parts: a free part (when it has six rigid body modes), a partially fixed part (when the number of rigid body modes is less than six), and a full fixed part (when there are no rigid body modes).

This chapter contains the following topics:

- **Natural Frequency**
- **Natural Modes**
- **Defining a Modal Analysis**

# 9.1 Natural Frequency

**Learning Objective**

Understand natural vibration and natural frequency.

All objects vibrate, when hit, struck, plucked or otherwise disturbed. When an object vibrates, it tends to do so at a specific frequency or set of frequencies. For example, it could be a guitar string or a tuning fork.

The frequency or frequencies at which an object tends to vibrate when disturbed is called the *characteristic* or *natural frequency* of the object.

If a dynamic load is applied to a model close to its natural frequency, the model exhibits a larger than normal oscillation. This phenomenon is called *resonance*. Without proper damping, the resonance can become uncontrollable and cause the model to collapse.

Natural frequencies are numbered (1st, 2nd, 3rd, etc.), with the 1st natural frequency being the lowest. The 1st natural frequency is sometimes called the *fundamental frequency* of an object.

*Resonance occurs when the frequency of the forced vibrations approaches or coincides with the natural frequency of the system.*

Modal analysis in Creo Simulate predicts the natural frequencies of your model so that you can determine whether or not the applied dynamic loads might cause resonance. The results of a modal analysis also help to determine whether a model requires more or less damping to prevent failure. Use a modal analysis to find the resonant frequencies for a structure under specific constraints.

# 9.2 Natural Modes

**Learning Objective**

Understand natural modes of vibration.

An object vibrating at a natural frequency creates a physical deformation, or shape, of the object. This shape is called the *natural mode* of vibration.

Using Creo Simulate, you can visualize these shapes and the frequency that is associated with them. Four mode shapes are shown in Figure 9–1. By viewing mode shapes, you can determine how a part reacts to different frequencies.

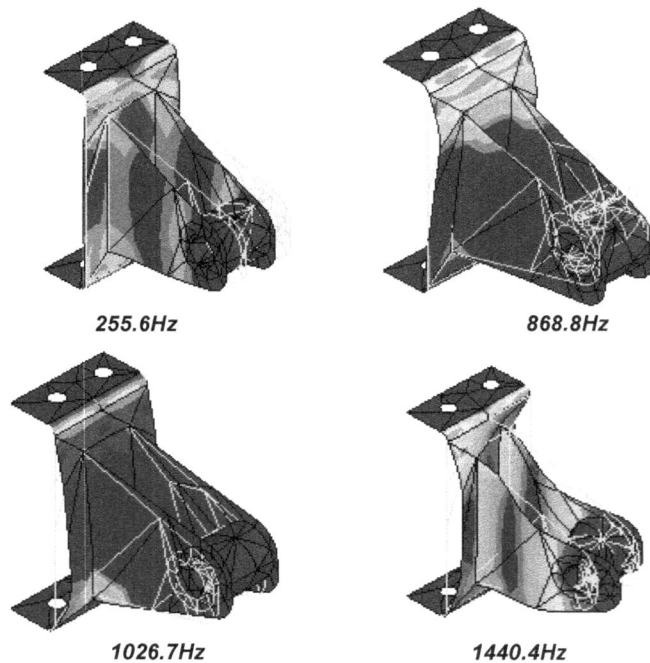

*255.6Hz*                    *868.8Hz*

*1026.7Hz*                   *1440.4Hz*

**Figure 9–1**

Note that the equation solved in Modal analysis is the equation of dynamic equilibrium (i.e., Newton's equation) with no loads included in the analysis. Therefore, the mode shapes are essentially dimensionless. When mode shapes are displayed in Creo Simulate, only some imaginary magnitudes are displayed, which are scaled to an arbitrary value.

# 9.3 Defining a Modal Analysis

**Learning Objective**

Understand how to create a modal analysis.

Modal analysis parameters are defined in the Modal Analysis Definition dialog box, as shown in Figure 9–2.

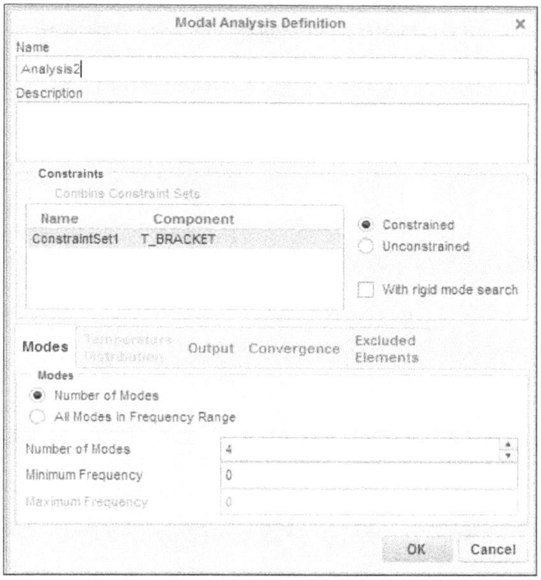

**Figure 9–2**

The options in the Modal Analysis dialog box are as follows:

| Option | Description |
|---|---|
| **Name** | Enter a name for the analysis. |
| **Description** | Enter a description of the analysis (optional). |
| **Constraints** | Enables you to define the constraint set using the following options: |
| **Constrained** | Select a constraint set, if one is available. |
| **Unconstrained** | Solves an unconstrained or under-constrained model. |
| **With rigid mode search** | Use when solving an unconstrained or under-constrained model, if you want to visualize the rigid body modes. Creo Simulate reports any rigid body modes that it finds. |

| | | |
|---|---|---|
| **Output** | | Define the output for the analysis. This tab contains the following options: |
| | **Calculate** | Select the stresses, rotations, and/or reactions to calculated quantity values. |
| | **Plot** | Enter a plotting grid density. Creo Simulate calculates and displays quantity values at the intersection of the grid lines on each element. |
| **Convergence** | | Select a convergence method using the Method drop-down list in the *Convergence* tab. |
| **Modes** | | Define the modes for the analysis in the *Modes* tab. This tab contains the following options: |
| | **Number of Modes** | Specifies the number of modes and frequencies for Creo Simulate to calculate. |
| | **All Modes in Frequency Range** | Requests the calculation of all modes within a frequency range in the *Min Frequency* and *Max Frequency* fields. |
| | **Minimum Frequency** | Specify the minimum frequency of a frequency range. You can only specify this if the **All Modes in Frequency Range** option is selected. |
| | **Maximum Frequency** | Specify the maximum frequency of a frequency range. You can only specify this if the **All Modes in Frequency Range** option is selected. |

# Practice 9a

# Modal Analysis of a Bracket

**Learning Objectives**

✓ Set up and run a modal analysis.

✓ Display the results.

*A modal analysis enables you to find the natural frequencies and corresponding natural modes of the bracket under a specific constraint set.*

In this practice, you will set up and run a modal analysis on a bracket model, as shown in Figure 9–3. You will use the shell idealization to represent the thin sections of the model.

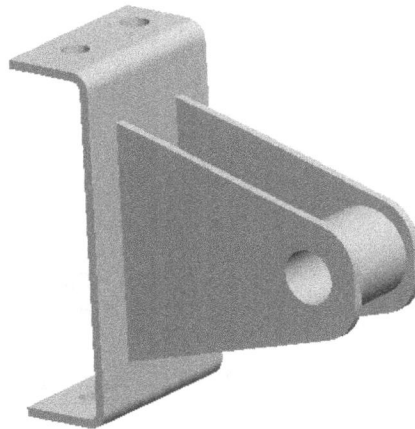

**Figure 9–3**

## Modeling Tasks

### Task 1 - Open the part.

1. Open **modal_hook_1.prt** in Creo Parametric. The unshaded part displays as shown in Figure 9–4.

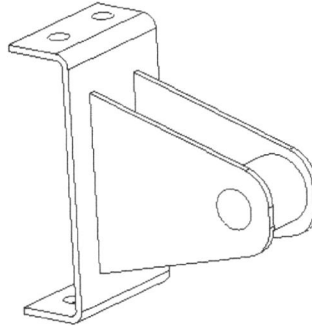

**Figure 9–4**

2. Ensure that the unit system is set to **mmNs**.

3. Select **Applications>Simulate**. Ensure that the **Structure** mode is active.

### Task 2 - Apply the material.

*The model's material properties should be as stated.*

1. Assign **STEEL** to the model. The following values are the default material properties for HS-low-alloy steel (STEEL):

   - Poisson = 0.27
   - Young's modulus = 199948 N/mm2
   - Coeff of thermal expansion = 1.17e-5 /C
   - Density = 7.82708e-9 tonne/mm^3

### Task 3 - Define the shell elements.

1. In the *Refine Model* tab, expand the Shell Pair drop-down list and select **Detect Shell Pairs**. The Auto Detect Shell Pairs dialog box opens as shown in Figure 9–5.

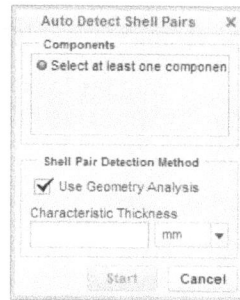

**Figure 9–5**

*The wall thickness in this part is 5mm.*

2.  In the *Characteristic Thickness* field, enter **6** and click

    Start . Creo Simulate runs the automatic detection algorithm and closes the Auto Detect Shell Pairs dialog box.

3.  In the *Refine Model* tab, in the *AutoGEM* area, click ⬛ to open the Simulation Geometry dialog box. Accept the default

    options and click Apply . The model displays as shown in Figure 9–6.

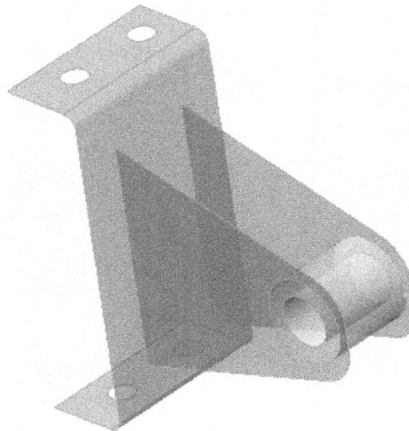

**Figure 9–6**

Verify that the boss is displayed in grey (this is the uncompressed area), while the thin-walled sections are displayed in green (these are the shell pairs compressed to a midsurface).

4.  Click Close in the Simulation Geometry dialog box.

## Task 4 - Apply the constraints.

In this task, you will apply constraints to the top and bottom surfaces of the bracket, as shown in Figure 9–7.

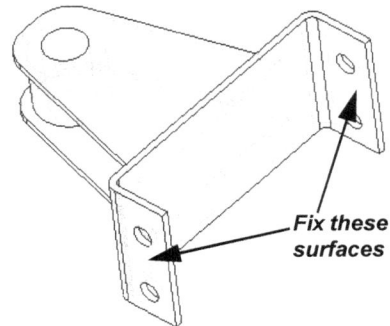

Fix these
surfaces

**Figure 9–7**

1. Click 🖾. The Constraint dialog box opens.

2. In the *Name* field, enter **surface_fix**.

3. Constrain the surfaces shown in Figure 9–7 in all of the Translations and Rotations. The model displays as shown in Figure 9–8.

**Figure 9–8**

## Task 5 - Mesh the model.

1. Mesh the model using the **All with Properties** option.

*The shell elements (Tri and Quad) are displayed in green and the 3D solid elements (Tetra) are displayed in blue.*

2. The model displays as shown in Figure 9–9.

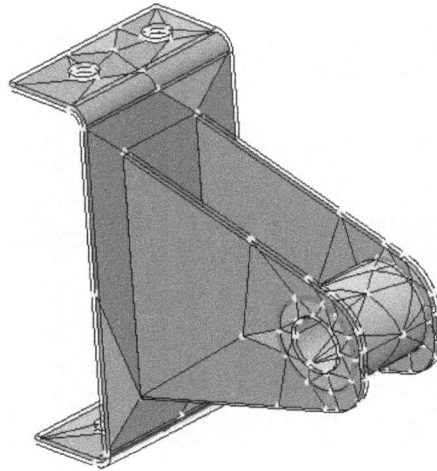

**Figure 9–9**

3. Close the AutoGEM dialog box and save the mesh.

## Summary

In the previous tasks, you created the simulation entities required to analyze your model. In the following tasks, you will specify the analysis type and convergence method and run the analysis.

## Analysis Tasks

### Task 6 - Run a Quick Check analysis.

In this task, the model is analyzed using the **Quick Check** convergence option, which checks for errors.

1. In the Analyses and Design Studies dialog box, select **File> New Modal**. The Modal Analysis Definition dialog box opens as shown in Figure 9–10.

*The objective of a modal study is to ensure that the system does not have a resonant frequency near the operating frequency.*

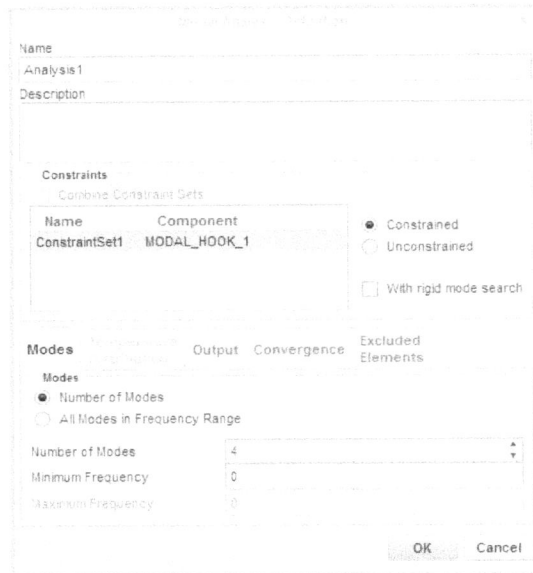

**Figure 9–10**

2. In the *Name* field, enter **modal_hook**.

3. (Optional) In the *Description* field, enter a description of the analysis.

4. In the *Constraints* area, accept the defaults.

*Select the* **Unconstrained** *and* **With rigid mode search** *options when you are not sure if your model is fully constrained.*

5. In the *Number of Modes* field, enter **6**.

6. Select the *Convergence* tab, expand the Method drop-down list and select **Quick Check**.

7. Click    OK    to accept the selections and close the Modal Analysis Definition dialog box.

8. Check the validity of the model and run the analysis. The run should complete without any errors.

## Task 7 - Run a Multi-Pass Adaptive analysis.

In this task, the model is analyzed using the **Multi-Pass Adaptive** convergence option.

*The solution converges on frequency.*

1. Change the convergence method to **Multi-Pass Adaptive**. In the *Polynomial Order* field, enter **9**. In the *Limits* area, in the *Percent Convergence* field, and accept the defaults.

2. Run the analysis.

3. In the Analyses and Design Studies dialog box, click ▦. In the Run Status window that displays (as shown in Figure 9–11), extract the following information.

```
Number of Modes: 6

Mode   Frequency (Hz)   Convergence
----   --------------   -----------
   1   2.607665e+02        3.0%
   2   9.401390e+02        7.5%
   3   1.015977e+03        8.4%
   4   1.467314e+03        3.3%
   5   1.723053e+03        3.6%
   6   1.821113e+03        3.9%
```

**Figure 9–11**

Note the convergence percentage for the six modes. The solution converges on the frequency (you set the convergence in Step 1 of this task). The convergence was obtained on pass six.

## Results Tasks

## Task 8 - Display the results.

In this task, you will create, animate, and display four Displacement Magnitude fringe plots for the first four modes of vibration.

1. In the Analyses and Design Studies dialog box, click [icon]. The Result Window Definition dialog box opens as shown in Figure 9–12.

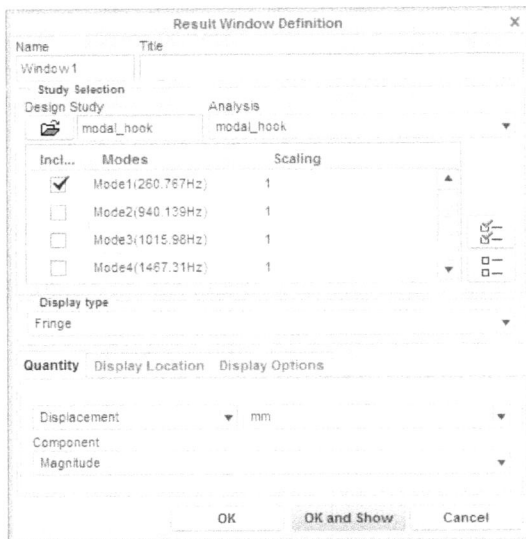

**Figure 9–12**

2. In the *Name* field, enter **mode1_window** and in the *Title* field, enter **mode_1**.

3. Select the *Display Options* tab and enter the information shown in Figure 9–13.

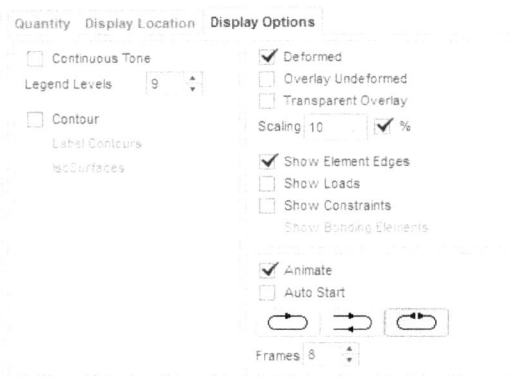

**Figure 9–13**

4. Display the result plot. Step through the animation to the frame shown in Figure 9–14.

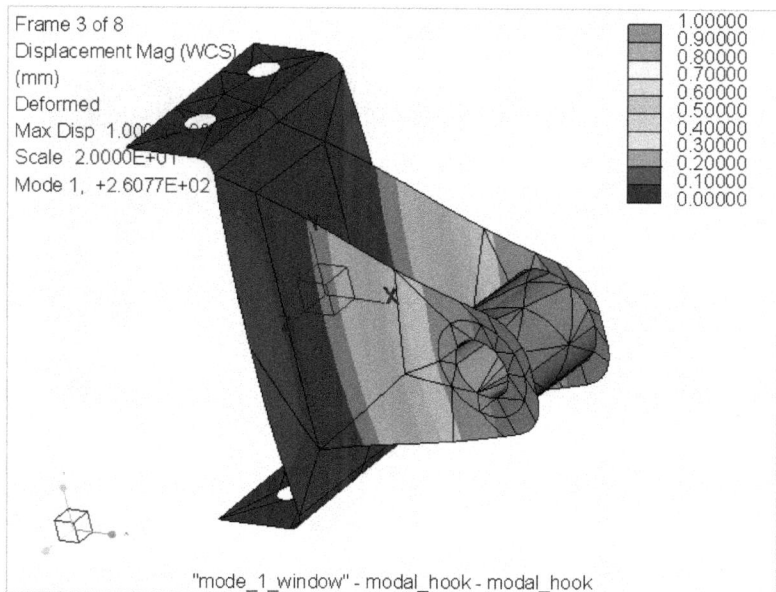

Figure 9–14

5. Create, animate, and display a Displacement Magnitude for mode 2. In the *Name* field, enter **mode2_window** and in the *Title* field, enter mode_2.

6. In the *Include* column, select the second checkbox as shown in Figure 9–15, and clear the first checkbox.

| Include | Modes | Scaling | |
|---|---|---|---|
| ☐ | Mode1(260.767Hz) | 1 | ▲ |
| ✓ | Mode2(940.139Hz) | 1 | |
| ☐ | Mode3(1015.98Hz) | 1 | |
| ☐ | Mode4(1467.31Hz) | 1 | ▼ |

Figure 9–15

7. Display the **mode_2** fringe plot. Step through the animation to the frame shown in Figure 9–16.

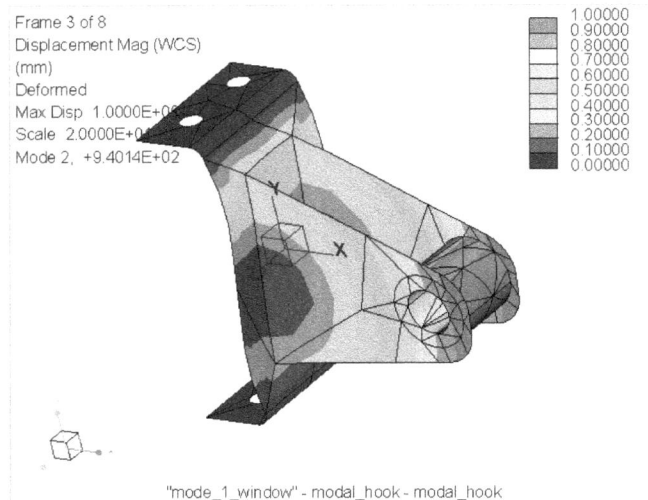

Frame 3 of 8
Displacement Mag (WCS)
(mm)
Deformed
Max Disp 1.0000E+0
Scale 2.0000E+0
Mode 2, +9.4014E+02

1.00000
0.90000
0.80000
0.70000
0.60000
0.50000
0.40000
0.30000
0.20000
0.10000
0.00000

"mode_1_window" - modal_hook - modal_hook

Figure 9–16

8. Create, animate, and display a Displacement Magnitude for mode 3. In the *Name* field, enter **mode3_window**, and in the *Title* field, enter **mode_3**.

9. In the *Include* column, select the third checkbox and clear the second checkbox.

10. Display the **mode_3** fringe plot. Step through the animation to the frame shown in Figure 9–17.

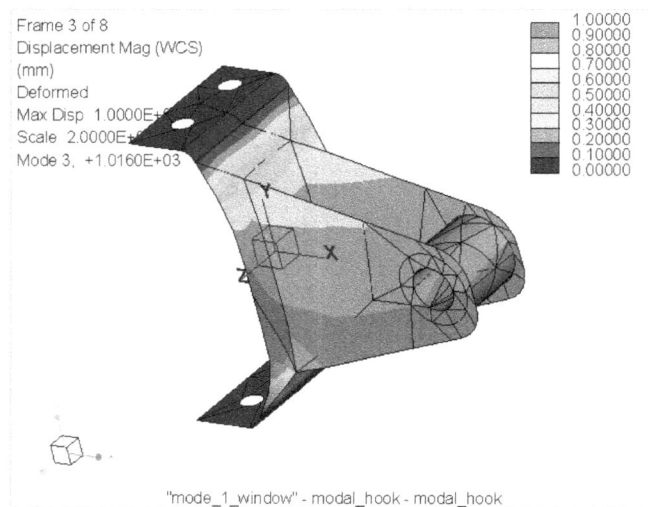

Frame 3 of 8
Displacement Mag (WCS)
(mm)
Deformed
Max Disp 1.0000E+
Scale 2.0000E+
Mode 3, +1.0160E+03

1.00000
0.90000
0.80000
0.70000
0.60000
0.50000
0.40000
0.30000
0.20000
0.10000
0.00000

"mode_1_window" - modal_hook - modal_hook

Figure 9–17

11. Create, animate, and display a Displacement Magnitude for mode 4. In the *Name* field, enter **mode4_window** and in the *Title* field enter **mode_4**.

12. In the *Include* column, select the fourth checkbox and clear the third checkbox.

13. Display the **mode_4** fringe plot. Step through the animation to the frame shown in Figure 9–18.

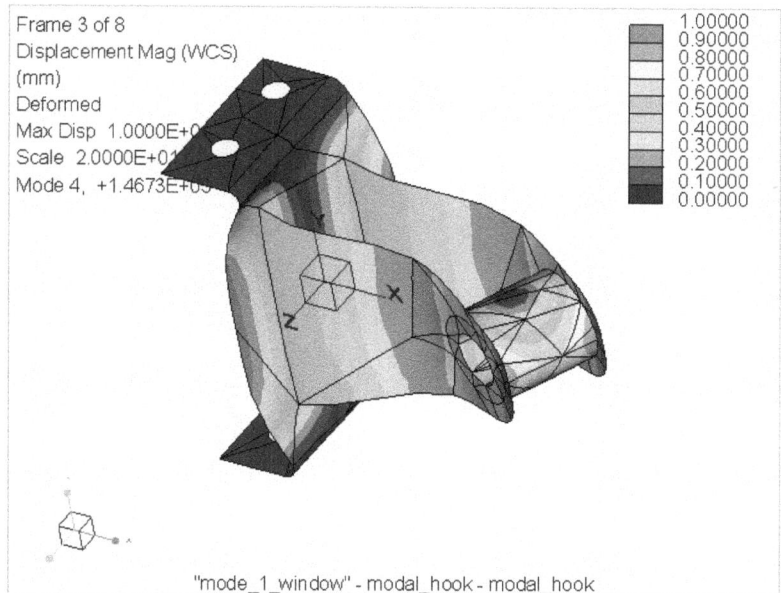

**Figure 9–18**

14. Exit the Results. Save and close the model.

## Task 9 - (Optional) Set up and run a new analysis.

1. Delete the mesh.

2. Delete the mid-surface shells.

3. Mesh the model with only 3D solid elements.

4. Set up and run a new Multi-Pass Adaptive analysis. Enter a different name for the analysis. In the *Polynomial Order* field, enter **9**. In the *Limits* area and *Converge on* area, in the *Percent Convergence* field, accept the defaults.

5. Compare the results.

# Chapter 10

## Welds, Springs, and Masses

Idealizations are used to simplify your model and shorten your analysis time. Three other useful idealizations are: welds, springs, and masses.

This chapter contains the following topics:

- **Weld Connections**
- **Springs**
- **Masses**

# 10.1 Weld Connections

**Learning Objectives**

✓ Understand how to create spot weld connections.

✓ Understand how to create end weld connections.

✓ Understand how to create perimeter weld connections.

Weld connections are analysis features that are intended to bridge gaps that occur during the midsurface compression of shell assemblies. The four types of weld connections available in Creo Simulate are: Spot Welds, End Welds, Perimeter Welds, and Weld Feature welds.

**Spot Welds**

Spot welds connect parts at datum point locations that you specify. An example of an assembly suitable for using spot welds is shown in Figure 10–1.

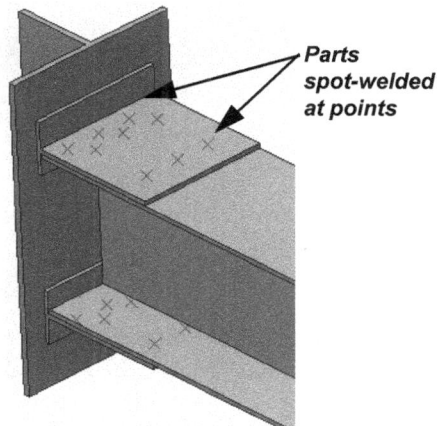

*Parts spot-welded at points*

**Figure 10–1**

A spot weld in Creo Simulate is modeled with a beam element with a round cross-section. This idealization accurately transfers forces from one part to another. However, stress values close to the spot welds might not be accurate.

The following conditions are required for successful spot welds:

• The surfaces being connected by the weld must be within 15° of being parallel to each other.

- One of the surfaces being connected must have datum points that define spot weld locations.

Use the following steps to create a spot weld:

1. In the *Connections* area, click ⌐.
2. Expand the Type drop-down list and select **Spot Weld**.
3. Select the two surfaces that you want to connect.
4. Select the datum points where the spot welds are going to be created.
5. Enter the diameter of the weld.
6. In the Materials dialog box, select the material of the weld.

## End Welds

End welds are used to connect plates that are joined at right or oblique angles, such as in T or L configurations. An example of an assembly suitable for using end welds is shown in Figure 10–2.

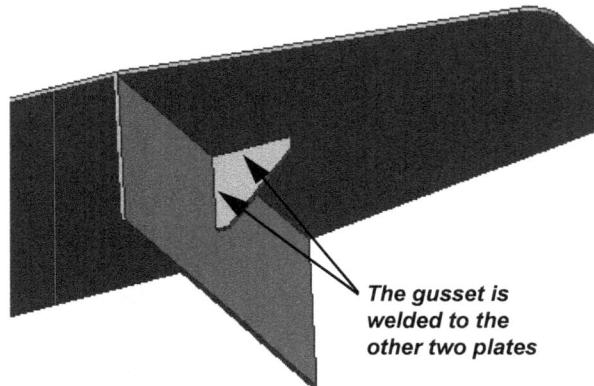

The gusset is welded to the other two plates

**Figure 10–2**

When an end weld is created, Creo Simulate creates shell elements to extend the mesh from one plate to join the mesh of a base plate.

Use the following steps to create an end weld:

1. In the *Connections* area, click ⌐.
2. Expand the Type drop-down list and select **End Weld**.
3. Select the surfaces to be welded.

# Perimeter Welds

*Curved plates can be used with perimeter welds.*

Perimeter welds are used to connect plates that are parallel to one another, along the perimeter of one plate. An example of an assembly suitable for using a perimeter weld is shown in Figure 10–3.

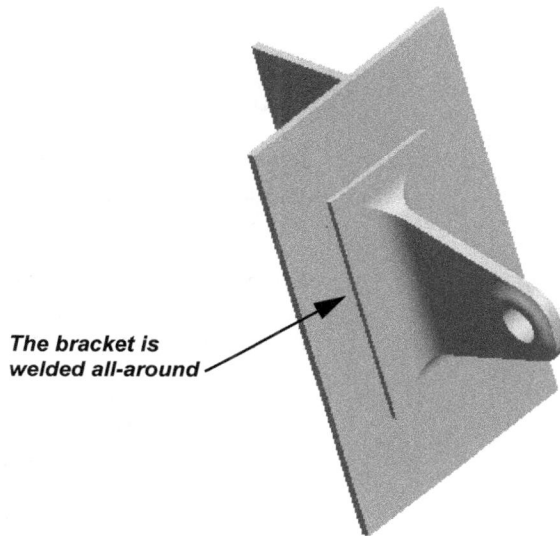

**The bracket is welded all-around**

**Figure 10–3**

Creo Simulate automatically creates a series of new surfaces to extend the edges of one plate to the surface of the other. Shell elements are created on these surfaces.

Use the following steps to create a perimeter weld:

1. In the Connections area, click ⌐.
2. Expand the Type drop-down list and select **Perimeter Weld**.
3. Select the doubler surface on which you want to place the weld.
4. Select the base surface to which to extend the weld.
5. Select the doubler surface's edges that you want to weld.
6. Enter the thickness of the shell elements that represent the perimeter weld.
7. Select a material for the weld.

# 10.2 Springs

**Learning Objectives**

Understand springs in Creo Simulate.

Understand how to create springs.

Spring elements are one-dimentsional idealizations that are intended to simulate the various elastic components in your model without specifying their geometrical shape.

*Non-linear springs require an Advanced Creo Simulate license.*

Springs in Creo Simulate can be linear (constant stiffness) or non-linear (variable stiffness). Springs can connect one point to the ground (fixed) or connect two points.

In the example shown in Figure 10–4 one spring connects two points (a point on the frame and the mass point) and a fixed to the ground spring supports the frame at the top.

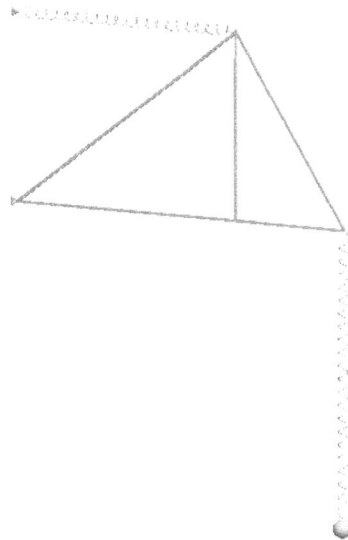

**Figure 10–4**

*Advanced springs require an Advanced Creo Simulate license.*

In Creo Simulate, you can create three types of springs: Simple, Advanced, and To Ground. Simple and Advanced springs can have any orientation, which is defined by selecting two points. Ground springs are always parallel to a coordinate system, such as WCS.

Use the following steps to create a spring:

1. In the *Idealizations* area, click ≋. The Spring Definition dialog box opens as shown in Figure 10–5.

*You cannot create zero length simple springs.*

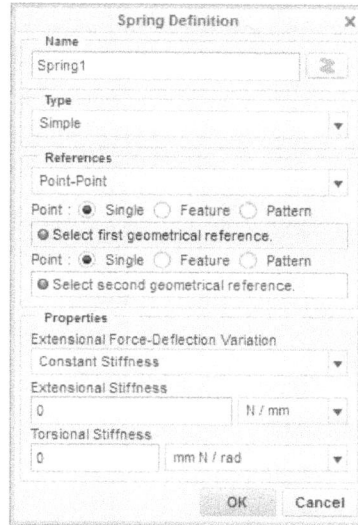

**Figure 10–5**

The options in the Spring Definition dialog box are as follows:

| Option | Description |
|---|---|
| **Name** | Enter the name of the spring or use the default name. |
| **References** | Selects geometry references. The following types of geometry references are available: **Point-Point**, **Point-Surface**, **Point-Edge**, and **Point-Point Pairs**. |
| **Type** | Selects the type of the spring. The following types of springs are available: **Simple**, **Advanced**, and **To Ground**. |
| **Extensional Force-Deflection Variation** | Selects a linear or non-linear spring:<br>• Constant Stiffness (linear spring)<br>• Force-Deflection Curve (non-linear spring) |
| **Extensional Stiffness** | Defines the extensional stiffness, (i.e., resistance to stretch) of your spring. |
| **Torsional Stiffness** | Defines torsional stiffness (i.e., resistance to twist) of your spring. |

## Stiffness

Simple springs only have two stiffness properties:

- **Extensional Stiffness:** Acting along the line connecting the two points.

- **Torsional Stiffness:** Acting about the line connecting the two points.

Advanced and To Ground springs require stiffness attributes to be defined in the Spring Properties Definition dialog box, as shown in Figure 10–6.

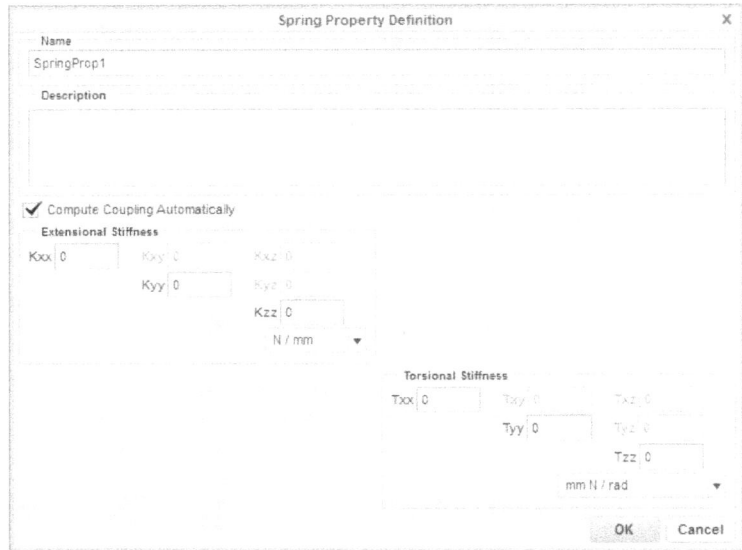

**Figure 10–6**

The options in the Spring Properties Definition dialog box are as follows:

| Box | Description |
| --- | --- |
| **Set Name** | Enter the name of the spring stiffness. |
| **Description** | (Optional) Enter the description of the spring stiffness. |
| **Extensional** | Enter the stiffness for the principal axes in the *Kxx*, *Kyy*, and *Kzz* fields. |
| **Torsional** | Enter the stiffness for the rotation around the principal axes in the *Txx*, *Tyy*, and *Tzz* fields. |

## Orientation

The spring principal axes, used to specify $K_{xx}$, $K_{yy}$, etc. stiffness directions in the Spring Properties Definition dialog box, are defined as follows:

- **To Ground spring:** The principal axes are aligned with the axes of the selected coordinate system (the default is WCS).

- **Advanced spring:** The X-principal axis is always along the line between the two points, the Y-axis direction is specified by the user (as is done for Beam elements), and the Z-axis direction is obtained as a cross-product of X-axis by the Y-axis.

# 10.3 Masses

**Learning Objectives**

Understand mass elements in Creo Simulate.

Understand how to create mass elements.

*You can attach a mass to a solid, shell, or beam.*

Mass elements are idealizations that are intended to simulate the mass properties of various components in your model, without specifying the component's geometrical shape. For example, a mass element might be used to simulate the weight of the engine attached to the truck frame, without actually specifying the engine's geometry.

*Advanced masses require an Advanced Creo Simulate license.*

Masses in Creo Simulate can be **Simple** or **Advanced**. Simple masses only have translational inertia, while Advanced masses can be assigned rotational inertia (i.e., moments of inertia) as well.

Use the following steps to create a mass:

*Select **Advanced** in the Type drop-down list to create an advanced mass.*

1. In the *Idealizations* area, click 🏋. The Mass Definition dialog box opens as shown in Figure 10–7.

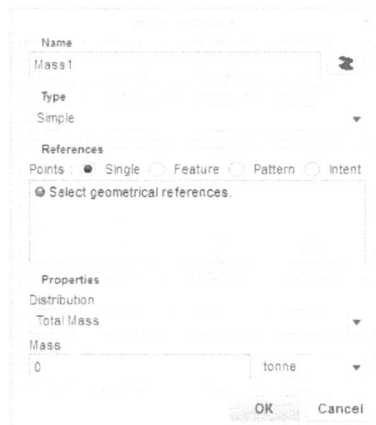

**Figure 10–7**

2. Enter the *Name*.
3. Expand the Type drop-down list and select **Simple** or **Advanced**.
4. Select the *References* (datum points).
5. Select the *Distribution* (**Total Mass** or **Mass Per Point**).
6. Enter the mass value.

# Practice 10a

# Spot Welds

**Learning Objectives**

- Create spot weld connections.

- Set up a spot welded FEA model analysis.

- Display the results of the analysis.

*Use the **Spot Weld** option for the small bolts, screws, and rivets in your model, and for the spot welds.*

In this practice, you will set up and run a spot welded model using the **Spot Weld** option. The assembly model is shown in Figure 10–8. The assembly model consists of four parts. You will use shell idealizations to model the parts.

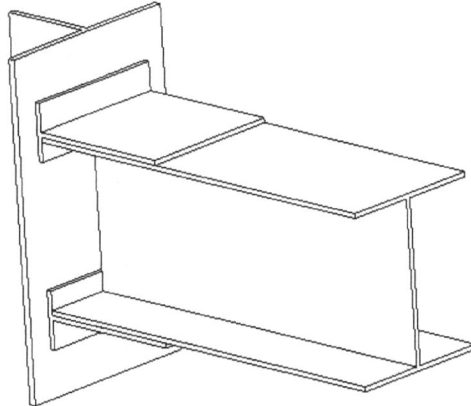

**Figure 10–8**

## Modeling Tasks

### Task 1 - Open the assembly.

1. Open **spot_weld.asm** in Creo Parametric. The model displays as shown in Figure 10–9.

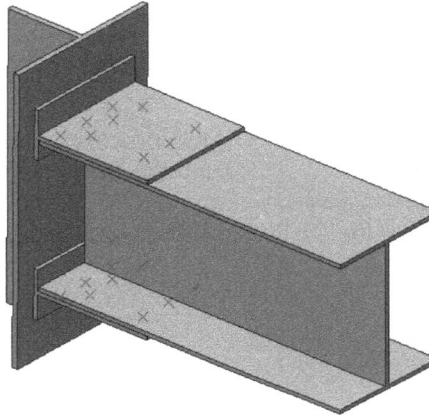

**Figure 10–9**

2. Ensure that the unit system is set to **mmNs**.

### Task 2 - Launch Creo Simulate.

1. Select **Applications>Simulate** to launch Creo Simulate.

2. Click 🖳 and clear the **Display AutoGEM Controls** option to hide the **HardPnt** icons.

*The Free Default Interface ensures that the parts are not bonded over the mated surfaces.*

3. Click 🗔 . Expand the Default Interface drop-down list and select **Free** as shown in Figure 10–10.

**Figure 10–10**

4. Click OK .

## Task 3 - Define shell pairs.

1. In the *Refine Model* tab, expand the Shell Pair drop-down list, and select **Detect Shell Pairs**. The Auto Detect Shell Pairs dialog box opens as shown in Figure 10–11.

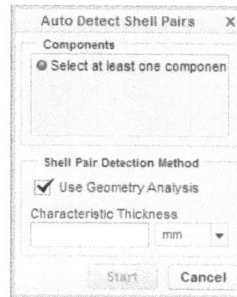

**Figure 10–11**

2. Select all four parts in the assembly (hold down <Ctrl> to multi-select).

3. In the *Characteristic Thickness* field, enter **8**. The Auto Detect Shell Pairs dialog box opens as shown in Figure 10–12.

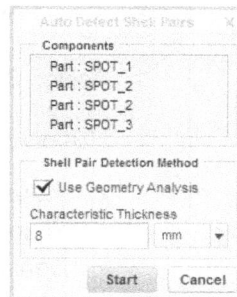

**Figure 10–12**

4. Click Start . Creo Simulate runs the automatic detection algorithm and closes the Auto Detect Shell Pairs dialog box.

5. Check the Model Tree. There should be nine shell pairs in the Model Tree on the assembly level.

6. In the *Refine Model* tab, in the *AutoGEM* area, click ⬚ to open the Simulation Geometry dialog box.

7. Accept the default options and click   Apply  . The model displays as shown in Figure 10–13. Ensure that all of the surfaces are highlighted in green, and that no elements in the model are displayed in a different color.

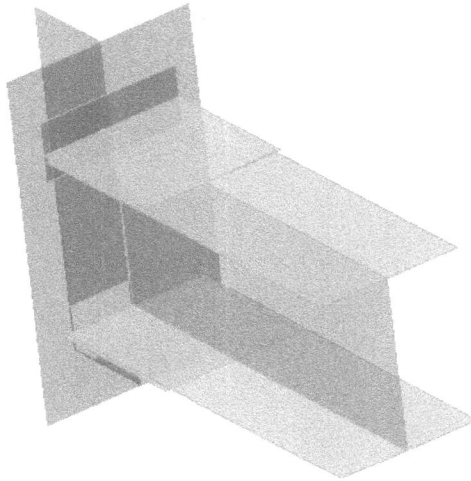

**Figure 10–13**

8. Click   Close   to close the Simulation Geometry dialog box.

## Task 4 - Apply the material.

*The model's material properties should be as stated.*

1. Assign **STEEL** to the assembly parts as the material. The following values are the default material properties for HS-low-alloy steel (STEEL):

   * Poisson = 0.27
   * Young's modulus = 199948 MPa
   * Density = 7.82708e-9 tonne/mm3

## Task 5 - Create spot weld connections.

In this task, you will connect the plates using the **Spot Weld** option.

1. In the *Connections* area, click   . The Weld Definition dialog box opens.

2. Expand the Type drop-down list and select **Spot Weld**.

3. Select the surfaces shown in Figure 10–14 as the *References* for the weld.

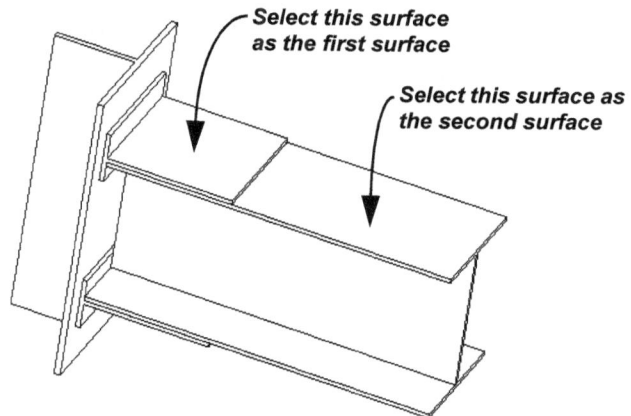

*Select this surface as the first surface*

*Select this surface as the second surface*

**Figure 10–14**

4. In the *Properties* area, select **Feature** option and select **PNT0**. Six points (PNT0 to PNT5) are highlighted, since they were created as one feature in Creo Parametric.

5. For the diameter, enter **10**.

6. For the weld material, select **STEEL**. The Weld Definition dialog box opens as shown in Figure 10–15.

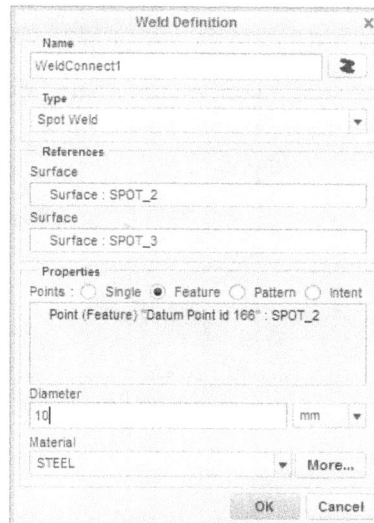

**Figure 10–15**

7. Click ⬚OK⬚ to close the Weld Definition dialog box. **Spot Weld** icons display as shown in Figure 10–16.

8. Repeat Steps 1 to 7 for the other side as shown in Figure 10–16.

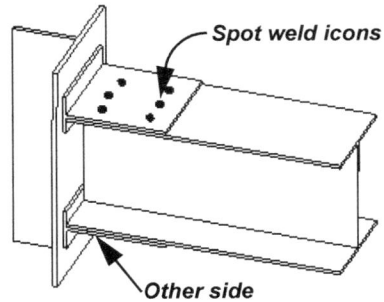

**Figure 10–16**

9. Repeat Steps 1 to 7 to create spot welds between the surfaces shown in Figure 10–17. Select **PNT6** when selecting the datum point feature.

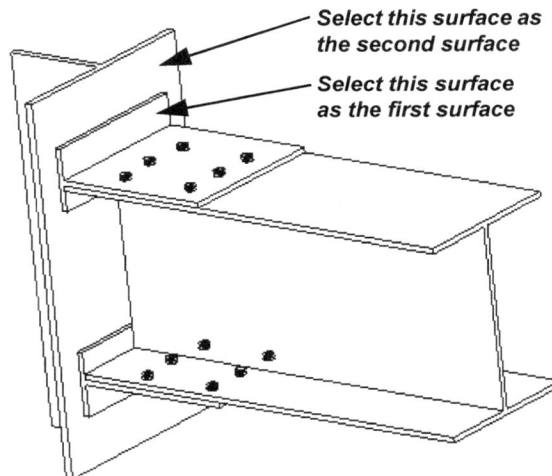

**Figure 10–17**

10. Repeat Steps 1 to 7 for the other side as shown in Figure 10–18.

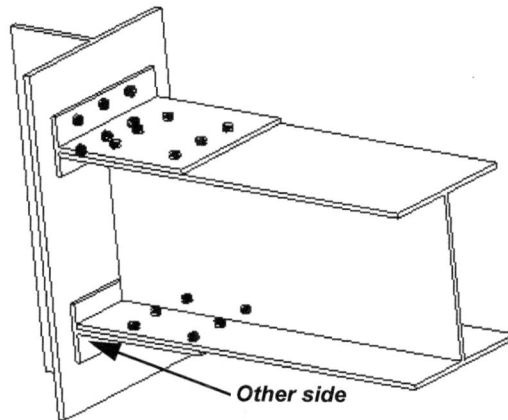

**Other side**

Figure 10–18

## Task 6 - Mesh the model.

1. Click ⬚ to open the AutoGEM dialog box. Accept **All with Properties** and click `Create`.

2. Close the AutoGEM Summary and Diagnostics dialog boxes when the meshing finishes. The model displays as shown in Figure 10–19.

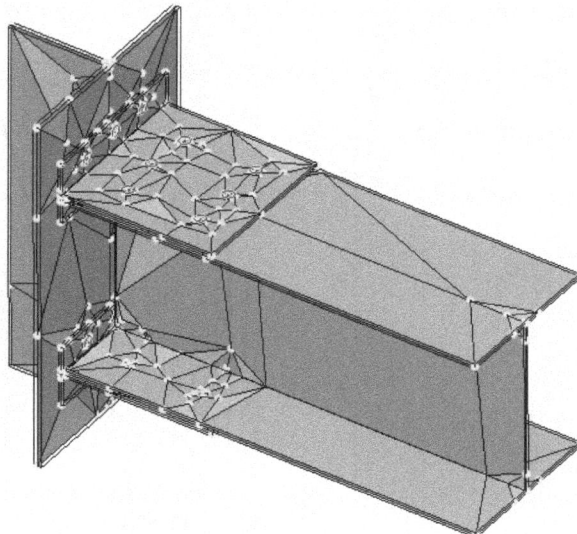

Figure 10–19

3. Zoom in on any spot weld in the model, such as the one shown in Figure 10–20.

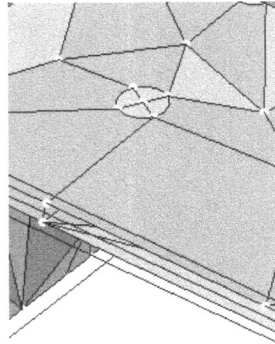

**Figure 10–20**

Note the small circular regions Creo Simulate created around each spot weld. The diameter of each region is the spot weld diameter that you entered in the Weld Definition dialog box.

4. Select the FRONT view and zoom in on the model to note in the gaps between the midsurfaces, such as those shown in Figure 10–21.

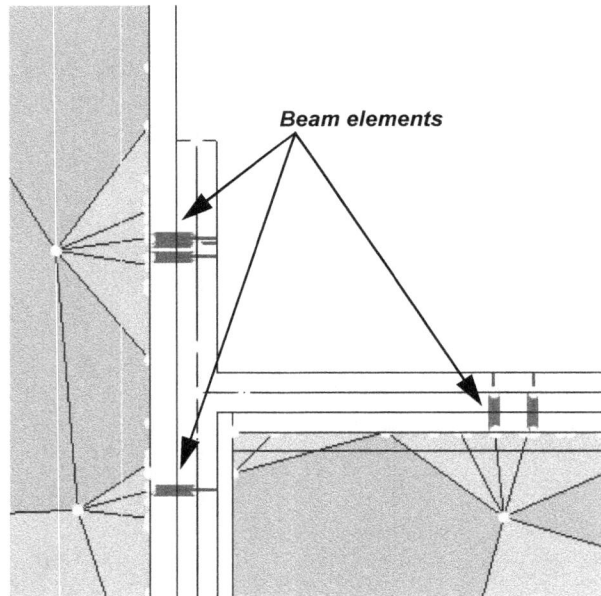

*Beam elements*

**Figure 10–21**

Note the beam elements (purple lines) between the parts. These are the elements that Creo Simulate automatically created to connect the midsurfaces at the spot weld points.

5. Close the AutoGEM dialog box and save the mesh.

## Task 7 - Apply loads.

1. In the X-direction, apply a load of **1000** on the edges (apply it to the edges rather than to the end surface) as shown in Figure 10–22. For the name of the load, enter **edge_load**.

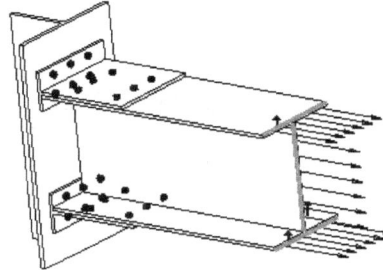

Figure 10–22

## Task 8 - Apply the constraints.

1. Constrain the model edges (fixed translation and rotation) as shown in Figure 10–23 (constrain the edges rather than the end surfaces). For the name of the constraint, enter **edge_constraints**.

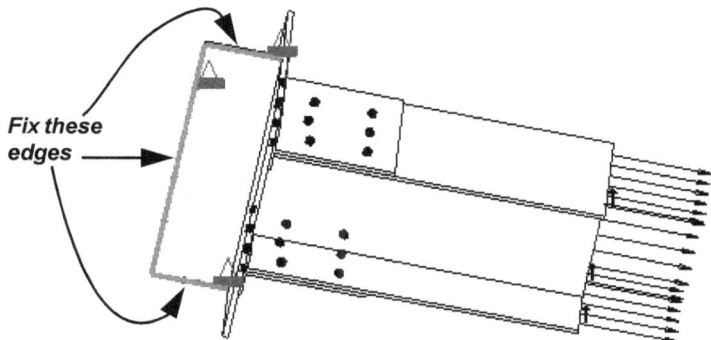

Fix these edges →

Figure 10–23

## Analysis Tasks

### Task 9 - Set up and run an analysis.

1. Set up a Multi-Pass Adaptive analysis. For the *Name*, enter **spot_weld**. In the *Polynomial Order* field, enter **9**. In the *Limits* area, in the *Percent Convergence* field, enter **10**.

2. Run the analysis.

3. In the Analyses and Design Studies dialog box, click [icon] and extract the following information from the Run Status window:

   - Analysis converges on pass nine.
   - Stress error is 1.2% of the maximum principal stress, as shown in Figure 10–24.

```
RMS Stress Error Estimates:

Load Set          Stress Error  % of Max Prin Str
----------------  ------------  -----------------
LoadSet1          7.26e-01        1.2% of  6.20e+01

Resource Check                       (15:36:31)
   Elapsed Time    (sec):     66.11
   CPU Time        (sec):     54.27
   Memory Usage    (kb):     624023
   Wrk Dir Dsk Usage (kb):    68850

The analysis converged to within 10% on
edge displacement, element strain energy,
and global RMS stress.
```

**Figure 10–24**

## Results Tasks

### Task 10 - Display the results.

In this task, you will create and display a von Mises stress fringe plot and a deformation animation for the model to verify the applied boundary conditions.

1. Create the deformation animation plot.

2. Start the animation. The applied boundary conditions behave correctly.

3. Create the undeformed von Mises stress fringe plot. Clear all of the **Include contributions from beams** options. Change the *Legend minimum* to **0** and *maximum* to **5**. The result plot displays as shown in Figure 10–25.

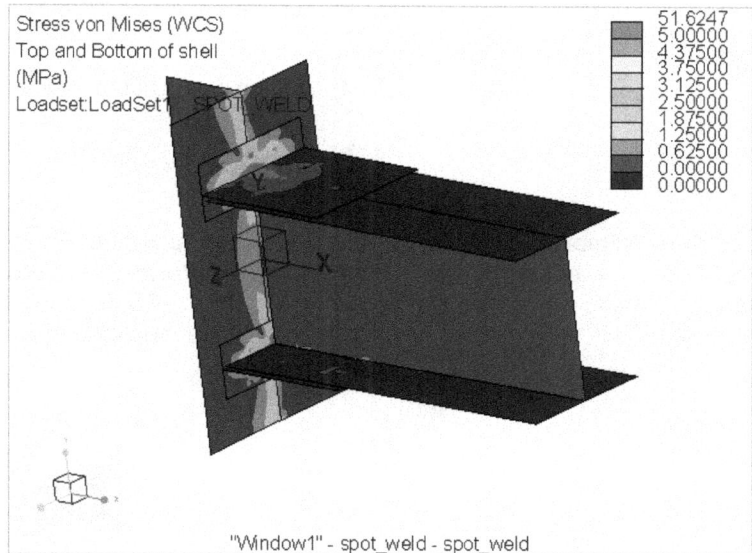

Stress von Mises (WCS)
Top and Bottom of shell
(MPa)
Loadset:LoadSet1   SPOT WELD

51.6247
5.00000
4.37500
3.75000
3.12500
2.50000
1.87500
1.25000
0.62500
0.00000
0.00000

"Window1" - spot_weld - spot_weld

**Figure 10–25**

4. Locate and examine high stress areas in the model, particularly the welds and the adjacent areas. If a high stress area is located at the weld, a more detailed analysis should be performed, such as using the 3D solid model type.

5. Exit the Results. Save and close the model.

# Practice 10b

# Perimeter Welds

**Learning Objectives**

- Create Perimeter Weld connections.

- Set up a continuous welded FEA model analysis.

- Display the results.

*Use the **Perimeter Weld** option to connect parallel plates.*

In this practice, you will set up and run a continuously welded model, using the **Perimeter Weld** option. The assembly model is shown in Figure 10–26. It consists of a beam plate and a hook plate. You will use idealization to shell the plates shown in Figure 10–26.

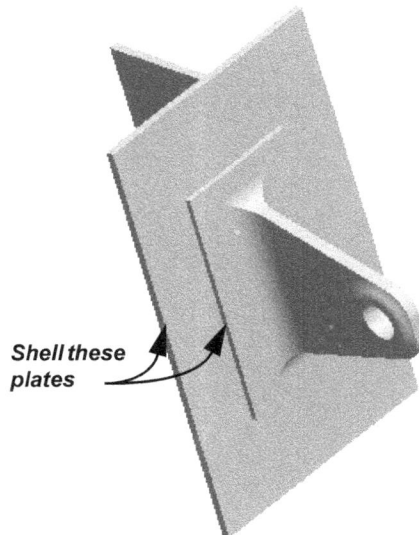

**Shell these plates**

**Figure 10–26**

## Modeling Tasks

### Task 1 - Open the model.

1. Open **weld_1.asm** in Creo Parametric. The assembly displays as shown in Figure 10–27.

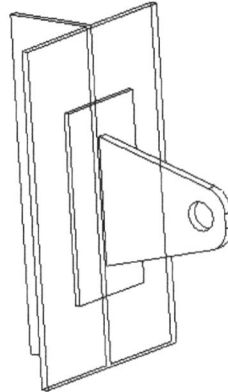

**Figure 10–27**

### Task 2 - Launch Creo Simulate.

1. Select **Applications>Simulate** to launch Creo Simulate.

*The Free Default Interface ensures that the parts are not bonded over the mated surfaces.*

2. Click ⬚. Expand the Default Interface drop-down list and select **Free**, as shown in Figure 10–28.

**Figure 10–28**

3. Click OK.

## Task 3 - Define the shell pairs.

1. In the *Refine Model* tab, expand the Shell Pair drop-down list and select **Detect Shell Pairs**. The Auto Detect Shell Pairs dialog box opens as shown in Figure 10–29.

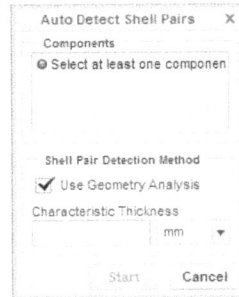

**Figure 10–29**

2. Select all of the parts in the assembly (hold down <Ctrl> to multi-select).

3. In the *Characteristic Thickness* field, enter **10**. The Auto Detect Shell Pairs dialog box opens as shown in Figure 10–30.

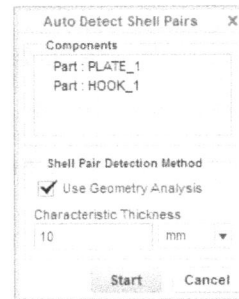

**Figure 10–30**

4. Click **Start**. Creo Simulate runs the automatic detection algorithm and closes the Auto Detect Shell Pairs dialog box.

5. There should be four shell pairs in the Model Tree on the assembly level.

6. In the *Refine Model* tab, in the *AutoGEM* area, click ⬚ to open the Simulation Geometry dialog box.

7. Accept the default options and click Apply . The model displays as shown in Figure 10–31. Ensure that all of the surfaces are highlighted in green, and that no elements in the model are displayed in different colors.

**Figure 10–31**

8. Click Close to close the Simulation Geometry dialog box.

## Task 4 - Apply the material.

*The model's material properties should be as stated.*

1. Assign **STEEL** as the material to the assembly parts. The following values are the default material properties for HS-low-alloy steel (STEEL):

- Poisson = 0.27
- Young's modulus = 199948 MPa
- Density = 7.82708e-9 tonne/mm3

## Task 5 - Create the weld connections.

*For perpendicular plates, use the **End Weld** option.*

In this task, you will connect the two plates using the **Perimeter Weld** option.

1. In the *Connections* area, click ⌐. The Weld Definition dialog box opens.

2. Expand the Type drop-down list and select **Perimeter Weld**.

3. Select the top surfaces of **hook_1** as the doubler surface from which to extend, as shown in Figure 10–32.

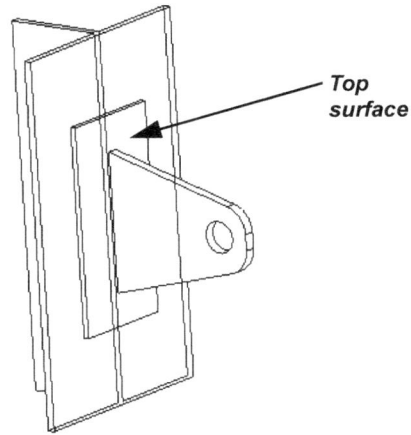

**Figure 10–32**

4. Select the **plate_1** top surface as the base surface to which to extend, as shown in Figure 10–33.

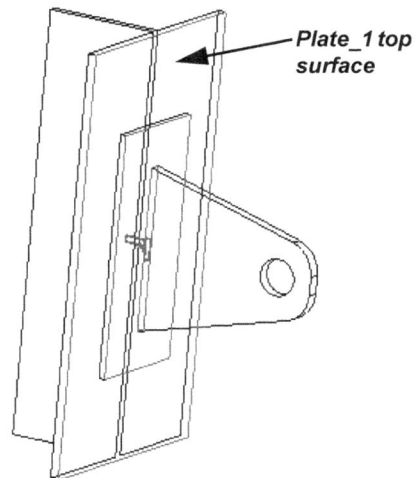

**Figure 10–33**

5. Select the four edges of the **hook top** surface as the edges of the doubler to define the weld location, as shown in Figure 10–34. Hold down <Ctrl> to select all four edges.

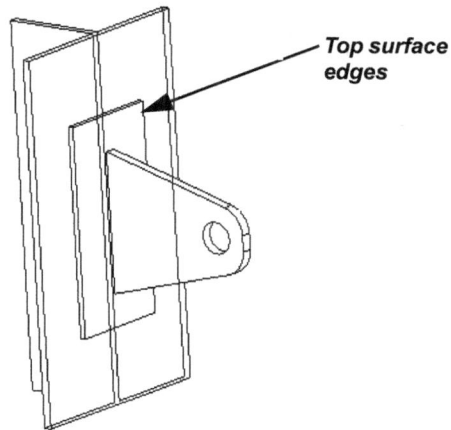

Figure 10–34

6. To use the same thickness as the plates for the thickness of the weld, enter **7.00**.

7. Expand the Material drop-down list and accept the default. The Weld Definition dialog box opens as shown in Figure 10–35.

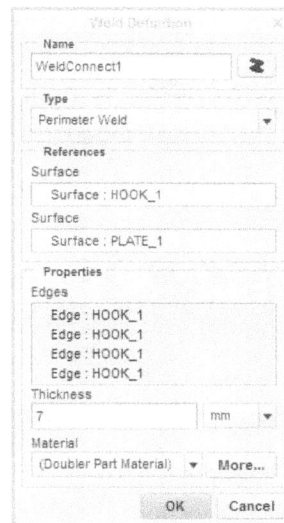

Figure 10–35

8. Click ОК to finish. Highlight the Connections heading in the Model Tree. The **Perimeter Weld** icon displays as shown in Figure 10–36.

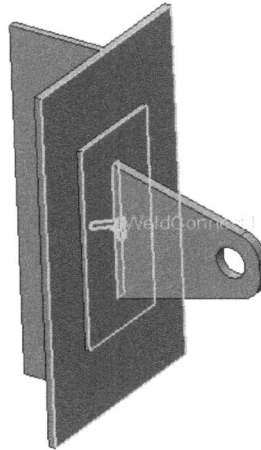

**Figure 10–36**

## Task 6 - Mesh the model.

1. Click [icon] to open the AutoGEM dialog box. Accept **All with Properties** and click Create.

2. Close the AutoGEM Summary and Diagnostics dialog boxes when the meshing finishes. The model displays as shown in Figure 10–37.

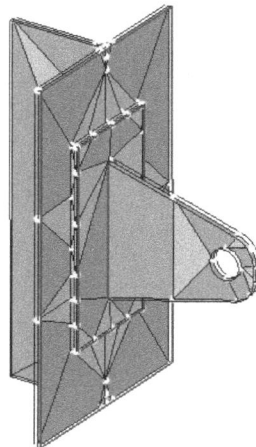

**Figure 10–37**

3. Zoom in on any perimeter weld area in the model, such as shown in Figure 10–38.

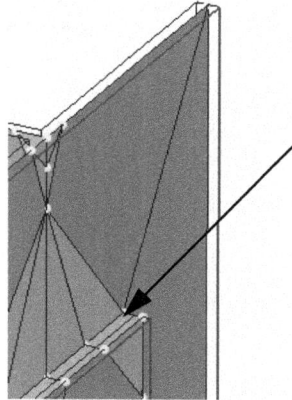

**Figure 10–38**

Note the shell elements that extend from the hook part edges to the base plate part. These are the elements that Creo Simulate automatically created to simulate the perimeter weld.

4. Close the AutoGEM dialog box and save the mesh.

---
**Task 7 - Apply the loads.**
---

1. Apply a force of **-8000** in the WCS's Y-direction to the hook's hole edge, as shown in Figure 10–39. For the name of the force, enter **hook_force**.

*In the Force area in the dialog box, select the **Components** option.*

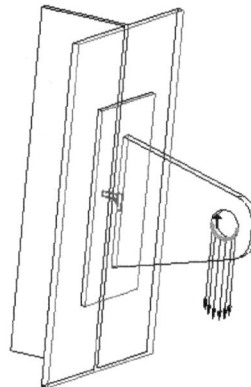

**Figure 10–39**

## Task 8 - Apply the constraints.

1. Constrain the edges of **plate_1** (fixed translation and rotation), as shown in Figure 10–40.

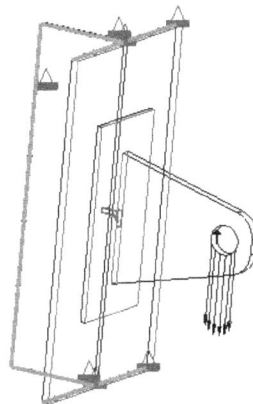

**Figure 10–40**

## Analysis Tasks

## Task 9 - Set up and run an analysis.

1. Set up a Single-Pass Adaptive analysis. For the name of the analysis, enter **weld_1**.

2. Run the analysis.

3. In the Analyses and Design Studies dialog box, click 🖿 and extract the following information from the Run Status window:

   - The RMS Stress error is 11.5% of the maximum principal stress, as shown in Figure 10–41.

```
RMS Stress Error Estimates:

Load Set          Stress Error   % of Max Prin Str
----------------- ------------   -----------------
LoadSet1          6.68e+01        11.5% of  5.80e+02
```

**Figure 10–41**

## Results Tasks

### Task 10 - Display the results.

In this task, you will create and display a von Mises stress fringe plot and deformation animation for the model. This verifies the applied boundary conditions.

1. Create the deformation animation plot and start the animation. The applied boundary conditions behave correctly.

2. Create the deformed von Mises stress fringe plot shown in Figure 10–42.

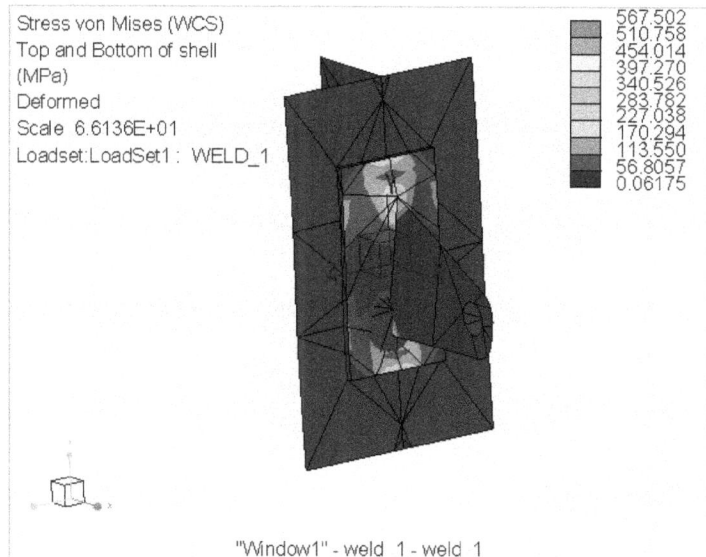

**Figure 10–42**

3. Locate and examine the high stress areas in the model, particularly the welds and the adjacent areas. If a high stress area is located at the weld, a more detailed analysis should be performed, such as using the 3D solid model type.

4. Exit the Results. Save and close the model.

# Practice 10c | Springs and Masses Analysis

**Learning Objectives**

✅ Create the beam elements.

✅ Create the spring elements.

✅ Create the mass element.

✅ Set up, run, and analyze an FEA model using masses and spring idealizations.

✅ Display the results.

In this practice, you will use spring and mass idealizations to set up and run an analysis on the model shown in Figure 10–43. The model is composed of beams and two springs. The ends of one beam and one spring are fixed, as shown in Figure 10–43. The beam joints are rigid. A mass is supported by another spring. The only load on the system is due to gravity. You will define three user-defined displacement point measures to determine the displacement of the frame at these points.

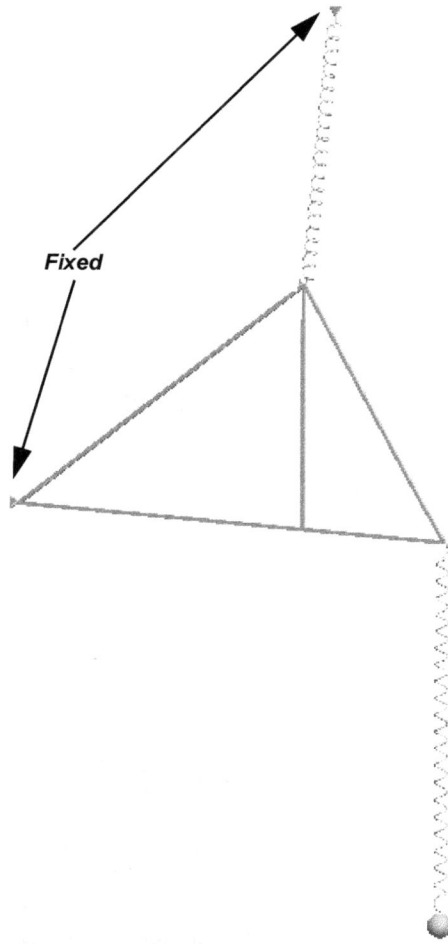

*Fixed*

**Figure 10–43**

The FEA model is shown in Figure 10–44.

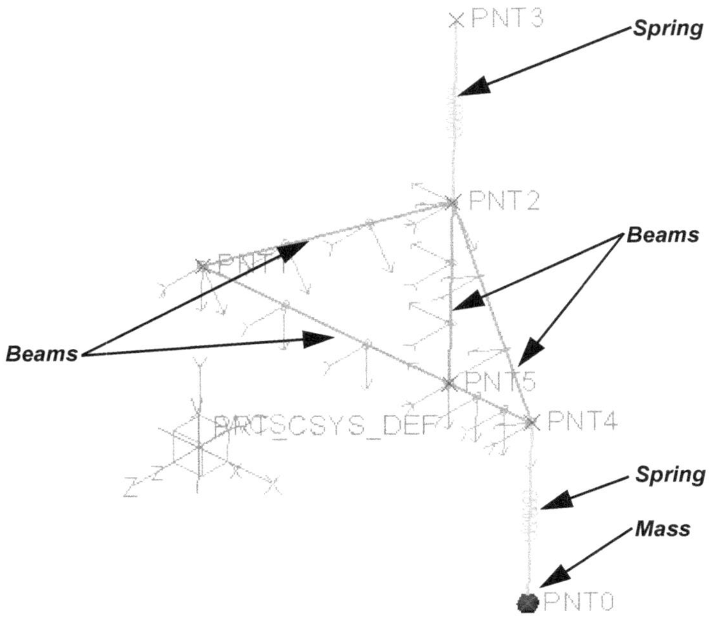

**Figure 10–44**

## Modeling Tasks

## Task 1 - Open the model.

1. Open **frame_1.prt** in Creo Parametric. The part displays as shown in Figure 10–45, with the datum planes and datum points turned on.

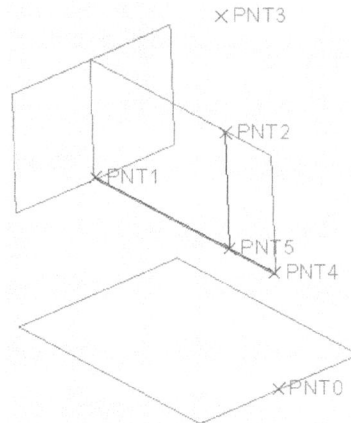

**Figure 10–45**

2. Ensure the unit system is set to **IPS**.

3. Select **Applications>Simulate** to launch Creo Simulate.

---

### Task 2 - Create three beam elements on datum curves.

---

1. Click ![icon] . The Beam Definition dialog box opens.

2. In the *Name* field, enter **beam_curves**.

3. Select the curves shown in Figure 10–46.

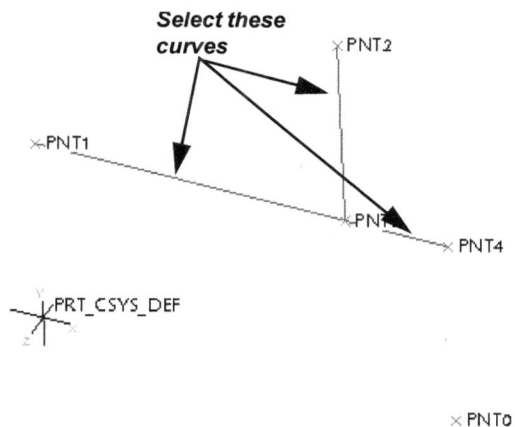

**Figure 10–46**

4. Assign **STEEL** as the material to the beams. The following values are the default material properties for HS-low-alloy steel (STEEL):

  • Poisson = 0.27
  • Young's modulus = 2.9e7 psi
  • Density = 0.0007324 lbf sec^2 /in^4

5. In the *Orientation* area, in the *X* field, enter **0**, in the *Y* field, enter **0**, and in the *Z* field, enter **1**.

6. Next to the Beam Section drop-down list, click  More... . In the Beam Sections dialog box, click  New... . The Beam Section Definition dialog box opens.

7. For the name of the section, enter **hollow_section**.

8. For the beam section, assign the **Hollow Circle**.

9. For the external radius, enter **0.5** and for the internal radius, enter **0.2**.

10. Return to the Beam Definition dialog box.

11. Click  OK  to create the beams. The model displays as shown in Figure 10–47.

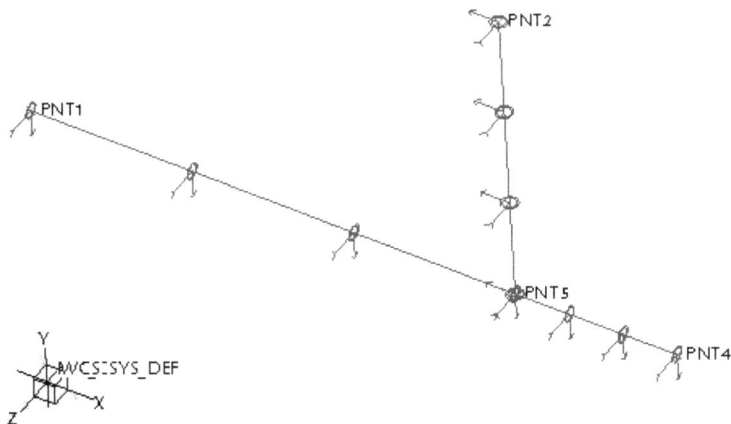

**Figure 10–47**

**Task 3 - Create two beam elements on datum points.**

1. Click 🗗. The Beam Definition dialog box opens.

2. In the *Name* field, enter **beam1_2**.

3. Expand the References drop-down list and select **Point-Point**.

4. Select **PNT1** and **PNT2**.

5. For the material for the beam, select **STEEL**.

6. In the *Y Direction* area, in the *X* field, enter **0**, in the Y field, enter **0**, and in the *Z* field, enter **1**.

7. Accept the default **hollow_section** beam section.

8. Click ___OK___ to create the beam. The model displays as shown in Figure 10–48.

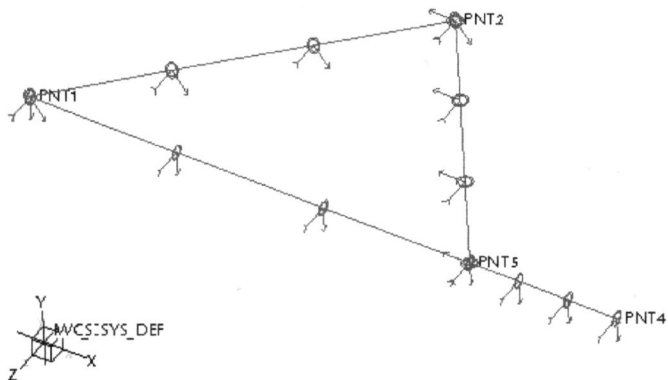

**Figure 10–48**

9. Repeat Steps 1 to 8 to create a beam element between PNT2 and PNT4. For the name of the beam, enter **beam2_4**. The model displays as shown in Figure 10–49.

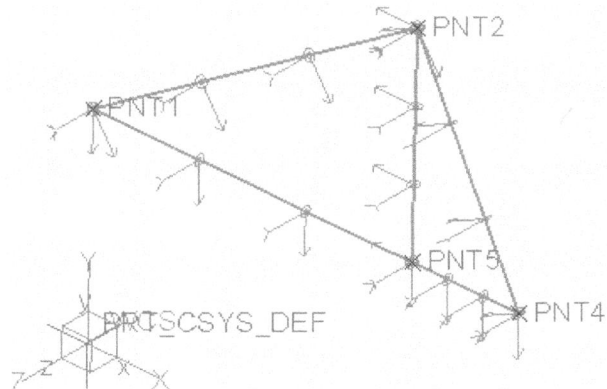

**Figure 10–49**

## Task 4 - Create the spring elements.

In this task, you will create two spring elements: one between PNT2 and PNT3 and another between PNT0 and PNT4.

1. In the *Idealizations* area, click ⬚. The Spring Definition dialog box opens as shown in Figure 10–50.

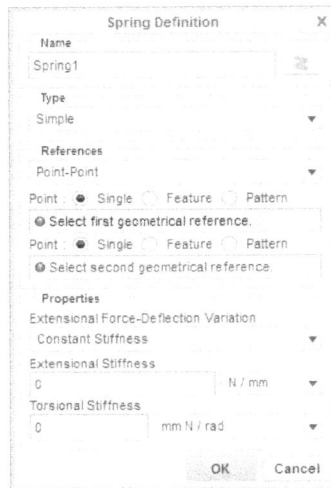

**Figure 10–50**

2. In the *Name* field, enter **Spring2_3**.

3. Expand the References drop-down list and accept the default option.

4. Select **PNT2** and **PNT3**.

5. In the *Extensional Stiffness* field, enter **2500**.

6. Click ⬜ OK ⬜ in the Spring Definition dialog box. A **Spring** icon displays between PNT2 and PNT3, as shown in Figure 10–51.

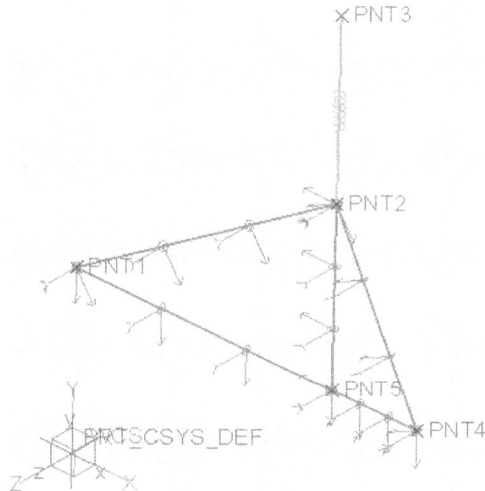

**Figure 10–51**

7. In the *Idealizations* area, click 🌀. The Spring Definition dialog box opens.

8. In the *Name* field, enter **Spring0_4**.

9. Expand the References drop-down list and accept the default option.

10. Select the **PNT0** and **PNT4**.

11. In the *Extensional Stiffness* field, enter **1500**.

12. Click ___OK___ in the Spring Definition dialog box. A **Spring** icon displays between PNT0 and PNT4, as shown in Figure 10–52.

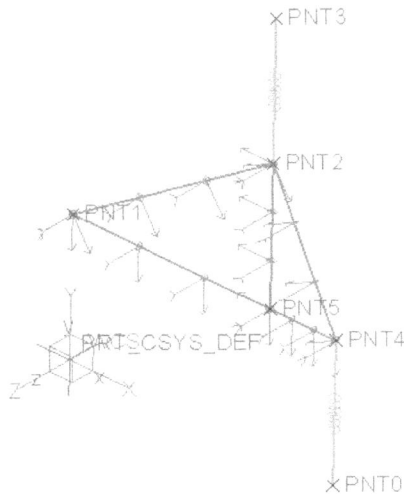

**Figure 10–52**

## Task 5 - Create the mass element on PNT0.

1. In the *Idealizations* area, click ⚖. The Mass Definition dialog box opens as shown in Figure 10–53.

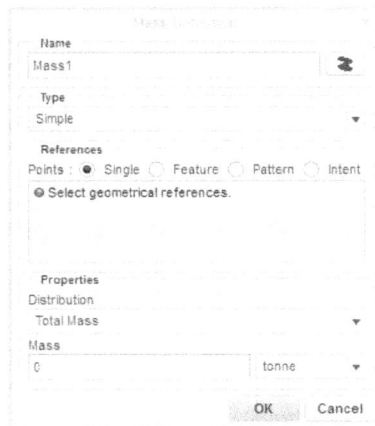

**Figure 10–53**

2. In the *Name* field, enter **mass_1**.

3. Select **PNT0**.

4. In the *Mass* field, enter **10**.

5. Click ⬜ OK . The **Mass** icon displays at PNT0, as shown in Figure 10–54.

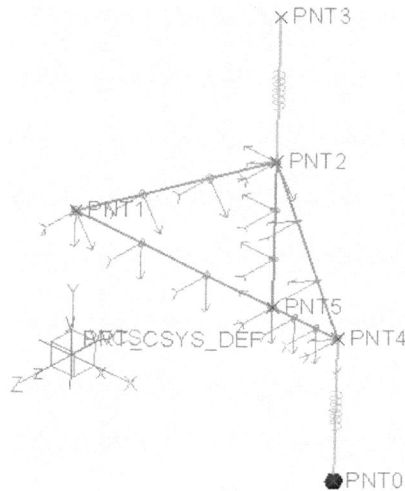

**Figure 10–54**

## Task 6 - Apply the gravity load to the model.

1. Click ⬜. The Gravity dialog box opens.

2. In the *Name* field, enter **gravity**.

3. For *Member of Set*, accept the default **LoadSet1** option.

*The gravity load is related to the WCS.*

4. In the dialog box, in the *Acceleration* area, in the *Y* field, enter **-386**.

5. Click  OK  to finish defining the gravity load. The model displays as shown in Figure 10–55.

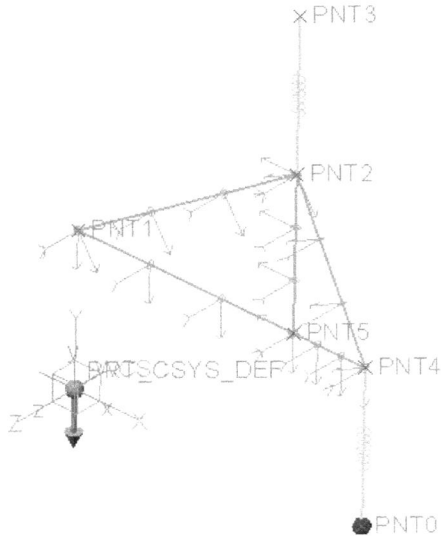

**Figure 10–55**

## Task 7 - Apply the constraints.

*The beams are cantilevered out from a wall.*

In this task, you will apply the constraints to PNT3, PNT1, and PNT0.

1. For the name of the constraint for PNT3 and PNT1, enter **const1**. Fix all of the degrees of freedom.

2. For the name of the constraint for PNT0, enter **const2**. Fix it so that it only moves in the Y-direction. The model displays as shown in Figure 10–56.

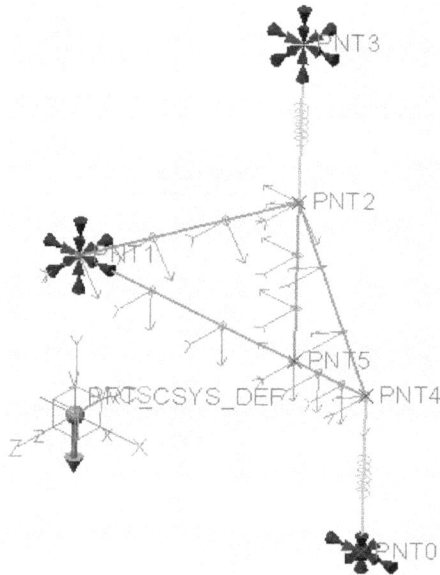

**Figure 10–56**

## Task 8 - Define the measures.

1. Set up three user-defined measures. Three displacement measures are created for PNT0, PNT2, and PNT4 in the Y-direction.

2. Name the measures **PNT0**, **PNT2** and **PNT4**.

## Summary

In the previous tasks, you created the simulation entities needed to analyze your model. In the following tasks, you will set the analysis type and the convergence method and run the analysis.

## Analysis Tasks

## Task 9 - Set up and run an analysis.

1. Set up a Multi-Pass Adaptive analysis. In the *Polynomial Order* field, enter **9** and in the *Limits* area, in the *Percent Convergence* field, enter **10**.

2. For the name of the analysis, enter **frame**.

3. Run the analysis.

4. Extract the following information from the Run Status window:

   • The pass number on which the analysis converged.
   • The values obtained for the user-defined measures.

## Results Tasks

## Task 10 - Display the results.

In this task, you will create and display a deformation animation for the model to verify the applied boundary conditions.

1. Create the Displacement Magnitude animation plot. The deformation at Frame 5 displays as shown in Figure 10–57.

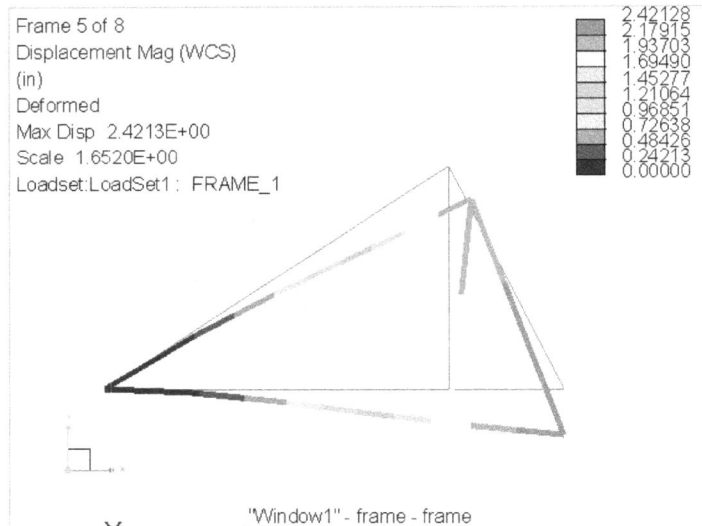

Frame 5 of 8
Displacement Mag (WCS)
(in)
Deformed
Max Disp  2.4213E+00
Scale  1.6520E+00
Loadset:LoadSet1 :  FRAME_1

2.42128
2.17915
1.93703
1.69490
1.45277
1.21064
0.96851
0.72638
0.48426
0.24213
0.00000

"Window1" - frame - frame

**Figure 10–57**

2. Start the animation. Do the applied boundary conditions behave correctly?

3. Exit the Results. Save and close the model.

# Chapter 11

## Fasteners and Rigid Links

When analyzing mechanical assemblies, a proper simulation of the connections and various interactions between the parts is of critical importance.

This chapter contains the following topics:

- **Rigid Links**
- **Fasteners**

# 11.1 Rigid Links

**Learning Objectives**

Understand rigid links in Creo Simulate.

Understand how to create rigid links.

A Rigid Link connects geometric entities in your model, such as surfaces, edges, or points, so they remain rigidly connected during the analysis. Rigid Links are useful for the idealization of a moving rigid structure attached to the model to be analyzed. The movement of the rigid structure might be part of the loading and specified by the user, or might be produced by loading on the main part of the model.

An example is shown in Figure 11–1. The heat sink/integrated circuit (HS/IC) package is bonded to the printed circuit board (PCB). The heat sink is made of aluminum, therefore, it is much stiffer than the thin PCB, which is made of plastic. The task is to determine the natural frequencies and natural modes of vibration for the assembly, using Modal analysis in Creo Simulate.

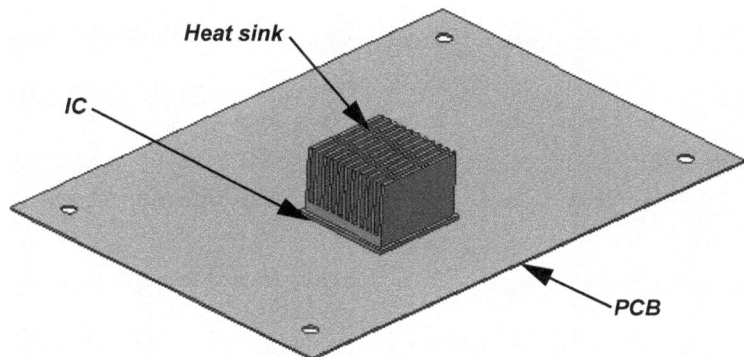

**Figure 11–1**

It is critical to preserve all of the masses in the system in the Modal analysis. Therefore, the mass of the HS/IC package must be included in the simulation. One option might be to model the mass by meshing the HS/IC package with solid elements and applying the material. However, a more computationally efficient approach would be to simulate the mass of the HS/IC package with a concentrated Mass located at the CoG of the package, then connecting the Mass with the PCB using a Rigid Link, as shown in Figure 11–2.

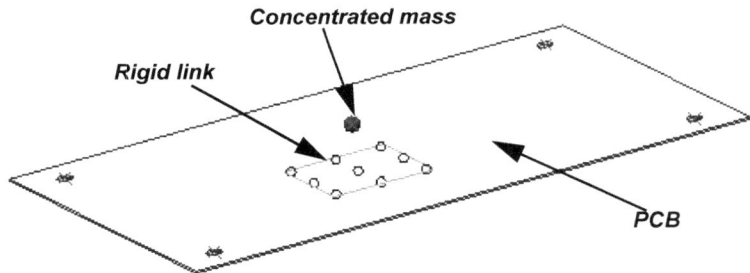

**Figure 11–2**

Additionally, rigid links can be used to connect two or more parts at selected surfaces.

When using rigid links, you should be aware of the following:

- The connected entities move together as one rigid body.

- The connected entities cannot deform, but the rigid body can move as a whole.

**Creating Rigid Links**

Use the following steps to create a rigid link:

1. In the *Refine Model* tab, click [icon] to open the Rigid Link Definition dialog box as shown in Figure 11–3.

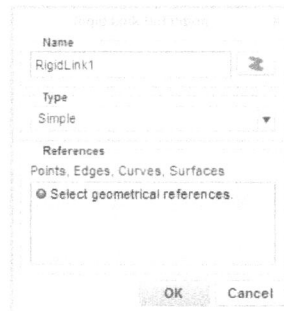

**Figure 11–3**

2. (Optional) Enter a name.
3. Expand the Type drop-down list and select **Simple** or **Advanced**.

   - The Advanced type enables you to control the independent degrees of freedom. Requires an Advanced Creo Simulate license.

4. Select the geometrical entities to connect (hold down <Ctrl> to multi-select).

   - You can connect the surfaces or edges of your model with a free point that is not otherwise associated with the model geometry.

5. Click   OK   .

# 11.2 Fasteners

**Learning Objectives**

Understand fastener connections in Creo Simulate.

Understand how to create fastener connections.

Fasteners in Creo Simulate simulate bolt or screw connections joining any two parts in an assembly. The connection is intended to simulate the load path within the assembly, as well as the amount of load carried by each bolt or screw.

**Prerequisites**

The model with fastener connections must meet the following conditions:

• The model must be an assembly. Any given fastener must pass through two separate components.

• The two holes participating in a fastener definition must be cylindrical and perpendicular to the part surface. The holes must have approximately the same diameter.

• There should not be any intervening geometry in the fastener's path. An example of an intervening geometry is shown in Figure 11–4.

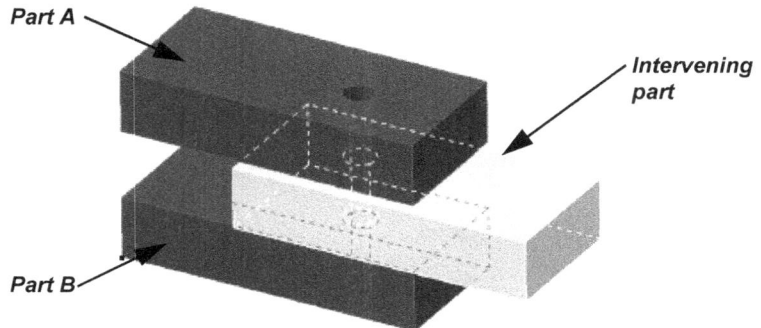

Figure 11–4

**Part Separation**

In the real world, the parts connected together by a fastener are not typically bonded over the entire interface surface, yet they do not interpenetrate when a preload or external load is applied.

To ensure that the surfaces are not bonded, Creo Simulate automatically creates a Free Interface between the two parts participating in the fastener definition.

To ensure that the two parts do not interpenetrate, you can use either of the following methods:

- Define the Contact Interface between the parts (note that the Contact Interface in this case overrides the automatic Free Interface). This method is the most accurate, but requires longer computation time due to the non-linear nature of the Contact Interface.

- Enable Creo Simulate to automatically use a separation spring to ensure non-penetration. This method has faster computation times, but does not permit the parts to separate, even if they would naturally do so under the applied loading.

If the automatic separation method is used, the following is done by Creo Simulate behind the scenes:

- Two annular separation areas on the contacting surfaces are automatically created, as shown in Figure 11–5. The outer diameter of the separation areas is called the *Separation Test Diameter*.

- A very stiff distributed linear spring (called the *Separation Spring*) is created between the annular areas. The stiffness of the spring ensures that the parts do not interpenetrate within the separation areas. However, since the separation spring is a linear spring, it does not let the parts separate, even if they are supposed to, under the given loading.

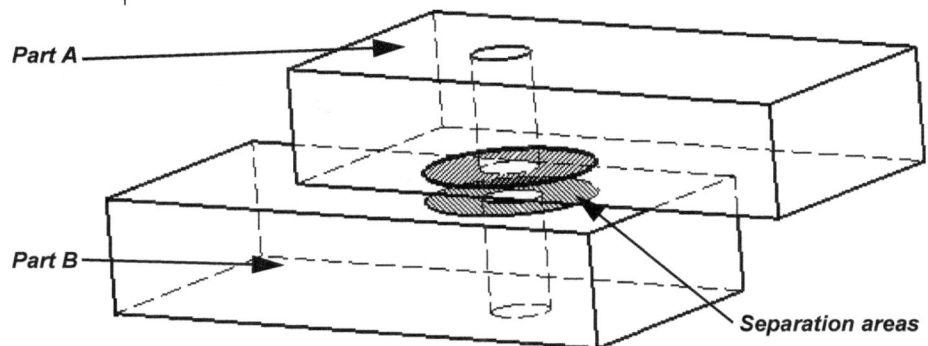

Part A

Part B

Separation areas

**Figure 11–5**

If you use the separation spring method to ensure the non-penetration of the fastened parts, it is strongly recommended that after the analysis run, you verify that all of the separation springs are in compression. If some separation springs are found to be in tension, they should be turned off, and the analysis re-run.

## Fastener Preload

Creo Simulate models the fastener preload by applying enforced displacements, so the nut and bolt head areas move toward each other, which tightens the parts together. Ideally, the amount of this prescribed displacement should produce axial force in the fastener that is equal to the required preload.

The distance that the nut and bolt head areas should move toward each other to produce the required preload is a complex mechanical and mathematical problem, whose solution depends on various factors (such as model geometry, fastener geometry, material properties, etc.). Creo Simulate must make certain simplified assumptions regarding the joined parts' stiffnesses. Therefore, it never gets the preload quite right. In fact, the actual fastener preload might substantially differ from the one entered in the Fastener Definition dialog box.

Therefore, running the analysis twice is recommended if an accurate fastener preload is required:

- In the first analysis run, apply only fastener preloads, and do not apply any external loads in the model. Compare the resulting reactions in the fasteners with the applied preloads, and calculate the correction coefficients for each fastener. For example, if a 100N preload was applied to a fastener and the reaction came out as 80N, the correction coefficient is 100/80 = 1.25

- In the second analysis run, multiply all of the preloads by their respective correction coefficients, so that the actual preloads are as required. Apply all of the external loads as well.

## Creating Fasteners

Use the following steps to create a Fastener:

1. In the *Refine Model* tab, click ⚜ to open the Fastener Definition dialog box as shown in Figure 11–6.

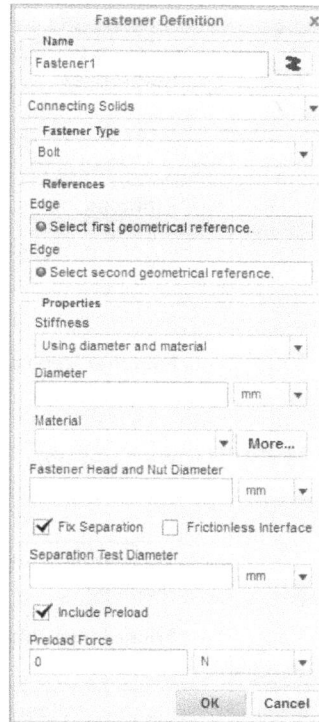

**Figure 11–6**

2. (Optional) Enter a fastener name.
3. Select **Connecting Solids** or **Connecting Shells**.
4. Select the **Fastener Type**.
5. Selected the fastener **References.**
6. In the *Properties* area, select the required options as shown in the following tables.
7. Click OK to complete.

| Option | Description |
|---|---|
| **Connecting Solids** | Creates a fastener connecting two solid parts. |
| **Connecting Shells** | Creates a fastener connecting two shell parts. |

| Fastener Type | • **Bolt:** The first edge you select is associated with the head of the bolt, and the second edge is associated with the nut.<br>• **Screw:** The first edge you select is associated with the head of the screw, and the second edge is associated with the other end of the screw. |
|---|---|
| References | For the **Connecting Solids** type, select the circular edges of the holes. For the **Connecting Shells** type, select either the hole edges or the datum points. |
| Stiffness | • **Using diameter and material:** Defines the fastener stiffness using the fastener diameter and material.<br>• **Using spring stiffness property:** Defines the fastener stiffness using a spring property. |
| Fastener Head and Nut Diameter | Defines the head and nut diameter for the fastener. For screws, there is no nut, so the value applies to the screw head. |
| Fix Separation | Creates a separation spring to prevent interpenetration of the parts over the annular separation areas. |
| Separation Test Diameter | Defines the diameter of the annular separation areas. |
| Frictionless Interface | If enabled, the parts are permitted to slide in a tangential direction over the separation areas. |
| Include Preload | Enables a preload for the fastener. Not available for the **Connecting Shells** type. |
| Preload Force | Defines the tensile force in the fastener that results from tightening the bolt or screw. |

## Fastener Measures

Creo Simulate automatically creates several measures for each fastener. The fastener measures are as follows:

| Measure | Description |
|---|---|
| axial_force | Axial force in a fastener. |
| axial_stress | Axial stress in a fastener. Calculated for the specified fastener diameter. |
| shear_force | Shear force for a fastener. |
| shear_stress | Shear stress in a fastener. Calculated for the specified fastener diameter. |

| bending_moment | Bending moment in a fastener. |
| --- | --- |
| bending_stress | Bending stress in a fastener. Calculated for the specified fastener diameter. |
| torsion_moment | Torsional moment in a fastener. Calculated if **Frictionless Interface** is enabled. |
| torsion_stress | Torsional stress in a fastener. Calculated for the specified fastener diameter. |
| sep_stress | Normal stress over the separation area. |
| intf_bend_momt | Bending moment calculated for the separation area. |
| intf_norm_forc | Normal force in the separation area. |
| intf_shr_forc | Shear force in the separation area. |
| intf_tors_momt | Torsional moment over the separation area. |

# Practice 11a | Modal Analysis of a PCB Assembly

**Learning Objectives**

✓ Understand how to create Masses.

✓ Understand how to create Rigid Links.

✓ Set up and run a Modal analysis.

In this practice, you will set up and run a Modal analysis for a PCB assembly as shown in Figure 11–7. The PCB is made of plastic, while the heat sink is made of aluminum and is much stiffer than the PCB. You will use a Mass and a Rigid Link to model the heat sink and the IC package.

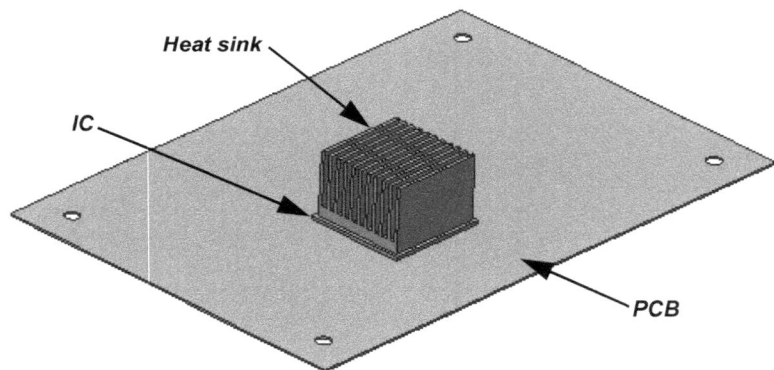

**Figure 11–7**

## Modeling Tasks

### Task 1 - Open the part in Creo Parametric.

1. Open **pcb.asm** assembly in Creo Parametric. The model displays as shown in Figure 11–8.

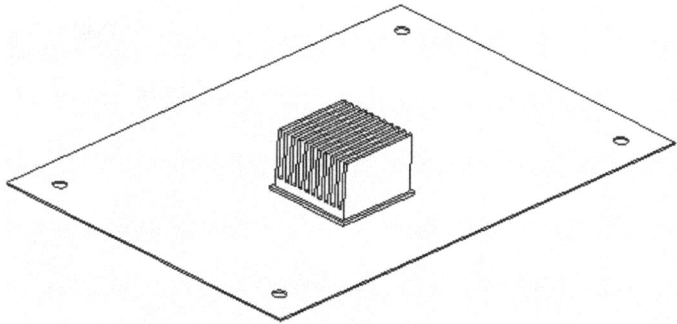

**Figure 11–8**

2.  Ensure that the unit system is set to **mmNs**.

## Task 2 - Create a simplified representation.

The heat sink/IC package is simulated with a mass and a rigid link. In this task, you will create a simplified representation to exclude the heat sink and the IC geometry from the analysis model.

1.  In the *View* tab, click 🖿 . The View Manager dialog box opens as shown in Figure 11–9.

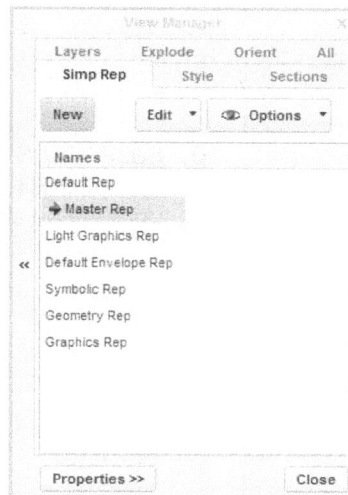

**Figure 11–9**

2. Click <sup>New...</sup> . Rename the new representation as **AnslRep** and press <Enter>. The Edit:ANLSREP dialog box opens as shown in Figure 11–10.

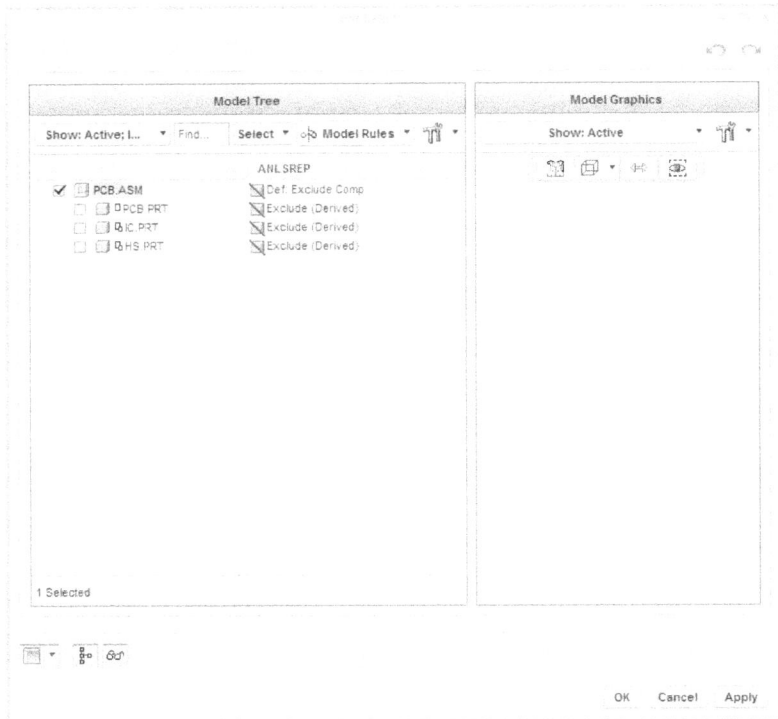

**Figure 11–10**

3. Set **PCB.ASM** and **PCB.PRT** to **Master Rep**, and **IC.PRT** and **HS.PRT** to **Exclude**. The Edit:ANLSREP dialog box updates as shown in Figure 11–11.

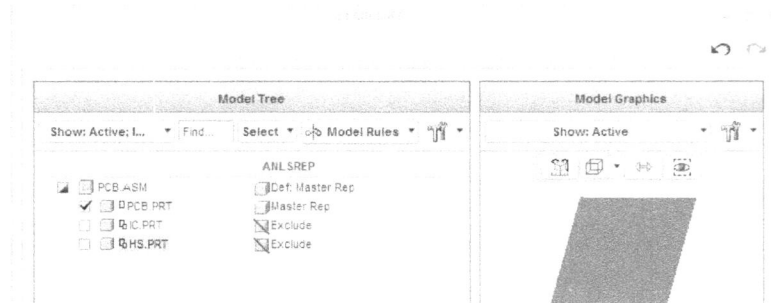

**Figure 11–11**

4. Click OK and Close to finish. The model displays as shown in Figure 11–12.

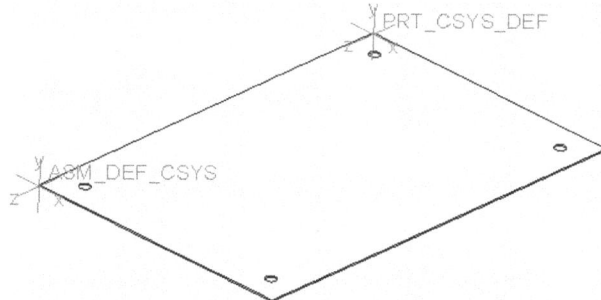

**Figure 11–12**

## Task 3 - Launch Creo Simulate.

1. Select **Applications>Simulate** to launch the Creo Simulate environment.

## Task 4 - Apply the material.

*The model's material properties should be as stated.*

1. Assign **NYLON** to the PCB part. The following values are the default material properties for NYLON:

- Poisson = 0.4
- Young's modulus = 4000.34 MPa
- Coeff of thermal expansion = 7.9992e-5 /C
- Density = 1.20014e-9 tonne/mm^3

## Task 5 - Create a surface region.

In this task, you will create a surface region to model the area over which the heat sink/IC package is bonded to the PCB.

1. Create a sketch on the top surface of the PCB (in the Y-direction up) with the dimensions shown in Figure 11–13.

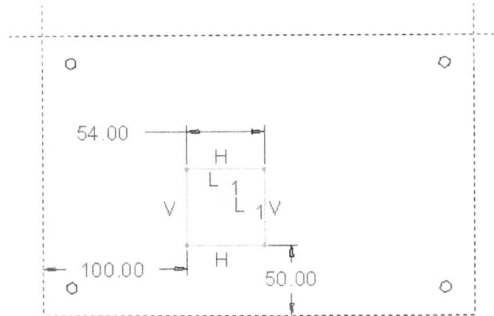

**Figure 11–13**

2. The model displays as shown in Figure 11–14.

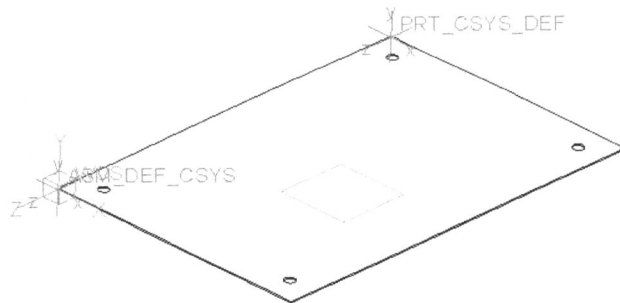

**Figure 11–14**

3. In the *Refine Model* tab, click [icon].

4. In the Select a Component dialog box, select the **PCB** part and click OK . The Surface Region dashboard displays as shown in Figure 11–15.

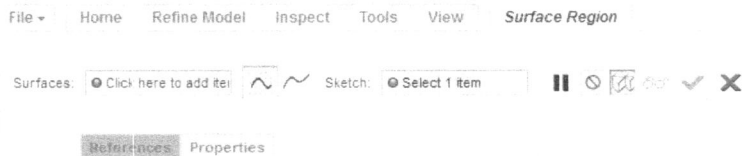

**Figure 11–15**

5. Activate the *Surfaces* field and select the top surface of the PCB.

6. Click ∿, activate the *Chain* field, and select the sketch. The model displays as shown in Figure 11–16.

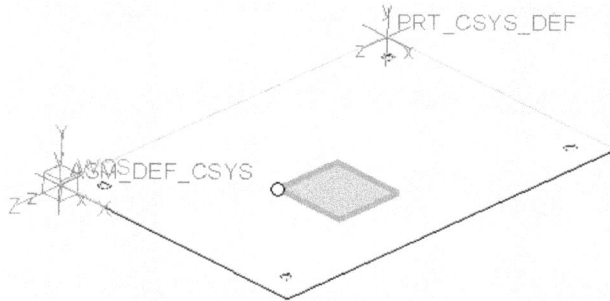

**Figure 11–16**

7. Click ✔ to complete the surface region.

---

**Task 6 - Create shell pairs.**

---

*The PCB thickness is 1mm.*

1. Define the shell pairs using the **Automatic Detection** tool, with a *Characteristic Thickness* of **1.1**.

---

**Task 7 - Create a datum point.**

---

In this task, you will create an assembly datum point located at the CoG of the heat sink/IC package.

1. Expand the Point drop-down list and click ⁺⁄⁎ (Offset Coordinate System).

2. Click OK in the Select a Component dialog box.

*You can use **File> Prepare>Model Properties** to calculate the CoG coordinates.*

3. In the Datum Point dialog box that opens, select **ASM_DEF_CSYS** as the reference, and enter the new point coordinates as shown in Figure 11–17.

| | Name | X Axis | Y Axis | Z Axis |
|---|---|---|---|---|
| 1 | APNT0 | 123.00 | 15.00 | -127.00 |

**Figure 11–17**

4. Click **OK** to finish.

## Task 8 - Create a rigid link.

In this task, you will create a rigid link to connect the CoG of the heat sink/IC assembly with the surface region on the PCB.

1. In the *Refine Model* tab, click 🗐. The Rigid Link Definition dialog box opens as shown in Figure 11–18.

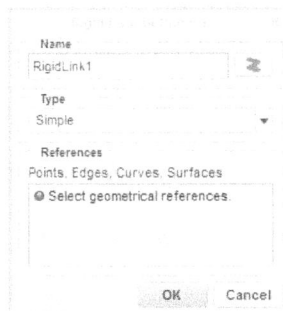

**Figure 11–18**

2. Select both the **APNT0** point and the surface region (hold down <Ctrl> to multi-select). Click  OK  to finish. The model displays as shown in Figure 11–19.

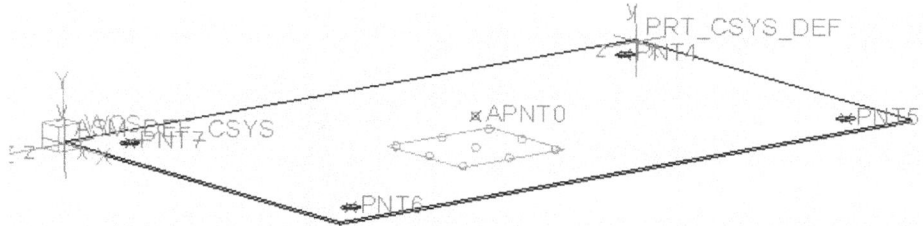

**Figure 11–19**

## Task 9 - Create a mass.

1. Click  . The Mass Definition dialog box opens as shown in Figure 11–20.

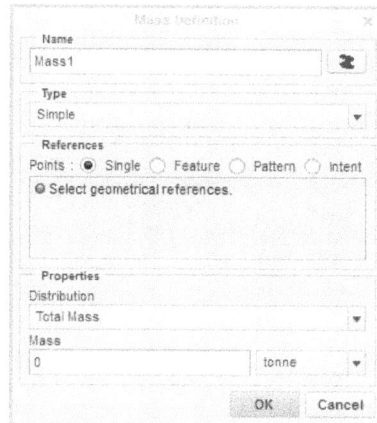

**Figure 11–20**

*The mass of the heat sink/IC package is 130g, (i.e., 1.3e-4 tonne).*

2. For the *Name*, enter **HS** and in the *Mass* field, enter **1.3e-4**. For the *Reference*, select the **APNT0** point. The Mass Definition dialog box opens as shown in Figure 11–21.

**Figure 11–21**

3. Click ___OK___ . The model opens as shown in Figure 11–22.

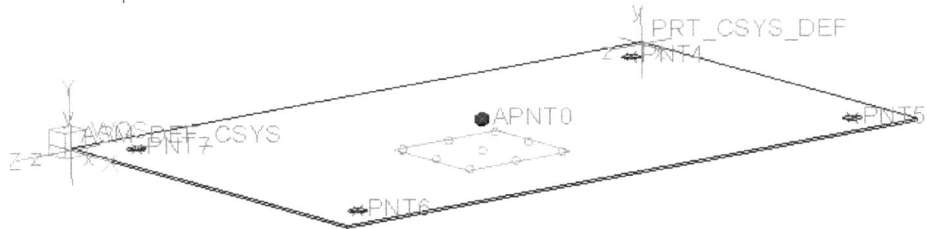

**Figure 11–22**

## Task 10 - Apply constraints.

1. Constrain the edges of the four holes in all of the translations. The model displays as shown in Figure 11–23.

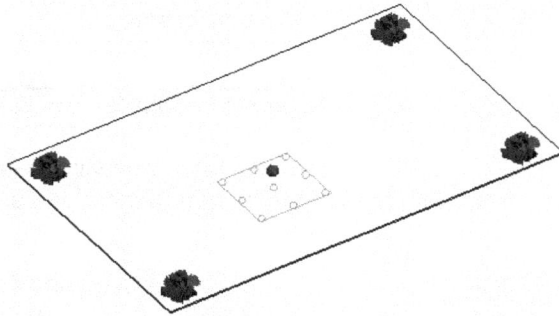

Figure 11–23

## Analysis Tasks

### Task 11 - Set up and run a Modal analysis

1. In the Analyses and Design Studies dialog box, click ⬜
   and select **File>New Modal**. The Modal Analysis Definition
   dialog box opens as shown in Figure 11–24.

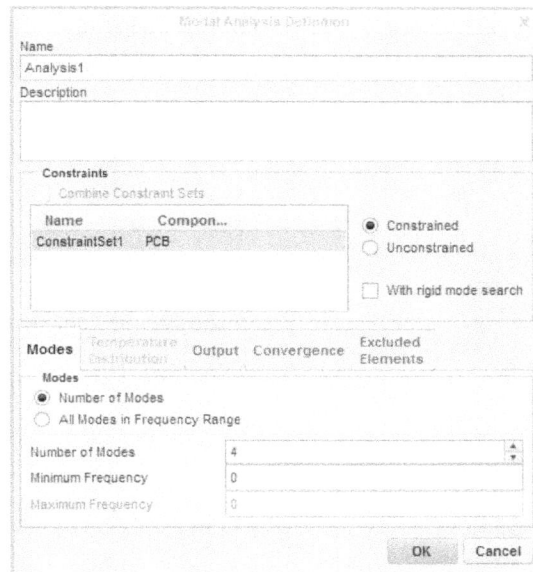

Figure 11–24

2. For the analysis name, enter **PCB**. Accept all of the other
   defaults and click ⬜ OK .

3. Run the analysis.

## Results Tasks

## Task 12 - Display the results.

In this task, you will create and animate the Displacement Magnitude fringe plots for the calculated modes of vibration.

1. In the Analyses and Design Studies dialog box, click [icon]. The Result Window Definition dialog box opens as shown in Figure 11–25.

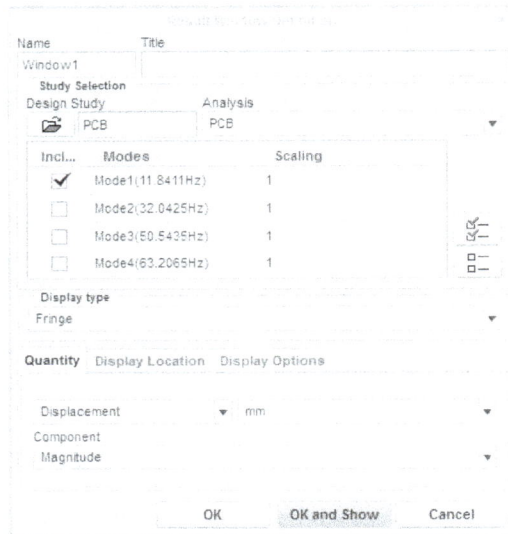

**Figure 11–25**

2. In the *Name* field, enter **mode1**.

3. Select the *Display Options* tab and select the required options as shown in Figure 11–26.

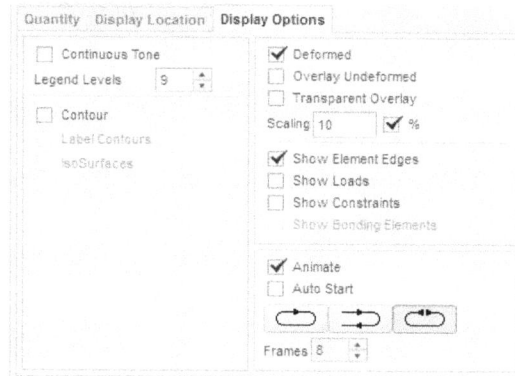

**Figure 11–26**

4. Display and animate the result plot. Step through the animation to the Frame 3, as shown in Figure 11–27.

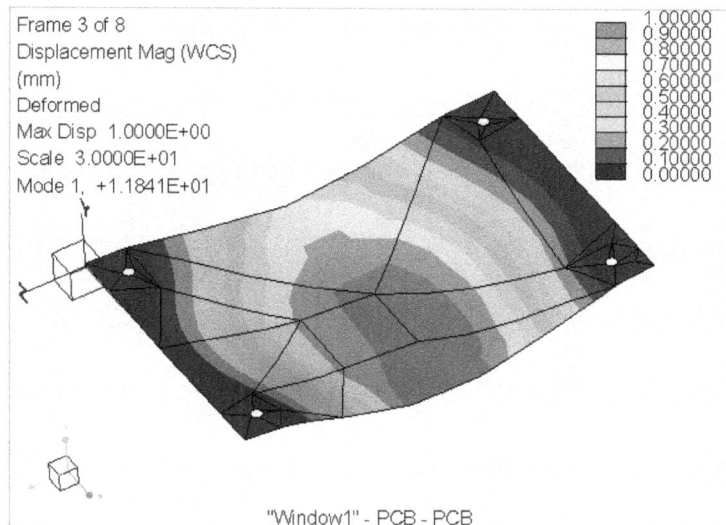

Frame 3 of 8
Displacement Mag (WCS)
(mm)
Deformed
Max Disp 1.0000E+00
Scale 3.0000E+01
Mode 1, +1.1841E+01

1.00000
0.90000
0.80000
0.70000
0.60000
0.50000
0.40000
0.30000
0.20000
0.10000
0.00000

"Window1" - PCB - PCB

**Figure 11–27**

Note that the surface region area remains flat through the deformation. The area has been rendered effectively undeformable, due to the Rigid Link applied to the surface region.

5. Create, animate, and display the Displacement Magnitude plot for the mode 2. In the *Name* field, enter **mode2**.

6. In the *Include* column, select the second checkbox (as shown in Figure 11–28), and clear the first checkbox.

| Incl... | Modes | Scaling |
|---|---|---|
| ☐ | Mode1(11.8411Hz) | 1 |
| ✓ | Mode2(32.0425Hz) | 1 |
| ☐ | Mode3(50.5435Hz) | 1 |
| ☐ | Mode4(63.2065Hz) | 1 |

**Figure 11–28**

7. Display the **mode_2** fringe plot. Step through the animation to the Frame 3, as shown in Figure 11–29.

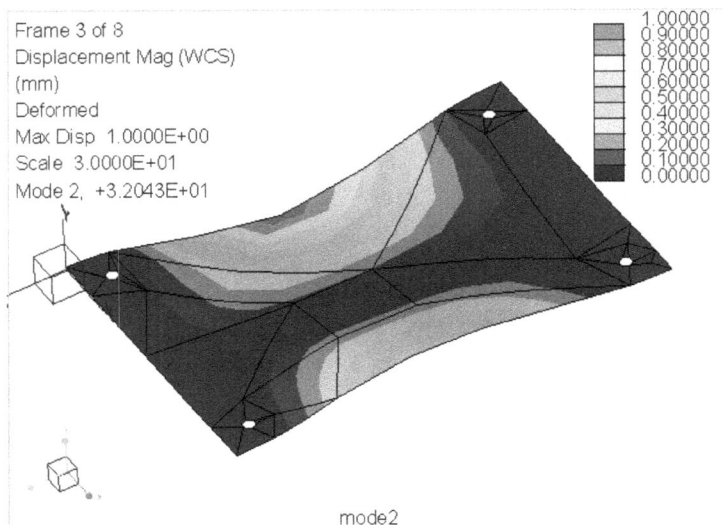

```
Frame 3 of 8
Displacement Mag (WCS)
(mm)
Deformed
Max Disp  1.0000E+00
Scale  3.0000E+01
Mode 2,  +3.2043E+01
```

```
1.00000
0.90000
0.80000
0.70000
0.60000
0.50000
0.40000
0.30000
0.20000
0.10000
0.00000
```

mode2

**Figure 11–29**

8. Create, animate, and display the Displacement Magnitude plots for Modes 3 and 4. Examine the motion of the surface region area in all of the animations.

9. Exit the Results. Save and close the model.

# Practice 11b

# Static Analysis of a Mixed Solid/Shell/Beam Model

### Learning Objectives

- Use a combination of Solids, Shells, and Beams in an analysis model.

- Connect a Beam to a Solid using a rigid link.

In this practice, you will set up and run a static analysis of a bracket assembly as shown in Figure 11–30. The shaft is press-fit into the bracket.

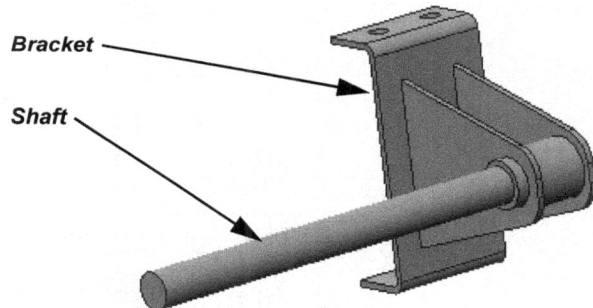

**Bracket**

**Shaft**

**Figure 11–30**

You will use the following idealizations for the parts in the model:

- The shaft is modeled with a beam.

- The cylindrical boss, into which the shaft is press-fit, is modeled with solids.

- The bracket is modeled with shells.

You will connect the beam to the solid using a rigid link.

## Modeling Tasks

### Task 1 - Open the assembly.

1. Open **bracket_shaft.asm** in Creo Parametric. The unshaded model displays as shown in Figure 11–31.

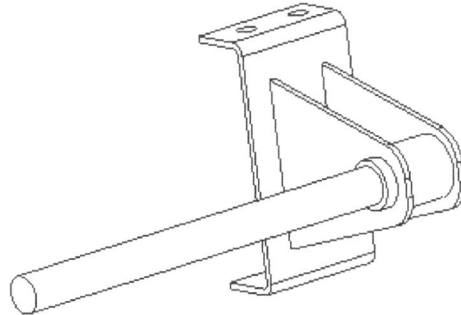

**Figure 11–31**

2. Switch to the Simulate application.

### Task 2 - Create a beam idealization.

1. Open **shaft.prt** in a new window.

2. Create two datum points as shown in Figure 11–32.

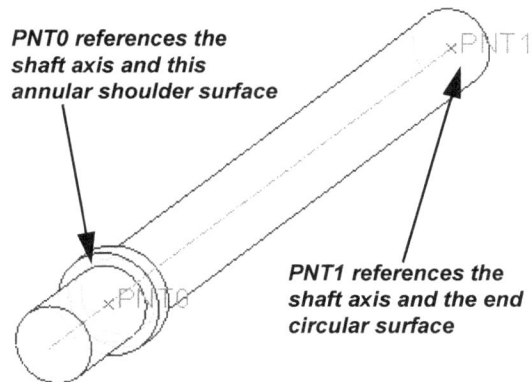

*PNT0 references the shaft axis and this annular shoulder surface*

*PNT1 references the shaft axis and the end circular surface*

**Figure 11–32**

3. Save and close **shaft.prt**. Return to the assembly window. The assembly model displays as shown in Figure 11–33.

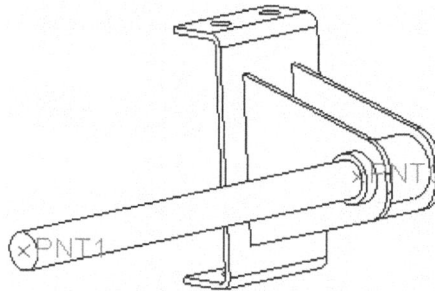

**Figure 11–33**

4.  In the *Refine Model* tab, click . The Beam Definition
    dialog box opens as shown in Figure 11–34.

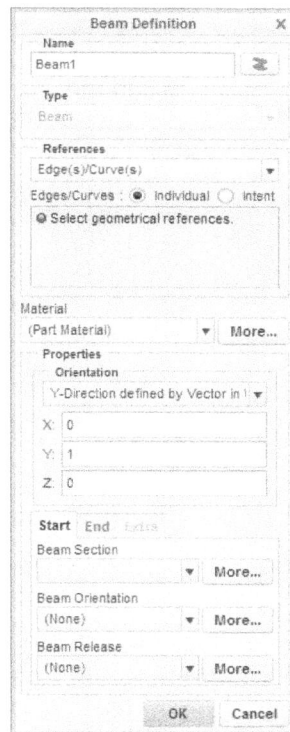

**Figure 11–34**

5.  In the *Name* field, enter **beam_shaft**.

6.  Expand the References drop-down list and select
    **Point-Point**.

7.  Select **PNT0** and **PNT1**.

*The model's material properties should be as stated.*

8. In the *Material* area, click  More…  . The Materials dialog box opens.

9. In the *Materials in Library* area, select **STEEL**. Click  ▶▶  to transfer STEEL to the *Materials in Model* area.

10. Select **Edit>Properties** to check the material properties. The following values are the default material properties for HS-low-alloy steel (STEEL):

   • Poisson = 0.27
   • Young's modulus = 199948 MPa

11. Click  OK  in the Material Definition dialog box and in the Materials dialog box. STEEL displays in the *Material* area in the Beam Definition dialog box.

12. In the *Orientation* area, accept the default X-, Y-, and Z-values.

13. Next to the Beam Section drop-down list, click  More…  . The Beam Sections dialog box opens as shown in Figure 11–35.

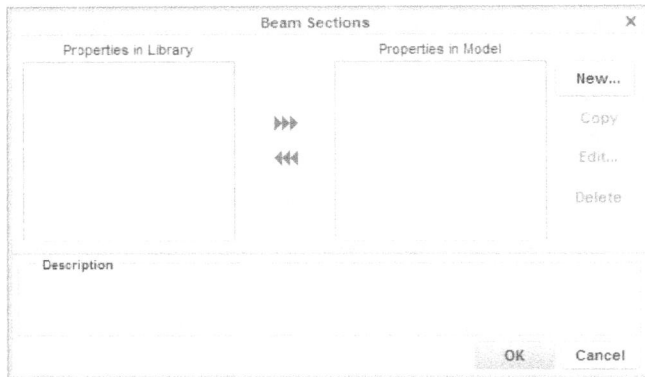

**Figure 11–35**

14. Click  New…  . The Beam Section Definition dialog box opens as shown in Figure 11–36.

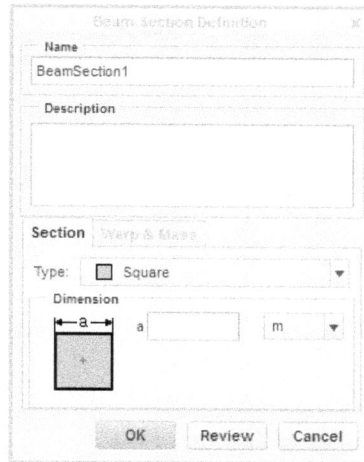

**Figure 11–36**

15. In the *Name* field, enter **circ_section**.

16. Expand the Type drop-down list and select **Solid Circle**. In the *R* field, enter **15**, as shown in Figure 11–37.

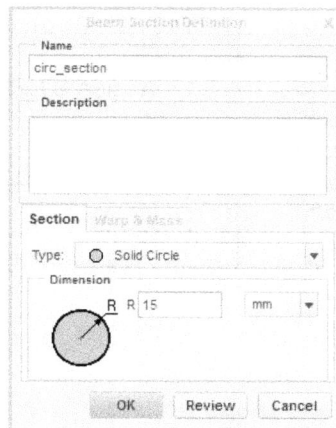

**Figure 11–37**

17. Click ___OK___ twice to close the Beam Section Definition dialog box and the Beam Sections dialog box.

18. Click ⬚ OK to close the Beam Definition dialog box. The model displays as shown in Figure 11–38.

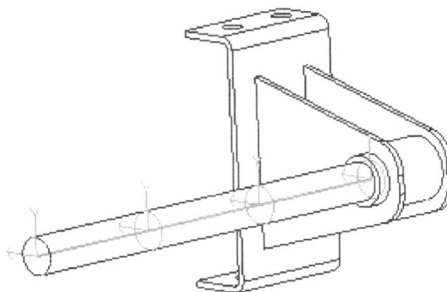

**Figure 11–38**

## Task 3 - Create shell pairs.

*The bracket thickness is 5mm.*

1. Use the **Automatic Detection** tool with the *Characteristic Thickness* set to **6** to define the shell pairs for the bracket part.

## Task 4 - Apply the material.

*Applying material to the shaft part is not needed. In Task 2, the material was applied to the beam that models the shaft.*

1. Assign **STEEL** to the bracket part only.

## Task 5 - Mesh the model.

1. Mesh the model using the **All with Properties** option. The mesh displays as shown in Figure 11–39.

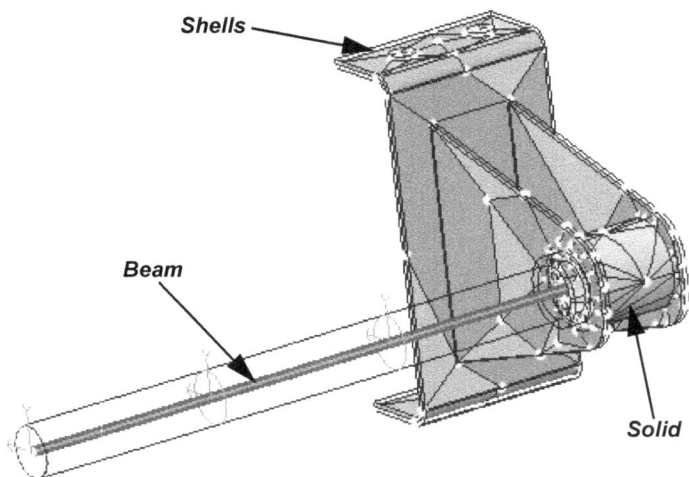

**Figure 11–39**

Note that the shaft has been meshed as a beam (purple line), the circular boss has been meshed with solids (blue), and the rest of the bracket has been meshed with shells (green).

2. Exit the AutoGEM dialog box without saving the mesh.

## Task 6 - Create a rigid link.

In this task, you will create a rigid link to connect the end of the beam to the inside surface of the hole in the bracket.

1. In the *Refine Model* tab, click ⌗. The Rigid Link Definition dialog box opens as shown in Figure 11–40.

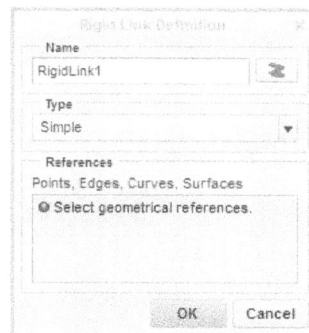

Figure 11–40

2. Select both the PNT0 point and the inside surface of the hole into which the shaft is inserted (hold down <Ctrl> to multi-select). Use the **Pick from List** option to select the surface of the hole.

3. Click OK to finish. The model displays as shown in Figure 11–41.

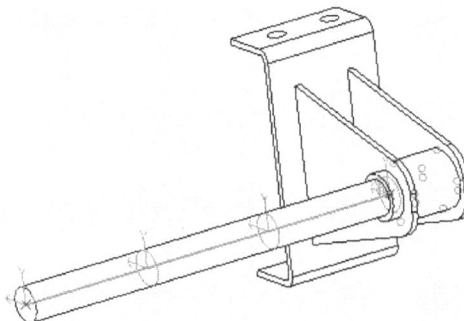

Figure 11–41

## Task 7 - Apply loads and constraints.

1. Apply force 200N to the PNT1 point in negative Y-direction.

2. Constrain the edges of the four holes in the bracket part in all of the translations.

3. The model displays as shown in Figure 11–42.

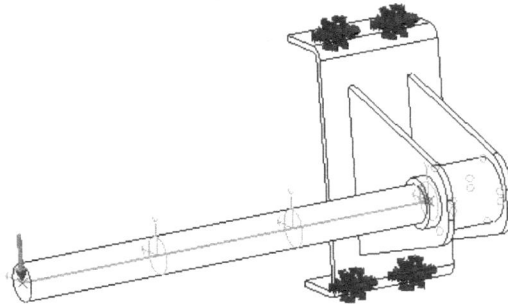

**Figure 11–42**

### Analysis Tasks

## Task 8 - Set up and run a static analysis.

1. Set up a Multi-Pass Adaptive static analysis. For the *Name*, enter **bracket_shaft**. In the *Polynomial Order* field, enter **9** and in the *Limits* area, in the *Percent Convergence* field, enter **10**.

2. Run the analysis.

3. In the Analyses and Design Studies dialog box, click ▤ and extract the following information from the Run Status window:

   • Analysis converges on pass 9.
   • Stress error is 14.7% of the maximum principal stress, as shown in Figure 11–43.

```
RMS Stress Error Estimates:

Load Set          Stress Error   % of Max Prin Str
---------------   ------------   -----------------
LoadSet1          6.35e+00       14.7% of  4.33e+01
```

**Figure 11–43**

## Results Tasks

### Task 9 - Display the results.

In this task, you will create and display a von Mises stress fringe plot and a deformation animation for the model to verify the applied boundary conditions.

1. Create the displacement magnitude animation plot.

2. Start the animation. Verify whether the applied boundary conditions behave correctly.

3. Create an undeformed von Mises stress fringe plot. Change the *Legend minimum* to **0** and *maximum* to **40**. The result plot displays as shown in Figure 11–44.

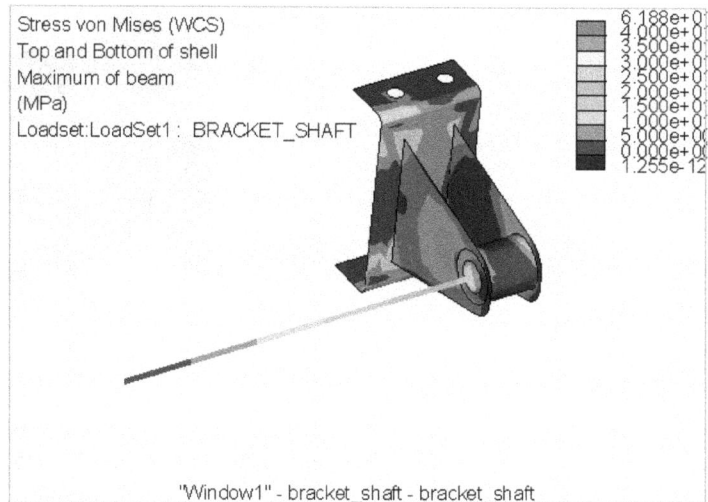

**Figure 11–44**

4. Locate and examine the high stress areas in the model.

5. Exit the Results. Save and close the model.

| Practice 11c | **Fasteners with Preload** |

**Learning Objectives**

✓ Understand how to create bolted connections in solid models.

✓ Understand how to apply bolt preload.

✓ Understand how to control and adjust preload accuracy.

In this practice, you will set up and run a static analysis of the assembly shown in Figure 11–45. The two plates in the assembly are bolted together through the three holes, with a preload of 500N on each bolt.

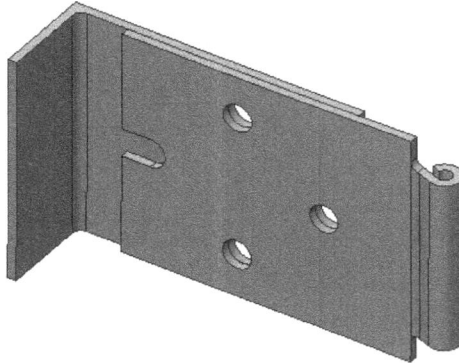

**Figure 11–45**

You will use the Fastener connection to model the bolted joints. You will solve the model in two iterations:

- In the first analysis, you will only apply preloads on the bolts, without applying any other loads in the model. The objective of this analysis is to check how accurately the preloads are simulated, and to correct the amount of preload applied, if needed.

- In the second and final analysis, you will solve the model with the corrected preloads, and with all of the other loads in the model fully applied.

## Modeling Tasks

### Task 1 - Open the model.

1. Open **fastener_ex1.asm** in Creo Parametric. The unshaded model displays as shown in Figure 11–46.

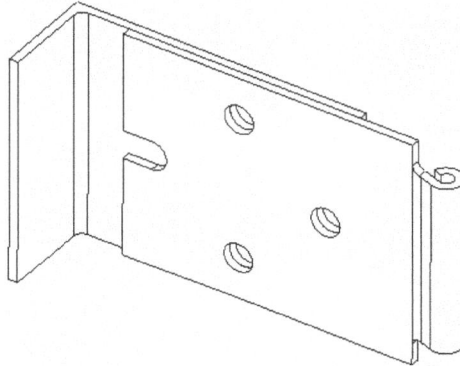

**Figure 11–46**

2. Select **Applications>Simulate** to switch to the Simulate environment.

### Task 2 - Apply the material.

*The material properties should be as stated.*

1. Assign **STEEL** to both parts. The following values are the default material properties for HS-low-alloy steel (STEEL):

   - Poisson = 0.27
   - Young's modulus = 199948 MPa

## Task 3 - Create the fasteners.

1. In the *Refine Model* tab, click ⬚. The Fastener Definition dialog box opens as shown in Figure 11–47.

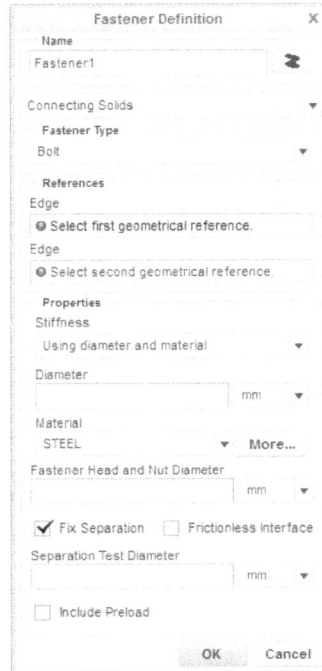

**Figure 11–47**

2. Select the circular edge of the top hole in the **hinge2** part as the first reference, as shown in Figure 11–48.

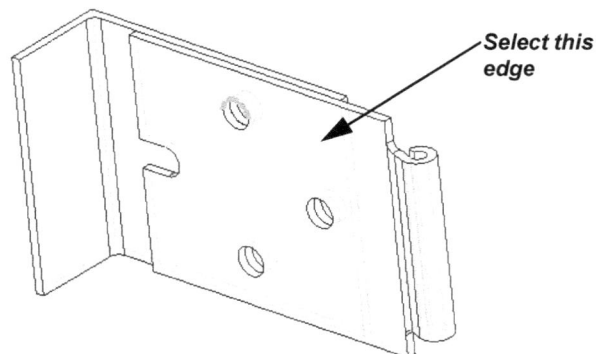

**Figure 11–48**

3. Select the circular edge of the top hole in the **plate** part as the second reference, as shown in Figure 11–49.

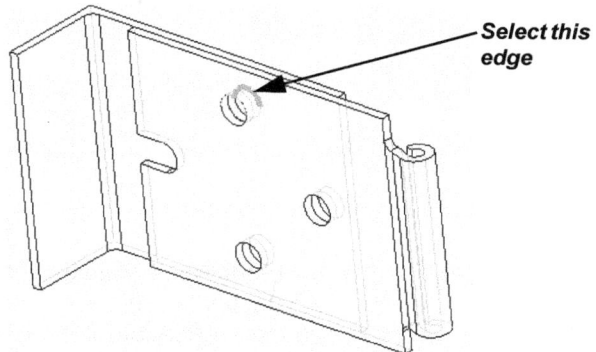

Select this edge

Figure 11–49

4. Select the **Include Preload** option. In the *Preload Force* field, enter **500**. The Fastener Definition dialog box opens as shown in Figure 11–50.

Figure 11–50

5. Click OK . A warning message box displays as shown in Figure 11–51, and the two contacting surfaces are highlighted.

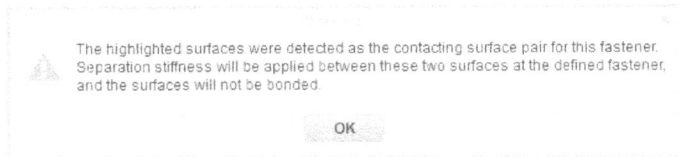

> ⚠ The highlighted surfaces were detected as the contacting surface pair for this fastener. Separation stiffness will be applied between these two surfaces at the defined fastener, and the surfaces will not be bonded.
>
> OK

**Figure 11–51**

Note that the message in the box prompts you that the two contacting surfaces will not be bonded during the analysis, due to the application of the Fastener.

6. Click OK to close the message box. The model displays as shown in Figure 11–52.

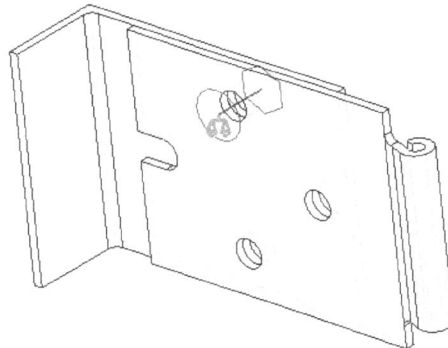

**Figure 11–52**

7. Repeat Steps 1 to 6 to create Fasteners in the second and the third holes, as shown in Figure 11–53.

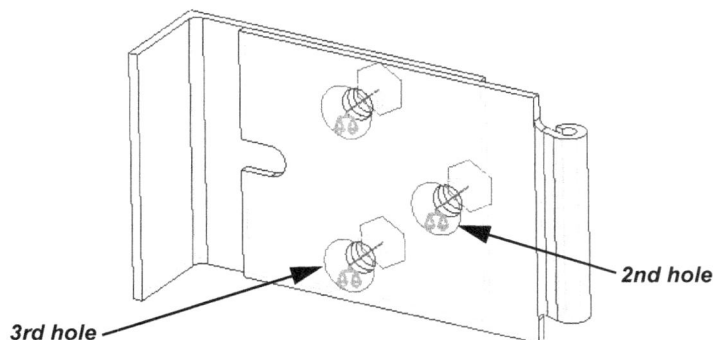

*2nd hole*

*3rd hole*

**Figure 11–53**

## Task 4 - Apply the constraints.

1. Constrain the surface shown in Figure 11–54 in all of the translations.

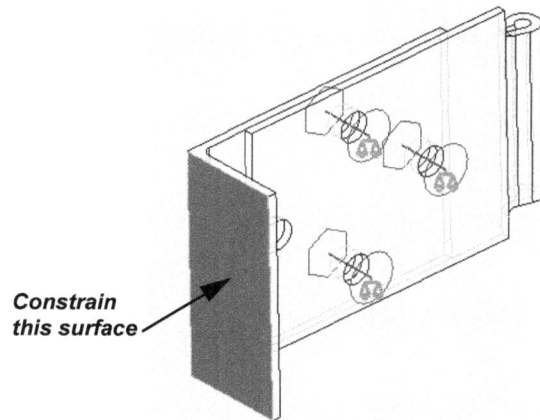

**Constrain this surface**

**Figure 11–54**

## Analysis Tasks

## Task 5 - Set up and run a static analysis.

In the preliminary analysis run, you will solve the model without having any external loads applied.

1. Set up a new static analysis, named **fastener1_preload**, with the options shown in Figure 11–55.

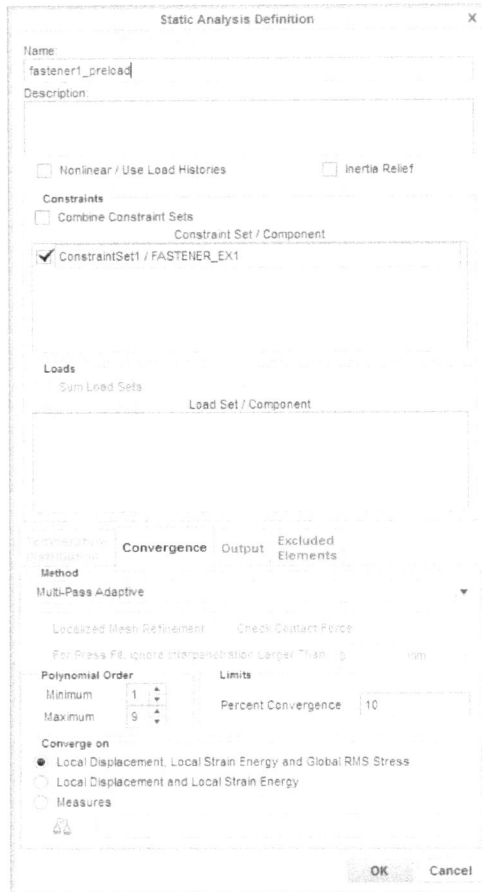

**Figure 11–55**

2. Run the analysis. It should converge on pass 6.

## Task 6 - Check the fastener axial forces.

Since no external loads were applied in this analysis run, the force in the fasteners must be equal to the preloads that you applied in Task 3.

1. In the Analyses and Design Studies dialog box, click [icon] to open the Run Status window, and scroll down to the *Measures* area.

2.  Extract the axial forces in the fasteners, as shown in Figure 11–56.

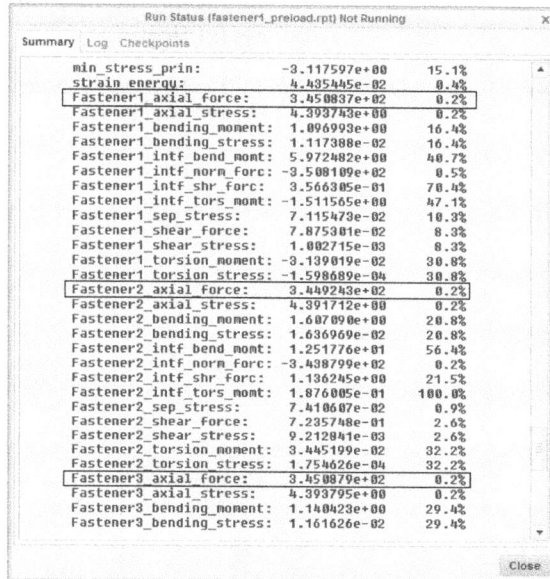

```
                    Run Status (fastener1_preload.rpt) Not Running                    ✕

Summary  Log  Checkpoints

        min_stress_prin:         -3.117597e+00      15.1%    ▲
        strain_energy:            4.435445e-02       0.4%
   ┌─── Fastener1_axial_force:     3.450837e+02       0.2% ───┐
        Fastener1_axial_stress:   4.393743e+00       0.2%
        Fastener1_bending_moment: 1.096993e+00      16.4%
        Fastener1_bending_stress: 1.117388e-02      16.4%
        Fastener1_intf_bend_mont: 5.972482e+00      40.7%
        Fastener1_intf_norm_forc: -3.508109e+02      0.5%
        Fastener1_intf_shr_forc:  3.566305e-01      70.4%
        Fastener1_intf_tors_mont: -1.511565e+00     47.1%
        Fastener1_sep_stress:     7.115473e-02      10.3%
        Fastener1_shear_force:    7.875301e-02       8.3%
        Fastener1_shear_stress:   1.002715e-03       8.3%
        Fastener1_torsion_moment: -3.139019e-02     30.8%
        Fastener1_torsion_stress: -1.598689e-04     30.8%
   ┌─── Fastener2_axial_force:     3.449243e+02       0.2% ───┐
        Fastener2_axial_stress:   4.391712e+00       0.2%
        Fastener2_bending_moment: 1.607090e+00      20.8%
        Fastener2_bending_stress: 1.636969e-02      20.8%
        Fastener2_intf_bend_mont: 1.251776e+01      56.4%
        Fastener2_intf_norm_forc: -3.438799e+02      0.2%
        Fastener2_intf_shr_forc:  1.136245e+00      21.5%
        Fastener2_intf_tors_mont: 1.876005e-01     100.0%
        Fastener2_sep_stress:     7.410607e-02       0.9%
        Fastener2_shear_force:    7.235748e-01       2.6%
        Fastener2_shear_stress:   9.212041e-03       2.6%
        Fastener2_torsion_moment: 3.445199e-02      32.2%
        Fastener2_torsion_stress: 1.754626e-04      32.2%
   ┌─── Fastener3_axial_force:     3.450879e+02       0.2% ───┐
        Fastener3_axial_stress:   4.393795e+00       0.2%
        Fastener3_bending_moment: 1.140423e+00      29.4%
        Fastener3_bending_stress: 1.161626e-02      29.4%    ▼

                                                              Close
```

**Figure 11–56**

Note that Creo Simulate did not get the preloads quite right. The required preloads were 500N, while the actual axial forces in the bolts are approximately 345N. In the next tasks, you will correct the preloads, apply the external loads, and re-run the analysis.

3.  Close the Run Status window and the Analyses and Design Studies dialog box.

## Modeling Tasks

## Task 7 - Calculate the preload correction coefficients.

1.  Calculate the preload correction coefficients as the <desired preload> divided by the <actual axial force>. The correction coefficient summary is as follows:

| Fastener | Desired Preload | Actual Axial Force | Correction Coeff |
|----------|-----------------|--------------------|--------------------|
| Fastener1 | 500N | 345.1N | 1.449 |
| Fastener2 | 500N | 344.9N | 1.450 |
| Fastener3 | 500N | 345.1N | 1.449 |

**Task 8 - Apply the corrected preloads.**

1. In the Model Tree, right-click on Fastener1 and select **Edit Definition**.

*500N x 1.449 = 724.5N*

2. In the *Preload Force* field, enter **724.5**, as shown in Figure 11–57.

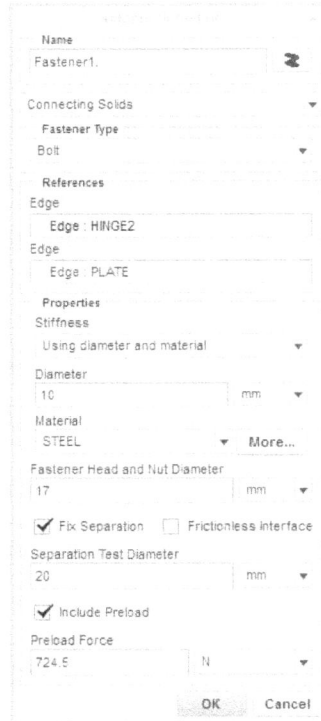

**Figure 11–57**

3. Click ___ OK ___ to finish. Click ___ OK ___ in the warning message box that displays.

4. Repeat Steps 1 to 3 and correct the preload values for the other two fasteners as follows:

   • Fastener2: **725**
   • Fastener3: **724.5**

## Task 9 - Apply the external loads.

1. Apply the force 100N in the Z-direction to the surface shown in Figure 11–58.

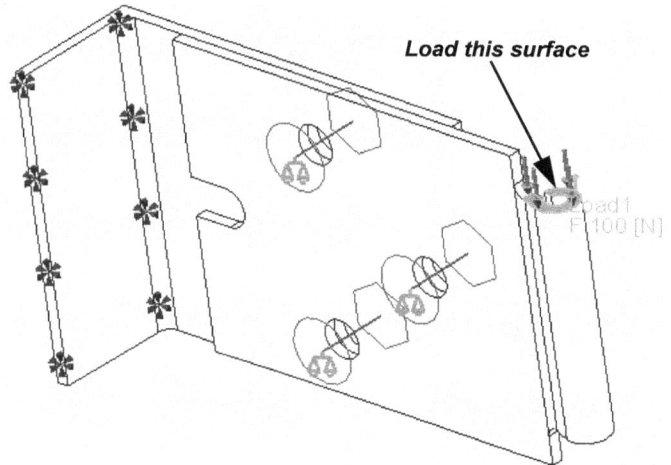

**Load this surface**

**Figure 11–58**

## Analysis Tasks

## Task 10 - Re-run the analysis.

1. Open the **fastener1_preload** analysis to edit it.

2. Select the **LoadSet1/FASTENER_EX1** option, as shown in Figure 11–59. This ensures that the external loads are now included in the analysis.

**Figure 11–59**

3. Run the analysis.

## Results Tasks

## Task 11 - Animate the model deformation.

1. Create the displacement magnitude animation plot.

2. Start the animation. Verify whether the applied boundary conditions behave correctly.

3. Step to Frame 5 of the animation. The result plot displays as shown in Figure 11–60.

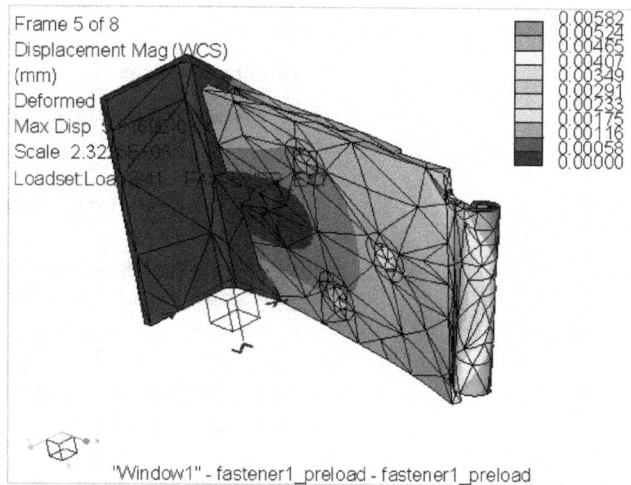

Figure 11–60

## Task 12 - Display the stress plot.

1. Create a deformed von Mises stress fringe plot. The result plot displays as shown in Figure 11–61.

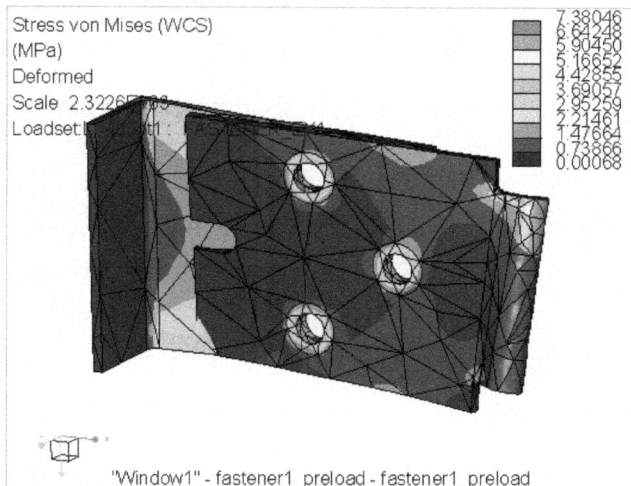

Figure 11–61

2. Examine the areas of maximum stress. Note the higher stresses around the bolt holes, caused by the preloads.

3. Exit the Results. Save and close the model.

# Practice 11d

# Handling Surface Separation Issues When Using Fasteners

**Learning Objectives**

Understand how to create fastened connections in solid models.

Understand how to check fastener interface forces.

Understand how to ensure the correct separation of assembly components.

In this practice, you will set up and run a static analysis of the assembly shown in Figure 11–62. The two parts are screwed together using the four holes in the flanges, with a 50N preload.

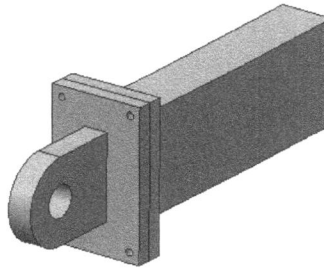

**Figure 11–62**

**Modeling Tasks**

**Task 1 - Open the model.**

1.  Open **fastener_ex2.asm** in Creo Parametric. The unshaded model displays as shown in Figure 11–63.

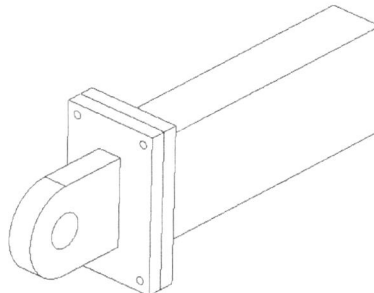

**Figure 11–63**

2. Select **Applications>Simulate** to switch to the Simulate environment.

## Task 2 - Apply the material.

*The material properties should be as stated.*

1. Assign **STEEL** to both parts. The following values are the default material properties for HS-low-alloy steel (STEEL):

   - Poisson = 0.27
   - Young's modulus = 199948 MPa

## Task 3 - Create the fasteners.

1. In the *Refine Model* tab, click ⚇ . The Fastener Definition dialog box opens as shown in Figure 11–64.

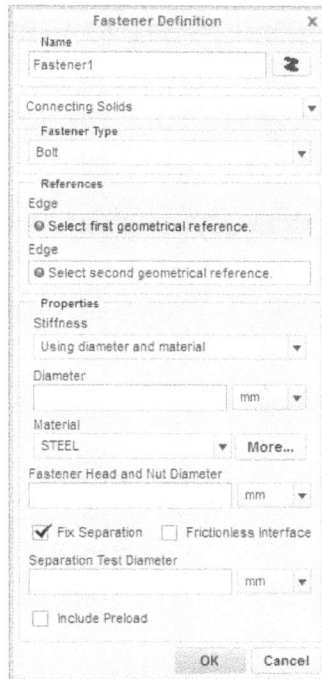

**Figure 11–64**

2. Select the circular edge of the top left hole in the **part2** part as the first reference, as shown in Figure 11–65.

*Select this edge*

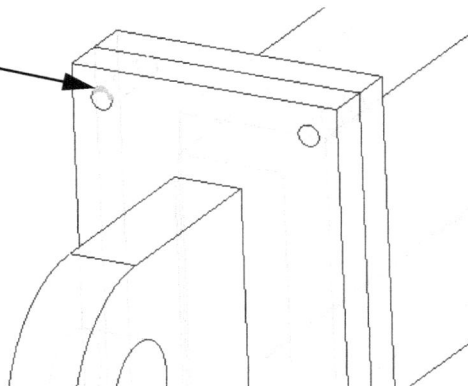

**Figure 11–65**

3. Select the circular edge of the top left hole in the **part1** part as the second reference, as shown in Figure 11–66.

*Select this edge*

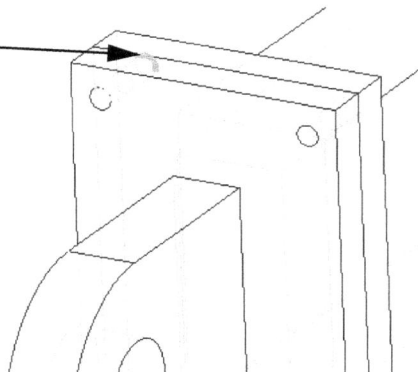

**Figure 11–66**

4. Select the **Include Preload** option. In the *Preload Force* field, enter **50**. The Fastener Definition dialog box opens as shown in Figure 11–67.

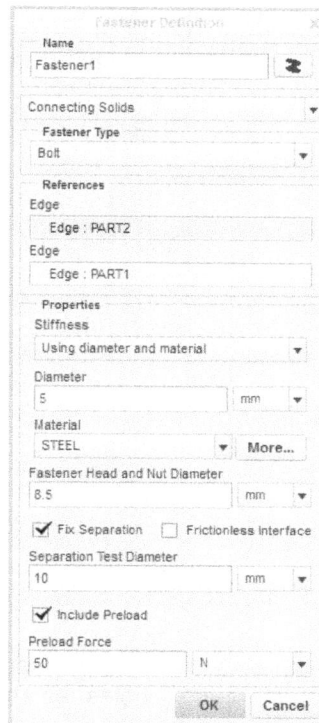

**Figure 11–67**

5. Click ___OK___ . A warning message box displays as shown in Figure 11–68, and the two contacting surfaces are highlighted.

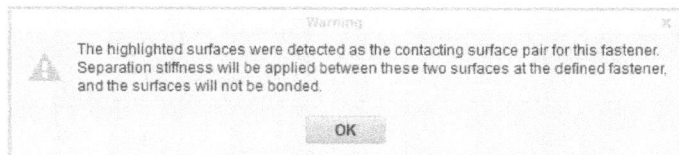

**Figure 11–68**

Note that the message in the box prompts you that the two contacting surfaces will not be bonded, due to the application of the Fastener.

6. Click OK to close the message box. The model displays as shown in Figure 11–69.

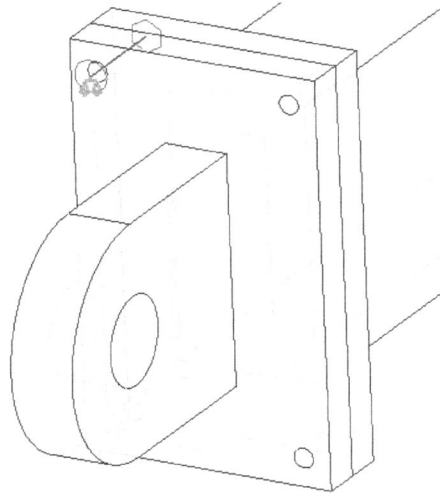

**Figure 11–69**

7. Repeat Steps 1 to 6 to create Fasteners in the remaining holes, as shown in Figure 11–70.

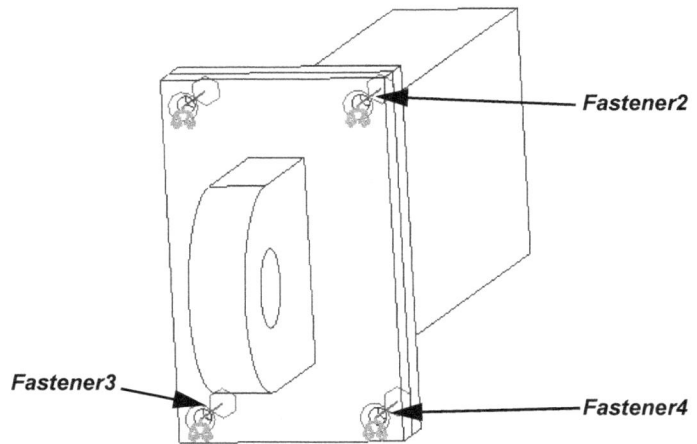

**Figure 11–70**

## Task 4 - Apply the constraints.

1. Constrain the surface shown in Figure 11–71 in all of the translations.

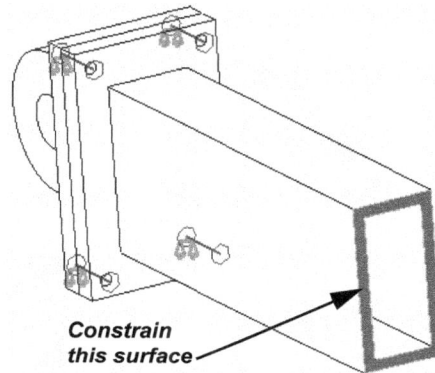

**Constrain this surface**

**Figure 11–71**

## Task 5 - Apply the loads.

1. Apply the force **-150** in Y-direction and **150** in Z-direction to the large hole, as shown in Figure 11–72.

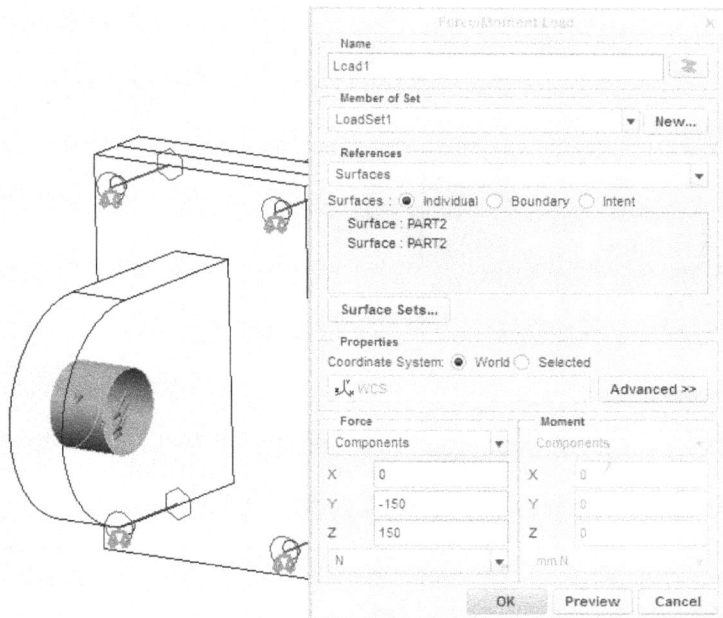

**Figure 11–72**

## Analysis Tasks

### Task 6 - Set up and run a static analysis.

1. Set up a Single-Pass Adaptive static analysis, named **fastener2**.

2. Run the analysis. Wait until the Diagnostics message box displays, but do not close it yet.

### Task 7 - Check the fastener separation status.

1. In the Diagnostics box, note that a warning message for Fastener1 and Fastener2 is displayed, prompting you that *The fix separation option for the fastener is preventing the parts from separating at locations where they should separate*, as shown in Figure 11–73. Close the Diagnostics box.

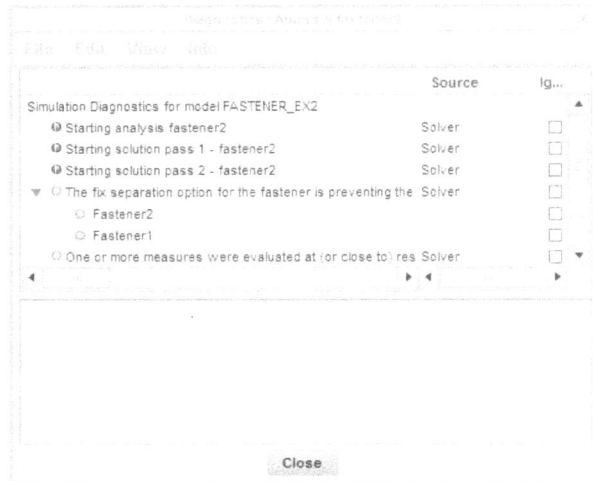

**Figure 11–73**

2. In the Analyses and Design Studies dialog box, click ▤ to open the Run Status window, and scroll down to the *Measures* area.

3. Extract the interface normal force (**intf_norm_forc**) measures for the fasteners, as shown in Figure 11–74.

```
strain_energy:              7.292276e-01
Fastener1_axial_force:      4.529812e+01
Fastener1_axial_stress:     2.307014e+00
Fastener1_bending_moment:   6.865612e+00
Fastener1_bending_stress:   5.594604e-01
Fastener1_intf_bend_momt:   3.199798e+02
Fastener1_intf_norm_forc:   1.608217e+01
Fastener1_intf_shr_forc:    2.435009e+01
Fastener1_intf_tors_momt:  -1.028432e+01
Fastener1_sep_stress:       1.810677e+00
Fastener1_shear_force:      8.614838e-02
Fastener1_shear_stress:     4.387501e-03
Fastener1_torsion_moment:  -2.151270e-01
Fastener1_torsion_stress:  -8.765061e-03
Fastener2_axial_force:      4.554334e+01
Fastener2_axial_stress:     2.319503e+00
Fastener2_bending_moment:   7.102301e+00
Fastener2_bending_stress:   5.787476e-01
Fastener2_intf_bend_momt:   3.793069e+02
Fastener2_intf_norm_forc:   2.624168e+01
Fastener2_intf_shr_forc:    2.433684e+01
Fastener2_intf_tors_momt:   1.633449e+01
Fastener2_sep_stress:       2.270193e+00
Fastener2_shear_force:      1.077921e-01
Fastener2_shear_stress:     5.489808e-03
Fastener2_torsion_moment:   1.926583e-01
Fastener2_torsion_stress:   7.849607e-03
Fastener3_axial_force:      3.887604e+01
Fastener3_axial_stress:     1.979940e+00
Fastener3_bending_moment:   9.191899e-01
Fastener3_bending_stress:   7.490233e-02
Fastener3_intf_bend_momt:   4.828646e+01
Fastener3_intf_norm_forc:  -3.413930e+01
Fastener3_intf_shr_forc:    1.796287e+01
Fastener3_intf_tors_momt:  -7.481879e+00
Fastener3_sep_stress:       2.270193e+00
Fastener3_shear_force:      8.405609e-02
Fastener3_shear_stress:     4.280941e-03
Fastener3_torsion_moment:  -1.424883e-01
Fastener3_torsion_stress:  -5.805497e-03
Fastener4_axial_force:      3.913205e+01
Fastener4_axial_stress:     1.992979e+00
Fastener4_bending_moment:   8.562922e-01
Fastener4_bending_stress:   6.977696e-02
Fastener4_intf_bend_momt:   4.071611e+01
Fastener4_intf_norm_forc:  -2.927688e+01
Fastener4_intf_shr_forc:    1.331091e+01
```

**Figure 11–74**

Note the following:

- The interface forces for the two bottom fasteners (Fastener3 and Fastener4) are negative. This means the separation springs in those two fasteners act in compression (i.e., they prevent the parts from inter-penetrating in that area) as they should, given the loading in the model.

- The interface forces for the top two fasteners (Fastener1 and Fastener2) are positive. This means the separation springs there act in tension (i.e., they incorrectly hold the parts together in that area, while the parts should actually be slightly separate). This is because the preload in the top fasteners is exceeded by the axial force induced by the loading in the model.

You will later correct the separation option for the top two fasteners to enable the parts to naturally separate at the top of the flange.

## Results Tasks

## Task 8 - Display the model deformation.

1. Create and display the displacement magnitude deformed plot.

2. Examine the deformation as shown in Figure 11–75. Note that the parts are kept in contact at the top of the flange, as predicted by the interface force signs obtained in Task 7.

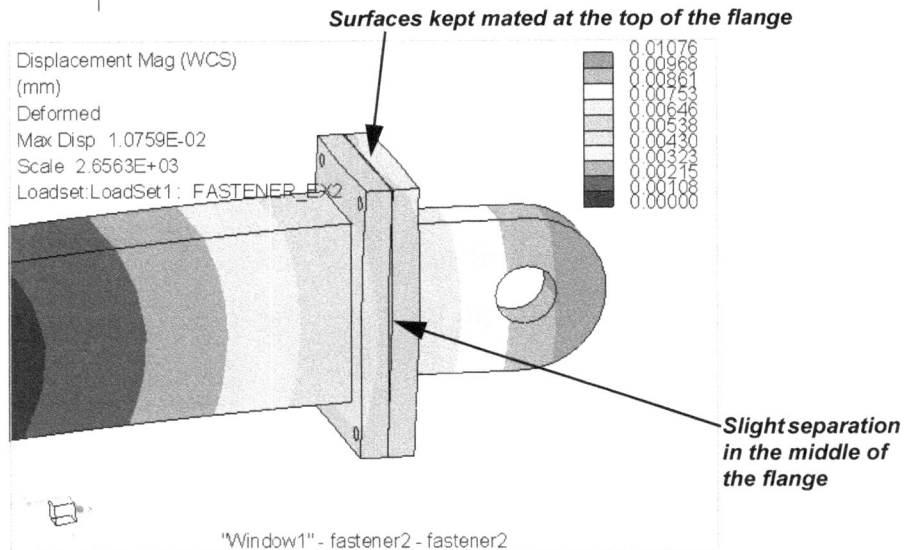

**Surfaces kept mated at the top of the flange**

Displacement Mag (WCS)
(mm)
Deformed
Max Disp 1.0759E-02
Scale 2.6563E+03
Loadset:LoadSet1: FASTENER_EX2

0.01076
0.00968
0.00861
0.00753
0.00646
0.00538
0.00430
0.00323
0.00215
0.00108
0.00000

**Slight separation in the middle of the flange**

"Window1" - fastener2 - fastener2

**Figure 11–75**

3. Exit the Results. Close the Analyses and Design Studies dialog box.

## Modeling Tasks

## Task 9 - Remove the separation springs.

In this task, you will remove the separation springs from the top two fasteners, to enable the surfaces to separate in that area once the force in the fastener exceeds the preload.

1. In the Model Tree, right-click on Fastener1 and select **Edit Definition**.

2. Clear the **Fix Separation** option, as shown in Figure 11–76.

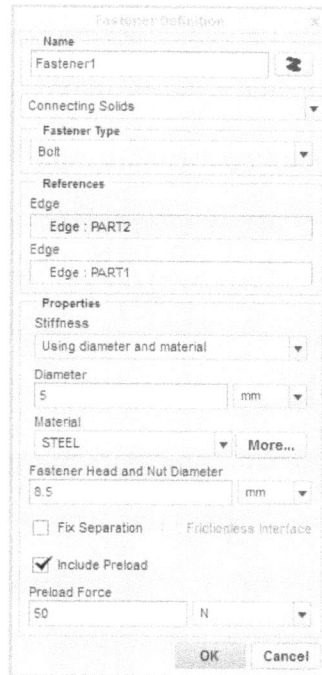

**Figure 11–76**

3. Click OK to finish. Click OK in the warning message box that displays.

4. Repeat Steps 1 to 3 for Fastener2.

## Analysis Tasks

### Task 10 - Re-run the analysis.

1. Run the **fastener2** analysis again.

2. Wait until the Diagnostics message box displays. Note that it no longer displays a warning message about the fasteners.

## Task 11 - Check the fastener separation status.

1. In the Analyses and Design Studies dialog box, click ▤ to open the Run Status window, and scroll down to the *Measures* area, as shown in Figure 11–77.

```
strain_energy:               8.118546e-01
Fastener1_axial_force:       8.313264e+01
Fastener1_axial_stress:      4.233911e+00
Fastener1_bending_moment:    2.442257e+01
Fastener1_bending_stress:    1.990130e+00
Fastener1_shear_force:       2.648446e+00
Fastener1_shear_stress:      1.348842e-01
Fastener1_torsion_moment:   -1.613125e-01
Fastener1_torsion_stress:   -6.572464e-03
Fastener2_axial_force:       8.274841e+01
Fastener2_axial_stress:      4.214342e+00
Fastener2_bending_moment:    2.422279e+01
Fastener2_bending_stress:    1.973851e+00
Fastener2_shear_force:       2.740669e+00
Fastener2_shear_stress:      1.395811e-01
Fastener2_torsion_moment:    2.382917e-01
Fastener2_torsion_stress:    9.708876e-03
Fastener3_axial_force:       3.909487e+01
Fastener3_axial_stress:      1.991085e+00
Fastener3_bending_moment:    1.638910e+00
Fastener3_bending_stress:    1.335504e-01
Fastener3_intf_bend_momt:    7.502779e+01
Fastener3_intf_norm_forc:   -3.219723e+01
Fastener3_intf_shr_forc:     3.482253e+01
Fastener3_intf_tors_momt:   -1.470505e+01
Fastener3_sep_stress:        2.650585e-01
Fastener3_shear_force:       1.555568e-01
Fastener3_shear_stress:      7.922444e-03
Fastener3_torsion_moment:   -2.539130e-01
Fastener3_torsion_stress:   -1.034534e-02
Fastener4_axial_force:       3.958728e+01
Fastener4_axial_stress:      2.016164e+00
Fastener4_bending_moment:    1.455147e+00
Fastener4_bending_stress:    1.185761e-01
Fastener4_intf_bend_momt:    6.491271e+01
Fastener4_intf_norm_forc:   -2.975363e+01
Fastener4_intf_shr_forc:     3.340145e+01
Fastener4_intf_tors_momt:    1.468434e+01
Fastener4_sep_stress:        3.578018e-01
Fastener4_shear_force:       1.493445e-01
Fastener4_shear_stress:      7.606051e-03
Fastener4_torsion_moment:    2.625024e-01
Fastener4_torsion_stress:    1.069531e-02
```

**Figure 11–77**

Note the following:

- The axial forces in Fastener1 and Fastener2 are approximately 83N, which exceeds the 50N preload.

- The interface normal forces in Fastener3 and Fastener4 are negative.

2. Close the Run Status box.

## Results Tasks

### Task 12 - Animate the model deformation.

1. Create the displacement magnitude animation plot.

2. Start the animation. Verify whether the applied boundary conditions behave correctly.

3. Step to Frame 5 of the animation. The result plot displays as shown in Figure 11–78. Note that the parts are now slightly separate at the top of the flange, which is correct.

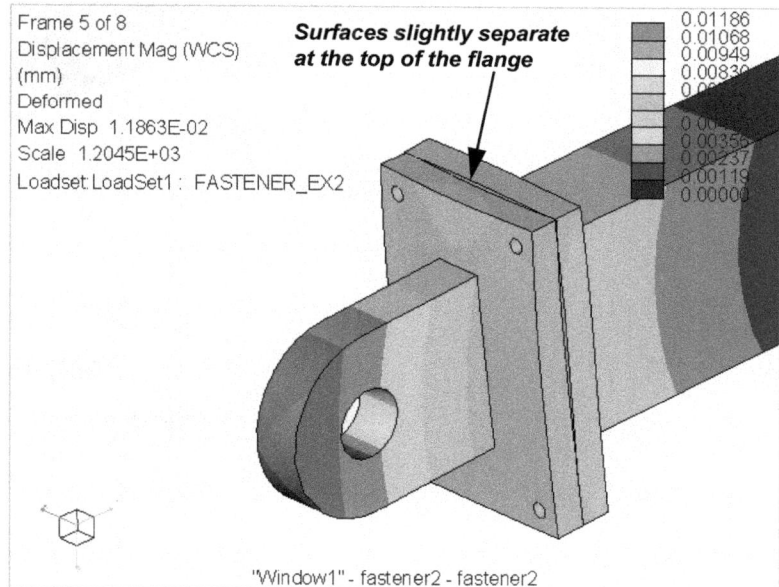

Figure 11–78

## Task 13 - Display the stress plot.

1. Create a deformed von Mises stress fringe plot. The result plot displays as shown in Figure 11–79.

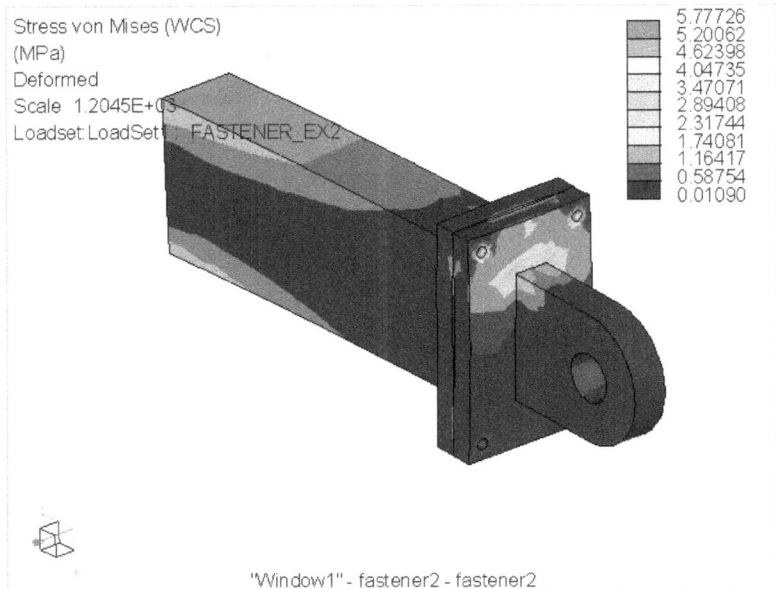

Stress von Mises (WCS)
(MPa)
Deformed
Scale 1.2045E+03
Loadset: LoadSet1: FASTENER_EX2

5.77726
5.20062
4.62398
4.04735
3.47071
2.89408
2.31744
1.74081
1.16417
0.58754
0.01090

"Window1" - fastener2 - fastener2

**Figure 11–79**

2. Exit the Results. Save and close the model.

# Chapter 12

## Buckling Analysis

In mechanical design, a column is defined as any member that is loaded in compression. In certain cases, the maximum load a column can sustain is determined by stiffness of the column, rather than by the yield stress of its material.

This chapter contains the following topics:

- **Theory of Buckling**
- **Creo Simulate Buckling Analysis**

# 12.1 Theory of Buckling

**Learning Objective**

Understand the concepts of the buckling analysis.

Buckling analysis predicts the magnitude of the load at which the loss of stability under compressive loads might occur. It is an important analysis for slender structures that are subject to large compressive stresses. For example, these could be structural columns or posts, bridge trusses, submarine hulls, etc.

Buckling might occur at stresses well below the yield stress. This is called *elastic buckling*. Therefore, it is important to analyze such structures for both stress and buckling.

In the example shown in Figure 12–1, a long slender column AB, of length (L) is constrained at end A and loaded with a centrally compressive load P at end B.

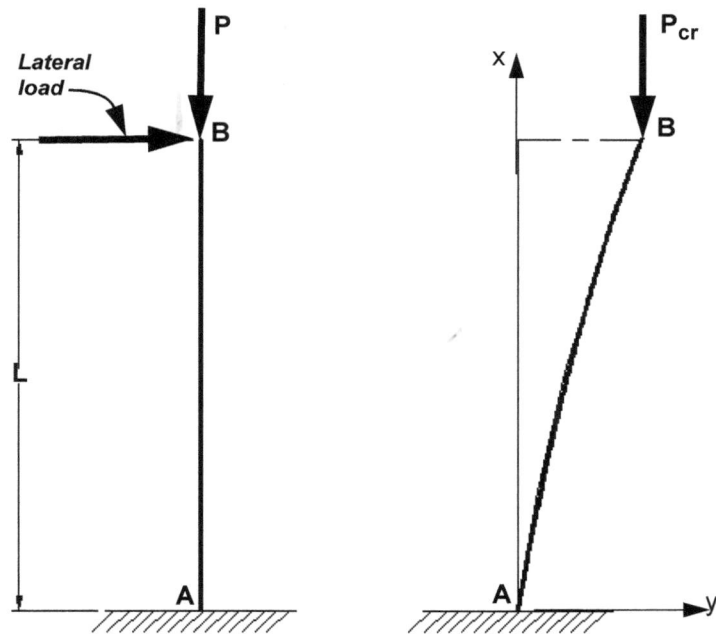

**Figure 12–1**

Assume that the column has the following characteristics:

- Perfectly straight

- Uniform cross-section

- Homogeneous

- Behaves elastically

When load P is small, the compressive column is laterally stable if end B is pushed slightly to one side. The column returns to its straight form as the lateral force is removed. As load P gradually increases, the straight form of the column becomes unstable and the column, if pushed to one side, remains there even if the lateral load is removed. This occurrence is called *buckling* and the value of the load at which this occurs is called the *critical load* ($P_{cr}$).

# 12.2 Creo Simulate Buckling Analysis

**Learning Objective**

Understand how to create a buckling analysis in Creo Simulate.

*The buckling analysis in Creo Simulate is only available for 3D solid models.*

The Creo Simulate buckling analysis is a linear or eigenvalue type of buckling analysis. The analysis predicts the critical load under which the structure is neutrally stable. The analysis solution is presented as a load factor called the *Buckling Load Factor* (BLF) and a corresponding buckling mode shape.

To produce a critical buckling load ($P_{cr}$), the applied load set is multiplied by the BLF:

$$P_{cr} = BLF \times P_{applied}$$

Therefore, the BLF is a safety factor for the structure against buckling. A BLF less than 1.0 indicates that the structure is predicted to buckle under the applied load.

The buckling mode shape indicates how the structure deforms at the onset of buckling. The number one mode shape is most likely to be the only one to occur. Therefore, be sure to verify your design for mode 1 as shown in Figure 12–2.

```
Number of Modes: 3

Mode     B. L. F.      Convergence
----   ------------    -----------
   1    1.106302e+01       0.0%
   2    1.695276e+01       0.0%
   3    9.939256e+01       0.4%
```

**Figure 12–2**

The linear buckling analysis provides a useful first order approximation of the critical buckling load for designers and generally produces results that are not conservative (the theory calculates a higher critical load than is actually observed in experiments). It also assumes that the initial loading on the model does not change the geometry. Therefore, it is recommended that you use generous safety factors.

Use the following steps to perform a buckling analysis:

1. Set up the model.
2. Assign material properties to the model.
3. Apply boundary conditions to the model (i.e., loads or constraints).
4. Create a static analysis.

   A static analysis must be defined before a buckling analysis can be created because the structure stiffness used in the buckling analysis is obtained from the static analysis. Therefore, the accuracy of the buckling analysis directly relates to the accuracy of the static analysis. You need to set a tight convergence criteria on the RMS stress, displacement, and strain energy.

5. Create a buckling analysis.
6. Run the buckling analysis.
7. Interpret the results.

To calculate the stresses and displacements on the structure at the critical buckling load, multiply the original compressive load by the smallest positive BLF, and rerun the static analysis.

# Practice 12a | Buckling Analysis of a Pole

**Learning Objectives**

✓ Understand how to set up and run a Buckling analysis.

✓ Understand how to determine the Buckling Load Factor.

✓ Understand how to visualize the Buckling modes.

In this practice, you will set up and run a buckling design analysis on a long slender pole, as shown in Figure 12–3. The pole has a rectangular cross-section (2 x 2) and is 13ft long.

**Figure 12–3**

**Modeling Tasks**

**Task 1 - Open the part.**

1. Open **buckle_pole.prt** in Creo Parametric. The part displays as shown in Figure 12–4.

**Figure 12–4**

2. Ensure that the unit system is set to **IPS**.

3. Select **Applications>Simulate**.

## Task 2 - Apply the loads.

1. Apply a total and uniform force of **-1000** in the X-direction to the pole's hole surface, as shown in Figure 12–5.

*The X-direction is relative to the WCS.*

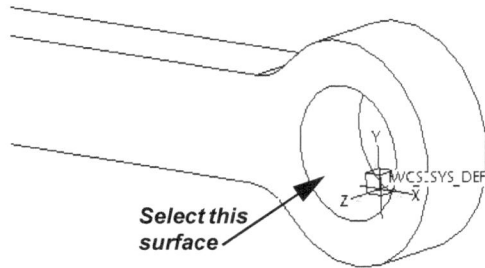

**Figure 12–5**

2. Name the load **buckle_f**. The model displays as shown in Figure 12–6.

*The load values are turned off.*

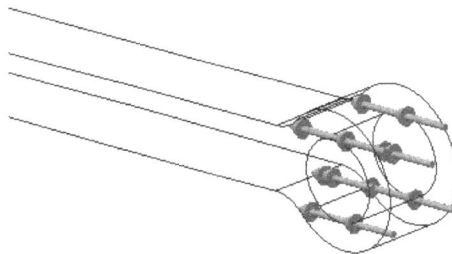

**Figure 12–6**

## Task 3 - Apply the constraints.

1. Fully constrain the hole on the other end of the pole (all of the translations), as shown in Figure 12–7.

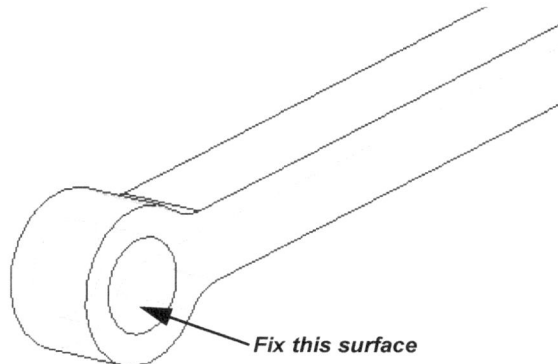

**Figure 12–7**

2. Name the constraint **pole_const**. The model displays as shown in Figure 12–8.

*The constraint values are turned off.*

**Figure 12–8**

### Task 4 - Apply the material.

1. Assign **STEEL** to the **buckle_pole** part. The following values are the default material properties for HS-low-alloy steel (STEEL):

   • Poisson = 0.27
   • Young's modulus = 2.9e+07 psi
   • Density = 0.0007324 lbf sec^2/in^4

### Analysis Tasks

### Task 5 - Set up an analysis.

In this task, you will set up a static analysis and a buckling analysis.

1. Click  . The Analyses and Design Studies dialog box opens.

2. Select **File>New Static**. The Static Analysis Definition dialog box opens.

3. For the analysis name, enter **static_pole**. In the Static Analysis Definition dialog box, select the options shown in Figure 12–9.

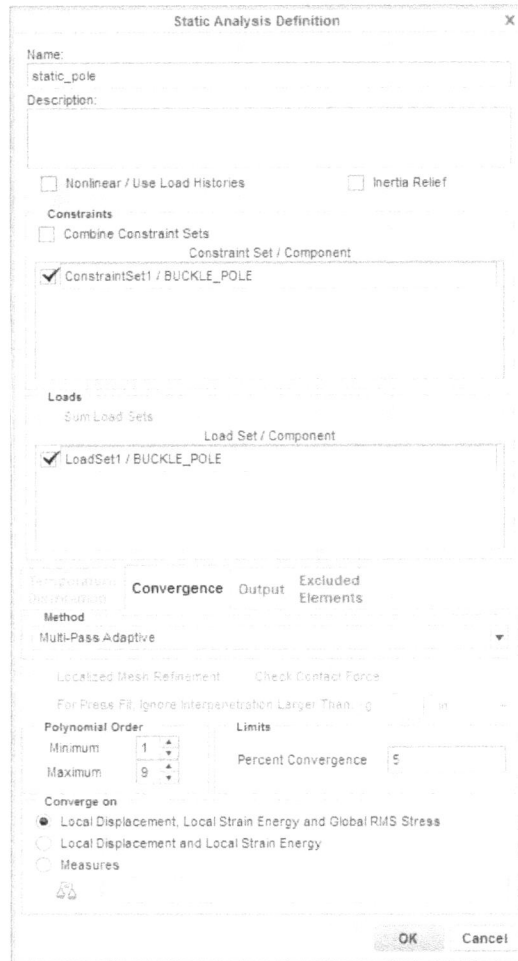

**Figure 12–9**

4. Click ⬛ OK . The Analyses and Design Studies dialog box opens.

5. Select **File>New Buckling**. The Buckling Analysis Definition dialog box opens as shown in Figure 12–10.

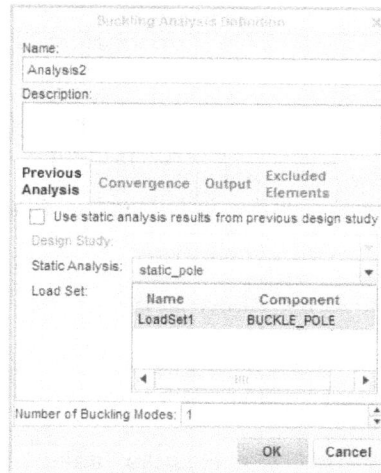

**Figure 12–10**

6. In the *Name* field, enter **buckle_pole**.

7. In the *Number of Buckling Modes* field, enter **3**.

8. Select the *Convergence* tab and enter the information shown in Figure 12–11.

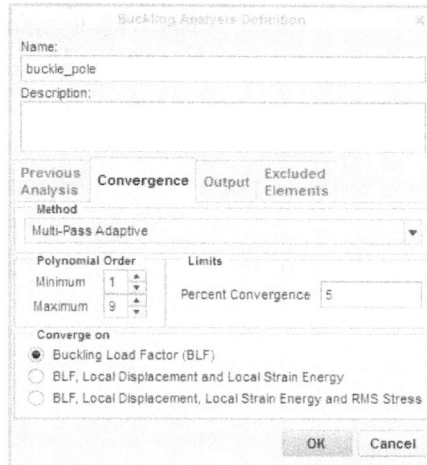

**Figure 12–11**

9. Click OK .

10. Run the buckle_pole analysis.

11. In the Analyses and Design Studies dialog box, click 🗐 . The Run Status window displays.

12. Scroll through the Runs Status window to display the analysis information. Note that the static_pole analysis was automatically run before the buckle_pole analysis.

13. Locate the BLF values in the Run Status dialog box when the run is complete, as shown in Figure 12–12.

```
Number of Modes: 3

Mode    B. L. F.     Convergence
----    ------------  ----------
   1   1.106302e+01      0.0%
   2   1.695276e+01      0.0%
   3   9.939256e+01      0.4%
```

**Figure 12–12**

## Results Tasks

## Task 6 - Display the results.

In this task, you will create and display three deformation animation fringe plots of the three buckling modes.

1. In the Analyses and Design Studies dialog box, click 📋 . The Result Window Definition dialog box opens as shown in Figure 12–13.

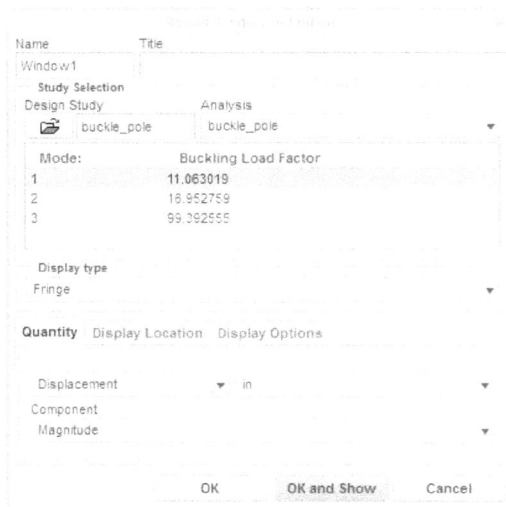

**Figure 12–13**

2. Ensure that Mode 1 is highlighted. In the Display Options tab, select **Deformed**, **Overlay Undeformed**, and **Animate**. Click

   OK and Show . The Displacement Magnitude result plot at Frame 3 displays as shown in Figure 12–14.

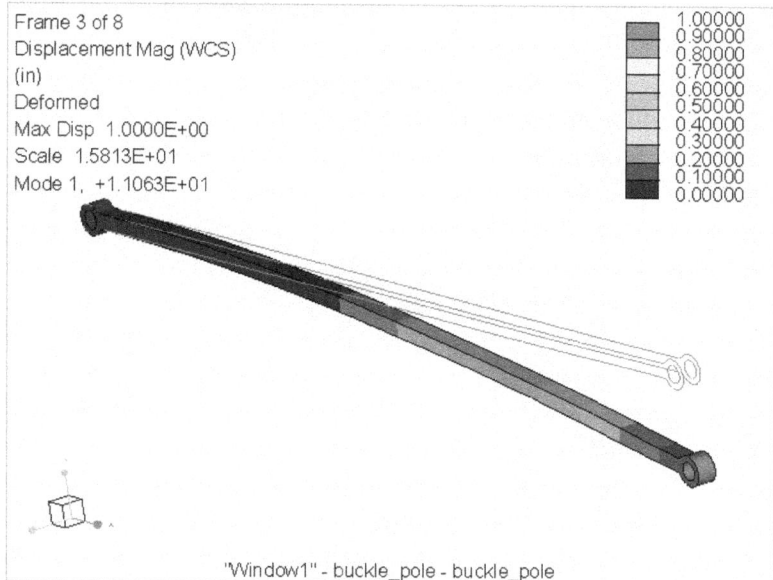

Frame 3 of 8
Displacement Mag (WCS)
(in)
Deformed
Max Disp 1.0000E+00
Scale 1.5813E+01
Mode 1, +1.1063E+01

1.00000
0.90000
0.80000
0.70000
0.60000
0.50000
0.40000
0.30000
0.20000
0.10000
0.00000

"Window1" - buckle_pole - buckle_pole

**Figure 12–14**

3. Click 🖼. Repeat Step 2 to display and animate Buckling modes 2 and 3.

4. Exit the Results. Save and close the model.

# Appendix A

## Basics of Structural Analysis

This chapter contains the following topics:

- **Quantities and Units**
- **Newton's Laws**

# A.1 Quantities and Units

**Fundamental Quantities**

The fundamental quantities of solid mechanics are: Length, Mass, and Time.

**Derived Quantities**

The derived quantities of solid mechanics are: Force, Moment, Weight, Stress, Velocity, and Acceleration.

**Units**

Units must be consistent to perform valid calculations. The appropriate units for common quantities of the English and Metric systems are as follows:

| Quantity | English Units | Metric Units |
|---|---|---|
| length | Inch, in | Millimeter, mm |
| time | Second, s | Second, s |
| mass | Slug $$\left(1\,\text{slug} = \frac{1\,\text{lbf}}{386.4\,\text{in}\,/\,\text{s}^2}\right)$$ | Tonne, t $(1\text{t} = 1\text{Mg} = 1\text{x}10^6\text{g})$ |
| velocity | in/s | mm/s |
| acceleration | in/s$^2$ | mm/s$^2$ |
| force | Pound, lbf | Newton, N |
| moment | Inch-pound, in lb | Newton-millimeter, N mm |
| weight | Pound, lbf | Newton, N |
| stress | Pounds per square inch, psi | Newton per square millimeter, N/mm$^2$ <br> Megapascal, Mpa $(1\text{Mpa} = 1\text{N}\,/\,\text{mm}^2)$ |

# A.2 Newton's Laws

Newton's three laws of motion are as follows:

1. An object in motion or at rest stays in motion or at rest unless acted on by an external force.
2. For every action there is an equal and opposite reaction.
3. Force = mass * acceleration ($F = ma$).

## Implications of Newton's Laws on Structural Analysis

A body remains stationary or in uniform motion in a straight line unless it is made to change that state by external forces. This is a fundamental assumption when performing a structural Linear Static analysis.

Static implies that there is no movement. It is assumed that the structure being analyzed is not free to move in any direction. Sufficient constraints must be applied to the model to remove all six rigid body degrees of freedom.

**Equilibrium & Free-Body Diagrams**

Free-body diagrams and equilibrium equations determine the load paths in a structure. Mathematically, this provides six equilibrium equations. The sum of the forces in each direction must equal zero and the sum of the moments in each direction must equal zero.

An example of a cantilever beam is shown in Figure A–1.

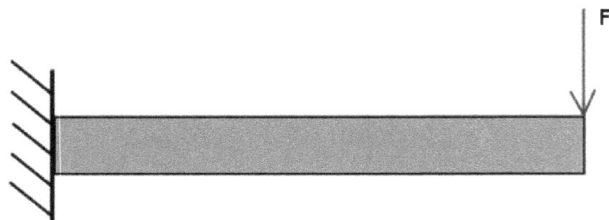

Figure A–1

Reactions to a force (F) must exist at the constraints, as shown in Figure A–2.

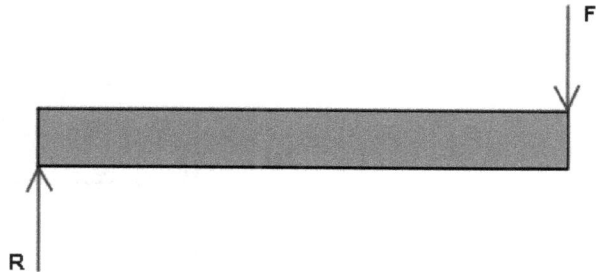

**Figure A–2**

For equilibrium to exist, the following equation must hold:

$R = -F$

This can be verified mathematically with the following equation:

$R + F = 0$

## Moments

If the constraint is a hinge, the entire beam rotates because a hinge cannot react to a moment. A simple hinge would not remove the rotational rigid body degree of freedom. However, a fully fixed constraint can react to moments and you can easily calculate its magnitude.

The ability to calculate the moments acting on and within a structure is useful. Bending often accounts for a part's maximum stress. Therefore, being able to perform a quick hand calculation to validate an analysis model is helpful.

A moment is calculated at a specific location and defined by the following calculation:

*FORCE x DISTANCE*

An applied force (F) causes moments on a structure as it moves away from the reaction force (R). Alternatively, you pure moments might be applied to the structure. Pure moments are transmitted through the system with a constant magnitude.

For static equilibrium to hold for the beam shown in Figure A–3, the sum of moments must equal zero.

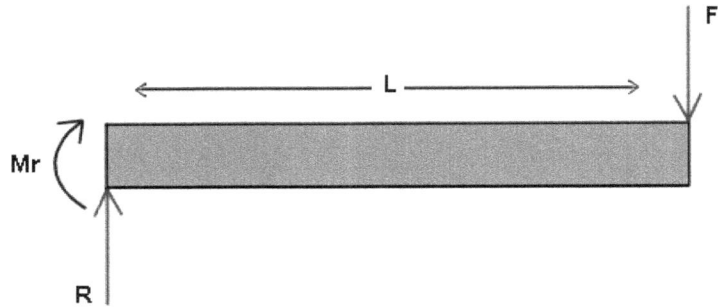

**Figure A–3**

If a moment is positive in the clockwise direction, the sum of the moments is as follows:

$(F \times L) + Mr = 0$

Since the net moment is being calculated at the location of the reaction force (R) the reaction force itself produces no moment. Therefore, the following equation holds:

$Mr = -(F \times L)$

Another example is shown in Figure A–4.

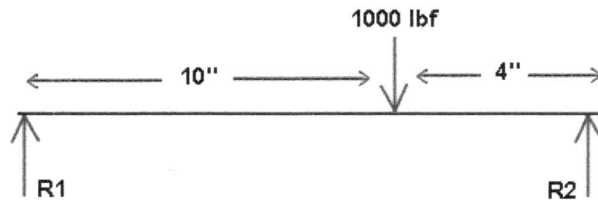

**Figure A–4**

This beam is supported (pinned) at both ends. Reaction forces exist when an external force is applied. For equilibrium to exist, the following equation must hold (vertical up is considered positive):

$R1 + R2 - 1000 = 0$

This single equation is not enough to determine the values of R1 and R2. An additional equation from the equilibrium of moments must be used. The following equation calculates the sum of the moments at the location of R1 (clockwise is considered positive):

$(R1 \times 0) + (1000 \times 10) - (R2 \times 14) = 0$

Using the force and moment equilibrium equations, the values for R1and R2 are calculated as follows:

$R2 = 714.3 \, lbf$

$R1 = 1000 - 714.3 = 285.7 \, lbf$

In addition to determining reaction loads, engineers typically calculate the shear and moment diagrams for beams. The moment at a beam's cross-section, in conjunction with linear-elastic beam theory, is used to determine the beam bending stresses.

Shears and moments are calculated at a beam cross-section location similar to the way reaction loads were determined. Consider the beam segment on only one side of the cross-section. Imagine the location of the cross-section as a fixed constraint. The beam diagram displays as shown in Figure A–5.

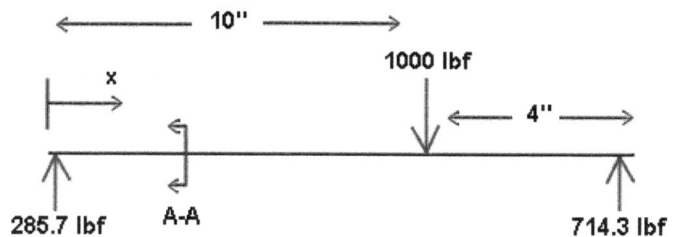

**Figure A–5**

The only the beam portion to the left of section A-A is shown in Figure A–6.

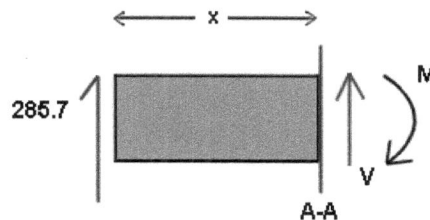

**Figure A–6**

The value of V is calculated using the following equation:

$285.7 + V = 0$

Therefore,

$M = -285.7x \, in \cdot lbf$

The value of M is calculated using the following equation:

$285.7x + M = 0$

Therefore,

$M = -285.7x\ in \cdot lbf$

If X is greater than 10in, the equations change due to the extra force. The following equations then apply:

$285.7 - 1000 + V = 0$

Therefore,

$V = 714.3\ lbf$

$285.7x - 1000\ (x - 10) + M = 0$

$M = 1000\ (x - 10) - 285.7x$

Therefore,

$M = 714.3x - 10000\ in \cdot lbf$

These results can be displayed graphically by creating shear and bending moment diagrams, as shown in Figure A–7.

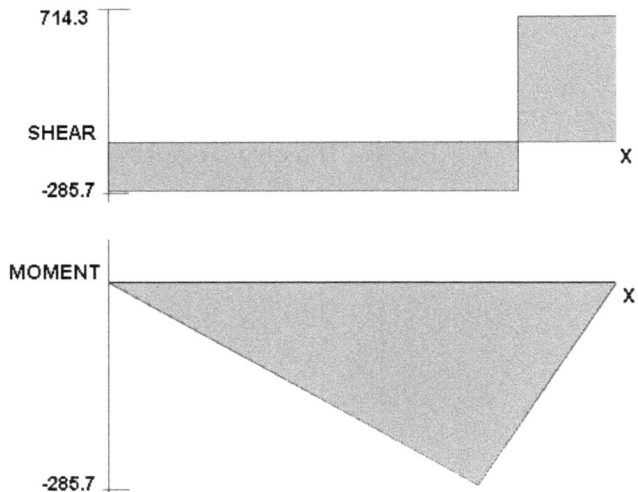

**Figure A–7**

Graphically, the maximum moment for this beam is directly under the applied load. The value of the moment, in conjunction with the beam bending equation, can be used to calculate the stresses in the beam.

Note that you cannot calculate reaction loads for every structure using only equilibrium. The beam diagram shown in Figure A–8 is similar to the case that you just solved. However, the ends have been fixed instead of pinned.

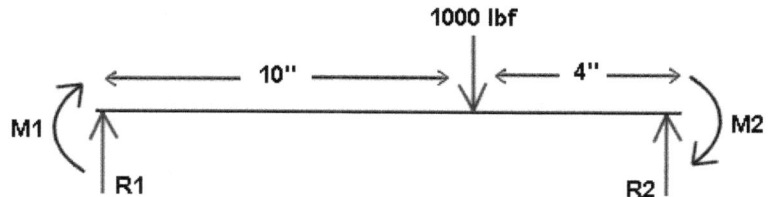

**Figure A–8**

Two additional unknowns now represent the moments transmitted through the ends of the beam: M1 and M2. A total of four unknowns now exist, but two equilibrium equations are available for each plane.

The following force and moment equilibrium equations (at R1) can be written:

$$R1 + R2 = 1000$$

$$M1 + 10(1000) - 14R2 + M2 = 0$$

These equations cannot be solved uniquely. Even if you try creating another moment equation at R2, the following equation results:

$$M1 + 14R1 - 4(1000) + M2 = 0$$

$$R1 - 1000 - R2$$

Therefore,

$$M1 + 14000 - 14R2 - 4000 + M2 = 0$$

$$M1 + 10000 - 14R2 + M2 = 0$$

The final equation is the same equation that you arrived at earlier. Therefore, creating another moment equation at R2 does not help. This problem is actually solvable by hand but requires additional equations that take into account the stiffness of the structure (elasticity theory). As problems become more complex, the only feasible approach often involves the use of numerical computer methods.

So far, only simple beams in a single plane have been considered. One of the most valuable uses for understanding the equilibrium equations is being able to calculate the reaction loads between different components in an assembly. This skill enables you to analyze single components from an assembly rather than attempting to model the entire structure.

## Stresses

The most basic definition of stress is as follows:

$$\text{STRESS} = \frac{\text{FORCE}}{\text{AREA}}$$

Or,

$$\sigma = \frac{F}{A}$$

An example of a tensile test specimen is shown in Figure A–9.

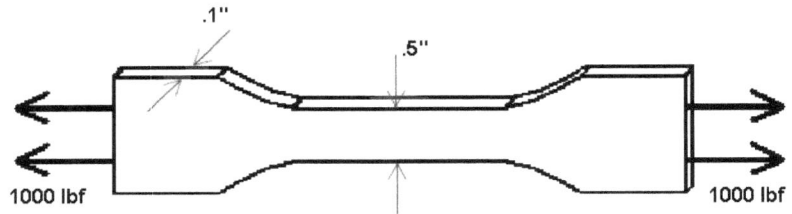

**Figure A–9**

The following properties apply:

$F = 1000\ lbf$

$A = 0.1 \times 0.5 = 0.05\ in^2$

Therefore,

$\sigma = 1000 \S 0.05$

$(\sigma = 20000)\ psi\ (20\ ksi)$

Once a stress has been determined, it can be used to predict the safety of the part, by comparing the stress in the part with the material's strength. A material's yield strength and ultimate strength are typically used for comparison. The yield strength is the amount of stress that a material can sustain before suffering permanent deformation, and the ultimate strength is the stress at which the material ruptures in tension.

Material properties can be displayed using a Stress-Strain diagram, as shown in Figure A–10. Strain relates to the displacements of the structure and is defined as follows:

$$STRAIN = \frac{CHANGE\,IN\,LENGTH}{LENGTH}$$

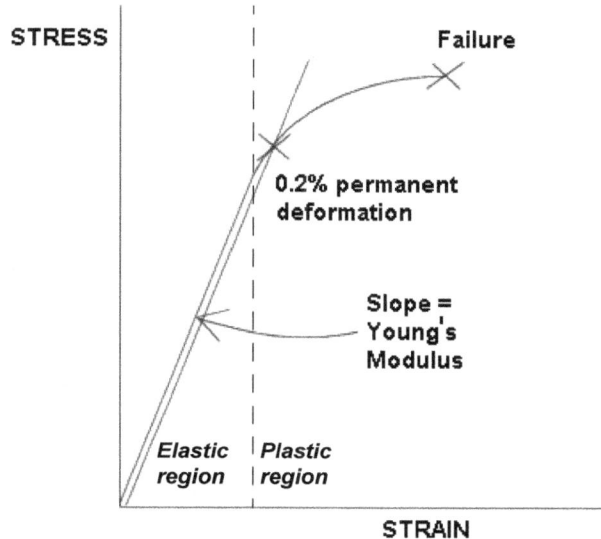

**Figure A–10**

Note that the initial portion of the curve is a straight line. This is called the *elastic* region. Linear static analysis assumes that the material is *only* being used in its elastic region. The slope of the curve is Young's Modulus, E. By generally accepted standards, the yield strength is determined to be the stress level at which a 0.2% permanent deformation is seen in the material. The ultimate strength is the maximum stress level that is obtained before failure.

The graph shown in Figure A–10 is an idealization. In reality, metals have an essentially linear first segment, but some materials (e.g., plastics or rubbers) do not. Although linear analysis makes the fundamental assumption of the linear material properties, it is still used frequently with plastics and other materials. To be more accurate, a non-linear analysis could be performed, but this is much more complex and costly. It is often quite acceptable to approximate a material's behavior as linear because a valuable insight into the component's behavior can still be obtained.

# 3D Stresses

So far, only the case of uniaxial stress has been considered. 3D has many components of stress, as shown in Figure A–11.

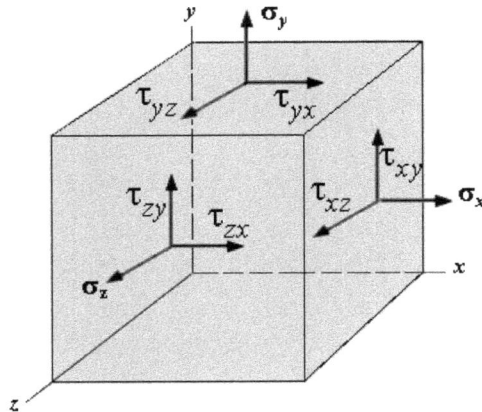

**Figure A–11**

$\sigma$ indicates a normal stress parallel to and acting on the plane denoted by the subscript. $\tau$ indicates a shear stress acting on the plane denoted by the first subscript and parallel to the plane denoted by the second subscript.

At any point in the component, you can visualize an infinitely smaller cube. Each face of the cube can react to a tensile stress normal to its surface and shear stresses in the other two perpendicular directions. To satisfy the equilibrium of the cube,

$\tau_{xy} = \tau_{yx}, \tau_{xz} = \tau_{zx}, \tau_{yz} = \tau_{zy}$.

With multiple stress components, a single value can no longer be compared against a material's yield strength. Furthermore, if the cube is reoriented (i.e., a different coordinate system is used), the stress values change. Consider the 2D example shown in Figure A–12.

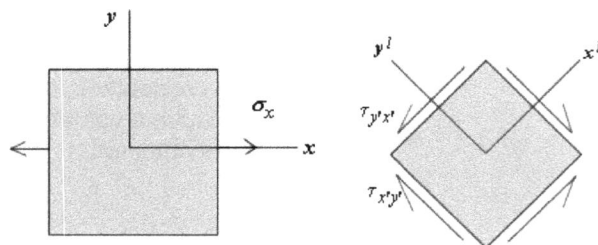

**Figure A–12**

Only a normal stress is shown on the left in Figure A–12. If the coordinate system is rotated, at least some of the stress in the new system must be reacted in shear. In fact, the normal stresses that must also be present to balance the vertical compression, are not shown on the right in Figure A–12.

Therefore, you cannot simply take a stress value from an arbitrary coordinate system. It is possible to find a coordinate system in which all of the stresses can be expressed as pure normal stresses through trigonometry). This is called the *Principal Coordinate System*, and the stresses expressed in that system are called the *Principal Stresses*. In 3D, three principal stresses are denoted (1, 2, and 3), which are usually arranged in a decreasing order of magnitude.

## Failure Theories

Figure A–13 shows three common failure theories:

- Maximum Principal Stress theory

- Maximum Shear Stress (Tresca) theory

- von Mises Stress theory

Each theory tries to predict yielding in a general stress state.

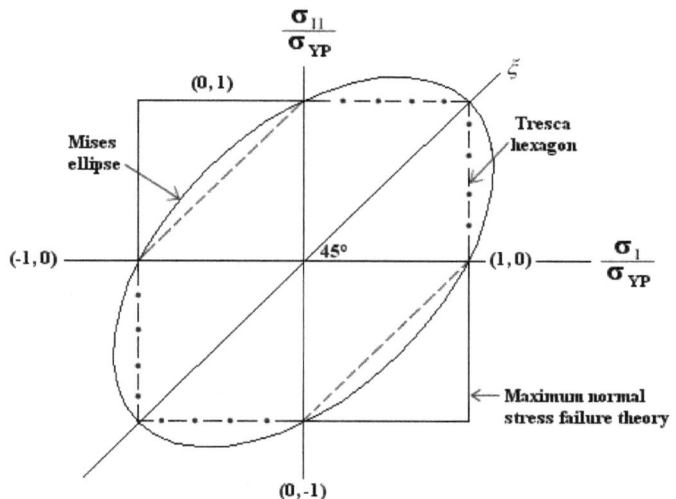

**Figure A–13**

The Maximum Principal Stress theory states that when the maximum principal stress exceeds the material's yield point, the material yields. The Maximum Shear Stress theory was proposed later when it was understood that yielding resulted from shearing between atoms of the solid. Finally, the von Mises Stress theory (also called *Distortion Energy* or *Effective Stress*) was determined to most closely match the experimental results for ductile isotropic materials.

In most cases, you should compare the calculated von Mises stress to the yield of the material to judge whether a component is capable of withstanding the applied loads without experiencing a permanent plastic deformation.

# Appendix B

## Poisson's Ratio Project

This chapter contains the following topics:

- **Poisson's Ratio**

# B.1 Poisson's Ratio

When a plate is subject to simple tension, the length of the plate increases in the load direction, but decreases in the dimensions that are perpendicular to the load. The ratio of the strain in the lateral direction to the axial direction is defined as *Poisson's ratio*.

*i.e.* *Poisson's ratio* $= \dfrac{unit\ lateral\ contraction}{unit\ axial\ elongation}$

*Poisson's ratio is a constant for a given material within its range of elastic behavior (e.g., structural steel = 0.3 approx.).*

The following example demonstrates how Poisson's ratio affects a rectangular (14x8) steel plate that is 0.2 thick, has one hole, and is under a simple tension of 20000lbs. You analyze the plate with a shell model.

You set up and run two standard design studies with different boundary conditions to indicate the Poisson's ratio effect on the analysis results.

The plate model with hole dimensions is shown in Figure B–1.

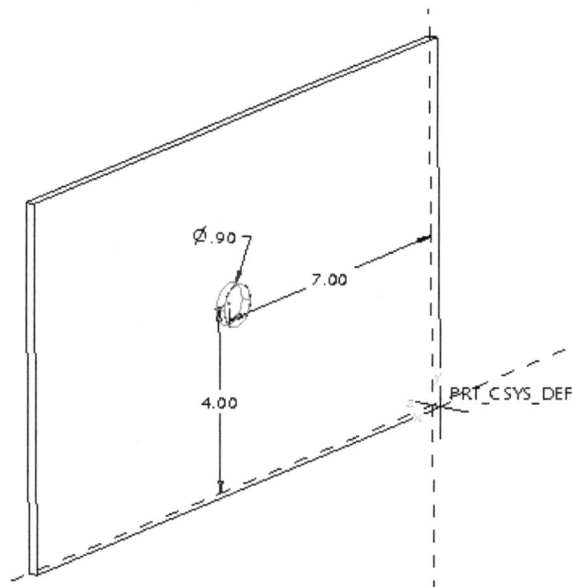

**Figure B–1**

## Modeling Tasks

### Task 1 - Open poisson_part in Creo Parametric and launch Creo Simulate.

1. Open **poisson_part.prt**. The part displays as shown in Figure B–2.

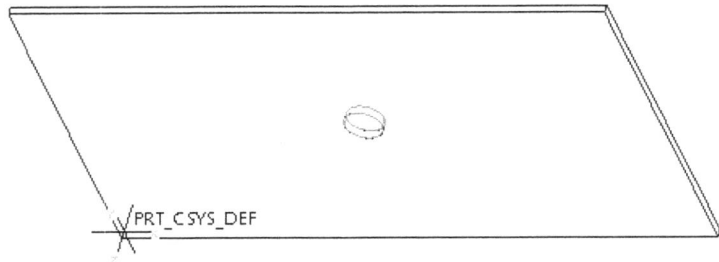

**Figure B–2**

2. Ensure that the unit system is set to **IPS**.

3. Launch Creo Simulate.

### Task 2 - Apply the material.

*The model's material properties should be as stated.*

1. Assign **STEEL** to the model. The following values are the default material properties for HS-low-alloy steel (STEEL):

   - Poisson = 0.27
   - Young's modulus = 2.9e+07 psi

### Task 3 - Define the shell pairs.

*The plate thickness is 0.2 inches.*

1. Use the **Automatic Detection** tool, with the *Characteristic Thickness* of **0.25** to define the shell pairs.

## Task 4 - Apply the loads.

1. Apply a tensile load of **20000** lbs to the edge shown in Figure B–3.

*The model shown in Figure B–3 is reoriented for clarity.*

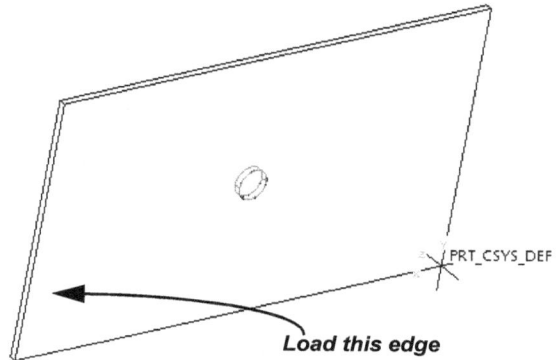

Figure B–3

## Task 5 - Apply the constraints.

1. Constrain the edges shown in Figure B–4, using the following values:

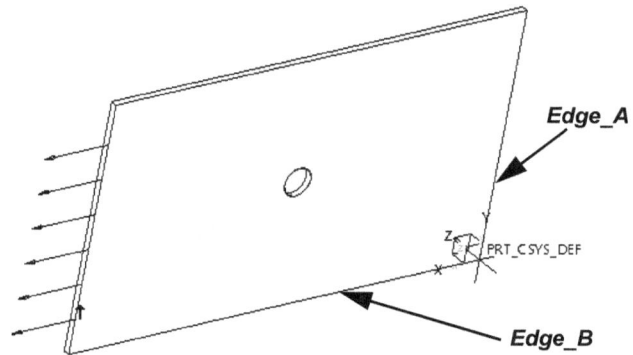

Figure B–4

| Constraint Set | Edge_A | Edge_B | Description |
|---|---|---|---|
| **const_1** | Fixed in all translations and rotations. | Free in all translations and rotations. | The constraint set does not permit the plate to decrease in dimensions perpendicular to the applied load along edge_A. This edge is said to be over-constrained. |

| const_2 | Fixed in X- and Z-directions. Free in Y-direction. Fixed in all rotations | Fixed in Y-direction only | The constraint set does not constrain edge_A in the Y-direction and edge_B in the X-direction. This permits the plate to decrease in dimensions perpendicular to the applied load, which causes in more realistic results. |

The model displays as shown in Figure B–5.

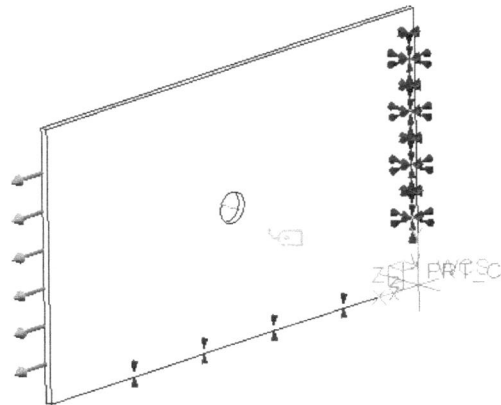

Figure B–5

## Analysis Tasks

## Task 6 - Set up the analysis.

1.  Set up the following:

    - A multipass analysis **Max. P order = 9** with a convergence of **1%**. Name the analysis **p_1**. Select **const_1** as the constraint set.
    - A multipass analysis **Max. P order = 9** with a convergence of **1%**. Name the analysis **p_2**. Select **const_2** as the constraint set.

## Task 7 - Run the analysis.

1.  Run both analyses.

2. Once the analyses have finished, open the run status and note the following details:

- Maximum von Mises stress in the p_1 analysis = 38.20ksi (approx.)
- Maximum von Mises stress in the p_2 analysis= 36.74ksi (approx.)

## Results Tasks

## Task 8 - Display the results.

1. Create and display the following:

- A deformed fringe color plot of the von Mises stress for analysis **p_1**, as shown in Figure B–6.
- A deformed fringe color plot of the von Mises stress for analysis **p_2**, as shown in Figure B–7.

The constraint set **const_1** in Figure B–6 does not permit the plate to decrease in dimensions perpendicular to the applied load. This model is said to be overconstrained. Note that the deformation of the plate is restricted and that the plate is not permitted to contract freely in the Y-direction. Therefore, the arched top and bottom edges display.

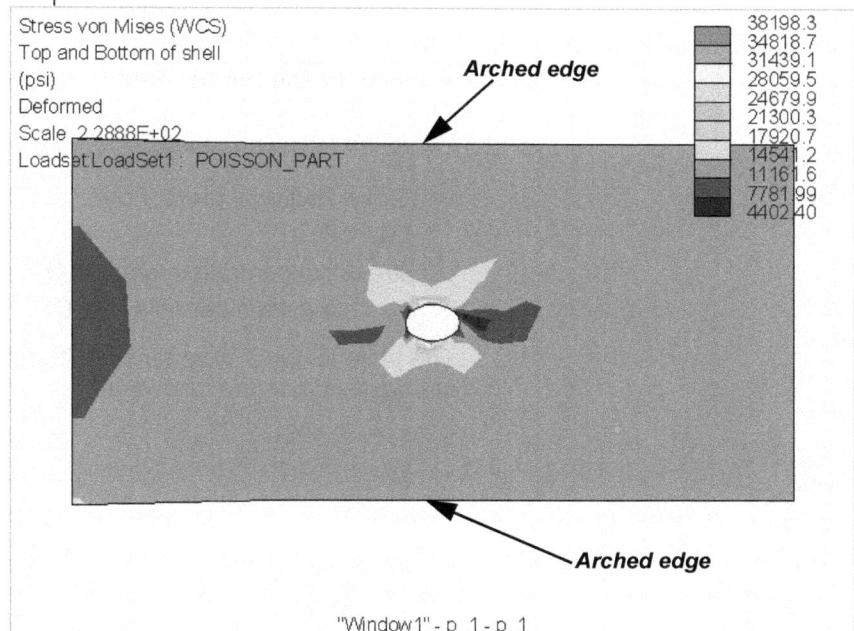

Stress von Mises (WCS)
Top and Bottom of shell
(psi)
Deformed
Scale 2.2888E+02
Loadset:LoadSet1 : POISSON_PART

*Arched edge*

*Arched edge*

38198.3
34818.7
31439.1
28059.5
24679.9
21300.3
17920.7
14541.2
11161.6
7781.99
4402.40

"Window1" - p_1 - p_1

**Figure B–6**

The constraint set **const_2** in Figure B–7 does not constrain edge_A in the Y-direction and edge_B in the X-direction. This permits the plate dimensions to decrease in the Y-direction. Note that the deformation of the plate is uniform.

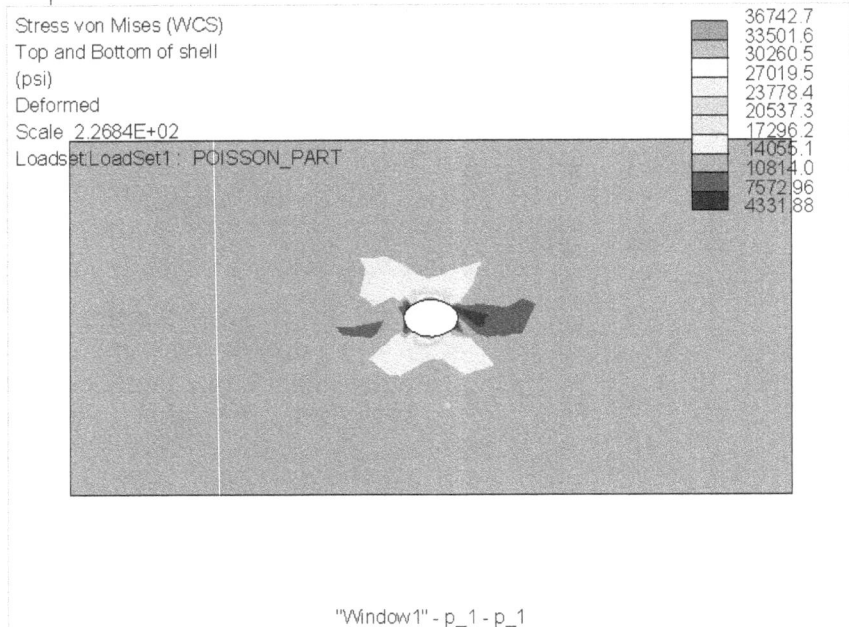

"Window1" - p_1 - p_1

**Figure B–7**

## Task 9 - Verify the results with hand calculations.

1. Verify the following results:

    - Cross-sectional area of plate at hole = (8 - 0.9)(0.2) = 1.42 in$^2$
    - Stress concentration factor for hole = 2.62
    - $\sigma_1$ = max. stress at hole = (2.62)(20000)/(1.42) = 36.9ksi

    The plate is under pure tension. Therefore, the principal stresses include the following:

    - $\sigma_1$ = 36.9ksi
    - $\sigma_2$ = 0
    - $\sigma_3$ = 0
    - von Mises stress = $\{[(\sigma_1 - \sigma_2)^2 + (\sigma_2 - \sigma_3)^2 + (\sigma_3 - \sigma_1)^2]/2\}^{1/2}$ = 36.9 ksi

2. A comparison of the hand-calculated maximum von Mises value with the values obtained from the FEA analysis is as follows:

| Method | vm (ksi) | Error% |
|---|---|---|
| Hand-calculated | 36.9 | 0.00 |
| Analysis [P_1] | 38.20 | 3.5 |
| Analysis [P_1] | 36.74 | 0.4 |

Although the values are close and comparable to each other, the constraint set **const_1** has over-constrained the plate and the deformation of the plate is not uniform due to the effect of the Poisson's ratio.

# Appendix C

## Verification and Practice Examples Set 1

This chapter contains the following topics:

- **Structural Analysis**

# C.1 Structural Analysis

In each of the following cases, create the Creo Parametric model and use the techniques learned in the previous practices to perform the appropriate analysis. Compare the results obtained with the following theoretical values. Note that the theory values also use approximations.

| Case | Description | Theory | Creo Simulate | Error % |
|------|-------------|--------|---------------|---------|
| 1A | Cantilever Beam - Bending | $\delta_{max} = .1167$ in <br> $\sigma_{max} = 39.4$ ksi | | |
| 1B | Cantilever Beam - Gravity | $\delta_{max} = 1.7 \times 10^{-4}$ in <br> $\sigma_{max} = 76.54$ psi | | |
| 2A | Plate w/ Hole - Tension | $\sigma_{max} = 14.6$ ksi | | |
| 2B | Plate w/ Hole - Bending | $\sigma_{max} = 34.7$ ksi | | |
| 3A | Step. Cir. Bar - Tension | $\sigma_{max} = 2.14$ ksi | | |
| 3B | Step. Cir. Bar - Bending | $\sigma_{max} = 1.56$ ksi | | |
| 3C | Step. Cir. Bar - Torsion | $\tau_{max} = 682.45$ psi | | |
| 4A | Loaded Hole in Plate | $\sigma_{max} = 9.98$ ksi | | |

# Case 1 - Cantilevered I-Beam

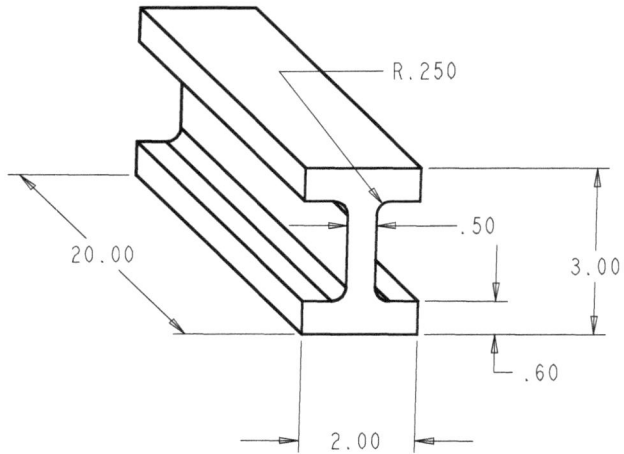

R.250

.50

20.00

3.00

.60

2.00

**Figure C–1**

## Loadcase A

- One end: **Immovable**

- The other end: **5000 lbf shear** (in the stiffer bending direction)

- Material: **Steel**

- Idealize the model with beam elements.

- Young's modulus: **E = 3.0e7**

- Poisson's ratio: $\nu$ **= 0.30**

- Mass density: **7.5e-4**

- Bending moment of inertia: **I = 3.8094 in$^4$**

## Loadcase A Analytical Solution

$$\text{maximum deflection, } \delta_{max} = \frac{F \times L^3}{3 \times E \times I}$$

$$= \frac{5000 \times (20)^3}{3 \times (3 \times 10^7) \times 3.8094}$$

$$= \textbf{0.1167 in}$$

$$\text{maximum stress, } \sigma_{max} = \frac{M \times y}{I}$$

$$= \frac{5000 \times 20 \times 1.5}{3.8094}$$

$$= \textbf{39.4 ksi}$$

## Loadcase B

- One end: **Immovable, 1G gravity load (386.4 in/s$^2$)**

- Cross-sectional area: **A = 3.35365**

- Idealize the model with beam elements.

## Loadcase B Analytical Solution

$$w = \text{mass density} \times A \times G$$

$$= (7.5 \times 10^{-4}) \times 3.35365 \times 386.4$$

$$= \textbf{0.9719 lbf/in}$$

$$\text{maximum deflection, } \delta_{max} = \frac{w \times L^4}{8 \times E \times I}$$

$$= \frac{0.9719 \times (20)^4}{8 \times (3 \times 10^7) \times 3.8094}$$

$$= \textbf{1.7} \times \textbf{10}^{-4} \textbf{in}$$

$$M = \frac{w \times L^2}{2}$$

$$= \frac{0.9719 \times (20)^2}{2}$$

$$= \textbf{194.38 in} \cdot \textbf{lbf}$$

$$\text{maximum stress, } \sigma_{max} = \frac{M \times y}{I}$$

$$= \frac{194.38 \times 1.5}{3.8094}$$

$$= \textbf{76.54 psi}$$

# Case 1 - Plate with a Hole

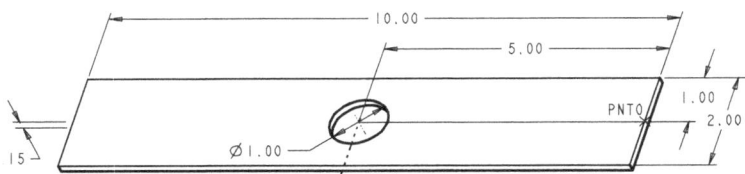

**Figure C–2**

## Loadcase A

- One end: **Immovable**
- The other end: **tensile load of 1000 lbf**
- **w=2**
- **d=1**

## Loadcase A Analytical Solution

$$\sigma_0 = \frac{1000}{(2-1) \times 0.15}$$
$$= 6667 \text{ psi}$$

$$\frac{d}{w} = 0.5$$

$$K_t = 2.19$$

$$\sigma_{max} = \sigma_0 \times K_t$$
$$= 6667 \times 2.19$$
$$= \textbf{14.6 ksi}$$

## Loadcase B

- One end: **Immovable**
- The other end: **Bending moment of 100 in lbf**

## Loadcase B Analytical Solution

$$I = \frac{(2-1) \times (0.15)^3}{12}$$
$$= 2.8125 \times 10^{-4}$$

$$\sigma_0 = \frac{100 \times 0.075}{2.8125 \times 10^{-4}}$$

$$K_t = 1.3$$

$$\sigma_{max} = \textbf{34.7 ksi}$$

## Case 1 - Stepped Circular Bar

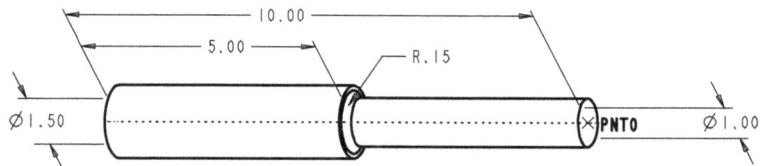

**Figure C–3**

### Loadcase A

- Large end: **Immovable**

- Small end: **1000 lbf tension**

### Loadcase A Analytical Solution

$$\sigma_0 = \frac{F}{A}$$

$$= \frac{1000}{\left(\pi \times (1)^2 \middle/ 4\right)}$$

$$= 1273 \text{ psi}$$

$$\frac{D}{d} = 1.5$$

$$\frac{r}{d} = 0.15$$

$$K_t = 1.68$$

$$\sigma_{max} = \textbf{2.14 ksi}$$

## Loadcase B

- Large end: **Immovable**

- Small end: **100 in·lbf bending**

## Loadcase B Analytical Solution

$$\sigma_0 = \frac{M \times y}{I}$$

$$= \textbf{1018.6 psi}$$

$$K_t = 1.53$$

$$\sigma_{max} = \textbf{1.56 ksi}$$

## Loadcase C

- Large end: **Immovable**

- Small end: **100 in lbf torsion**

## Loadcase C Analytical Solution

$$\tau_0 = \frac{T \times c}{J}$$

$$= \frac{100 \times 0.5}{\left( \pi \times 1^4 \big/ 32 \right)}$$

$$= 509.3 \, \text{psi}$$

$$K_s = 1.34$$

$$\tau_{max} = \textbf{682.45 psi}$$

# Case 1 - Loaded Plate with Hole

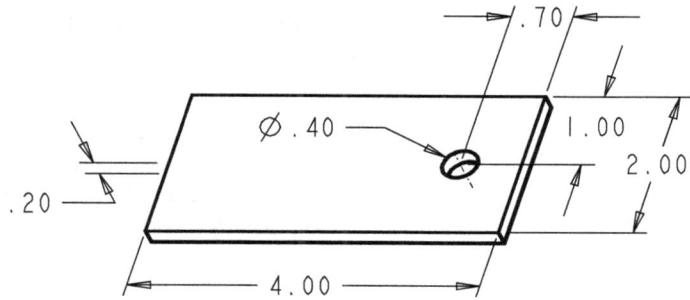

**Figure C–4**

## Loadcase A

- End farthest from hole: **Immovable**

- Bearing load in hole of 500 lbf directed towards nearest end of plate.

$$w = 2$$
$$t = 0.2$$
$$h = 0.70$$
$$d = 0.40$$

## Loadcase A Analytical Solution

$$\sigma_0 = 500 \times (2 - 0.40) \times 0.2$$
$$= 1.56 \text{ ksi}$$

$$d/w = 0.2$$

$$h/w = 0.35$$

$$K_t = 6.1$$

$$\sigma_{max} = \textbf{9.98 ksi}$$

# Practice C1

# Structural Analysis Examples - Set 2

In this practice, in each of the following cases, you will create the Creo Parametric model and use the techniques learned in the previous practices to perform the appropriate analysis. For each model, define the material as steel with the following properties:

- Young's modulus: **E = 3.0e7**

- Poisson's ratio: **ν = 0.30**

- Mass density: **7.5e-4**

## Case 1 - Straight Beams

Beams are usually quite easy to solve, but care must be taken when applying boundary conditions. For these straight beam examples, build a 10" long beam with 0.5"x1.0" cross-section, as shown in Figure C–5.

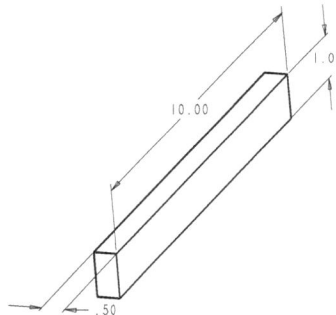

**Figure C–5**

### Loadcase A - Fixed-Fixed Beam

1. Apply Immovable constraints to the two ends of the beam.

2. Apply a **200 lbf/in$^2$** uniform load as the *Load Per Unit* normal to the top of the beam. This equals a **100lbf/in** load along the beam.

3. Solve the model. Compare the results to the table in Loadcase B - All Edges Fixed – Concentrated Load, Step 5.

## Loadcase B - Pinned-Pinned Beam

In this case, do not use beam elements. Mesh the model with 3D solid elements. To create a pinned connection, you must constrain a curve. Solid analyses do not have an associated moment carrying degrees of freedom. A constrained line is free to spin about the line as required for a pin joint.

1. In Creo Parametric, create a straight datum curve at each end of the beam, as shown in Figure C–6.

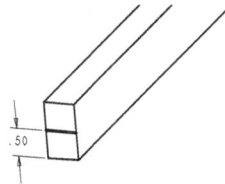

.50

**Figure C–6**

2. Constrain the curves as **Immovable**.

3. Apply a **200 lbf/in$^2$** pressure. This is equivalent to the **200 lbf/in$^2$** uniform load (*Load Per Unit*) in Loadcase A.

4. Solve the model. Compare the results to the table in Loadcase B - All Edges Fixed – Concentrated Load, Step 5.

## Case 2 - Rectangular Plate

Boundary conditions for plates must be modeled similar to those used for simply supported pinned beam-ends. For these rectangular plate examples, build the following model.

1. Build a 10in x 5in x 0.5in plate. The part displays as shown in Figure C–7.

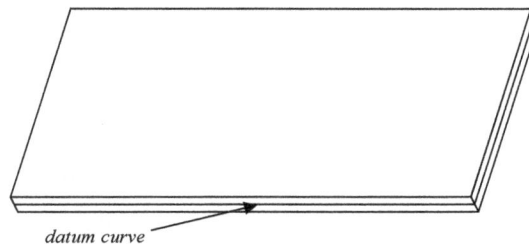

*datum curve*

**Figure C–7**

## Loadcase A - All Edges pinned – Distributed Load

1. Create datum curves on the four sides.

2. Make the four curves **Immovable** to simulate simple support.

3. Apply a downward **100lbf/in$^2$** *Load Per Unit* normal to the top surface.

4. Solve the model. Compare the results to the table in Loadcase B - All Edges Fixed – Concentrated Load, Step 5.

## Loadcase B - All Edges Fixed – Concentrated Load

1. In Creo Parametric, sketch a circular datum curve centered on the top of the plate with a radius of **0.5**.

2. Create a Surface Region using the circular datum curve.

3. Set all four side surfaces as **Immovable**.

4. Apply a *Total Force* of **10000lbf** to the small surface region (normal to surface). The loading should display as shown in Figure C–8.

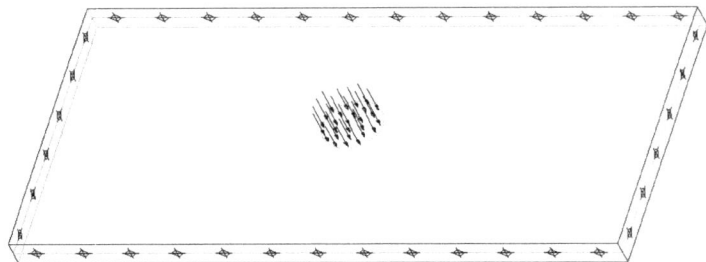

**Figure C–8**

5. Solve the model. Compare the results to the following table.

| Case | Quantity | Roark 6$^{th}$ Ed. | Pro/MECHANICA |
|------|----------|--------------------|----------------|
| 1a | Max. Y Disp | -2.083e-3 | |
| | Max. Stress | 10000 | |
| | Stress at Mid Beam | 5000 | |
| 1b | Max. Y Disp | -.0104 | |
| | Max. Stress | 15000 | |
| 2a | Horz. Disp at left end neutral axis | .69 | |
| 2b | Horz. Disp at left end neutral axis | 1.58 | |

# Appendix D

## Conversion Factors

This chapter contains the following topics:

- **Conversion Factors**

# D.1 Conversion Factors

| To Convert From | To | Multiply By |
|---|---|---|
| degree (angle) | radian (rad) | 1.745329e-2 |
| foot | meter | 3.048e-1 |
| ft/min | m/sec | 5.080e-3 |
| ft/sec | m/sec | 3.048e-1 |
| ft/sec^2 | m/sec^2 | 3.048e-1 |
| ft-lbf | joule | 1.355818 |
| ft-lbf/sec | watt | 1.355818 |
| horsepower | watt | 7.456999e2 |
| inch | meter | 2.54e-2 |
| km/h | m/sec | 2.777778e-1 |
| kW-h | joule | 3.6e6 |
| kip (1000lb) | N (newton) | 4.448222e3 |
| litter | m^3 | 1e-3 |
| mile | m | 1.609344e3 |
| ounce-force | N | 2.780139e-1o |
| zf-in | N-m | 7.061552e-3 |
| pound (lb) | Kg | 4.535924e-1 |
| slug-ft^2 | Kg-m^2 | 4.214011e-2 |
| lb/ft^3 | Kg/m^3 | 1.601846e1 |
| lbf (pound-force) | N | 4.448222 |
| lbf-ft | N-m | 1.335818 |
| lbf-in | N-m | 1.129848e-1 |
| lbf/ft | N/m | 1.459390e1 |
| lbf/ft^2 | Pa (pascal) | 4.788026e1 |
| lbf/in | N/m | 1.751268e2 |
| lbf/in^2 (psi) | Pa | 6.894757e3 |
| slug | Kg | 1.45939e1 |
| slug/ft^3 | Kg/m^3 | 5.153788e2 |
| ton (2000lb) | Kg | 9.071847e2 |
| W-h | joule | 3.6e3 |

www.ingramcontent.com/pod-product-compliance
Lightning Source LLC
Chambersburg PA
CB-IW080345220326
41598CB00030B/4611